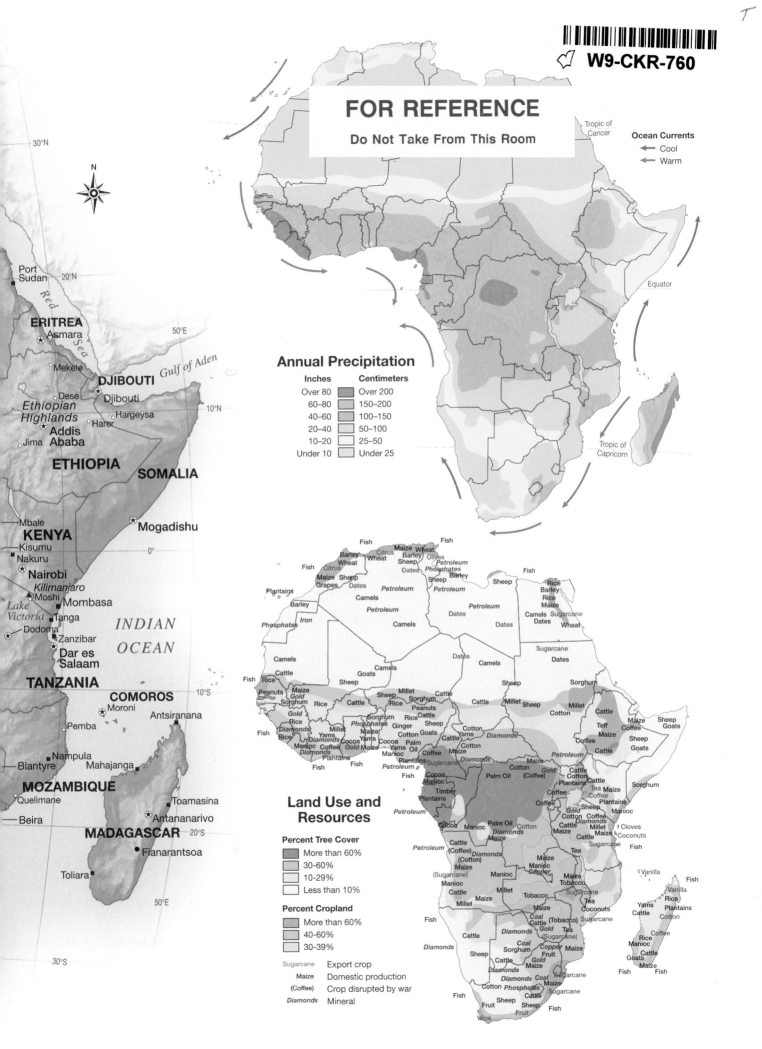

W9-CKR-760

Annual Precipitation

Inches	Centimeters
Over 80	Over 200
60–80	150–200
40–60	100–150
20–40	50–100
10–20	25–50
Under 10	Under 25

Ocean Currents
← Cool
← Warm

Tropic of Cancer

Equator

Tropic of Capricorn

Land Use and Resources

Percent Tree Cover
- More than 60%
- 30-60%
- 10-29%
- Less than 10%

Percent Cropland
- More than 60%
- 40-60%
- 30-39%

Sugarcane	Export crop
Maize	Domestic production
(Coffee)	Crop disrupted by war
Diamonds	Mineral

(Regional map labels, left side:)

Port Sudan
Red Sea
ERITREA — Asmara
Mekele
DJIBOUTI — Djibouti
Ethiopian Highlands
Dese
Gulf of Aden
Hargeysa
Harer
Addis Ababa
Jima
ETHIOPIA
SOMALIA
Mogadishu
Mbale
KENYA
Kisumu
Nakuru
Nairobi
Kilimanjaro
Moshi — Mombasa
Lake Victoria
Dodoma — Tanga
Zanzibar
Dar es Salaam
TANZANIA
INDIAN OCEAN
COMOROS
Moroni
Antsiranana
Pemba
Nampula
Blantyre
Mahajanga
MOZAMBIQUE
Quelimane
Toamasina
Beira
Antananarivo
MADAGASCAR
Fianarantsoa
Toliara

NEW ENCYCLOPEDIA OF

AFRICA

NEW ENCYCLOPEDIA OF

AFRICA

Volume 5

Taboo and Sin–Zubayr
Index

John Middleton

EDITOR IN CHIEF

Joseph C. Miller

EDITOR

CHARLES SCRIBNER'S SONS
A part of Gale, Cengage Learning

Detroit • New York • San Francisco • New Haven, Conn • Waterville, Maine • London

New Encyclopedia of Africa

John Middleton, Editor in Chief
Joseph C. Miller, Editor

© 2008 Gale, a part of Cengage Learning

For more information, contact
Charles Scribner's Sons
A part of Gale, Cengage Learning
27500 Drake Rd.
Farmington Hills, MI 48331-3535
Or you can visit our Internet site at
gale.cengage.com

For permission to use material from this product, submit your request via Web at http://www.gale-edit.com/permissions, or you may download our Permissions Request form and submit your request by fax or mail to:

Permissions Department
Gale
27500 Drake Rd.
Farmington Hills, MI 48331-3535
Permissions Hotline:
248-699-8006 or 800-877-4253 ext. 8006
Fax: 248-699-8074 or 800-762-4058

Since this page cannot legibly accommodate all copyright notices, the credits constitute an extension of the copyright notice.

While every effort has been made to ensure the reliability of the information presented in this publication, Gale, a part of Cengage Learning does not guarantee the accuracy of the data contained herein. Gale accepts no payment for listing; and inclusion in the publication of any organization, agency, institution, publication, service, or individual does not imply endorsement of the editors or publisher. Errors brought to the attention of the publisher and verified to the satisfaction of the publisher will be corrected in future editions.

NEW ENCYCLOPEDIA OF AFRICA

John Middleton, editor in chief ; Joseph C. Miller, editor.
    p. cm.
        Includes bibliographical references and index.
        ISBN 978-0-684-31454-9 (set : alk. paper)
        ISBN 978-0-684-31455-6 (vol. 1 : alk. paper)
        ISBN 978-0-684-31456-3 (vol. 2 : alk. paper)
        ISBN 978-0-684-31457-0 (vol. 3 : alk. paper)
        ISBN 978-0-684-31458-7 (vol. 4 : alk. paper)
        ISBN 978-0-684-31459-4 (vol. 5 : alk. paper)
        Africa—Encyclopedias. Middleton, John, 1921- Miller, Joseph Calder.
        Title.

DT2.N48 2008
960.03—dc22
        2007021746

ISBN-10:

0-684-31454-1 (set)
0-684-31455-X (vol. 1)
0-684-31456-8 (vol. 2)
0-684-31457-6 (vol. 3)
0-684-31458-4 (vol. 4)
0-684-31459-2 (vol. 5)

This title is also available as an e-book.
ISBN-13: 978-0-684-31557-7; ISBN-10: 0-684-31557-2
Contact your Gale representative for ordering information.

Printed in the United States of America
2 3 4 5 6 7 14 13 12 11 10 09 08

EDITORIAL BOARD

Joseph Harris
Howard University
Historian

Goran Hyden
University of Florida
Political scientist,
East Africa

Ali Mazrui
State University of New York,
Binghamton
Political scientist,
East Africa

Sally Falk Moore
Harvard University
Anthropologist, lawyer, East
Africa

V. Y. Mudimbe
Duke University
Philosopher, novelist, poet,
Central Africa

Roland Oliver
School of Oriental and African
Studies, University of London
Historian

Abdul Sheriff
Zanzibar Indian Ocean Research
Institute
Historian, East Africa

Wim Van Binsbergen
University of Leiden,
Netherlands
Anthropologist, philosopher,
Southern Africa

Jan Vansina
University of Wisconsin
Historian, Central Africa

CONSULTANTS

Kelly Askew
University of Michigan
Anthropologist, musicologist,
East Africa

Karin Barber
University of Birmingham
Historian, West Africa

Julia Clancy-Smith
University of Arizona
Historian, North Africa

Mamadou Diouf
Columbia University
Anthropologist, historian, West
Africa

Toyin Falola
University of Texas, Austin
Historian, West Africa

Richard Fardon
School of Oriental and African
Studies, University of London
Anthropologist, Central Africa

Gillian Feeley-Harnik
University of Michigan
Anthropologist, Madagascar

Peter Geschiere
University of Amsterdam
Anthropologist, Central Africa

Michelle Gilbert
Sarah Lawrence College
Art historian, West Africa

Jane Guyer
Johns Hopkins University
Historian, West Africa

Andrew Hill
Yale University
Paleontologist, East Africa

Michael Lambek
University of Toronto
Anthropologist, East Africa

George Nelson
University of Liverpool
Medicine, East/West Africa

Kimani Njogu
Twaweza Communications,
Nairobi
Director, linguist, East Africa

John Peel
School of Oriental and African
Studies, University of
London
Anthropologist, West Africa

Paul Richards
Wageningen University and
Research Centre,
Netherlands
Geographer, West Africa

Janet Roitman
University of Paris
Anthropologist,
Central Africa

Parker Shipton
Boston University
Anthropologist, East Africa

Thomas Spear
University of Wisconsin
Historian, East Africa

Dorothy Woodson
Yale University
Librarian, Africa

TABOO AND SIN. The general idea of sin does not present any particular problem in comparative religion. A sin is a wicked act that transgresses the laws of God. Its contrast sets are crime, a wicked act which incurs the penalty of law, and vice, a disapproved habit of life that may lead to sin and lawbreaking. Sins are not usually illegal, and, vice versa, breaking the law is not necessarily sinful. Vice is a moral term; crime is defined and punishable by law; sin is defined in religious doctrine. It is a deliberate act, committed knowingly, and it has a clear moral content. *Taboo* is a Polynesian word that means a forbidden action or a general prohibition against touching or approaching a thing. For example, in Polynesia it was taboo for anyone to touch the head of a chief, even by mistake. Food and sex taboos are important African examples. Like sin, taboo is also a term for a transgression, but unlike sin, the moral content of the rule may be hard to see.

Sinners may be seen to prosper. If they sin and repent, they may be forgiven and get away scot free, or if they do receive divine punishment it may be postponed to the hereafter. Theories of sin vary according to the theory of the person: in some religions people are reincarnated from previous existence, in which case they may be expiating past sins, or they may carry with them a predetermined tendency to sin. Medieval Christianity paid much attention to divine retribution in the afterlife, developing descriptions of hell, purgatory, and heaven in terms of a perfectly just and exact divine retribution for vice and virtue. Repentance

should lead to purification administered in priestly rituals. The theology of sin is clearly a means of social control.

The idea of taboo also controls moral behavior, but the control is depersonalized: it is not linked inherently to any doctrine of personality or to afterlife or prenatal existence. It tends to be focused on a forbidden intrusion into a sacred place or a forbidden contact. In central Africa taboos protect pregnant women and small babies from even indirect contact with adulterers: an adulterer who eats food cooked on the same fire or who shares salt with the mother endangers the life of the child. In this case the taboo breaker is the woman putting herself or her child at risk, and the adulterer seems to go unpunished. More generally, taboo breakers can expect to be punished in their lifetime. As with sin, the punishing effects may fall on the individual, or on his or her kin, or on the whole community. This part of the belief mobilizes other people to monitor correct behavior. Neighbors are going to be affected if a taboo is broken, and so they take an interest in its being kept.

Repentance is not necessary for canceling broken taboos, because intention is not involved. Whether the act was deliberate or inadvertent, there has to be some way to expiate it, a way to cancel its effects. Purification in both sin and taboo is a ritual that reintegrates the offender into the community. Both sin and taboo, to that extent, are liable to be treated as matters of public concern and seen as offences against the community which has been endangered. Among the Leele of Zaire the birth of twins was surrounded with danger because twins were a specific, powerful divine intervention into the normal course of human fertility. Not just at birth, but all their lives, taboos surrounded the person of twins; what one should call "taboos of respect" had to be observed if a twin arrived as a stranger in a village, otherwise the hunting would not prosper until the rite of twin-entry had been performed.

When the sense of community weakens, sins become private and taboos disappear. In English there is no noun for the forbidden state or for the forbidden thing. In the centuries-old process of privatizing sin, eradicating purgatory, and losing any lively conception of hell, one has come to suppose that taboo is a concept completely foreign to the English speaking, and so one adopts the foreign word, "taboo." Although the word generally fits into a system of religious doctrines, the English speaking tend to apply it to trivial secular contexts. For example, it has been said to be taboo to talk about death or sex at dinner; walking on lawns in public places or smoking in restaurants might be taboo. These usages emphasize the impersonal and inadvertent aspects of the word. They also illustrate the attempt to control knowledge and to uphold rights of property which are typical of taboos. But using the word for minor breaches of etiquette diminishes and distorts the meaning of an idea that is as central to all religions, including those of sub-Saharan Africa, as the idea of sin.

Sinners may meet their retribution in their lifetime or in a hereafter. In the Bible when the widow's son fell ill and was at death's door, she feared that she was being punished for her sins (1 Kings 17:18). In the Western Christian tradition some sins have popularly been thought to entail automatic physical consequences that punish the sinner. There was an idea in Europe that certain sins would bring about instant retribution, particularly the sin of oath-breaking. The expression that emphasizes the truth of an oath: "I swear I am telling the truth, so strike me dead!" is a relic of a belief that a perjured oath taker would be killed on the spot by a thunderbolt. Most of the examples of taboos in Africa are of this type, in which automatic punishments fall on the heads of wrongdoers. Sometimes the wrongs are hard to connect with the moral code, as for instance taboos

surrounding the birth of twins; others show the moral implications more easily, as for example the sexual taboos that punish adultery with the death of babies or incest with leprosy. Respect taboos, such as taboos against insulting high office, uphold the political system as surely as sexual taboos uphold the institution of the family.

One way of presenting taboo is as a system of rules that keeps two different spheres, the divine order and the order of nature, apart, so that if the taboo is breached the mixing of the two spheres produces disastrous results. This description is only impressionistic, since in most religions there are no two completely separate spheres. With an immanent God who exists within the natural world, taboo is just as much part of the order of nature as earth and water, and the physical elements are just as much part of the divine order. The disjunction between nature and divinity established in the development of secular science and education in the Renaissance makes it difficult to understand taboo. This is because one encounters it in foreign cultures as an impersonal force: a taboo works by its own power; no spiritual being has to intervene to make it effective.

A question of credibility fascinated the first explorers and missionaries who wanted to understand African religions. To them it was perfectly credible that a curse should be feared and be believed to have bad effects. Prophecies also, and sins, might plausibly be expected to bring misfortune because of the implicit reference to a divine scrutiny and a divine power to direct misfortune where it would punish evildoers. Taboos presented problems because they looked like isolated beliefs about how the world is, equivalent to a belief in the pull of gravity or the effects of climate. For example, taboos that connected illness directly to immorality sound too like a failure of scientific reasoning or an absurd attempt to use misfortune to coerce behavior. Why should anyone believe that incest produces skin disease, or adultery a perilous childbirth? Both are common beliefs in Africa. Or why should eating swine's flesh or contact with corpses be strictly avoided, as in Judaism? Outsiders to the culture can see no connection. Ridicule used to be poured on the idea that breach of dietary taboos might cause illness, as if they were based on mistaken nutritional science.

Such interpretations fall beside the point when taboo is classed, as it should be, along with prophecy, curses, and blessings, as an intrinsic part of a theistic universe. Just as it makes sense for a worshiper to believe in the real power of curses, sins, and blessings, so it makes sense for the worshiper to believe that God set up a human society and protected it by making real dangers attend on the breach of divine laws.

For reasons that connect religions with mortality one has no problem understanding curses. For one, if a curse is effective in destroying the good fortune of the curser's enemy it is because some spiritual being ensures that it works. One understands very well that an insulted father or elder, or a debtor or poor man, if treated unjustly, may utter a curse against the wrongdoer, and when misfortune later falls on the object of the curse it can be taken for granted that God made it efficacious. Likewise for prophecy: one has no problem understanding that the seer who foretells a good or bad event is able to look into the future by virtue of a divinely given calling. The same is true of blessings. The theistic background to these beliefs makes them susceptible of an easy religious explanation. Theists would have no difficulty in believing that God would intervene to support curses and blessings, and endow some people with prophetic powers.

Curses and blessings engage moral judgment as well: one expects good behavior to be rewarded and bad behavior to be punished, so it is very credible that a just God should make sure that penalties and rewards are distributed fairly. For the same sort of reason, beliefs that correspond to the Christian idea of sin are intuitively unproblematic. The sin is an offense against God, who may forgive it or may be angry enough to punish it.

Taboo is in a different class: a belief in disaster following inexorably on the breach of specified rules, it works within the created physical world without implying any special divine intervention. Further problems arise when taboo is presented as if it were a sin against God's law, but one that has no moral aspect: how can God be angry or punish an act that is completely inadvertent and does no harm to anyone? What sort of God makes laws that have no sense? The common, but wrong, idea that taboos are senseless is what makes them difficult to interpret.

When observed carefully, the rules whose breach constitute taboo usually carry an indirect moral implication. Quite often they have an important function for maintaining the community's customs. What one might regard as three separate orders may be combined in the system of taboo: the natural order, the divine order, and the social order. The surface structure of taboo involves only two things: the infraction of a rule, witting or unwitting, and the certain penalty; but under this simple scheme lies a third assumption: that the world was made to behave in this way and is sustained in its efficacy by God. Taboo depends on a divine order, or rather it is how the divine order is maintained. Thus has the universe been created, and thus has it been furnished with an armory that automatically punishes the sinner as surely as fire burns, water drowns, and weights fall.

To have a full understanding of taboo, imagine a universe that is built as an abstract model of moral values and religious and social symbols and fully sensitized to human behavior. In this responsive universe the whole conceivable range of good deeds and acts of respect and piety would automatically bring down blessings, and all injustices, insults, and disregard for symbolic distinctions would bring down punishments. The world of Homer would seem something like this. From the extreme case one can set out some of the variant forms. In some religions the automatic operation of taboo is expected to be intelligible: if one has broken a taboo unwittingly, it is supposed that one could and should have known the offense. In other religions there are so many taboos and their connection with social life is so tenuous that no one can be expected to look out for them in advance. Only when tripped by a misfortune and after consulting a diviner does the normal person discover that a taboo has been breached, finding that one has walked inadvertently on a dog's grave, for example, or touched a corpse.

The question, Why do people believe in taboos? is answered after considering these other questions: Who makes taboos? How can they be cancelled? Taboo essentially combines the idea of defilement and punishment, to be cured by purification. So where does the idea of defilement come from? Religions vary greatly in their interest in defilement. Laws for purification meet a collective concern to reconcile and to reincorporate the defiler or to make an example of him. A community that is highly individualistic, where each member is free to join or go away at any time, will have little interest in either defilement or purification. The reason for believing in the dangers of taboo or defilement is the holding of important shared values. So, for example, if something about the religion is held to be vulnerable, speaking irreverently is declared a sin or a taboo, and the agreement on blasphemy makes it easy to rally around the demand for repentance and penalty. If the outraged consensus is mustered to protect the king the sense of outrage focuses on lèse-majesté; if mustered against perjury, the sanctity of the oath and the courts is protected.

Taboo is not a difficult system to live with if there are plenty of simple purifications. Taboo is not static. When the common good ceases to have a hold on the public conscience and the old taboos fall into ridicule, new ones grow up to protect the new focus of concern. When strong communal control gives way to individually contested control of power, communal taboos transform into an honor system; a blot on the family honor can become a curse for the following generations. If hierarchy transforms into an egalitarian community, the taboos upholding stratification lose credibility and those that protect the boundary acquire additional force. Taboo is an intelligible system. It shifts with the desire of people to protect the things that matter, and it shifts with changes in values.

See also **Divination and Oracles; Law; Philosophy and the Study of Africa; Religion and Ritual.**

BIBLIOGRAPHY

Douglas, Mary. *Purity and Danger: An Analysis of Concepts of Pollution and Taboo.* London: Ark Paperbacks, 1984.

Duffy, Eamon. *The Stripping of the Altars: Traditional Religion in England, 1400–c. 1580.* New Haven, CT: Yale University Press, 2005.

Le Goff, Jacques. *The Birth of Purgatory.* Chicago: University of Chicago Press, 1986.

McDannell, Colleen, and Bernard Lang. *Heaven: A History.* New Haven, CT: Yale University Press, 1988.

Steiner, Franz. *Taboo.* London: Cohen & West, 1956.

Walker, Daniel P. *The Decline of Hell: Seventeenth-Century Discussions of Eternal Torment.* Chicago: University of Chicago Press, 1964.

MARY DOUGLAS

TAFAWA BALEWA, ABUBAKAR

(1912–1966). Born in Bauchi Province south of the Muslim Hausa regions in what is now central Nigeria to a non-Fulani, nonroyal family (unlike most of the early elite of the northern Hausa emirates), Alhaji Abubakar Tafawa Balewa was educated at Katsina Higher College in the heart of the Hausa area of the colony. He was appointed a schoolmaster in 1933 and in the same year married Hafsatu (Zainab), the daughter of a Fulani Islamic judge. Following her death in childbirth, Abubakar was to make no less than six marriages. In 1934 his novel *Shaihu Umar*, the romanticized travels of a Hausa teacher, was published as one of the prize-winning entries in a competition for creative writing in the Hausa language. Forty years on, it was to be both dramatized and filmed.

Yet neither teaching nor literature was to become Balewa's career; it was in politics that he attained the pinnacle of fame and admiration. He cofounded the Bauchi General Improvement Union in 1943 and was nominated to the Northern Legislature in 1946. There he advanced his reformist views against emirate authoritarianism. In 1949 he was promoted to the still largely European cadre of education officers, and his career was confirmed. Returned as a member of the Nigerian legislature for Bauchi Province in both the regional (1951) and federal (1954) elections and chosen as vice president of the dominant Northern People's Congress, Abubakar was given the portfolio of central minister of works in 1952 and of transport in 1954. In 1957 he became prime minister of the Federation and was knighted in 1960.

During the 1960s, Nigeria's final nationalist decade, Abubakar was known for his balanced judgment, the transparency of his honesty and modesty, and the widespread respect that his leadership of the evolving and volatile Federation earned him, internationally as well as domestically. But the responsibility of leading such a fractious and fragile state as Nigeria in the early 1960s

Abubakar Tafawa Balewa (1912–1966) at an African Summit Conference, 1963. Tafawa Balewa, prime minister of Nigeria, was a trained teacher who encouraged the formation of the Organization of African Unity. A university is named in his honor in Bauchi, his birthplace. © BETTMANN/CORBIS

imposed its strain and left the conscientious Abubakar with continual worries.

Domestically, each general election and national census resulted in cries of foul play. In holding the sensitive regions of the Federation together, Abubakar had not only the personal antagonisms of southern nationalist leaders Benjamin Nnamdi Azikiwe and Obafemi Awolowo to contend with, but also the authoritarianism of his own party's leader, the northern elite's Ahmadu Bello. International issues such as the place of apartheid South Africa in the British Commonwealth, France's atom bomb test in the Sahara, the Congo upheaval, Rhodesia's Unilateral Declaration of Independence, and the scrapping of the defense pact between Nigeria and Britain all severely tested Abubakar's qualities as a statesman.

His steadfast resolution saved the country from disintegration in the political crisis in 1964, when, refusing to be stampeded by the president's lack of confidence in him, Abubakar broke the threatening constitutional deadlock by assembling a broad-based government, following the partially boycotted general election. His bold initiative enabled the Federation to survive—at least for another twelve months. But the salvation was short-lived. On the eve of January 15, 1966, a bloody mutiny erupted. Abubakar was abducted and assassinated; to this day it is unclear how far his murder was an integral part of the original plot.

For subsequent generations, Abubakar has lived on as a rare example of the postcolonial African statesman and the epitome of the *honnête homme* of Hausa culture. His place in Nigeria's history as its first, final, and finest prime minister remains unchallenged.

See also **Awolowo, Obafemi; Azikiwe, Benjamin Nnamdi; Bello, Ahmadu.**

BIBLIOGRAPHY

Balewa, Alhaji Abubakar Tafawa. *Mr. Prime Minister: A Selection of Speeches.* Lagos, Nigeria: Federal Ministry of Information, 1964.

Clark, Trevor. *A Right Honourable Gentleman: Abubakar from the Black Rock.* Zaria: Hudahuda, 1991.

Kirk-Greene, Anthony H. M. *Mutumin Kirkii: The Concept of the Good Man in Hausa.* Bloomington: Indiana University, 1974.

Sklar, Richard L. *Nigerian Political Parties: Power in Emergent African Nations.* Princeton, NJ: Princeton University Press, 1963.

Whitaker, C. S. "Three Perspectives on Hierarchy: Political Thought and Leadership in Northern Nigeria." *Journal of Commonwealth Political Studies* 3 (1965): 1–19.

ANTHONY KIRK-GREENE

TANGIER. The city of Tangier (*Tanja* in Arabic; *Tanger* in French) is one of Morocco's principal ports, with an urban population of 669,685 in 2004. A port city has existed on the site since Punic times, when it was already called Tingi. Due to the city's strategic location on the Atlantic side of the Straits of Gibraltar, it has been contested and occupied by great powers throughout its history. In Roman times Tangier was the capital of Mauritania Tingitana, an imperial province. The city and its hinterland remained under Roman rule until it fell to the Vandals in 429 CE. It reverted to Byzantine control from 534 to 682 and then passed to the Visigoths of Spain, which ruled it until the Muslim conquest in 702. From the eighth to thirteenth centuries Muslim maritime power was at its height in the Straits region and the port city thrived, serving for both commercial and naval expeditions. This era of the city's history culminated with the career of its best-known son, Ibn Battuta, the erudite world traveler of the fourteenth century.

The rise of powerful maritime states in Christian Europe placed Tangier on the front line of many wars. The Portuguese, in control of Ceuta since 1415, seized it in 1471. Both presidios passed to the Spanish when Portugal lost its sovereignty (1580–1640). In 1661 the Portuguese ceded Tangier, along with Mumbai in India, to the English crown. A resurgent Morocco under Sultan Moulay Isma' initiated a lengthy blockade of the city. Tangier finally fell to the Moroccans in 1684, though the English destroyed both the city and the port before abandoning it. In 1923, after years of stalemate among the European powers, Tangier was declared an "international city," under the joint administration of France, Spain, Great Britain, and Italy, a status it kept until Morocco's accession to independence in 1956. International Tangier acquired a reputation as a haven for Western artists, libertines, and spies, and the era is represented in the works of such authors as Paul Bowles, William Burroughs, Mohamed Choukri, and Jean Genet. Since independence, Tangier has become an industrial city and radio transmission center. Its port and international airport harbor industrial free trade and export processing zones, an entirely new container port is as of 2007 being built at a location twenty-one miles to the east, and there is renewed discussion of building a rail tunnel beneath the straits to Spain.

See also **Morocco; Morocco, History of (1000 to 1900); Muslim Northern Africa, History of (641 to 1500 CE).**

BIBLIOGRAPHY

Stuart, Graham H. *The International City of Tangier*, 2nd edition. Stanford, CA: Stanford University Press, 1955.

Vaidon, Lawdom. *Tangier: A Different Way*. Metuchen, NJ: Scarecrow Press, 1977.

ERIC S. ROSS

TANZANIA

This entry includes the following articles:
GEOGRAPHY AND ECONOMY
SOCIETY AND CULTURE
HISTORY AND POLITICS

GEOGRAPHY AND ECONOMY

Tanzania is located on the east coast of Africa just south of the equator and includes the islands of Zanzibar, Mafia, and Pemba. Colonial occupation by Germany (German East Africa, 1885–1917) and Great Britain (Tanganyika, 1919–1961) superimposed boundaries on roughly 120 different language groups. The modern territorial configuration is the result of a 1964 revolt against the Zanzibar sultanate that led to a union of the islands with mainland Tanganyika (Tanzania, 1964–). With a total land area of 587,258 square miles and a population of 36.8 million people in 2005, it is both the largest and most populous country in East Africa.

Tanzania has three basic physiographic regions, the coastal plain, highlands in the north and south, and the interior plateau. Within this broad classification are notable geographic features including Mount Kilimanjaro—Africa's highest point at 19,340 feet—and the Great Rift Valley. The fault zones associated with the rift have been inundated to form a series of major lakes including Tanganyika and Nyasa. The five major river systems, the Pangani, Wami, Rufiji, Ruvu, and Ruvuma, all drain into the Indian Ocean.

Rainfall is highly variable, spatially and temporally, due to topography and the seasonal shifts in winds produced by the movement of the Inter-Tropical Convergence Zone. The northern part of the country experiences a bimodal rainfall regime, with peaks in October to December and March to May, while the rest of the country has a unimodal regime with a peak in December to April. Mean annual rainfall varies from more than 59 inches in parts of the southern highlands to less than 20 inches over much of the interior plateau.

Tanzania's population is unevenly distributed, with most settlement located in three areas—the Indian Ocean coast, lake region, and northern and southern highlands—leaving vast areas of the interior sparsely populated. Though the majority of the

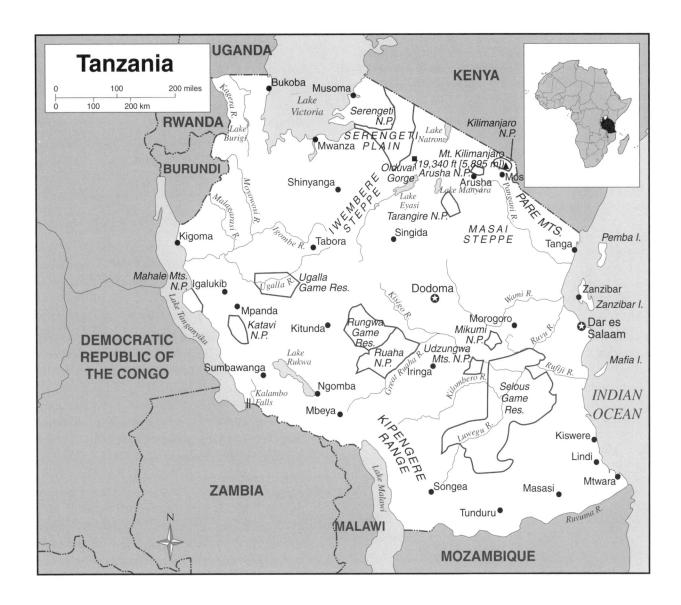

population is rural, urbanization has accelerated since the late twentieth century, swelling the country's largest cities such as Dar es Salaam, Arusha, and Dodoma. The natural rate of population increase is near 2 percent and life expectancy, below fifty years, is declining, due largely to a national HIV/AIDS infection rate estimated at 11 percent.

Colonialism reoriented the region's ancient Indian Ocean trade and promoted new agricultural export commodities such as sisal, tea, coffee, tobacco, and cotton. The fuller incorporation of Tanzania into the world economy led to the establishment of an African peasant class and regional differentiation, two processes that continue to influence Tanzania's economic development. In an effort to concentrate African labor in agriculture, British colonial policy restricted African involvement in the professions and deemphasized African education.

At independence Tanzania thus had few university graduates, highly uneven regional development, and an economy heavily dependent on the export of a few agricultural commodities. The manufacturing sector was insignificant and confined to the processing of agricultural commodities. In the early twenty-first century the economy remained dependent on agriculture, employing 85 percent of its workforce and accounting for 75 percent of its exports, principally coffee, cotton, cashew nuts, tea, sisal, and tobacco.

In the 1970s and 1980s Tanzania's economy experienced a series of external shocks, notably the 1973 and 1979 oil shocks and declining world market prices for agricultural commodities. Internally, the single-party socialist state pursued a policy of self reliance, announced in the 1967 Arusha Declaration. The general policy thrust discouraged private investment, promoted import substitution industrialization and state ownership of manufacturing, and established state monopsonies for agricultural commodities. The combined external and internal forces led to declining terms of trade, rising external debt, and a falling per capita gross domestic product (GDP).

In the midst of economic decline and rising debt, Tanzania signed an agreement with the International Monetary Fund (IMF) in 1985 to implement the national Economic Recovery Program. Since then the state has committed itself to a series of structural adjustment programs, abandoned socialist development policies, and promoted privatization, foreign investment, currency devaluation, and the reduction of state expenditures.

The successes and failures of two decades of neoliberal economic development policies continue to be debated. On the one hand, manufacturing grew 6.3 percent per annum from 1996 to 2004. Real GDP growth increased significantly and inflation was brought under control. Foreign direct investment also increased, the bulk of which was directed toward tourism and mining. As a result, tourism has become the second largest source of foreign exchange after agriculture, and mining has been growing at 15.5 percent per annum.

On the other hand, Tanzania remains one of the least developed countries in the world, with a per capita GDP of $800. Debt has risen sharply, far outpacing GDP growth. In 1999 the IMF deemed Tanzania's debt to be "unsustainable," and designated it a "highly indebted poor country," making it eligible for debt relief. Nevertheless, total external debt reached $7.9 billion in 2004, while an estimated 40 to 50 percent of the population still lives below poverty level.

See also **Colonial Policies and Practices; Dar es Salaam; Debt and Credit; Disease: HIV/AIDS, Social and Political Aspects; Ecosystems; International Monetary Fund.**

BIBLIOGRAPHY

Berry, L., ed. *Tanzania in Maps.* London: University of London Press, 1971.

Forster, Peter G., and Sam Maghimbi, eds. *Agrarian Economy: State and Society in Contemporary Tanzania.* Aldershot, U.K.: Ashgate, 1999.

Iliffe, John. *A Modern History of Tanganyika.* Cambridge, U.K.: Cambridge University Press, 1979.

Szirmai, Adam, and Paul Lapperre, eds. *The Industrial Experience of Tanzania.* New York: Palgrave, 2001.

RODERICK P. NEUMANN

SOCIETY AND CULTURES

The East African nation of Tanzania, just as most African nation states, encompasses many different cultures and peoples. It developed as an entity out of the colonial era. In the case of Tanzania, almost uniquely, the political process of creation continued after the end of colonial rule. Mainland Tanzania became independent as Tanganyika in 1961, and the offshore island state of Zanzibar followed in 1963. The two merged to form Tanzania in 1964 after a bloody revolution on the Isles (Zanzibar and Pemba). The formal lines on the map that were created in the late nineteenth century by Europeans bound together peoples, cultures, languages, and precolonial states into a new political entity. Yet these components of the new colony had social and economic elements of coherence that preceded the declaration of colonial rule. The merger of previously separate colonies-become-nations both reactivated older patterns of cultural and economic interaction between coast and interior and magnified the diversity already present in each of the two states.

The peoples of Tanzania have built their cultures and societies both on the ways they provided subsistence for themselves and on the historical movements of people, ideas, and things across the landscape. Their diversity reflects long-term processes of social and economic development within the particular landscapes of the region. The languages of Tanzania come from all four of the major indigenous language families found in Africa, making the country one of the few areas in Africa with such diversity.

Of the approximately 120 different languages spoken in Tanzania, the largest number comes from the Bantu subbranch of the Niger–Congo language family. Small communities such as the Sandawe and Hadza still speak the oldest languages found in the area, those of the Khoesan family. Speakers of Cushitic languages, part of the great Afro–Asiatic family centered to the north in Ethiopia and beyond, such as the Iraqw and Burunge, brought cattle keeping and agriculture into the region as early as 3000 BCE. At about 1000 BCE, Bantu speakers entered the northwest corner of the region. There, encountering cereal-growing speakers of languages of the fourth major grouping in Africa, Nilo–Saharan, the Bantu speakers developed a new synthesis of agriculture, animal husbandry, and iron working that enabled them to create daughter languages of the Bantu subfamily across the region and beyond. In the early twenty-first century, the majority of Tanzanians come from communities whose indigenous tongue belongs to the Bantu family.

Over the last 1,000 years, speakers of Nilotic languages of the Nilo-Saharan group—Luo and the Maasai language, Maa—have moved further into the territory. Over the course of these millennia, incoming Bantu speakers made local accommodations with the older communities they found in the area, and all dug in and developed reasonably stable social strategies and cultural expressions, as well as connections with neighbors of complementing adaptations that allowed for the development of larger scale political, economic, and cultural inter-action. These processes of immigration, and the immigrants' languages, have continued into recent times, with continuing adaptations by the old local communities. Indian language-speakers, Arabs, Portuguese mariners, and German and English col-onizers have all left their marks.

The majority of Tanzania's peoples have prac-ticed agriculture as their main mode of subsistence, developing highly refined and varied types according to the environments they utilize. In better-watered higher elevations, such as the Kagera region west of Lake Victoria-Nyanza, Mt. Kilimanjaro, Mt. Meru, the Usambaras, the Pare, and the Uluguru moun-tains, residents combine intensive cultivation of bananas on permanent fields with cattle keeping and the production of modern cash crops such as coffee and tea. In the drier plains surrounding these northern highlands and stretching into central Tanzania, the Sukuma, the Nyamwezi, and the Gogo combined cattle keeping with extensive cultivation of grain crops such as sorghum, millet, and maize. In the southwestern Fipa highlands of the country, fertile land allows for the production of a wide variety of crops. Along the Indian Ocean coast, the presence of tsetse flies that carry sleeping sickness often prevented the keeping of livestock, but farmers there could cultivate rice and coconuts.

The Cushitic-speaking communities live in the plains and highlands of northern Tanzania and share subsistence strategies with their Bantu-speak-ing neighbors. The Khoesan-speaking Sandawe and Hadza communities both rely more heavily on for-aging, along with Maa-speaking Dorobo groups. Maa-speaking communities occupy the low-lying dry plains of the southern Great Rift Valley from Kenya well into central and eastern Tanzania. They focus their economic—and hence social and polit-ical—strategies on keeping cattle; however, a num-ber of Maa-speaking communities, including the Arusha of Mt. Meru, have colonized wetter, higher areas and taken up settled agriculture. Historically, individuals often moved between communities and their associated life-ways. Ethnicity, as biography, remained fluid and situational in many contexts, and communities consequently contained individ-uals of many different background who were able to contribute diverse knowledge and experiences to the others.

Cultural conventions within these communities varied with languages and landscapes. Although patrilineal descent remained by and large a general organizing principle for most communities, some reckoned kinship through the mother's side, such as the Luguru, Sagaru, and Kaguru. Most, though, accounted primary kinship through the father's line. In some cases, communities, as amongst the Luguru, determined access to land through mem-bership in clans, large groups of people claiming a more remote sort of descent from a distant ances-tor, and these sorts of allegiance acquired political overtones. Others organized themselves in groups of more immediate kin: lineages tracing descent from a known ancestor only a few generations removed. For purposes transcending the divisions of unilineal descent, many turned to age sets. The Maasai practiced the most famous form of age-set organization, with all males passing through stages of social identities from junior warrior to senior elder and females having similar, although appropriately different, stages. All the individuals of each age cohort—set—passed through each stage together. Many Bantu-speaking communities exchanged personnel with Maasai and eventually adopted their practices so that the Gogo and the Chagga developed age sets that mirrored Maasai practices.

In almost all societies, some form of coming-of-age ritual marked puberty and thus the transition to young adulthood for both males and females. *Jando*, the Swahili term for these rituals, usually included isolation and teaching of the youth by elders, and often also included circumcision to mark readiness for reproductive contributions to the community. For females, variations of the Swahili *nyago* rituals provided the same type of teaching (although genital cutting was less common for females). Marriage usually followed and represented not just the union of the two individuals involved but of the entire families behind them.

Although almost all Tanzanian societies practiced patriarchy, thereby lodging community and political authority in males, and also patrilocality, thus removing young women from their own groups of kin to live with their husband and his male relatives, even those who traced descent and hence lineage membership through females (matrilineally), married women could usually call on the continued support of their family and eventually their grown children. Women also participated in spirit possession and other ritual groups as a way of building social support mechanisms in the communities where they found themselves married. Most societies allowed men to form as many alliances through multiple marriages (polygyny) as they could, but in general only this sort of influence remained the preserve of wealthy, politically prominent, and often senior men. Families raised children to think of all the members of their parents'—mother's or father's—kin group, often quite a large number of people, as responsible for them. Again, in Swahili and many other Bantu languages, people extended the terms for brother, father, mother, and sister to cover almost any such relative of the proper generation and gender.

Tanzanian societies developed a great range of political systems. Many recognized primarily localized authority, where chiefs, as Europeans called them, led communities ranging in size from the hundreds to the tens of thousands. Leaders, such as the *Watemi* of the Gogo and the Nyamwezi, held sway over territories in which they ritually controlled the rains and ruled more as first among other senior males than as a separate, singular, arbitrary power. In other areas, clans united to centralized authority over wider territories under a single representative of the group, a kind of king. The basis of the leader's exclusive authority lay both in the person's ability to marshal military force and in the claims of the king (as the Kilindi rulers of the Usambara mountains) to be able to heal the land and thus to bring rains, fruitful harvests, and fertile women to the area. In short, authority throughout most of Tanzania lay with those who held ritual power to bring harmony between the human community and the spiritized environments in which they lived. Religious practices centered both on maintaining this harmony against those who would disturb it: greedy or antisocial, disloyal individuals often called witches in English; and propagating ancestral spirits that could bring favor within the domains of the groups of kin.

Islam came to the Indian Ocean coast along the trade routes that reached back many centuries, and in the nineteenth century, Swahili traders carried Islam far inland along the trade routes that tapped ivory and slaves from the regions beyond Lake Tanganyika, the western boundary of the modern nation. In the nineteenth and especially the twentieth centuries, Christianity arrived with the European missionaries who led the way toward colonial conquests and then helped consolidate early colonial rule. Both monotheistic religions gained adherents in the local converts who shaped the practice of these universal faiths to local conditions and the communities formed around them.

THE SWAHILI NATION—MODERNITY IN TANZANIA

Out of this historic social and cultural diversity, what eventually could be thought of as a Tanzanian culture was created by the people of the colony, then country, over the course of the twentieth century. The British, who took over the part of German East Africa that became Tanganyika after World War I, followed German practice in making

Swahili the language of government. They also instituted a version of their colonial strategy of Indirect Rule that placed local traditional rulers in the role of government administrators. These "Native Authorities" were sometimes individuals who sought to mediate between state and people, and hence commanded the loyalty of the people for whom they were responsible to colonial district officers. Others were ambitious collaborators often rejected by the local communities. The rigidities of colonial rule in Tanganyika through these quasi-ethnic strategies reified ethnic boundaries that had previously been permeable collaborations through and among which individuals could move according to collective needs and individual opportunities. They also created a class of neotraditional chiefs who had a vested interest in promoting those divisions. However, in Tanganyika, unlike many other British colonies, the use of Swahili on top of these local political institutions promoted a solidarity on the colonial, and then national, level that had the potential to overcome the divisive effects of this tribalism. The British required that all schools use Swahili language as a medium of instruction.

The anticolonial nationalist movement that developed in the colony during the 1950s built on this rather narrow base of shared culture by emphasizing not just Pan-Africanism but also Swahili as a unifying factor. When Julius Nyerere led Tanganyika to independence, his movement—the Tanganyika African National Union (TANU)—and government promoted *Ujamaa na Kujitegemea*, Socialism and Self-Reliance, as keys to national integration and economic development. On Zanzibar, independence came amidst a struggle between a land-owning Arab elite who saw the Isles as an Arab nation, and an African majority, many descended from slaves brought from the communities of the Tanganyikan interior, who saw it as an African one. A bloody revolt against the Arab sultan's government in 1964, almost immediately after the British had left, resulted in a radical government and a merger with the descendants of former kin in Tanganyika to form the nation of Tanzania.

Ujamaa succeeded in promoting a sense of national unity even as it proved a failure as economic policy. People across the country did not forget their origins but rather participated in an ongoing dialogue about the meaning of nationality as an extension of those loyalties. The Swahili language serves as the glue for the whole project. Yet, although some have spoken of the creation of Tanzania as the Swahili nation, across the mainland Swahili itself remains an almost pejorative term used to talk of outsiders, thus implying dominance by coastal politicians. At the same time, Tanzanians increasingly practice culture in Swahili. The modern mass media, newspapers, radio, and television, reach across the nation in Swahili. *Taarab*, a coastal musical style particularly associated with Zanzibar, has almost become the musical style of the whole country. Meanwhile popular forms of music including *dansi* and *Bongo flava*—hip-hop performed in Swahili—find national audiences.

Despite the creation of this common discourse of popular culture, sharp social and cultural cleavages exist in Tanzanian society in the early twenty-first century. Formally, Tanzania has committed itself to promoting gender equity within the national sphere. Women have equal access to education and many have risen to high positions in government and in the private sector; however, patriarchal attitudes still permeate both local society and legal institutions. Most prominently among the divisive issues, at least to some on the Isles, remains the question of the union between the mainland and Zanzibar. Religious divisions also remain potential sources of conflict. The population seems evenly divided between Christians and Muslims, and on occasion conflict has broken out between opposing members of the two communities of faith. The general poverty of the country means that social cohesion remains fragile. Yet after forty years of national independence, the priorities drawing Tanzanians together have proved stronger than the ones dividing them.

See also **Bantu, Eastern, Southern, and Western, History of (1000 BCE to 1500); Christianity; Ethnicity; Islam; Kingship; Kinship and Descent; Languages; Marriage Systems; Nyerere, Julius Kambarage; Production Strategies: Agriculture; Spirit Possession; Warfare; Witchcraft.**

BIBLIOGRAPHY

Askew, Kelly. *Performing the Nation: Swahili Music and Cultural Politics in Tanzania*. Chicago: University of Chicago Press, 2002.

United Republic of Tanzania

Population:	39,384,223 (2007 est.)
Area:	945,087 sq. km (364,900 sq. mi.)
Official languages:	Kiswahili, English
National currency:	Tanzanian shilling
Principal religions:	Christian 45%, Muslim 45%, indigenous 10%
Capital:	legislative capital: Dodoma (est. pop. 324,427 in 2002); executive capital: Dar es Salaam (est. pop. 637,573 in 2002)
Other urban centers:	Arusha, Mwanza, Dodoma, Mbeya, Mtwara, Stonetown, Zanzibar
Annual rainfall:	508–1,498 mm (20–59 in.), varying by region
Principal geographical features:	*Mountains:* Mount Kilimanjaro, Mount Meru, Mount Rugwe, Pare Range, Usambara Range, Livingstone Mountains, Kipengere Range, Poroto Range, Ufipa Highlands, Uluguru Mountains, Matengo Highlands *Lakes:* Victoria-Nyanza, Tanganyika, Rukwa, Eyasi, Manyara, Natron *Rivers:* Pangani, Wami, Mkondoa, Ruvu (Kingani), Rufiji, Ruaha, Kilombero, Mbaragendu, Matandu, Mbemkuru, Lewugu, Lukuledi, Ruvuma, Kagera, Mori, Mara, Malagarasi, Songwe, Ruhuhu *Islands:* Zanzibar, Pemba, Mafia *Other:* Great Rift Valley, Olduvai Gorge, Ngorongoro Crater
Economy:	*GDP per capita:* US$800 (2006)
Principal products and exports:	*Agricultural:* coffee, sisal, tea, cotton, pyrethrum (insecticide made from chrysanthemums), cashew nuts, tobacco, cloves, corn, wheat, cassava (tapioca), bananas, fruits, vegetables, cattle, sheep, goats *Manufacturing:* agricultural processing (sugar, beer, cigarettes, sisal twine), salt, soda ash; cement, oil refining, shoes, apparel, wood products, fertilizer *Mining:* diamonds, gold, gemstones, iron ore, phosphate, coal, copper, zinc, cobalt, lead, salt Tourism, centering on the country's numerous game reserves, is important to the economy.
Government:	In 1961 Tanganyika became independent from a UN trusteeship administered by the United Kingdom. Zanzibar gained independence from the United Kingdom in 1963. Tanganyika and Zanzibar united in 1964. Constitutions 1960, 1965, 1977. Zanzibari constitution, 1985. Multiparty democracy. President elected by universal suffrage for 5-year term. 274-member unicameral National Assembly, 232 seats filled by direct election, part of the remainder filled by presidential appointment and the rest designated by law for specific officials. President appoints prime minister and chooses cabinet from among members of the National Assembly. For purposes of local government there are 26 regions, headed by regional commissioners, appointed from the ranks of the National Assembly; 60 mainland districts and 9 areas (on Zanzibar), headed by district or area councils; and villages headed by village development committees.
Heads of state since independence:	1961–1985: President Julius Nyerere (prime minister of Tanganyika until republic proclaimed in 1962) 1985–1995: President Ali Hassan Mwinyi 1995–2005: President Benjamin Mkapa 2005–: President Jakaya Kikwete
Armed forces:	President is commander in chief. Conscription enlistment for 2-year terms. *Army:* 45,000 *Navy:* 1,000 *Air force:* 3,600 *Paramilitary:* 14,000 *Reserves:* 85,000
Transportation:	*Rail:* 3,569 km (2,213 mi.) *Roads:* 78,891 km (49,021 mi.), 9% paved *Ports:* Bukoba, Dar es Salaam, Kigoma, Musoma, Mwanza, Tanga, Zanzibar *National airlines:* Air Tanzania, Zanzibar Airways, Alliance *Airports:* International facilities at Dar es Salaam, Kilimanjaro, Zanzibar. Over 100 small airports and airstrips.
Media:	3 daily newspapers: *Daily News, Uhuru, Kipanga.* Publishers include the Tanzania Publishing House and a branch of the East African Literature Bureau. Radio services provided by Radio Tanzania and Voice of Tanzania Zanzibar. 23 radio stations, 3 television stations.
Literacy and education:	*Total literacy rate:* 78.2% (2006). Education is free, universal, and compulsory for ages 7–14. Postsecondary education provided by University of Dar es Salaam and other institutions.

Feierman, Steven. *Peasant Intellectuals: Anthropology and History in Tanzania.* Madison: University of Wisconsin Press, 1990.

Fair, Laura. *Pastimes and Politics: Culture, Community, and Identity in Post-Abolition Urban Zanzibar, 1890–1945.* Athens: Ohio University Press, 2001.

Geiger, Susan. *TANU Women: Gender and Culture in the Making of Tanganyikan Nationalism, 1955–1965.* Portsmouth, NH: Heinemann, 1997.

Giblin, James L. *A History of the Excluded: Making Family a Refuge from State in Twentieth-Century Tanzania,* with Blandina Kaduma Giblin. Oxford: James Currey;

Dar es Salaam, Tanzania: Mkuki na Nyota; Athens: Ohio University Press, 2005.

Hodgson, Dorothy L. *Once Intrepid Warriors: Gender, Ethnicity, and The Cultural Politics of Maasai Development*. Bloomington: Indiana University Press, 2001.

Iliffe, John. *A Modern History of Tanganyika*. Cambridge, U.K.: Cambridge University Press, 1979.

Maddox, Gregory H., with Ernest M. Kongola. *Practicing History in Central Tanzania: Writing, Memory, and Performance*. Portsmouth, NH: Heinemann, 2006.

Maddox, Gregory, and James L. Giblin, eds. *In Search of a Nation: Histories of Authority and Dissidence from Tanzania*. Oxford and Athens, OH: James Currey and Ohio University Press, Eastern African Studies Series, 2005.

Spear, Thomas, and Richard Waller, eds. *Being Maasai*. Athens: Ohio University Press, 1992.

GREGORY H. MADDOX

HISTORY AND POLITICS

With a surface area of 364,900 square miles and a population of 39.4 million, Tanzania is located on the east coast of Africa. It is hugged by the Indian Ocean on the East, and bordered by Kenya and Uganda to the North; Rwanda, Burundi, and Democratic Republic of the Congo (DRC) to the West; and Malawi, Zambia, and Mozambique to the South. According to 2004 statistics, annual per capita income is estimated at $320 and gross domestic product (GDP) growth at 6.3 percent.

The United Republic of Tanzania is composed of the Tanzania mainland and Zanzibar Islands. The mainland first became a recognized territory in 1884 in the wake of the Berlin Conference when it was ceded to Germany, becoming Deutsch Ouest Afrika which, at that time, incorporated Rwanda, Burundi, and an area of Northern Mozambique.

It should be noted that German control over this territory was rather tenuous. The colonial authority was therefore brutal relying heavily on forced labor to produce colonial crops such as cotton. These policies were deeply resented by the people leading to open rebellion in 1905. This rebellion, which lasted from 1905 to 1907 came to be known as the Maji Maji Rebellion. Starting at the coast, the rebellion quickly spread across the southern part of the territory, joining a number of ethnic groups in a common struggle against

foreign rule. This insurrection is remembered as the strongest resistance against German rule in Africa. The resistance led to the general weakening or German imperial rule and its eventual collapse after World War I. This experience was to inspire the nationalist struggle against British rule after World War II.

After World War I and the defeat of Germany, Tanganyika was brought under a League of Nations trusteeship to be administered by the United Kingdom. Zanzibar was at that time under the sultanate of Oman and a protectorate of the United Kingdom.

The nationalist struggles for independence in Tanganyika and Zanzibar were closely linked. The Tanganyika African National Union, led by Julius Kambarage Nyerere (1922–1999) in Tanganyika, and the Afro-Shiraz Party, led by Abeid Amani Karume (1905–1972) in Zanzibar, collaborated in strategies and tactics against British rule throughout the 1950s. To a large extent this prepared the ground for the future union between Tanganyika and Zanzibar to form the United Republic of Tanzania.

Tanganyika gained independence in 1961 under the Tanganyika African National Union (TANU) led by Julius Nyerere after an election in which it had overwhelmingly defeated the competing political parties. The losing parties were later banned when Tanganyika became a constitutional one-party state in 1965. Tanganyika was joined by Zanzibar to form the United Republic of Tanzania in 1964 after the latter became independent in 1963 and overthrew the sultanate in a revolution led by the Afro-Shiraz Party (ASP) under Abeid Amani Karume.

The origins of the union have remained controversial. The union and Zanzibar governments have maintained that the union was entered in the long-enduring spirit of Pan-Africanism and African unity that had spurred their collaboration in the nationalist struggles. Skeptics have argued that the fledgling ASP revolutionary government in Zanzibar was seeking protection from a sultan-sponsored or -backed counterrevolution in the islands. Alternatively, others have argued that the mainland (Tanganyika) was seeking to tame and control the revolution in its own interests. Yet others have argued that Tanganyika had collaborated with the United States in the latter's quest to prevent the establishment of another Cuba off the East African coast. Whatever the reasons, negotiations leading to the union culminated in the signing of the Articles of Union in April 1964, within two months of the revolution in Zanzibar.

From the formation of the union the two political parties enjoyed the monopoly of political power after the declaration of a constitutional one-party state. TANU monopolized politics on the mainland while ASP remained the sole party in Zanzibar. To consolidate their grip on power and remove the anomaly of two parties in a constitutional one-party state, the two merged in 1976 forming the hitherto dominant political party Chama cha Mapinduzi (CCM).

Tanzania has been through two major phases in its historical development. The first phase (1961–1985) was socialist in orientation while the second (1985–present) is liberalist. In the first phase economically the country followed a policy of socialism and self-reliance (popularly known as *ujamaa*) until early 1982 when it reluctantly embarked upon economic liberalization. Under the policy of ujamaa the state was the major actor in the economy stressing communal production in agriculture and the establishment of state enterprises in industry and commerce. The outcome was mixed. Agricultural production was partly disrupted by the policy of forced villagization adopted in the early 1970s. State enterprises faltered and in a lot of cases progressively depended on state subsidies, forcing state deficit spending and fuelling inflation. Attempts to rectify this situation from internal resources were not successful.

Meanwhile the economy stagnated with declines in agricultural and industrial output. The volume and value of exports declined, precipitating a major shortage in foreign earnings and a rise in foreign debt, forcing a devaluation of the Tanzania shilling. The economy came under severe stress forcing the government to seek the assistance of the International Monetary Fund (IMF) and World Bank in addressing some of the structural problems in the economy. This eventually resulted in an agreement with the IMF and the launching of an economic recovery program in 1985. Among other things this program entailed devaluation, price decontrol, reduction of the state sector, balancing the budget, and privatization. This, in effect, marked the end of the ujamaa phase and launched the country onto the liberalization phase that has continued into the early twenty-first century.

Pressures for economic reforms largely emanated from international financial institutions. These pressures were initially resisted by the government under Nyerere's presidency, particularly in the 1970s. During the difficult negotiations between Tanzania and the IMF toward the end of the 1970s, for example, Tanzania maintained its commitment to ujamaa policies. When the IMF insisted on stringent conditionalities of devaluation and austerity in government spending at the expense of welfare gains such as education, health, and potable water, Nyerere vehemently protested: "Who elected the IMF to be the Finance Ministry for every country in the world?" By 1985, however, he was forced to step down as president and in 1990 he also relinquished the chair of the party.

By the beginning of the 1990s the IMF/World Bank policies had produced more negative than positive results. On the positive side growth in output had risen from 2 percent in 1980 to 4.4 percent in 1990. However this recovery was concentrated in agriculture although world prices for traditional agricultural exports were declining probably because of increased global output in relatively saturated markets. Industrial output was declining with a shift of investment from production to commerce. Social services had suffered a precipitous decline. Inflation had grown by 30 percent, fueling corruption and embezzlement in government and parastatals. The road network had broken down. Corruption became rampant and endemic.

It is generally acknowledged that under the Arusha Declaration literacy rates and school attendance soared, schools and health centers increased, and peoples' incomes and quality of life improved. At the time of independence in 1961, the British left the country with 85 percent illiteracy, two engineers, and twelve doctors. By 1985 Tanzania had 99 percent literacy and thousands of engineers and doctors. In 1988 Tanzania's per-capita income was $280 but had declined to $140 in 1998. Enrollment in schools plummeted to 63 percent and conditions in health and other services deteriorated. It is instructive to note that even as the

CCM spearheads the liberalization/privatization policies socialism remains entrenched in the constitution.

Politically, during the ujamaa phase, the country was under constitutional one-party rule dominated by TANU and ASP and later CCM. This changed in 1992 when the constitution was amended restoring multiparty democracy. From a political point of view, the ujamaa policy contributed toward consolidating national unity, patriotism, and raising Tanzania's stature in the region as the leading benefactor of the liberation movements in southern Africa. This was, however, accomplished through authoritarian rule, which muzzled any political dissent and obstructed meaningful political participation, resulting in political exclusion and the weakening of civil society.

The 1980s not only ushered in the liberalization and privatization of the economy but also saw concurrent demands for political liberalization begin to grow and crystallize organizationally. These latter demands were largely internal, emanating from different political groups, some of which were critical of economic liberalization but almost all of which were calling for more open political space in the form of a multiparty political system. Among those leading the call for political liberalization was Nyerere who, having realized that the wind of democratization was a worldwide phenomenon, cautioned his party to lead the transition or be engulfed by the democratization wave.

These demands were initially vigorously resisted by the ruling party and the government but President Mwinyi, who had succeeded Nyerere in 1985 as president and in 1990 as chairman of CCM, finally yielded to the pressures. In 1990 the government set up a Commission on One Party or Many Parties headed by then Chief Justice Francis Nyalali. Within nine months the commission produced a report recommending, inter alia, the restoration of a multiparty system, the reduction of the powers of the president, the repealing of repressive laws, and the rewriting the constitution.

Of all these recommendations only the reinstatement of multipartism was adopted by the government The others were ignored. The government responded by initiating a controlled transition in which the CCM has been controlling the players, process, path and pace. But the failure to implement most of the Nyalali recommendations, and particularly the adoption of a new constitution, continues to generate considerable acrimony between the ruling party and the opposition.

Tanzania needs to address the constitutional challenge to ensure not only that there is a continuous dialogue between all political actors but also that this dialogue creates an environment in which meaningful political competition is established. This is perhaps the greatest challenge facing Tanzania in the years ahead as it emerges from decades of single-party rule and seeks to establish a stable democracy.

See also **Colonial Policies and Practices; Economic Systems; International Monetary Fund; Nyerere, Julius Kambarage; Production Strategies; Socialism and Postsocialisms; World Bank; Zanzibar.**

BIBLIOGRAPHY

Baregu, Mwesiga. "The Rise and Fall of the One-Party State in Tanzania." In *Economic Change and Political Liberalization in Sub-Saharan Africa*, ed. Jennifer A. Widner. Baltimore, MD: Johns Hopkins University Press, 1994.

Coulson, Andrew. *Tanzania: A Political Economy.* Cambridge, U.K.: Cambridge University Press, 1982.

Nyerere, Julius. *Freedom and Socialism.* New York: Oxford University Press, 1968.

Sivji, Issa. *Law, State and the Working Class in Tanzania.* London: James Currey, 1984.

Mwesiga Baregu

TATOOING. *See* **Body Adornment and Clothing.**

TAYLOR, CHARLES GAHNHAY

(1948–). The president of Liberia 1997 to 2003, Charles Taylor was born on January 28, 1948, in Arthington, Liberia, to Nelson (a lawyer and judge) and Zoe Taylor. He was educated in Monrovia and attended college in the United States, receiving a degree in economic theory at Bentley College (Massachusetts) in 1977. After graduation he remained in the United States, working with the Union of Liberian Associations

Liberian president Charles Taylor (1948–), left, being escorted by UN personnel to a plane departing for the Hague, June 20, 2006. After being charged with eleven counts of war crimes for allegedly helping rebels in the Sierra Leone civil war, he tried to escape from the Nigerian seaside home where he was living in exile in March 2006. He was caught a day later and returned to the United Nations in Sierra Leone. © SPECIAL COURT FOR SIERRA LEONE HANDOUT/EPA/CORBIS

in the Americas. He led a protest against Liberia's then-president, William Tolbert, when the latter visited New York in 1979. President Tolbert suggested that Taylor bring his talents to Liberia, and in the following year, Taylor returned home.

Within months of Taylor's return, President Tolbert was assassinated by rebel insurgents led by Samuel K. Doe. Taylor managed to secure a position in the ministry of finance, and he was accused of embezzlement of nearly one million dollars. In October 1983 he fled to avoid arrest, turning up in Plymouth, Massachusetts. There he was arrested and held for extradition, but he escaped and fled to Libya. Five years later, he returned to Liberia at the head of the National Patriotic

Front of Liberia (NPFL), intending to challenge Doe's rule.

The NPFL forces unseated Doe, who was executed in 1990, but the organization had split into two factions, one led by Taylor, the other by Prince Yormie Johnson. The victory over Doe led directly into a new civil war that left 200,000 people dead and another million displaced by the violence. In 1995 a peace accord was finally reached. Elections were held in 1997, which Taylor won with more than seventy percent of the vote. His administration was charged with corruption, and he was personally accused of supporting insurgent violence in neighboring Sierra Leone. In Liberia, the Liberians United for Reconciliation and Democracy (LURD) formed to militarily challenge Taylor's rule. The resulting civil war lasted through 2003.

International pressure against Taylor became overwhelming, and he was indicted by a U.N. tribunal for war crimes and crimes against humanity. He finally left Liberia to take refuge in Nigeria, whose president Olusegun Obasanjo has offered protection. The United Nations' indictment remains outstanding, as do other criminal charges against him.

See also **Liberia: History and Politics; Obasanjo, Olusegun; United Nations.**

BIBLIOGRAPHY

Levitt, Jeremy I. *The Evolution of Deadly Conflict in Liberia: From "Paternaltarianism" to State Collapse.* Durham, NC: Carolina Academic Press, 2005.

Obunleye, Bayo. *Behind Rebel Line: Anatomy of Charles Taylor's Hostage Camps.* Enugu, Nigeria: Delta of Nigeria, 1995.

Yoder, John Charles. *Popular Political Culture, Civil Society, and State Crisis in Liberia.* Lewiston, NY: Edwin Mellen Press, 2003.

NANCY GRATTON

Empress Taytu of Abyssinia (c. 1851–1918). When Menelik II's health began to decline, his wife, Empress Taytu, began to make decisions for the country that angered rivals and favored family members. HULTON ARCHIVE/GETTY IMAGES

TAYTU, EMPRESS (c. 1851–1918).

The wife of Menelik II, who ruled Ethiopia from 1889 to 1913, Taytu Betel was born in Gondär to one of Ethiopia's most noble families. She traced her descent back to the founders of the Solomonid Dynasty. She was married and divorced four times before finally marrying King Sahle Maryam of Shewa in 1883. When Ethiopia's emperor, Yohannes IV (1868–1889) was killed in battle, Sahle Maryam succeeded him to the throne. He took the name Menelik II and Taytu Betel became empress.

Taytu exerted a strong, conservative influence on the conduct of imperial affairs. She opposed Westernizing trends in Ethiopia, and was personally implicated in the breakdown of talks with Italy regarding that nation's involvement in Ethiopian affairs, particularly Italy's desire to annex the northern province of Eritrea. When Italy invaded Ethiopia from the north, Taitu joined her husband in leading the army to oppose the incursion. At the Battle of Adwa (1896) the Italians were routed, and Ethiopia declared its full independence.

Menelik II courted the good opinion of the public, so Taytu was often the one to announce difficult or unpopular decisions. Thus she preserved her husband's popularity at the expense of her own. When Menelik grew ill in 1902, she took full control of the government. A resentful public accused her of nepotism and corruption, and she was ultimately forced to cede power to Lij Iyasu, Menelik II's grandson and presumptive heir to the throne, in 1910.

Taytu was ordered to confine her activities to the care of her husband. At his death, of a stroke, she was banished to the town of Entoto, but continued meddling in politics. She is believed to have conspired in the overthrow of Iyasu, whom she saw as hostile, and in the installation of her stepdaughter, Zauditu (with whom she was close), as empress in 1916. Upon her death in 1918 her body was brought to Addis Ababa and interred beside her husband at the Baeta Le Mariam Monastery.

See also **Ethiopia and the Horn, History of (1600 to 1910); Ethiopia, Modern; Menelik II; Queens and Queen Mothers.**

BIBLIOGRAPHY

Prouty, Chris. *Empress Taytu and Menelik II: Ethiopia 1833–1910.* Trenton, NJ: Red Sea Press, 1986.

NANCY E. GRATTON

TECHNOLOGICAL SPECIALIZATION PERIOD, HISTORY OF (C. 19,000 TO 5,000 BCE).

During the fourteen millennia from 19,000 to 5000 BCE, a succession of transforming shifts in economy and culture redirected the course of human history, not just in Africa, but worldwide.

The opening period of this span, the era of Last Glacial Maximum, 19,000–12,000 BCE, brought catastrophic reversals of fortune to many regions of the earth. The glaciers of the northern hemisphere pushed much farther south in Europe and North America. In Europe, human populations survived only in a few habitable refuge areas. The whole of the vast Siberian regions of Asia became uninhabitable and were abandoned by human beings. In Africa, a period of climates far drier and significantly cooler than those at present took hold across much of the continent. The Sahara expanded several hundred miles farther south than it is in the early twenty-first century, becoming hyperarid and entirely uninhabitable. The rain forests of Africa survived only in remnant areas at the east and west sides of the Congo Basin and in one or two parts of West Africa. Recent studies suggest that, even in Africa, the areas of more favorable climate became population refugia. One such notable region seems to have lain in and around the southeastern Ethiopian highlands. Others may have been in West Africa and in parts of the Congo Basin.

The Last Glacial Maximum was also the prelude to a new age of sweeping demographic and cultural transformation across Africa. After 12,000 BCE

another massive climatic shift began. It took place in two stages, with an initial period of warmer, wetter climates taking hold in the northern hemisphere between about 12,000 and 10,800 BCE. Climatic conditions deteriorated again during the Younger Dryas period, from around 10,800 to 8500 BCE. But from 8500 onward there came a long return to warmer, wetter conditions all across the continent. The Sahara became, as it had not been for more than 60,000 years, a sweep of mixed steppe and grassland environments. Rain forest reexpanded across the Congo Basin, and the rain forests of West Africa joined together in one coastal hinterland belt that extended 100 to 150 miles farther inland than it does today. Climatic amelioration opened up Africa to the regrowth of human population and to vast new population expansions, most notably the resettlement of the Sahara after a more than 40,000-year hiatus.

The regions of northeastern Africa surrounding the southern Ethiopian highlands became a major source of new cultural expansions in the millennia following the close of the Ice Age. All four of the major language families of Africa—Afrasian (Afro-Asiatic), Khoesan, Nilo-Saharan, and Niger-Kordofanian—are most plausibly argued to have originated there. The ancestral languages (or protolanguages) of these families were each likely spoken in the period preceding 11,000 BCE and following the end of the Last Glacial Maximum. The speakers of each protolanguage lived by hunting and gathering. In other words, their societies existed before the eras of the cultivation of crops or the raising of livestock. In addition, the proto-Khoesan, proto-Afrasian, and proto-Nilo-Saharan peoples—and possibly the proto-Niger-Kordofanian, as well—each used bows and arrows. In Africa, these weapons date at least as early as 13,000–11,000 BCE. The climatic amelioration at the end of the Last Glacial Maximum, it may be suggested, opened the way to the expansion of each language family widely across Africa.

The proto-Afrasian society most likely resided in the Ethiopian highlands by or before 13,000 BCE. Some Afrasian-speaking peoples then spread northward to Egypt possibly as early as 12,000 BCE. One offshoot of this settlement, a people who spoke the language ancestral to the much later Semitic languages of the Middle East, soon after this time crossed the Sinai Peninsula into the Palestine-Syria regions. The most probable archaeological correlation of this ancestral Semitic settlement is with the Mushabian culture that spread from northern Egypt into the Levant shortly before 10,000 BCE. In the ninth millennium BCE, a further westward expansion of Afrasian peoples across the northern half of the Sahara took place. These communities, which have been linked to the makers of the widespread Capsian archaeological tradition of the northern Sahara, spoke languages ancestral to those of the latter-day Berbers of the Sahara and North Africa and to those of the Chadic peoples, who live in the present-day Lake Chad region south of the Sahara.

The proto-Khoesan society is best placed in northern East Africa, immediately south of the Ethiopian highlands. In the period following 13,000 BCE, Khoesan languages came to be spoken across much of eastern Africa and, after 8000 BCE, across all of southern Africa as well. The spread of this cultural tradition and language family appears to correlate with the spread of different varieties of the Eastern African Microlithic (or Wilton) archaeological complex.

A third major African language family, Nilo-Saharan, originated along the western margins of the southern Ethiopian highlands. Before 8500 BCE, Nilo-Saharan peoples had established themselves widely in the areas surrounding the middle Nile River.

Proto-Niger-Kordofanian, the ancestor language of the fourth major African language family, may also have been spoken in the Middle Nile Basin, but if so in areas just to the west of the Nile River. Speakers of languages of the western branch of Niger-Kordofanian, Niger-Congo, moved far west to the savannas of West Africa at a period that is still uncertain. From 8500 to 5000 BCE, speakers of the Niger-Congo languages extended their territories into most of West Africa. After 3000 BCE, the expansion of the Bantu subgroup of Niger-Congo spread this language family and its ancient cultural tradition through the Congo Basin and, since 500 BCE, across a majority of eastern and southern Africa.

Along with population growth and expansion, the end of the Last Glacial Maximum set off an era of deep change in many aspects of culture. In several regions of Africa, people developed more

Some of the many varieties of Sorghum bicolor grown during the rainy season in North Cameroon. African farmers domesticated this grain crop, important today in such far-flung parts of the world as north China and the American Middle West, sometime before 5000 BCE. COURTESY OF NICHOLAS DAVID

specialized and more productive technologies of gathering and hunting to cope with or to take advantage of the new plant and animal environments. In northeastern Africa, for example, Afrasian communities turned to the intensive collection of wild grains sometime before 8500 BCE and so were able to take particular advantage of the great expansion of grassland in the far eastern and northern Sahara. Nilo-Saharan peoples along the Nile, in contrast, turned to an intensive exploitation of aquatic food resources, using harpoons and new fishing techniques. After 8500 BCE, their descendants settled all across the southern half of the Sahara, as rivers began to flow in those regions and new lakes swelled in size. Other closely related Nilo-Saharan communities took an alternative tack: they moved northward with the advance of grassland and steppe into the eastern Sahara and became wild grain collectors, as had their Afrasian neighbors.

The Khoesan societies resisted many of these trends. They responded to the changing environmental opportunities by adopting a fully microlithic stone tool technology and developing eclectic and flexible new methods of foraging, adaptable to a great variety of savanna and steppe environments. They seem everywhere to have retained the small band structure of the previous historical age,

50,000 BP to 19,000 BCE, and, if the example of the modern-day Hadza of Tanzania is any guide, relied on coalitions of close female relations as the social focus of the band.

In contrast, population growth must have been a much more crucial factor for peoples of the other three African language families. Among Afrasian, Nilo-Saharan, and Niger-Kordofanian peoples, there arose early a new kind of institution, unilineal kinship, capable of binding together a much bigger group of people than a small gathering and hunting band. Unilineal kin groups existed among these societies either already at the period when the proto-languages were still spoken or came into being in the immediately succeeding eras. In unilineal systems of descent, people belong to lineages or clans. Lineages and clans are social alliances that arise when local communities grow large enough in size that allegiance to one's close kin no longer suffices to sustain cooperative relations. People who belong to a lineage or clan claim descent from a common ancestor who lived many generations before. In expanding the claim of kinship to wider groups of people than their own close relatives, people extend the duties of cooperation and hospitality required by kinship to a larger community than a band. Apparently, among Afrasian, Nilo-Saharan, and Niger-Kordofanian peoples, the climatic amelioration of the post-Ice Age era led to the emergence of hamlet- or village-sized local residential units and to more sedentary kinds of gathering and hunting, and thus to the need for the more inclusive social groupings that unilineal kinship provides.

Historians have suggested that, in each case, the earliest clans and lineages among these peoples were governed by matrilineal rules of descent. Considering that the common basis of band cohesion among human beings of the period before the end of the Last Glacial Maximum is likely to have been the coalition of close female kin, this outcome is hardly surprising. A local band organized around a core group of women related to each other as sisters, daughters, and mothers is an already matrilocal residential group, bound together by the descent of the women of the coalition from the same grandmother or great-grandmother. The development of a matrilineage or matriclan structure was simply the expansion of the female coalition into a larger matrilocal group, whose common female ancestor lived significantly farther back in the past than a grandmother or great-grandmother. Matrilocal residence would have been carried over into the new matrilineal kinship system and probably would have remained customary everywhere in Africa for thousands of years.

As Christine Ahmed-Saidi has discovered in studying the history of farming communities of the past 2,000 years in East-Central Africa, the continuing existence of female kin coalitions is compatible with membership in a wider matriclan or matrilineage. Such female coalitions may well therefore have persisted as subunits within the matrilineal clans and lineages of the early Afrasian, Nilo-Saharan, and Niger-Kordofanian peoples. In East-Central Africa down to the twentieth century CE, these female coalitions remained the social units to which young men had to go to obtain wives. The men gained approval as suitors by undertaking many months or even years of bride service to the group, carrying out chores and assisting in the work of the women's households. Female matrikin coalitions backed up their social authority through their control over the initiation of their daughters into womanhood and over their daughters' access to the tools and symbols of adulthood, and through ritual sanctions, the most important and ancient of which were the rules of mother-in-law avoidance directed at sons-in-law.

Nearly everywhere in Africa, patrilineal descent and patrilocal residence did not begin to replace matrilineal descent and matrilocal residence until after 5000 BCE and, usually, not until long after that time. Large regions of the continent—including most of the southern savanna belt from Angola to Mozambique, along with scattered areas in West Africa, East Africa, Eritrea, and Sudan—remain matrilineal in descent even now. The single possible early exception may have been peoples of the Cushitic branch of the Afrasian family, whose territories in the early twenty-first century extend from the southeast corner of Egypt through the Horn of Africa to central Tanzania in the south. This grouping of societies may have become patrilineal as early as the period 8000–5000 BCE.

With the sweeping social changes of the era from 12,000 to 5000 BCE came major changes in ideas and beliefs. The shamanistic type of religion characteristic of most human societies from 50,000 BP to 19,000 BCE declined greatly in importance after 8500. Only among Khoesan people has this type of belief system continued to prevail—not surprisingly, because the Khoesan, after all, maintained down to recent centuries the small local band organization typical of 50,000 BP to 19,000 BCE.

Shamanism still existed, it seems likely, among the early Nilo-Saharan peoples of 13,000–8500 BCE, but by probably the eighth millennium a new belief system, Sudanic religion, had taken hold among most Nilo-Saharan groups. This religion was monotheistic, with one God or Divinity overseeing existence. The Sudanic belief system spread from the Nilo-Saharans to the Cushitic peoples of the Horn of Africa before 5000 BCE.

Shamanism persisted down to relatively recent times among the peoples of the Nuba Mountains of Sudan, who spoke languages of the Kordofanian branch of the Niger-Congo family. The peoples of the Niger-Congo branch of the family, however, developed a new and different religion by the period 9000–8000 BCE. The Niger-Congo religion recognized three levels of spirit: the Creator God, who after creating the world no longer actively engaged with it; individual spirits whose realms were particular local territories, such as the watershed of a particular stream; and the spirits of the ancestors. Everywhere, by far the most important and active concern in Niger-Congo religious observance was the ancestors.

As far back as the proto-Afrasian period, Afrasian societies followed a still different belief system that we call *henotheism*. In henotheism, the people who belong to a particular clan or regional group of related clans have their own particular clan deity. Their primary religious duties are to their own deity, although they also recognize that other clans or clan groups have their own distinct deities. Remnants of these henotheistic beliefs lasted, for example, down to the predynastic era among the ancient Egyptians, who were cultural descendants of the proto-Afrasians. Under the early pharaohs of Egypt, as part of the political unification of their domains at the end of the fourth millennium BCE, the local deities of the different nomes were brought into a common religious pantheon, thus converting the henotheism of predynastic Egypt into the polytheistic religion of early dynastic Egypt.

Art changed but did not lose its salience in the new religious environments. The archaeologist Augustine Holl has argued that the extensive rock art of the Sahara, so notable from 8000 BCE onward, evoked ceremonies of adolescent initiation and not shamanism, despite its clearly ritual symbolism. In Niger-Congo societies, wood sculptures of the spirits of the ancestors, scholars believe, became the newly important artistic form. A related art form was the carving of masks, important in ceremonies of all kinds, including rites of passage of young people to adulthood. After the Niger-Congo societies took up agriculture, masks figured importantly as well in the ceremonies of planting and harvest. In sharp contrast, right up to the early twentieth century, the Khoesan peoples in both East Africa and southern Africa, who preserved a shamanistic belief system, maintained in their rock art the ancient human ritual focus on the trance experiences of the shamans.

After 8500 BCE a new series of changes, both in subsistence practices—in the ways people get

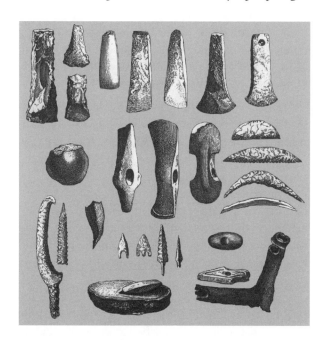

Assorted stone tools used by prehistoric man. Tools include axes along the top; arrowheads on the second row from the bottom. Polished stone ax technology widely came into use in West Africa between 6000 and 3000 BCE, as agricultural ways of life became established in those regions. SHEILA TERRY/PHOTO RESEARCHERS INC. IMAGE TAKEN FROM BILDER ATLAS.

food—and in tool technology, began to unfold in Africa. As in a number of other distant parts of world, so also in Africa the period 8500–5000 BCE was the Age of Agricultural Invention. The cultivation of crops and the raising of animals for food had ultimately revolutionary consequences for human culture and society. The reason is simple: the new subsistence technologies had the potential to multiply many times over the quantities of food that people could obtain from the same amount of land by gathering and hunting.

In Africa, sometime around 8500 BCE, those Nilo-Saharan people who had previously been wild grain collectors in the eastern Sahara began the earliest deliberate raising of cattle in all of world history. Between 7500 and 5000 BCE, three further developments raised agricultural invention to a new level of historical salience in Africa. One was the addition by the Nilo-Saharan cattle raisers of cultivated crops, such as sorghum, to their subsistence repertory. A second crucial change was the expansion, between 6000 and 5000 BCE, of these Nilo-Saharan farmers and cattle raisers across the southern Sahara and the Sahel belt of Africa, as far west as the Inland Delta of the Niger River, bringing their new economy to all those regions. The third transformative development of the era was the separate invention of a different agricultural system, based on the raising of yams and a variety of other crops, by the Niger-Congo peoples of West Africa.

Three major African technological breakthroughs accompanied the new developments in subsistence between 9000 and 5000 BCE. Most notably, Nilo-Saharan peoples of the southern Sahara invented pottery sometime before 8500 BCE. In so doing, they became the earliest inventors of ceramic technology in world history. Both the cattle-raising Nilo-Saharans and the related Nilo-Saharan peoples who followed aquatic-based livelihoods in the ninth millennium BCE participated in this invention. A second major technological advance of the era was the development among both Nilo-Saharan and Niger-Congo peoples of techniques for making polished stone tools, in particular, the polished stone axes useful in clearing fields for the cultivation of crops.

A third striking invention was cotton-weaving technology, created by Nilo-Saharan-speaking peoples living in the eastern Sudan of Africa between about 6000 and 5000 BCE. Archaeologists find spindlewhorls for spinning cotton thread in the habitation sites of this time, revealing that these communities had begun to domesticate the indigenous African cotton species and to embark on their own development of cotton textile technology, separate from the equally early invention of this technology far off in India. Possibly equally early, Niger-Congo inhabitants of high-rainfall areas of West Africa invented a distinct loom technology of their own, designed to produce a different textile—raffia cloth, woven from the fibers of the raffia palm.

Wherever people adopted the raising of crops and animals between 9000 and 5000 BCE, whether in Africa or elsewhere in the world, these new practices led to growth in the size of local communities and to the gradual growth of human population overall. Demographic growth further entrenched the reliance of people on unilineal institutions of kinship because, increasingly, such institutions provided individuals with built-in support groups in societies consisting of numerous lineages and clans. Together, these various developments in kinship, belief, technology, subsistence, and demography laid the historical foundations for the emergence in Africa after 5000 BCE of new kinds of political institutions, the earliest forms of social stratification, the first towns and the first states, and new directions of technological innovation.

See also **Archaeology and Prehistory; Ceramics; Desertification, Reactions to, History of (c. 5000 to 1000 BCE); Early Human Society, History of (c. 50,000 BP to 19,000 BCE); Ecosystems: Savannas; Kinship and Descent; Languages.**

BIBLIOGRAPHY

Ahmed-Saidi, Christine. *Before Eve Was Eve.* Ph.D. diss. University of California at Los Angeles, 1996.

Ehret, Christopher. "Sudanic Civilization." In *Agricultural and Pastoral Societies in Ancient and Classical History,* ed. Michael Adas. Philadelphia: Temple University Press, for the American Historical Association, 2001.

Ehret, Christopher. *The Civilizations of Africa: A History to 1800.* Charlottesville: University of Virginia Press, 2002.

Ehret, Christopher. "History in the Sahara: Society and Economy in the Early Holocene." In *History and the Testimony of Language.* Berkeley: University of California Press, 2007.

Holl, Augustin. *Saharan Rock Art.* Lanham, MD: Rowman and Littlefield, 2004.

Kuper, Rudolph, and Stefan Kröpelin. "Climate-Controlled Holocene Occupation in the Sahara: Motor of Africa's Evolution." *Science* 313 (August 11, 2006): 803–807.

Lewis-Williams, J. David. *A Cosmos in Stone: Interpreting Religion and Society through Rock Art.* Walnut Creek, CA: AltaMira Press, 2002.

Wendorf, Fred, and Romuald Schild. "Nabta Playa and Its Role in Northeastern African History." *Anthropological Archaeology* 20 (1998): 97–123.

CHRISTOPHER EHRET

TELEVISION. *See* **Media: Radio and TV.**

TEMPELS, PLACIED (1906–1977). Placied Tempels was a Franciscan missionary and the author of *La philosophie bantoue* and the founder of the Jamaa, a charismatic religious movement that developed inside the Catholic church in Zaire in the 1950s. Tempels maintained that the "Bantu," an ethnicization of the speakers of many distinct modern languages in central, eastern, and southern Africa, like all "peoples," have "a complete positive philosophy" concerning human beings, their surroundings, the felicitous and adverse events they experience, and life, death, and the hereafter. He identified "vital force" as the fundamental notion of being in Bantu ontology—a being that is constitutively interconnected and interdependent with ancestors and descendants.

The Jamaa grew out of Tempels's firsthand insights into the Bantu worldview. It developed through intense, face-to-face interaction between Tempels, a small group of his Franciscan colleagues who belonged to the movement and were his charismatic lieutenants, and the African lay women and men who constituted the core membership of the Jamaa. These lay members typically came from urban, industrial backgrounds; they ranged in age from thirty to fifty years old; and they were usually initiated into the Jamaa as couples. One of the most distinctive features of the movement is that it emerged and evolved inside of an ecclesia, to which it brought core Bantu-African beliefs, values, symbols, and rites. In turn, the location of the

Jamaa inside the church, and the way its members participated in and were influenced by a Christian vision, profoundly transformed basic attitudes and behaviors integrally associated with African patterns of kinship, magic, and religion.

In response to the growing disquietude about the Jamaa on the part of the Catholic bishops of the Congo, Tempels was confined in 1963 to his convent in Hasselt, Belgium, by his Franciscan superiors. In the last phase of his life, he witnessed from a distance a greater structuration and regulation of the Jamaa by a 1971 Congo/Zaire government ordinance that applied to all religious movements, and by a set of statutes and bylaws issued by the Jamaa in 1974, which were required by the bishop of Lubumbashi.

The Jamaa—Tempels's most significant contribution—has survived his death. To our knowledge, it currently exists in three forms: a remnant of the original Jamaa; a Jamaa domesticated by the Catholic hierarchy; and an "underground" Jamaa, called Katete.

See also **Christianity.**

BIBLIOGRAPHY

De Craemer, Willy. *The Jamaa and the Church: A Bantu Catholic Movement in Zaire.* Oxford: Clarendon Press, 1977.

Tempels, Placied. *La philosophie bantoue*, 2nd edition, trans. A. Rubbens. Paris: Présence africaine, 1961.

WILLY DE CRAEMER

TÉTOUAN. Built as a fortress five centuries ago, Tétouan, in Berber originally *Tittawin*, meaning "springs of water," is one of Morocco's most flourishing commercial and cultural cities. Its five centuries of history are clearly reflected in the medina's urban structure, architecture, traditional society, culture, and arts. Of Moroccan cities, Tétouan is one of the closest to Europe and is connected to other parts of Morocco by land and air. It includes three historical sections that complement each other: the five-century-old Islamic medina classified by the United Nations Education, Scientific, and Cultural Organization (UNESCO) as a world cultural heritage city in

1997; the early-twentieth-century Spanish colonial town; and the urban areas that developed since Morocco's independence in 1956.

The population of Tétouan in 2007 is approximately 600,000. Historically its inhabitants included numerous ethnic groups such as the Andalusians and the Arab and Berber tribes of northern Morocco. The city's historical contact with European countries, especially Spain, has always been important. Tétouan's population is highly diverse. Factors like immigration to Tétouan from different parts of Morocco and from Morocco to Europe have had a tremendous impact on it.

Tétouan has always been strategically important because of its privileged geographical location, situated on the edge of Mount Dersa in the Rif Mountains and overlooking the plains of Martil, which stretch for six miles to the Mediterranean coast. Built by Andalusian emigrants from Granada, Tétouan developed as a strategic fortress and trading center. Its military confrontations with the Portuguese and the Spaniards and its commercial maritime relations with the main Mediterranean ports enabled Tétouan to emerge as an important commercial link between the internal trading cities in Morocco and Europe.

Important events in Tétouan's history include its conquest by the Spanish army in 1860, which had drastic financial consequences, and its becoming the capital of the Spanish Protectorate in Morocco from 1912 to 1956.

In the first decade of the 2000s Tétouan is experiencing profound economic, social, and cultural transformation. New economic projects, infrastructure of roads and highways, and numerous tourist projects will introduce significant changes in its urban features and lifestyle. Because of its strategic situation, Tétouan receives large numbers of immigrants from different parts of Morocco, which explains its increasing population and the great pressure on its growing economy. The road between Tétouan and Ceuta, a Spanish enclave in North Africa, is one of Morocco's busiest roads. Tétouan's strategic location will enable it to play an important role in the development of the provinces of North Morocco in the coming years.

See also **Colonial Policies and Practices: Spanish; Morocco; Morocco: History of (1000 to 1900).**

BIBLIOGRAPHY

Benaboud, Mhammad, ed. *Tétouan Capitale Méditerranée.* Rabat: Publications de l'Association Tétouan Asmir, 2004.

MHAMMAD BENABOUD

TÉWODROS (c. 1820–1868). Born around 1820 to Amhara noble parents, Téwodros was originally named Kasa. He was educated at monasteries and began his independent career in the early 1840s as a *shefta*, or bandit. In 1852 he launched a military campaign that, three years later, brought him to coronation as emperor of a fractured, weak Ethiopian state, when he took the apocalyptic regal name Téwodros. He promised to revive the monarchy and reunite the country, which, since the 1770s, had collapsed into a cluster of warring fiefdoms. His initial successes foundered on entrenched

CANEDI

Râs Kassà (o Teodoro).

Téwodros II (c. 1820–1868). Emperor of Ethiopia Téwodros is considered to be the first ruler of modern Ethiopia.

local interests. His hopes of introducing Western technology were foiled by the disinterest of the British, to whom he turned for help.

The British failure to acknowledge a letter of friendship, written in 1862, led Téwodros to imprison their consul and a number of other foreigners. The result was a British expedition to the emperor's fortress of Maqdala and Téwodros's death by suicide on April 13, 1868. The first of Ethiopia's modern rulers, Téwodros began the process of national reunification and pioneered the use of the modern vernacular, Amharic, over the classical literary language, Ge'ez. He remains a popular figure in poetry and prose in modern Ethiopia, of particular appeal to the young and the radical.

See also **Ethiopia and the Horn, History of (1600 to 1910); Warfare.**

BIBLIOGRAPHY

Rubenson, Sven. *King of Kings: Tewodros of Ethiopia.* Addis Ababa: Haile Sellassie I University in association with Oxford University Press, 1966.

Zaneb. *The Chronicle of King Theodore of Abyssinia,* ed. Enno Littmann. New York: Charles Scribner's Sons, 1902.

DONALD E. CRUMMEY

TEXTILES. The cultural and economic significance of woven textiles and cloths produced by other techniques in Africa cannot be overestimated. Throughout the continent there are highly developed ideas of personal modesty and appropriate self-presentation that are intricately bound up with issues that include but are not limited to age, gender, social role, and religious affiliation. Both locally produced and imported cloths play key roles in these processes of establishing and maintaining social identities alongside other factors such as demeanor and deportment, jewelry, and in some cases body modification. In highland Ethiopia both men and women wear lightweight white cotton shawls called *shamma*, often with a border or *tibeb* of supplementary weft float patterns in silk or rayon. The precise way in which a *shamma* is worn can express the wearer's sadness, respect, confidence and at least a dozen other attitudes, while the width and elaboration of the *tibeb* is indicative of rank and wealth. The details of these ideas are usually locally specific, with their own processes of continuity and change, but in many cases they also draw on and interact with broader themes.

Since the Islamic jihads of the eighteenth and early nineteenth centuries, tailored and embroidered robes have become the predominant forms of prestige male dress across much of West Africa from Senegal to Cameroon, often displacing older forms such as wrapped cloth worn toga-style. Nevertheless, in areas such as southern Ghana wrapped kente cloths remain, and in some Yoruba areas of southwestern Nigeria one can still see a few important men at ceremonies wearing an indigo dyed wrapper cloth on top of a tailored robe.

At the same time the different paths taken to establish social identities within groups and the distinct textiles and other cloths forms that have developed in the course of these processes sometimes allowed differences between groups to become expressed through the use of textiles and dress. In most situations the expression of ethnic identities is a secondary aspect of the use of cloths in all forms. Senior Asante men and women attending a local chieftaincy ceremony may gain prestige by wearing *kente* cloths in part because they demonstrate a sense of Asante tradition that in the early twenty-first century is considered important, but they are not wearing them primarily to express the fact that they are Asante. However, in the wider context of a nationwide event, where people from other regions of Ghana also have important roles, dressing in that way explicitly affirms an Asante origin.

The economic significance of textiles in much of Africa is as great as their cultural role. In some regions of West Africa strips of woven cotton served as a currency well into the twentieth century, while squares of raffia cloth played a similar role in earlier centuries in coastal areas of the Congo and Angola. In Luanda in the seventeenth century the Portuguese colonial authorities tried to establish control over this cloth as a money by stamping each raffia sheet with an authorizing mark. Among the Lele and the Kuba further inland, raffia cloth was a kind of ritual currency suitable for paying certain social obligations between individuals and lineages rather than for everyday transactions.

Since the first contact with Europe in the sixteenth century, the trade of fabrics has played a key economic role. By some estimates, more than 50 percent of the (European) value of Africans' purchases from the Atlantic trade was textiles, mostly Indian cottons. Africans traded to acquire special and distinctively textured or patterned textiles—brocade, damask or silk fabrics, red cotton cloths, and the like. Europeans generally acquired African fabrics only to exchange them for slaves several hundred miles away. Handmade indigo dyed wrappers woven by Yoruba women were purchased by European traders from the Ijebu Yoruba and the Edo at Bénin (Nigeria) and sold for slaves in both Ghana and Congo. Cloths woven under Portuguese supervision by slaves on the Cape Verde archipelago were highly valued on the Guinea Coast. Africans themselves also traded textiles over long distances to meet highly specific local demands.

CLOTH PRODUCTION IN AFRICA

Barkcloth, which is beaten from the bark of a ficus tree (*Ficus natalensis*) is not a textile in the strict sense, but in much of central and parts of eastern Africa barkcloth filled the same role of bodily coverage and cultural expression as textiles elsewhere. Production of woven textiles, both for domestic use and for market trade, employed, and in some areas continues to employ thousands of men and women. Although the techniques of weaving have not changed, twenty-first-century textiles often look different from those produced earlier: weavers incorporate finer, industrially manufactured threads of intense colors to make possible a variety of new visual creations. In some cases, such as the wool and cotton blankets of the West African Sahel, these new materials have transformed what were previously very long-lasting styles. In other cases, for instance the Yoruba narrow-strip woven cloth known as *aso oke*, they have merely added new impetus to what were already highly dynamic and fashion-oriented styles.

Weaving has a long history in all of north and west Africa, Ethiopia, and coastal East Africa, along with many areas of Central Africa. In southern Africa it could be found in some locales but died out more than a hundred years ago.

Scholars of African textiles have classified the great diversity of loom types found on the continent on the basis of the number of heddles used. A heddle is a device for separating the longitudinal or warp threads held in tension by a loom into two groups, upper and lower, forming a vertical gap, called a shed, and thus allowing the passage of crosswise or weft threads between them. Double heddle looms incorporate a foot peddle for alternating the shed and thus allowing faster weaving. Among the double heddle looms found in Africa are various urban north African looms, the narrow strip loom found throughout West Africa, tripod looms in Sierra Leone and Liberia, a loom probably of Indian origin in Ethiopia and Somalia, and a number of looms in Madagascar. With the exception of Madagascar, only male weavers operated all these looms until recent decades.

On a single heddle loom alternate warp threads only are attached to the heddle and a set of sticks is manipulated to create the two sheds. Vertically mounted single heddle looms are used by Berber women in north Africa, by women in Togo, Bénin, Nigeria, and western Cameroon, and by men weaving raffia in southeast Nigeria and Central Africa. Horizontally mounted, single heddle mounted horizontally looms are used by Berber women, by men in North Cameroon, and the neighboring Benue Valley of Nigeria, and by women to produce silk *lambas* in Madagascar.

Each loom type has its own history, much of which can no longer be recovered. Although the spread of Islam promoted the trade in textiles within Africa and was an important factor in modifying modes of dress (as has been Christianity), earlier accounts that regarded contacts with Muslim northern Africa as sufficient explanation for the introduction of weaving south of the Sahara are greatly oversimplistic.

WEAVING IN WEST AFRICA

The oldest known textiles are nine fragments found in a king's grave at Igbo Ukwu (southeastern Nigeria), dating to the ninth century CE, well before Islam reached the region. Finds of very early textiles were also made in the Sahel (burial caves of the Tellem in the Bandiagara cliff in Mali). These cotton and wool fragments, found in great quantities, date back to the eleventh century CE. Analysis of thirteenth-century textile fragments recovered from a cistern in Benin City show complex decorative techniques were already in use. Shortly before 1655, the oldest complete extant African textiles from historical times—two gowns—made their way to Ulm, Germany.

Textile fibers that have been known for ages are cotton, wool, wild silk, bast, and raffia. Such industrially produced fibers as rayon or lurex play an important role in the textile trade. Weaving areas that are still active include both rural Berber and urban traditions in Morocco and Tunisia, various groups in Egypt, *shamma* weavers in highland Ethiopia, and numerous West African peoples. In the interior delta of the Niger river in Mali, Fulani men weave woolen *kaasa* covers and *Truearkila* blankets that in the past were important in the kola nut trade with Ghana and Sierra Leone. The Dogon substitute an indigo and white cotton blanket for the corpse of an important man in commemorative funerary rites.

In Beledougou (western Mali), Bamana women, in a labor-intensive process, paint cloth with a specially prepared mud to produce *bogolan fini*, or mud cloth, worn locally by hunters, musicians, and newly excised young women, and which has more recently become popular with tourists. Mandjak weavers in Senegambia and Guinea-Bissau, specialize in richly decorated, colorful cloths that urban women like to wear as *pagnes* (French for "wrapper cloths"). The weft-float patterns of synthetic silk, rayon, or lurex are woven with the aid of twenty-four or more supplementary heddles—a technical specialty distinctive to the region and derived from Portuguese influence in Cape Verde.

In Côte d'Ivoire the Dyula, particularly in the northern town of Kong, were important in diffusing weaving techniques such as warp *ikat*, currently a specialty of the Baule. The Guro and Senufo also weave a variety of finely patterned textiles, while in the south of the country the Dida produce small tie-dyed raffia cloths in shades of brown and red. In southern Ghana and Togo, *kente* cloths are famous. These large cloths, woven by Ewe and Asante weavers, are among the best known African textiles worldwide and still play an important role in Ghanaian ceremonial dress. A specialty known only to the Asante are *adinkra* cloths with black stamped motifs.

In southern Nigeria, Yoruba men, and since the 1990s increasing numbers of women, weave *aso oke* strip cloth that is fashionable for wear on special occasions throughout West Africa. Since the mid-1990s women cloth traders who encouraged Ghanaian weavers to work for the Nigerian market have blended aspects of Ewe traditions into the mix of *aso oke* designs. While Yoruba women have largely abandoned the vertical single heddle loom, it still flourishes in the Ebira town of Okene and is found in smaller numbers among the Hausa, Nupe, and Igbo, particularly at Akwete.

As recently as the 1930s, more than forty ethnic groups in the Democratic Republic of the Congo wove raffia, but by the early twenty-first century the great textile artisans were found in the ethnic groups of the kingdom of Kuba the southwestern part of the country. Simply put, two types of these textiles can be distinguished: small, richly decorated rectangular pieces, and long skirts. Raffia is woven exclusively by men, the small rectangles are decorated by women, but the long skirts consisting of many rectangles sewn together are decorated by men also depending on whether the skirt is for a man or a woman. As this final example suggests, textile production traditions frequently involved a complex interplay of gender-specific roles.

INDIGO IN WEST AFRICA

Indigo dyeing is an early biotechnology that was practiced in western Sudan (Mali) more than one thousand years ago and has played a key part in the evolution of textile design throughout West Africa. There were three main centers. Among the Yoruba women, dyers specialized in *adire* cloths produced by applying a cassava-based paste as a resist in a batik technique. Among the Hausa (northern Nigeria), indigo dyeing was practiced by men, (tie-dyeing was not important historically). Operating on a large scale as an export industry until the mid-twentieth century, their main products were lluxury robes and veils of very narrow strip cloth beaten with extra indigo paste to produce a metallic glaze that was highly prized by Tuareg nobles to the north. Among the Soninke and Wolof (Mali, Senegal), dyeing is practiced by women. A specialty of these dyers is extremely fine reserves with embroidery. The most important dyeing centers in the early twenty-first century are Kayes, Mali, and Labé, Guinea.

TEXTILE IMPORTS AND LOCAL MANUFACTURE

There is a long history of imports of luxury textiles through the trans-Saharan caravan trade, the Indian Ocean and Mediterranean trade networks, and since the sixteenth century via European coastal trade. Africans had very precise ideas about what cloths they desired, and these imports largely complemented rather than displaced domestic production. From the late nineteenth century larger quantities of lower value European, Indian, and more recently Chinese textiles were imported and these, along with the products of local industrial manufacture have replaced locally woven cloths for everyday wear in most parts of Africa. Imported cloths provided a stimulus for the development of some distinctive local traditions, such as the appliqué flags of Fante *Asafo* companies in coastal Ghana or the bead decorated blankets of the Ndebele in South Africa. Other types of cloth have been developed specifically to supply African markets, most notably the resin-resist "African wax" prints worn throughout sub-Saharan Africa and the pictorial *kanga* of the Swahili coast in the East.

See also **Art; Benin City; Body Adornment and Clothing; Money; Slave Trades.**

BIBLIOGRAPHY

Bolland, Rita. *Tellem Textiles: Archaeological Finds from Burial Caves in Mali's Bandiagara Cliff.* Amsterdam: Royal Tropical Institute, 1991.

Gilfoy, Peggy Stoltz. *Patterns of Life: West-African Strip-Weaving Traditions.* Washington, DC: Smithsonian Institution Press, 1987.

Idiens, Dale, and K. G. Ponting, eds. *Textiles of Africa.* Bath, U.K.: Pasold Research Fund, 1980.

Kriger, C. E. *Cloth in West African History.* Lanham: Altamira 2006.

Kusimba, C. M.; J. C. Odland; and B. Bronson; eds. *Unwrapping the Textile Traditions of Madagascar.* Los Angeles: Fowler Museum of Cultural History, 2004.

Lamb, Venice. *West African Weaving.* London: Shell, 1975.

Lamb, Venice, and Alastair Lamb. *Au Cameroun: Weaving—Tissage.* Hertingfordbury, U.K.: Roxford, 1981.

Lamb, Venice, and Alastair Lamb. *Sierra Leone Weaving.* Hertingfordbury, U.K.: Roxford, 1984.

Lamb, Venice, and Judy Holms. *Nigerian Weaving.* Roxford, U.K.: H.A. and V.A. Lamb, 1980.

Paydar, Niloo Imami, and Ivo Grammet, eds. *The Fabric of Moroccan Life* Indianapolis: Indianapolis Museum of Art, 2002.

Perani, Judith, and Norma H.Wolff. *Cloth, Dress and Art Patronage in Africa* Oxford: Berg, 1999.

Picton, John, and John Mack. *African Textiles,* 2nd edition. London: British Museum Press, 1989.

Ross, Doran H. *Wrapped in Pride: Ghanaian Kente and African American Identity.* Los Angeles: UCLA Fowler Museum of Cultural History, 1998.

Schädler, Karl-Ferdinand. *Weaving in Africa South of the Sahara.* Munich: Prestel, 1987.

Smithsonian Institution. *History, Design, and Craft in West African Strip-Woven Cloth.* Papers presented at a symposium organized by the National Museum of African Art, February 18–19, 1988.

Spring, Christopher, and Julie Hudson. *North African Textiles.* London: British Museum Press, 1995.

BERNHARD GARDI
REVISED BY DUNCAN CLARKE

THEATER

This entry includes the following articles:
ANGLOPHONE CENTRAL AND EASTERN AFRICA
ANGLOPHONE WESTERN AFRICA
FRANCOPHONE AFRICA
NORTHERN AFRICA
SOUTHERN AFRICA

ANGLOPHONE CENTRAL AND EASTERN AFRICA

Theater includes displays of suspenseful actions that are representations of events, in the real or supernatural world, before an audience—as well as certain forms of ritual, dance, and other performing arts. The term also refers to a space reserved for dramatic performances. Viewed as such, theater has been part and parcel of human existence, though manifested in different ways at specific historical moments. For instance, precolonial theater in eastern and Central Africa was collective, anonymous, participatory, and attuned to the people's rhythm of life. It came alive in a variety of social and cultural activities, such as birth, initiation, hunting, marriage, spirit-possession rituals, and death-related activities. Most of the indigenous theater forms were, however, suppressed during the colonial era, which generally denigrated non-Western cultures, especially in the efforts to introduce Christianity into the region. The main reason for this suppression was that cultural theatrical activities were perceived as the symbolic paths to the indigenous people's religious and moral base.

With the onset of colonialism, economic and political disputes were manifested in cultural reaffirmation. For instance, among the Gikuyu the tensions surrounding the practice of female circumcision, and its accompanying songs and dances, were replayed theatrically in central Kenya from 1928 to 1931 through the Muthirigu dances. Related precolonial dramatic forms were reactivated during the Mau Mau revolt of liberation. In addition, in northwestern Zambia the Makisi masquerade theater, which was originally performed during the initiation of boys, took a semi-commercial twist within the colonial setup, and in southern Mozambique the possession rituals of African spirits, such as Ndau and Ngoni, started incorporating foreigners in their portrayal of life. Similar innovations were made in the Gule wa Mkulu masquerade of the Nyau among the Chewa of Malawi, eastern Zambia, and Mozambique. The Eritrea community-based Theatre Project has been in existence since 1995 as part of national reconstruction after the thirty-year war with Ethiopia. The Project seeks to nurture Eritrean cultures through theater in indigenous languages, suppressed by Italian and English colonialism between 1890 and 1952. Evidently, performing arts in the region have continued to capture the changing patterns of life in the colonial and postcolonial era.

With the introduction of formal education, literary theater was incorporated into the curriculum, and between the 1920s and 1930s in eastern and Central Africa, formal colonialism made it imperative that exclusive European social spots be established in major colonial cities such as Mombasa, Nairobi, Dar es Salaam, Salisbury (present-day Harare), and Kampala. Consequently, cultural and leisure theaters were created in those areas that had a strong settler community. Permanent theaters such as the Kenya National Theatre in Nairobi, the Lusaka Theatre Club, and the Little Theatre clubs in Mombasa and Dar es Salaam, as symbols of cultural solidarity and group cohesion, were established. The main function of the theater clubs in their exclusiveness was to facilitate the self-definition of the European expatriate population in an African context. The dramas performed in the exclusive expatriate clubs were mainly productions from the European classical canon and domestic romantic comedies.

Mobile film units were established not only to provide entertainment in the townships but also to explain British policy and politico-military practice to the colonial subjects. Radio drama was imported and censored for an African audience. Theater for development, though occasionally utilizing precolonial dramatic forms, tended to be didactic and was especially geared toward the transmission of information on agriculture, primary health care, savings, loans, and tax collection. For instance, in Nyasaland (present-day Malawi) plays were performed in the 1930s at Ndirande Welfare Club in Blantyre to promote health care, and in the 1950s the interracial play *The False Friend* was performed to encourage progressive farming. In many cases, colonial lifestyles were parodied in theater. The Sajeni (Sergeant) masks in Northern Rhodesia (present-day Zambia), the militaristic mimes of the Beni dances in eastern Africa, the Kalela dances in Northern Rhodesia, the Malipenga in Nyasaland, and the work songs in Mozambique, were artistic responses to colonial culture.

Although the region is vibrant with drama, most theater activities are urban and school-based. Efforts are made to reach the rural areas through the free-traveling theater and popular theater movements. Moreover, the Annual Schools Drama Festival and the Music Festival have become crucial aspects of the region's educational system. In Kenya such theater groups as Miujiza Theatre Workshop Productions, the Theatre Company, Mbalamwezi Players, Igiza Productions, Chelepe Arts, Phoenix Players, Kenya Drama in Education Association, and the Eastleigh Drama Clubs are active. These Nairobi-based groups perform at the Kenya National Theatre established in 1953, Rahimtula Trust Building, the British Council, Goethe Institute, French Cultural Center, the Professional Centre, the Godown Arts Centre, the University of Nairobi Education Theatre, and Creative Arts Center at Kenyatta University. Performances in the rural areas occur in community social Halls, streets, market places, and bars.

Radio and television stations carry popular drama programs and health-related soap operas such as the award-winning 216-episode *Ushikwapo Shikamana* (If assisted assist yourself), scripted by Kimani Njogu and Ezekiel Kazungu and broadcast on national radio between 1986 and 1989; the 1993–1995 family harmony serial *Kuelewana ni Kuzungumza* (Dialogue is the basis of understanding), scripted by Kimani Njogu and Rocha Chimerah, and produced by Tom Kazungu for the national radio; *Tushauriane* (Let us advise each other), scripted by Felix Osodo and broadcast on national television between 1986 and 1987; and the Tanzanian *Twende na Wakati* (Let us go with the times), produced by Rose Haji and broadcast on national radio between 1993 and 1997. Some of these health-related soap operas follow the entertainment-education methodology advocated by the Mexican Miguel Sabido and used by the Population Communications International, New York, and Johns Hopkins University Center for Communication Programs in the transmission of messages for behavior change. A crucial component of that methodology is research conducted to develop the educational themes and social values to be encouraged or discouraged. The soap opera in the region has a strong following because, apparently, viewers relate to the experiences of the characters and receive immediate and anticipated gratification after the completion of the subplots or the sequence.

African playwrights have a strong desire to participate in social change through their art. The popular theater movement in the region, which has borrowed from the indigenous performing arts and the South American experience, especially as encapsulated in the writings of the Brazilian educator Paulo Freire and Augusto Boal, attempts to utilize theater for consciousness raising while proceeding from the premise that socioeconomic and political problems stem from a given social order that can be reversed.

Community theater is vibrant in the region. Kamirithu Community Educational and Cultural Centre that led to the detention of the Kenyan novelist and playwright Ngũgĩ wa Thiong'o (b. 1938) set in motion a series of similar experiments in Zimbabwe, Botswana, Tanzania, and Uganda. Ngũgĩ explores the contradictions, tensions, and struggles in the political and cultural terrain of a neocolony in the plays *Ngaahika Ndeenda* (I will marry when I want, 1980); *Trial of Dedan Kimathi* (1976, written with Micere Mugo), on Kenya's freedom struggle; *Maitu*

Njugira (Mother sing for me), yet to be a published opera; and *The Black Hermit* (1968). In the *Black Hermit* Ngũgĩ also addresses the issue of ethnic loyalty in Africa.

Francis Imbuga (b. 1947) has explored the issues of betrayal, greed, political intolerance, obsession with power, and the tensions between "traditional" and modern ways of life in postcolonial Kenya in most of his plays.

Most Tanzanian plays are in Swahili, the country's national language, and theater has over the years been used for mass mobilization, especially in the implementation of government projects. Ebrahim Hussein and Penina Mlama have published plays that capture historical and political events in the region. Hussein has published *Kinjeketile* (1967), which is based on the 1905–1907 Maji-Maji rebellion against German rule, as well as other plays that depict the postcolonial condition in Africa. Equally, Said Ahmed Mohamed has explored the politics of betrayal and the relationship between rulers and the ruled especially in *Kivuli Kinaishi* (1990) and *Amezidi* (1995).

In *Amezidi*, Said Ahmed examines Africa's depressed economic situation and dependence, including the relationship between African countries and financial institutions in the West. The theater arts department at the University of Dar es Salaam, Bagamoyo College of Art, and independent performing groups work together to enrich drama and theater in Tanzania. Most of the issues discussed in Tanzanian theater include the colonial and postcolonial experience, the status of women in a changing social, cultural, and political environment, corruption among the political and economic elite, and the relationship between African nations and the West. In addition, the Tanzanian government has consciously utilized theater for social development in a significant way.

The playwrights Stephen Chifunyise and Kabwe Kasoma have persisted in criticizing government policy and practice. Kasoma's plays—including *The Black Mamba* trilogy (1973), on the rise of Kenneth Kaunda to power and his achievements as the first president of Zambia, *The Long Arm of the Law* (1968), on Copperbelt township life, *Distortion, The Fools Marry* (performed at Chikwakwa Theatre in Lusaka on June 11, 1960), *Lobengula, Mankenda,* and *Katongo Chala*—all show his commitment not only to theater but also to the role that artists can play in changing the political and social direction of their countries. This is the same spirit that guides University of Zambia Dramatic Society (UNZADRAMS) in its performances. Victor Eleame Musinga in *The Tragedy of Mr. No Balance* (1974) attempts to show how individuals make opportunities where none seem to exist. Similarly, the Ethiopian playwright Tse-gaye Gabre-Medhim is committed to the representation of historical events and cultural tensions in his country in order to help shape it.

Theater is a very popular activity in Ugandan schools and in Kampala, especially through the efforts of professionals at Makerere University. The most popular plays in Luganda have been written by Wycliffe Kiyingi, who has scripted numerous stage, radio, and television plays and set up a traveling theater group. He contributed to the Makerere free-traveling theater movement of the mid-1960s. The drama group Theatre Ltd., founded in 1970, included people from various academic and theatrical backgrounds, such as David Rubadiri, Rose Mbowa, Robert Serumaga, Wycliffe Kiyingi, and Byron Kawadwa. Kawadwa also founded the Kampala City Players in 1964 and contributed significantly to popularizing theater in Luganda by creating socially committed theater based on indigenous performance styles. His semioperatic plays such as *St. Charles Lwanga* and *Oluyimba Lwa Wankoko* (The son of Wankoko) were very popular.

Idi Amin's coup of 1971 destabilized theater activities as Okot p'Bitek, David Rubadiri, and John Ruganda went into exile. John Ruganda has written *The Burdens* (1972), *Black Mamba* (1973), *Echoes of Silence* (1986), and *The Floods* (1980). Kawadwa was killed by Amin in 1977, and Robert Serumaga, author of *The Elephants* (1969), *A Play* (1974), and *Majangwa* (1974), died on the battlefield while attempting to liberate his country.

Such groups as the Kampala Shining Star Association, the Kayaayu Film Players, the Kintu Players, and the Baganda Cultural and Dramatic Society continued to function despite the many political difficulties they were encountering. Under the government of Yoweri Museveni, theater has again found a place to flourish. Most of the plays performed at the Uganda National Theatre are in Luganda. There are also plays by Alex Mukulu, who published *Ten Years of Banana*

(1993), on dictatorship. Traveling theater has continued over the years to take music, drama, and dance to different parts of the country for educational and entertainment purposes. Significantly, in the early 2000s there has been a profusion of semi-professional theater groups, such as Black Pearls, Teamline, Afri-Talent, and Ba Kayimbira. There has also been a growth of private theaters in the whole region. Generally, theater in eastern and Central Africa aspires to be socially relevant.

See also **Amin Dada, Idi; Dar es Salaam; Film and Cinema; Literature; Mombasa; Museveni, Yoweri; Ngũgĩ wa Thiong'o; Popular Culture: Central Africa; Popular Culture: Eastern Africa.**

BIBLIOGRAPHY

Banham, Martin, et al. *African Theatre in Development.* Oxford: James Currey, 1999.

Barber, Karin. "Popular Arts in Africa." *African Studies Review* 30, no. 3 (1987): 1–78.

Etherton, Michael. *The Development of African Drama.* London: Hutchison University Library for Africa, 1982.

Kerr, David. *African Popular Theater: From Pre-Colonial Times to the Present Day.* London: James Currey, 1995.

Mlama, Penina Muhando. *Culture and Development: The Popular Theatre Approach in Africa.* Uppsala, Sweden: Scandinavian Institute of African Studies, 1991.

Wambua, Kawive. "Creating a Counter Culture through Theatre." *Jahazi: Culture, Arts and Performance* 1, no. 1 (2006): 23–27.

KIMANI NJOGU

ANGLOPHONE WESTERN AFRICA

Theater is one of the major cultural institutions in West Africa that did not suffer a major setback in spite of colonialism. Theater in western Africa is the most vibrant and profuse on the entire continent.

TRADITIONAL THEATER

The epithet "traditional" is used advisedly to refer to indigenous performances that existed before the impact of colonialism and that continues to play an important role in the artistic life of communities, alongside the modern theater. It includes secular forms and recreational activities such as the storytelling *(Anansesem)* performances of the Akan of Ghana; the secular and religious motifs which are found in festivals such as the *kundum* festival (among the Ahanta of Ghana); the *okumkpa* festival of the Afikpo (Nigeria); the elaborate and spectacular masquerades that one finds in Sierra Leone, Nigeria, and Ghana; and the *Apidan* various theater forms of the Yoruba (Nigeria).

There has been intransigence on the part of some scholars in accepting certain African traditional performances as "drama" because of the relative lack of a "linguistic content" and a well-defined plot, and the multigeneric nature of the performances. Drama as a distinct social phenomenon has always existed in traditional African societies, largely in the form of opera, ballet, mime, and verbal performance.

Irrespective of the society in which it is found, traditional African theater is characterized by a number of common features: it is nonscripted (examples include the *apidan* and the *okumkpa*); song, music, and dance are preponderant (as in *anansesem*, and in the *kotéba* of Mali, to use an example from Francophone Africa); an assortment of stereotypical character types rather than individuals are portrayed (such as the prostitute, the deceitful merchant, and foreigners or "outsiders," as one finds in the *apidan*); and political and social institutions are ridiculed. (Corrupt chiefs and mercenary prophets of foreign religions are frequently subjects of attack, as in the *apidan*, the *okumkpa*, and the plays of the Ekong society of the Ibibio.)

MODERN THEATER

Modern western African theater takes its inspiration from both the traditional theater and the theater of the West as introduced by missionaries and colonialists. The bulk of the plays written come from Ghana and Nigeria.

The Ghanaian theater was started by nationalists who were not professional playwrights. Their major preoccupation was to remove the shackles of Britain's cultural imperialism from the Gold Coast (as Ghana was known before independence). Thus, the plays of the period were mainly philosophical and satirical in outlook. Ferdinand Kwasi Fiawoo's (1891–1969) *The Fifth Landing Stage* (1943) and Joseph Boakye Danquah's (1895–1965) *The Third Woman* (1943) explore Ewe and Akan philosophies, while Kobina Sakyi's (1892–1956) *The Blinkards* (1974) satirizes the Gold Coast elite for its slavish imitation of British habits.

The modern Ghanaian theater in English came into fruition with the works of Efua Theodora Sutherland (1924–1996) and Joe de Graft (1924–1978). Both were instrumental in the establishment of the Ghana School of Music, Dance, and Drama (now the School of Performing Arts at the University of Ghana). A playwright and a director, Sutherland was interested in researching and experimenting with the rich theatrical traditions of the Akan, especially the *anansesem* (Ananse stories). This interest was reflected in her collaboration with the people of Atwia-Ekumfi in building a community theater, known as Kodzi dan (storytelling house), and also in her major play, *The Marriage of Anansewa* (1975). This play explores the resources of the *anansesem* tradition: a narrator, songs (*mboguo* used for delineation of character, the depiction of mood and atmosphere, and the creation of suspense), dance, and the character of Ananse (the Spider) in dealing with the themes of national unity, greed, and avarice. Other plays by Sutherland include *Foriwa* (1967) and *Edufa* (1969). *Foriwa* deals with the theme of national reconstruction, while *Edufa* explores the dangers involved in the insatiable desire for wealth.

Joe de Graft's plays, mainly *Sons and Daughters* (1964), *Through a Film Darkly* (1970), and *Muntu* (1977), deal with domestic tensions as a result of social transformations in modern Ghana. For example, in *Sons and Daughters* de Graft, through the character Maanan, defends the visual and performing arts in Ghana against the myopic elites of the day, represented by James Ofosu, a lawyer.

After the pioneering works of Sutherland and de Graft came a new generation of playwrights, namely Ama Ata Aidoo (b. 1942), Asiedu Yirenkyi (b. 1945), and Mohammed ben Abdallah (b. 1944). Of the three, Aidoo is the most internationally recognized as a playwright and novelist. All three held ministerial appointments in the Provisional National Defense Council (PNDC) regime (1981–1992) of Jerry Rawlings.

Aidoo's *The Dilemma of a Ghost* (1965) explores the theme of the clash of cultures, represented by the marriage of Ato (a Ghanaian male) to Eulalie (an American woman). Her greatest achievement, however, is in *Anowa* (1969). Considered one of the finest plays on the continent, it examines the impact of the transatlantic slave trade on the psyche of the people of the Gold Coast during the 1870s. Anowa, the heroine of the play, confronts her patriarchal society and questions its involvement in the traffic of human beings.

Yirenkyi's reputation rests on a collection titled *Kivuli and Other Plays* (1980). *Kivuli* deals with the mundane theme of marital problems; *another play in this collection, Amma Pranaa*, employs the techniques of *anansesem*; and *a third, Blood and Tears*, is a bitter satire on the incompetence and hypocrisy of the new Ghanaian middle class represented by the character Charles Brown.

Abdallah has published six plays to date, all of which have been staged by Abibigroma (the resident theater company of the School of Performing Arts). The major ones are *The Fall of Kumbi* (1989), which deals with the fall of the ancient Ghana empire, and its precursor, *The Trial of Mallam Ilya* (1987), which examines in epic proportions the political and social repercussions of the overthrow of Kwame Nkrumah. Other theater practitioners worthy of mention in Ghana include directors Sandy Arkhurst and John Djisenu, playwright and critic Martin Owusu (author of *The Sudden Return and Other Plays*, 1973), Yaw Asare, and Efo Kodjo Mawugbe.

Nigeria, the most populous country in Africa, has produced over half the continent's output of dramatic literature. Until the late twentieth century, the theater was dominated by the literary giant Wole Soyinka (b. 1934), along with John Pepper Clark-Bekederemo (b. 1935) and Ola Rotimi (1938–2000).

Playwright, poet, novelist, critic, and winner of the Nobel Prize for Literature (1986), Soyinka's prominence in the world of drama stems from his use of Yoruba religion and folklore, his establishment of a theory of Yoruba-African tragedy, and his scathing attacks against despotic regimes in Africa. Soyinka has been imprisoned by the Nigerian authorities at least twice, and in the mid-1990s fled Nigeria to live in Paris for his personal safety. His major plays, in which he explores Yoruba metaphysics, include *The Road* (1965), *Death and the King's Horseman* (1975), and *A Dance of the Forests* (1963), which he was commissioned to write as part of Nigeria's independence celebrations in 1960. His satiric comedies include *The Lion and the Jewel* (1963), *The Trials of Brother Jero* (1964), and *A Play of Giants* (1984), in which he excoriates African dictators such as Idi Amin Dada (Uganda) and Jean-Bédel Bokassa (Central African Republic), as well as the two superpowers (the United States and the former Soviet Union). In his play *King Baabu* (2002), Soyinka also pens a scathing indictment of Nigeria's Abacha regime.

Clark-Bekederemo—poet, novelist, playwright, and critic—comes from the Niger Delta area of Nigeria. Consequently, his plays are set in and deal with the riverine culture of the area. His earlier plays, principally *Song of a Goat* (1961) and *Ozidi* (1966), deal with the need to sacrifice the pride and self-esteem of the individual in favor of the continued health and growth of the entire community. His trilogy, *The Bikoroa Plays* (1985), offers an insight into Nigerian social and political life from the beginning of the colonial period to the new Nigeria of the 1950s.

Rotimi is best known for his plays *The Gods Are Not to Blame* (1971) and *Our Husband Has Gone Mad Again* (1977). But his importance in Anglophone West African theater lies in the fact that he is the only major playwright to have specialized in the genre of the historical play. His first such play, *Kurumi* (1971), deals with the internecine wars of the Yoruba around the nineteenth century, while the play *Ovonramwen Nogbaisi* (1974) deconstructs colonial history in order to redeem the distorted view of Ovonramwem as a brutal despot.

In the mid-1970s, a new generation of playwrights emerged in Nigeria. Their vision is more radical, and they are even bolder in their use of and experimentation with traditional forms. Prominent among them are Zulu Sofola (1935–1995), Tess Onwueme (b. 1943), Femi Osofisan (b. 1946), Kole Omotoso (b. 1943), Bode Sowande (b. 1948), and Stella Oyedepo (b. 1951). In plays such as *Once Upon Four Robbers* (Osofisan, 1980); *Wazobia* (Onwueme, 1988); and *Worshippers of the Naira* (Oyedepo, 1994), the vast resources of the African theater are fully exploited.

Although Ghana and Nigeria dominate the Anglophone literary theater in West Africa, perhaps, it useful to note the contributions of two minority traditions in the region: Anglophone Cameroon and Sierra Leone. The Cameroonian theater of English expression is dominated by

Bate Besong and Bule Butake, whose works have consistently brought them into conflict with the Cameroonian authorities. Unfortunately, the rich theatrical resources in most Sierra Leonean traditional ceremonies, such as the Poro initiation rites, have not given rise to an equivalent output in dramatic literature. With the exception of the pioneering works of Raymond Sarif Easmon (*Dear Parent and Ogre*, 1964) and the politically relevant plays of Yulissa Amadu Maddy, the theater has remained a very marginal activity in the cultural life of the country.

POPULAR THEATER

The Yoruba Traveling Theater of Nigeria, the Krio theater in Sierra Leone, and the Concert Party of Ghana are prime examples of popular theater in Anglophone western Africa. This lively theater draws its inspiration from both the traditional and the modern theaters. It uses the indigenous languages of the area, deals with topical issues, and blends the performance with live music.

The Yoruba Traveling Theater reached its maturity and its era of commercial success with Hubert Ogunde (1916–1990), who formed the African Music Research Party in 1946. His plays *Tiger's Empire* (1946) and *Mr. Devil's Money* were great successes. Ogunde was banned from performing in the Western Region for two years because of his famous play *Yoruba Ronu* (Yorubas, think!) in 1964. Before his death, Ogunde played the role of Johnson's father-in-law in the film version of Joyce Cary's *Mister Johnson* (1947) in 1990. Other personalities of the traveling theater are Duro Ladipo (1931–1978), Kola Ogunmola (1925–1973), and Moses Olaiya Adejumo (b. 1936), popularly known as Baba Sala, who has made the bold innovation of using film and video as part of his repertory.

The Ghanaian Concert Party tradition was started by a Mr. Yalley, a headteacher of Sekondi, in 1918. Yalley's performances made use of jokes, songs, and dances. He also wore fancy dresses, wigs, false moustaches, and the white makeup of a minstrel. His shows were performed in English and catered to the urban elite of his day. However, the Concert Party as it operates now, performing in Akan, using guitar band music, and touring all parts of the country, was the hallmark of E. K. Nyame, who formed the Akan Trio in 1952. Two important but contradictory phenomena took place in the 1990s. While the Ghanaian government has sought to break the chasm between the African theater and its diasporaic counterparts by instituting the biannual Pan African Festival of Arts (Panafest), the concert parties, partly to reach a wider Ghanaian audience both at home and abroad, have taken advantage of the latest technology by recording some of their performances on DVDs, thereby unwittingly breaching the audience-actor intimacy—a hallmark of the tradition.

The Krio theater of Sierra Leone is not as developed and versatile as its counterparts in Ghana and Nigeria. Krio theaters are mainly concentrated in Freetown and its environs. The leading practitioners are Charlie Haffner, Yulisa Amadu Maddy, and Dele Charley. The uniqueness of Krio theater is in its dance-drama, which is performed in a nonverbal mode.

See also **Aidoo, Ama Ata; Bokassa, Jean-Bédel; Literature: Oral; Nkrumah, Francis Nwia Kofi; Ogunde, Hubert Adedeji; Popular Culture: Western Africa; Rawlings, Jerry; Soyinka, Wole.**

BIBLIOGRAPHY

Anyidoho, Kofi, and James Gibbs, eds. *FonTomFrom: Contemporary Ghanaian Literature, Theater, and Film.* Atlanta, GA: Rodopi, 2000.

Bame, Kwabena N. *Come to Laugh: African Traditional Theater in Ghana.* New York: Lilian Barber, 1985.

Banham, Martin, ed. *A History of Theatre in Africa.* Cambridge, U.K.: Cambridge University Press, 2004.

Banham, Martin; Errol Hill; and George Woodyard; eds. *The Cambridge Guide to African and Caribbean Theatre.* Cambridge, U.K.: Cambridge University Press, 1994.

Barber, Karin; John Collins; and Alan Ricard. *West African Popular Theater.* Bloomington: Indiana University Press, 1997.

Cole, Catherine M. *Ghana's Concert Party Theater.* Bloomington: Indiana University Press, 2001.

Conteh-Morgan, John, and Tejumola Olaniyan, eds. *African Drama and Performance.* Bloomington: Indiana University Press, 2004.

Dunton, Chris. *Make Man Talk True: Nigerian Drama in English Since 1970.* New York: Hans Zell, 1992.

Etherton, Michael. *The Development of African Drama.* London: Hutchinson, 1982.

Gotrick, Kacke. *Apidan Theatre and Modern Drama: A Study in a Traditional Yoruba Theatre and Its Influence on Modern Drama by Yoruba Playwrights.* Stockholm: Almqvist and Wiksell International, 1984.

ALEX O. BOATENG

FRANCOPHONE AFRICA

AFRICAN CULTURE AND THEATRICAL EXPRESSION

Society dictates the nature of local artistic productions. Precolonial sub-Saharan Africa's society never had a generic term for dramatic performances and never created a space for them. Actors were usually anonymous, and productions consisted of all forms of dramatic expressions (such as pantomime, dance, music, poetry, and mask dance). But although Africans did not name their theater, they lived it, as an essential cultural expression. Their productions ranged from ritual ceremonies to collective spontaneous rejoicing intended for a wide rural audience.

Rites refers to the various religious ceremonies in use in a community. These ceremonies are regulated, that is, their words and gestures (which have sacred and symbolic significance) follow prescriptions set by those participating in the ritual. In traditional Africa, rites are rooted in religion; people use ritual to get in touch with their spiritual roots, establishing ties that go unrecognized in the course of daily life.

Every aspect of a ritual has a symbolic signification that is part of a concrete language that can be transformed into a theatrical performance. The performance of this language creates a space that is symbolic or mythic. It is a place where people meet, as officiating masters and as participants. It is also the meeting place of the human and the divine, through prayer. In his study *Rituel et pré-théâtre* (1965), André Schaeffner (1895–1980) demonstrates that prayer is more than a sentimental act. He shows that it is necessary to achieve contact with the divine.

In ritual, each participant has the opportunity to specialize in a role. In Côte d'Ivoire, the team led by Wéréwéré Liking (b. 1950) of Cameroon and Marie-José Hourantier of France placed great importance on the readaptation of ritual by modern theater in Africa. In this same way, Wole Soyinka has used Yoruba ritual in his work.

Hourantier's production of Wéréwéré Liking's *La puissance de Um* (1970) was an attempt to restore the effectiveness of ritual. It was an effort to control the performance by reproducing the Bassa initiation schema that involves a five-pointed star. In recent years, inspired by the West African tradition, Wéréwéré Liking has put together a Pan-African epic *Sogolon* that also draws on Mandingue rituals.

THE IMPORTANCE OF DANCE

In Africa, dance is the most important mode of artistic expression. Music, whether instrumental or vocal, is always associated with a recitation or with choreography. Dance enhances religious rituals. Hunting tribes used figurative dance to ask forgiveness of the spirit of the animal whose physical form they were about to kill.

Dance is often part of a theatrical performance. It is stylized in such a way that its beauty is (more or less) independent of its meaning. In some cases, dancers add to music a dialogue that transforms the dance into a true dramatic performance.

Human beings can discover their bodies through dance, and can enter into a physical communion with liberty. Dance involves the themes of life and human feeling. African dance is more than just uncontrolled spontaneity. It is a harmonious combination of lines and movements imperceptibly linked to technique and is therefore a fundamental theatrical form of expression.

Although African dance is the art of movement, it does not leave the earth. Feet held close together are used to pound the soil continuously. There are several kinds of dance steps: *échappés* (escapes), *relevés* (high steps), and *assemblés* (steps in which the feet are brought together). The Bugereb, a Dyula dance practiced in Senegal, is one example of an assemblé. In it the feet hit the earth alternately, and then together.

Masques (ceremonies involving masks) reaffirm the role of myths in daily life. They sensibly reinvigorate nature and society simultaneously. The masks are sculpted to receive spirits. Sometimes they feature both human and animal traits. Thus the mask transforms the body of the dancer, who nevertheless retains his or her individuality and who acts as a living medium that incarnates the other being that is momentarily represented.

Occasionally, masques present comic and satiric elements in ritual ceremonies. During these ceremonies, the masques are presented as true spectacles that express the richness of African choreography and music.

Expressive movement, gesture, and even possession are all tied to music and rhythm. Dance is naturally accompanied by music; it is music that permits the dancer to find his or her steps. Of all the arts, it is probably music that most directly affects us. It is therefore not surprising that music accompanies most rituals. Music is tied to dance and sustains direct emotional participation. It can relax tension by calming; a crisis may dissolve in dance. The tom-tom is the instrument most often used. A frenetic, rhythmic instrument, it is easily incorporated in a great variety of instrumental ensembles.

Music and dance join to create an emotional state favorable to possession and trance. They also play an essential role in the ceremony of exorcism, which is called Ndëp among the Wolof of Senegal.

Black African dramaturgy is a synthesis that integrates the expressive possibilities of body and word and excludes neither. In this universe, theater involves words, gestures, and music, each contributing intimately to dramatic expression.

SECULAR EXPRESSION

In addition to religious ceremonies, Africans have developed a repertoire of collective celebrations whose object was the transposition of manners. These spectacles are lyric, musical, and dramatic. They represent ordinary people on the stage and appeal to a large rural public in which the spectacles find their roots.

The narrative exists in all African oral literature. It has a wide variety of dramatic characteristics. It relies on an oral narration that is, above all, a theatrical performance. In this narrative theater, the narrator is an actor. The narrator employs all dramatic resources, acting out, alone, a multitude of roles both human and animal. Several specialists in African theater have researched the narrative. One good example is Bernard Zadi Zaourou (b. 1938) of the Didiga company (of the *Groupe de Recherches des Traditions Orales*) in Abidjan. *L'os de Mor Lam* (1977), by Birago Diop (1906–1989), initiated this research.

The Koteba (giant snail) is a traditional performance in Mali that is composed of two parts. The first employs chants, rhythm, and dance. There is a sort of rhythmic prelude that joins chant, movement, and mime. The audience spontaneously becomes, in turn, actors, dancers, and a live stage set. The second part consists of short plays and skits improvised by the Kotedenw (children of the snail). These make up a comedy of manners that makes fun of stock characters such as the blind man, the miser, the leper, and others. The official theater company of Mali is called the National Koteba; this organization strives to preserve the techniques of the traditional Koteba. There are numerous traditional ceremonies of this type, including the *simb* (play of the false lion) of Senegal and the *xaxar*, a reception for the second, third, or fourth wife of a Wolof man.

The actors in secular festivities must be masters of their craft. They must be able to dance, sing, and mime. Among the Wolof, for example, are professionals such as the *mband-katt* and *taaxuraan-katt* who are itinerant entertainers, similar to the jugglers in medieval Europe. They perform in the marketplace, in the street, or in specially designated areas. All are specialists who work with instruments such as the tom-tom and the kora. Suleyman Coly has a central place for the griot in *Waramba* (a play co-produced with the Renaud Barrault Theater in September 1991). Niangora Porquet in Abidjan created the griotique, which was inspired by the techniques of the African griot.

GENESIS AND EVOLUTION OF MODERN THEATER

Modern African theater was born in the colonial school system. Students, who were usually interns, performed short plays at end-of-year festivals. Even the missionaries, who were hostile to pagan ceremonies, organized celebrations at Christmas and Easter. These early performances were inspired by European theater. It was not until the creation of the *École Normale des Instituteurs* in Saint-Louis, Senegal, in 1903 and the arrival of George Hardy in 1913 that true theater began, and only in the 1930s that a form of theater specifically recognized as African appeared. It was named indigenous theater and began at the *École Normale William Ponty* in Senegal.

At William Ponty, headmaster George Hardy, who was followed by Jean-Louis Monod and Albert Charton, understood the educational value of theater and encouraged creativity. At the end of the 1932–1933 school year, a play written by Dahomean students, *Bayol et Behanzin*, was performed along with a Molière farce. This is the first known example of African Francophone theater.

Charles Béart of the École Primaire Supérieure in Bingerville, Côte d'Ivoire, was also a force in the creation of indigenous theater. With the arrival of Béart as a professor at the Ponty school in 1935, theater soared to new heights. Professors asked their pupils to look to their own traditional culture for subjects of plays. The costumes, pulled out of personal wardrobes at the time of performance, consisted of loincloths and boubou shirts taken from real life. Plays started and ended with chanting and dancing.

In 1935, the elite of Dakar (some 1,000 spectators) attended a performance of *Election of the King* (of the Dahomeans) at the Chamber of Commerce. The theater of the Ponty school reached its apogee in the 1936–1937 school year. Students from Côte d'Ivoire presented *Assemien, roi de Sanvi*, and students from Guinea Conakry performed *Le Capitaine Peroz et Samory à Bissandougou*. The Ponty troupe was invited to the international exposition in Paris in 1937 and gave two performances at the Theéâaftre des Champs Elysées.

After 1949, which marked the end of the Ponty theater, African theater found a new orientation. New prime movers, such as the Guinean Fodeba Keita, a schoolteacher from Ponty, denounced colonial policy. This new theater encountered opposition from the colonial authorities, but Africans who went to France for higher education would demonstrate the vitality of this theater in Paris.

After 1960 the majority of African nations gained independence. Theater developed differently in each country. Senegal was particularly privileged to have the Daniel Sorano National Theater. Many actors from the national conservatory joined this theater, which had one of the best acting troupes in the world. After Senegal, Côte d'Ivoire was famous for its dramatic art. Its National Institute of Arts contained an important theatrical laboratory. Throughout Africa the new orientation of theater toward the valorization of traditional culture ensured public loyalty and support.

DRAMATIC TEXTS

It is possible to divide African repertory plays into three categories. The first is historical plays, by far the most important. These are reenactments of the lives of important people in African history, with the aim of rehabilitating them through modern myths. The most famous include *La mort de Chaka*, by Seydou Badian (b. 1928; 1962), *Une saison au Congo*, by Aimé Césaire, and *L'exil d'Albouri*, by Cheik Aliou Ndao (1972). The second category is those plays that satirize current political rulers, such as *Le président*, by Maxime Ndebeka or *Le destin glorieux du Maréchal Nnikon Nniku, prince qu'on sort* (1979) by Tchicaya U Tam' si (1931–1988). Finally there are plays that deal with social situations, such as *Trois prétendants, un mari* (1964), by Guillaume Oyono-Mbia and *Monsieur Thogô Gnini* (1965), by Bernard Dadié (b. 1916).

The means of expression of this essentially political and social theater reveal that the traditional ceremonies have survived colonization. In speech, these plays use oral discourse (maxims, symbols, proverbs, and repetition), silences that signal stage direction, interjections, and apostrophes. Images suggest the local environment. Ndao uses the savanna bestiary: the lion (symbol of greatness); the hyena (contempt); and the boa and owl (wildlife). In the plays there is a constant use of couplets and refrains from local songs within the French text. The switching between spoken and sung passages is reminiscent of the sung fables in the local oral literature.

African political theater focuses upon great historical figures such as Albouri, Christophe, Shaka Zulu, Patrice Lumumba, and Lat Dyor Diop. These characters are often tragic figures, divided between their vision of the world and the reality of their situations. In addition, there are the secondary characters derived from the traditional imaginations, such as the griot and the ritual officiant. Their role in the play is derived from social status. The griot is the most eloquent. He is the life of the play, giving it music, mimicry, and dance. The presence of the ritual officiant permits the display of fetishes such as animal horns, masks, and skulls.

Ritual and incantations plunge the spectator into the magical universe as a participant in simulations of ritual ceremonies. Plays use social concepts and the traditional family to weave relationships between these characters and dramatic situations. Thus, the plays explore the clash of cultures. Stagecraft—the procedures and effects by which drama is realized on the stage—most clearly demonstrates the traditional character of the spectacle.

The atmosphere of religious and recreational ceremonies is reproduced through emotion, mysticism, and humor in a universe where tragedy exists side by side with laughter, and where mimicry and dance are in sympathy. It is a harmonious, fairy-tale tableau that almost overflows the stage. In the plays of Fodeba Keita, the language of choreography reinforces the text. Few plays leave out cadence, song, and dance. Rhythm becomes a connection between the stage and the audience. The music that comes out of cultural tradition is familiar to the audience. In Europe, the theater borrowed the idea of incidental music from the cinema. In Africa, incidental music is an essential part of the production.

EUROPEAN CULTURE AND AFRICAN THEATER

Most African playwrights were molded in the European manner, as was the educated African public. It is therefore no surprise that modern African theater borrows from the best of European theater. The administration of African theaters is structured similarly to European theater administration. The Sorano Theater in Dakar is a state theater. The state administers it through a director general. The troupe has a staff that includes a manager, a reading committee, a director, a stage manager, and a set designer.

In European theaters, two worlds are placed in opposition: a room full of spectators on the one hand, and on the other, the stage with a set where the actors perform. This structure reinforces both text and action. It optimizes legibility and facilitates comprehension. The classic organization of African plays is very clear. There is exposition; tension, which rises through the third or fourth act; and a denouement of the crisis or catastrophe arising in the final acts. The frame, the closed universe, is never totally absent. Fate appears as an overwhelming force. African theater, however, has not appropriated all the trends of modern European theatrical literature—the innovations of Eugène Ionesco's (1909–1994) theater of the absurd or Samuel Beckett's (1906–1989) avant-garde theater, for example. As one of the most recognizable leaders of the African avant-garde movement, the Congolese Playwright Sony Labou Tansi has imposed a new tone with his group the Rocado Zulu Theatre (founded in Brazzaville in 1979). For example in *La parenthèse de sang* (1978), he shows the absurdity of killing and death.

There are two dominant trends in contemporary set design. One is a trend toward abstraction and symbolism, and the other is a trend toward realism. The two trends are directly opposed. African set design has often oscillated between naturalism and symbolism, even though the set must always adapt to African realities. African set design has always been influenced by realism. The set must seem real to sustain the fiction, and it must also help the actor identify with the character by having the actor interact with the atmosphere and the objects associated with the character. Historical plays require a detailed reconstruction of royal paraphernalia down to the smallest detail, names of historic figures, and authentic songs, dances, and rites. The objects used and costumes worn, often considered to be objects of mystical power, assist the actor in a more than material way. They aid the actor in spiritually, helping the actor be the character. There is a communion between set and play, actor and audience.

Africa adopted a European-style theater building, linked to the culture of the European bourgeoisie and characterized by the division between stage and audience, the hierarchicalization of spectators by ticket price, the separation of roles between playwright and actor, the administrative system, and so on. By its architecture and urban location, African theater reflects bourgeois culture. For example, the Daniel Sorano Theater in Dakar is one of the most luxurious rooms in all of Africa, though the proscenium does not lend itself to historical plays and must sometimes be adapted to involve the spectator.

There are several schools of thought concerning the craft of acting. The theory of direct identification relies on the actor's identification with his or her role and sincere expression of emotion. The theory of distancing sees identification as a form of hallucination, not to be trusted, and seeks to produce art controlled by the intellect. Finally, there is a theory that relies on the actor's gestures. The theater of gesture, in the tradition of Antonin Artaud (1896–1948), is revered in Africa. The body of the actor becomes the source and the instrument of the language of gesture. In Africa, bodily expression, especially through dance, is seen as playing a crucial role in the art of theater.

The African actor must always identify with his or her role, to reach to the roots of ritual, but especially in historical tragedies where the actor plays a personage of mythic proportions. Douta Seck, an actor who played the part of Christophe to much critical acclaim, saw himself as a horse of genius, that is, a kind of priest of tradition, dealing with supernatural, sacred forces.

THE AFRICAN AESTHETIC AND THE THEATER

According to Prosper Compaore in *Théâtre africain* (1990), the true practitioners of African theater know that African cultures do not recognize the artificial dichotomy between art and society. Thus, Bertolt Brecht (1898–1956) has no followers in Africa, even though some of his plays were performed or adapted in Africa. *The Exception and the Rule* and *The Threepenny Opera* were produced by Gaoussou Diawara of the National Institute of the Arts in Bamako, Mali in 1984 and 1985.

In African theater, audiences are not made up of passive observers. The audience participates in the metamorphosis of actor into character. Thus, one must include the spectator when considering African theater. The audience loses its individuality and becomes a mass persona in a continuing dialectic between set and house. The unceasing rhythm, chants, and dance bring the actors and the public together.

See also Césaire, Aimé; Dakar; Dance; Keita, Fodeba; Literature: Oral; Lumumba, Patrice; Masks and Masquerades; Music; Religion and Ritual; Saint-Louis; Shaka Zulu; Sony Labou Tansi; Spirit Possession.

BIBLIOGRAPHY

Actes du colloque de Mohammedia. Casablanca, Morocco: Wallada, 1990.

Actes du colloque sur le théâtre négro-africain. Paris: Présence africaine, 1971.

Carpentier, Peter. "Théâtre in East and West Africa." *Drama* (Spring 1963): 30–32.

Cook, David. "Theatre Goes to the People." *Transition* 25 (1966): 23–33.

Cornevin, Robert. *Le théâtre noir en Afrique et à Madagascar*. Paris: Le Livre africain, 1970.

Diop, Alioune Oumy. *Le théâtra traditionnel au Sénégal*. Dakar, Senegal: Nouvelles Editions africaines du Sénégal, 1990.

Fiangor, Rogo Koffi M. *Le Théâtre africain francophone: analyse de l'écriture, de l'évolution et des apports interculturels*. Paris: L'Harmattan, 2002.

Hourantier, Marie-José. *Du rituel au théâtre rituel*. Paris; Editions L'Harmattan, 1984.

Jukpor, Bernard K'Anene. *Etude sur la satire dans le theater ouest-africain francophone*. Paris: L'Harmattan, 1995.

Laude, Jean. *The Arts of Black Africa*, trans. Jean Decock. Berkeley: University of California Press, 1971.

Meissalloux, Claude. "A farce villageoise à la ville: Le Kotéba de Bamako." *Présence africaine* 52 (1954): 27–50.

Ngandu, Pius Nkashama. *Théâtres et scenes de spectacle: etudes sur les dramaturgies et les arts gestuels*. Paris: L'Harmattan, 1993.

Rouget, Gilbert. *La musique et la transe*. Paris: Gallimard, 1980.

Schipperr, Mineke. *Théâtre et société en Afrique*. Dakar, Senegal: n.p., 1984.

Théâtre africain, Théâtres africains?: Actes du colloque sur le théâtre africain. École Normale Supérieure, Bamako, 14–18 novembre 1988. Paris: Editions Silex, 1990.

BASSIROU DIENG
REVISED BY ANDRÉ N. SIAMUNDELE

NORTHERN AFRICA

Northern African theater exists in a liminal space, between East and West. It is a fusion of Western theatrical traditions and the Arabic performance traditions. The hybrid nature of such a theater is evident in the way popular performance behavior such as *al-halqa* (a circle of storytelling) has been transposed from public squares and marketplaces such as Marrakesh's Jemaa el-Fna, or Cairo's Ataba, to modern theater buildings. Al-halqa has a managed environment that is strictly opposed to the Eurocentric closed theatrical institution. Its audience is called upon "to drift" spontaneously

Performance of Tayeb Saddiki's _Al-fil wasarawil_ (Elephants and pants). The play was conceived within the tradition of _Ibsat_ and _al-halqa_, and performed by Masrah al-karma. _Ibsat_ is a traditional performance that appeared in Morocco in the eighteenth century in Marrakesh.
PHOTOGRAPH BY KHALID AMINE

into an arc surrounding the performance from all sides. The space required by the _hlayqi_ (the maker of spectacle) is not a specific space, and the timing of the performance is any time. No fourth wall with hypnotic fields is erected between stage and auditorium, for such binary opposition does not exist in al-halqa. All the marketplace or Medina gates can be transformed into a stage; and the entire circle is a playing area, as open as its repertoire of narratives and dances.

In order to retrieve this performance tradition, theater in north Africa has become more and more improvisational and self-reflexive, even as such retrieval is still negotiated within the paradoxical parameters of appropriating and disappropriating the Western models. This effort started with the call for an original/autochthonous Egyptian/Arabic theater by Youssef Idriss (1927–1991). His writings on theater mainly published in _al-katib_ journal in the mid-1960s form a body of theatrical manifestos for a new theatrical enterprise. His masterpiece titled _Al-Farafir: The Flipflaps_ (1964) is still considered an exceptional reference text with a strong aura of authority all over north Africa. This fame, in turn, has led some to the "worship of ancestors," and to a ceaseless quest for purity in the name of "authentic"

Arabic theater (a tendency that is part of political Pan-Arabism). The reality, however, is that these so-called indigenous performing traditions are cultural constructs that change time and again and are transformed according to the inner dynamics of folk traditions that are adaptive, fluid, and changing. Although these performances have been of great artistic delight as social dramas, they have not developed into a theatrical activity similar to western theater.

A hybrid theatrical tradition has, however, been established by the Moroccan Tayeb Saddiki, not only in Morocco but in all North Africa. His play titled _Diwan sidi abderrahman al-majdub_ (The collection of Master Abderrahman al-majdub, 1967) is a play conceived in an open public place that is also hybrid in the way it holds up a mirror to the performance itself almost in the same way as the Comedia dell'arte. The play's structure is circular rather than linear. It is situated in Jemaa el-Fna, an open site of orature that is also a space of hybridity. The first scenes of al-majdub production are designed to draw the audience's attention to the making of al-halqa and its circular architecture. On-stage actors transcribe the circular form of al-halqa through a series of comic acrobatic games and mimetic body language. They serve as audiences for each other as the narrator (the story teller) gives space to his little halqa. The halqa of al-majdub represents the Moroccan popular poet as a Shakespearean fool, giving voice to wisdom in a corrupt social order. The effects of such an absurd situation are comic, yet redemptive leading to a collective catharsis.

Saddiki's play *Maqamat Badia Ezzamane El-Hamadani* marks another turning point in Moroccan theater as it restores the performative qualities of maqamat's narrativity back to the Moroccan and Arab stage. The play takes place in an open public square. At the outset, Saddiki's narrator announces that it can be any of the famous Arab squares: It can be Al-Halfaouin of Tunis, or Harun Arrachid's square in Baghdad, or the Green Ataba of Cairo, or even our magical Jemaa el-Fna in Marrakesh. Then the two prominent bsat personae playfully call the attention of their audiences. Other actors play audiences too while preparing to adapt one the roles. Like most halqa's of the bsat tradition, the performance lacks an organic thematic unity, for it is fragmented into little furjas (performances) or halqas that have only one common aspect: the master narrator. In the first furja, Issa Bnou Hicham tells the story of his friend, poet Abdoul Fath Al-Iskandari whom he surprisingly runs into in one of the halqas of Baghdad. Aboul Fath justifies his present situation as a performer and condemns the decadent spirit of his society. The second furja is composed of five maqamas (long narrative poems) wherein the two friends Issa Bnou Hicham and Aboul Fath Al Iskandari have more stories performed in the bsat's halqa. All these stories are derived from the maqamas, yet theatricalized as fragmented little performances.

Saddiki's fragmentation strategy is rooted in the dynamics of the halqa and its fluidity as far as the unity of subject is concerned. A recent bsat performance in Morocco is a play titled *Lbsaytiya* (The bsat people), performed in the National Festival of Theater in July 2006 by one of Marrakesh's most prominent theater companies, Warchat Ibdae Drama. *Lbsaytiya*, however, reproduces the same spirit of fragmented furja. The whole performance is inspired by the magical spell of Jemaa el-Fna, as lbsaytiya agree to present their various bsat performances in the square of Jemaa el-Fna.

The Algerian Abdelkader Alloula (1929–1994), who performed some of his plays in Morocco, remains the most significant Maghrebi artist, besides Saddiki, to use al-halqa. Alloula directed all his creative energy in the last decade of his life to develop a theatrical methodology drawn from the Algerian halqa called *al-quwal*. Alloula's theater is formed, thus, through the condensation of social Gestus (a Brechtean device that consists of drawing attention to the social status of characters), reflecting the points of views adopted by personas through physical expression, intonation and other kinesics features. Occasionally, the manifestations of Gestus are extremely complicated and contradictory as the verbal word alone does not help in highlighting these whole complications. That is why the Alloulian actor must give his role the necessary concentration so that he/she does not fail in conveying the picture with all its dimensions. Through the estrangement of theatrical semiosis and its displacement from conventional dramatic constructions, Alloula's aim is not only to renew the viewer's perception of what is presented on the halqa's stage, but also to transcend the cognitive value in order to introduce a latent, yet a strong desire to reconstruct the present reality. Regarding this, Alloula's theatrical techniques are much politicized. Alloula's theater is rooted in situations marked by tension and extracted from critical historical moments. It highlights the contradictions existing between individual and collective preferences in postcolonial Algeria.

Alloula has experimented with al-halqa's techniques in his last five works: *Al-goual* (1980), *Al-Ajouad* (1985), *Al-litham* (1989), *At-tufahu* (1992), and *Arlukan khadimu as-sayyedayni* (1993). Alloula's *Al-Ajouad*, a play that was performed in the Moroccan Festival of Amateur Theater in 1987, exemplifies the artistic exchanges between the Maghreb countries. Every scene of *Al-Ajouad* is related to a major character presented, on the one hand through epic narration, and on the other hand, through dramatic acting. The aesthetic criss-crossing of narrative and dramatic lines becomes a characteristic feature of the Alloulian theatrical enterprise. Alloula relies on the actor narrator (a total actor) "with his stick and ornamented clothing" to relate events, sing the praises of the characters rooted in the popular conscience, and incarnate some scenes through playing roles. Most characters in *Al-Ajouad* hold modest jobs and suffer from marginalization and poverty. Yet they

Performance of Tangier playwright Zobeir Ben Bouchta's *Lalla Jmila.* The play was performed in Tangier in the theatrical season of 2004 by the Ibn Khaldoun Theatre Company. Lalla Jmila is the play's main character. The project was subsidized by the Ministry of Culture and selected in the official competition of the national festival in Mekunes. PHOTOGRAPH BY KHALID AMINE are unique in their self-esteem and resolute desire to aspire for a better future.

In summary, the hybrid nature of North African theater emerged as a result of cultural negotiations between self and other, East and West, tradition and modernity. It is a postcolonial theater that is located at the crossroads and a continuum of intersections, encounters, and negotiations. The outcome is a complex palimpsest that highlights the importance of cultural exchange and hybridity rather than the essentialist quest for the pure and original.

See also **Art, Regional Styles: Northern Africa; Cairo; Marrakesh; Media: Cinema; Tunis.**

BIBLIOGRAPHY

Aziza, Mohammed. *Al-Islam wa-lmasrah* [Islam and theater]. Riad: Uyoun al-maqalat, 1987.

Berrchid, Abdelkrim. *Al-masrah al-ihtifaliy* [Festive theater]. Trablus: Adar al-Jamahiria, 1990.

Carlson, Marvin, ed. *The Arab Oedipus.* New York: Martin E. Segal Theatre Center Publications, 2005.

Hamdan, Mas'd. *Poetics, Politics and Protest in Arab Theatre.* Brighton: Sussex Academic Press, 2006.

Kolk, Mieke, ed. *The Performance of the Comic in Arabic Theater.* Belgim: Documenta, 2005.

Mniai, Hassan. *Abhat fi al-masrah al-magrebiy* [Studies in Moroccan theater]. Meknes: Voix de Meknes, 1974.

Mniai, Hassan. *Huna al-masrah al- 'arabiy -huna ba'du t-tajaliyatihi* [Here is Arabic theater, here are some of its features]. Meknes: Safir, 1990.

'Orsan, Ali Okla. *Adawahir al-masrahiya inda al-arab* [The Arabs' theatrical phenomena]. Damascus: The Union of Arab Writers, 1985.

Saddiki, Tayeb. *Maqamat Badiaa Ezzamane El-Hamadani* [An entertaining bsat]. Kenitra: Boukili Publications, 1998.

KHALID AMINE

SOUTHERN AFRICA

Any description of precolonial performance is inevitably limited and largely dependent on the residue of such performance forms in the late nineteenth and twentieth centuries. Early theater scholarship across the world has tended to focus almost exclusively on the institutionalized theater systems and the canon of literary drama, ignoring indigenous usage in most countries and not much interested in interactive and communal forms. The result is a historical record in

which most of the indigenous cultural expression in southern Africa is overshadowed by imported European plays and conventions, which by the end of the nineteenth century had become the cultural norm. Performance practice was similarly affected, for the early missionaries and colonial rulers, with Christian values and morality, frowned on all indigenous pagan practices and performances. Inextricably related to this was that the European, and particularly British, way of life—purveyed through the missionary schools and churches, often using dramatized Bible sketches and religious sermons to do so—ironically mirrored and perhaps replaced the didactic role played by much of the spurned indigenous performance. It would only be by the mid-twentieth century that both theater scholars and practitioners in Namibia, Zimbabwe, Malawi, Swaziland, Lesotho, Mozambique, Botswana, and South Africa would gradually come to question this one-sided view, and begin to value and use indigenous forms for artistic, social, political, and economic development programs on the subcontinent.

PRECOLONIAL THEATER AND PERFORMANCE

Prior to European settlement in the seventeenth century, Africans practiced an array of theatrical performance forms, including dramatized songs and enacted ritual narratives. The oldest forms are found with the nomadic communities that roamed over the semidesert terrain of much of Botswana, Namibia, and the Cape Province for thousands of years. The Khoesan ceremonial and ritualistic dramas and dances, for example, have a long history dated by anthropologists at over six thousand years. The various Bantu peoples have similar performance forms, such as the Xhosa *intsomi* and the Zulu *inganekwane*, storytelling practices that are still performed today. The same is true of their extensive dance and music traditions.

From the early linguists and anthropologists to twentieth century musical anthropologists and the oral literature movement, there have always conscious efforts to document, preserve, and, if possible, revive these old traditions. Some forms have survived into the twenty-first century in adapted or hybridized styles. A number of artists, for example, such as storyteller Gcina Mhlope (b. 1959), consciously seek to revive such traditions in performance, teaching the form and even making it a mainstream art form. The role of the praise poet in particular was revitalized in the 1970–1990 period of cultural and armed resistance with the so-called struggle poets and singers. These performers received significant international recognition during the inauguration of Nelson Mandela as president. On occasion, elements from indigenous forms have been adapted to suit immediate circumstances, frequently featuring in the hybrid contemporary plays, dance, and music that evolved from the late 1940s onward, to become a dominant feature of the theater after 1970.

COLONIAL THEATER IN SOUTH AFRICA

Besides a number of earlier contacts and smaller settlements, the first formal European colonization occurred in the Cape in 1652, when Dutch settlers came and introduced the first of a series of new cultural norms and traditions which would dominate the region for more than three centuries. Under the Dutch (1652 to 1799) there was little record of formal theater, but they brought powerful educational traditions from Holland, notably the so-called *rederykerskamers*, a system of social clubs aimed at cultural, moral, and educational upliftment that was maintained throughout much of the British colonial period (1799–1910), as well. Indirectly this became the basis for the dominant Afrikaans language theater, itself crucial for the evolution of a state-supported theatrical system that produced a vast canon of new theatrical works over the course of the twentieth century.

However, formal institutionalized theater only came with the British annexation of the region. As in all its colonies, the British administrators encouraged amateur theater in the garrisons and among the civilians and supported visits by professional companies, a tradition that provided the key models for local theater makers—both descendants of European immigrants and aspirant indigenous African thespians. The works produced were in the colonial languages (English, Dutch, Portuguese, and German), performed by local amateurs (often aided by men from the local garrisons), and augmented by visiting professional companies from the mother countries. Initially they did very little locally written work as most of the material was standard European texts, including a great deal of Shakespeare—both in the original language and translated. What was original was usually a short

topical prologue or epilogue, or a musical skit of some sort. One of the best-known examples is the bilingual skit *Kaatje Kekkelbek, or Life among the Hottentots*, devised in Grahamstown by Andrew Geddes Bain (1797–1864) and Frederick Rex in about 1844.

The first substantial body of indigenous plays came in the second half of the nineteenth century as a direct result of the British presence, its expansionist tactics, and the resulting Anglo-Boer War (also known as the South African War). These plays were largely written in Dutch and later in Kitchen Dutch (or Afrikaans), not only by the descendents of the original white settlers, but also the Dutch-speaking slaves from Dutch east India and the mixed-race descendents of liaisons between the various peoples in the Cape. A slave called Majiet, for example, wrote protest plays for performance in the slave lodge, whereas Dutch and French writers such as Suasso de Lima, Boniface, and Melt Brink (1842–1925) produced short one-act farces and satires for performance by amateurs and schools. Later, more serious writers concerned with the identity of the Dutch/Afrikaans-speaking population began writing ponderous nationalistic works on the history and struggles of the Afrikaner peoples of the subcontinent. This tradition of playwriting would blossom and bear significant fruits in the twentieth century, particularly under the apartheid regime, as such work was seen as essential for the evolution of an Afrikaner identity.

THE EARLY TWENTIETH CENTURY

Although many Afrikaans plays had been written by the early twentieth century and more were being penned to be taken on tour of the rural areas from 1925 onward, only a few indigenously written English plays had been produced in the nineteenth century. However, some English playwrights did emerge in the early years of the twentieth century, the more successful being Stephen Black, who wrote popular farces such as *Helena's Hope* (1906), satirizing the multiracial Cape Town society. A truly local tradition of writing in English would only be established in the 1960s, when the political situation provided increasing rationalization for serious theater focused on local sociopolitical issues. This cultural boycott deprived the country of access to the best of European and American theater and opened a market for local work.

Among the indigenous black population, theatrical performance was initially limited to the traditional performance forms—dance, song, and narrative. Gradually, under the tutelage of missionary schools and other European organizations, a hybrid blend of indigenous and European forms began to emerge, prompting local playwriting. For example, in Malawi there were sporadic attempts to establish such a playwriting tradition in the 1950s. Little of substance occurred until the University of Malawi sponsored the Chancellor College Travelling Theatre, in which Chichewa-language plays that were created through participatory research and performance began to supplant English-language plays. With this development, the potential of theater in adult education began to be realized; by the mid-1990s there was an active industry in theater-in-education.

In South Africa the Anglo-American influence on playwriting in black communities was evident early, in works such as the first published Xhosa drama (Guybon Sinxo's *Debeza's Baboons*, 1927) and in Herbert Dhlomo's (1907–1956) *The Girl Who Killed to Save: Nonqause the Liberator* (1936), the first play by a black person published in English. Based on a Xhosa legend, it is in the style of English sentimental comedy and melodrama.

Whereas black middle-class theater before the 1960s reflects a taste for European dramatic literature, a popular form of theater was emerging among working-class black people. Esau Mtetwa founded the first black professional troupe, called Lucky Stars, in Natal in 1926 and toured the country, putting on popular sketches and plays in the vernacular that were based on Zulu legends and customs. This trend was hastened when the 1930s and 1940s combination of economic depression and drought forced white and black rural farmers to seek a livelihood in the rapidly expanding mining towns and cities. Because of the quick growth of economically depressed mixed race areas and a growing number of slum areas in the cities, many ethnic groupings were eroded, particularly among Africans. This led to an increasing synthesis of ethnic performance traditions with the worker theater as well as models of performance from the West, especially America. Eventually this gave rise to successful combinations of ethnic and jazz music with ethnic and international dance. For example, in

1959 the musical *King Kong*, about the rise and fall of a heavyweight boxer, was first produced in Johannesburg and brought African musicians and actors to the attention of the theater establishment there and in London and New York; it also provided an example for many aspiring actors and directors who saw in it the commercial and artistic possibilities of the musical play that blended indigenous and imported conventions.

THE RISE OF RESISTANCE THEATER AND THEATER FOR DEVELOPMENT

In Zimbabwe, the colonial imposition of European traditions was resisted for many years, but during the 1970s a burgeoning of antisettler resistance art provided perhaps the most important stimulus to black artists. In the years since political liberation, radio and television have provided platforms for the work of writers such as Stephen Chifunyise and Thompson Tsodzo (b. 1952). But perhaps the most important and original drama has been produced by the community-based theater movement that the Zimbabwe Foundation for Education with Production organized. This organization spawned work that is currently best represented by grassroots community organizations and the University of Zimbabwe's undergraduate courses in drama.

The former British protectorates of Lesotho and Botswana have in many ways been tied to the political economy of South Africa, and it is not surprising that their cultural development has run parallel in many ways. Thematic concerns of playwrights have ranged from the obvious theme of oppression by colonial settlers to long-standing concerns with marriage and polygamy, superstition, and modernization, and have included contemporary issues emanating from the effects of apartheid. The first play written and published in Setswana (the major indigenous language of Botswana) was *Motsasele* by Leetile Raditladi (1910–1971) in 1937. But the most famous achievement in Botswana's theatrical history (though not without its detractors) has been the theater-for-development project *Laedza batanani* (*The Sun Has Risen, Come Out and Work*, 1974), in which theater became the medium for a massive education project.

The first play written and published in Lesotho was *Sek'ona sa joala* (*A Calabash of Beer*) by

Twentyman Mofokeng in 1939; in the 1980–2000 period the best-known Basotho playwright was and remains Zakes Mda (b. 1948), whose plays have been translated into many languages. His award-winning play *The Hill* (1979) dealt with the effects of apartheid migrant labor on rural societies, and many of his subsequent works commented incisively on the uneasy coexistence of first- and third-world societies on the subcontinent. His prophetic short play *We Shall Sing for the Fatherland* is an excellent example of this theme. In the 1970s the National University of Lesotho established a flourishing theater-for-development industry in which theater companies tour rural areas and assist in adult education, including the teaching of literacy. Zakes Mda became one of the key theorists of this movement and published his doctorate on the field.

Theater in Swaziland is best known through the work of a woman who is neither Swazi nor a playwright. Anthropologist Hilda Kuper's (1911–1992) *A Witch in My Heart* (1970) presents a view of the role of women in Swazi society that has not been matched by the work of any Swazi writer. In Swaziland there exist many types of indigenous performance, which take the form of ceremonies and rituals, but there was not by the mid-1990s a developed theater tradition.

In Namibia, theater-for-development was important during the early 1970s, though the South African state-funded South West African Performing Arts Council imported South African work. It also produced and toured a great deal of classical and European fare in Afrikaans, English, and German. After independence this group became the Namibian National Theatre, which is still active.

The influence of the liberation war was strongly felt in Mozambique and the songs and poetry of the war years were widely used in the work of practitioners involved in making theater through participatory research and performance, with some early theater based on a vaudeville tradition. In 1971 a Portuguese director, Norberto Barroca, staged a play by Lindo Lhongo called *The Newlyweds; or, Dramatic Consultation on the Bride Price* that explored the transition from tribal customs to a contemporary urban and political context, using traditional forms of performance to examine themes of change and continuity. In general, however, theater did not develop in Mozambique to an extent comparable with that in some other countries of the region. This is possibly due to the extent of repressive colonial rule there and to the devastation caused by decades of war.

Although theater-for-development increasingly became the defining form of African theater, such projects did not have the same prominence in South Africa. However, interactive theater processes were sometimes used there for educative purposes. In the late 1970s for example, drama in education (creative dramatics) and theater in education were introduced as a means of awakening the conscience of the youth, and in the 1980s trade union workers' theater became an important tool to foster union solidarity and to develop political awareness among black workers. Much of this latter work was linked to Brechtian theories and Boal's notions of forum theater, all crucial elements in the later political theater. In the late 1980s and early 1990s a form of theater-for-development began to emerge under the new dispensation, to focus on social issues such as the AIDS pandemic, violent crime, rape, nation building, and voter education for the formerly disenfranchised masses—and much government funding and private sponsorship has gone into this.

STATE-FUNDED AND COMMERCIAL THEATER AT MID-CENTURY

White Afrikaans-language theater was privileged from the start, for it was not only a political tool serving the Afrikaans language and the Afrikaner nation, but the artists had a captive audience, as they were working in a dominant local language of European heritage for a population trained to value European cultural forms. This was strengthened by the Nationalist government's direct subsidies of theater, initially through the bilingual (Afrikaans and English) state-funded National Theatre Organization (1947–1962), then through four bilingual provincial performing arts councils that evolved from it (1963–1993). These institutions produced a flood of theatrical work by local theater makers, including some outspoken critics of apartheid such as André P. Brink (b. 1935), Bartho Smit (1924–1986), and Adam Small. Plays such as Smit's *Christine* (1971) and Small's *Kanna hy kô Huistoe* (*Kanna Comes Home*) interrogated the racist value systems in the country, and as a result ran foul of censorship laws.

In the 1970s a more overt form of resistance developed among Afrikaans-speaking youth, notably through a powerful Afrikaans cabaret movement initiated by Hennie Aucamp (b. 1934) and involving the growing Afrikaans alternative rock music movement. During the 1980s–1990s, its impetus was primarily anarchic and political, expressing abhorrence of and resistance against the regime, culminating in *Piekniek by Dingaan* (*Picnic with Dingane*) in 1989. As a form, cabaret still exists but has lost its edge as the apartheid specter faded, and has reverted to more nostalgic blend of musical presentation and stand-up theater.

A number of white English theater makers also found employment in this subsidized theater in the early years, among them the renowned lighting designer and theater manager Mannie Manim, who later co-founded the Market Theatre, and authors Guy Butler (1918–2001) and James Ambrose Brown. The new work focused exclusively on South African themes and sought to develop a distinctively South African idiom. However, few writers would achieve the sustained success of the key Afrikaans dramatists until the 1990s, and none the international stature of Athol Fugard (b. 1932).

Alongside the state-funded system, there has been a strong commercial theater industry in the country, including touring companies playing the Empire in the late nineteenth and early twentieth century. These included vast conglomerates such as African Consolidated Theatres that sponsored theaters and productions throughout the Union, many smaller urban companies performing European and American fare (such as Leonard Rayne and Brian Brooke), and local touring companies of mainly Afrikaans-speaking actor-managers, notably the charismatic and bilingual André Huguenet (d. 1961). This continued to flourish with entrepreneurs such as Taubie Kushlick and Pieter Toerien (b. 1945), who produced primarily American and British hits that managed to bypass the international playwright's boycott in the 1970s and 1980s. In the early post-apartheid years, the world opened up for the country to finally welcome international theatrical hits from Broadway, the West End, and the European capitals, and especially the large-scale musicals such as *Les Miserables*, *Phantom of the Opera*, and,

ironically, *The Lion King*. They have since become the bread and butter of the upscale commercial theaters run by Pieter Toerien and others.

By the 1950s, some of these entrepreneurs felt compelled to do more politically relevant work: antiracist plays from Europe and America, as well as indigenous anti-apartheid plays, such as Basil Warner's *Try for White* (1958) and Lewis Sowden's (1903–1974) *Kimberley Train* (1959). However, the tighter censorship and racial laws of the 1960s soon put a virtual end to the latter trend.

A special category has for long been the African musical, a viable product for export. Besides the influential but hybrid *King Kong*, it was the so-called tribal musicals that made the real money. Despite being criticized as inauthentic and exploiting indigenous culture for commercial gain, these productions created work and training opportunities for many performers excluded from the state system. Gibson Kente (1932–2004), one of these, developed his own theatrical style based on the *King Kong* format, and become the country's most successful entrepreneur. He not only turned black citizens into theatergoers but also popularized his township musical to such an extent that it would be snapped up and adapted by the political movements of the 1970s and 1980s. Other prominent African musicals were *Ipi-Tombi*, a collaborative effort produced by Bertha Egnos (b. 1913), and Welcome Msomi's *Umabatha*—a Zulu adaptation of *Macbeth*—which achieved critical acclaim in 1972 at the World Theatre Season in London. In the 1980s David Kramer (b. 1951) and Taliep Petersen's (1950–2006) collaboration on the successful Coloured musical *District Six–The Musical* (1987) ran for years, and the spectacular musicals of Mbongeni Ngema (b. 1955) dominated the 1990s with *Sarafina!*, *Magic at 4:00 A.M.* and *The Zulu*. Another international success is Richard Loring's (1917–2005) *African Footprint* (2004).

This entire midcentury growth period was substantially supported by state investment in the founding of a range of drama training institutions at the various universities. Initially however, with two exceptions, these were limited to white students and it was only in the 1980s that free access was available to all—which meant alternative training methods had to be found.

THEATER AND RESISTANCE

By the late 1950s, frustration with the politics and the arts system had set in among theater makers and artists across language and cultural divides. A search began for ways to coordinate and support black and multiracial work and to offer training for new performers and artists, and for alternative venues and forms of theater making. A key early example was Union Artists, which not only supported and mentored many artists but also were responsible for the influential *King Kong* project. By the 1970s a radical increase in national and international resistance to apartheid and the burgeoning Black Consciousness movement spearheaded radical changes in black resistance politics, stressing cultural liberation through an alternative black South African aesthetic. Militant political plays and performance events emerged from groups such as Peoples' Experimental Theatre and the Theatre Council of Natal. Both groups were charged and brought to trial in 1974–1975 under the Terrorism Act for their involvement in the dissemination of subversive plays and literature. This in turn led to a radical shift toward political theater and what became known as black theater by writers such as Fatima Dike (b. 1948), Maishe Maponya (b. 1951), and Matsemela Manaka (b. 1956), as evidenced in Fatima Dike's *The First South African* and Maponya's *The Hungry Earth* (1981).

At the same time, a number of younger white and black activist-theater makers began to work together and important multicultural fringe groups emerged. Even within the state system of performing arts councils, Ken Leach, Pieter Fourie (b. 1940), Francois Swart and others sought to put on subversive work in experimental venues.

The most crucial factor, however, was the founding of a number of independent venues in the 1970s, the most influential being the Space Theatre in Cape Town (1972) and the Market Theatre in Johannesburg (1976). Focusing on developing theater projects that addressed the cultural contradictions of South African life, these venues found ways to circumvent the racial laws. Among the new works that were being produced were Athol Fugard's steady stream of trenchant plays, beginning with *Blood Knot* and including his masterpieces (*Boesman and Lena*, *Master Harold and the Boys*, *The Road to Mecca*). His simple but compelling neonaturalism became the model for a substantial

number of young theater makers to add their voices to the clamor for change in the 1980s. Paul Slabolepszy, Anthony Akerman, Pieter-Dirk Uys (b. 1945), Deon Opperman, Reza de Wet, and others began to produce significant new work, led by Slabolepszy's *Saturday Night at the Palace* and leading to De Wet's award-winning Gothic dramas about the Afrikaner psyche. Another phenomenon was the rise of the satirist and stand-up comedian as political activist. Notable examples include the immensely effective Pieter-Dirk Uys and his alter ego, Evita Bezuidenhout, with constantly updated shows such as *Hell is for Whites Only* and *Adapt or Dye*.

Another important factor was the distinct shift toward a new style of improvised political theater in which the previously neglected African traditions become dominant. Inspired by the early improvised work of Theatre Workshop '71 (*The Women of Crossroads*), John Kani (b. 1943), Winston Ntshona (b. 1941), Athol Fugard (*The Island*, *Sizwe Bansi is Dead*), and the innovative improvisational work of Barney Simon, the plays tended to incorporate aspects of precolonial African genres into their more formal structures and blend these with the new urban cultural experiences of their audiences. The seminal *Woza Albert* (1981) and Ngema's *Asinamali* (1985) by Barney Simon, Mbongeni Ngema and Percy Mtwa, and Junction Avenue Theatre's groundbreaking *Sophiatown* (1986), best epitomize this. By the late 1990s and the first decade of the twenty-first century, a large number of producers had evolved the hybrid play into a distinctive South African form. Among this later work are such haunting works as William Kentridge (b. 1955) and the Handspring Puppet Company's unique adaptations of world classics (*Woyzeck on the Highfeld*, 1992 and *Faustus in Africa*, 1995), Mark Fleishman, the Magnet Theatre Company and Jazzart's sensitive collaboration based on Khoesan performance traditions (*Rain in a Dead Man's Footsteps*, 2003), David Kramer and Taliep Petersen's anthropological journey into the slave and Khoesan history (*Ghoema*, 2005) and Brett Bailey and the Third World Bunfight company's satirical look at colonial preconceptions about Africa (*Ipi Zombie*, 1996, *iMumbo Jumbo*, 1997, and *Big Dada*, 2003).

THE FESTIVAL CIRCUIT

From a structural point of view, the most important facet of the post-1994 period has been the rise of the festival culture in southern Africa. The oldest and best known is the annual National Arts Festival in Grahamstown that was founded in 1974 to support the embattled English language and culture. For long the only national festival, it soon went beyond its parochial boundaries to encompass all cultures in the country and to provide an indication of emerging trends in the whole subcontinent. More than thirty years later it is a twelve-day international festival with fifty thousand attendees seeing more than five hundred theater events.

In the 1990s the fall of the apartheid regime opened the field for formerly excluded artists, and closed down the state-funded companies, thus putting pressure on artists to create their own work. At the same time, formerly protected cultures had to look after their own survival and development. This led to the founding of a series of arts festivals, beginning with the annual Oudtshoorn Festival dedicated to the now-embattled Afrikaans language and culture. Within a few years this began to rival the Grahamstown festival in size, and ever more festivals came, catering to a variety of cultures, languages, economic situations, and cultural tastes. Growing exponentially, the year 2004 saw more than 150 local festivals in the country, and at least forty significant arts and cultural festivals being aggressively advertised across the country. This includes a state-supported Mayibuye festival of African arts in Bloemfontein. The festivals have become the core of the industry and in many ways constitute the annual theatrical season.

It is apparent from the work showcased here that the old formulas of both European-style formulas and the aggressive agit-prop style of anti-apartheid theater were being adapted and even debunked, and that theater practitioners were seeking new forms, methods, and themes that are expressive of the new African psyche and context. Since 1994 therefore there has been an increasing focus on the struggle for identity and nationhood, the search for peace, and the exploration of notions of memory and forgiveness—issues most notably symbolized by the Truth and Reconciliation Commission and endemic to works such as *Ubu and the Truth Commission* (1997) by Jane Taylor, William Kentridge, and the Handspring Puppet Company, *Die Jogger* (*The Jogger*, 1997) by André P. Brink, and *Die Toneelstuk* (*The Play* 2001) by

Breyten Breytenbach (b. 1939). Notable too are the many plays focusing on healing of the wounds of the past, from Athol Fugard's *My Children! My Africa!* (1989) and *Valley Song* (1995) to such festival works as *Peace Shall Prevail; Now Is the Time for Reconciliation; People Like Us,* and *Unity,* and John Kani's thought-provoking *Nothing but the Truth* (2002).

From a history of precolonial performance followed by colonial subjugation, in which indigenous practices were suppressed or marginalized, to its resurgence in the form of politically motivated theater and drama, practitioners of drama and theater in southern Africa have finally cast off some of the more restrictive European models and the declamatory political style of the struggle period, and finally have begun to use a variety of hybridization processes to firmly establish a distinctive and nuanced regional cultural identity.

See also **Apartheid; Cape Town; Colonial Policies and Practices; Education, School; Festivals and Carnivals; Fugard, Athol; Literature; Mandela, Nelson; Music; Popular Culture: Southern Africa.**

BIBLIOGRAPHY

Coplan, David B. *In Township Tonight: South Africa's Black City Music and Theatre.* Johannesburg, South Africa: Ravan Press, 1985.

Davis, Geoffrey, and Anne Fuchs, eds. *Theatre and Change in South Africa.* Amsterdam: Harwood Academic Publishers, 1996.

Gunner, Liz, ed. *Politics and Performance: Theatre, Poetry, and Song in Southern Africa.* Johannesburg, South Africa: Witwatersrand University Press, 1994.

Hauptfleisch, Temple. *Theatre and Society in South African. Reflections in a Fractured Mirror.* Pretoria, South Africa: J. L. van Schaik Academic, 1997.

Hauptfleisch, Temple, and Ian Steadman, eds. *South African Theatre: Four Plays and an Introduction.* Pretoria, South Africa: HAUM Educational Publishers, 1984.

International Defence and Aid Fund for Southern Africa. *Black Theatre in South Africa.* London: International Defence and Aid Fund, 1976.

Kamlongera, Christopher. "Theatre for Development: The Case of Malawi." *Theatre Research International* 7, no. 2 (1982): 207–222.

Kavanagh, Robert Mshengu, ed. *South African People's Plays: Ons phola hi.* London: Heinemann, 1982.

Kavanagh, Robert Mshengu, ed. *Theatre and Cultural Struggle in South Africa.* London: Zed Books, 1985.

Kruger, Loren. *The Drama of South Africa. Plays, Pageants and Publics since 1910.* London: Routledge, 1999.

Mda, Zakes. "Current Trends in Theatre-for-Development in South Africa." In *Writing South Africa,* ed. Derrick Attridge and Rosemary Jolly. Cambridge, U.K.: Cambridge University Press 1998.

Orkin, Martin. *Drama and the South African State.* Manchester, U.K.: Manchester University Press, 1991.

Popular Theatre Committee, Institute of Adult Education, University College of Botswana. *Laedza batanani: Organising Popular Theatre: The* Laedza Batanani *Experience, 1974–1977.* Gaborone, Botswana: n.p., 1978.

Solberg, Rolf, ed. *Alternative Theatre in South Africa: Talks with Prime Movers since the 1970s.* Pietermaritzburg, South Africa: Hadeda Books, 1999.

Solberg, Rolf, ed. *South African Theatre in the Melting Pot. Trends and Developments at the Turn of the Millennium.* Grahamstown, South Africa: Institute for the Study of English in Africa, 2003.

Von Kotze, Astrid. *Organise and Act: The Natal Workers' Theatre Movement, 1983–1987.* Durban, South Africa: Culture and Working Life, 1988.

TEMPLE HAUPTFLEISCH
EDWIN HEES

THEOLOGY. *See* **Christianity; Islam; Judaism in Africa; Philosophy; Religion and Ritual.**

THUKU, HARRY (1895–1970). The Kenyan nationalist leader and first president of the East African Association, Harry Thuku was born into a poor family in Mbari ya-Gathirimu in northern Kenya and left home at the age of twelve to attend a Gospel Mission Society school, where he learned to read and write. At sixteen, he left the school for Nairobi; there, he found employment at the Standard Bank of South Africa as a messenger, before he was convicted of fraud and sent to prison. Released in 1913, he worked as a clerk counting huts before he joined the *Leader of British East Africa* newspaper as a compositor and was exposed to the world of politics.

Thuku took particular issue with the system of forced labor in Africa. At the time, it was commonplace for Africans, dependent on an economy dominated by colonial powers, to consign themselves to a system in which they were obliged to do whatever manual labor was designated for them by Europeans. Given a common, low wage and required to pay taxes to the colonial government for the "privilege" of getting work, Africans found themselves unable to control their circumstances, with no way of gaining access to the realm of power and production. This system was institutionalized in 1919, when each African seeking employment was required to carry a *kipande*, a container holding registration papers regarding the availability for work of the person bearing the documents.

By fiat of the colonial government, taxes levied on African workers increased while wages were lowered. Discontent grew, and Kenyans formed their first political organization, the Young Kikuyu Association, after a 1921 meeting in a Nairobi suburb where objections to the labor system were discussed. The organization soon became the East African Association (EAA), which established branches throughout Kenya. With Thuku as the organization's first president, they sent letters of protest to the colonial secretary in London while they organized meetings in Kenya to protest the allocation of the majority of fertile land in Kenya to Europeans.

In 1922 Thuku was arrested for his involvement with the EAA. To protest his arrest, the EEA organized demonstrations throughout Kenya, and twenty people at the gathering in Nairobi were killed by colonial troops. Authorities, fearing further uprising, deported Thuku to Mombasa, then to Kismayu Island, and later to Marsabit in the remote north. He spent almost nine years in detention there, using his time to learn about agriculture. He returned home in 1930, and immediately began work on his own farm, which became one of the wealthiest in Kenya at his time. Later in life, Thuku was the first African director of the Kenya Planters Coffee Union (KPCU). He lived to see Kenya independent in 1963 and died on June 14, 1970.

See also **Colonial Policies and Practices; Kenya; Labor: Conscript and Forced.**

BIBLIOGRAPHY

King, Kenneth, ed. *Harry Thuku: An Autobiography.* Nairobi, Kenya: Oxford University Press, 1971.

SARAH VALDEZ

TIJANI, AHMAD (1737–1815).

Ahmad Tijani was a Muslim mystic and founder of a Sufi order, the Tijaniyya. Born in 'Ayn Madi in southwestern Algeria, Tijani studied the Islamic mystical Way in Fez (Morocco). During a prolonged visit to Egypt and Arabia in 1772–1778, primarily for the pilgrimage, he received authorization to propagate the Khalwatiyya Sufi order. But after his return to Algeria, Tijani announced in 1782 or 1783 that he had received a waking vision of the prophet Muhammad, who had authorized him to begin an independent mission of spiritual guidance and had communicated special prayer litanies to him. In 1789 he moved to Fez, perhaps virtually exiled by the Ottoman authorities in Algeria, and remained there until his death.

Although Tijani found favor at the Moroccan court, there was considerable opposition from scholarly circles to his claims of direct prophetic guidance. Indeed, although his teachings have spread widely in northern and western Africa, there has always been strong opposition to his claims that he was the highest-ranking saint of all ages (*qutb al-aqtab*) and that more merit accrues from reciting certain Tijani litanies (notably the *salat al-fatih*) than reciting the Qur'an. His claim of unique authority from the prophet Muhammad led him to forbid his followers from having recourse to the saints of any other order; this has produced friction between Tijanis and other Sufis, and sometimes violence. He left no manual of his teachings, but a disciple, 'Ali Harazim ibn Barada, compiled what he claimed was an account of his life and teachings, the *Jawahir al-Ma'ani*, though this has been shown to be, at least in part, a plagiarism of an earlier source.

See also **Fez; Islam; Prophetic Movements.**

BIBLIOGRAPHY

Abun Nasr, Jamil. *The Tijaniyya: A Sufi Order in the Modern World*. New York: Oxford University Press, 1965.

Paden, John N. *Religion and Political Culture in Kano*. Berkeley: University of California Press, 1973.

Triaud, Jean-Louis, and David Robinson, eds. *La Tijâniyya: Une confrérie musulmane à la conquête de l'Afrique*. Paris: Karthala, 2000.

JOHN HUNWICK

TIMBUKTU.

A historic city in Mali, Timbuktu (*Tombouctou* in French) is located six miles north of the Niger River, at the southern edge of the Sahara. Timbuktu, most likely a Berber toponym, was founded in the eleventh or twelfth century as a trading center where a trans-Saharan camel caravan route connected with the Niger River commercial network. The city rose to prominence in the fourteenth century, when it was one of the principal cities of the Empire of Mali and its main "port" on the Sahara. It is at that time that the trading city began to acquire a reputation for Islamic scholarship, exemplified by its Sankora mosque-university. In 1468 Timbuktu fell to the Songhay Empire. The city's intellectual and commercial elite enjoyed an uneasy relationship with Songhay's rulers and some sought refuge in Walāta, a city beyond the western border of the empire. In 1591 the Moroccan army occupied Timbuktu and many of its clerics and scholars, such as Ahmad Baba, were exiled to Marrakesh.

Thereafter, civic authority rested with the *arma*, a group descended from Moroccan officers married to Songhay women and allied with regional Tuareq tribal leaders. The *arma* regime lasted until the late eighteenth century. During that time the trans-Saharan trade routes responsible for the city's wealth declined irremediably yet the city continued to produce scholars such as 'Abd al-Rahman al-Sa'di (d. 1655) and Mahmud Al-Ka'ti (d. 1664). Cultural and intellectual activities continued into the first half of the nineteenth century, under the Kunta shaykhs who established the Qadiriyya Sufi order there. The Kunta managed Timbuktu's relations with the *dina* of Masina (1818–1862) and then with the Tukulor-Tijânî empire until the French occupied it in 1894. In the early twenty-first century the city (population 32,000 in 1998) is a regional administrative center and one of Mali's main tourist destinations, famous for its adobe architecture and the thousands of Arabic-language manuscripts that attest to past intellectual accomplishments. In 1988 Timbuktu and its libraries were listed as a United Nations Education, Scientific, and Cultural Organization (UNESCO) world heritage site.

See also **Mansa Musa; Marrakesh; Niger River; Slave Trades; Sunni 'Ali; Walāta.**

Minaret of Sankore Mosque. Sankore is one of Timbuktu's three historic Friday mosques. The mosque is probably as old as the city itself. In the fifteenth and sixteenth centuries, it functioned as a university and its scholars were highly regarded. Like much of the historic city, this minaret is built of adobe and has a highly tapered, pyramidal form characteristic of the Sudanic architectural style. PHOTOGRAPH BY JOHN A. SHOUP, AL AKHAWAYN UNIVERSITY

BIBLIOGRAPHY

Abitbol, Michel. *Tombouctou et les Arma* [Timbuktu and the Arma]. Paris: G.-P. Maisonneuve & Larose, 1979.

Cissoko, Sékéné Mody. *Tombouctou et l'Empire Songhay: épanouissement du Soudan Nigérien aux XVe–XVIe siècles* [Timbuktu and the Songhay Empire: The flourishing of Sudanic Niger in the 15th–16th centuries]. Dakar: Nouvelles éditions africaines, 1975.

Saad, Elias N. *Social History of Timbuktu: The Role of Muslim Scholars and Notables, 1400–1900.* Cambridge, U.K.: Cambridge University Press, 1983.

ERIC S. ROSS

TIME RECKONING AND CALENDARS. The ways in which people reckon time in small-scale, nonliterate African communities with simple technologies are in some ways familiar to those who live in modern industrial societies, but in other ways are surprisingly different. This entry examines traditional methods of time reckoning in African societies, and discusses to what extent the notions of time involved differ from modern concepts of time. Indigenous systems of time reckoning in Africa were often not recorded and have in the twenty-first century been largely displaced by Western and Islamic forms, so that information on traditional systems is quite poor.

TIME DIVISIONS OF THE DAY
The day typically begins either at dawn or sunset, and its divisions are based on the position of the sun and on the most important social activities. Those of the Konso of Ethiopia are as in Table 1.

Divisions of a typical Konso day	
Sunrise	pirtoota
Sunrise until the sun is well up	teikanta
Period around mid-morning	kutata
From then until early afternoon	kuiatakuta, (big, full day)
Mid-day meal	pifa,
Early to later afternoon	kalakalla
Late afternoon	harsheta akalakalla
When the cattle return home from grazing	kakalsiima
Twilight	shishiipa (and sunset)
Sunset	dumateta
Evening (includes twilight and sunset)	kalapta
When it becomes quite dark	shishiipa'akuta
Suppertime	etowa
Night	halketa

Table 1.

These time divisions, some of which overlap, are quite sufficient to coordinate ordinary social activities: the Western clock-time based on fixed hours is only necessary for the highly organized social world of schools and offices, and for calculating the time that employees work in a factory or business.

Systems of time reckoning that include the hours of darkness only appeared where regular astronomical observations were made throughout the night, as in ancient Egypt where the idea of the 24-hour day first developed. While in some societies of sub-Saharan Africa a few men might make observations of the night sky, this did not lead their society to adopt official systems of time reckoning for the night. Paul Bohannan's observations on the Tiv of Nigeria apply generally:

> Tiv are much less specific about time during the night. The time between dusk and about 10 o'clock is called "sitting together" (*teman imôngo*). After that follows "the middle of the night" (*helatô tugh*), which overlaps with "the time of the first sleep" (*icin i mnya môm*); "the time of the second sleep" (*acin a mnya ahar*) is about 3:00 AM or a bit later. The pre-dawn breeze (*kiishi*) gives its name to the period just before dawn. (317).

Days are counted in relation to weeks and even months, but only in the rarest cases do people ever keep count of the number of days in the year.

YEARLY CALENDARS

The most important system of time reckoning, however, is the yearly calendar, and in Africa this is based on seasonal activities. A standard example of the calendar of a farming people is provided by the Konso in Table 2.

This type of system of named months is not normally found among hunter-gatherers, whose only form of time reckoning tends to be the sequence of foraging activities themselves throughout the year. But while it is often supposed that a calendar of named months is essential for agriculture and planning its seasonal work, this is quite untrue. For the practical purposes of farming, people know quite well what they have to do throughout the agricultural year, and can easily give a list of these activities in chronological order if asked to do so, as in the case of the Konso calendar. Sowing, in particular, has to be coordinated with the weather, which of course varies from year to year, while for predicting the seasons people can observe natural signs such as the Pleiades, which are associated with the coming of the rains, and the rising positions of the sun on the horizon throughout the year.

The Konso calendar

Seasons	Months	Main activities
Bona	Jan/Feb **Oypa**	*xayshima*: preparation of the ground, especially uprooting old sorghum stalks and burning rubbish. Some crop sowing.
Katana/ Sorora	Feb/Mar **Sakanokama**	*ayla*: sowing of crops. Rains begin.
Katana/ Sorora	Mar/Apr **Murano**	*arma saasaha*: first weeding. Rains continue.
Katana/ Sorora	Apr/May **Pillelo**	*armafaya*: main weeding. Rains continue.
Katana/ Sorora	May/June **Hari**	*olapa*: last weeding. *epalta*: bird scaring. Crops begin to ripen.
Masana	June/July **Tola**	Crops continue ripening.
Masana	July/Aug **Orxolasha**	*fera*: harvest begins. Cooler and cloudier.
Masana	Aug/Sept **Sessaysha**	*fera*: harvest continues.
Hakayta	Sept/Oct **Partupota**	*xayshima*: preparation of the ground. Ratooning* of cut sorghum roots. Small rains begin.
Hakayta	Oct/Nov **Kiisha**	*arma*: weeding.
Hakayta	Nov/Dec **Olintela**	*fera*: harvest of ratoon* crops. Small rains end.
Bona	Dec/Jan **Porinka**	*fera*: harvesting of cotton. Preparation of ground and uprooting of sorghum stalks.

(* ratooning is a second sprouting of a crop such as sorghum)

Table 2.

Auspicious and inauspicious months of the Konso year

Month	Dates	Good/Bad
Oypa	January/February	+
Sakanokama	February/March	+
Murano	March/April	−
Pillelo	April/May	+
Hari	May/June	−
Tola	June/July	+
Orxolasha	July/August	+
Sessaysha	August/September	−
Partupota	September/October	+
Kiisha	October/November	−
Olintela	November/December	+
Porinka	December/January	−

Table 3.

So the practical significance of calendars can easily be exaggerated. Even where people like the Konso do have named months; unlike individuals in Western societies they are not continually thinking about which one it is, and when asked the name of the current month, they may not know and have to reflect about it or ask someone else. The primary use of named months is actually for coordinating social events and as a guide to when religious ceremonies should be performed, but since religious ceremonies are fundamentally concerned with good harvests and the health and fertility of men and beasts, there is a need for these calendars to be linked in a permanent way to the seasons and to agricultural activities. As a result some months may be considered auspicious for religious ceremonies, while others are inauspicious (see Table 3).

Calendars are therefore a very important part of the people's general system of classification and sense of cosmic order, and neighboring societies in the East Cushitic language group have a roughly similar pattern of auspicious and inauspicious months to those of the Konso.

THE LUNAR PROBLEM

There is a basic problem in coordinating the lunar months with the solar year: the lunar year is approximately 11¼ days shorter than the solar year, because each lunation (period from one new moon to the next) is 29½ days so that a sequence of 12 lunar months is only 354 days, not 365¼. This means that after 3 solar years a lunar calendar will have advanced about 1 month in relation to a fixed solar calendar. The ancient Egyptians roughly solved this by ignoring the moon entirely and establishing a purely solar calendar of 12 months each of 30 days, with 5 extra days at the end of the year, giving 365 days. This advanced by 1 day every 4 years in relation to the actual solar year, because the ¼ day was omitted, but was nevertheless fairly stable in the short term. But calendars of the Konso type, which are very common in Africa, are called luni-solar because they attempt to coordinate the months with the solar year, and this means that, unlike the Egyptian calendar, they have to be corrected about every three years.

The Borana of East Africa have a highly sophisticated method of solving the lunar problem by the use of the stars in conjunction with the phases of the moon, but this is unique in Africa, and a much more usual method is to repeat one of the months when necessary, which in the Konso case is Oypa: the rains are supposed to begin in Sakanokama, but if they do not then Sakanokama is treated as if it were still Oypa. Since all the Konso can observe the lateness of the rains for themselves there is no problem of who orders the repetition of Oypa, or how consensus is obtained. The Konso weather pattern, in which December and January are regularly dry and the rains, if they come at all, arrive by April, makes this mode of correcting the calendar feasible. Consider, for example, condition A, in which the rains come on time in all or even most successive years. This would mean that Oypa was not repeated sufficiently often to correct the calendar—about every three years. It would by then have advanced to January and since this month, like December, is regularly a very dry month Oypa would have to be repeated and would thus correct the calendar.

Second, consider condition B, in which Oypa is repeated too often after a succession of very dry years. In this case the end of Oypa would be delayed until March or even April, when again there is regularly a high rainfall, and so would not be repeated until it had fallen back into its proper place. The end of Oypa will therefore fluctuate within the solar year between January and March, but usually ending at some time in February just before the great rains, thus maintaining the calendar in a fairly stable approximation to the solar year.

The Konso, like most other nonliterate peoples, had no idea that there is a solar year of 365 days, and a lunar cycle of 354 days, with one cycle moving faster than the other. They did not count the number of days in the year at all, and although they now know that the Amharic calendar has 365 days, do not consider this superior to their own, but simply a difference of custom. Their only interest is in keeping the standard months roughly aligned with the seasons.

Another very common method is to have a calendar of thirteen months, and to leave out the thirteenth month until it is needed—this essentially achieves the same thing as repeating a month. Again, the Nupe of Nigeria start their year with the month that marks the beginning of the rainy season: "From the beginning of the rains the people count twelve, thirteen, or sometimes fourteen months until the new rains break. The last month of the old year (i.e. the 13th or 14th month) is then identified with the first month of the new year" (Nadel, 409).

Although the year in many societies is often considered to start with some important event such as the rains, people may also disagree about when the year should begin; or there may be agricultural, legal, and ritual years beginning in different months. It is also quite possible for people to have the notion of a year comprising the seasons and a sequence of months, but not be sure how many months it has.

While it may be generally believed that there are 30 days between each new moon, the practical observation of the new moon is difficult; reckoning tends to become uncertain at the end of each month, so that if the new moon appears on the 29th day people will say that they must have miscounted. Within the month, the waxing and waning phases of the moon are extremely important, so that months are typically divided into halves, before and after each full moon, and the counting of days occurs within each half. (The waxing and waning periods of the moon are also often magically significant.)

SOCIAL STRUCTURE AND TIME RECKONING
A number of African societies also make arbitrary subdivisions of the month into weeks. The seven-day week originated in Babylonia as the closest whole-day equivalent to the four phases of the

moon and was adopted by Judaism, and ultimately by Christianity and Islam, which spread the idea throughout Africa. But there were indigenous African weeks, notably in East and West Africa, where they were based on local cycles of four or five markets arranged so that people would be within walking distance of at least one of them in the week. The four-day market cycle of some of the East Cushitic peoples, and the five-day cycle of the Yoruba are examples.

Market cycles are examples of how the social structure, rather than the natural world, may provide the basis for time reckoning, and social time reckoning allows people to conceptualize sequences of events covering many years. In kingdoms people may use sequences of kings and the events of their reigns. Among the Baganda:

> Periods of time were marked by the reigns of the kings, called the *mirembe* of each king; *mirembe* signifies the time of peace enjoyed during the reign of the king, after the anarchy and disturbance which were rife during the interregnum between the death of one king and the appointment of his successor. The events falling in the reign of a particular king were fixed chronologically by the wars in which he was engaged or, if there was no war, by the hill upon which the king lived at the time, before he moved his capital to another hill. By this method of marking time the people were able to tell within a few weeks when an event had happened, or when a person had been born. (Roscoe, 37)

Societies with formal age-set systems could use these as a guide to the sequence of past events, especially where the sets were based on successive generations. The Konso did this on the basis of an 18-year cycle, as in Table 4.

Time reckoning by age-sets

Sets	Dates
Orxasha	pre-1845
Kayala	1845–1863
Onayla	1863–1881
Qadasha	1881–1899
Qawasha	1899–1917
Qasha	1917–1935
Arapala	1935–1953
Fulasi	1953–1971

Table 4.

Battles and other significant events could be related to this sequence of sets, and they also kept a record of age-set ceremonies by a series of stones in a sacred wood, from which they knew that the system had begun in 1593 (in our chronology). The related Borana had an even more remarkable age system with a cycle of eight generations covering 280 years, and which for learned men provided the framework in which historical events were ordered. But other societies could use age-set systems in a quite different way, to produce an entirely closed and arbitrary scheme of the past, and an extreme case is that of the Pokot of East Africa:

[F]or the Pokot the past, the present, and the future are encompassed, not only for the individual but for the whole nation, by eight age-sets whose names are repeated through time in the same cyclical order. No point in the cycle, no age-set name, may be used to mark the beginning....Within this cycle, and through the sole use of age-set names, no event may be dated more than three generations ago. It may come, then, as no surprise that the repetition of the names of the age-set cycle is equivalent to a recapitulation of tribal history. Each age-set is linked with a number of events, events whose form will recur when this age-set name is repeated. The history of the Pokot (I am tempted to say of man, the history of his actions since he assumed his definitive human form), is encompassed by the cycle of eight age-sets. Only the appearance of the gods, and their acts of creation, lie, in terms of time, beyond the confines of this cycle. Divine history (at least before the creation of man) is open-ended, social history is cyclical. (Peristiany, 183)

Just as age-sets could form closed systems of time reckoning, so could kinship structures:

[T]he Nuer system of lineages may be considered a fixed system, there being a constant number of steps between living persons and the founder of their clan and the lineages having a constant position relative to one another. However many generations succeed one another the depth and range of lineages does not increase.... How shallow is Nuer time may be judged from the fact that the tree under which mankind came into being was still standing in Western Nuerland a few years ago! (Evans-Pritchard, 107–108)

THE ISLAMIC CALENDAR

Absolute systems of dating based on a specific historical event are entirely absent in traditional sub-Saharan Africa, and where they exist are the result of Christian or Islamic influence. The Islamic era is calculated from the migration, Hidjra, of Muhammad from Mecca to Medina in 622 CE, and was formally instituted in 638 CE. Official and important events in Muslim history have subsequently been dated on this basis, but the years of the AH (*Anno Hegirae*) chronology are actually lunar and not solar years. In 632 CE (AH 10) Muhammad decreed that the religious life of Muslims should be based on a purely lunar calendar, deliberately unrelated to the actual seasons with which the pagan festivals had been closely linked. Each month begins with the local sighting of the new moon, but the last day of the month cannot be predicted; the only exception is that the month of Ramadan cannot last longer than 30 days even if the new moon has not been seen. The result, of course, is that the lunar months are in a constantly changing relation with the seasons, that takes a cycle of 32½ years to complete.

The needs of agriculture, taxation, and astronomy, however, have continued to be met by the use of solar calendars, or by local luni-solar calendars, and the seven-day week remained an integral part of the Muslim calendar, which eventually became standard in North Africa and the other regions of the continent, such as northern Nigeria and Somalia, to which Islam also spread. In the absence of an absolute dating system of this sort it is therefore especially difficult for individuals to keep an accurate count of their ages, even in societies with age-set systems, and so physical and social maturity rather than actual years are the relevant criteria of personal age in traditional African societies.

THINKING ABOUT TIME

Time reckoning in Africa, whether associated with natural or social processes, is based on sequences of actual events: these may be cyclical, such as the seasons, the phases of the moon, the daily movements of the sun, the human life cycle from birth to death, and the succession of the generations; or linear, such as events in the life of the individual and his society. This dependence on *sequences* of events has important consequences for African notions of time.

First, it means that time reckoning is qualitative, not quantitative. That is, specific events are located in relation to other events, such as "that village had not yet moved when my youngest son was born," or "the Government came after I had been circumcised, but before I married." Time *intervals* are also incommensurable with one another:

> For the Tiv time is divided by natural and social events into different sorts of periods, but since the events often belong to different logical series there is little attempt to correlate the different sorts of division of time. Tiv make no attempt to correlate moons with markets or either with agricultural activities or seasons. If one asks how many moons there are in a year, the answer varies between ten and eighteen; if one asks the number of markets in a moon, the answer varies between three and eighteen, and of the number of days in a moon, between ten and fifty. (Bohannan, 257)

So sequences of standard events do not form quantifiable series like the hours of a 24-hour clock: one cannot say that three twilights equal one morning, or that from first light to the going out into the fields is the same amount of time as from the coming back of the cattle until supper time. The same is true of divisions of the year, even if they are expressed in named months:

> [The Nuer] have very limited means of reckoning the relative duration of periods of time intervening between events, since they have few, and not well-defined or systematized, units of time.… It is true that the year is divided into twelve units, but Nuer do not reckon in them as fractions of a unit. They may be able to state in what month occurred, but it is with great difficulty that they reckon the relations between events in abstract numerical symbols. They think much more easily in terms of activities and in terms of successions of activities and in terms of social structure and of structural differences than in pure units of time. (Evans-Pritchard, 103–104)

Because time is represented in terms of different sequences of unquantifiable events and of social structures such as generations or age-sets, time is not therefore understood as a universal standard of measurement that is the same everywhere, a chronology, but instead is broken up into different sequences of local events. Without a set of objectively defined, quantifiable and commensurable units, these qualitative sequences of events may have gaps in which time ceases to be reckoned, they may proceed at different rates in different places, so that there is no reason to think that a day here is the same as a day anywhere else, and time may seem to speed up or slow down. It is not therefore uniform, continuous, or homogeneous.

Homogeneous time is common to the whole universe, and not localized or subjective; in continuous time the present is only one moment in a single process in which there are no gaps, while uniform time flows at the same rate.

Second, because this notion of time is tied to sequences of events, speed as such is irrelevant; one cannot compare the speeds of different sequences in relation to a common standard of time—chronologically—and the only thing that matters is the *order* in which events occur and their relative position to one another, so that they are like the static landmarks on a journey or a path. The series ABCDEFGHIJ could equally well stand for a path with landmarks or for a sequence of events, and what is important are things like *order* (A before D before H); *inclusion* (B between A and C); and *proximity* (H next to I and G, but not J or F). So J and A are far from E, while C and G are near, but there is no way of measuring how near or far independently of the series itself, since distance or length of time can only be specified in terms of the number of intervening elements in a sequence. This kind of space is called "topological" space, and it provides a very good model of African concepts of time as well.

The time concepts of the Iraqw of Tanzania, for example, are basically topological. While they have words for years, months, and days, they only use these sequentially, not chronologically:

> They do not use these standards of measurement comparatively to produce a general concept of uniform time, a chronology, that is, against which all events may be compared. Years, months, days, and hours are partitions of the flow of time, and in the way we use the term here, are topological. The creation of a uniform (e.g., Euclidean) space or a uniform time standard (e.g., a chronology) requires a logical act that the Iraqw do not perform. (Thornton, 171)

This spatialized conception of time occurs very widely, as among the Lugbara of Uganda, where "a man, his family and his lineage are in the centre of a field of social relations, which extends both in space and time" (Middleton, 230). Greater remoteness in time is comparable to greater geographical remoteness, and remoteness in both cases is correlated with strangeness, whether of the pre-human culture heroes, or alien monsters, as shown in Figure 1.

Without an absolute chronology such as the Common Era of modern Western culture, based

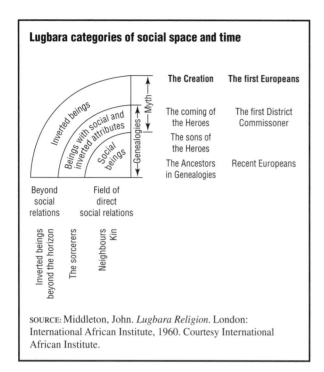

Lugbara categories of social space and time

The Creation | The first Europeans

The coming of the Heroes | The first District Commissoner

The sons of the Heroes

The Ancestors in Genealogies | Recent Europeans

SOURCE: Middleton, John. *Lugbara Religion.* London: International African Institute, 1960. Courtesy International African Institute.

Figure 1.

on solar years and subdivided into equally stable months, days, hours, minutes and seconds, and without the experience of clocks and having to compare different processes going at different speeds, it is impossible to go beyond a static "topological time" to abstract the measurement of temporal process from the details of specific sequences of events processes, and to represent time as homogeneous, continuous, and uniform.

THE SIGNIFICANCE OF THE PAST

One can also consider events, especially human activities, in relation to whether they are completed, still in process, or not yet begun. In this sense events or activities that are complete, or "perfect," are more real than those that are unfinished, and very much more so than those not yet started. In traditional societies with simple technologies, therefore, where temporal interests are focused on social activities, the past will have much more normative significance than the future, since it is the past that has provided the basic social institutions, and social relations have been established in the past. In oral cultures, therefore, people look to the past for their basic orientation rather than to what has still to come into being. For them, history

does not move forward toward a goal still in the future, but rather it points to the roots of their existence such as the origin of the world, the creation of humankind, the formation of their history and traditions, and the coming into being of their society. The future is therefore unreal not only because it contains no events, but because it has no religious or normative significance. Of course, it is possible to project a sequence of markets, seasons, age-sets, or generations into the future and discuss what will happen in so many of these units from now, but in general if Africans speak of the future it is in terms of the completion of events that have already begun to take place.

It is primarily the literate civilizations that envisage total cosmic processes, such as cycles of growth and destruction, or some linear process leading from the creation of the world to an ultimate judgement and grand finale of history. Nor is there, in traditional African thought, any idea of an indefinite process of evolutionary change leading to a perfect mode of social organization, or an ideal condition of society located in the future, and toward which one should devote one's efforts.

See also **Anthropology and the Study of Africa; King Lists and Chronologies; Philosophy.**

BIBLIOGRAPHY

Bohannan, Paul. "Concepts of Time among the Tiv of Nigeria." *Southwestern Journal of Anthropology* 9, no. 3 (1953): 251–262.

Booth, N. S. "Time and Change in African Traditional Thought." *Journal of Religion in Africa* 7, no. 2 (1975): 81–91.

Dux, G. *Die Zeit in der Geschichte.* Frankfurt am Main: Suhrkamp, 1992.

Eickelman, Dale F. "Time in a Complex Society: A Moroccan Example." *Ethnology* 16 (1977): 39–55.

Evans-Pritchard, E. E. *The Nuer: A Description of the Modes of Livelihood and Political Institutions of a Nilotic People.* Oxford: Clarendon Press, 1940.

Hallpike, C. R. *The Konso of Ethiopia: A Study of the Values of a Cushitic People.* Oxford: Clarendon Press, 1972.

Hallpike, C. R. *The Foundations of Primitive Thought.* Oxford: Clarendon Press, 1979.

Legesse, Asmarom. *Gada: Three Approaches to the Study of African Society.* New York: Free Press, 1973.

Mbiti, John S. *African Religion and Philosophy,* 2nd edition. London: Heineman, 1969.

Middleton, John. *Lugbara Religion*. London: International African Institute, 1960.

Nadel, S. F. *A Black Byzantium: The Kingdom of Nupe in Nigeria*. London: International African Institute, 1942.

Nilsson, Martin P. *Primitive Time-Reckoning*. Lund, Sweden: C.W.K. Gleerup, 1920.

Peristiany, J. G. "The Ideal and the Actual: The Role of Prophets in the Pokot Political System." In *Studies in Social Anthropology*, ed. J. H. M. Beattie and R. G. Lienhardt. Oxford: Clarendon Press, 1975.

Roscoe, John. *The Baganda*. London: Macmillan, 1911.

Thornton, Robert J. *Space, Time, and Culture among the Iraqw of Tanzania*. New York: Academic Press, 1980.

C. R. HALLPIKE

TINUBU, MADAME (1805–1887).

Madame Tinubu flourished as both a trader and a politician in Abeokuta, Badagri, and Lagos, three nineteenth-century southwestern Nigerian towns that exploited their proximity to the sea and trade with the Europeans. Born in Abeokuta, Tinubu moved to Badagri about 1832, when she married Adele, a prince, and later king, of Lagos. As a trader, Tinubu supplied local products in exchange for a variety of European imports. As a politician, she was deeply involved in the Lagos dynastic struggles. She grew wealthy and powerful, but was bitterly resented by rivals.

Tinubu encountered a crisis in Lagos during the 1850s stemming from her prominence in both trade and politics. The British, who had established an initial presence along the coast, had begun to interfere in local politics in a way that threatened Tinubu and many others. To the British, she was a terror who promoted the slave trade that they were heavily committed to ending. Expelled from Lagos in 1856, she returned to Abeokuta, where she rebuilt her trade and became involved in local politics and warfare. For her distinguished service, she was given the leading female title, *iyalode*.

Tinubu has become a legend in modern times. In Abeokuta, her tomb is a tourist attraction and a plaza bears her name. In Lagos, the names of a major street and square keep her memory alive.

See also **Abeokuta; Slave Trades; Women: Women and Trade.**

BIBLIOGRAPHY

Biobaku, Saburi Olade. *The Egba and Their Neighbours, 1842–1872*. Oxford: Clarendon Press, 1957.

Smith, Robert Sydney. *The Lagos Consulate, 1851–1861*. Berkeley, University of California Press, 1979.

Yemitan, Oladipo. *Madame Tinubu, Merchant and King-Maker*. Ibadan, Nigeria: University Press, 1987.

TOYIN FALOLA

TIPPU TIP (1837–1905).

Tippu Tip was the popular name of Hamed bin Muhammed el-Murjebi, the best-known of the many nineteenth-century Arab and Swahili traders in the Great Lakes and Upper Congo region of Central Africa. The sultanate of Zanzibar, particularly under Sultan Barghash ibn Saʿid (ruled 1870–1888), had taken over the centuries-old Swahili commerce with the interior that carried ivory and slaves to the coast and returned to the interior with cloth and beads. One interior trade route for this commerce was from Kilwa, then dealing mainly in slaves with the French of Réunion to Lake Mweru and beyond, and another route, dealing mainly in ivory, from Bagamoyo and Zanzibar to Lake Tanganyika. The area served by the latter route became divided into two main spheres of influence: that of the Nywamwezi chief Mirambo in what was later Central Tanganyika, and that of Tippu Tip in the region beyond the lake in the Upper Congo-Maniema region, opened later. These two men became virtually independent rulers, or warlords, although they remained dependent commercially upon Zanzibar, which supplied them not only with goods but also with the arms and ammunition that they used to maintain their positions.

Mirambo later lost the support of Sultan Barghash. The sultan had placed his trust in Tippu Tip, a fellow Arab, to control the far interior on his behalf against the predatory agents of King Léopold's African International Association, represented there by Henry Morton Stanley. The latter planned to export the ivory of the region westward, down the Congo River, whereas Barghash appointed Tippu Tip to retain the east coast monopoly through Zanzibar.

Tippu Tip built up an immense satrapy on the Upper Congo that extended as far as Stanley

Tippu Tip (1837–1905). Slaveholder and trader Tippu Tip helped many western explorers, including Henry Morton Stanley, with their travels in Africa. CORBIS

domination over a large area and depended on a temporary monopoly of firearms. Some were not indigenous Africans and thus had no ties with local groups and chiefs; they depended on support from uprooted and detribalized Africans such as the *ruga ruga* and other nineteenth-century refugees in what is now Tanzania. Most of these rulers were little more than small-scale warlords, but some, such as both Tippu Tip and Mirambo, achieved a certain amount of political stability and imposed a kind of order over areas torn by slave trading and other brutal forms of exploitation. Their empires were short-lived, taken over by more powerful European colonizers who either subdued or destroyed them in the 1890s and 1900s, when the rulers' power stood in the way of imperial consolidation.

See also **Barghash Ibn Saʿid; Ivory; Mirambo; Slave Trades: Atlantic, Central Africa; Stanley, Henry Morton.**

BIBLIOGRAPHY

Brode, Heinrich. *Tippoo Tib: The Story of His Career in Central Africa*. Trans. H. Havelock. London: Arnold, 1907.

Farrant, Leda. *Tippu Tip and the East African Slave Trade*. New York: St. Martin's Press, 1975.

Renault, François. *Tippo Tip: un potentat arabe en Afrique centrale au XIXe siècle*. Paris: Société française d'histoire d'outre-mer, 1987.

Tippoo Tip. *Maisha ya Hamed bin Muhammed el Murjebi yaani Tippu Tip*. Trans. Wilfred Howell Whiteley. Kampala, Nairobi, 1966.

JOHN MIDDLETON

Falls (present-day Boyoma Falls), where he was in direct contact with Stanley and other Europeans working for Léopold. He was appointed official Zanzibar governor (*wali*) of the Upper Congo and Manyema, and for some years he achieved a *modus vivendi* between the Belgians and Zanzibar. Tippu Tip's authority, although dependent ultimately on his military strength, was far-reaching: he administered a personal sort of justice—appointed his own officials and subgovernors from among the many Arab traders who lived in the region—and established some kind of peace between among the many local groups and their chiefs who competed for a share of the lucrative commerce. Tippu Tip returned to Zanzibar in 1891 and died there in 1905.

Tippu Tip was an example of a not uncommon figure in nineteenth-century African history, the upstart entrepreneur who established political

TOGO

This entry includes the following articles:
GEOGRAPHY AND ECONOMY
SOCIETY AND CULTURES
HISTORY AND POLITICS

GEOGRAPHY AND ECONOMY

A small country in West Africa, Togo occupies a unique place in the ecological sub-region. The Togo coastal strip lies in the sole break in the forested swath that runs from southern Senegal in the west to northern Angola in the southwest. The relationship between its geographical and ecological positions, however, is entirely coincidental. Its international borders and economic activities stem from its complicated colonial history.

GEOGRAPHY

Covering a total area (land and inland water) of 21,925 square miles, Togo extends 365 miles inland, forty miles wide at the Atlantic coast and ninety miles wide at its widest point. It is bordered by Ghana on the west, Burkina Faso to the north, and Bénin to the east.

Togo consists of six geographical regions. The coastal region is low-lying, with a sandy beach backed by the Tokoin plateau, marsh, and the Lake Togo lagoon. The Tokoin (Watchi) Plateau extends about twenty miles inland at an elevation of 200 to 300 feet to the northeast, a higher tableland is drained by the Mono, Haho, Sio, and tributaries. The Atakora massif stretches diagonally across Togo from the town of Kpalime northeast, at different points it is known as the Danyi and Akposso Plateau, Fetish massif, Fazao mountain, Tchaoudjo massif and Kabye mountains. The highest point is the Pic d'Agou at 3,937 feet. North of the mountain range is the Oti plateau, a savanna land drained by the river of the same name. A higher, semiarid region extends to the northern border.

The climate is mostly tropical and humid, though the dry, desert winds of the Harmattan blow south from December to early February, bringing cooler weather and little moisture. Annual temperatures vary between 75 and 98 degrees Fahrenheit in the south and 65 to 100 degrees Fahrenheit in the north. The thirty Togolese ethnic groups are found in all parts of the country, most notably in the capital Lomé (the estimated population in 2000 was 1 million), which is situated on the border with Ghana.

The current population of Togo is estimated by the United Nations to be 5.7 million, with growth at approximately 3.5 percent per annum, though the last government census dates from 1981. One-fifth of the population lives in the capital. Kara, the second largest city, has approximately 200,000 inhabitants. Population density reached approximately 173 per square mile in 1991, with 75 percent in rural villages.

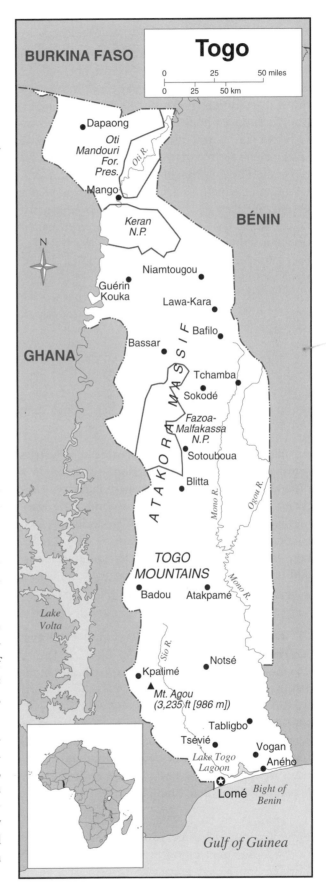

ECONOMY

Agriculture provides the mainstay of the economy, employing close to four-fifths of the active population. Farmers grow food for subsistence and for sale. Private property exists in Togo alongside traditional community custodianship and land is bought and sold under both systems. Private ownership of land began during the German period, as small parcels were purchased for commerce and for missions. The French continued this policy of gentle aggrandizement, but in the post-independence period this pattern was complicated by the president's illegal seizure and redistribution of plantations owned by his opponents. Thus, much land in the south, and particularly in the capital Lomé, remains the site of intense litigation, which takes place in the civil courts. Warnings are often written in red on the walls of land parcels to deter sale or deception.

Agricultural and manufactured products are sold both retail and wholesale in shops and markets. The informal economy is significant and is found in every town and village market, including the Assigamé (Grand Marché) in Lomé.

The 1990s saw most government industries privatized. Phosphate production, operated as a monopoly, remains Togo's largest industry; electricity production is a distant second. The once highly favored banking sector is declining, and tourism is insignificant. Togo has a small oil refinery, and animal husbandry, telecommunications, and information technology are growth industries. Togo has very high use of Internet and email services per capita.

Togo's stagnant, underdeveloped economy, suffering from an aid boycott in 2007, is largely dependent on agricultural exports. In the mid-1990s, more than 50 percent of Togo's exports were of four primary products: coffee, cocoa, cotton, and phosphates. Until the reconstruction of ports in Cotonou and Lagos, Lomé was one of the busiest on the coast. The roads and rail infrastructure are rapidly declining, however, despite the launching of the Free Trade Zone in 1989.

France is by far Togo's largest trading partner. Fifty percent of imports from France are consumption goods, a minority of which is re-exported to Burkina and Niger. Forty-two percent of imports are of equipment, building and agricultural supplies. Togo imports all its petroleum needs.

Customary divisions of labor generally do not still hold in Togo, though men do most heavy construction work. Women perform almost all other manual labor in towns and villages, though less machine work, and control small-scale market commerce. Child labor is ubiquitous, and since 1996 numerous incidents of child slavery have been exposed. Girls are more likely to work than go to school in much of Togo.

Individuals who have had post-secondary school education usually occupy professional positions. Successful business people may or may not have formal education, but often have relatives, friends, or patrons who have helped finance their establishments.

See also **Agriculture; Children and Childhood; Climate; Education: University and College; Slavery and Servile Institutions.**

BIBLIOGRAPHY

Agier, Michel. *Commerce et sociabilité: les négociants soudanais du quartier zongo de Lomé (Togo)* [Commerce and sociability: Sahelian merchants in Lomé's Zongo (Togo)]. Paris: Editions de l'Orstom, 1983.

Comhaire-Sylvain, Suzanne. *Femmes de Lomé* [The women of Lomé]. St. Augustin: Steyler Verlag, 1982.

Decalo, Samuel. *Historical Dictionary of Togo*, 3rd edition. Baltimore, MD: Scarecrow Press, 1996.

Marguerat, Yves. *Population, migrations, urbanisation au Togo et en Afrique noire: articles et documents (1981–1993)* [Population, migration, and urbanization in Togo and Africa: Articles and documents (1981–1993)]. Lomé: Presses de l'Université du Bénin, 1994.

Piot, Charles. *Remotely Global: Village Modernity in West Africa*. Chicago: University of Chicago Press, 1999.

BENJAMIN LAWRANCE

SOCIETY AND CULTURES

Togo was first colonized by Germany in 1884, then by Britain and France under international treaty. The United Nations (UN) administered the region and named the Togoland areas trusteeships in 1946. On April 27, 1960, French Togoland became the independent Republic of Togo.

During the interwar period several organizations, including the Cercles des Amitiés Françaises, the Duawo, and the Bund der deutschen Togo-länder, organized and militated in public and private against French rule. The Cercles became the Committee for Togolese Unity Party (CUT), under the leadership of Sylvanus Epiphanio Olympio. In a UN-sponsored election, the CUT won control of the legislature and Olympio became the country's first president on April 27, 1960.

During Togo's first years of independence, Ewe peoples from the south dominated the government. But the Kabyé and other northern groups dominated the army. In 1963 a group of northern army officers assassinated Olympio. Until the dictatorship of Gnassingbe Eyadema, the southern Ewe culture predominated in all realms of life and was second only to the influence of France. After 1967, however, Eyadema deigned to redress the southern bias in cultural, political, and social life, and to this end created *authenticité*, modeled on the program of Zaire's dictator Mobutu Sese Seko. This movement attempted to highlight the many diverse cultures of Togo, but resulted in reducing them to two only, that of the north and the south. Since the 1990s the idea of Togolese nationhood has become submerged by that of Kabyé ethnicity.

Ethnic tensions are minimal, despite the persistent murmurings of certain politicians. Political strife came to a head in 1991–1994, resulting in south-against-north violence. Despite concomitant refugees and resettlement, Togo's thirty ethnic groups continue to mix and intermarry throughout the country.

FOOD AND CUSTOMS

Togolese usually have two or three meals per day, each consisting largely of a starch product, such as cassava, sorghum, maize, millet, yams, or plantains. A hot, spicy sauce is served with midday or evening meals, consisting of a protein, like fish, goat, beans, or beef and often rich in palm (red) oil or peanut paste. Fruits and vegetables, though readily available, are eaten more by the bourgeoisie.

Food and drink—such as beer, gin, and *sodabi*—are all important ceremonial items. Throughout the north, food, beer, and sacrificed animals are offered to spirits and consumed by those in attendance. In the south, alcohol is often the key ingredient. Among wealthy middle-class Togolese the usual French three- or four-course meal is always served at functions.

Private property exists in Togo alongside traditional community custodianship and land is bought and sold under both systems. Much land in the south, and particularly in the capital Lomé, remains the site of intense litigation, which takes place in the civil courts. Warnings are often written in red on the walls of land parcels to deter sale or deception.

Agricultural and manufactured products are sold both retail and wholesale in shops and markets. The informal economy is significant and is found in every town and village market, including the *assigamé* (Grand Marché) in Lomé.

Customary divisions of labor generally do not still hold in Togo, although men do most heavy construction work. Women perform almost all other manual labor in towns and villages, though less machine work, and control small market commerce. Child labor is ubiquitous, and in 1996 and 1998 several incidents of child slavery were exposed. Girls are more likely to work than go to school in much of Togo.

Professional positions are usually occupied by individuals who have had postsecondary school education. Successful businesspeople may or may not have formal education, but often have relatives, friends, or patrons who helped finance their establishment.

SOCIAL STRATIFICATION

Togolese society is divided along traditional and nontraditional lines. The traditional elite includes "kings" and paramount chiefs and voodoo priests. The modern elite includes government functionaries, businessmen, and the educated. Poor rural families often send their children for schooling or employment to relatives living in the cities. During the colonial period all but the simplest clothing was considered a social distinguishing factor in villages, while brick houses and cars were the items that denoted social standing in towns. Since the mid- to late twentieth century, wealthy villagers can afford tin roofs and some even telephones, while in the cities, large houses, cable television, Western dress, and restaurant dining are hallmarks of success.

FAMILY, KINSHIP, AND SOCIALIZATION

Women, although having attained legal equality, remain unequal in all walks of life. Women and men are kept apart in most social gatherings. Women usually eat after men but before children. Discrimination against women in employment is common practice and widespread. Women have little place in political life and less in government programs, though there is a ministry allocated to women's and family affairs. Only women descended from ruling families, successful businesswomen, or the few women politicians enjoy privileges equal to that of men, more won than granted. One interesting exception is that of the Mama/Nana Benz, so-named after the wealth accrued from the capital's markets, and their penchant for Mercedes Benz automobiles.

Traditional systems of social organization are significant in the daily lives of Togolese. Kinship systems provide networks for support and are visible during all major life-cycle ceremonies. Marriage practices vary throughout Togo according to the ethnic group, though organized religions and the state have altered the ceremonies of even the most secluded villages. Social disapproval of ethnic exogamy is lessening, though the government unofficially discourages it. Marriage law follows French legal statutes and requires an appearance before a magistrate for all state apparatuses to be in effect. Customary marriage, without state sanction, is still widespread. The payment of bridewealth remains important throughout Togo. Polygyny is decreasing, though unofficial relationships uphold its role.

The basic family structure is extended, although nuclear family units are increasingly commonplace in urban areas. In most cases, the man is the supreme head of the household. In the absence of the husband, the wife's senior brother holds sway. The extended family has a redistributive economic base.

Inheritance laws follow French legal statutes in the case of a legal marriage. In the event of a customary marriage only, customary inheritance laws are enforced. Most ethnic groups in Togo are patrilineal by tradition or have become so as a consequence of colonization.

Kinship is largely patrilineal throughout Togo and remains powerful even among Westernized, urban populations. Village and neighborhood chiefs remain integral to local dispute resolution.

Infants are cared for by the mother and female members of the household, including servants. Among some ethnic groups infants are exposed to the father only eight days after birth. Until the age of five, children remain at home. Initiation ceremonies occur from this age and throughout adolescence. After the age of five, all children can commence school, providing the family can pay the school fees. On average boys are three times more likely to complete primary schooling than girls. Secondary schooling is more common in the south, and numerous private and public schools offer the French baccalaureate system. Often children are sent abroad during strikes.

RELIGION

Since the inception of colonialism, French law has protected freedom of religious worship. The French interpreted this to include polytheistic African religions, and this perhaps partly accounts for the popularity of traditional voodoo cults and rituals. Throughout the country many different forms of Christianity and Islam are practiced. Roman Catholicism is the most prevalent Christian denomination. Islam is virtually paramount in the north. Since the 1990s various American Baptist sects, the Assemblies of God, Mormons, Jehovah's Witnesses, and Eckankar have been making inroads.

Religious officials, whether Catholic priests or voodoo *sofo*, are held in the highest esteem in both rural and urban settings. They are always invited to bless traditional ceremonies as well as building projects or any new initiative. Traditional healers are also held in high regard and, in the wake of the HIV/AIDS epidemic, are gaining popularity.

A Togolese funeral is the most important event of a person's life. Wildly extravagant by Western standards, funeral celebrations are a daily occurrence. Marching bands, choirs, football tournaments, banquets, and stately services are as fundamental to the Togolese funeral as an expensively decorated coffin. Funerals often take place over a month or more. If the person dies in an accident, however, or some other sudden tragedy (AIDS for example), this is considered a "hot death" and the funeral services are concluded more quickly.

See also **Christianity; Colonial Policies and Practices; Eyadema, Gnassingbe (Étienne); Islam; Kinship and Affinity; Kinship and Descent; Marriage**

République Togolaise (Republic of Togo)

Population:	5,701,579 (2007 est.)
Area:	56,785 sq. km (21,925 sq. mi.)
Official language:	French
Languages:	French, Ewe, Kabre, Cotocoli, Hausa
National currency:	CFA franc
Principal religions:	animist 33%, Christian 47%, Muslim 14%, other 6%
Capital:	Lomé (est. pop. 850,000 in 2006)
Other urban centers:	Sokodé, Palimé, Atakpamé, Bassari, Tsévié, Anécho, Sansanné-Mango, Bafilo, Taligbo
Annual rainfall:	ranges from 1,020 mm (40 in.) in the north to 1,780 mm (70 in.) in the south
Principal geographical features:	*Mountains:* Chaine du Togo, Mount Agou *Lakes:* Lac Togo (an inland lagoon) *Rivers:* Oti, Kara, Mô, Anié, Ogou, Mono, Haho, Zio, Alabo, Aka
Economy:	*GDP per capita:* US$1,700 (2006)
Principal products and exports:	*Agricultural:* coffee, cocoa, cotton, yams, cassava (tapioca), corn, beans, rice, millet, sorghum, livestock, fish *Manufacturing:* agricultural processing, cement, handicrafts, textiles, beverages *Mining:* phosphates, limestone, marble, iron ore, bauxite, some uranium, gold, diamonds
Government:	The territory currently occupied by Togo was initially part of land claimed by Germany and split between the British and the French in 1914. Modern Togo is that portion that was administered by France under a League of Nations mandate (later a UN trusteeship). Independence, 1960. Constitutions approved in 1961 and 1963, suspended in 1967. New constitution approved in 1979, replaced in 1992. Republic. President elected for 5-year term by universal suffrage. 81-seat unicameral Assemblée Nationale elected by universal suffrage. President appoints prime minister. President and prime minister appoint Council of Ministers. For purposes of local government, there are 30 prefectures.
Heads of state since independence:	1960–1963: President Sylvanus Olympio 1963–1967: President Nicolas Grunitzky 1967–2005: President General Gnassingbe Eyadema 2005–: President Faure Gnassingbe
Armed forces:	President is commander in chief. *Army:* 6,500 *Navy:* 200 *Air force:* 250 *Paramilitary:* 1,000
Transportation:	*Rail:* 568 km (353 mi.), maintained by the Société Nationale des Chemins de Fer Togolais *Roads:* 7,547 km (4,679 mi.), 24% paved *Ports:* Lome, Kpémé *National airline:* Air Togo makes internal flights and has service to Lagos. Togo has a 7% share in Air Afrique. *Airports:* International facilities at Lomé. Smaller airports at Sokode, Sansomé-Mango, and Niamtougou. 5 other smaller airports.
Media:	Main periodicals: *La Nouvelle Marche, Togo-Presse, Courrier du Golfe, Forum Hebdo, La Parole, Kpakpa Désenchanté, La Tribune des Démocrates.* Principal publisher is the state-owned Établissements des Éditions du Togo Radiodiffusion du Togo and Radio Lomé provide radio service. Télévision Togolaise provides television service.
Literacy and education:	*Total literacy rate:* Male: 75%; female: 47% (2006). Postsecondary education is provided by the Université du Bénin at Lomé; Institut National des Sciences de l'Éducation; Institut Universitaire de Technologie, de Santé, et des Science Biologiques; École Nationale d'Administration; Institut Togolais des Sciences Humaines; Technical College; and through scholarships to French universities.

Systems; Mobutu Sese Seko; Olympio, Sylvanus Epiphanio; Postcolonialism; Production Strategies; Women: Women and the Law.

BIBLIOGRAPHY

Lawrance, Benjamin N. *Locality, Mobility and 'Nation': Peri-Urban Colonialism in Togo's Eweland, 1900–1960.* Rochester, NY: University of Rochester Press, 2007.

Piot, Charles. *Remotely Global: Village Modernity in West Africa.* Chicago: University of Chicago Press, 1999.

Rosenthal, Judy. *Possession, Ecstasy and the Law in Ewe Voodoo.* Charlottesville: University of Virginia Press, 1998.

BENJAMIN LAWRANCE

HISTORY AND POLITICS

The German Reich annexed Togo as a *Schutzgebiet* (protectorate) in 1884. By 1900 German colonial control stretched the length and breadth of modern Togo and the German colonial capital had been moved from Zébé to Lomé. While the extension of colonial authority was a brutal military process with fierce resistance from the Kotokoli, the Kabye, and the Konkomba, once occupation was complete, a system of roads and railroads, built by German money and forced labor, facilitated the economic exploitation of the territory. British, French, and African troops invaded and captured German Togoland in 1914. For the duration of the war, British troops controlled much of the Ewe region, also reuniting the Konkomba kingdoms.

The League of Nations mandates officially began in 1922, with one third under British control and two-thirds under the administration of France. The Ewe sub-groups were further divided by the border, while the Konkomba regained unity under their capital Yendi. Many smaller groups such as the Akposso were severed from their farmlands. During the mandate the French forced large numbers of Kabye to settle in the center and south, officially to reduce overcrowding, but really to provide cheap labor reserves for plantations and industrialization. During the same period the capital grew rapidly and all of Togo's ethnic groups and religions gained a foothold in the historically Ewe region. The main administrative developments of this period included increased centralization, the enhancement and invention of traditional chiefly authorities, and the entrenchment of political authority among the Ewe-speaking elite.

The anticolonial movement began in earnest in the 1930s. Two popular protests, a market women's revolt in 1933 and the suppression of a pro-German lobby group Bund der Deutschen Togoländer, are considered formative moments for anticolonial sentiment. After these incidents the French enjoined elite Togolese to form a Cercle des Amitiés Françaises to counter resistance murmurings. Sylvanus Epiphanio Olympio, the organization's first vice president, ultimately turned the group into a pro-independence party, the Comité de l'Unité Togolaise (CUT), by 1945. The CUT sparred with a rival, conservative group led by future president Nicolas Grunitzky, but ultimately prevailed. After a United Nations–sponsored plebiscite that resulted in British Togoland joining the Republic of Ghana upon independence in 1957, French Togoland followed suit with elections to the French Union in 1958 paving the way for the independent République Togolaise in 1960.

With independence the Ewe sub-groups, led by President Olympio, sought to quickly replace the French administrative cadre. Olympio's initial pan-African and pluralist concerns gave way to authoritarianism and arbitrariness. With greater literacy and economic resources, including a monopoly on cocoa, cotton and coffee sales, the Ewe elite were overrepresented in government and administration. Even during the French occupation, however, northern groups, such as the Kabye and Kotokoli, represented more than eighty percent of the armed forces. This ethnically imbalanced distribution of political and military capital set the stage for sub-Saharan Africa's first coup d'état. Olympio was murdered as he attempted to scale the wall of the U.S. embassy in 1963.

A second coup in 1967 ended southern dominance, and the Kabyé Colonel Gnassingbe (Étienne) Eyadema (1937–2005) became president. Eyadema oversaw a program of redistribution of economic resources, as large numbers of northerners entered the political and administrative arena, in turn redirecting a substantial percentage north. The creation of a one party state under the rule of the Rassemblement du Peuple Togolais (RPT) provided Eyadema with the classic tool of postcolonial prebendalism. During the late 1970s, taking his lead from Mobutu, the former dictator of Zaire, Eyadema launched a program of "authenticité" that essentialized ethnic identities, but further exacerbated the north-south division. Inflated primary export prices coupled with a tourism boom meant that Togo had briefly a very buoyant economy. By the late 1980s, however, economic stagnation caused by enormous international debt prefigured Togo's current social and political turmoil.

North-South ethnic tensions occasionally flared into violence in the 1990s, although official and unofficial political propaganda and the stated platform of political parties greatly exaggerate existing cleavages. During 1991–1992, a democratic revolution that modeled itself on the 1991 constitutional convention dethroning Matthieu Kérékou of Bénin, resulted in the brief loss of the presidency by Eyadema and ended the RPT-led one-party dictatorship. Hundreds of thousands of Kabyé fled north to escape political violence in the south, and at the same time southerners fled to neighboring Ghana and Bénin. Western embassies closed and expatriates and donors were evacuated. Eyadéma, with the aid of French military hardware and political support, soon reasserted his control in a violent bloodbath. Southerners, almost exclusively Ewe-speakers, continued to be exposed to brutality and harassment, but rule in the North was also ensured by violence and intimidation.

Eyadema succeeded in regaining limited political legitimacy in Western eyes via the ballot box in 1993, but the fraud and violence of the 1998 presidential election sealed his status as Africa's pariah. The fraudulent legislative elections of 2002 provided the RPT with a supermajority, and the party subsequently changed the constitution to permit the president to run for a third consecutive term in 2003. With the removal of these limits, Eyadema was free to stand again and did so, winning the elections on June 1 with 57.2 percent of the vote. Another change reduced the minimum age of the president from forty-five to thirty-five years. As Eyadema's son Faure Gnassingbé was thirty-five at the time, many believed he was paving the way for a dynastic succession.

In the early twenty-first century both Amnesty International and the United Nations Commission on Human Rights have led investigations into alleged human rights abuses. Repeated attempts to convene assembly elections have failed and Western donors have linked their return to the establishment of peaceful, democratic civil society. On February 5, 2005, Eyadema died of a massive heart attack. At the time of his death, he was Africa's longest serving ruler and dictator. His son Faure Gnassingbé immediately seized power with the help of the military, just as the next in line (the president of the National Assembly) was visiting neighboring Bénin. Gnassingbé pushed through a quick constitutional change, a move that was denounced as a military coup by the population and the international community.

Under heavy pressure from ECOWAS and the international community, Faure stepped down on February 25 and was replaced by Bonfoh Abbass, second head of the parliament until the presidential elections of April 24, 2005. The elections were marred with violence and fraud. Most observers estimate at least 800 people were murdered by police and the military. At least 40,000 people continue to reside as refugees in Ghana and Bénin. When the president of the National Electoral Commission announced the result that Faure Gnassingbé had won 60 percent of the vote, she immediately fled the country. By most accounts Gnassingbé continues the politically repressive policies of his late father.

See also **Colonial Policies and Practices; Economic Community of West African States (ECOWAS); Eyadema, Gnassingbe (Étienne); Olympio, Sylvanus Epiphanio.**

BIBLIOGRAPHY

Bouraima, Nouridine, and Yves Marguerat. *La population du Togo en 1981: premières observations sur les résultats provisoires du recensement de novembre 1981* [The populations of Togo in 1981: First observations of the provisional results of the census of November 1981]. Lomé: République togolaise, Ministère du plan, de l'industrie et de la réforme administrative, Direction de la statistique, 1983.

Cornevin, Robert. *Histoire du Togo*, 3rd edition. Paris: Berger-Levrault, 1969.

Decalo, Samuel, *Historical Dictionary of Togo*, 3rd edition. Baltimore, MD: Scarecrow Press, 1996.

Lawrance, Benjamin N. *Locality, Mobility and "Nation": Peri-Urban Urban Colonialism in Togo's Eweland, 1900–1960.* Rochester, NY: University of Rochester Press, 2007.

Marguerat, Yves. *Population, migrations, urbanisation au Togo et en Afrique noire: articles et documents (1981–1993).* Lomé: Presses de l'Université du Bénin, 1994.

Piot, Charles. *Remotely Global: Village Modernity in West Africa.* Chicago: Chicago University Press, 1999.

BENJAMIN LAWRANCE

TOMBALBAYE, FRANÇOIS-NGARTA

(1918–1975). Born in Bessada, in southern Chad (Moyen-Chari), and educated by Protestant missionaries, François-Ngarta Tombalbaye found employment as a secondary school teacher in Fort-Archambault (present-day Sarh) and Fort-Lamy (present-day N'Djamena). In 1946 he took part in the creation of the Parti Progressiste Tchadien (PPT), the Chadian branch of the pan-French-African Rassemblement Démocratique Africain (RDA), and later became president of the first Chadian trade union, Union des Syndicats Autonomes du Tchad (USAT). In 1952 he was elected deputy from Chad to the French National Assembly; reelected in 1957, he subsequently served as vice president of the Grand Conseil de l'Afrique Équatoriale Française. After serving as Chad's prime minister under the 1958 Loi-Cadre framing of the transition of France's colonies in Africa toward independence, he was elected president of the Republic on the eve of independence on August 11, 1960.

From then on, his overriding concern was to promote the interests of the Christian south—and particularly those of his own group of origin, the Sara—at the expense of the Muslim north of his country, such as neighboring Sudan (and also Nigeria), divided along religious and ethnic lines reflecting their straddling of the edge of the Sahara desert. By ruthlessly eliminating his opponents from the north, he sowed the seeds of the rebellion that erupted there in 1965 and eventually led to his demise. France's military involvement on behalf of his regime proved utterly ineffectual against the guerrilla tactics of the Front for the Liberation of Chad (FROLINAT) that was aided by its Islamic neighbor to the north, Libya. Nor did Tombalbaye's cultural revolution, patterned along the lines of Mobutu Sese Seko's doctrine of authenticity, succeed in restoring national unity. The resurrection of the Yondo ceremony—a long-abandoned and, as Tombalbaye's deep facial scars testified, not always pleasant initiation rite—had the opposite effect, causing wholesale defections among the rank and file of his party, the Mouvement National pour la Révolution Culturelle et Sociale (MNRCS), which grew out of the PPT. He was faced with a no-win situation in the north and growing political tensions in the south; disaffection also spread to the military.

On April 13, 1975, a group of army men and gendarmes led by Captain Wadal Abdelkader Kamougue (b. 1939) surrounded Tombalbaye's residence and summoned him to surrender. Resisting arrest, Tombalbaye was shot dead in his living room; he was subsequently buried in the north, hundreds of miles from the capital. Nineteen years later, on April 13, 1994, at the request of the Chadian National Conference, Tombalbaye's remains were transferred to Bessada, his native village in the south, and handed over to members of his family in the

Chad president and prime minister François-Ngarta Tombalbaye (1918–1975) at a news conference, June 18, 1963. Tombalbaye's face shows ceremonial tribe scars while visiting Paris after attending the Addis Ababa Conference of African Heads of State. © BETTMANN/CORBIS

course of a ceremony attended by Chadian president Idriss Déby.

See also **Chad; Christianity: Overview.**

BIBLIOGRAPHY

Buijtenhuijs, Robert. *Le Frolinat et les révoltes populaires du Tchad, 1965–1976.* The Hague: Mouton Publishers, 1978.

Lanne, Bernard. "Plaidoyer pour Tombalbaye." *Le Mois en Afrique,* nos. 249–250, 251–252 (1986).

Magnant, Jean-Pierre. "Tchad: Crise de l'état ou crise de gouvernement?" In *États d'Afrique noire: Formations, mécanismes, et crise,* ed. Jean-François Médard. Paris: Karthala, 1991.

RÉNE LEMARCHAND

TOMBOUCTOU. *See* **Timbuktu.**

TOURÉ, AMADOU TOUMANI

(1948–). Amadou Toumani Touré was born in Mapti, Mali. He attended primary school in his hometown and secondary school in Bamako, the Malian capital. Touré entered the army and joined the Parachute Corps. He received training in the Soviet Union and France and in 1984 became the corps' commander.

After troops of the Malian military dictator Moussa Traoré (b. 1936) killed more than one hundred pro-democracy demonstrators in 1991, Touré led a coup that overthrew Traoré. Serving as temporary head of state, Touré led a transition to democracy that included the adoption of a constitution that created a multiparty political system. In 1992 he stepped down from his post after a new president was elected. After leaving office, Touré engaged in various humanitarian missions to improve health care in Mali and promote regional peace, often in coordination with the Carter Center of former U.S. president Jimmy Carter.

In 2002 Touré ran for president of Mali. He had no party affiliation but was backed by a coalition of opposition parties. He led the first election round with 28 percent of the vote and then won the runoff with 64 percent of the ballots. His five-year term as president began in June 2002.

As president Touré improved Mali's relations with the United States and worked toward a market economy. But he also sharply attacked U.S. subsidies for American cotton farmers, which, he said, undercut the cotton exports of Mali, the largest producer of cotton in sub-Saharan Africa. Building roads, providing clean water to all Malians, and the eradicating disease were primary goals of Touré. In the spring of 2006 his army put down a brief uprising over economic aid issues by nomadic Tuareg tribes in Mali's northern desert.

See also **Mali: History and Politics; Warfare: Internal Revolts.**

Amadou Toumani Touré (1948–). The president of Mali arrives at the opening ceremony of the tenth Francophone Summit in Ouagadougou, Burkina Faso, November 2004. Despite having no party affiliation, Touré was elected to the presidency in June 2002. © AP Images

BIBLIOGRAPHY

Bingen, R. James; David Robinson; and John M. Staatz; eds. *Democracy and Development in Mali.* East Lansing: Michigan State University Press, 2000.

Touré, Amadou Toumani, and Blaise Compaoré. "Your Farm Subsidies Are Strangling Us." *New York Times,* July 11, 2003.

MICHAEL LEVINE

TOURÉ, SAMORI (1830–1900). Samori

Touré was born along the upper Milo River, one of the headwaters of the Niger, at a time of significant economic, political, and cultural change in the far western African savannas. By 1867 he had started his major state-building enterprise, which was to transform the southern parts of these grassy woodlands.

Although the transatlantic slave trade was ending, its legacy of militarization of African societies, increased commerce, and rapid social and cultural change had disturbed the upper Milo Valley. The upper Milo and Niger Valleys had been important long-distance trade routes linking the Atlantic ports on the Guinea coast to the vast expanse of the sudanic interior. Along these routes passed slaves, gold, desert salt, dried fish, and cloth from the interior. These were sold for imported firearms, cloth, and utensils from the coast and for kola nuts from the forest. Increased commerce through this region encouraged smaller polities (Malinke: *kafu*) to jostle for greater territorial control. Military activity yielded more conflict and captives, which fed the trade in slaves both to the coast and through the interior, where demand was great for labor to increase production of goods for regional and long-distance trade.

The African merchants who plied these routes often settled at strategic points, forming a commercial diaspora. Many were Malinke and were called Dyula. Originally Muslim, the Dyula usually developed mutually advantageous relationships with the dominant political groups among whom they settled. In some cases, these accommodations led them to abandon Islam. Such was the case with Touré's family. However, increasing Islamic militancy in nearby Futa Jallon, in Konya (in the border region between present-day Guinea and Côte d'Ivoire), and in the wider sudanic zone at the end of the eighteenth and early nineteenth centuries encouraged the Dyula of upper Guinea toward increased political and military activity as Muslims. Touré's fortunes were directly associated with these trends.

In the 1850s, Touré participated in the military adventures of two competing *kafu*. Having learned the arts of war, he allied himself with his maternal kin, who were also engaged in state building. He became the military leader (*keletigi*) and transformed the local warriors into disciplined cavalry and infantry units, using imported horses and firearms acquired through his Dyula commercial connections. Touré's tactical and organizational

innovations contributed to his growing political strength. Around 1874, he moved his followers to Bisandugu and declared himself *faama* (king).

Aware that his new military power rested upon sustained commercial ties, Touré expanded his state toward the goldfields of Buré and the commercial center of Kankan. Organizing a vast territorial empire, which his state had become, required more than military might. In 1886–1887, Touré embraced Islam, changed his title to *almami*, and declared a theocracy. He required the conversion of all his subjects to Islam. In April 1887, he began a crucial campaign against the Kenedugu kingdom. His armies laid siege to Sikasso, the capital. The siege lasted until August 1888, when Touré was forced to abandon his efforts and confront a new enemy, the French then advancing militarily inland from Senegal, and unrest within his empire.

Since 1881, the French military commander Lieutenant Colonel Gustave Borgnis-Desbordes had built a line of forts stretching from Kayes on the upper Senegal River to Bamako on the Niger River. The French expanded along a corridor that traversed the Umarian empire to the north, the Muslim state of Futa Jallon to the south, and Touré's state to the southeast. French forces collided with Touré's army in February 1882, at the town of Kenyeran on the upper Niger; Touré's warriors forced the French to retreat. The two sides kept apart until the French started to build a fort at Bamako late in 1882. In April 1883 Touré's forces fought the French near there at Weyanko. Touré's forces won the initial encounter; but ten days later, the French soundly defeated them. The battle sobered both Touré who now appreciated the decisive French firepower, and the French, who recognized their vulnerability at the edge of an uncertain supply route. The two forces did not clash again until 1885, when Touré sought a decisive victory against the ever-expanding French presence in the goldfields of Buré. He forced the French to retreat, but their superior firepower prevented their defeat. Touré reluctantly signed a treaty of peace and commerce with the French on March 28, 1886; sent his son, Karamogo, to France; and turned his attention to Sikasso. On March 26, 1887, he signed an amendment to the 1886 peace treaty that ceded the left bank of the Niger to the French and established an ill-defined protectorate.

The abortive siege of Sikasso was the turning point in Touré's fortunes. Making successful war gave cohesion to African warrior states such as his. Failure to continue to seize booty led to a rapid disintegration of the uneasy collaboration of war leaders that constituted the state. The long siege of Sikasso ushered in an acute crisis. The heartland of Touré's empire rose in rebellion against his imposition of Islam, the theocracy, and the failure to provide booty. Moreover, under Colonel Joseph Simon Gallieni (1886–1888) and Major Louis Archinard (1888–1891), the French resumed aggressive territorial expansion.

Early in 1888, Touré reorganized his army, acquired modern repeating rifles, and instituted a form of bureaucratic centralism over tactics and supply. He recruited actively among Africans who had served the French or the British and could train his armies in European warfare. He organized workshops in which his ironworkers copied imported rifles. Despite his political and military consolidations, growing French incursions into his territories threatened his power and his resources. In 1892, Touré decided to strike eastward. To arrest further French incursions, he ordered all inhabitants of his kingdom to destroy their villages, take their food, and follow his army.

Between 1893 and 1898, Touré conquered an immense area between the Sassandra and Volta Rivers, stretching from Seguela in the west to Wa in the east. In the process, his state was transformed from a polity that had developed in response to local and regional situations into an empire of conquest. Touré had hoped to move into a region where neither the French nor the British were active. Rather than finding refuge, he and his warriors were caught between the French and British armies in Nigeria, among African populations that rebelled constantly against him. Touré's campaigns in the eastern empire unleashed the final, massive waves of enslavement in this region. When the French stormed Sikasso in May 1898, Touré decided to return to the high country of his birth. He ordered his twelve thousand troops and one hundred thousand civilians to return to Guinea. Famine and desertion plagued his forces. When the French finally captured him on September 29, 1898, he led only a bedraggled and hungry band of warriors and civilians. Touré was deported to Ndjolé, Gabon, where he died of pneumonia on June 2, 1900.

See also **Colonialism and Imperialism; Islam; Military Organizations; Slave Trades.**

BIBLIOGRAPHY

Camara, Kémoko. *L'Almamy Samory Touré: Grand capitaine et grand administrateur.* Conakry, Guinea: Secretariat d'etat à la recherche scientifique, Institut des traditions populaires, 1970.

Fofana, Khalil I. *L'Almami Samori Touré Empereur: Récit historique.* Paris: Présence africaine, 1998.

Freestone, Basil. *The Horsemen from Beyond.* London: D. Dobson, 1981.

Person, Yves. *Samori: Une revolution dyula.* 3 vols. Nîmes, France, 1969–1971.

Person, Yves. "Guinea-Samori." Trans. Joan White. In *West African Resistance: The Military Response to Colonial Occupation,* ed. Michael Crowder. London: Hutchinson, 1978.

RICHARD ROBERTS

TOURÉ, SÉKOU (1922–1984).

Long after the nations of modern Africa gained their independence, Sékou Touré still evokes strong reactions. He was, for some, an opponent of French colonization, a supporter of pan-Africanism, and a leader in Guinea's independence movement; yet, to others he was a Marxist ideologue and ruthless dictator. Born to a modest Faranah (upper Guinean) family, he had little education. However, he was soon recognized for his oratorical and leadership skills. He acquired some Qur'anic learning and attended the Georges Poiret School in Conakry for a year. He practiced many trades before choosing commerce. He obtained a job in the postal administration and soon became both a trade unionist and a politician. He cofounded the Rassemblement Démocratique Africain (RDA) in 1947 and was active in the local section of that party, the Parti Démocratique de Guinée, becoming its secretary-general in 1952. In 1956 he created the Confédération Nationale des Travailleurs Africains, a labor union that maintained its autonomy with regard to the French union federation, the Confédération Générale des Travailleurs. Later he established other grades unions in French West Africa.

Touré mobilized the Guinean populace with anticolonialist rhetoric, denunciations of administrative chiefs appointed by the French rulers of the

Sékou Touré (1922–1984). Between 1965 and 1975, Touré, president of the Republic of Guinea, cut all ties between Guinea and France, its former colonial power. CORBIS

colony, and appeals to those on the margins of society (such as slaves, youth, and women). From this period, in order to establish his party and to assert himself against the maneuvers of colonial authorities, who would not hesitate to falsify elections, he used authoritarian means to eliminate those who opposed him. Several stages characterized his political rise, relating both to his personal strategy and to French reforms. He organized his first strike in 1945 and was briefly imprisoned in 1947. He led his first successful general strike in 1953 and in the same year was elected to the Guinean territorial assembly. He was elected mayor of Conakry in 1955 and served as a deputy to the French National Assembly in 1956. He became vice president of the Government Council in 1957, as the French created institutions in anticipation of independence. In the referendum of 1958, providing for the establishment of a French community of African quasi-colonies, he came out in favor of immediate independence with the famous statement, "We prefer poverty in freedom to opulence in slavery." With an overwhelming vote of about 95 percent, Guinea became the first French colony in sub-Saharan Africa to become fully independent. Touré became the first president of the new republic and remained president until his death twenty-six years later.

The harshness of France's reaction to Guinea's independence forced Touré to radicalize his anti-imperialist rhetoric and to turn to the Eastern bloc for economic aid and technical assistance. As a result, the republic became a one-party state with abolition of civil rights, nationalization of industry and commerce, and agricultural collectivization. Touré trapped Guinea in a cycle of increasingly radical Marxist theory that led to greater opposition, which in turn brought about greater repression and overwhelming misery. Outside threats, real (as in 1970, when Portuguese mercenaries and Guinean opposition forces invaded) or invented, were used to justify constant police surveillance and the cultivation of informants. There were between ten thousand and thirty thousand victims of the police state, and massive numbers of Guineans went into exile—over 1 million, or about one-fifth of the population.

The resumption of diplomatic ties with France in 1975 (they had been cut off in 1964) was followed in 1978 by economic liberalization resulting from demonstrations by women, a weak economy, rural resistance, and external pressure. The continuation of the liberalization of the economy was strengthened after Touré's death in 1984 in—ironically, perhaps—a hospital in Cleveland, Ohio. It was a strange place of death for an opponent of both capitalism and imperialism.

See also **Colonial Policies and Practices; Labor: Trades Unions and Associations; Political Systems.**

BIBLIOGRAPHY

Adamolekum, Lapido. *Sékou Touré's Guinea: An Experiment in Nation Building.* London: Methuen, 1976.

Diallo, Amadou. *La mort de Diallo Telli.* Paris: Karthala, 1983.

Jeanjean, Maurice. *Sékou Touré: Un totalitarisme africain.* Paris: Harmattan, 2004.

Kaké, Ibrahim Baba. *Sékou Touré. Le héros et le tyran.* Paris: Groupe Jeune Afrique, 1987.

Suret-Canale, Jean. *La république de Guinée.* Paris: Éditions socials, 1970.

ODILE GOERG

TOURISM. The word "tourism" in the African context refers to visiting peoples and places in Africa for recreation, to observe or hunt animals, or to widen one's experience of peoples and places that are culturally different, strange, or exotic. There have been three main historical periods in African tourism, in all of which most tourists have come from countries outside Africa. It has been an aspect of colonialism and globalization, a form of trade and exploitation, and the exchange of the beauty and interest of African lands and peoples for non-African money.

HISTORICAL PERIODS OF TOURISM

The first period was that of the late nineteenth-century travel of Europeans, mainly to Egypt and the Nile, an extension of the eighteenth-century Grand Tour. Travel was also to South Africa, Tunisia, Morocco, Algeria, the Atlantic islands, and other places then considered cultural extensions of Europe but possessing a safe exoticism, to be distinguished as distinct from the more dangerous exploration that opened the "unknown" in Africa to European knowledge.

The second period, between the two world wars, included to a greater extent than before the pursuit of big game: shooting rare animals for trophies in the form of animal heads, horns, and skins, a pattern long found among hunting parties in Europe and India. Other trophies included photographs and art items made by African artists for local use rather than specifically for sale to visitors, many being stolen from shrines and royal palaces. Most tourists of this period were wealthy Europeans and North Americans who could afford the great expense and time needed for the journey. The word tourism was rarely used, the preferred word being "travel," or local terms such as "safari."

The third period, since World War II, has been the period of mass tourism. As passenger sea transport between Europe and Africa declined and air transport took its place, travel became cheaper, and mass package tours lasting only a week or two rather than the earlier period of months became possible and popular. Tourism has become the fastest growing world business, linked to the provision of hotels, facilities for rapid and easy local transport, and the growth of guided itineraries. Most tourists have been less wealthy and less socially exclusive than those of the earlier periods, and the killing of animals less usual, indeed often prohibited by the host governments. That most tourists have come from countries with hard currencies has led to the tourism business being strongly supported by independent African governments: several African countries (including the Gambia, Kenya, Mauritius, Réunion, Seychelles, and, until recently, Zimbabwe) obtain a major part of their income from tourism. Trophies usually comprise photographs and art objects made specifically for sale to tourists, rather than for local use.

CAUSES AND EFFECTS OF TOURISM

Tourism has had different histories, aims, and consequences in different parts of the continent. The most visited countries in recent years have been South Africa (with six million tourists), Tunisia, Egypt, Morocco, Zimbabwe (until 2006), Kenya (with a quarter of all European tourists coming to Africa), Tanzania, and the Indian Ocean islands. Western and central Africa have been well behind. The most popular countries for mass tourism for the British, these countries contain areas with near-European climates; English or French are widely spoken and may be the official languages; the main tourist companies are British, American, or French, or have close commercial ties with them. Most of the countries have or until recently have had easy availability of wild animals for shooting or photographing. They also have the provision of hotels catering for tourist rather than local clienteles, the existence of safe beaches and tourist camps, and carefully maintained personal security; many have world-famous sites such as Great Zimbabwe or the Pyramids of early Egypt.

Tourists who visit Africa to experience wildlife, especially big game, probably form the single largest category. Much of it remains similar to the classic big-game safari, except that the former upper-class connection has gone, and animals may almost everywhere be shot only by camera, with photographs taking the place as trophies of the former heads and skins of slaughtered beasts. A form of tourism that is important for island and coastal regions is maritime tourism by cruise ship. The ships are floating hotels, tourist activities essentially being short visits to the larger ports and their neighborhoods.

In most of these countries their colonial past is emphasized to encourage tourists to see themselves as linked to that past rather than merely being modern strangers: to travel in time may be held as important and interesting as to travel in space. Many modern tourists do not see themselves as explorers to little-known lands but as visiting former colonies where they may see themselves as almost rightful possessors and even as imagined reincarnations of former upper-class colonial rulers and settlers, thereby continuing the formerly widespread view of Africans as culturally and socially inferior peoples.

Besides the mythicizing of history and time is the redrawing of historical and politically actual space. The maps of these countries are, as it were, redrafted by tourists and centered on carefully delineated game reserves, safe beaches, exotic and ancient towns, and impressive areas such as the Great Rift Valley in eastern Africa. The present-day urban, industrial, and agricultural cores inhabited by these countries' citizens are largely omitted in favor of scenically beautiful areas occupied by wild animals and by meticulously defined romantic figures of traditional Africans living (or supposedly so) outside modern cities, and so considered to be purely traditional natives, unpolluted by the modern world. The best-known examples are probably the Maasai of Kenya and the Zulu of South Africa. The tourist companies rewrite colonial history to show such groups as central to the area, the economically crucial urban and industrial inhabitants being omitted from tourist gaze and experience.

THE TWO SIDES OF THE TOURIST COIN

The tourist industry has many local economic and cultural effects. These include the exploitation of local people, who themselves gain only a small part of the income from tourism, almost all of which goes to entrepreneurs and African governments. There is also the offensiveness of much tourist behavior from tourists' ignorance of local and traditional values and cultures, and the continuation of former colonialist attitudes by many non-African tourists who regard themselves as members of a global elite and enjoy their perceived economic and believed cultural superiority over Africans.

Non-African tourist companies no longer hold a monopoly in this industry. African participation is increasingly economically important and profitable, although African entrepreneurs are less able to control the linked businesses of hotel ownership and air travel and can take part at only the lower levels of the industry, such as using tourists as a source of at least some wealth and status in return for personal, guiding, sexual, and other services. Tourism is often informally linked to casual prostitution, and many host areas are widely known as sites where marriages may occur between tourists and their hosts—the former mostly female visitors and the latter mostly men seeking tourist women who might take them back to their own countries, a recognized form of out-migration. Other areas are notorious as host areas for sex tours in which the tourists openly seek prostitutes, whether women, men, or children.

As might be expected, the exploitation of the local by the global is frequently disguised as noneconomic. A widespread tourist form is the so-called ecotourism in which tourists claim not to harm the environment. By constructing game parks and the like, the governments of these countries can claim to be in the vanguard of the green ecological movement: profit can be dressed as ecological purity (there are also many private game parks in South Africa that claim the same). There is also social or humanitarian tourism, in which tourists claim not to seek the primitive African (usually meaning a poor and socially and culturally inferior African) but rather to present a morally correct and nonexploitative face. But they are easily exploited by the tourist companies, African or non-African, local dance groups, artists, and the like, all of whom are well able to support the many African and non-African game experts, art historians, and saviors of the primitive found throughout the continent.

A factor rather little considered by travel agents, who construct much of the ideology of tourism, is a wish to undertake what resembles a religious pilgrimage by constructing a landscape of fantasy occupied by noble animals and simple peoples, visiting an innocent world that lies outside the everyday one of commerce and class and race antagonism of the industrialized countries. Many tourists identify with an idealized colonial past (hardly the historical reality): it is no coincidence that the most visited countries of Africa are those with a past of colonial white settlement, of which a history is invented and supported by an immense industry of novels, travel books, films, photographs, and the like, all intended to shape the present as a continuation of an idealized or mythicized past.

In brief, African tourism is both a form of exploitation of Africa by the outside world, a means by which the inhabitants of an impoverished continent attempt to join and profit from the presence of wealthy visitors from that world, and part of tourists' dream of the moral and eternal innocence of a believed world beyond their own.

See also **Prostitution; Transportation; Travel and Exploration; Wildlife; Zimbabwe, Great.**

BIBLIOGRAPHY

Brunerr, E. M. "The Maasai and the Lion King: Authenticity, Nationalism, and Globalization in African Tourism." *American Ethnologist* 28, no. 4 (2001): 881–908.

Gamble, W. P. *Tourism and Development in Africa.* London: Murray, 1989.

Middleton, John. "Aspects of Tourism in Kenya." *Anthropology Southern Africa* 27, nos. 3 and 4 (2004).

Popović, Vojislav. *Tourism in Eastern Africa.* Munich: Weltforum Verlag, 1972.

Sumich, Jason. "'Looking for the Other': Tourism, Power, and Identity in Zanzibar." *Anthropology Southern Africa* 23, nos. 1 and 2 (2002): 39–45.

JOHN MIDDLETON

TOWNS. *See* **Urbanism and Urbanization.**

TRACEY, HUGH (1903–1977). Born in England, Hugh Tracey was sent to Southern Rhodesia in 1920 to work on his brother's farm where his fascination with the music and folklore of Karanga farm workers led him to take a group of Karanga men to Johannesburg to be recorded by Columbia, London in 1929, thus producing the first-ever recording of the indigenous music of Southern Rhodesia. In the following years he developed his diverse abilities as an engineer, researcher, writer, publisher, lecturer, and broadcaster. Encouraged to carry on with the survey, collect and classify aspect of his work, he received funding from a Carnegie Fellowship, which allowed him, from June 1932 to July 1933, to record over 600 items on aluminum discs.

For twelve years (1936–1947) Tracey took up broadcasting as a profession. In 1940 he began extensive research on Chopi xylophone orchestras in Mozambique. He formed the African Music Society in 1948 and began publishing its newsletter. He went on to found the International Library of African Music and its annual journal *African Music*

Hugh Tracey (1903–1977) playing kalimba. Tracey was the founder of the International Library of African Music. The kalimba is one of the many instruments of the various cultures of sub-Saharan Africa he documented during his four-decade-long career as a pioneer researcher of African music. COURTESY OF INTERNATIONAL LIBRARY OF AFRICAN MUSIC, RHODES UNIVERSITY in 1954. From recordings made on nineteen field trips throughout sub-Saharan Africa, he produced the widely acclaimed *Music of Africa* (25 LPs) and *Sound of Africa* (218) LP series. Notable publications include *Chopi Musicians* (1948) and *Dances of the Witswatersrand Gold Mines* (1952).

See also **Popular Culture: Southern Africa.**

BIBLIOGRAPHY

Tracey, Hugh. *Catalogue the Sound of Africa Series.* Vol 1. Roodeport: International Library of African Music, 1973.

DIANE THRAM

TRADE, NATIONAL AND INTERNATIONAL SYSTEMS.

Because economic prosperity has so far eluded most of the African continent, the role of international trade in African development has been at the forefront of public debates by development policy makers, analysts and researchers since the 1950s. Although it is well established, based on empirical evidence observed over many centuries, that greater openness to trade and enhanced integration into global markets is associated with higher income growth, the degree of openness and integration or marginalization of African economies is still a matter of dispute. Due to its dualist economic structures, significant parts of African economies have in all times been exposed to the rest of the world through trade, while some other parts have been locked into self subsistence and self reliance.

Although due to the growing worldwide demand for slaves, it was only during the fifteenth through nineteenth centuries that Africa's trade with the rest of the world reached its apogee, yet there is ample evidence that Africa has been trading with the rest of the world since the earliest times.

SLAVE TRADE

During the transatlantic slave trade period, which lasted about four centuries and led to the transportation of about 20 million Africans from Africa to the Americas, it is estimated that Portugal transported about 40 percent of slaves, thanks to its initial two hundred years' monopoly on the export of slaves. Britain, France, Spain, and Netherlands transported the rest. The slave trade had three legs. The first leg was the export of goods (cowrie shells used as money, beads, salt, sugar, brandy, horses, and guns) from Europe to Africa. The second leg witnessed the transportation of slaves from Africa to the Americas. The third leg was the return to Europe with the produce from the slave labor (cotton, sugar, tobacco and rum). Until the nineteenth century, difference in income per capita across countries was marginal and started to widen only with the industrial revolution. The slave trade period corresponding income growth rate was close to zero.

COLONIAL TRADE

During the early years of the colonial period, coastal areas of colonies were strategic provisioning centers, and ports of defense, at a time when control of high seas was essential for military superiority and domination. Africa's coastal areas, and progressively its interior lands, were subsequently used as sources of raw agriculture and mining materials, and outlets for colonial expansion. Trade within each colonial space was strictly controlled, with widespread prohibitions and colonial monopolistic markets.

POSTCOLONIAL TRADE

During the postcolonial period, and following accession of most African countries to independence during the 1950s and 1960s, the colonial trade system that prevailed in the colonial period continued unabated. Trade was characterized by production of primary products and commodities in the colonies and production of industrial goods in Europe. Colonial corporations from England, France, Portugal and Spain shaped trade, investments, consumption patterns and labor markets in African countries. Dependency theorists (including Paul Baran, Andre Gunder Frank, T. Dos Santos, and Samir Amin) contend that the chronic underdevelopment and poverty of third world countries could be explained to a large extent through the dynamics of the international trade system, which is characterized by "unequal exchange," exploitation of colonies, heavy penetration of foreign capital in minerals, plantations, light manufacturing sectors, and consumption patterns influenced by developed countries.

POSTINDEPENDENCE TRADE POLICIES

Due to the frailties of newly independent African state institutions and the limited domestic capacity at independence, and in the midst of the Cold War, the newly independent states emphasized inward oriented import substitution industrialization based on widespread use of tariff and non-tariff barriers to reduce external competition faced by large scale state-owned enterprises. These inward oriented trade policies led to slower growth, lagging investments, fiscal and trade deficits, chronic poverty, and persistent inequalities. These problems were exacerbated by the 1973 and 1979 oil shocks, raising debts, political instability, and dependence on foreign aid. In response to the deteriorating situation, structural reforms were launched in the early 1980s, in three phases. The first phase focused on macroeconomic stabilization. The second phase focused on supply side policies, The third phase focused on poverty alleviation including targeted social programs and safety nets. Trade and trade policy issues were at the front and center of all three phases. In recognition of the role of trade for growth, a greater emphasis is being put on trade facilitation at the borders, export diversification and competitiveness at global levels.

AFRICA IN THE GLOBAL ECONOMY AT THE START OF THE TWENTY-FIRST CENTURY

Although trade accounts for a sizeable part of each African country's gross domestic product (54.7% average in 2004), sub-Saharan Africa's shares of world trade and investment declined progressively to negligible proportions at the dusk of the twentieth century. Because the typical African country has a substantial exposure to the rest of the world through external trade, trade policy can have significant impact on sub-Saharan development prospects. Based on the early 1980s diagnostic on the causes of African stagnation, which attributed much of the fault of African's poor economic performance in the 1970s.to misguided trade policies; trade reforms carried great weight in many policy reforms implemented by African countries since the early 1980s.

IS THE AFRICAN CONTINENT OVERTRADING OR UNDERTRADING WITH THE REST OF THE WORLD?

There are presently two conflicting views with distinct policy implications on the state of Africa's integration into global markets.

The First View. According to this view, a look at the evolution of simple integration indicators (e.g., decline of Africa's share of world exports) supports the popular impression that Africa is progressively disintegrating or marginalizing from world trade [marginalization-from-trade hypothesis], and has simply missed the opportunities offered by globalization. This is evidenced by the dramatic decline of Africa's shares of world exports and imports: SSA's' shares of world exports declined from 2.5 percent in 1980 to 0.9 percent in 1999 while SSA's shares of world imports also fell from 2.1 percent to 1 percent in 1999. Similarly, Africa's shares of trade in commodities declined from about 8 percent in 1980 to only 4.4 percent in 2000. This dismal performance was achieved despite tariff preferences granted by rich countries under various preferential schemes.

This first view contends that Africa's economic marginalization and dismal economic performance is the result of its relatively isolationist policies and closed economies as well as geographical factors such as access to sea (for no fewer than fourteen economies representing a third of Africa population) and tropical climate. Contrary to other parts of the world and particularly Asia, Africa's exports (in volume) grew less rapidly than GDP, while the African continent did not participate in increased opportunities for foreign direct investments available on world markets during the post–World War II golden age of fastest economic growth of all times (1950–1973).

Although for the last four decades of the twentieth century, SSA countries had an interest in regional integration to accelerate their industrialization and growth as evidenced by the largest number of regional integration organizations globally, only 10 percent of African exports were intraregional (traded to other African countries) while 68 percent of exports from countries in Western Europe were exported to other Western European countries, and similarly 40 percent of North American exports were exported to other countries in North America. Too often, the only tangible result of regional agreements (RI) in Africa has been the creation of bloated bureaucracies, and most African RI have failed to make a significant contribution in any substantive way to rapid and sustainable growth of African economies. In the absence of full-fledged trade liberalization at the global level given low progress on multilateral trade negotiations, it is estimated that trade liberalization within SSA alone could increase intra-SSA trade by 54 percent. This increase could account for more than 36 percent of welfare gains that SSA stands to gain as a result of global trade liberalization.

The question is therefore not whether or not Africa should integrate into global economy but rather what should be the most effective form of its integration. It is contended that with better policies, Africa could trade more, attract more capital flows, and benefit immensely from full integration into the world economy, as it is well established that export and income are very closely related, and trade openness offers new opportunities including expanded markets, acquisition of new and efficient production methods and technologies, new ideas, and increased level of factor productivity. Policy implications derived from this view call for an emphasis on policy measures to expand trade opportunities.

The Second View. The first view (marginalization-from-trade hypothesis) has been challenged in recent academic research by a second view showing that Africa overall has not been left behind. This view holds that Africa does not trade too little, and the continent trades just as much as can be expected given the underlying key determinants of trade (country income, size, and geography based on econometric gravity models). According to this second view, SSA is not poor for lack of access to markets, and foreign protectionism is not responsible for poor trade and economic performance in SSA. Instead, the region is poor because of a litany of factors including lack of democracy, political instability, lack of efficient institutions (rule of law, strong property rights, lower corruption and better governance) and poor policies that are a hindrance for markets to flourish. Of the policies necessary to unleash Africa's huge economic potential and accelerate poverty reduction, trade policy is central as SSA continue to be one of the most protectionist regions in the world. Based on most recent data analysis, although the rich countries reduced their applied tariff by 84 percent between 1983 and 2003 in the context of the Uruguay round, SSA countries reduced theirs by only 20 percent. While it has become well established that countries with greater freedom to trade tend to grow faster than countries that restrict trade, non tariff protection in the poorest

countries of SSA is still four times greater than non tariff protection in rich countries. Whereas average trade tariffs declined significantly in SSA in the 1990s, they are still among the highest in the world and SSA remains one of the world's most protectionist regions, even though African leaders urge an end to protectionist and subsidy policies in the developed world. This relatively high level of African protectionism explains to a large extent why trade among Africa countries remains relatively low. Policy implications of this second view call for the need to take into account possible causality between growth and other determinants.

The contention that Africa has disintegrated from world trade is therefore called into question through the use of new econometric techniques. There is some evidence that countries in Anglophone Africa (Eastern and Southern Africa) are reversing the trend of Africa disintegration particularly in their trade with advanced counties. The African marginalization-from-trade hypothesis seems, however, to be valid only for the group of Central and Western African countries (Francophone Africa). Most recent research suggests that Francophone countries are currently underexploiting their trading opportunities and have over time witnessed disintegration, particularly in their trade with technologically advanced countries. This relatively low performance of Francophone Africa (West and Central) compared to Anglophone Africa (East and Southern Africa) might be explained by higher trade related transaction costs, greater inefficiencies in key infrastructures services, and currency arrangements (particularly prior to 1994 CFA currency devaluation) which penalize exports.

CONCLUSION

Historically, no other part of the world has achieved rapid, sustained economic growth while disconnected from the world economy. Therefore, economists tend to agree that enhancing African integration into global markets to reap the benefits of globalization is a sine qua non condition for accelerated prosperity creation in Africa. With continued improvement of macroeconomic environment, an essential precondition for sustained growth, other key complementary policy elements include the stability and integrity of legal systems, improved governance, reduced regulations for private sector development, better infrastructure, greater regional integration, and enhanced trade facilitation.

See also **Cold War; Colonial Policies and Practices; Debt and Credit; Economic Systems; Globalization; Postcolonialism; Slave Trades.**

BIBLIOGRAPHY

Cline, William. *Trade Policy and Global Poverty.* Washington, DC: Institute for International Economics, 2004.

Coe, David, and Alexander Hoffmaister. "North-South Trade: Is Africa Unusual?" *Journal of African Economies* 8, no. 2 (July 1999): 228–256.

Helpman, Elhanan. *The Mystery of Economic Growth.* Cambridge, MA: Harvard University Press, 2004.

Lewis, Peter, ed. *Africa: Dilemmas of Development and Change.* Boulder, CO: Westview Press, 1998.

Maddison, Angus. *The World Economy: A Millennial Perspective.* Paris: Development Center of the Organisation for Economic Co-operation and Development, 2006.

Subramanian, Arvind, and Natalia T. Tamirisa. "Is Africa Integrated in the Global Economy?" *IMF Staff Papers* 50, no. 3 (2003).

Oyejide, T. Ademola. "Trade Liberalization, Regional Integration, and African Development in the Context of Structural adjustment." In *African Voices on Structural Adjustment*, ed. Thankdika Mkandiwire and Charles C. Soludo. Trenton, NJ: Africa World Press, 2003.

World Bank. *Can Africa Claim the Twenty-First Century?* Washington, DC: World Bank, 2000.

SALOMON SAMEN

TRADE UNIONS.   *See* **Labor: Trades Unions** and Associations.

TRADITION, ORAL.   *See* **Literature: Oral.**

TRANSPORTATION

This entry includes the following articles:
OVERVIEW
AIR
CARAVAN
RAILWAYS
RIVER
SHIPPING AND PORTS

OVERVIEW

When discussing transportation in Africa in the twenty-first century, it is appropriate to focus on issues and initiatives. A plan is in place to advance the aims and interventions that were part of the two decades of transport improvement programs managed under United Nations auspices in the 1980s and 1990s. Foreign multinational agencies are working closely with African partners to derive better results than previously from transport projects, and to match them more closely with broader development objectives.

Africa's transport heritage is not particularly auspicious. The essential challenges have been familiar to commentators over many decades and appear timeless and resistant to resolution. Major problems are the expense of transport (twice as high as in some Asian developing countries), and the geographical unevenness of good quality transport service. In low traffic volume rural areas there is often only very limited access to even underprovided public transport: more than 66 percent of Africans live further than one mile from an all-season road. Statistics about roadside waiting time for delayed and postponed scheduled bus service are not available.

In many places public transport service is slow, overcrowded, and erratic. Dangerous road transport is occasioned by driver wage schemes that encourage overloading and speeding on potholed and unmarked roads. As on land, dangerous air and inland water transport derives from weak regulation, poor law enforcement, and harsh operating conditions. There is underinvestment everywhere in all modes of transport used by poor people. Long lines of vehicles form at inadequately served public transport terminals and at docks and cross-border customs posts.

Mobility inequalities are startling: in Africa's capital cities gleaming latest-model imported motor cars cruise past pedestrians whose onerous long-distance walking consumes time and energy that could be used more productively. Donkey carts and hand carts crowd urban streets where traffic segregation has collapsed. Transport made vulnerable by underinvestment and war is particularly prone to damage by extreme weather events. Haphazard and make-do transport caricatures Africa with good reason. Worst of all, thousands of Africans die (between 62,000 and 82,000 in 2000) or are injured each year on inadequately lit and badly marked, narrow roads: shamed by the world's highest per capita rate of traffic deaths (28 per hundred thousand people), Africa accounts for twice as many (10%) of the world's road fatalities than its share (less than 5%) of the world's registered vehicles.

The enormous challenge of starting to reverse African transport problems is the task of a new grouping of several development agencies and lenders working under the umbrella of the sub-Saharan African Transport Policy Program. Here, multilateral foreign financial, technical, and managerial assistance continues to replace the corporate and nationalist transport programs of the past. The endeavor is to learn from a fragmented and disappointing transport investment and aid record. So far, postcolonial transport investment in Africa has only created short-lived and piecemeal improvements in a few places for a few privileged people.

Previous transport interventions in Africa have tended to focus on engineering improvements that link more places, carry more people and commodities, and quicken transport. Some prestige infrastructure projects had more of a symbolic purpose. Accommodating these interventions to the geographical and cultural diversity of Africa proved difficult, not least in circumstances of declining public funding and regional rivalry. Disjointed country- and mode-specific planning and provision contributed to ineffectiveness. The domination of public monopolies in transport ownership and management concealed subsidies and other inefficiencies.

Current transport interventions in Africa are focused on making transport more effective and affordable. The aim is to help African economies become more competitive globally and to help Africans overcome their poverty. The target is also facilitation of improved mobility at levels that are fiscally and environmentally sustainable: injudicious road building can aggravate poverty by harming agricultural self-sufficiency and ecological integrity.

Physical transport provision is being aligned carefully with other steps. Improving transport while simultaneously creating jobs is an obvious instance of appropriate transport planning and investment: in the rural roads sector for instance, awarding building and maintenance contracts to

local work parties generates wages, crease a sense of ownership and responsibility, can restore dignity to unemployed people, and can empower women (who shoulder two-thirds of the rural transport burden). Using local materials and simple hand tools is cost effective and environmentally appropriate in the context of designing, building, and maintaining roads to service affordable and sustainable non-motorized local transport in the impoverished African countryside.

For some years there have been efforts in Africa to commercialize public transport. Easing private sector investment in transport is one way of encouraging enterprising and efficient transport resource management: awarding operating concessions to specialist road constructors and managers, and to specialist rail builders and operators, has not yet yielded the results expected, Africa's airports and 80 major sea ports (which conduct more than 90% of the continent's overseas trade) remain outside the private sector.

A notable step forward in twenty-first century transport programming in Africa is its alignment with nontransport goals. Notably, the New Partnership for Africa's Development (NEPAD) has leant its political support to using transport as a way of integrating African economies so as to enlarge internal markets and achieve economies of scale in production and circulation. Key here is the project to create transit corridors without the borders and barriers that slow trade and raise the costs of commerce. Harmonizing transport and trade practices on roads and waterways that link maritime states to the continent's fifteen landlocked countries would increase Africa's competitive access to continental and global markets, and spur economic growth. Focusing transport investment at selected regional transport hubs is intended to yield better returns than spreading investment more thinly: superior services and facilities at a few maritime, rail, and air centers can expedite traffic handling and eliminate wasteful over-provision and unnecessary competition.

Transport is also being used as a lever to help achieve the United Nations Millennium Development goals in Africa. Improved transport is clearly able to assist eradication of extreme poverty and hunger, attainment of universal completion of primary schooling and gender equality, reduction of child and maternal mortality rates, curtailment of the spread of communicable diseases, and improvement of access to work opportunities for the poorest people. For example, better and more affordable transport will allow more Africans to access educational and health care opportunities, will allow distribution of medical services and distribution of emergency humanitarian food and medical supplies. Transport workforce education and training will slow the transmission of HIV/AIDS at transit and transfer points and at transport construction sites, and curb the consequent loss of social capital in the transport sector and in the continent's primary transport corridors.

The institutional and organizational reform that supports the new thinking about transport intervention in Africa includes the gesture of holding public consultation exercises in Africa, establishing multilingual local secretariats, and simplifying the bewildering multiplication of more-or-less opaque transport agencies and subagencies of the late twentieth century. On a managerial level, steps are being taken to operationalize and standardize data collection for monitoring transport conditions and transport improvements across the continent. Training Africans to operate transport services and projects is an important long-term capacitation exercise. There is also a shift toward a style of participatory transport planning that creates opportunities for civil society to become involved in solving public transport problems, not least women's transport needs.

The current efforts to rehabilitate and restructure African transportation are ambitious. Their deliberate integration with other pro-poor and growth initiatives gives them a greater chance of success than some of their less coherent predecessors. African transport may indeed be on the threshold of a new era. Plan implementation, adherence and momentum will be crucial if the grand intentions are to touch and improve the lives of millions of African farmers, entrepreneurs, commuters, mothers, and school children who face variously inaccessible, unaffordable, unreliable, and unsafe transport.

See also **Aid and Development; Labor; United Nations; Urbanism and Urbanization.**

BIBLIOGRAPHY

Bryceson, D. F., et al. "Livelihoods, Daily Mobility and Poverty in Sub-Saharan Africa." *Transport Reviews* 23, no. 2 (2003): 177–196.

Goldstein, A. "Infrastructure Development and Regulatory Reform in Sub-Saharan Africa, the Case of Air Transport." *World Economy* 24, no. 2 (2001): 221–248.

Gysels, M., et al. "Truck Drivers, Middlemen and Commercial Sex Workers: AIDS and the Mediation of Sex in South West Uganda." *AIDS Care* 13, no. 3 (2001): 373–385.

Howe, J. "'Filling the Middle': Uganda's Appropriate Transport Services." *Transport Reviews* 23, no. 2 (2003): 161–176.

Jones, Jim A. *Industrial Labor in the Colonial World: Workers of the Chemin de Fer Dakar-Niger, 1881–1963.* Portsmouth, NH: Heinemann, 2002.

Koster, J. H., and M. de Langen. *Low-Cost Mobility in African Cities.* Proceedings of the Velomondial-World Bank Expert Group Meeting, Delft, The Netherlands, June 12–23, 2000. UNESCO-IHE, 2001.

Martinez, A. J. T. "Road Maintenance Policies in Sub-Saharan Africa: Unsolved Problems and Acting Strategies." *Transport Policy* 8 (2001): 257–265.

Mashiri, P. "Managing 'Face' in Urban Public Transport: Polite Request Strategies in Commuter Omnibus Discourse in Harare." *Zambezia* 28, no. 1 (2001): 85–95.

Monson, J. *Freedom Railway to Ordinary Train: A Rural History of TAZARA.* Portsmouth, NH: Heinemann, 2006.

Mutambirwa, C., and B. J. Turton. "Air Transport Operations and Policy in Zimbabwe, 1980–1998." *Journal of Transport Geography* 8, no. 1 (2000): 67–76.

Njoh, A. J. "Transportation Infrastructure and Economic Development in Sub-Saharan Africa." *Public Works Management and Policy* 4, no. 4 (2000): 286–296.

Porter, G. "Living in a Walking World: Rural Mobility and Social Equity Issues in Sub-Saharan Africa." *World Development* 30 (2002): 285–300.

Wilkie, D. S., et al. "Roads, Development and Conservation in the Congo Basin." *Conservation Biology* 14 (2000): 1614–1622.

GORDON PIRIE

AIR

Much of African air transport remains isolated from the transformation of the global aviation industry by competition, privatization, and deregulation. Little has been realized from plans for a liberalized African air transport policy, set out in the 1988 Yamoussoukro Declaration, reaffirmed in 1994 and followed by the Yamoussoukro Decision in 1999, which is (in principle if not yet reality) implementable and enforceable. In 2005 the African Union again failed to reach agreement on an implementation date, largely because of fears concerning the impact of competition on national airlines. Due to this protectionism, expansion of air services between African countries remains restricted. Although there are notable exceptions, such as Kenya Airlines, many African carriers are still wholly or partially state-owned, and moves toward privatization are constrained by financial losses and debts.

The historical development of air transport in Africa, allied to widespread poverty and warfare, ensures that many of the factors impacting on the demand for, and supply of, airline services are external to the continent. Africa's air transport networks largely evolved under colonialism, while independence led to the creation of a plethora of small state-owned national carriers. The balance of demand for air transport still remains located outside the continent although regional and domestic traffic typically accounts for between 30 to 50 percent of the market. Although demand for air transport is growing at a rate higher than the world average, Africa accounts for less than 5 percent of global airline activity and only 3 percent of aircraft departures.

While almost every country in Africa supports a national carrier, most have limited networks and resources to add to their lack of global presence. Only South African Airways (SAA) (34), Egyptair (69), and Royal Air Maroc (RAM) (85) were included in the world's leading 100 airline companies (by revenues) in 2005, according to an August 2006 issue of *Airline Business*. Such problems of scale are compounded by a lack of cooperation between the various state-owned airlines. Air Afrique, originally established in 1961 by the 11 Yaoundé Treaty states, collapsed in 2001. There are, however, encouraging signs of foreign investment in African airlines. RAM is the majority shareholder in Air Senegal International, Virgin Atlantic owns 49 percent of Virgin Nigeria Airways, while Kenya Airlines is 26 percent owned by KLM. Comair in South Africa is a British Airways franchisee. Only Kenya Airlines and SAA, however, are affiliated to global airline global alliances (2006). Trade with Europe, tourism, and VFR traffic are the primary generators of air traffic into Africa (IATA, 2006). The Republic of South Africa is the dominant business destination, and SAA has reconfigured its network in the post-apartheid era to reflect the country's increasingly prominent role within the continent. Nigeria also generates significant business traffic, not least because of oil. According to the World Trade Organization, in 2004, 31 million tourists arrived by air, virtually all in North, East, and South Africa.

Political fragmentation and the failure to develop collaborative ventures has produced a plethora of international airports, some of which support only a few relatively low-frequency scheduled connections to Europe or the Middle East, where Paris, Brussels, London, and Dubai are the most frequently served cities. The most important African international airports include Addis Ababa, Cairo, Nairobi, Dakar, and Casablanca, but only Johannesburg (83), the dominant intercontinental hub in southern Africa, was listed in the world's top 100 airports in 2005 (by passengers carried), according to a June 2006 issue of *Airline Business*. The limited charter market is almost entirely controlled by European companies. While the bulk of air cargo is carried as belly-hold freight in passenger aircraft, few African airlines operate dedicated freighters and international cargo services, mostly handling perishable commodities such as foodstuffs and flowers, are often flown by European-based carriers.

International services within Africa also tend to be restricted in scope and frequency. Five separate regional concentrations can be identified: North Africa, centered on Casablanca, Algiers, Tripoli, and Cairo; a dispersed network in West Africa; Southern Africa focusing on Johannesburg and Cape Town; East Africa, converging on Addis Ababa and Nairobi; and the Indian Ocean islands. Although these regional complexes remain poorly connected to each other, east-west linkages being particularly limited both in absolute number and frequency, both Ethiopian Airlines and Kenya Airways are developing their intra-African networks. Domestic passenger services are also restricted, their provision reflecting factors such as variations in tourism, distribution of urban centers, business demand, and levels of disposable income. The largest networks are in South Africa, Kenya, Nigeria, and the Maghreb states. Numerous third-level operators provide nonscheduled services for the tourist industry and aid agencies.

See also **Addis Ababa; Cairo; Casablanca; Dakar; Johannesburg; Nairobi; Tourism; Tripoli; Urbanism and Urbanization.**

BIBLIOGRAPHY

Abeyratne, R. "Implications of the Yamoussoukro Decision on African aviation." *Air and Space Law* 28 (2003): 280–293.

Airline Business. "Aiports." *Airline Business* 22, no. 6 (2006): 50–60.

Airline Business. "The World Airline Rankings." *Airline Business* 22, no. 8 (2006): 58–86.

Doganis, R. *The Airline Business in the 21st Century.* London: Routledge, 2001.

IATA. *Passenger and Freight Forecast, 2005–2009.* Montreal: IATA, 2006.

Pirie, G. "Passenger Traffic in the 1930s on British Imperial Air Routes: Refinement and Revision." *Journal of Transport History* 25 (2004): 66–84.

Pirie, G. "'Africanization' of South Africa's International Air Links, 1994–2003." *Journal of Transport Geography* 14 (2006): 3–14.

World Tourism Organization. *Tourism Market Trends 2004—Africa.* Madrid: World Tourism Organization, 2005.

BRIAN GRAHAM

CARAVAN

One institution—the caravan—dominated land transportation in Africa prior to the twentieth century. Caravans took different forms depending on prevailing socioeconomic and environmental conditions. In most regions caravans consisted of human porters, although in the Sahara Desert, the Sahel, and some other savanna and mountain landscapes, for example in Ethiopia and Maasailand, pack animals such as camels and donkeys were utilized. In vast regions of West, Central, East, and Southern Africa, porterage was ubiquitous and caravans were typically the major employers of labor, free or slave, outside agriculture.

The high cost of transportation has always made economic development difficult in Africa. In the twelfth century the Arab geographer Idrisi recorded for the East Africa coast that, as there were no pack animals among these people they had to carry the objects for the cities where they buy and sell. This was to be the case up until early colonial times. The use of draft and pack animals was virtually precluded by the presence of the trypanosome-carrying tsetse fly in broad belts of woodland that stretched across the savannas of West, Central, and eastern Africa. Domestic animals with little immunity to the parasite, such as donkeys, asses, horses and oxen, died of sleeping sickness within days of infection. For this same reason wheeled transportation was also not feasible, a further impediment being the absence of good roads except in areas of high population density such as Asante and Buganda. The solution was for the mobilization of human labor, especially where complex systems of local and regional trade emerged relatively early, for example, in Hausaland, the Akan region, and south-central Africa.

Human porterage is inefficient compared with modern mechanical forms of transportation. The economics of porterage tended to work against trade in bulky staples such as grain due to the relatively small weights that even fit professional carriers could manage. The high costs of rations and wages were also impediments. Yet given African realities, porterage was economically rational. In times of famine, porters sometimes took grain up to 120 miles to regions experiencing shortages. In normal times caravans moved high-value and low-bulk goods such as cloth, iron goods, guns, kola nuts, tobacco, and ivory. Slaves and livestock walked themselves to market. In most cases, pioneering caravaneers were peoples of the interior: the Soninke, Hausa, and Mande of West Africa, the Bisa, Yao, Kamba, Sumbwa, and Nyamwezi of East Africa, and the Chokwe, Chikunda, and Kololo farther south. Such peoples lay strategically across exchange systems, for example between livestock breeders and producers of iron. Thus the long-distance caravan systems of the eighteenth and nineteenth centuries were the offspring of local and regional trading patterns.

During the early stages the role of women in local trade and small-scale caravan operation was particularly important, for example, amongst the N'yanja of Malawi, the Kamba, and the salt caravans to Lake Eyasi of Tanzania's Sukuma. International trade was a motor for the emergence of more specialized caravan systems as regional trade systems merged to create vast networks stretching across the continent. For example, the Nyamwezi and Sumbwa of present-day Tanzania, stimulated by news of the demand for ivory at the coast, crossed Lake Malawi to reach the Luangwa Valley in Zambia to exploit the great elephant herds. By the second half of the eighteenth century they were organizing caravans to coastal towns such as Kilwa Kivinje, Mbwa Maji, Pangani, and then Bagamoyo. In time they created a vast trading and laboring diaspora, stretching from Zanzibar to Nyangwe on the Congo River, and from Katanga (Shaba) to Bunyoro. They dominated the East and Central African trade routes, organizing their own large caravans that set out from trading chiefdoms such as Unyanyembe (present-day Tabora) and the capitals of the empire builder, Mirambo.

The Nyamwezi, porters and traders par excellence, also worked on a wage basis for African Arab caravan operators from the Swahili coast. The latter were never able to supersede their rivals, despite the fame of great coastal traders and caravan operators such as Tippu Tip, Rumaliza, Said Habib, and others. The coast men were typically funded by Indian financiers based at Zanzibar and Bagamoyo, and frequently in debt to them. Rapidly increasing ivory exports due to the spread of middle-class consumption in Europe and North America, and African demand for mass-produced cloth and guns, were the motors of the caravan system. The increasingly favorable balance of trade drove an expanding elephant frontier into the center of the continent and large caravans of up to 3,000 members took longer and longer journeys between sources of supply and markets. On the opposite coast from the Portuguese sphere the *pombeiros* of Benguela and other towns, portrayed in Angolan novelist Pepetela's book *Yeke*, fulfilled a similar role to the African Arabs.

Specialist caravan workers increasingly engaged in migrant or itinerant labor, sometimes signing up for a new journey on the completion of a safari. On the Gold Coast and in Yorubaland, as well as in East Africa, professional porters, guards, guides, and headmen staffed the caravans. Most porters remained connected to their rural homes, but while on safari they were a mobile workforce with its own widely recognized customs, ethics, and codes of honor. While traveling they were almost a proletariat, completely separated as they were from their home communities and agricultural subsistence. They were dependent on their wages, typically paid in fixed units of cloth, and rations were supplied in

kind or, more frequently, in the small currency of the region. Porters invested their wages and perhaps profits from small scale trade in agriculture, cattle, slaves, and bride price. As caravan labor became specialized, the caravan business followed suit. Specialist recruitment agencies and caravan outfitters emerged. In East Africa the best known was operated by the Khoja, Sewa Haji, who plowed back some of his profits into hospitals for sick porters. More often, large traders or entrepreneurial chiefs managed recruitment, either through patron client networks or direct recruitment in the towns and villages in commercialized regions. An alternative was to hire headmen who would deliver their own porter gangs.

The caravan system was a primary force in changing the infrastructure of trade and urbanization. Port cities, market towns, and caravanserais rose and fell according to the dynamics of the caravan system. Routes changed depending on the availability of food supplies, political conditions, and economic calculations. A feature of the routes was the emergence of trading and caravanning diasporas, notably those of Mande, Soninke, and Hausa speakers in West Africa and the Nyamwezi, and Swahili in the east. New urban centers such as Ujiji (on Lake Tanganyika), Tabora, and Bagamoyo were creatures of the caravans. In Yoruba towns like Ife and Ibadan and in the Akan region specialized quarters were reserved for Hausa traders of cloth and kola nuts. In some regions the caravan infrastructure was shaped by the hajj. Muslim pilgrims from many parts of West Africa and the Horn often merged with commercial ventures, the West Africans crossing Darfur, a caravan crossroads, to the Nile Valley, whereas those from the Muslim fringe of Ethiopia and Somalia trekked to the Red Sea ports through Harar and other Muslim towns.

Porters carried loads either on their heads or their shoulders. Loads were specially packaged (in Zanzibar this itself was a task for skilled packers) to be of a standard weight and size. Elephant tusks, being frequently heavy, were the prerogative of the porter elite, and in East Africa Herculean porters might carry a tusk weighing 120 pounds over 600 miles to the coast. Wages, paid either per month or per journey, were usually disbursed in fixed units of cloth or other currency. In East Africa the standard unit was the *doti merikani*—four-meter lengths of plain American calico—although wages were calculated in Maria Theresa thalers. Professional slave porters in the Imerina kingdom on Madagascar frequently struck for higher wages, as did the Islamicized slave and freed slave *Waungwana* of the East African coast. Most commonly resistance to poor wages and conditions was expressed through desertion, either en masse or in drabs and drabs. The threat of desertion by professional porters served to discipline naïve caravan operators, as the balance of power often lay with their men. Nyamwezi porters when deserting typically left their loads behind, minus any owed wages. To steal was a disgrace. Indeed, the earliest colonial labor legislation of Kenya and Zanzibar contained customary provisions derived from the norms of East African caravan culture ensuring standard loads, punishments for infractions, rest periods, and rations.

At the same time caravans were mobile villages. Women and children often traveled with their men. In East Africa as well as in the Sudan, so-called caravan marriages replaced more formal relationships. Women fleeing slavery or unwanted marriages frequently found a new vocation and relative freedom in the caravans, much decried by nineteenth-century missionaries. Many caravan operators found that the presence of women increased the productivity of their porters and reduced incidents of sickness. Typically, women carried food and the comforts of the camp whereas their partners managed the standard loads of between sixty and seventy-five pounds. In some cases, for example among the Manyema, women themselves carried heavy loads on their backs.

Caravans were not only a form of transportation. Just as significantly they were the prime movers of new forms of culture and socioeconomic organization into remote regions. With the caravans went Islam and Christianity, as well as some aspects of older African cosmologies. Indeed, early European missionaries and explorers were forced to adapt to the realities of caravan travel as hundreds of diaries and journals attest. New forms of expressionist culture, especially music, dance, clothing, and personal ornamentation, swept up and down the caravan routes, not only from the coasts to the interior, but from the interior to the port towns and even beyond to the maritime world of the Atlantic and Indian Oceans. Indeed, professional porters of the long-distance caravans held much in common with merchant mariners of the world of sail.

The safari experience stimulated stories, songs, and poems, told and retold to rapt audiences at caravan stops and market towns. Ritual joking relationships (*utani* in Kiswahili) crossed the East African savanna and the Senegambia/Mali region in the west. An institution derived from the kin and clan relationships, *utani* linked peoples from vastly different backgrounds in relationships of hospitality and mutual aid. Along the central caravan route between Ujiji and Bagamoyo, the Nyamwezi were joking partners with no less than thirty-one different ethnic groups. *Utani* lubricated relationships among porters of differing origins, and between caravan personnel and host communities. *Utani* was perfectly suited as a readily available cultural concept for adaptation to the liminal situations regularly encountered by caravan porters. Finally, specialist caravan traders and porters brought the world of the market to regions hitherto not exposed. Ideas of entrepreneurship, profit, and wage labor were integral to the caravan business amongst the Soninke of Mauritania and Mali, the coastal peoples of the Gold Coast (Ghana), and the Nyamwezi. Wherever they went, such peoples stimulated innovative ideas and cultural change, introduced new goods (such as firearms, mass-produced textiles) and crops (white rice and tobacco), and contributed to emerging intersocietal cultures.

See also **Congo River; Disease: Viral and Infectious; Ivory; Labor; Livestock: Domestication; Marriage Systems; Pilgrimages: Islamic; Sahara Desert; Textiles; Tippu Tip; Trade, National and International Systems; Urbanism and Urbanization.**

BIBLIOGRAPHY

Campbell, Gwyn. "Labour and the Transport Problem in Imperial Madagascar, 1810–1895." *Journal of African History* 21 (1980): 341–356.

Coquery-Vidrovitch, Catherine, and Paul E. Lovejoy, eds. *The Workers of African Trade.* Beverley Hills, CA: Sage Publications, 1985.

Isaacman, Allen, and Barbara Isaacman. *Slavery and Beyond: The Making of Men and Chikunda Ethnic Identities in the Unstable World of South-Central Africa, 1750–1920.* Portsmouth, NH: Heinemann, 2004.

Lovejoy, Paul E. *Caravans of Kola: The Hausa Kola Trade 1700–1900*. Zaria, Nigeria: Ahmadu Bello University Press Ltd., 1980.

Manchuelle, Francois. *Willing Migrants: Soninke Labor Diasporas, 1848–1960*. Athens: Ohio University Press, 1997.

Northrup, David. *Beyond the Bend in the River: African Labor in Eastern Zaire, 1865–1940*. Athens: Ohio University Press, 1988.

Ogunremi, Gabriel Ogundeji. *Counting the Camels: The Economics of Transportation in Pre-Industrial Nigeria* New York: NOK Publishers International, 1982.

Rockel, Stephen J. *Carriers of Culture: Labor on the Road in Nineteenth-Century East Africa*. Portsmouth, NH: Heinemann, 2006.

STEVEN ROCKEL

RAILWAYS

Rail transport was generally viewed in the nineteenth and early twentieth centuries as one of the crucial factors that could bring about tropical Africa's economic development. For instance, a prominent colonialist stated that the development of the African continent is impossible without railways, and has awaited their advent. When eventually railways arrived and took hold of the continent, they brought about revolutionary economic, political, and social changes.

Prior to the colonization of Africa and the construction of railways in the region, the means of transport included pack animals, waterways and water transportation, and human porterage. They were adequate for the needs of precolonial African political economy. However, with the rapid development and modernization of the economy from the nineteenth century through colonization, the traditional modes of transport proved expensive, slow, and inefficient for the volume of goods and number of people to be carried. This was particularly so for the human porterage mode of transport.

It was against this backdrop of transport inadequacies that private commercial interests started agitating for railway development in Africa in the first half of the nineteenth century. But nothing happened by way of railway construction until toward the end of that century, when major European powers that in the past had been hesitant to be drawn into formal colonization of Africa and the attendant construction of railways changed

their minds. This was because of the heightened rivalry among European powers, especially after the Berlin Conference of 1884–1885.

To register their presence in territories that had been acquired, and to ensure that important export commodities—agricultural crops and minerals—were not diverted by rival European traders and powers, each European state began constructing competing railway lines across the continent. Thus began the phenomenon of railway imperialism in Africa. However, this imperialism was not without costs to the continent.

Although the construction of railways brought many advantages, such as increased transportation efficiency, urbanization, increased agricultural and mineral production, reduced cost of transport, and the provision of a genuine alternative to the degrading human porterage, it equally brought many problems. These included a new relations of production (capitalism), underdevelopment, regional inequality, destruction of peasant agriculture, huge debts caused by loans secured to construct the railways, economic dependency, promotion of wage labor, marginalization of African peasant farmers, rural poverty, labor migration, and the creation of cheap labor reserves.

RAILWAY DEVELOPMENT

The first railway line was constructed from the Cape in South Africa in 1859. This modest beginning was later followed by massive railway developments in the region—the consequence of the discovery of diamonds in Kimberley in 1870. This pattern of railway construction that was dependent on the discovery of mineral resources was subsequently replicated across sub-Saharan Africa from the late nineteenth century to the second half of the twentieth century. Such railways were constructed in Belgian Congo (present-day Democratic Republic of the Congo, or DRC), Rhodesia (present-day Zimbabwe), Bechuanaland (Botswana), Mozambique, Angola, Gold Coast (Ghana), Nigeria, Sierra Leone, Liberia, and Uganda.

However, it was not only for the exploitation of mineral resources that railways were constructed. Some were primarily built because of military, administrative, strategic, and political reasons. For others, they were built to accelerate the production and transportation of agricultural products. It was for this reason that the Sierra Leone Railway was constructed to the oil palm producing regions. Similarly the Kumasi-to-Accra line was constructed to connect the cocoa areas. In Nigeria, the Kano-to-Lagos railway was to stimulate cotton production, and it later served as a catalyst for the cocoa and groundnut producing areas. Furthermore, some railways were constructed to serve as important transport links to some of the prominent and navigable African rivers such as the Senegal, Niger, Benue, Congo, and Zambezi.

One important point to note is that, more often than not, non mineral-related railways could not pay their way. Also, most of the railways were no-frills lines; built with shoestring budgets, they were mostly single lines laid with light steel rails. As much as possible, physical obstacles along their routes were avoided. Hence, the overwhelming majority of Africa's railways—apart from South Africa and North Africa, which had well integrated railways comparable to those in Europe and America—are characterized by sharp curves, steep gradients, and roundabout routes. Thus on the whole, train speeds were restricted and there were limits to the capacities of goods and passengers they could carry. Another major feature of railroad construction in Africa, especially in the late nineteenth century and early twentieth century, was the extensive use of forced labor in most parts of the continent as Mason and Ousmene have clearly shown in their works on the controversial issue.

By the 1930s, the main structure of Africa's railway network had developed. In the next two decades, there were few railway extensions built, but no major constructions. Meanwhile, during this latter period rail transport started experiencing stiff competition from road transport vis-à-vis passenger service and short-distance, less-bulky freight transportation. However, in the long-haul freight sector, rail transport had no rivals as it could carry bulk freight—agricultural products and mineral resources, the backbones of African economy—over great distances, and at cheaper costs than road transport. It thus profited greatly from this peculiar freight from the mid-1940s to the early 1960s. Such gains were also aided by the construction of new railway lines in many colonial territories from the second half of the 1950s to the 1970s. Some of the countries and territories where new railways were constructed include Nigeria, Gabon, Kenya, Angola, Mozambique, Ghana, Democratic Republic of the Congo, Tanzania, and Uganda.

POSTINDEPENDENCE RAILWAY DEVELOPMENTS

In addition, from the 1970s onward, more railways were constructed for the exploitation of mineral resources. These railway developments continued the colonial vertical construction patterns that were designed to transport minerals and agricultural products from the interior to the coast. There were few lateral lines although some did exist in Ghana, Tanzania, and DRC. The longest of these was the 404-mile Nouadhibour-to-F'Derik-and-Tazadit iron deposit railway in Mauritania, which was opened in 1963. Also in 1963, another iron line was opened in Liberia to connect the town of Buchanan to the Mount Nimba iron mines.

However, the most important railway development at this time was that of the 1,156-mile Kapiri Mposhi (Zambia)-to-Dar es Salaam (Tanzania): the Tanzam Railway. First conceived during the colonial period, it was not built before the 1970s due to lack of justifiable economic reason. However, when the Ian Smith (b. 1919) regime in Rhodesia (present-day Zimbabwe) imposed a blockage on the movement of goods to and from landlocked Zambia that would pass through Rhodesian ports, Zambia and Tanzania both approached China, which not only provided a US$400 million loan for the project but also constructed the international railway line that opened in 1975.

This modernization program of African railways of the 1960s and 1970s could have continued to the next decade and beyond except for two reasons. First, according to *United Nations, UN Transport and Communications Decade for Africa*, the World Bank and the United Nations advised African nations to stop further modernization programs and concentrate instead on modernizing road transport. The nations were told they should only maintain the existing railway infrastructure. Second, from the late 1970s onward, Africa started experiencing serious economic crises that led the continent into huge foreign debts. To bail out African nations from their economic morass, the World Bank and the International Monetary Fund (IMF) recommended that African leaders adopt the Structural Adjustment Program (SAP) under which African nations were obliged to implement specific economic reforms that included the liberalization of the economies, removal of tariffs and controls, devaluation of the national currencies, and privatization of state institutions and corporations such as those managing the railways.

The consequences of these reforms were that, one, there was reduced funding of the railway authorities by the various governments—hitherto their main financiers. Two, due to the devaluation of the currencies, the importation of machinery, spare parts, locomotives, rolling stocks, steel rails, and communication equipment (in the case of the railway industry) became costly to procure from abroad. Thus many railways in Africa fell into disrepair. To compound an already serious situation, some of the inherited antiquated railways were destroyed by the many conflicts that have engulfed the continent since independence in the early 1960s.

GLOBALIZATION AND RAILWAY DEVELOPMENT

It was in this context of bleak future prospect of rail transport in Africa that some observers began trumpeting the complete end of rail transport in Africa. However, with the ever-increasing impact of economic globalization on the continent and the attendant foreign investment prospect, the privatization of African railways that started imperceptibly in the mid-1990s has, since the beginning of the new millennium, accelerated rapidly. The impetus for these developments is the keen interest shown by Western multinational corporations and the Chinese, Korean, Japanese, Taiwanese, and South African governments and institutions in investing in the rail sector. Already these investors have entered into negotiations and, by 2007, were on the verge of clinching many deals under which dilapidated rail infrastructure was to be replaced and modernized.

For instance, the South African railway company, Spoornet, has invested capital in some East and Southern African railways. In addition, it has many railway management contracts in Democratic Republic of the Congo and Tanzania. Apart from Spoornet, a group of Canadian investors, the East African Railway Development Corporation, has gained many concessions to manage railways in Tanzania, Kenya, Uganda, and Zambia.

Meanwhile, in West Africa, Nigeria in late 2006 embarked on a twenty-five-year reorganization and modernization program for its nearly dead railway industry. As a first step, in November 2006 the country embarked on the first phase of the project: the construction of the 628-mile double-track standard-gauge railway line from Lagos to Kano. The cost of this first phase is US$8.3 billion, and is to be covered by loans from the Chinese government and other foreign investors.

Thus, it would appear that the future of rail transport in Africa is brighter and more promising in the twenty-first century than it was in the closing decades of the twentieth. However, the success of any railway modernization in Africa will depend on many factors, which, if not properly handled, could still scuttle the march of progress. Chief among these is political and economic stability on the continent. Unless this is achieved over a long period of time, foreign investors are likely to be scared away from investing in the industry. Secondly, the African economy must continue to grow in leaps and bounds so that it will be able to produce the necessary volume of goods and the right number of passengers needed for a commercially viable railway industry.

See also **Accra; Agriculture; Colonial Policies and Practices; Dar es Salaam; Economic History; Globalization; International Monetary Fund; Kano; Kumasi; Labor: Conscript and Forced; Lagos; Metals and Minerals; United Nations; Urbanism and Urbanization; World Bank.**

BIBLIOGRAPHY

Arnold, Guy. *A Guide to African Political & Economic Development.* London: Fitzroy Dearborn, 2001.

Christopher, A. J. *Colonial Africa.* Totowa, NJ: Barnes and Noble, 1984.

Davis Clarence, and Kenneth E. Wilburn, eds. *Railway Imperialism.* New York: Greenwood Press, 1991.

Hilling, David. *Transport and Developing Countries.* London: Routledge, 1996.

Konczacki, Z. A., and J. M. Konczacki, eds. *An Economic History of Tropical Africa,* Vol. II. London: Frank Cass, 1977.

Mason, M. "Working on the Railway: Forced Labor in Northern Nigeria, 1907–1912." In *African Labor History,* ed. Gutkind, P.W., R. Cohen, and J. Copans. London: Sage Publications, 1978.

O'Connor, Anthony. *Railways and Development in Uganda.* Oxford: Oxford University Press, 1965.

O'Connor, Anthony. "New Railway Construction and the Pattern of Economic Development in Uganda."

Transactions of the Institute of British Geographers 36 (1965): 21–30.

Ousmane, S. *God's Bits of Wood*. London: Heinemann, 1995.

Pedersen, Poul O. *The Changing Structure of Transport under Trade Liberalisation and Globalization and Its Impact on African Development*. Copenhagen, Denmark: Centre for Development Research, 2000.

Pirie, Gordon. "The Decivilizing Rails: Railways and Underdevelopment in Southern Africa." *Tidschrift voor Economische en Sociale Geografie* 73, no. 4 (1982): 221–228.

Simon, David. *Transport and Development in the Third World*. London: Routledge, 1996.

Udo, Reuben K. *The Human Geography of Tropical Africa*. Exeter, U.K.: Heinemann Educational Books, 1982.

United Nations, UN Transport and Communications Decade for Africa 1978–88, Vol. 1: Global Strategy and Plan of Action, First Phase, 1980–83. Addis Ababa, Ethiopia: United Nations Economic and Social Council, May 1979.

TOKUNBO AYOOLA

RIVER

Unlike the great rivers on other continents the majestic rivers of Africa were not historic waterways from the ocean to the interior. Near the mouth of all the major rivers of Africa, except the Senegal and the Gambia, the navigable passage upriver was blocked by a series of cataracts over which the broad placid flowing rivers tumbled down from the African plateau to a narrow coastal plain. These natural obstacles beyond the estuaries of African rivers prevented the sixteenth-century Portuguese and later British and French mariners from easily penetrating into the interior of Africa by ship, which forestalled the discovery of much of Africa until the nineteenth century and then by arduous journeys on foot through swamps, savannas, and rainforests. The Nile, the world's longest river (4,238 miles), and the only major river flowing south to north, is blocked by six cataracts, the first at Aswan, 800 miles from the Mediterranean Sea. Navigation on the Niger (2,604 miles) is disrupted by the Bussa Rapids above its confluence with the Benue River, and on the Congo (Zaire, 2,718 miles) plunges through a series of cataracts cut in deep canyons to a short coastal plain and the Atlantic Ocean at the small village of Muanda. After crossing the coastal plain from the Indian Ocean (1,600 miles), the Cabora Bassa Rapids prevent the Zambezi from becoming a waterway to the interior. All of these cataracts have been made more permanent by hydroelectric dams—the Aswan High Dam on the Nile, the Kainji Dam at Bussa on the Niger, and the Cabora Bassa Dam on the Zambezi.

Once above the cataracts the Nile, Niger, and Congo rivers are broad and navigable for more than a thousand miles, but the Zambezi has never been a major artery for transportation, limited to relatively short stretches between the Cabora Bassa Rapids, the Batoka Gorge, and Victoria Falls. Historically the Africans have always used the rivers for transportation. The dynastic Egyptians developed a well-organized system by which their boats would sail upstream before the steady north wind from Asia to return downstream on the current. Between its upper delta to the Bussa Rapids the Niger is navigable for more than a thousand miles and historically the major artery for trade, passengers, and war in the traditional pirogues. From its massive delta, known as the Oil Rivers, the Niger is navigable to its confluence with the Benue (Bénoué), and then for another 500 miles up its major tributary and is a major artery for trade and passengers by fleets of canoes, barges, and steamers. Similarly, the Congo flows uninterrupted downstream from Stanley Falls at Kisangani 1,000 miles to Kinshasa. This stretch of the Congo has historically been a major waterway for transportation fed by a vast network embracing 9,000 miles of navigable tributaries in Central Africa. Although not major rivers, the Senegal (1,020 miles) and Gambia are navigable for 300 miles and 302 miles respectively. The Gambia (700 miles) is the finest of all African rivers. It is the only African waterway easily accessible to oceangoing shipping and the major artery for transportation in the Republic of the Gambia.

See also **Congo River; Kinshasa; Kisangani; Niger River; Nile River; Travel and Exploration.**

BIBLIOGRAPHY

Bovill, Edward W. *The Niger Explored*. New York: Oxford University Press, 1968.

Collins, Robert O. *The Nile*. New Haven, CT: Yale University Press, 2002.

Coppinger, Mike, and Jumbo Williams. *The Zambezi: River of Africa*. London: New Holland, 1991.

Forbath, Peter. *The River Congo: The Discovery, Exploration, and Exploitation of the World's Most Dramatic River.* New York: Harper and Row, 1977.

ROBERT COLLINS

SHIPPING AND PORTS

In conformity with global trends, some 90 percent of Africa's foreign trade is channeled through the ports and conveyed by liner shipping. Cargoes constitute the bulk of freight with passengers being a minuscule proportion of the total traffic. Ports are, therefore, critical to the overseas trade and internal economies of the individual countries, including the landlocked ones.

African ports have the following general features. First, they are located on a long coastline that is generally lacking in natural indentation. Hence, there are only a few natural harbors. Second, the ports vary in size and economic importance. Third, in addition to the few natural ports, several artificial ports have also been created for economic and strategic interests. Fourth, the ports are multifunctional urban centers with considerable human population. Fifth, they are aligned with inland transport networks, especially railway lines. Sixth, though some ports were created as outlets for single commodities, such as crude and refined oil, iron ore, phosphate, or timber, most African ports handle miscellaneous exports and imports. Seventh, important inland ports along major rivers and lakes convey a portion of the traffic of the African hinterland. Finally, various colonial and post-independence governments have developed the modern ports at great financial cost.

THE DEVELOPMENT OF AFRICAN PORTS

Four major phases may be identified in the development of African ports since the period before European colonial rule in the nineteenth century. However, the Republic of South Africa, where Dutch settlers had established a colony at the Cape in the mid-seventeenth century, is an exception. The first stage, which antedated formal European colonial rule, was that of the rudimentary fishing or trading ports that had poor transport links with the hinterland. Such ports were mainly undeveloped trade outlets, primarily along lagoons and river estuaries. The second stage was transitional in that the European presence was just being established through trade and informal political rule. Links with Europe were fostered and the ports began to function as potential urban centers and increasingly important commercial centers. The third stage was the heyday of colonial rule, when rail and road links were fully established between the ports and the hinterland. The ports also served as capital cities of the emerging colonial administration. Finally, in the period since independence, new ports have been developed and old ones expanded. Rural dwellers drifted to the emergent port cities, which also became centers of commercial activity and import substitution industrialization. The ports handle increasing volumes of exports, such as tin and iron ore, diamonds, gold, timber, phosphates, crude oil, and forest produce, and a wide variety of foreign imports.

Huge capital and engineering skills have been committed to the development of old and new ports since the nineteenth century. Even at natural harbors, such as Dakar, Freetown, Lobito, and Durban, such commitments were required to make the ports accessible to oceangoing shipping. This was obligatory at ports sheltered from the sea by lagoons and shallow entrances. Hundreds of thousands of tons of stone were railed from Abeokuta, some sixty miles to the north, for harbor works at Lagos (Nigeria) by the *pierre perdue* method. Port development there consisted of the construction of moles, the dredging of the approach channels, the lengthening of the quays, and the removal of the bar at the mouth of the harbor, known as the bugbear of the bight. Altogether, port engineering works at Lagos and Port Harcourt, an artificial port in eastern Nigeria, between 1892 and 1939 increased the depth of the port's entrance and provided ample berthing facilities for oceangoing vessels. However, the projects burdened the finances of the Nigerian colony with huge debts accruing from loans raised in the metropolitan country, Britain. The Nigerian example was replicated at other African countries, notably Durban in South Africa, Tema and Takoradi in Ghana, and Mombasa in Kenya. However, investment in port development did not always justify the outlay in terms of traffic and financial returns.

A striking feature of port development in Africa from the late nineteenth century until the end of the twentieth was the coordination of harbor works with rail and road development. Indeed, rail links coupled with developed hinterlands determined the fortunes of African ports. Cape Town and Durban in South Africa, Dakar in Senegal, Mombasa in Kenya, Dar es Salaam in Tanzania, Lagos and Port Harcourt in Nigeria, and Douala in Cameroon became preeminent in their respective countries largely because of their rail connections with their hinterlands. Rail transport gave the ports access to large urban centers and sources of traffic, cut costs of transportation, and gave a decisive advantage over potential or actual rivals in terms of access to a greater share of the traffic of a contested hinterland. Lagos gained such an edge over the Niger Delta ports in the contest for the traffic of Northern Nigeria after direct rail links were established between it and Kano in 1912. The latter consequently declined or even became extinct. In the context of such inter-port competition within or across national boundaries, ports that had superior transport links, or that had access to a rich hinterland, superseded their rivals. This accounted for the edge that Durban had over other South African ports, and what allowed Lagos to be overwhelmingly superior to other Nigerian ports.

During the twentieth century, government policy, technological development, and global economic trends were crucial to the pattern and magnitude of port development. The oscillation between concentration and diffusion was the general pattern of development of African ports from the nineteenth century. Ports developed and declined in accordance with the growth or decline of the domestic and global economies. During an economic boom, African countries with multiple port outlets maintained a multiplicity of such outlets, whereas an economic slump, with the concomitant decrease in port throughput, led to the concentration of overseas trade at only a few ports. In addition, whereas port diffusion was a feature of peacetime trade, concentration was a wartime imperative as witnessed during the world wars of the twentieth century.

SHIPPING

The shipping business developed unevenly across Africa. Although the maritime countries of North and East Africa have recorded several centuries of indigenous seafaring across the Mediterranean and Indian Oceans, those of West Africa only engaged in local seafaring activities, in spite of the wide-ranging fishing activities of the Izon (Ijaw) and Ilaje of Nigeria, and the Ewe and Fante of Togo and Ghana, respectively. Generally, dhows and small fishing craft were in use on Africa's rivers, lakes, and seaways, and often over long distances. However, with the coming of the Europeans from the fifteenth century, sail, and later, steam ships facilitated the trans-Atlantic slave trade, and, from the late nineteenth century, the trade in forest produce. From the latter date, European shipping lines established regular services between Africa and the wider world, mainly Europe. In due course, they formed shipping conferences or rings that kept out African and foreign competitors and determined freight rates. These rates tended to be high, compared to other routes.

During the first half of the twentieth century, the dominant shipping lines were Britain's Elder Dempster, the German Woemann Linie, the French Chargeurs Reunis, and the Dutch West African Line. The American Bull Line played a minor role during the inter-war years. However, the two world wars eliminated German shipping and consolidated the hold of British and Allied shipping on the trade. In the second half of the twentieth century, African national lines competed unsuccessfully with the established foreign lines that continued to carry the preponderant proportion of Africa's maritime trade. Not even the intervention of the United Nations Conference on Trade and Development (UNCTAD), which produced a Liner Code that allocated favorable quotas of Africa's seaborne trade to indigenous lines during the 1970s, could tilt the balance in favor of African shipping lines. Lack of capacity, which government-assisted fleet development was meant to address, remained the bane of indigenous shipping in Africa.

Into the early twenty-first century, the indigenous share of African shipping has been insignificant even as national governments have played a key role in fleet development. Ghana, Nigeria, Cameroon, and Côte d'Ivoire, among others, established national shipping lines during the twentieth century with varying success. These were the products of the maritime nationalism in the aftermath of the countries' independence from European rule from the mid-1950s. However, by the late 1990s, these government-operated shipping lines had folded up in the wake of mismanagement and official corruption. In spite of the favorable environment created by the UNCTAD Liner Code, African national shipping lines failed to control a significant share of their overseas carrying trade. Though the Code gave national lines a statutory monopoly of their coastwise shipping and a statutory share of foreign trade, the freighters failed to establish a monopoly of the former or to carry any significant share of the latter because of the failure of their fleet development projects. Funds for fleet development were simply diverted to other uses.

The African shipping business is characterized by a preponderance of foreign ownership, unsuccessful government involvement in fleet development, the mismanagement of the maritime industry, and the low percentage of coastwise and passenger shipping. The bulk of African shipping focuses on long-sea trades with Europe, the Americas, and Asia. Passenger shipping is severely limited, as is coastwise traffic. However, passenger shipping, especially pleasure cruises, is a significant but by no means a significant proportion of shipping in South Africa. In addition, short-sea coastwise shipping is carried out in Senegal between the Casamance region and the capital, Dakar, by means of ferry boats, one of which had a fatal accident in 2002.

The fortunes of shipping in Africa have varied with the prevailing local and global economic conditions, the availability of freight, official policy, and the conditions of inland transport and harbor facilities. As the draught at the entrance of ports and availability of berthing and navigational facilities determine the capacity and number of vessels that could enter the harbor, port investment has sought to improve facilities. Port charges, too, determine the number and frequency of calls by ships, with ports such as Lagos achieving notoriety for their exorbitant tariffs. The introduction of containerization, with the attendant changes in shipbuilding and cargo-handling, has shaped the fortunes of African ports since the late twentieth century. Unitization of cargo and the creation of inland container depots in the hinterland of seaports have been facilitated by road, railway, and water transport. However, most African ports fall short of international standards in cargo handling, security, and customs administration, which affect shipping turnaround and the overall efficiency of port operations.

IMPACT OF SHIPPING AND PORTS

Ports and shipping have exerted significant social, economic, and political impact on African economies. Port cities constitute the connecting points between land and sea transport, and their urban life and culture differ in many respects from those of their hinterland counterparts. African port cities have served as capital cities and administrative centers, and are major industrial and commercial centers of the countries in which they exist. The sheer magnitude of their port traffic and the location of commercial enterprises and industries in their immediate vicinity make port cities growth poles in the local and wider settings.

As commercial and industrial hubs, port cities represent a large pool of producers and consumers. Indeed, many African port cities have large retail sectors, where women dominate the local economy. Conversely, the maritime labor market is male-dominated, given the nature of work aboard ships and at the quays. Dock and offshore laborers are recruited from proximate and distant communities. Until the mid-twentieth century, the Kru of Liberia were the specialist maritime workers in Africa. They were the dominant group of African mariners that served on board the ships of European liners that link Africa with the rest of the world. Accordingly, they registered significant social and cultural impact on their host communities along the West African coastline.

Given their multiple functions, African port cities are melting pots of cultures and civilizations, where people of diverse cultural and social backgrounds interact across racial, ethnic, and religious boundaries. Many African ports have a sprinkling of half-caste offspring of interracial liaisons, and the cities also witness criminal activities that are often perpetrated by the crews of visiting ships. Prostitution, sexually transmitted diseases, youth deviance, and avant-garde culture have also been associated with port cities.

African port cities are centers of political and social struggles, where political parties, labor unions, newspapers, and various pressure groups expose the views of various groups and communities. Lagos,

Shipping and ports. Thousands of rail and port workers from a government company, Transnet, march in Durban, South Africa, February 1, 2006, after a failure of the negotiations to restructure Transnet. Close to 100,000 workers downed tools costing the government a loss of close to US$30 million over three days. Durban harbor is the busiest port in Africa. STR/AFP/Getty Images

Durban, Dakar, and Mombasa, among other African port cities, exemplify the problems of population explosion, including unregulated urban and suburban development, increased crime, ethnic and communal disturbances, and strikes. Since the early twentieth century, maritime and railway workers' unions at the major ports have been at the vanguard of labor activism, often involving industrial action, to press for better working conditions or to articulate wider political and social issues.

Ports have exerted a considerable impact on the external trade and domestic economies of African states since the colonial period, when the African nation-states were formally integrated into the world economy as appendages of the imperial countries. The colonial economies were essentially small and heavily dependent upon their primary produce exports and were, accordingly, oriented toward the seaports, which were the termini of rail, river, and road transport systems established during the period. At independence, African nation-states accounted for an insignificant proportion of global trade but they pursued nationalist economic policies, as contrasted with those favoring regional

economic integration, which further reduced their role as global economic actors. Worse still, many of these states are landlocked and the cost of transport from the coastal terminals to the hinterlands over several hundred miles has imposed huge burdens on their external trade and limited the rate of their economic growth. This was further aggravated by the nature of their produce, which was, in most cases, bulky, mainly unprocessed, and of low value.

Lack of direct access to seaports, the limited capacity of coastal terminals, and the inefficiency of port operators have continued to limit the growth of the external trade and domestic economies of most African countries. A striking example is Burkina Faso, a landlocked country whose seaboard outlet at Abidjan is nearly 746 miles away. The sheer distance and attendant transport costs, and the protracted political turbulence in the Ivorien hinterland of the port, have constrained the external trade and internal economic growth of Burkina Faso. Insecurity and inefficient port operations, epitomized by corruption, slow turnaround times, poor transshipment services, and red tape, also inhibit the conduct of trade (especially by landlocked countries) through the seaboard outlets. These constraints apply in varying degrees to countries such as Mali, Niger, Central African Republic, Rwanda, Burundi, Zimbabwe, Zambia, and Chad, which are dependent upon the major coastal outlets of their respective regions in Dakar, Abidjan, Lagos, Douala, Mombasa, Maputo, and Durban.

See also **Abeokuta; Abidjan; Accra; Bamako; Cape Town; Dakar; Dar es Salaam; Debt and Credit; Djibouti, Republic of; Douala; Economic History; Freetown; Geography and the Study of Africa; History of Africa; Kano; Lagos; Libreville; Lomé; Maputo; Mombasa; Nairobi; Nationalism; Port Harcourt; Porto Novo; Slave Trades; Timbuktu; Urbanism and Urbanization.**

BIBLIOGRAPHY

Davies, Peter N. *The Trade Makers: Elder Dempster in West Africa, 1852–1972, 1973–1989*, St. John's, Newfoundland: International Maritime Economic History Association, 2000.

Hoyle, Brian S. "Cityport Industrialization and Regional Development in Less-Developed Countries: The Tropical African Experience." In *Cityport Industrialization and Regional Development: Spatial Analysis and Planning Strategies*, eds. Brian S. Hoyle and D.A. Pinder, eds. Oxford: Pergamon, 1981.

Hoyle, Brian S., and D. Hilling, eds. *Seaports and Development in Tropical Africa*, London: Macmillan, 1970.

Iheduru, Okechukwu. C. *The Political Economy of International Shipping in Developing Countries*. Newark: University of Delaware Press, 1996.

Lumby, Anthony B. "The South African Economy and the Development of the Port of Durban during the Inter-War Years." *The Great Circle: Journal of the Australian Association for Maritime History* 13, no. 1 (1991): 21–34.

Olukoju, Ayodeji. *The "Liverpool" of West Africa: The Dynamics and Impact of Maritime Trade in Lagos, 1900–1950*. Trenton, NJ: Africa World Press, 2004.

AYODEJI OLUKOJU

TRANSVAAL. *See* **Cape Colony and Hinterland, History of (1600 to 1910); South Africa, Republic of.**

TRAVEL AND EXPLORATION

This entry includes the following articles:
ARAB
CHINESE
EUROPEAN (PRE-1500)
EUROPEAN (1500 TO 1800)
EUROPEAN (SINCE 1800)

ARAB

Muslims, Arabs, Berbers, Persians, Indians, and Chinese traveled to what they called the land of the blacks in the eight centuries prior to European oceanic exploration. These travels can be grouped into two main categories: the trans-Saharan overland routes between North and West Africa, and the maritime routes of the Red Sea and Persian Gulf that extended to East Africa, India, and beyond.

The earliest Muslim travelers to tropical regions of Africa were undoubtedly merchants and traders. This was the case of the Ibadi Berbers of North Africa who pioneered the trans-Saharan caravan routes to the western Sudan in the ninth century CE, as well as the Persian and Arab navigators from the Gulf who set up regular shipping routes to the East African coast, also in the ninth century. With the exception of al-Mas'udi (d. 956), author of *Meadows of Gold and Mines of Gems*, who visited the East African coast in 916, none of the early travelers left firsthand written accounts of their travels, and most of them remain anonymous. Nonetheless, the information they provided relating to trade routes, towns, and the type and value of goods traded, were fully described in the roads and kingdoms literary genre of the tenth century: Al-Mas'udi, al-Maqdisi (b. c. 945), and Ibn Hawqal (d. after 977). Moreover, travel was by no means one way. Once Islam had taken root in the sub-Saharan regions, African pilgrims began traveling to North Africa, Egypt, and Arabia. These pilgrims provided important sources of geographical, historical, and ethnographic information, some of which was incorporated into the works of such important Arab geographers and historians as al-Bakri (1014–1094), al-Idrisi (1100–c. 1165), and Ibn Khaldun.

The Malian emperor Mansa Wali (d. c. 1270), son of Sundiata (c. 1217–1255), was the first monarch to perform the *hajj* in Mecca sometime in the 1260s. He was followed at the end of the

Pilgrimage caravan to Mecca and ship crossing the Persian Gulf. Al-Hariri of Basra (1054–1122) is the author of a book called *Al-Maqamat* (The assemblies), part of the *adab* genre (rhymed prose and poetry), which was intended to entertain a sophisticated, educated audience. In the thirteenth century, the work was completed with a set of now-famous illustrations by Yahya ibn Mahmud al-Wasti, including the two shown here.

thirteenth century by Mansa Sakura (d. c. 1300), who was killed during the return journey, and then by Mansa Kankan Musa in 1324. Kankan Musa's pilgrimage had an especially lasting impact on knowledge of Africa in the Middle East and Europe. The Malian emperor and his retinue sojourned for a time in Cairo where they had high-level relations with the Mamluk court and where they liberally disbursed gold at the currency market. This visit was chronicled by al-ʿUmari (1300–1384), who recounted the two Atlantic exploration expeditions of Mansa Abu Bakr, Musa's predecessor. Kankan Musa's fame as the purveyor of fabulous quantities of gold also reached Europe. This emperor is portrayed, along with the Abyssinian *Negus* (king), on the 1375 Catalan map, and this helped orient Portugal's Atlantic expeditions of the following century.

The fourteenth and fifteenth centuries mark the heyday of Muslim scholarly travel in West Africa. Contrary to the merchants, the names, itineraries, and sometimes even the travel accounts of these scholars, jurists, and mystics are known. The most famous scholar-traveler of the period was Ibn Battuta, the Moroccan jurist who traveled the entire length and breadth of the Muslim world. In 1330–1331, after performing his first pilgrimage to Mecca, Ibn Battuta visited the Red Sea and Indian Ocean ports of Suwakin, Zaila, Mogadishu, Mombasa, and Kilwa. Twenty years later he undertook the last of his voyages, to Mali, and visited most of the cities of western Sudan (including Walāta, Niani—or Malli, the Malian capital—Timbuktu, Gao, and Takedda) in the process. His is the first full eyewitness account of these regions.

Another Moroccan jurist, al-Maghili (c. 1440–1505), had an impact on politics and Islamic society in western Sudan. Following his persecution of the Jews of Touat in the Sahara, al-Maghili pursued a career as legal consultant in the Hausa city-states of Katsina and Kano before joining the court of Askia Muhammad Turé (r. 1493–1538) in Gao about 1495. His rulings, or *fatwa*s, have survived and constitute an important primary source for the study of the Songhay Empire. A contemporary Egyptian jurist, al-Suyuti (c. 1445–1505), also impacted Islamic practice there. Askia Muhammad first met al-Suyuti in Cairo during his 1497 pilgrimage to Mecca. There ensued a lengthy correspondence on matters of faith and government, and al-Suyuti, who may or may not have actually traveled to Sudan, is credited with having introduced architectural innovations to the Songhay court, among other things.

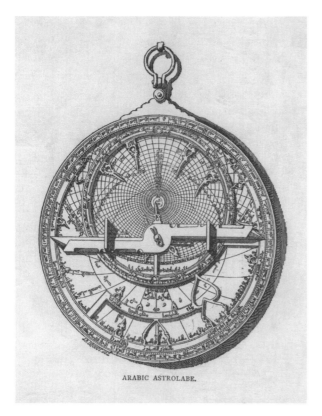

An Arabic astrolabe, c. 1450. HULTON ARCHIVE/GETTY IMAGES

This fecund period of trans-Saharan travel ends with the enigmatic figure of Leo Africanus. Born Hasan bin Muhammad al-Wazzan al-Ziati al-Gharnati, he was a Muslim refugee from Granada who grew up in Fez, Morocco. A trader and sometimes diplomat, he traveled to Timbuktu in 1509–1510 on behalf of the Moroccan sultan. Although the specifics of his West African travels are not clear, he is believed to have visited a number of other cities in the region in the years that followed. Many years later, as a convert to Catholicism and in the service of the Pope in Rome, he wrote his *Description of Africa* in Italian. The book was soon translated into French and Latin and it became a major source of knowledge of Africa in Europe.

Meanwhile, geographical knowledge of the East African coast was being advanced by a Chinese Muslim admiral, Zheng He (1371–1427). A member of China's Hui, or Muslim, ethnic group and descending from a line of scholars and civil servants from Yunan province, Zheng He was put in charge of the Ming Empire's treasure fleets. Beginning in 1417 he sailed this fleet to Mogadishu and at least as far as Malindi, and possibly even farther south. The account of his travels was written up in Chinese as *Eunuch Sanbao to the Western Ocean*. The possibility that Zheng He, or some other Arab or Indian navigators, had rounded the Cape of Good Hope and entered the Atlantic Ocean prior to Vasco da Gama's (c. 1469–1524) historic journey of 1498 is still being debated. What is certain is that, once da Gama entered the Indian Ocean, this Portuguese navigator relied on the knowledge and know-how of Muslim seafarers. In Malindi, Vasco da Gama enlisted the services of Ahmad ibn Majid (b. c. 1432) to pilot his ship to Calicut in India. Ibn Majid, born in Oman, was possibly the most famous seafarer of his day, having authored a major work on navigation entitled *The Book of Useful Information on the Principles and Rules of Navigation* (or *Kitab al-Fawa'id*), written in 1490. It is also reported that during his return voyage, Vasco da Gama used the nautical map of a certain Malem Cana, a Moor of Gujarat.

Beginning in the sixteenth century, European maritime expansion eclipsed the older trade routes of the Indian Ocean and the Sahara. Nonetheless, traders and scholars continued to travel them and to leave written records until the eve of colonial conquest. For instance, Ahmad Baba (1556–1627) was a leading scholar in Timbuktu. Following the Moroccan conquest of the city he was exiled to Marrakesh where he continued to write and to teach. Much later still was Aby Serur Mardochee (1826–1886), a rabbi and merchant from southern Morocco. Between 1858 and 1872 he and his younger brother were running the family business in Timbuktu. Later retired in French Algeria, Mardochee wrote about the experience.

See also **Baba, Ahmad; Cartography; Fez; Gama, Vasco da; Gao; Ibn Battuta, Muhammad ibn Abdullah; Ibn Khaldun, Abd al-Rahman; Judaism in Africa; Kano; Leo Africanus; Maghili; Muhammad ibn 'Abd al-Karim al-; Metals and Minerals: Gold and Silver; Mogadishu; Mombasa; Moors in African History; Niani; Pilgrimages, Islamic; Timbuktu; Walāta.**

BIBLIOGRAPHY

Blum, Charlotte, and Humphrey John Fisher. "Love for Three Oranges, or the *Askiya*'s Dilemma: The *Askiya*, al-Maghili, and Timbuktu, c. 1500 A.D." *Journal of African History* 34, no. 1 (1993): 65–91.

Brett, Michael. "Islam and Trade in the *Bilad al-Sudan*, Tenth-Eleventh Century A.D." *Journal of African History* 24, no. 4 (1983): 431–400.

Dreyer, Edward L. *Zheng He: China and the Oceans in the Early Ming, 1405–1433*. New York: Pearson Longman, 2007.

Dunn, Ross E. *The Adventures of Ibn Battuta: A Muslim Traveller of the Fourteenth Century*. Berkeley: University of California Press, 1986.

Hamdun, Said, and Noel King, trans. *Ibn Battuta in Black Africa*. London: Collings, 1975.

Hopkins, John Francis Price, and Nehemia Levtzion, eds. *Corpus of Early Arabic Sources for West African History*, 1st Markus Wiener Publishers edition. Princeton, NJ: Markus Wiener, 2000.

Hunwick, John O., ed. and trans. *Sharia in Songhay: The Replies of al-Maghili to the Questions of Askia al-Hajj Muhammad*. New York: Oxford University Press, 1985.

Masonen, Pekka, and Humphrey John Fisher. "Not Quite Venus from the Waves: The Almoravid Conquest of Ghana in the Modern Historiography of Western Africa." *History in Africa* 23 (1996): 197–232.

ERIC S. ROSS

CHINESE

Chinese contacts with Africa have to be understood within the context of the Indian Ocean trading system of antiquity and later periods, and two types of evidence—the historical and the archaeological—inform the picture. The presence of African sorghum in India and also western China as early as the late first millennium BCE attests to at least indirect, overland contact rather than directly via any maritime route. The first century CE historical source the *Periplus Maris Erythraei* points to contacts between Roman Egypt, eastern Africa and India; it is inconceivable that China, which had close relations with India, was not unaware of the east African coast and the Horn of Africa. Han dynasty (206 BCE–220 CE) records tell of the region of *Huang-Chi* described as an important trading center lying twelve months' journey, or "30,000 li" westward of China and which *could* be identified with Aksum (assuming that *Huang-Chi* is a rendition of the Aksumite ethnon *Agaz*). The exports of *Huang-Chi* included tortoise shell and ivory (known Aksumite exports at this time), and there is a story that a rhinoceros was brought to the court of the usurper Wang Mang (1–6 CE) as a gift from the ruler. A certain Gan Ying, a Chinese envoy to Rome, is said to have visited a place known as *Dou-Le* at the end of the first century CE and returned to China with a delegation from there. This *could* be a reference to the Aksumite port of Adulis, but neither account is wholly persuasive of an African identification.

In 2001 the scholar Wolbert Smidt drew readers' attention to a later eighth-century source of Du Huan, whose accounts of his travels (*Jingxingji*) tell of a visit to a country in Africa called Molin-guo, which Smidt identified as the lowlands of Eritrea and Somalia; to the south lay a country known as Laobosa, which he argued may be a corruption of the Arabic term *al Habasha*. There is scant archaeological evidence for Chinese-Aksumite contacts; Chinese material at Aksum *may* possibly be represented by a small forged iron and silver piece from Chamber D in the Tomb of the Brick Arches (third century CE).

More solid Chinese accounts of Africa appear during the T'ang dynasty (618–907 CE), and two toponyms demand particular attention. *Muâ-liěn*, according to Paul Wheatley (1975), occurs in five different sources dating from the ninth and tenth centuries and it has been variously identified as Mauretania (very doubtful) or more popularly as Malindi (Kenya coast), but the Russian scholar Vegus has suggested that a better identification taking into account mis-scribed ethnonyms should be Meroë in the Sudan. Another toponym, *Po-Pa-Li*, suggests a corruption of the Persian Barbarig, hence Berbera, the northern coasts of Somalia, but this region is not referred to again after the twelfth century. Clearly these accounts imply a second-hand knowledge of Africa, probably attained via Arab travellers. There is no evidence for direct contact between Africa and China at this time; from the later eighth–twelfth centuries, the Baghdad author al-Masudi commented that gold and ivory (the Chinese valued African ivory above its Indian counterpart) from Sofala (Mozambique) was conveyed to Oman and thence onward to India and China. It is also known that African Zanj slaves, mangrove poles, ambergris, and incense were much in demand in China. The Southern Sung period (1127–1279) saw a concerted expansion in overseas trade and there are now many references to Africa, especially in the reliable Chu-Fan-Chi (*Gazetteer of*

Foreigners) compiled by Chao Ju-Kua in circa 1225 CE, but again his reports of the peoples of the Horn and the eastern African coasts had probably been garnered from his contacts with Arab and Persian traders he met in China.

Archaeological evidence from sites along the eastern African coasts demonstrates that Chinese imports (ceramics and coins) were becoming significant during this period, especially at Kilwa (southern Tanzania), Manda, and Shanga (northern Kenya), where at the latter site Chinese stoneware is present throughout the sequence. Chinese maritime trading and exploration reached a peak during the Ming period (1368–1644); between 1405 and 1433 seven Chinese expeditions sailed to the "western Ocean" under the command of the eunuch Cheng-Ho (1371–1433). In 1415 during the fourth voyage elements of the fleet certainly attained the east African coast; a delegation from Kilwa returned with the fleet to China bringing a giraffe as a gift, and one of Cheng-Ho's captains, Fsei Hin, visited Mogadishu. The ships of the fifth voyage (1417–1419) and sixth voyage (1421–1422) maintained lucrative trade contacts with Africa. The main historical sources for this period include Fsei Hin's detailed notes on African topography, people, and climate—*Hsing'ch'a Sheng-lan* (Triumphant vision of the starry raft, 1436)—and Mao Yüan-i's *Wu-Pei-Chih* (Notes on military preparedness, seventeenth century).

The earliest Chinese map of Africa, the *Yü t'u* of Chu Ssŭ-pen, evidently based upon information gleaned from Arab sources, dates to the early fourteenth century and erroneously places Zanzibar (*Sang-Ku-Pa*) on the west coast. Marine charts from this period also show strong Arab influence. Chinese contacts with central-southern Africa from the thirteenth through the sixteenth centuries are also attested archaeologically by finds of celadon at the sites of Mapungubwe, Great Zimbabwe, and Dholo-Dhlo inter alia yet it is clear that they were never visited directly by Chinese merchants or travellers for by then-Chinese maritime domination of the Indian Ocean had been effectively challenged by the Portuguese.

See also **Adulis; Aksum; Cartography; Ivory; Metals and Minerals: Gold and Silver; Mogadishu; Slave Trades; Trade, National and International Systems; Zimbabwe, Great.**

BIBLIOGRAPHY

Duyvendak, Jan. *China's Discovery of Africa*. London: Arthur Probsthain, 1949.

Fiaccadori, Gianfranco. "Teofilo Indiano Pt 11." *Studi Classici e Orientali* 34 (1984): 271–308.

Hermann, A. "Ein alter Seeverkehr zwischen Abessinien und süd-China bis zum Beginn unserer Zeitrechnung." *Zeitschrift der Gesellschaft für Erdkunde* 10 (1913): 553–561.

Smidt, Wolbert. "A Chinese in the Nubian and Abyssinian Kingdoms (8th Century)." *Chroniques Yemenites* 9 (2001). Available from http://cy.revues.org/document33.html.

Wheatley, Paul. "Analecta Sino-Africana Recensa." In *East Africa and the Orient: Cultural Syntheses in Pre-colonial Times*, ed. H. Neville Chittick and Robert I. Rotberg. New York and London: Africana Publishing Company, 1975.

NIALL FINNERAN

EUROPEAN (PRE-1500)

Africa was recognized by ancient and medieval geographers as one of the three continents forming the human universe. However, direct contact and knowledge was historically limited to North Africa. The broad belt north of the Sahara Desert formed an integral part of the political, diplomatic, and economic life of the Mediterranean world. While the level of integration differed, North Africa was accessible to Europeans throughout the antiquity and medieval period through direct interaction, descriptive accounts, and oral geography.

In the second half of the first millennium CE, the fall of the Roman Empire, Muslim conquests, and the decline of cities and market economies in northwestern and central Europe weakened the contacts between largely Muslim North Africa and increasingly Christian Europe. However, the revival of intercontinental trade in the twelfth and thirteenth centuries brought European traders back to the North African shores. The key role of Mamluk Egypt in the Crusades and its mediation in the trade with the Indian Ocean further enhanced the commercial contact between the two shores of the Mediterranean Sea. The success of the reconquest and the subsequent aggressive policy of various Christian states, particularly Aragon and Genoa, led to an increase of diplomatic activity that generated additional need for travel. In the fourteenth and fifteenth centuries, European traders and diplomats traveled to all the major North African centers, from Agadir and Safi in Morocco, Tlemcen in modern Algeria, and Alexandria and Cairo in Egypt. The reach of Jewish merchants, who often acted as intermediaries for Christian partners, extended along the key trans-Saharan routes. In consequence, much commercial and political information on North Africa and the Saharan trade was readily available in the Christian Mediterranean, even if direct contact most often stopped at the northern boundary of the desert.

The knowledge of other parts of Africa was much more limited. While West Africa was known to be the source of the gold and slaves that found their way to the Mediterranean since at the latest the eighth century and a few individual Europeans were said to have visited the great trading cities of the Western Sudan, West Africa south of the Niger Bend was beyond the reach of direct knowledge of late medieval Europe. No contacts or information existed between Europe and Central and South Africa. Coastal East Africa, on the other hand, was embedded in European consciousness since antiquity, mostly in connection with the Solomon and Queen of Sheba narrative, and the sustained participation of the East African cities in the Indian Ocean trading. Their importance was so ingrained in European geographical awareness that they were incorporated into the supposed itineraries of both Infante Dom Pedro of Portugal (1420s), and Pero de Covilhã, dispatched to explore the trade in West Indian Ocean in the late fifteenth century.

Coastal Atlantic Africa, one of the hitherto most isolated regions of the continent, was the focus of European explorations in the fifteenth century. Members of the Portuguese royal house, particularly Infante Dom Henrique (Henry the Navigator) and his grandnephew, King Dom João II, sponsored a series of voyages that between 1434 and 1488 explored the vast coastline from Cape Bojador to the Cape of Good Hope, revealing the previously unknown extent and shape of the African continent.

Unlike the ill-fated 1291 voyage by the Vivaldi brothers, the fifteenth-century European explorers laid an expanding foundation for sustained contact with Atlantic Africa, spurred on by the prospect of profit and reward upon return. In the 1440s and 1450s, a series of expeditions headed by both Portuguese captains and Italian merchants progressed as far as modern Guinea-Bissau. The exploration of the Windward Coast (the Grain Coast as far as Sierra Leone) was completed in the 1460s. The 1470s saw a rapid progression along the Gulf of Guinea. In the early 1480s, Diogo Cão established contact with the kingdom of Kongo and explored the long coastal expanse of future Angola and northern Namibia. In 1487 Bartolomeu Dias not only reached the southernmost tip of Africa, but proved beyond doubt that the Atlantic and Indian Ocean were interconnected, opening the way for Vasco da Gama's 1498 arrival in India.

While the Portuguese largely remained confined to the coast, they nonetheless tried to gather as much information about the interior as possible, as witnessed by contemporary travelogues and reports (for example, Duarte Pacheco Pereira's *Esmeraldo de Situ Orbis* and Valentim Fernandes's compilation of written accounts and oral reports). They also made a sustained effort to establish diplomatic relations with West African rulers. While much of this diplomatic activity involved states within approximately sixty-two miles from the Atlantic coast, King Dom João II's missions to western Sudan in the 1480s reflected the keen interest the Portuguese had in the traditional heartland of West Africa. The hope that the Zaire River would provide a shortcut to the Indian Ocean, as well as the conversion of the ruling family of Kongo to Christianity, led to a spurt of explorations in the interior of west-central Africa in the late 1480s and 1490s. Finally, Vasco da Gama's voyage (1497–1499) circumnavigated southern Africa and reached the rich trading cities of East Africa, from Sofala to Mombasa and Melindi. However, the early goal of Portuguese explorations—to find an alternate route to the land of Prester John (Ethiopia)—was not realized until the early sixteenth century.

See also **Cartography; Gama, Vasco da; Judaism in Africa; Metals and Minerals: Gold and Silver; Mombasa; Queens and Queen Mothers; Sahara Desert; Slave Trades.**

BIBLIOGRAPHY

Elbl, Ivana, "Cross-Cultural Trade and Diplomacy, Portuguese Relations with West Africa, 1441–1521." *Journal of World History* 3 (1992): 165–204.

Fernandes, Valentim. *O Manuscrito "Valentim Fernandes,"* ed. António Baião. Lisbon: Academia Portuguesa da História, 1940.

Fernández-Armesto, Felipe. *Before Columbus: Exploration and Colonization from the Mediterranean to the Atlantic, 1229–1492.* Philadelphia: University of Philadelphia Press, 1987.

Pereira, Duarte Pacheco. *Esmeraldo de Situ Orbis,* ed. and trans. G. H. T. Kimble. London: Hakluyt Society, 1937.

Phillips, J.R.S. *The Medieval Expansion of Europe.* New York: Oxford University Press, 1988.

Thomaz, Luís Filipe. "Le Portugal et l'Afrique au XVe siècle: Les debuts de l'expansion." *Arquivos do Centro Cultural Português* 26 (1989): 161–256.

IVANA ELBL

EUROPEAN (1500 TO 1800)

The European exploration of the African coast had essentially been completed by 1514, but exploration of the interior hardly got under way until the 1790s. In the interim knowledge of sub-Saharan Africa grew sporadically but was confined mainly to a few commercially important places on the coast.

The account of Leo Africanus (1550), who visited the West Sudan twice between 1509 and 1513, remained the basis for knowledge of this interior region until the nineteenth century. Subsequent exploration was limited mainly to Senegambia. On the Gambia, following the lead set by the Portuguese, English traders reached the Barracunda Falls by 1651, and in 1689 Cornelius Hodges traveled overland from there to Bambuk. By this time the French were familiar with the Senegal as far up as the kingdom of Galam, and in 1700 they established a fort near the farthest navigable point of the river.

The only part of the North Africa interior to attract explorers was Egypt, where tourist-scholars (mainly French) pushed up the Nile, visiting Sennar in 1699 and producing two books on Upper Egypt in the 1780s. A few Europeans visited the Barbary states in the eighteenth century for diplomatic or commercial reasons, but most information on the North African interior came via the English and French consuls in Tripoli.

In Central Africa, Leo Africanus's contemporary, António Fernandes, explored the hinterland of Sofala (modern southern Mozambique) and visited gold mines in the lands of Mutapa (Monomatapa) from 1511 to 1514. A century later (1616), Gaspar Bocarro traveled from Quíloa to Tete on the Zambezi. In both cases exploration was followed by the creation of Portuguese bases on the Zambezi—first at Sena, later at Tete. There followed nearly two centuries in which no centrally directed exploration took place, but control and knowledge of the Zambezi Valley was consolidated. In 1798 Francisco José de Lacerda led an exploratory expedition from Tete to the court of the Kazembe on Lake Mweru. Five years earlier, starting from the opposite coast (Angola), Alexandre da Silva Teixeira had reached the Luvale country.

Eyewitness accounts of Ethiopia were provided by Francisco Alvarez, a member of the Portuguese embassy of 1520–1526; by Jesuit travelers in the period 1603–1633; by the Frenchman Charles Poncet, who visited the court at Gondär in 1699–1700; and by James Bruce, whose *Travels to Discover the Source of the Nile* (1790), describing experiences of 1769–1772, was a landmark in the history of travel writing.

The interior of the Cape of Good Hope was explored in the late seventeenth and early eighteenth centuries by *trekboers*, but not until the 1780s did reports on this exploration begin to appear in print. The authors included two Swedes—Andreas Sparrman (1783) and Carl Thunberg (1788–1793)—and a Frenchman, François Levaillant (1790).

The appearance of books such as these reflected a growth of public interest in Africa, particularly in London and Paris, during the last quarter of the eighteenth century. This in turn stimulated further exploration. With the support of the Association for Promoting the Discovery of the Interior Parts of Africa (the African Association), founded in London in 1788, James Watt and Matthew Winterbottom explored Fuuta Jallon and the Rio Nuñez (modern Guinea) in 1794; and in 1796 Mungo Park traveled to Segu (in modern Mali) on the Niger River.

Travel, however, was not necessarily the best way of extending knowledge. Some important travelers left no account, such as David van Nyendael, who visited the Asante kingdom (modern Ghana) in 1702, and two Italian priests who reportedly reached Katsina (in modern Nigeria) several years later. Others managed to report on the West Sudan without setting foot there—for example, the American John Ledyard, who died in Cairo on his way to western Africa in 1789. Yet significant advances in knowledge of Africa may be found in the work of scholars such as Luis del Mármol (*Descripcion general de Affrica*, 1573, 1599), Richard Hakluyt (*The Principall Navigations, Voiages, and Discoveries of the English Nation*, 1589), Olfert Dapper (*Naukeurige beschrijvinge der Afrikaensche gewesten*, 1668), and Hiob Ludolf (*Historia aethiopica*, 1681). These authors made use of written and oral information available in Europe, and their compilations created a popular genre of travel literature.

See also **Cartography; Geography and the Study of Africa; Leo Africanus; Niger River; Nile River; Tripoli; Zambezi River.**

BIBLIOGRAPHY

Alpern, Stanley B. *Guide to Original Sources for Precolonial Western Africa: An Updated and Expanded Supplement to Fage (1994)*. Madison: University of Wisconsin, African Studies Program, 2006.

Fernández-Armesto, Felipe, ed. *The Times Atlas of World Exploration*. New York: Times Books, 1991.

Hallett, Robin. *The Penetration of Africa: European Enterprise and Exploration Principally in Northern and Western Africa up to 1830*. Vol. 1. New York: Routledge and Kegan Paul, 1965.

Masonen, Pekka. *The Negroland Revisited: Discovery and Invention of the Sudanese Middle Ages*. Helsinki: The Finnish Academy of Science and Letters, 2000.

ADAM JONES

EUROPEAN (SINCE 1800)

Exploration of Africa gained considerably in momentum in the course of the nineteenth century, reflecting (and reflected in) a growth of public interest and enhanced technical possibilities. The kind of information sought by travelers varied widely, depending on the institutions that sponsored them as well as their personal inclinations. Whereas exotic flora and fauna had dominated much writing on Africa before 1800, thereafter information on geography and on African societies became more important. Yet as Mary Louise Pratt and others have argued, such "discoveries" often consisted not so much in uncovering something fully new as in "converting local knowledges into European knowledges."

For nineteenth-century explorers, North Africa served mainly as a gateway to the lands south of the Sahara, although travelers such as Heinrich Barth in the early 1850s and Gerhard Rohlfs in the early 1860s shed some further light on this region. Less spectacular, but of considerable importance as a contribution to knowledge, was the detailed scientific work conducted by French scholars in Egypt following Napoleon's invasion of 1798 and in Algeria in the period 1844–1867.

It was West Africa that dominated European explorers' interest in the first half of the nineteenth century. Mungo Park led his last expedition into West Africa in 1805 where he died on the middle Niger. In 1821–1822 Dixon Denham, Hugh Clapperton, and Walter Oudney crossed the Sahara to Lake Chad. Clapperton's servant, Richard Lander, returned to Africa three years later with his brother John and ascertained the lower course of the Niger. The most scholarly explorer to cover a large area of western Africa was Heinrich Barth, in 1850–1855. In 1869 Gustav Nachtigal led an embassy to Bornu and in the 1880s explored Togoland and the Cameroons.

The botanist William Burchell traveled in South Africa in 1811–1812; many later travelers there were big-game hunters such as William Cornwallis Harris, who in the 1830s traveled into Matabele country, and Roualeyn Gordon Cumming. David Livingstone was the key figure in exploring Africa south of the Equator in this period, driven by an implacable belief that his course was God-directed. From 1841 to 1853 he served in South Africa under the London Missionary Society. Then, accompanied by a party of Makololo, he embarked on an exploratory journey lasting three years, which included the European discovery of the Victoria Falls and a crossing of Africa from west to east (he was preceded in the latter by the Hungarian Ladislau Magyar). Virtually all of these explorers wrote of their travels, or books were posthumously compiled from their journals, but Livingstone's *Missionary Travels and Researches in South Africa* (1857), which reached nine editions, had a unique effect in turning attention to the continent. Believing in the Zambezi as the route to the interior for "Christianity and commerce," Livingstone returned to Africa in 1858.

In East Africa the missionaries Johannes Rebmann, Johann Ludwig Krapf (a notable linguist), and J. J. Erhardt brought accounts, in the 1840s, of Mounts Kilimanjaro and Kenya, and stories of a great interior lake. To establish whether these were indeed the fabled "Mountains of the Moon," and to discover the source of the Nile, the Royal Geographical Society sent an expedition in 1856. Its leader was Richard Francis Burton, who had already visited Mecca, disguised as a Muslim. It was his companion, John Hanning Speke, who found the source of the Nile in Lake Victoria; Burton disputed this, but Speke was asked by the Royal Geographical Society to undertake a further expedition to confirm his discovery. This, accompanied by James Augustus Grant, he did in 1860–1863. His claim was challenged by Burton, but before the two could engage in public debate, Speke was killed in a shooting accident in 1864. On their journey, Speke and Grant met Samuel White Baker, a resourceful hunter who explored and named Lake Albert, through which the White Nile flowed.

Doubts still remained about the source of the Nile, and it was nominally to solve these that Livingstone undertook his last expedition in 1866. Ill health and geographical uncertainty made this expedition a failure, ending with his death in 1873, but his "discovery" by the British-born American journalist Henry M. Stanley in 1871, the bringing of his body to the coast by a group of African followers, and the skilful editing of his *Last Journals* by Horace Waller (1874) contributed to building up a legend.

Verney Lovett Cameron, a naval officer sent to relieve Livingstone in 1873, continued across Africa after learning of his death and completed the first east-to-west crossing. From 1874 to 1877 Stanley too crossed Africa, tracing the course of the Congo River (partly explored from its mouth by James Tuckey in 1815) and then serving as the first administrator of what became the Congo Free State. In this capacity he became a rival of the Italian-born French explorer, Count Pierre Savorgnan de Brazza, who had explored the Oguwe River in Gabon and was the founder of the French Congo.

Other explorers in East Africa were Charles New, missionary and traveler, who died in 1875 after visiting Chagga territory; Joseph Thomson, the Scottish geologist who traveled without the customary casualties to Lake Rukwa and later explored Maasai country; Harry Hamilton Johnston, later an administrator but first in Africa as a naturalist in the Kilimanjaro area; Karl Peters, whose "Emin Pasha Relief Expedition" was a cloak for German imperialism; the Hungarian Count Samuel Teleki and the naval officer Ludwig von Hohnel, discoverers of Lakes Rudolf and Stefanie; and the American May French Sheldon, who traveled in a wickerwork palanquin during 1891. Georg Schweinfurth, botanist and ethnographer, penetrated the western Nile territories and confirmed the existence of the Central African pyigmies in the 1860s and 1870s.

The last notable European traveler in Africa in the nineteenth century was Mary Kingsley, whose *Travels in West Africa* (1897) describes journeys there in 1893 and 1894–1895. An outspoken critic of both missionary and government policy, she took the side of merchants trading in the area.

The large output of firsthand accounts of Africa from travelers—whether the robust adventure of Baker's *Albert N'Yanza* (1866), the precision and mordant style of Burton's *The Lake Regions of Central Africa* (1860), or Livingstone's vastly popular *Missionary Travels*— had far-reaching effects on popular images of Africa.

See also **Barth Heinrich; Gordon, Charles George; Livingstone, David; Nile River; Sahara Desert; Stanley, Henry Morton; Zambezi River.**

BIBLIOGRAPHY

Delpar, Helen, ed. *The Discoverers: An Encyclopedia of Explorers and Exploration.* New York: McGraw-Hill, 1980.

Fabian, Johannes. *Out of Our Minds: Reason and Madness in the Exploration of Central Africa.* Berkeley: University of California Press, 2000.

Fernández-Armesto, Felipe, ed. *The Times Atlas of World Exploration.* New York: Times Books/Harper Collins, 1991.

Lloyd, Christopher C. *The Search for the Niger.* London: Collins, 1973.

Severin, Timothy. *The African Adventure: Four Hundred Years of Exploration.* New York: Dutton, 1973.

Simpson, Donald H. *Dark Companions: The African Contribution to the European Exploration of East Africa.* London: Paul Elek, 1975.

DONALD H. SIMPSON
REVISED BY ADAM JONES

TRIBE AND TRIBALISM. In the twenty-first century few people refer to Africa and its peoples as "primitive" or "backward"; but many still hold that African people live in "tribes" and refer to their marriages, gods, or arts as "tribal," implicitly defining the word as being essentially "not like us," as living in small isolated communities that lack global technologies, as "indigenous" and relatively unaffected by the world outside Africa, and as being either barbarous, exotic, or romantically "noble."

In the African context the word "tribe" derives from the colonial period as denoting local territorial and cultural groups under the control of colonial administrations. It was borrowed from usage in India where it was used for peoples who were neither Hindu nor Muslim and so were considered inferior. In Africa administrators tried to make order out of the myriad small groups which they subjugated. Many of them were under the control of powerful African kingdoms but most were autonomous, varying in size from several million to only a few hundred people. They were typically clusters of people claiming common origins and cultures, speaking their own languages or dialects, marrying usually among themselves within their own boundaries, and with their own religious beliefs and practices. By categorizing them as individual "tribes" and so ignoring their internal differences and their complex ties with one another, and by amalgamating small ones and dividing large ones to make them all of an approximately similar size, their colonial rulers could treat them as equally subject to common overrule and law. When differences were recognized they were typically those useful for administration: some groups were considered more suitable than others for military recruitment or for industrial or demeaning labor, or defined simply as either pastoralists or as agriculturalists. Historians have often claimed that the colonial administrators "invented" "tribes."

This is a simplification: rather they gave existing groups and clusters new names for their own administrative convenience, names that in time came to be used by the people themselves.

The term also had a curiously ambivalent meaning: as well as being under colonial control, "tribal" peoples needed protection from the outside world, and to give that protection was often held to be one of the colonizers' responsibilities. Christian missionaries took it as their task to convert them, to "save" them from the moral evils thought to surround them. Tribal peoples were held to be of an original innocence, usually in remote areas away from the colonial cities, without industry (yet used as urban migrant laborers), despite their innocence usually considered warlike and dangerous, retaining as far as they could their own "customs." There was little reason to devote much effort to developing or "modernizing" them and as long as they paid their taxes and kept the peace they could safely be left alone. Administrations generally tried to retain local identities even while changing "indigenous" organizations and patterns of behavior, and local groups themselves usually tried to keep their "traditional" identities rather than forsake or change them, so as to retain a sense of cultural autonomy. The same process is seen in the early twenty-first century as local groups try to keep pride in their cultural identities against external modernization and nationalism, so that their "traditional" ethnic or "tribal" names often open them to accusations of old-fashioned "tribalism." Whereas new governments may try to "detribalize" their subjects, the latter may attempt to "retribalize" themselves.

At the same time tribal identity has never been and is not permanent for any group: it can be changed, dropped, or adopted as means to claim social identity and economic and political rights. Groups may divide or amalgamate with others, both processes often requiring the adoption of new "tribal" identities and names. Many South African groups of mixed European and non-European ancestry have long been known as "Cape Coloured" people, and there are similar identities among many groups of mixed Khoe and Bushmen, today often claiming primordial rights over land in Namibia and Botswana. In Kenya the many formerly distinct "tribes" of the Kavirondo area are known as a single cluster named Luhya;

and behind the Kenya coast the formerly distinct nine "tribes" are today known as a single group known as Mijikenda ("nine towns"). Both thereby claim new rights and greater power in the Kenya nation than before.

The word tribe was at one time also used by many anthropologists to isolate and define a particular type or level of political and organizational system. Much was made of an apparent tripartite classification of African societies, comprising bands, tribes, and kingdoms, an implicitly evolutionary series in which each type was distinguished by its productive economy and its level of political and community authority. In this *schema* tribes comprised the great majority of African societies, essentially those in the middle, and much effort was devoted to analyzing their immensely varied structures and organizations. One consequence was that anthropologists became associated with the study of this majority of middle-range societies, so that newly independent postcolonial governments often linked them with "tribalists" who were thought to oppose the newly powerful "nationalists": this tied nicely with the then-fashionable view of the discipline of anthropology as being intimately linked to colonialism. In addition, studies of modern African cities often referred to their immigrants as "tribesmen" in distinction to the "townsmen" who were their more permanent inhabitants. This simplistic view has long been discarded in the light of research showing that the distinction is essentially between the phases of men's and women's lives as they move between rural and urban residence rather than one of a timeless pattern of settlement and culture. In the twenty-first century the use of the terms tribe and tribalism to describe or define the people of Africa has virtually ended, although it is still often used by local politicians to refer to their supporters or their enemies.

See also **Anthropology, Social, and the Study of Africa; Colonial Policies and Practices; Ethnicity; Linguistics, Historical; Linguistics and the Study of Africa; Nationalism.**

BIBLIOGRAPHY

Amselle, Jean-Loup, and E. M'bokolo, eds. *Au Coeur de l'ethnie: Ethnies, tribalisme et etat en Afrique.* Paris: La Decouverte, 1985.

Barth, Frederik, ed. *Ethnic Groups and Boundaries: The Social Organization of Culture Difference.* Boston: Little Brown, 1969.

Epstein, A.L. *Politics in an Urban African Community.* Manchester, U.K.: Manchester University Press, 1958.

Vail, Leroy, ed. *The Creation of Tribalism in Southern Africa.* Oxford: James Currey, 1989.

JOHN MIDDLETON

TRIPOLI. Tripoli (in Arabic, *Tarabulus*) is the capital and largest city of the Socialist People's Libyan Arab Jamahiriya, with estimates of 1.3 to 1.7 million inhabitants in 2006. A Mediterranean coastal city founded by Phoenician traders in the seventh century BCE, Tripoli was ruled by Romans for 600 years, and was in turn controlled by the Vandals, Byzantines, Arabs, Sicilian Normans, Spanish, Knights of St. John, Ottomans, Italians, and British before becoming a joint capital with Benghazi in an independent Libya that began in December 1951 (and Tripoli became the single capital in 1970). Historically, the city was an important seaport and entrepôt for trans-Saharan trade, particularly for slaves and luxury goods such as ivory, gold, and ostrich feathers. Corsair pirates brought much wealth to Tripoli, until the city was bombarded by American and British ships at the beginning of the nineteenth century. The city traditionally was a mixture of Berbers, Arabs, Jews, Maltese, Greeks, sub-Saharan Africans (earlier as slaves), and by the twentieth century, Italians. After the discovery of oil in 1959 Tripoli became a center of industrialization and commerce, with increasing numbers of foreign workers. At the beginning of the twenty-first century Tripoli is emerging from its stark concrete apartment buildings and isolation as tourism fosters new hotels and foreign corporations open offices, even though huge billboards of Muammar Qadhdhafi throughout the city are reminders of the limits or the speed to which change takes place in the city.

See also **Libya; Qadhdhafi, Muammar.**

BIBLIOGRAPHY

Elkabir, Yassin Ali. *Migrants in Tripoli: A Case Study of Assimilation.* Pittsburgh: University Center for International Studies, University of Pittsburgh, 1980.

Rghei, Amer S., and Nelson, J. G. "The Conservation and Use of the Walled City of Tripoli." *Geographical Journal* 160, no. 2 (1994): 143–158.

MICHAEL E. BONINE

TROPICAL AND HUMID FORESTS.
See Ecosystems: Tropical and Humid Forests.

TRUTH COMMISSIONS.

Truth commissions—official, temporary bodies established to investigate a pattern of violations over a period of time, concluding with a final report and recommendations for reforms—have been created in more than thirty countries, dating to the mid-1970s. The late twentieth and early twenty-first centuries have revealed a remarkable increase in the number and type of such commissions being created around the world. Since the Truth and Reconciliation Commission of South Africa began work in 1995, attracting worldwide attention, the idea of a nonjudicial inquiry into past widespread abuses has caught the attention of new governments, victims groups, and human rights organizations in many countries, in a wide variety of contexts.

Many of these truth commissions have been created in Africa. The first modern truth commission was created by Idi Amin Dada in Uganda in 1974. This suffered significant political constraints, but succeeded in producing an important report. Other truth commissions have been created in the Democratic Republic of the Congo, Ghana, Liberia, Morocco, Nigeria, Sierra Leone, and Zimbabwe (where the government refused to release its report). Mozambique briefly considered the idea of a truth commission in the early 1990s, but decided against such a program. Burundi has agreed to a truth commission in its Arusha peace agreement, although it is not clear when and if such a body will be created.

The South African truth commission was unique in its ability to grant amnesty in exchange for truth. This arrangement was applicable only to those crimes shown to be politically motivated, and after full disclosure of relevant facts by the perpetrator, including responding to direct questions from the victims of their crimes. This resulted in many powerful, televised scenes of perpetrators admitting the details of their deeds. But despite the compelling nature of the South African experience, this amnesty-for-truth model is not likely to be appropriate elsewhere, in part because it will only be successful where perpetrators fear that they may be prosecuted if they do not confess and seek amnesty. More often than not, the national judicial system of postwar or postauthoritarian states is weak and severely compromised.

Typically, truth commissions are set up for a relatively short period of time: two or three years on average. They typically employ hundreds of staff as researchers, statement-takers, and investigators, and receive extensive, detailed information from thousands of victims and other witnesses. Some have been given subpoena powers, or the explicit right to gain access to government documents. Others have had to rely on voluntary cooperation not only of high-level officials but also direct perpetrators, sometimes in return for guarantees of confidentiality. Each truth commission is unique, and must be rooted in the realities and possibilities of its particular environment.

Truth commissions do not have the power to prosecute wrongdoers, but many have recommended that prosecutions take place, and some have shared their archives with the prosecuting authorities. Some have also chosen to publicly name those persons they conclude to be perpetrators of specific violations.

Where truth commissions have been proposed or created in contexts where an international or hybrid tribunal is under way, important procedural questions have been raised. In Sierra Leone, the question of the relationship between the truth commission and the Special Court for Sierra Leone was the subject of considerable discussion, and at times also a source of tension and misunderstanding. In other cases, however, the interplay between nonjudicial truth-seeking and prosecutions in court (whether a national, hybrid, or international court) has been much more explicit and intentional, and has led to the possibility of strengthened judicial accountability over time.

The compelling nature of public hearings by some truth commissions, notably South Africa's, has led a number of other commissions, including those in Ghana, Sierra Leone, and Liberia, to include a public hearings component in their work. The power of holding public hearings has been highlighted by recent experience, with proceedings often broadcast live on television and radio, bringing significantly increased attention to human rights concerns in the country. In Nigeria, for example, the public was absorbed for a full year in watching the truth commission's televised sessions.

The heightened global interest in truth commissions reflects, in part, a greater attention generally to the challenge of transitional justice after massive atrocity or abusive rule. Increasingly, countries emerging from a period of widespread rights violations are recognizing the importance of thinking broadly and holistically in designing justice policies. It is generally recognized that a justice policy based solely on criminal prosecutions will often leave many perpetrators untouched, many victims unheard, and many needs of society unmet. It is unlikely that national capacity will be sufficient to process thousands of accused persons in court. Policies that include both judicial and non-judicial approaches to justice offer greater possibilities of satisfying the wide range of needs and demands of a society facing the legacy of a brutal past.

See also **Amin Dada, Idi; Ghana; Liberia; Nigeria; Sierra Leone; South Africa, Republic of.**

BIBLIOGRAPHY

Boraine, Alex. *A Country Unmasked: Inside South Africa's Truth and Reconciliation Commission.* New York: Oxford University Press, 2000.

Hayner, Priscilla B. *Unspeakable Truths: Facing the Challenge of Truth Commissions.* New York and London: Routledge, 2001.

PRISCILLA HAYNER

TSETSE FLY. *See* **Agriculture: Pests and Pest Control.**

TSHOMBE, MOÏSE KAPENDA

(1917–1969). Born in the historic Lunda capital of Musumba in the Lualaba district of Katanga (Shaba) Province, Moïse Kapenda Tshombe was linked, through marriage, to the Lunda royal family. A Methodist, he completed his intermediate secondary education and trained to become a preacher and a teacher. He became a merchant like his father and a member of the African Middle Class, a business interest group. In 1958, he cofounded the Confédération des Associations Tribales du Katanga (Conakat), an organization that aimed to defend ethnic interests in the province.

The independence movement in the Belgian Congo, though centered in the distant colonial

Moïse Kapenda Tshombe (1917–1969) at a 1965 press conference. Tshombe's CONAKAT party ran on a platform of creating an independent Congo. When his party won control of Katanga, he and other leaders succeeded as Congo became an independent republic. TERRENCE SPENCER/ TIME LIFE PICTURES/GETTY IMAGES capital of Léopoldville, propelled Tshombe to the political forefront. In 1959 he became president of Conakat, held separatist views, and at the 1960 Brussels Round Table held to determine the Congo's political future unsuccessfully advocated a confederal system of government in which each province would have almost total autonomy. Through procedural maneuvering and the repression of the nationalist parties allied with the first prime minister of the independent Democratic Republic of the Congo, Patrice Lumumba, Tshombe was elected president of the Katanga provincial government in 1960. On July 11, 1960, eleven days after formal independence was granted to the country on June 30, 1960, he proclaimed Katanga's secession from the Lumumba-led central government. The secession triggered a series of events, including Lumumba's murder at Tshombe's headquarters by Tshombe's associates.

At the end of the secession in 1963 Tshombe was living in exile in Spain. In 1964 he was recalled to the Congo central government by President Joseph Kasavubu and was made prime minister in order to eradicate spreading Lumumbist popular rebellions. Using European and South African mercenaries, he accomplished this goal, only to be fired by Kasavubu. The political imbroglio that followed led to the military coup by Joseph Mobutu (later president Mobutu Sese Seko) and Tshombe's second exile in Europe. Tshombe tried to regain power by plotting a mercenary-led coup but was tricked by Mobutu's CIA-supplied intelligence services, kidnapped, and taken to Algeria, where he died in prison. He was buried in Belgium.

See also **Colonial Policies and Practices: Belgian; Congo, Republic of; Lumumba, Patrice; Mobutu Sese Seko.**

BIBLIOGRAPHY

Chomé, Jules. *Moïse Tshombe et l'escroquerie katangaise.* Brussels: Éditions de la Fondation J. Jacquemotte, 1966.

Hoskyns, Catherine. *The Congo since Independence: January 1960–December 1961.* London: Oxford University Press, 1965.

Tshombe, Moïse. *My Fifteen Months in Government,* trans. Lewis Barnays. Plano, TX: University of Plano, 1967.

S. N. SANGMPAM

TUBMAN, WILLIAM VACANARAT SHADRACH (1895–1971).

Considered to be the man who pushed Liberia into the modern era as president of that country from 1944 to 1971, William Vacanarat Shadrach Tubman was born at Harper, Cape Palmas, in southeastern Liberia on November 29, 1895. A descendant of American slaves who emigrated from Georgia in the nineteenth century, Tubman was born into the elite ruling class. He was educated at Cape Palmas Methodist Seminary and Cuttington College Divinity School, graduating in 1913. He studied law privately and was called to the bar in 1917.

Known as a "poor man's lawyer," he took cases virtually without recompense. Ambitious and personable, Tubman joined the conservative and dominant True Whig Party and in 1923 became the youngest senator in Liberia's history. In 1937 he was appointed an associate justice of the Supreme Court. In 1943 Tubman received the party nomination for president and was elected to that office on January 3, 1944. Although he imposed one-man rule, Tubman was generally a popular leader who is best remembered for his economic

William Tubman (1895–1971) at his desk in Monrovia, 1956. Tubman was elected president of Liberia seven times. He was a descendant of former American slaves who returned to Africa through the Maryland State Colonization Society. AFP/ GETTY IMAGES

development of Liberia, extending civil rights to Africans in the hinterland, and giving the vote to all Liberians. He was instrumental in formulating the principles of the Organization of African Unity in 1963. He died in office on July 23, 1971.

See also **Liberia: History and Politics.**

BIBLIOGRAPHY

Henries, A. Doris Banks. *A Biography of President William V. S. Tubman*. London: Macmillan, 1967.

Tubman, William V. S. *The Official Papers of William V. S. Tubman, President of the Republic of Liberia: Covering Addresses, Messages, Speeches, and Statements 1960–1967*, ed. E. Reginald Townsend. London: Longmans, 1968.

Wreh, Tuan. *The Love of Liberty: The Rule of President William V. S. Tubman in Liberia, 1944–1971*. London: C. Hurst, 1976.

ROBERT UTTARO

TUNIS. The capital and largest city of Tunisia, to which it has given its name, Tunis is located on a narrow isthmus between a coastal lagoon (now connected to the Mediterranean) and a shallow lake. The population of the metropolitan area was estimated at 2 million in 2006. As well as serving as political capital, Tunis is also Tunisia's principal financial, commercial, industrial, transport, cultural, and media center. Phoenicians established a town on the site in the eighth century BCE, but it remained overshadowed by its powerful neighbor, Carthage, until the Arab conquest in 695 CE. Tunis, already a trading center and port, became the capital of a small emirate in 1054 and then of the powerful Hafsid dynasty in 1228. Under the Hafsids the city experienced a period of unprecedented prosperity and intellectual flowering, powered in part by refugees from Andalusia (the best known of whom was Ibn Khaldûn).

In the sixteenth century, Tunis was on the front line of the wars between the Habsburgs and the Ottomans, falling definitively to the latter in 1574. Under Ottoman rule the city was a *beylik* (autonomous province). It was an active center of privateering thanks to the Barbary pirates, and attracted numerous European traders. The French

Aerial view of the city of Tunis. Tunis is both the capital and the largest city of Tunisia. The city is Tunisia's principal financial, commercial, industrial, transport, cultural, and media center. MARCH OF TIME/TIME LIFE PICTURES/GETTY IMAGES

occupied Tunis in 1881 and turned it into the capital of their Tunisian protectorate. A new, European city center was built between the old city and the port on the lagoon. Most of the institutions created since independence (1956) have been established either in the Hafsid- and Ottoman-era Casba quarters (now completely rebuilt), or else in vast new suburban districts to the north of the lagoon.

See also **Tunisia.**

BIBLIOGRAPHY

Micaud, Ellen C. "Urbanization, Urbanism and the Medina of Tunis." *International Journal of Middle East Studies* 9 (1978): 431–447.

Santelli, Serge. *Tunis: la ville et le creuset méditerranéen.* Paris: Les éditions du demi-cercle/CNRS éditions, 1995.

DAVID CHIDESTER

TUNISIA

This entry includes the following articles:
GEOGRAPHY AND ECONOMY
SOCIETY AND CULTURES
HISTORY AND POLITICS

GEOGRAPHY AND ECONOMY

Tunisia is the northernmost country in Africa. It occupies the plains and plateaus at the eastern end of the North African complex. It has an extensive Mediterranean coastline (713 miles) that has opened it up to influences from around the Mediterranean. The land area of the country is 63,170 square miles. Some areas in the south are below sea level, and the high point is Chambi Mountain at 5,065 feet. The country is divided in two by a low mountain chain, the "Dorsale," or backbone, that runs from southwest to northeast and also marks the division between the relatively well-watered north (more than fifteen inches annual rainfall, normally enough to produce a wheat crop) and the drier south. Cultivated land is about 30 percent of the total, and includes about 1,544 square miles under irrigation. The main crops are cereals (wheat) and tree crops such as olives, dates, and citrus. There is substantial animal husbandry, primarily of sheep. Coastal fishing employs a number of people.

During the colonial period (1881–1956) French and other European farmers took over much of the best farmland, but this was recovered after independence, when much of it was organized into agricultural cooperatives. Although Tunisia shifted away from socialism, large market-oriented farms using wage labor continue to dominate. From precolonial times, in good years Tunisia exported olive oil and wheat to Europe, and agricultural exports continue to be important.

Tunisia experimented with heavy industry in the early years of independence, but the main focus has turned to light industry, often tightly integrated into European markets (textiles and clothing, diamond cutting). In the early 2000s phosphates and chemicals are relatively important, and make substantial use of Tunisian raw materials. There is some oil and gas production.

Agriculture represents about 13 percent of gross domestic product (GDP), but occupies up to about 50 percent of the labor force, while industry represents about 32 percent of GDP with 23 percent of the labor force, and services represents 55 percent of GDP with about one-quarter of the labor force. GDP growth depends on the success of tourism and agriculture, the former affected by the international conjuncture and the latter by rainfall. In a good year it has been around 5 percent. The national labor confederation has played a strong role in domestic politics since the days of the independence struggle.

Tourism is an important service sector. It caters largely to European vacationers seeking a seaside holiday, though visits to Roman and Islamic monuments are organized. There is also an "informal" (untaxed) sector of undetermined size consisting of petty retailers and craftsmen. Tunisia has a well-developed network of weekly and daily markets that link the ecologically different parts of the country together. Many Tunisians work abroad, mostly in Europe, and some have settled there; there is a flow of remittances from these migrant workers.

In 2007 Tunisia's population was estimated at around 10 million. Most of the population and economic activity have been concentrated in the coastal area from Bizerte through Tunis to Gabes in the south. The country has been relatively successful at using family planning education to curb the growth of its population, so population growth rate is 1 percent, and the fertility rate is 1.74, both lower than most of its peer countries. The literacy rate is 74 percent (higher among men) and the life expectancy is seventy-five years. Communication has been enhanced by the introduction of cell phones, which now outnumber land lines by a ratio of 3:1.

The critical environmental problems for Tunisia are the shortage of natural fresh water resources and waste disposal. With the increasing population, Tunisia is well under the scarcity benchmark for water. Water conservation is an issue, and desalination cannot be far away. Raw sewage and other waste also degrade the available water, and the government has been investing in sewage treatment plants, especially where pollution threatens tourism. There is also concern for the linked problems of deforestation, desertification, overgrazing, and soil erosion. The oceans also suffer from pollution, and waste from the phosphate processing plants on the coast has turned the Gulf of Gabes into a marine desert. Tunisia is characterized by a growing and increasingly prosperous population in a somewhat fragile environment.

See also **Colonial Policies and Practices; Communication; Ecosystems; Production Strategies; Soils; Textiles; Tourism; Tunis; Water and Irrigation.**

BIBLIOGRAPHY

Murphy, Emma C. *Economic and Political Change in Tunisia: From Bourguiba To Ben Ali.* New York: St. Martin's Press, 1999.

Sethom, Hafedh. *Pouvoir urbain et paysannerie en Tunisie: qui sème le vent récolte la tempête.* Tunis: Cérès Productions, 1992.

Zartman, I. William, ed. *Tunisia: The Political Economy of Reform.* Boulder, CO: Lynne Rienner, 1991.

NICHOLAS S. HOPKINS

SOCIETY AND CULTURES

Over 98 percent of Tunisia's population of 10 million identify themselves as Arab Muslims of the Maliki rite, making Tunisia the most ethnically and religiously homogeneous country of the Arab Muslim world. The remainder of the population includes a small number of Berbers, the indigenous people of the country. They live predominantly on the island of Jerba or in villages and rural areas in the extreme southern part of the country. Among these are some speakers of the Berber language, although most also speak Arabic and French. Other groups include Algerians, Moroccans, and Libyans living and working in Tunisia. There is a small European population, mostly expatriates working in the country. Finally, especially in Tunis, there is a small but growing number of sub-Saharans without papers, hoping to be able to get to Europe.

The country has not always been characterized by such homogeneity. In 1946, ten years before the country's independence, the population of just over 3 million comprised Arab Muslims (88%), Tunisian Jews (2%), French (4.5%), and Italians (2.6%). Many of the non-Muslims lived in Tunis, and included among the French were many who were born Italian—Christian or Jewish—and Tunisian Jews who had been permitted to become naturalized French citizens. Tunisians are often quick to speak of their country as a historical crossroads and acknowledge the roles that many peoples and cultures—the Berbers, the Phoenicians, the Romans, the Arabs, the Italians, and the French, among others—have played in creating present-day Tunisia.

Many defining features of contemporary Tunisian society are direct consequences of the social, economic, and political policies of Habib Bourguiba, Tunisia's first president, who served from 1956 until 1987, and Zine el-Abidine Bin Ali, who has served as president since that time. Both men have been authoritarian leaders committed to a politics of modernization characterized by openness to the West while maintaining a sense of authenticity to or rootedness in the Arab/Islamic heritage.

Debates about many issues locate Tunisians along this continuum as they take positions seen as favoring increased globalization (a few decades earlier, such Tunisians favored modernity) with an eye toward Europe and France in particular, on the one hand, or a return to Tunisia's precolonial past with an eye toward the Middle East and increasingly political Islam, on the other. As in many one-party states where the government tightly controls numerous aspects of daily life—and for all practical purposes, Tunisia remains a one-party state, criticism of the government, if tolerated at all, can be indirectly expressed in the domain of religion. Specifically, whatever else they may be, expressions of religious devotion are popularly understood as critiques of the government and its policies, and public signs of devotion—for example, the wearing of conservative Islamic dress, including the hijab for women and long beards for men, and avid

participation in public prayers—become immediately suspect in the eyes of the government.

Predictably, many liberal critics of the Tunisian government's policies argue that the lack of democracy or freedom in the country encourages extremism expressed through the politicization of Islam. In contrast, supporters of such policies point to the country's stability and the steady improvement of the standard of living and general quality of life for those who are willing to accept the status quo as grounds for justifying what critics argue are violations of civil and human rights. Such discussions, however, take place *sotto voce* within the country or among expatriates or others outside its borders.

Tunisia is often heralded for its progress in many domains; chief among these is women's rights. Shortly after independence, a Personal Status Code was put in place that gave civil, rather than religious, courts jurisdiction over matters relating to women and the family, including marriage, divorce, and inheritance, while abolishing polygamy and granting women the right to seek divorce. Later laws have continued to strengthen the rights of women and children, and the role of women in public life continues to expand. Over a quarter of the country's judges are women, for example. Not all Tunisians, including some women, have been happy with these laws and the social changes they have brought. Those criticizing them generally long for a legal system based on a more traditional and conservative reading of Islamic law. Supporters of these changes understand them as reflections of Islamic values in the modern world. Both sides see themselves as representing the true nature of their faith. Thus, as in many countries, including the United States, religion becomes the terrain on which various political battles are fought.

Equally a result of earlier policies, Tunisia has a relatively highly educated, increasingly urbanized populace with a low birth rate; the average family size in 2004 was 4.1. There is likewise a growing middle class. At the same time, many educated young people are unable to find jobs commensurate with their level of education, a situation that encourages them to postpone marriage and leaves them feeling far less optimistic than earlier generations of Tunisians did.

Tunisian Republic

Population:	10,276,158 (2007 est.)
Area:	163,610 sq. km (63,170 sq. mi.)
Official language:	Arabic
Languages:	French, Arabic
National currency:	Tunisian dinar
Principal religions:	Muslim 98%, Christian 1%, Jewish 1%
Capital:	Tunis (est. pop. 728,453 in 2004)
Other urban centers:	Aryanah, Safaqis, Susah, at-Tadaman Dawwar Hishar
Annual rainfall:	432 mm (17 in.) in the north, 152 mm (6 in.) in the south
Principal geographical features:	*Mountains:* Atlas Mountains (range), Al-Qabail Mountains (range), Jebel ech Chambi *Rivers:* Medjerda *Lakes:* Chott el Djerid, Ichkeul, Tritonis, Tunis
Economy:	*GDP per capita:* US$8,800 (2006)
Principal products and exports:	*Agricultural:* olives, olive oil, grain, tomatoes, citrus fruit, sugar beets, dates, almonds, beef, dairy products *Manufacturing:* textiles, footwear, agribusiness, beverages *Mining:* petroleum, phosphate, iron ore *Tourism:* Tourism based on the Mediterranean climate is important to Tunisia's economy.
Government:	Independence from France, 1956. Constitution, 1959, revised 1988 and 2002. Republic. President elected for 5-year term (no term limits) by popular vote. Bicameral system consists of the Chamber of Deputies (189 members elected by popular vote for 5-year terms) and the Chamber of Advisors (126 seats: 85 members elected by municipal counselors, deputies, mayors, and professional associations and trade unions and 41 appointed by president; 6-year term). Prime minister appointed by president. For purposes of local government, there are 24 governates.
Heads of state since independence:	1956–1987: President Habib Bourguiba 1987–: President Zine el Abidine Ben Ali
Armed forces:	The Tunisian Armed Forces consist of an army, navy, and air force. President is commander in chief. Compulsory 12-month service.
Transportation:	*Rail:* 2,153 km (1,338 mi.) *Ports:* Bizerte, Gabes, La Goulette, Skhira *Roads:* 19,232 km (11,950 mi.), 66% paved *National airline:* Tunisair *Airports:* International facilities at Djerba, Gafsa, Monastir, Sfax, Tozeur, and Tunis. 24 other airports throughout the country.
Media:	Newspapers include *Al Horria, Essahafa, La Presse, Le Renouveau.* 27 radio stations, 26 television stations.
Literacy and education:	*Total literacy rate:* 74.3% (2006). Education is compulsory for ages 6–16. Postsecondary education provided by 12 universities and several technical and teacher-training institutes.

As it invested in education for its citizens, independent Tunisia similarly invested in an infrastructure that encouraged tourism, and tourism and remittances from workers living abroad in Europe or the Arab Gulf are the country's top sources of hard currency. Given Tunisia's history and these facts, it is not surprising that Tunisians generally value multilingualism. Tunisians speak Tunisian Arabic natively; they learn Modern Standard Arabic at school, where they also begin studying French in elementary school and English a few years later. Many Tunisians have picked up Italian from watching television; those, especially men, who live in areas frequented by tourists often speak other languages. Tunisians schooled even in the 1980s used French as a medium of instruction for math and science. Those schooled before independence might have studied Modern Standard Arabic as a foreign language. Thus, Tunisians of different generations have different relationships with the languages they speak, and those of different generations have had different kinds of educational experiences. Older educated Tunisians could have been educated in colonial schools, schools run by French religious orders, or colonial schools designed to educate Tunisians, whereas younger Tunisians will have, with rarest exception, attended Tunisian schools. The growth of a nationalized system of education now available to nearly all Tunisians using a single curriculum with Arabic as the language of instruction has helped foster a particular kind of nationalism, one markedly different from that experienced by earlier generations.

See also **Algeria; Bin Ali, Zine el-Abidine; Bourguiba; Habib bin 'Ali; Education, University and College: Northern Africa; Family; Human Rights; Immigration and Immigrant Groups: European; Judaism in Africa; Languages; Marriage Systems; Morocco; Nationalism; Women: Women and Law.**

BIBLIOGRAPHY

Charrad, Mounira M. *States and Women's Rights: The Making of Postcolonial Tunisia, Algeria, and Morocco.* Berkeley: University of California Press, 2001.

Geyer, Georgie Anne. *Tunisia: A Journey through a Country That Works.* London: Stacey International, 2003.

Perkins, Kenneth. *A History of Modern Tunisia.* New York: Cambridge University Press, 2004.

Sebag, Paul. *Histoire des Juifs de Tunisie: Des origines à nos jours.* Paris: L'Harmattan, 1991.

KEITH WALTERS

HISTORY AND POLITICS

France established a protectorate over Tunisia in 1881, while retaining the Husseini dynasty of local rulers, known as "beys." The protectorate was an extension of France's involvement in neighboring Algeria, and was part of a complex balancing act involving the Ottoman Empire, the nominal suzerains since 1574, Britain, and Italy. In practice Tunisia was treated like a colony for seventy-five years, and French and other European settlers were encouraged to take up farming and other occupations.

Soon a nationalist movement emerged, at first among intellectuals then among the wider population. The first organization was the Young Tunisians, followed by the Destour (Constitutional) Party in 1920. In 1934, some younger members of this party broke off and founded the "Néo-Destour" party under the leadership of Habib bin 'Ali Bourguiba.

World War II had considerable impact on Tunisia. France was defeated and occupied in 1940, and control over Tunisia was loosened. In the long winter of 1942–1943 Tunisia was the theater of combat between the Allies and the Axis powers. The uncertainty gave the reigning bey, Moncef, the chance to push his own ideas on Tunisian nationalism. But when the Gaullist French reestablished

control in 1943, they deposed Moncef, leaving Bourguiba later a freer hand.

The Néo-Destour party carried the flame of nationalism until Tunisian independence on March 20, 1956. Bourguiba and other members of the party were imprisoned and exiled from time to time. In the final years before independence there was some armed struggle, but on the entire Tunisian independence was negotiated. Bourguiba not only had to win independence from France, but he had to confront a more radical opponent, Salah Ben Youssef, as well as the remnants of the royal family. Ben Youssef was exiled and eliminated, and sixteen months after independence, on July 25, 1957, the last bey was deposed and Tunisia was declared a republic.

During the early years of independence, many reforms were promulgated. A new personal status code was issued, the religious courts were abolished, and an initial land reform was initiated. Tunisia also played a supportive role in the Algerian struggle for independence, and suffered cross-border attacks by the French. As an extension of this, in 1961 the Tunisians attempted to expel the French from their naval base at Bizerte, with considerable loss of life. After negotiations, Tunisia took over the base two years later.

In the 1960s Tunisia experimented with socialism. It was moving toward a widespread socialist reorganization through the cooperative movement when Bourguiba suddenly called a halt in 1969. The architect of the socialist policies, Ahmed Ben Saleh, fell into disgrace. Since the 1970s Tunisia has essentially been following a free-market system, although substantial state involvement in the economy remains. The establishment has adopted the policy of integrating the economy into the international system as much as possible, adapting Tunisian light industry to European and international rules, encouraging labor migration, and respecting the advice of the World Bank.

During this period an Islamic movement came into being, but was suppressed by the Bourguiba government in a context of considerable tension. Dissatisfaction with the manner of handling this challenge contributed to the removal of Bourguiba, ostensibly on health grounds, on November 7, 1987. He was replaced by Zine el-Abidine Bin Ali. Bin Ali had risen through the police and the security apparatus. He has been a consolidator after the charismatic

Bourguiba, and has routinized a highly structured system. A new constitution was approved in 2002.

Considerable economic success has been combined with political stability at the price of suppression of dissent, both religious and secular. Multiparty elections are regularly held but are manipulated, most notably by control of the candidates allowed to run.

Tunisia has historically had a strong labor movement, also reflecting connections with the international labor movement. At times the labor union has appeared as an alternative to the single party, but in the confrontations the party and the government bureaucracy have won out. At other times, the human rights movement also emerged as an alternative model, but it too has been blocked. Occasionally women have tried to organize alternatives to the party's women's movement, but have also not been able to establish themselves—in part because, although Tunisian legislation on women's personal status is progressive, attitudes toward independent women's movements are unsupportive.

The party that was created by Bourguiba in 1934 evolved into the single party of independence and continues with some name changes to be the dominant organized political force in the early twenty-first century. It is known as the "Rassemblement Constitutionnelle Démocratique" (Democratic Constitutional Rally). In the fifty years since independence the party and the government have coexisted, and are essentially two aspects of the same political establishment. The party allows for some kinds of debate that would be difficult in the bureaucratic context of the government, but at the same time it takes its lead from the key figures in the government, and notably the president. Debate outside this structure is constrained.

Bourguiba's leadership from the 1930s through the 1980s was critical to Tunisia's development. In his early years he was a proponent of modernization and rationalization, although he was not always as secular as his reputation. He was an eloquent speaker and was considered a charismatic leader who introduced or facilitated many changes in Tunisian society. While in the beginning the party and the political establishment were oriented to development, in the early 2000s a major concern is consolidation and security, along with improving economic conditions. Tunisia shares in many of these trends with neighboring Arab and non-Arab countries—socialism in the 1960s, an Islamic political alternative beginning in the 1980s, and the prominence of the security apparatus. The dominance and longevity of Bourguiba and the relative salience of the labor union give Tunisia its distinctiveness.

See also **Bin Ali, Zine el-Abidine; Bourguiba, Habib bin ʿAli; Nationalism; Socialism and Postsocialisms; Women: Women and the Law; World Bank; World War II.**

BIBLIOGRAPHY

King, Stephen J. *Liberalization against Democracy: The Local Politics of Economic Reform in Tunisia.* Bloomington: Indiana University Press, 2003.

Micaud, Charles A. *Tunisia: The Politics of Modernization.* New York and London: Praeger, 1964.

Perkins, Kenneth. *A History of Modern Tunisia.* Cambridge, U.K.: Cambridge University Press, 2004.

NICHOLAS S. HOPKINS

TURABI, HASAN ʿABD ALLAH AL-

(1932–). The Sudanese Islamist leader and lawyer Hasan ʿAbd Allah al-Turabi, from a well-known religious family in the Sudan Republic, was educated at Khartoum and the Sorbonne. After returning to the Sudan in 1962, he succeeded in uniting the various Islamist groups, through his leadership of a campaign for an Islamic constitution for the country. He served for a period as attorney general under President Jaafar al-Nimeiry (r. 1969–1985). He is credited with being the mastermind behind the coup that brought the Islamist regime of President Umar al-Beshir to power in June 1989.

Turabi aspires to play an international role as an Islamist leader—for example, attempting to mediate between Iraq and Kuwait just before the Gulf War, and establishing the Popular Arab Islamic Congress as a counterweight to the Organization of the Islamic Conference. His only formal position within al-Bashir's regime is speaker in the People's Assembly.

See also **Islam.**

Hasan al-Turabi speaks to his followers in Khartoum, May 7, 2000. The Sudanese political and religious leader protected Osama bin Laden when he based Al Qaeda operations in Sudan from 1990 to 1996 at Turabi's request. While in Sudan, bin Laden agreed to help build roads and fight Christian separatists in southern Sudan. SALAH OMAR/AFP/GETTY IMAGES

BIBLIOGRAPHY

Affendi, Abdel-wahab El. *Turabi's Revolution, Islam, and Power in Sudan.* London: Grey Seal, 1991.

R. S. O'FAHEY

TUTSI. *See* **Burundi; Rwanda.**

TUTU, DESMOND MPILO (1931–).
Born in Klerksdorp in the Transvaal, Desmond Mpilo Tutu became a high school teacher in 1955 after having graduated in 1953 from the Pretoria Bantu College. He obtained a Bachelor of Arts degree from the University of South Africa in 1958. After a serious illness, and under the influence of Father Trevor Huddleston of the Anglican Community of the Resurrection, Tutu studied for the priesthood at Saint Peter's College, Johannesburg. He was ordained deacon in 1960 and priest the following year. From 1962 to 1965 he studied at King's College, University of London, obtaining a bachelor's degree in divinity and a master's degree in theology. From 1967 to 1969 he lectured at the Federal Theological Seminary in Alice, Cape, and from 1970 to 1972, at the universities of Botswana, Lesotho, and Swaziland (in Roma, Lesotho). From 1972 to 1975 he was associate director of the Theological Education Fund of the World Council of Churches, based in England.

Desmond Tutu (1931–). Archbishop Tutu called for an economic boycott of South Africa after the Soweto Riots in 1976. In the early 2000s, he began working heavily in the fight against the global AIDS epidemic, even serving as honorary chair of the Global AIDS Alliance. GIANLUIGI GUERCIA/AFP/GETTY IMAGES

Having been elected Anglican dean of Johannesburg in 1975, he returned to South Africa. In 1976 he was consecrated bishop of Lesotho, but two years later he accepted appointment as the general secretary of the South African Council of Churches. During his tenure in this office he became an international spokesperson in the struggle against apartheid and was awarded the Nobel Peace Prize in 1984. The same year he was elected bishop of Johannesburg, and in 1986 he became archbishop of Cape Town. He retired from this office in June 1996. In January 1996 he was appointed the chairperson of the Commission on Truth and Reconciliation by President Nelson Mandela. Recipient of many honorary doctorates and other awards, Tutu was elected president of the All Africa Conference of Churches in 1987, and reelected to that office in 1993. After the ban against liberation movements was removed in South Africa in February 1990, Tutu played a major role in facilitating peace, reconciliation, and national reconstruction in South Africa. He was awarded the Sydney Peace Prize in 1999 in recognition of this work. He has contributed his reconciliation skills to the cause of the Palestinians, likening their treatment by Israel to a form of apartheid. In 2004, Tutu traveled to the United Kingdom to take up the post of visiting professor in post-conflict societies at London's Kings College, and in 2005 spoke out against the detention of suspected terrorists without trial at Guantanamo Bay, Cuba. Tutu is married to Leah Nomalizo Shenxane; the couple has four children.

See also **Apartheid; Huddleston, Trevor; Mandela, Nelson.**

BIBLIOGRAPHY

Primary Works

Hope and Suffering: Sermons and Speeches. Grand Rapids, MI: Eerdmans, 1984.

Crying in the Wilderness: The Struggle for Justice in South Africa, intro. and ed. John Webster. London: Mowbray, 1986.

Apartheid and the Dignity of Personhood. London: Center for the Study of Global Governance, London School of Economics, 1995.

Secondary Works

Du Boulay, Shirley. *Tutu: Voice of the Voiceless.* Grand Rapids, MI: Eerdmans, 1988.

Gish, Steven. *Desmond Tutu: A Biography.* Westport, CT: Greenwood Press, 2004.

Tlhagale, Buti, and Itumuleng Mosala. *Hammering Swords into Ploughshares: Essays in Honor of Archbishop Mpilo Desmond Tutu.* Grand Rapids, MI: Eerdmans, 1986.

JOHN W. DE GRUCHY

TUTUOLA, AMOS (1920–1997). The Nigerian writer Amos Tutuola was born in Abeokuta, Nigeria, and educated at a variety of institutions (including the Salvation Army School in Abeokuta, Lagos High School, and Anglican Central School in Abeokuta) before being forced to discontinue his schooling in 1939, when, following his father's death, his family was unable to pay his tuition fees. In 1940 he moved to Lagos, where he trained as a blacksmith and eventually found employment as a messenger in the colonial Department of Labor.

While at the Department of Labor, Tutuola began to compose versions of the Yoruba fables he had listened to as a child in Abeokuta. With the assistance of the United Society for Christian Literature, Tutuola secured Faber and Faber's interest in his first manuscript, *The Palm-Wine Drinkard and His Dead Palm-Wine Tapster in the Deads' Town* (1952). The text, a fabulous account of magical adventures and picaresque wandering that hybridizes the generic conventions of the novel and of oral folklore, was an instant success in the United Kingdom (it received a glowing review by Dylan Thomas). Tutuola's second book, *My Life in the Bush of Ghosts*, published in 1954, was equally well received in the U.K. and in the United States, where Tutuola has been identified as a founding figure of a Nigerian novelistic tradition. Nigerian opinion was, at first, less celebratory. Tutuola's disregard of the niceties of grammar and his willingness to represent a world animated by the spirits of a Yoruba cosmology troubled some Nigerian readers anxious to dispute representations of Africa that might be taken as primitive, rather than literarily primitivist.

Following the 1955 publication of *Simbi and the Satyr of the Dark Jungle*, Tutuola moved to Ibadan, where he took a position with the Nigerian Broadcasting Corporation and began work on a dramatic version of *The Palm-Wine Drinkard*. In the years that followed, Tutuola published several additional volumes (*The Brave African Huntress* appeared in 1958, *Feather Woman of the Jungle* in 1962, and *Ajaiyi and His Inherited Poverty* in 1967). In 1962 the Arts Theatre at the University of Ibadan staged a Yoruba version of *The Palm-Wine Drinkard*. The performance was very well received in Nigeria and is credited by Harold R. Collins, one of the first scholars to produce a book-length study of Tutuola's work, with securing Tutuola's reputation in his native country.

In 1981, Tutuola published another picaresque narrative, *The Witch-Herbalist of the Remote Town*, and five years later published a volume titled *Yoruba Folktales*, a work that seeks to document, rather than to embroider, an oral storytelling tradition. In his subsequent two books, *Pauper, Brawler, and Slanderer* (1987) and *The Village Witch Doctor and Other Stories* (1990), however, Tutuola reclaimed his signature style as the epic fabulist of Yoruba narrative. He died in Ibadan, Nigeria, on June 8, 1997.

See also **Literature; Theater.**

BIBLIOGRAPHY

Collins, Harold Reeves. *Amos Tutuola*. New York: Twayne, 1969.

Gera, Anjali. *Three Great African Novelists: Chinua Achebe, Wole Soyinka, and Amos Tutuola*. New Delhi: Creative Books, 2001.

Ikupasa, O'Mos. *Aspects of Yoruba Cosmology in Tutuola's Novels*. Kinshasa, Zaire: Centre de Recherches Pedagogiques, 1990.

Owomoyela, Oyekan. "Amos Tutuola." In *African Writers*, ed. C. Brian Cox. New York: Charles Scribner's Sons, 1997.

IAN BAUCOM

UBANGUI. *See* **Colonial Policies and Practices: French West and Equatorial Africa.**

UGANDA

This entry includes the following articles:
GEOGRAPHY AND ECONOMY
SOCIETY AND CULTURES
HISTORY AND POLITICS

GEOGRAPHY AND ECONOMY

The Republic of Uganda lies on the equator in East Africa and borders Kenya in the east, Sudan in the north, the Democratic Republic of the Congo (DRC) in the west, and Tanzania and Rwanda in the south. When the Uganda Protectorate was declared by Great Britain in 1894 the term *Uganda*—meaning "State of the Ganda people"—only included the Buganda kingdom. The term was subsequently retained as protectorate rights were extended to adjacent areas, culminating in the formal ratification of the Protectorate by the Uganda Order in Council of 1902. Following the incorporation of West Nile District into Uganda in 1914, and the transfer of Rudolf Province to Kenya in 1926, Uganda's modern borders were established.

GEOGRAPHY

Of Uganda's total area of 93,065 square miles, 16,988 square miles is open water and swampland, including Lake Victoria, Lake Albert, Lake Edward, and Lake Kyoga. The Victoria Nile emerges from Lake Victoria at Jinja and leaves Uganda to the north as the Albert Nile. Lake Kyoga in central Uganda is an approximate boundary between the Bantu-speaking south and the Nilotic and Central Sudanic language speakers in the north. The 2007 estimate population was 30.2 million.

Uganda's topography is dominated by the Central African plateau located between the eastern and western branches of the Great Rift Valley. This declines from 3,937 feet at Lake Victoria to 2,985 feet on the Sudan border. The eastern and western borders are mountainous; the Virunga (Mufumbira) Mountains border Rwanda and the Ruwenzori Range borders DRC (Mt. Stanley/Margherita PK., 16,763 feet), while a range of volcanic hills dominated by Mt. Elgon (14,178 feet) border Kenya.

Uganda has a tropical environment that is modified by its continental situation, the diversity of altitudes, and the presence of water bodies. Most of Uganda lies in the central zone of the tropical belt and has bimodal rainfall. The south and central regions experience heavier rains from March through May, and lighter rains from September through November (47–86 inches per year). In the north rainfall is less pronouncedly bimodal (31.5–51.5 inches per year), while the northeast has one yearly rainy period from March through April (under 51 inches). Mean annual temperatures range from 60 degrees Fahrenheit in the southwestern highlands to 77 degrees Fahrenheit in the northwest. Natural vegetation is heaviest in the south (tropical savanna with remnants of equatorial forests) and the rich soils and

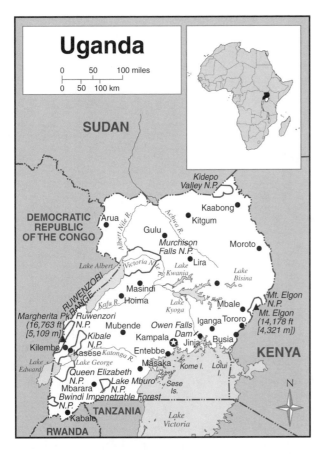

Uganda

0 50 100 miles

0 50 100 km

SUDAN

DEMOCRATIC
REPUBLIC
OF THE CONGO

Kidepo
Valley N.P.

Arua
Gulu
Kaabong
Kitgum

Murchison
Falls N.P.

Moroto

Albert Nile R.

Achwa R.

Lake Albert

Victoria Nile

Lake
Kwania

Lira

Lake
Bisina

RUWENZORI RANGE

Kafu R.

Masindi
Hoima

Lake
Kyoga

Mbale

Mt. Elgon
N.P.

Margherita Pk.
(16,763 ft
[5,109 m])

Ruwenzori
N.P.

Mubende

Owen Falls
Dam

Iganga
Tororo

Mt. Elgon
(14,178 ft
[4,321 m])

Kibale
N.P.

Kampala

Jinja

Busia

Kilembe

Kasese

Katonga R.

Entebbe

KENYA

Lake
Edward

Lake George

Masaka

Kome I.

Lolui
I.

Queen Elizabeth
N.P.

Lake Mburo
N.P.

Sese
Is.

Mbarara

Bwindi Impenetrable Forest
N.P.

Kabale

TANZANIA

Lake
Victoria

N

RWANDA

plentiful rainfall permit extensive agriculture; mostly the banana-coffee system. Vegetation thins to savanna in the north (banana-millet-cotton/tobacco system) and acacia and cactus on the dry plains in the northeast where pastoral economies are common.

ECONOMY

The declaration of the Uganda Protectorate was chiefly motivated by geo-political factors—especially gaining control over the headwaters of the Nile River—but once achieved it was necessary to generate revenue so that the Protectorate pay its way. Cotton, then in demand from Metropolitan interests seeking new sources of supply to circumvent high tariffs from Britain's traditional trading partners, was to facilitate both of these demands and played a central role in shaping the socioeconomic space of the Protectorate until World War II. Within the wider system of indirect rule, the colonial administration instituted and then utilized the Native Authority—comprising modified or invented chiefly political hierarchies—to enforce taxation of

the African populace, distribute cotton seed, and impel peasant farmers to plant cotton.

A policy of uneven development had, by the late 1920s, made the south and central regions the dominant areas of cotton cultivation and the north a labor reserve. The extension of the Uganda Railway from Mombassa to Kisumu (completed in 1901), and subsequently to Jinja (1928), allowed cotton to be transported to British textile mills without breaking bulk. Cotton was purchased, ginned, and exported in a milieu of increasingly pervasive regulation and monopolization. This circumscribed the spatial and economic opportunities open to the African population, a situation that was compounded by the dominance of Ugandan-Asians in the trading and marketing sectors.

Until the Colonial Welfare and Development Act of 1940, industrialization had been actively inhibited in Uganda to minimize competition, to preserve an idealized rural "tribal order," and to protect the cotton sector. However, following World War II the colonial administration instigated a program of state-led industrialization and modernization. The Owen Falls Dam at Jinja was completed in 1954, and a range of industries were established in partnership with the Uganda Development Corporation (established in 1952); textile mills, breweries, cement, and paper industries, and a plant for processing copper ore mined at Kilembe in western Uganda (closed in 1978). Much of the private industrial investment was made by the Uganda-Asian Madhvani and Mehta Corporations with capital accumulated in the small but important sugar sector. Following independence in 1962 there were a number of years of economic growth (gross domestic product growth averaging 5.8% between 1963 and 1971), but the 1971 military coup lead by Idi Amin Dada initiated two decades of industrial and wider economic collapse. The 1972 expulsion of the Asian population, the nationalization and plundering of industries, wider economic mismanagement, and increasing international isolation caused infrastructural decay, the collapse of the crop marketing systems, escalating inflation, and an increase in the size and penetration of a black market economy (*magendo*).

Coffee and food crop cultivation became more attractive to farmers as coffee prices increased and as payments to farmers for cotton by the monopolistic marketing boards became unreliable. Despite some economic stabilization resulting from the World Bank/International Monetary Fund (IMF) structural adjustment program implemented during the first years of the second Milton Obote government (1980–1985), the escalating so-called bush war with Yoweri Museveni's National Resistance Army led to renewed economic collapse. The takeover by Museveni's National Resistant Movement (NRM) in 1986 heralded a period of improved law and order, relative economic stability and liberalization in the traditionally more prosperous south and central regions, but continued instability and population displacements in the north due to the paramilitary actions of the Lords Resistance Army. The Economic Recovery Program (ERP) agreed upon between the IMF and the NRM government in 1987 included currency devaluation, civil service reform, deregulation of pricing and marketing controls, and privatization.

Although plagued by delays and irregularities, these measures have acted to stabilize the economy and have provided a more secure investment environment. The continued importance of the informal sector makes any accurate assessment of macroeconomic performance or real incomes problematic. The national economy remains vulnerable to fluctuations in international coffee prices, and poverty remains chronic in many areas. Agriculture remains the most important sector of the economy, and employs above 80 percent of Uganda's population. Chief primary sector exports are coffee, fish, tea, sugar, maize, cotton, and tobacco, and the most important industrial exports are textiles, beer, cement and steel products.

See also **Amin Dada, Idi; Colonial Policies and Practices; International Monetary Fund; Museveni, Yoweri; Nile River; Obote, Milton; Transportation: Railways; World Bank.**

BIBLIOGRAPHY

Bigsten, Arne, and Steve Kayizzi-Mugerwa. *Crisis, Adjustment and Growth in Uganda.* London: Macmillan, 1999.

Byerley, Andrew. *Becoming Jinja: The Production of Space and Making of Place in an African Industrial Town.* Stockholm: Almqvist and Wiksell, 2005.

Hansen, Holger Bernt, and Michael Twaddle, eds. *Uganda Now: Between Decay and Development.* Athens: Ohio University Press, 1988.

Hill, M. F. *Permanent Way: The Story of the Kenya and Uganda Railway.* Nairobi: East African Railways and Harbors, 1949.

Van Zwanenburg, R.M.A., with Anne King. *An Economic History of Kenya and Uganda. 1800–1970.* Atlantic Highlands, NJ: Humanities Press, 1975.

ANDREW BYERLEY

SOCIETY AND CULTURES

Uganda has 30 million people, of whom only 13 percent live in urban areas. National wealth is concentrated in the capital city Kampala and its immediate surrounding area. Uganda is one of the poorest nations, ranked 158 out of 174 nations by the United Nations Development Program Human Development Index. The backbone of the economy is the small-scale peasant producers dependent on subsistence farming and low-cash incomes. Uganda is completely dependent on foreign aid and has used some of it to achieve positive growth rates of between 5 and 10 percent and low annual inflation. Uganda has had its international debt cancelled and economic growth is reflected in the boom in land sales, housing construction, traffic congestion, numerous markets and supermarkets, and in the establishment of the Kampala Stock Exchange. However, the extensive squatter settlement slums and widespread unemployment and petty trading indicate that the benefits of development are unevenly distributed. The majority of people, both in rural and urban areas, live in grinding poverty. Economic and political success is biased toward those with considerable financial resources and good connections.

Recovery from the anarchy, violence, and poverty of the tumultuous years between 1971 and 1985 coincided with a new development paradigm, participatory development. Aid agencies insisted on funding self-help cooperatives. The result has been a proliferation of nongovernmental organizations (NGOs) defining local issues or associating with internationally identified fundable problems, ranging from war widows, orphans, human rights, and people living with HIV/AIDS. However, the efforts of grassroots civil society struggle to achieve sustainable development and are undermined by endemic corruption.

The hosting of the British flag on old Kampala Hill in 1893 by Captain Frederick Lugard put in motion the British colonization of Uganda started in 1890 by the Imperial British East African Company. On April 12, 1894, the *London Gazette* declared Uganda a British Protectorate and on April 21 a cartoon in *Punch*, the English humorous magazine, depicted a surprised John Bull discovering an abandoned baby Uganda on the doorstep. In other words Lugard's actions had forced colonial responsibility on the British government. The geographical entity had already been created during the Scramble for Africa at the 1885 Berlin Conference. Many people found themselves divided between Uganda and the present-day surrounding countries of Congo, Kenya, Rwanda, Burundi, Tanzania, and Sudan. The diversity in peoples and polities in nineteenth-century Uganda is illustrated in terms of languages and political structures. There were 200 political entities constituted by 62 groups with distinct languages and whose sizes varied from a few thousand (the Ik, Tapeth, and Pokot) to 1 million (Baganda). In the early 2000s there are only thirty-two spoken languages. The map in Figure 1 shows linguistic areas consisting of diverse ethnic groups.

Bantu speakers are in the South and include Banyarwanda, Bakiga, Banyankole, Baganda, Banyoro, Basoga, Bagwere, Basamia, Banyole, Bagisu, Bamba, and Bakonjo. The western Nilotic include Acholi, Jonam, Jopadhola, and the Langi who are thought to have converted from the eastern Nilotic groups, which include the Ik, Karamojong, Labwor, Tapeth, Iteso, Pokot, Kakwa, and Sebei; and the Sudanic groups of Lugbara and Madi. The Iteso, Kakwa, and Adhola are situated a distance from their linguistic category because of migration. One ethnic group not on the map is the Nubi who are Muslim urban dwellers and descendants of South Sudanese soldiers employed in the Protectorate service of subduing the Muslims and the Ganda King Mwanga. The official language of Uganda is English. Knowledge of Luganda is widespread. Swahili, previously used in the army and police and despised as the language of the coastal Arab slave traders, became a language of survival in the 1970s when confronted with violent, uneducated, and sometimes foreign soldiers.

Uganda politics and development reflect the consequences of colonial policies. The people living in the "fertile crescent" around Lake Victoria would grow cash crops with migrant labor provided by the people

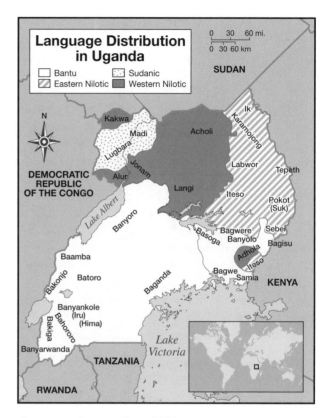

COURTESY OF CHRISTINE OBBO, 2006

in the north and southwest. This geographical division of labor led to uneven distribution of economic opportunities. Labor reserves were not production zones and further provided a reservoir for police and army recruitment. These divisions of labor and opportunities are often ignored by those who blame postcolonial conflicts entirely on ethnicity.

From Uganda's inception the dynamics of ethnicity and religion have had a great influence on political alliances and cleavages. The European missionaries, representing different religious orders, arrived in the early 1890s, bringing and passing on to their African converts religious antagonisms based on the historical struggles between Catholicism and Protestantism (French and British imports, respectively). Coexistence was achieved when different missionaries established churches, schools, and hospitals on different hills of the administrative capital Kampala. In 1962 when Uganda attained political independence from Britain, the Democratic Party, with a predominant Catholic membership, was vilified as antimonarchist by Baganda nationalists of Kabaka Yekka (The King Only) who later allied themselves with the Uganda People's Congress, seen as representing national

---

Republic of Uganda

Population:	30,262,610 (2007 est.)
Area:	241,038 sq. km (93,065 sq. mi.)
Official language:	English
Languages:	English, Luganda and Swahili, other Bantu and Nilotic languages
National currency:	Uganda shilling
Principal religions:	Christian 84% (Roman Catholic and Protestant), Muslim 12%
Capital:	Kampala (est. pop. 1,200,000 in 2002)
Other urban centers:	Jinja, Mbale, Mbarara, Masaka, Entebbe, Gulu, Fort Portal, Soroti
Annual rainfall:	varies from 2,250 mm (90 in.) near Lake Victoria to 400 mm (15 in.) in Karamoja Plains
Principal geographical features:	*Mountains:* Mt. Ruwenzori, Mt. Elgon, Mt. Margherita, Mt. Mufumbiro, Mt. Moroto *Lakes:* George, Edward, Kyoga, Albert, Victoria, Kwania, Salisbury, Bisinia *Rivers:* Victoria Nile (becomes Albert Nile), Katonga, Kafu, Aswa, Pager, Depeth-Okok, Mpologa-Malaba
Economy:	*GDP per capita:* US$1,900 (2006)
Principal products and exports:	*Agricultural:* coffee, tea, cotton, tobacco, cassava (tapioca), potatoes, corn, millet, pulses, cut flowers, beef, goat meat, milk, poultry *Manufacturing:* sugar processing, brewing, tobacco, cotton textiles, cement, steel production *Mining:* copper, phosphates, limestone, gold
Government:	Independence from the United Kingdom, 1962. Republic proclaimed, 1963. Independence constitution, 1961; suspended 1966; replaced, 1967. New constitution adopted, 1995. Under the new constitution, the president is directly elected by universal suffrage for 5-year term (first direct election of a president since independence). 276-seat Parliament of Uganda serves 5-year terms, 214 members elected by universal suffrage, 62 selected by electoral colleges. Prime minister is head of government. President appoints Cabinet. For purposes of local government there are 56 districts.
Heads of state since independence:	1962–1966: Prime Minister A. Milton Obote 1963: President Edward Mutesa II 1966–1971: President A. Milton Obote 1971–1979: President for Life Idi Amin 1979: President Yusuf Lule, chairman of the National Consultative Council (NCC) 1979–1980: President Godfrey Binaisa, chairman of the NCC 1980: Paulo Muwanga, chairman of the Military Commission of the National Front for the Liberation of Uganda 1980–1985: President A. Milton Obote 1985–1986: General Tito Okello, chairman of the Military Council 1986–: President Yoweri Museveni
Armed forces:	President is commander in chief. Voluntary enlistment. *Total armed forces (army, navy, air force):* 50,000
Transportation:	*Rail:* 1,241 km (769 mi.) *Roads:* 70,764 km (43,970 mi.), 23% paved *National airline:* Uganda Airlines *Airports:* Principal airport at Entebbe, second international facility at Arua. 29 smaller airports and airstrips throughout the country.
Media:	dailies, including *Financial Times, New Vision, The Star.* Publishers include Longman Press, Uganda Publishing House. Radio Uganda is state-owned. Uganda Television Service was founded in 1963. 40 radio stations, 9 television stations.
Literacy and education:	*Total literacy rate:* 70% (2003). Primary education reform begun in 1994. Postsecondary education provided at Makerere University, Makerere Institute for Social Research, Mbarara University of Science and Technology, Uganda Martyrs University, Uganda Polytechnic.

diversity. However, following the 1991 coup d'etat Muslims who had hitherto been marginalized in politics and education moved to the center and Christians faced persecution. Despite opportunistic conversions to Islam, Catholics continued to constitute about 50 percent of the population, followed by Protestants at 40 percent and Muslims at 10 percent. Both Christians and Muslims continue to seek help for health both from

biomedical practitioners and traditional healers, most of whom are mediums of traditional deities and spirits.

Migration, urbanization, education, and poverty have brought changes to some cultural practices but others have remained resistant or slow to change. The Sebei, Bagisu, and Muslims circumcise men and the former circumcise women. Increasingly circumcision candidates in towns are recruited through coercion. Ugandans usually have several names that provide religious, ethnic, clan, gender, and sometimes marital identity. Ideologically all Ugandan societies are patrilineal: Descent is traced through men. Despite the fact that poverty has meant that most young men can neither afford to pay bride wealth for marriage nor support families and young women voluntarily or involuntarily resign themselves to the status of unmarried mother, societies still adhere to the ideal of the patrilineal affiliation of children.

Uganda is in the throes of religious and cultural fundamentalism. Poverty and the AIDS epidemic have left people desperate for solace. Uganda is awash with foreign missionaries, the most prominent being U.S. and European born-again Christians. Uganda has been awarded $230 million from the U.S. government's emergency plan. The Ugandan government has shifted its HIV/AIDS prevention strategies to accommodate the United States government's faith-based abstinence-only funding policy. The moral "social vaccines" of abstinence and faithfulness (AB) are promoted over the apparently less virtuous condoms (C). Abstinence is not a choice for women because they are constrained by their inferior social status from exercising sexual and reproductive choice. While women do most of the productive work in the fields and in the urban streets, they lack economic power and this makes them vulnerable to HIV infection. Monogamous women are infected by their sole partners, their husbands. They cannot demand safer sexual practices or fidelity. Women need the power to use the ABC prevention methods individually or in combination as they best suit their circumstances.

In the 1990s Western aid donors lauded Uganda for setting the standard in Africa's fights against HIV/AIDS because infection rates had fallen from 18 percent in the 1980s to 6 percent in 2003. Infection rates have since risen to 7 percent for men and 9 percent for women. Cultural fundamentalists, who stress men's rights rather than their responsibilities, and churches, which stress the respectability of being a married woman, both aggressively promote marriage. The consequence is that men see marriage as a prophylaxis irrespective of their sexual history or promiscuous behavior, and women bear the brunt of infection.

There are high infections among women and young girls because of lack of political commitment to effective legislation and implementation of policies that promote the economic advancement or protection against sexual violence. In northern Uganda the Acholi have missed a decade of development because of the activities of Konyi's Lord's Resistance Army, which is supposed to fight the national army but in fact preys on young children, using girls as sex slaves and boys as soldiers.

See also **Disease: HIV/AIDS; Ethnicity; Kinship and Descent; Labor; Languages; Lugard, Frederick John Dealtry; Marriage Systems; Nongovernmental Organizations.**

BIBLIOGRAPHY

Action for Development (ACFODE). *Visible at Last: NGO Contribution to Women's Recognition in Uganda.* Kampala: ACFORDE, 1995.

Jorgensen, Jan Jelmert. *Uganda: A Modern History.* New York: St. Martin's Press, 1981.

Leggett, Ian L. *Uganda.* London: Oxfam, 2001.

Thomas, Harold B., and Robert Scott. *Uganda.* New York: Oxford University Press, 1949.

Trowell, Margaret, and Klaus P. Wachsman. *Tribal Crafts of Uganda.* New York: Oxford University Press, 1953.

CHRISTINE OBBO

HISTORY AND POLITICS

To understand the sociopolitical and historical developments in Uganda, it is important to situate the country's development trajectory beginning from the mid-1800s. Since Uganda was declared a British protectorate in 1894, there have been three major historical periods. These are the process of colonial conquest and rule, the formative years of colonialism (1900–1962), and the postcolonial rule and beyond. The imposition of colonial rule was an event characterized by resistance and collaboration through formation of ethnic and religious alliances prior to 1900, thus effectively defining which ethnic group got access to resources and which did not. The effects of the different ethnic alliances formed during the struggle against colonialism—for example, the Ganda formed an alliance with colonial conquerors against the Banyoro resistance—has had lasting economic and political bearings on Uganda's history. The subsequent 1900 Buganda

Agreement between Buganda's king (*Kabaka*) and the British colonial rulers set a parameter for land ownership because it did not only define who could own land but also how land was owned and where, which later affected the political spectrum in all of Uganda. Similarly, the period from 1900 to 1920 is also an important part of the historical developments in Uganda because it was during this period that cash-crop growing was institutionalized, although not by peaceful means. The postcolonial period (post-1962) was characterized by militarism, dictatorships, political instabilities, abuse of human rights, corruption, economic stagnation, civil wars, and the governmental implementation of neoliberal policies such as structural adjustment policies (SAPs) that, to some extent, determine the socioeconomic and political history the country then experienced.

THE PRECOLONIAL PERIOD

Many precolonial societies in Africa depended on individual communities arranged into small fiefdoms or kingdoms. In Uganda, these included the most recognizable and powerful kingdoms of Buganda, Bunyoro, Tooro, Ankole, and Busoga. The production relations of these communities were dependant on their sociocultural and political systems. In addition, other small, noncentralized societies, such as Bagishu and Bakiga, whose organization was based on clans and lineages, ensured that everyone in the community was well taken care of through either kinship or friendship networks. In all these communities, the feudal mode of production existed, with the rulers extracting tribute from the commoners via their appointed representatives or the heads of the clans.

The political and military strength of the kingdoms prior to the coming of the colonialists and explorers in the mid-1800s has been a subject of debate among scholars. The Bunyoro-Kitara empire was the largest, stretching across present-day western Kenya, northern Tanzania, and eastern Democratic Republic of the Congo. However, successive weak kings, a lack of effective control, and the numerous wars of resistance against colonial invaders reduced Bunyoro to a district size by the early twentieth century. The coming of the missionaries and their subsequent conversion of Ugandans to Christianity, especially around 1888–1892, fomented interreligious fighting, intrigue, and alliance formations.

These were between the Church Missionary Society members (Protestants) and the Roman Catholic White Fathers (Catholics) against traditionalists and a small number of Muslims and later against each other. Colonial conquest occurred near the end of the Industrial Revolution, and many European countries needed raw materials. The colonial powers therefore sought out areas that would be a cheap source of materials such as cotton, coffee, labor, and markets for their industrial products.

It is important to note that, prior to colonial rule, women and men had a special relationship in terms of their gender roles. Women grew food crops while men cleared land for cultivation, built houses, and performed other chores such as looking after domestic animals. Once in a while, regional specialization was occurred, for example, the Batooro specialized in copper works, the Banyoro developed iron works, the Ganda specialized in bark cloth and carpentry, and the Basoga specialized in canoe making. However, this specialization did not remove people from their subsistence livelihoods where men and young boys, for example, worked in salt mines, and women and young girls tended the gardens.

The exchange of goods and services took several forms, ranging from barter trade to cash transactions. This exchange of goods occurred within and between states or kingdoms, which was complimentary rather than competitive in nature. Substantial trade with the outside world did not begin until the early nineteenth century when increased demand for ivory on the east African coast forced Arab traders to venture deep inland. Since the Ganda settled along the long distance route, they were able to control interregional trade by acquiring gun power. A majority of the items exchanged were for personal use, such as ornaments, clothing (cotton), and guns. The weapons were later used to assert regional control and domination over neighboring communities and, because of transport limitations, only a few items reached Uganda. This made the cost of goods expensive in Uganda or even hard to obtain.

THE COLONIAL RULE

The period from 1900 to 1930 was a turning point in Uganda's political and economic history because it is during this time that the colonial government reorganized its sociopolitical and economic structure from a non-cash to a capitalist economy by introducing cash crops, compulsory labor requirements, and taxation. Road and railway construction became an important aspect if colonial powers were to exploit the interior, a vast area with many untapped resources that necessitated employing unskilled African laborers, especially in plantations. The period leading up to World War I was important in the institutionalization of the rapidly expanding plantation agriculture of crops such as coffee, tea, rubber, sugar, and cotton. Thus, the deployment of the contentious colonial economic policies not only defined what work people could engage in or not, but also confined people to particular livelihood patterns while participating in the cash economy.

POSTCOLONIAL ERA

The economic arrangement of the production system as defined by the colonial administrators did not fizzle out at independence on October 9, 1962, but continued to be the dominant mode of livelihood patterns in many parts of Uganda. Although the colonial regime established a plantation agricultural system in Uganda, the African farmer continued to be restricted and exploited as a peripheral producer. Uganda's politics increasingly became focused on divisions based on ethnicity and religious beliefs, and the socioeconomic and political sphere fell into decline and waste. Beginning with the postindependence government in 1962–1966, Uganda implemented development projects based on the European and North American planning models where the emphasis is on adopting one particular production system, depending on climate and location. The 1966 government crisis in which the prime minister abrogated the constitution and Uganda became a republic, and the period 1966–1971, did not severely affect the government service provision. Centralized planning, supervised by the central government, continued to guide the development process. However, ethnic and religious divides created much discontent and mistrust of the government, resulting in the 1971 military coup.

The coup, led by dictator Idi Amin, and the period 1971–1979 when he was in control, were turning points in Uganda's history. It regenerated the general socioeconomic and political development that Uganda had made over the years. With the declaration of economic war in 1972, all Ugandans of Asian origin controlling major portions of the country's economic

activities at the time were unwelcome and subsequently expelled. This led to the diminishing of Uganda's economic status with no possibility of recovery.

The period following the collapse of Idi Amin's regime, 1979–1986, was characterized by continued turmoil, violations of human rights—including the killing of innocent people—mismanagement of the economy, and guerrilla warfare. The government under Apollo Milton Obote could have implemented a recovery and rehabilitation program after the chaos of the 1970s, but instead it became a replica of what the dictator Amin had created while in control of the country. The army, led by General Tito Okello (1914–1996), overthrew President Obote in 1985. This gave the rebels of Yoweri Museveni, a former guerrilla leader, an advantage to take over government from Okello on January 26, 1986. From 1986, however, with a new government headed by Museveni, Uganda started on the path to reconstruction and rehabilitation with new promise of security, peace, and development.

While Museveni came to power as a self-professed Marxist, multilateral bodies such as the World Bank and International Monetary Fund (IMF) forced his government to change to liberal economic policies. However, Museveni has been overzealous with liberalizing public assets and attracting foreign investors. Therefore, such policies have not translated into serious development. Politically, since Museveni came to power through a guerrilla war, many other groups, including the Lords Resistance Army operating in northern Uganda, wanted to emulate his example. This did not happen because Museveni entrenched himself into power through control of the army and stifling opposition groups. Economically, during the period from the late 1980s through the 1990s, Uganda became what the international financial institutions (IFIs) considered a model country in its implementation of SAPs that aimed at stabilizing and revamping the economy.

UGANDA AND STRUCTURAL ADJUSTMENT POLICIES

Although by the end of the 1960s Uganda had made great strides in improving nationals' livelihoods, the 1970s and 1980s reversed many of the achievements. Apart from undemocratic governance, the 1980s saw the implementation of SAPs and their conditionalities. The different SAP conditions imposed by the World Bank and the IMF on Uganda placed the country in a subordinate position in the world arena. Some of the conditions included cuts in funding to social services, the introduction of cost sharing in education and health services, devaluation of the currency, removal of subsidies to farmers, increased exports, reduced imports, and a commitment to payment of international debts. Scholars argue that the language used in SAP conditions is reminiscent of the colonial regimes. The unfortunate reality, however, is that Uganda has focused on organizing workshops and seminars for good governance and capacity building, in which the elite members of government bureaucratic institutions take a large percentage of the funds and the remainder goes to expatriate workers, rather than focusing on using the borrowed resources to truly advance.

Though SAPs are supposed to be advantageous to the implementing nation, the long-term impact on people's livelihoods has been disastrous. For example, privatization introduced under SAPs only helped the elite government officials and those politically connected to reap benefits. Instead of playing regulatory roles under privatization, government employees, both national and local, collude with officials (who are supposed to regulate) to engage in corrupt practices. It is not surprising to find that government officials own most of the privatized companies. Thus, instead of the SAP policies benefiting people, they mainly benefit the corrupt officials, and exacerbate poverty levels. Therefore, poverty and a sense of powerlessness in terms of material well-being among the people seem to shape the sociopolitical and economic history in Uganda.

See also **Amin Dada, Idi; Christianity; Colonial Policies and Practices; Colonialism and Imperialism; Government; Human Rights; International Monetary Fund; Islam; Kagwa, Apolo; Lugard, Frederick John Dealtry; Museveni, Yoweri; Nyerere, Julius Kambarage; Obote, Milton; Political Systems; Stanley, Henry Morton; Warfare: Internal Revolts; World Bank.**

BIBLIOGRAPHY

Fuller, Thomas. "African Labor and Training in the Uganda Colonial Economy." *The International Journal of African Historical Studies* 10, no. 1 (1977): 77–95.

Jørgensen, Jan Jelmert. *Uganda: A Modern History.* London: Helm, 1981.

Kaberuka, Will. *The Political Economy of Uganda 1890–1979.* New York: Vantage Press, 1990.

Kasozi, Abdu Basajjabaka Kawalya. *The Social Origins of Violence in Uganda, 1964–1985.* Montreal, Canada: McGill-Queen's University Press, 1994.

Mamdani, Mohamood. *Politics and Class Formation in Uganda.* New York: Monthly Review Press, 1976.

Mkandwire, Thandika. "Globalization, Equity and Social Development." *African Sociological Review* 6, no. 1 (2002): 115–132.

Muhumuza, William. "The Paradox of Pursuing Anti-Poverty Strategies under Structural Adjustment Reforms in Uganda." *The Journal of Social, Political and Economic Studies* 27, no. 3 (2002): 271–306.

Taylor, Thomas. "The Struggle for Economic Control of Uganda, 1919–1922: Formulation of an Economic Policy." *The International Journal of African Historical Studies* 11, no.1 (1978): 1–31.

Taylor, Thomas. "The Establishment of a European Plantation Sector within the Emerging Colonial Economy of Uganda, 1902–1919." *The International Journal of African Historical Studies* 19, no. 1 (1986): 35–58.

Twaddle, Michael. *Kakungulu and the Creation of Uganda, 1868-1928.* London: James Currey, 1993.

ANDREW ELLIAS STATE

'UMAR IBN SA'ID TAL (c. 1794–1864).

'Umar ibn Sa'id Tal exerted a profound influence on the spread of Islam and one of its brotherhoods, the Tijaniyya, across a broad swath of West Africa. Through his writing, charisma, and military achievements, and through his descendants, he remains a prominent figure for Muslims in Senegal, Guinea, Mali, and other parts of West Africa.

'Umar was born in the valley of the Senegal River at Halwar, near the town of Podor (1794 and 1797 are the dates of birth most frequently advanced). His father was a local cleric and teacher in a Muslim society dominated by the Fulani (Fulbe) people, who played leading roles in the spread of introducing Islam across West Africa in the eighteenth and nineteenth centuries.

The young 'Umar showed a strong aptitude for learning as he pursued his clerical training in the conventional peripatetic pattern. In addition to his studies in Islamic law, theology, and literature, he accepted initiation into the Sufi brotherhood called the Tijaniyya that had begun in the late eighteenth century in Algeria and Morocco. ʿUmar then made the pilgrimage to Mecca and Medina; he fulfilled this obligation in three successive years (1828–1830). During this time, his initiation into the Tijaniyya was reaffirmed, and he was authorized to spread the brotherhood in West Africa.

ʿUmar spent significant time in most of the main Muslim centers of West Africa during his studies and his pilgrimages, particularly in the areas where Fulani Muslims had taken power through the jihad or holy war in the preceding decades: the imamate of Fuuta Jallon, the caliphate of Hamdullahi or Masina, and the Sokoto Caliphate. ʿUmar spent the 1840s in Fuuta Jallon developing a loyal group of disciples. During this period he wrote his major work, *Al-Rimah*, an important resource for Tijaniyya in the early twenty-first century.

Between 1852 and his death in 1864, ʿUmar enlisted his disciples and many other Muslims in a jihad against the predominantly non-Muslim kingdoms in the upper Senegal and middle Niger River valleys. Most of his recruits were Fulani from the areas of Fuuta Jallon, Fuuta Toro, and Senegambia; most of his opponents were Mandinka and Bambara living in the western part of present-day Mali.

In 1862 ʿUmar went beyond his mission of destroying the structures of paganism when he issued an ultimatum to the neighboring Islamic theocracy of Hamdullahi to cease its support of the Bambara regime of Segu, his declared enemy. He conquered this Fulani Muslim regime, but its inhabitants soon joined forces with an influential Timbuktu cleric, Ahmad al-Bakkay, overturned the new ʿUmarian regime, and brought ʿUmar's life to an end in 1864.

ʿUmar left his imprint on the societies of Senegal, Guinea, and Mali. His works, especially *Al-Rimah*, are widely used in Tijaniyya teaching. Many of his descendants are well placed in the elite political and religious classes. In Senegal he is remembered as a hero of Islamic expansion and resistance to the French, whereas many in Mali see him as an invader who destroyed indigenous states and weakened their social structures.

See also **Islam.**

BIBLIOGRAPHY

Ly-Tall, Madina. *Un Islam militant en Afrique de l'Ouest au XIXe siècle.* Paris: Harmattan, 1991.

Robinson, David. *The Holy War of Umar Tal: The Western Sudan in the Mid-Nineteenth Century.* Oxford: Clarendon Press, 1985.

Willis, John Ralph. *In the Path of Allah: The Passion of al-Hajj ʿUmar: An Essay into the Nature of Charisma in Islam* London: F. Cass, 1989.

DAVID ROBINSON

UNDERDEVELOPMENT. *See* Economic History.

UNEMPLOYMENT. *See* Labor.

UNITED NATIONS

This entry includes the following articles:
AFRICA IN THE UNITED NATIONS
UNITED NATIONS IN AFRICA

AFRICA IN THE UNITED NATIONS

When the United Nations (UN) was established following the end of World War II in 1945, much of sub-Saharan Africa was firmly in the grip of European colonialism. Liberia, Ethiopia, and the Republic of South Africa enjoy the distinction of being the only three African states that were among the original fifty sovereign states that signed the UN charter in San Francisco in June 1945. "With this Charter," President Harry Truman reminded the signatories, "the world can begin to look forward to the time when all worthy human beings may be permitted to live decently as free people" (Schlesinger, p. 293). That journey toward the freedom for all peoples began earnestly for the United Nations and, within a decade, the UN midwifed the birth of Ghana as the first African nation to emerge from European colonialism in 1957. Since then, Africa has remained a visible component of the sixty-year efforts of the United

Nations to actualize the purposes enshrined in Article 1 of the charter. This entry examines Africa's contributions to two aspects of UN activities and goals: (1) decolonization and socioeconomic justice; and (2) collective security.

DECOLONIZATION AND SOCIOECONOMIC JUSTICE

Africa was the epicenter of the long and tortuous global struggle to end formal colonialism. Although the formal colonization of Africa was relatively brief, between 1885 and the 1960s, its devastating effects have lingered on longer here than anywhere else. The reason, according to some scholars, is the near *sui generis* character of the deep-seated racism upon which African colonization was predicated. In his study of the Congo, for instance, Martin Ewans ascertained that the vast majority of European colonial administrators had such a low opinion of Africans as a race that, he concluded: "It is a legitimate criticism of all the colonial powers in Africa that none of them seriously envisaged a progress to self-rule until it was too late in the day to avoid what became a 'scramble out of Africa.' " (2002, 242). Self-government did occur, mostly peacefully, throughout Africa, and the new states joined the United Nations where they helped keep global attention on the problem of racism and decolonization from being consumed by Cold War politics.

Led by their nationalist elites, such as Kwame Nkrumah and Julius Nyerere, Africa's new states used the UN platform to mobilize international opinion and action against colonialism and white supremacist rule in southern Africa. As Nkrumah envisioned it, no single African state could be truly independent until the rest of the continent was free. The new states pursued this cause by building bridges and issue-based coalitions with other numbers of the United Nations, especially the newly independent states of Asia and the Middle East and the older states of South America and the Caribbean whose numbers had altered the size and demographic character of the General Assembly. In the General Assembly, these groups formed a visible and predictable voting bloc, becoming the Group of 77 (G-77) by the 1970s when socioeconomic justice and fair commodity prices led them to demand for a new international economic order.

The success of the G-77 in pressing the issue of socioeconomic justice through the United Nations Conference on Trade and Development (UNCTAD) emboldened the group to demand greater UN action to end the remnants of colonialism and white supremacist regimes in southern Africa. By far the greatest challenge posed to the group was the Republic of South Africa, which was deepening and extending the application of apartheid, a policy of separate development on the basis of race that was launched in 1948, not only at home but also to neighboring Namibia. Since the Sharpeville Massacre of 1960 that set off events that resulted in the arrest, trial, and imprisonment of Nelson Mandela and other leaders of the African National Congress, the strategy of African states at the UN had been to weaken the support that Pretoria gets from key Western states and, through the agencies of the UN, get the international community to apply maximum pressure on Pretoria to abandon its apartheid policy.

The increased power of Africa's oil-exporting countries, especially Nigeria, Algeria, and Libya from 1973 onward, was quickly converted into political capital within the G-77. Throughout the 1970s, the African group at the United Nations, backed by their G-77 allies and the Scandinavian states, successfully pressed the issue of economic sanctions, mandatory arms, and oil embargo against South Africa at the General Assembly and the Security Council. By 1975, the diplomatic isolation of South Africa had been virtually achieved with the effective exclusion of Pretoria from "all the organs of the United Nations" (United Nations 1994, 30). Two years later, in 1977, the Security Council imposed a mandatory arms embargo on South Africa. By 1980, southern Rhodesia became independent as Zimbabwe, and for the next decade African states and their allies turned their attention toward generating grassroots support within Western states for divestment of big corporations from South Africa. This focus paid off and thus was born the divestment movement.

The movement's biggest prize came in 1985, when the United States Congress overrode President Ronald Reagan's veto to pass into law the Comprehensive Anti-Apartheid Act, which made it illegal for American companies to conduct business in South Africa. Less than five years later, in February 1990, the government of South Africa released Nelson Mandela, its most famous prisoner and the living symbol of the anti-apartheid struggle.

In the same year, Pretoria abandoned its much-touted mandate of South West Africa, paving the way for Namibia's independence in March 1990. Finally, in April 1994, South Africans of all races buried apartheid when they went to the polls and overwhelmingly elected Nelson Mandela, leader of the African National Congress (ANC), as president of South Africa. This remarkably peaceful transition has allowed a united South Africa to take its place in the comity of nations as it struggles, not without difficulties, to meet the socio-economic aspirations of its diverse population.

COLLECTIVE SECURITY

The fragility of African states at independence was hardly in doubt. Unprepared for self-government by the various mandatory powers, Africa's postcolonial state elites realized that they would become especially susceptible to even the weakest forms of sociopolitical and/or economic turbulence. Their response to this danger was to seek collective means to protect themselves against such shocks by coalescing around international organizations and regimes, such as the Organization of African Unity (OAU). This is the very essence of Nkrumah's vision and his relentless efforts to build solidarity between African, Arab, Caribbean, Asian, and Latin American states in the United Nations.

For African elites, the real test of the promises and limits of collective security advocacy came very early and, not unpredictably, in the Congo, which presented the worst example of paternalism and benign neglect ever exhibited by a mandatory power. Congo was overexploited and severely underdeveloped by Belgium, its mandatory power. According to the United Nations, "few Congolese studied beyond the secondary level and, at the time of independence, there were among them 17 university graduates and no doctors, lawyers or engineers" (1990, 216). Therefore, state capacity was a problem from the beginning, and it affected all aspects of society, especially in the vital area of national security. According to Ernest Lefever, Congo's "*Force Publique,* which in 1960 was a 25,000-man national security force combining the functions of an army and a police . . . was entirely officered by 1,100 Europeans, mainly Belgians" (1965, 9). The rest, of course, were "largely illiterate Congolese troops." More significantly, Lefever poignantly observed that the Congolese soldier

was "loyal neither to state nor nation" and that no significant changes in the functions or command structure of the Force were planned or anticipated" (10).

Within one week of gaining independence on June 30, 1960, trouble erupted in the Congo when the African soldiers of the Congolese Army mutinied against their Belgian officers. In the weeks that followed, the rebellion spread rather quickly throughout Congo, including the strategic and mineral-rich province of Katanga. In panic, much of Congo's European population fled to the relative safety of Leopoldville, where Belgian troops were still stationed. Unable and unwilling to meet Brussels's demand for firm government action to stem the mutiny, Prime Minister Patrice Lumumba, whose "communist sympathies" had long been noted by Brussels and Washington, lost the confidence of Belgian authorities who, with the United States, sought regime change in Leopoldville. By July 10, Belgium had deployed upwards of 10,000 troops throughout the Congo ostensibly to protect its citizens and maintain law and order, but in reality to effect its policy of regime change (Lefever 1965, 11–14). In doing so, however, it embarked upon a collision course with Lumumba's nationalist government, which was committed to asserting its powers.

The response of the nationalist government to the events was predictable, even if detrimental to the long-term stability of the Congo. On July 9, the president and commander-in-chief of the Congolese Armed Forces, Joseph Kasavubu, acting in concert with Prime Minister Lumumba, announced the dismissal of General Janssens, alongside other European senior officers of the Force Publique. The move, which was designed to Africanize the army and pacify the mutinous native soldiers, resulted in the elevation of a native, Victor Lundula, as commander of the army, and Joseph Mobutu as army chief of staff. The president and prime minister also changed the official name of the army from the Force Publique to Armée Nationale Congolese (Congolese National Army).

None of these changes, however, was enough to stop Congo from spiraling toward complete anarchy. Indeed, the declaration of the secession of the province of Katanga on July 11 by its premier, Moise Tshombe, triggered a political and constitutional crisis that hastened the demise of the Congo. The day after, in what was to be their last major political act together as Congo's constituted authority, President

Kasavubu and Prime Minister Lumumba requested the assistance of the United Nations to avert a complete breakdown of law and order in the Congo. The request was granted by the Security Council via resolution 143, and UN peacekeepers began arriving Congo on July 15 under the umbrella of the United Nations Operation in the Congo (ONUC). At its height, ONUC comprised some 20,000 troops and several thousand civilian personnel, but it was resoundingly ineffective and utterly dysfunctional. Under its watch, Congo would disintegrate into armed enclaves as ONUC leadership clung to the principle of "neutrality," which few believed. On September 14, Colonel Mobutu formally sacked the fledgling but unstable democratic government. The subsequent assassination of Prime Minister Lumumba and the rise of Mobutu as the military and political henchman of the Congo—all with the tacit support of some western powers and the much vaunted Central Intelligence Agency (CIA)—brought the complexities of Cold War politics to Africa.

More significantly for the future, the failure of ONUC had an unsavory effect on African elites insofar as it ingrained in their consciousness a deep-seated suspicion of UN peacekeeping operations in their states. That suspicion, which continued through the 1990s with the failure of high profile UN operations in Somalia during 1992–1994, was tragically cemented by the genocide that occurred in Rwanda in 1994 under the watch of the United Nations Assistance Mission in Rwanda (UNAMIR). As has been noted by Romeo Dallaire, the Canadian-born commander of UNAMIR whose valiant efforts to stop the genocide was thwarted by the politics and bureaucratic culture of the United Nations, this particular episode of genocide was made even sadder by the fact that it was preventable and stoppable (Dallaire and Power 2004, Barnett 2002). Remarkably, these failures happened with Africans at the helm of affairs at the United Nations: UN Secretary-General Boutros Boutros-Ghali (Egypt), and Kofi Annan (Ghana), head of UN Department of Peacekeeping Operations (DPKO) and secretary-general, 1996–2006. This fact has somewhat diluted the power of racism as the explanation for the failure of collective security in Africa since the Congo crisis.

Faced with the threat of destabilization, African states have responded to these UN failures by focusing on internal mechanisms for collective security. For example, when conflict broke out in Liberia and Sierra Leone in the 1990s, members of the Economic Community of West African States (ECOWAS) assembled a regional peacekeeping force to contain the conflicts. In an incident that is eerily similar to ONUC, Samuel Doe—the embattled president who was at the center of the conflict in Liberia—was abducted by rebel forces from the headquarters of ECOWAS peacekeepers in Monrovia and was later tortured and assassinated. The similarities did not end there. In both West Africa and southern Africa, the various attempts at peace-maintenance in their regions by ECOWAS and SADC, respectively, proved to be no more successful than the efforts by the United Nations. In fact, according to some scholars, these regional attempts at collective security may have prolonged and exacerbated the crises in their regions.

In conclusion, the combination of UN failures in collective security under the leadership of two Africans—Boutros-Ghali and Annan—and the glaring weaknesses of Africa's home-grown collective security mechanisms have helped to weaken the appeal of racism as the explanation for the relative failure of the United Nations in Africa. This shift in emphasis has helped focus attention toward creative partnerships between the United Nations, African regional organizations, and non-governmental organizations whose resources and goodwill are essential to creating a sustainable peace. This realization, even if belated for the many innocent lives that have been lost needlessly, may well be Africa's greatest contribution yet to the emergence of a United Nations that is both efficient and responsive to the needs of all the peoples of the world.

See also **Annan, Kofi; Cold War; Decolonization; Economic Community of West African States (ECOWAS); Lumumba, Patrice; Mandela, Nelson; Mobutu Sese Seko; Nkrumah, Francis Nwia Kofi; Nyerere, Julius Kambarage; Organization of African Unity; Postcolonialism; Tshombe, Moïse Kapenda.**

BIBLIOGRAPHY

Adibe, Clement E. "The Liberian Conflict and the ECOWAS-UN Partnership." *Third World Quarterly* 18, no. 3 (1997): 471–488.

Baghwati, Jagdish, ed. *The New International Economic Order: The North-South Debate.* Cambridge, MA: MIT Press, 1977.

Barnett, Michael. *Eyewitness to a Genocide: The United Nations and Rwanda.* Ithaca, N.Y.: Cornell University Press, 2002.

Berman, Eric, and Katie Sams. *Peacekeeping in Africa: Capabilities and Culpabilities.* Geneva: United Nations Institute for Disarmament Research, 2000.

Dallaire, Romeo, and Samantha Power. *Shake Hands with the Devil: The Failure of Humanity in Rwanda.* New York: Carroll and Graff, 2004.

Ewans, Martin. *European Atrocity, African Catastrophe: Leopold II, the Congo Free State and its Aftermath.* London: Routledge Curzon, 2002.

Lefever, Ernest. *Crisis in the Congo: A United Nations Force in Action.* Washington, DC: The Brookings Institution, 1965.

United Nations. *The Blue Helmets: A Review of United Nations Peace-Keeping.* New York: United Nations Department of Public Information, 1990.

United Nations. *The United Nations and Apartheid, 1948–1994.* New York: United Nations Department of Public Information, 1994.

CLEMENT EME ADIBE

UNITED NATIONS IN AFRICA

Anyone interested in the extent to which the United Nations (UN) has changed in scope and function since its founding need look no further than the role of the organization in Africa. Three African states were among the fifty-one that signed the United Nations Charter at its inception. In the early twenty-first century, African states easily comprise one-quarter of the UN's total membership and African issues are a factor in virtually every UN organ and associated agency. Originally intended to address interstate conflict, the UN has since become a major player in intrastate conflict, especially in Africa. Roughly half of all current UN peacekeeping operations are in Africa and three-quarters of all UN troops are deployed in Africa, making the continent a core issue area for the United Nations.

Africa has been the location of some of the UN's most significant failures as well as some important successes. In 1960, the UN Security Council authorized a UN operation in the Congo in order to assist the newly independent government. The subsequent collapse of the government and the secession attempt by Katanga meant that the UN mission soon found itself in the midst of a civil war. The Security Council's determination not to accept Katangan secession, and the inability of the UN operation to stop the civil war generated deep political rifts that nearly tore the organization apart.

Later failures in Somalia and Rwanda in the early 1990s are symbolic of the difficulties the UN encountered in living up to what was perceived to be its post–Cold War potential. At the vanguard of its new willingness to respond to humanitarian crises the UN's third mission in Somalia eventually left the country little better off than when it arrived. And in Rwanda, the UN's failure to respond to the genocide has left a lasting legacy of shame. In the context of the UN's significant commitment to Bosnia and then Kosovo, Somalia and Rwanda also became symbolic of concerns about double standards. Why was the West so willing and able to commit significant resources and political will to the Balkans but not to Africa?

UN involvement with Namibia began when the territory passed from the League of Nations mandate system to the UN's trusteeship system in 1946. Under the League system, in 1920 South Africa was given a mandate to administer the territory. Their refusal to accept the transfer of the territory to the UN set in motion many years of stalemate and negotiation involving almost every organ of the UN at one time or another. The end of the Cold War provided the opening for the implementation of a 1978 Security Council resolution establishing a transitional plan. In 1989, under the auspices of a UN peacekeeping operation, South African troops withdrew from the country and democratic elections led to the establishment of a new government. The UN has also been successful in other areas of Africa, including hard fought and perhaps tenuous progress in a number of conflict situations in West Africa. The UN Security Council's response rate, however, remains inconsistent. As of 2007, the inability of the Council to agree on any significant response to the situation in the Darfur region reveals that the need for political will among the key players of the Security Council remains a critical factor.

While increasing its own activities in response to conflict in Africa, the UN encouraged and supported African regional organizations in taking a

South African UN peacekeepers look at a Congolese soldier walking past their truck in Bunia, Democratic Republic of Congo, February 2005. Security at the time in the area and surroundings had been on the increase following the ambush and killing of nine Bangladesh soldiers three days earlier by local militiamen. Simon Maina/AFP/Getty Images

greater role. Under the banner African solutions for African problems this change helps to spread the burden of the response to conflict and opens up the possibility that states in the region with more knowledge of the actors and issues of the conflict may be able to have greater impact in bringing about a solution. On the other hand, a heavier reliance on regional actors sometimes means that the burden is being shared with or simply shifted to actors with far less in the way of capacity to deal with conflict situations than UN troops. In addition, the very fact that they are also of the region in which the conflict is occurring means that they may have their own political agendas to pursue. These dilemmas have played out in conflict situations in Africa with mixed results. The UN has worked with the Economic Community of West African States (ECOWAS) with some degree of success in that region, and with the African Union in a variety of different conflict scenarios. The ability of the Sudanese government, however, to resist international action on Darfur by allowing African Union troops, who are experiencing significant difficulties in carrying out their mission, while refusing UN

troops reveals that additional actors opens up the possibility for delay and resistance as much as it holds the potential for mutually reinforcing efforts involving regional actors and the UN.

Boutros Boutros-Ghali and then Kofi Annan played a significant role as Africans in the role of secretary-general of the United Nations. Under Kofi Annan in particular, African issues rose to become a central theme for the organization and he led the way in ensuring that the focus was proactive and multi-dimensional. In 1998, reflecting the amount of time and resources the UN was spending on African conflict Secretary-General Annan issued a report on the causes of conflict and the promotion of durable peace and sustainable development in Africa. The report prompted the creation of ad hoc working groups on conflict in Africa in the Security Council, the General Assembly and the Economic and Social Council (ECOSOC) along with a number of other institutional mechanisms. In 2003, the secretary-general established the Office of the Special Advisor on Africa. The special advisor works to enhance international support for security and development in Africa, assists the secretary-general in improving

War-torn Sudanese town receives supplies. Sudanese form a long line at an aid distribution point to receive food, mosquito nets, and clothes from the Islamic relief organization that manages the Internally Displaced Persons (IDPs) camp of Krinding-2, on the outskirts of the western town of El-Geneina, close to the border with Chad, October 2004. CRIS BOURONCLE/AFP/GETTY IMAGES

the coherence of UN support for Africa, and facilitates deliberations on the New Partnership for Africa's Development (NEPAD). These goals are also pursued by various other UN agencies such as the Economic Commission for Africa and the United Nations Education, Scientific and Cultural Organization (UNESCO), which prioritizes Africa in its activities. In addition, the General Assembly takes on issues of specific importance to Africa. In 2001, for example, the General Assembly held a special session on HIV/AIDS.

See also **Annan, Kofi; Cold War; Disease: HIV/AIDS, Social and Political Aspects; Economic Community of West African States (ECOWAS); Education, School; Healing and Health Care; Namibia; Organization of African Unity; Rwanda; Somalia; Sudan: Wars; Warfare: Civil Wars.**

BIBLIOGRAPHY

Boulden, Jane, ed. *Dealing with Conflict in Africa, the United Nations and Regional Organizations.* New York: Palgrave, 2003.

Laremont, Ricardo Rene. *The Causes of War and the Consequences of Peacekeeping in Africa.* Westport, CT: Greenwood, 2001.

Souaré, Issaka K. *Africa in the United Nations System, 1945–2005.* London: Adonis and Abbey, 2006.

JANE BOULDEN

UPPER VOLTA. *See* **Burkina Faso.**

URBANISM AND URBANIZATION

This entry includes the following articles:
OVERVIEW
PREHISTORIC
HISTORIC
INDEPENDENCE ERA
HOUSING

OVERVIEW

Until the last two decades of the twentieth century, scholars thought that sub-Saharan Africa would continue to be overwhelmingly rural and that urbanization was not a problem because it was associated with modernization and industrialization. Both sub-Saharan governments and international donor agencies fostered rural development and agriculturally based strategies without paying attention to the rapid rates of urbanization. In the twenty-first century, urbanization has been added to the long list of potentially devastating development problems that must be addressed. The fundamental problem is that urban populations are growing very fast while economic growth and the development transformations necessary to support the expanding populations and enhance the quality of urban life are not occurring as rapidly.

Issues of urban management can be discussed and properly understood only in the wider context of national urbanization policies. The need for active urbanization policies is greater in sub-Saharan Africa than in other parts of the world because the growth of population is high while the rates of economic growth are low and the role of government is more pervasive than elsewhere. The sub-Saharan governments clearly face serious problems in managing their rapidly growing urban centers.

Urbanization is bringing about economic and political changes that affect the ways in which sub-Saharan Africans organize spatially and subsist economically. The challenge to sub-Saharan Africa's development process is to manage the changes. The potential contributions of urban centers to national development need to be realized if the past gains in agricultural production are to be consolidated. Urbanization provides the production efficiencies that support off-farm employment, the focus of both political and economic decentralization policies, and principal sites for the processing and marketing of agricultural products. The patterns in which the urban population settles in the twenty-first century will dictate the standard of living for both urban and rural areas and the possibilities of improving that standard for years to come. A commitment to an explicit urban policy calls for expanding the activity of international donors, which have an important role to play in supporting the efforts of public, private, and informal sectors of urban areas to provide credit, land, and infrastructure to low-income families.

Small and intermediate urban centers are at the core of the long-term relationship between urbanization and agricultural development and will play a key role in sub-Saharan Africa's urbanization. The interdependence of urban and rural populations in the region is striking, with a positive correlation between improved urban infrastructure and rising agricultural productivity. Support should be given to both. Intermediate and small urban centers should be supported by investment in physical and social infrastructure on the basis of their growth potential.

Urban services can be provided efficiently only if there is a partnership between central and local governments and between the public and private sectors, with greater responsibilities being given to the local government and the private sector than has generally been the case. Decentralization makes better use of local human, financial, and physical resources and offers the possibility for more effective resource mobilization, self-sustaining development projects that better reflect local needs, and increased citizen participation in decision making in both the rural and urban areas.

Sub-Saharan Africa is facing three problems simultaneously: rapid population growth, declining agricultural productivity, and massive migration to urban areas. The urban economies have not been able to absorb the large number of rural migrants. Ethnic conflicts and wars, natural disasters, and desertification have increased the rate of urbanization. Literacy campaigns and vocational training have doubtless stimulated the rural-to-urban migration. To slow it down, three types of policies must be pursued. The first aims at encouraging the rural economy. The second encourages the growth of small and intermediate urban centers. The third maintains the growth of large or primary urban centers.

TRENDS AND PROSPECTS

Urbanization has not been an entirely modern development in sub-Saharan Africa. The capitals of some precolonial kingdoms date back to the tenth and eleventh centuries. However, many of sub-Saharan Africa's major urban centers developed only at the end of the nineteenth and the beginning of the twentieth centuries, and most of them remained small for several decades. Since World War II, the pace of urbanization has accelerated markedly and is expected to continue to do so for some time to come.

Precolonial Urbanization. The earliest urban centers in sub-Saharan Africa were probably built between the eleventh and eighth centuries BCE in eastern and western Africa. But the majority of these urban centers were associated with divine kingship and so their rise and decline depended on the life of the ruler. However, the majority of African urban centers were founded from the early sixteenth to the late nineteenth centuries, when there was substantial European trade with sub-Saharan Africa. It is important to distinguish between the "old" and the "new" forms of urban centers, between precolonial, colonial, and postcolonial urbanization.

Although sub-Saharan Africa is noted for its ancient urban centers (through the first century CE), the precolonial era had a number of urban centers. This is especially true in western Africa and parts of Central, eastern, and southern Africa. The precolonial urban centers were not of the same "urbanness" as the modern ones because the former retained their traditional forms, function, and structure, whereas the latter possessed most of the features of an "urban place" in the Western sense of the term. The medieval urban centers in western Africa, Central Africa, and along the coast of eastern and southern Africa came into being around the tenth century. They were closely associated with Islam, which aggressively established trade routes resulting in the building of caravan towns that later became urban centers. Thus, the urban centers in sub-Saharan Africa have a mixture of Islamic and traditional African elements. The majority of these were built of impermanent materials.

European colonizers helped to build early trading posts and forts by creating the trade routes that influenced the urban morphology even before colonization of the continent. During the early stages of colonization, Europeans penetrated the interior of sub-Saharan Africa, and the substitution of ocean transport for caravans hastened the decline or disappearance of the majority of precolonial urban centers. Those that survived the spatial onslaught emerged as a "colonial settlement" with essentially two central business districts—one traditional and one modern.

Colonial Urbanization. The imposition of Western European influence (later culminating in colonial rule) over Africa gave rise to some important urban centers. Founded between the sixteenth and twentieth centuries, they were either new settlements serving as the administrative and trading centers of the colonial powers or upgraded centers predating the colonial period. Other urban areas developed in the course of the exploitation of natural resources, including Kumasi (gold), Enugu (tin and coal), and the copper and diamond urban center of Elisabethville (present-day Lubumbashi). Thus, as the colonial powers established their hegemony over sub-Saharan Africa, urban centers emerged as administrative centers, regional markets, and foci of transport networks. The colonial administrations established peaceful conditions, introduced the money economy that helped to link sub-Saharan Africa to world markets, and initiated the general changes associated with increased agricultural production and industrial development. All of these combined to increase the growth of urbanization.

European urbanization in sub-Saharan Africa began with small forts and trading posts in the sixteenth century. These early urban centers included Rufisque, Senegal; Kayes, Mali; Bissau, Guinea-Bissau; Lagos, Nigeria; Luanda and Benguela, Angola; Cape Town, Republic of South Africa; Conakry, Guinea; Sekondi-Takoradi, Cape Coast; and Accra, Ghana.

The majority of the urban centers in the interior of Africa were founded during the last quarter of the nineteenth century and the first quarter of the twentieth century. Since the few industrial jobs were concentrated in them, they were magnets for the rural population. The populations of most of the colonial urban centers were originally characterized by adult males, but over time the composition became less different from that of the country as a whole. This male predominance continued until the beginning of the postcolonial era, when African families were allowed to reside legally in the urban areas. The postcolonial era is the most important stage in African urbanization.

Postcolonial Urbanization. Sub-Saharan Africa remains essentially at the frontier of the urbanization and spatial transformations witnessed by the rest of the world during the twentieth century. The region still is mostly rural in a world where the majority of the population was living in urban centers by the end of the twentieth century. Sub-Saharan Africa has few very large urban centers, and its population growth rate is still increasing. Except for southern Africa, the sub-Saharan region is at the threshold of an urban transformation of major proportions because of the combination of low levels of urbanization and high rates of urban growth. The ingredients for such transformation are minimal levels of urbanization, low degrees of urban concentration, high and increasing rates of population and urban growth, uneven distribution of population and resources, increasing efforts to achieve national integration, and highly centralized political systems. If past experience is any indication, such conditions point to major tendencies toward spatial polarization with increasing urban concentration and widening regional inequalities.

Sub-Saharan Africa is the world's least urbanized region, in terms of the proportion of the population living in urban centers. At the beginning of the twenty-first century, only 30.5 percent of the total population is living in such centers. But this proportion ranges from 6 percent in Rwanda to 82.5 percent in Djibouti. Despite the generally low levels of urbanization, sub-Saharan Africa is experiencing the highest rates of urbanization in the world, averaging nearly 4.4 percent per annum. The annual average rate of urbanization is not expected to decrease to 3.3 percent until after 2025. Although sub-Saharan Africa is the least urbanized region, its urban growth will continue to be the most rapid in the world. In the 1970s and 1980s, the population growth was in the range of 4.3 to 4.9 percent. This is twice the rate of the more developed countries (MDCs) and the world average. Moreover, whereas urban growth rates have been falling secularly both in the world as a whole and in less developed countries (LDCs) in general, this is not the case in sub-Saharan Africa.

The rapid growth of urban centers in sub-Saharan Africa represents a major aspect of the social demographic changes that were experienced during the twentieth century. Most sub-Saharan countries have pursued a policy of urbanization as a means of achieving a modern level of technology. This policy is based on the notion that the degree of urbanization is a yardstick for measuring the level of industrialization, modernization, and socioeconomic development. However, these attributes of urbanization are lacking in sub-Saharan Africa. Instead, the countries there have become

Percentage of population living in urban areas: 1970, 1980, 1994, and 2025				
Region	1970	1980	1994	2025
World	36.6	39.4	44.8	61.1
More-developed countries	67.5	71.3	74.7	84.0
Less-developed countries	25.1	29.2	37.0	57.0
Sub-Saharan Africa	20.0	25.0	30.5	50.5
Asia	21.0	26.7	32.4	54.0
Latin America	57.4	65.1	73.7	84.7
Oceania	70.8	71.2	70.3	84.8

SOURCE: United Nations, *World Urbanization Prospects: The 1994 Revision,* ST/ESA/SER.A/150 (New York, 1995), pp. 784–785.

Table 1.

victims of a strong rural-urban migration that has often led to an average growth rate as high as 6 percent per annum, more than double the average national growth rate.

The urban population in sub-Saharan Africa increased from 14.7 percent in 1950 to 30.5 percent in 1994, and is likely to reach 50.5 percent by 2025 (see Table 1). In 1950, eight of every ten urban sub-Saharan Africans resided in small and intermediate urban centers. By 2015 it is expected that more than half of the urban population will still be residing in such urban centers. Low levels of urbanization characterize most of sub-Saharan Africa except southern Africa. By 1980, 25 percent of sub-Saharan Africa's population lived in urban areas; this figure was just behind Asia (26.7%), but much less than half that of Latin America (65.1%) and that of the MDCs (71.3%). Thus, by 2025 the projected proportion of Latin America's urban population (84.7%) will be close to the level attained by MDCs (84%) but far ahead of sub-Saharan Africa's 50.5 percent. This startling forecast assumes a gradual decline in the annual rate of urban growth from about 4.5 percent per annum in 1950–1955 to about 3.3 percent per annum by 2020–2025. The rate of growth in sub-Saharan Africa reached a peak of 4.9 percent per annum in 1960–1965 and has started to taper off rather slowly.

Until the 1990s Africa was characterized by the absence of any urban center with 10 million or

Percentage of population growth in rural areas and urban growth: sub-Saharan countries with at least half of their population growth in ruual areas

	1965–1970		1990–1995	
	Percentage of all growth in rural areas	Urban growth rate	Percentage of all growth in rural areas	Urban growth rate
Eastern Africa	79	6.2	62	5.4
Burundi	96	3.4	85	6.6
Comoros	57	6.1	54	5.7
Eritrea	79	5.1	73	4.4
Ethiopia	83	4.9	79	4.7
Kenya	80	6.9	52	6.8
Madagascar	72	5.0	54	5.8
Malawi	85	6.8	77	6.2
Rwanda	94	7.7	90	4.2
Somalia	73	3.3	51	2.5
Uganda	85	8.1	80	5.7
United Rep. Tanzania	84	7.9	53	6.1
Zambia	27	8.1	50	3.5
Central Africa	46	5.7	54	4.5
Angola	54	5.1	48	6.3
Chad	59	7.2	72	3.6
Zaire	42	5.8	65	3.9
Southern Africa	50	2.9	36	3.1
Lesotho	71	8.0	51	6.2
Western Africa	60	5.4	40	5.2
Bénin	50	7.3	55	4.6
Gambia	75	4.8	61	6.2
Mali	71	4.7	55	5.7
Niger	79	7.0	73	5.6
Togo	79	7.3	55	4.8

SOURCE: United Nations, *World Urbanization Prospects: The 1994 Revision,* ST/ESA/SER.A/150 (New York, 1995), p. 30.

Table 2.

more inhabitants. The first urban center to achieve this size was Lagos, in 1995; 4.1 percent of the African urban population lived in Lagos that year. The second class of urban centers, those with a population of 5 million to 10 million, held 6.4 percent of the African urban population in 1970. After the expected disappearance of the second-level urban centers, through movement into the group of 10 million or more, the number of the latter is expected to reach 11 million by 2015. At that time, they will contain 11.9 percent of the urban population, or 68 million persons. The percentage of Africans living in urban centers with 1 million to 5 million inhabitants rose from 10.5 percent in 1950 to 21.3 percent in 1990; it is expected to remain at about that level until 2015 (20.8%). Beginning from the relatively modest 84 million urban residents in 1970, sub-Saharan Africa had 240 million urban dwellers in 1995, expected to increase to 804 million by 2025.

Because of the extremely large population base in rural areas, sub-Saharan countries have to absorb large numbers of rural migrants while struggling with rapid urbanization. In 1990–1995, more than half of the population growth in eastern and Central Africa was in rural areas. The share of rural growth in total population growth is even larger in some countries. Table 2 lists African countries that experienced at least half of their population growth in rural areas in 1990–1995, along with the urban growth rates. In eastern Africa, Rwanda, one of the two least urbanized countries in the world, had the highest percentage of rural population growth (90%). It was followed by Burundi, Uganda, Ethiopia, Malawi, and Eritrea. All those countries had urban growth rates of more than 4 percent per annum between 1990 and 1995. They also were characterized by low levels of urbanization. (Less than one-third of the population resided in urban areas.) More than half of the population growth is expected to take place in rural areas in Burundi and Rwanda between 2020 and 2025. In Central Africa, Chad and Zaire experienced at least 65 percent of their population growth in rural areas

Percentage of population growth in urban areas, selected years

	1950	1960	1970	1980	1990	2000	2010	2025
Sub-Saharan Africa	14.7	18.4	23.0	27.3	31.8	37.3	43.8	53.8
Eastern Africa	5.3	7.4	10.4	14.6	19.2	24.6	30.7	41.2
Central Africa	14.2	17.9	24.8	28.1	31.0	35.9	42.9	54.0
Southern Africa	38.2	41.9	43.6	44.5	46.2	50.7	57.3	66.6
Western Africa	10.3	14.5	19.6	25.8	32.8	40.6	48.5	59.2

SOURCE: United Nations, *World Urbanization Prospects: The 1994 Revision,* ST/ESA/SER.A/150 (New York, 1995), pp. 78–79.

Table 3.

during 1990–1995. Lesotho in southern Africa also had more than half of its population growth in rural areas in 1990–1995; Niger, with 73 percent, recorded the highest percentage of population growth in rural areas in western Africa.

The most urbanized sub-Saharan African region in 1995 was southern Africa (48%). Western Africa (36%) and Central Africa (33%) were in between, and eastern Africa had the lowest level (21%). This order of urbanization levels is projected to be maintained until 2025 (see Table 3). By 2025, 66.6 percent of the population of southern Africa is expected to be living in urban centers; the figures for eastern and western Africa are projected to be 41.2 and 59.2 percent, respectively.

Some countries exhibit very low levels of urbanization (less than 10% of the population of Burundi and Rwanda live in urban areas), but in others more than 80 percent of the population resides in urban areas (Djibouti, 83%). In Burundi, Eritrea, Malawi, Niger, Rwanda, and Uganda—all of them but Eritrea classified by the United Nations as least developed—the urbanization level was under 20 percent in 1994.

The annual average rates of growth of urban populations in eastern and western Africa are the highest in Africa. Although the rates for both are on the decline, they were around 6 percent per annum during most of the 1970s and are unlikely to go down to around 4 percent until after 2005. In southern Africa, natural population increase will be the dominant factor in the growth of urbanization, whereas in western and eastern Africa, which have some of the fastest-growing urban centers in the world, rural-urban migration and urban natural increase will be the most significant factors in the growth of urban centers.

REGIONAL VARIATIONS

Western Africa. Western Africa has an indigenous tradition of the "African metropolis," which developed a complex pattern of rural-urban interdependence. In addition, a number of established urban centers, such as Kano and Kumasi, prospered in western Africa for many years. The majority of the urban centers in Anglophone and Francophone western Africa, however, were established during the colonial period. Among individual countries, the highest proportion of urban population in 1995 was in Cape Verde (54.3%), followed by Mauritania (53.8%) and Liberia (45.0%). Those showing the lowest percentages of urbanization in 1995 were Niger (17.0%), Guinea-Bissau (22.2%), the British island of St. Helena (26.9%), and Burkina Faso (27.2%). The remaining ten countries have proportions between 30 and 44 percent. In most countries of western Africa, the growth rate of the urban population in 1990–1995 was four times that of the overall population growth. The corresponding average annual rate of change of the urban population as a proportion of the total for 1990–1995 is also very high. The highest was recorded by Burkina Faso at 8.44% the lowest was 1.18 percent in Senegal.

Central Africa. Historically, this region has had the second lowest level of urbanization in Africa. But the rate of urbanization has increased; in 1995 it was 33.2 percent urban, compared to 14.2 percent in 1950. The average annual rate of change in the proportion of the population that is urban is generally very high for all countries except in Zaire for the period 1990–1995. However, there were pronounced intercountry differences. In 1995 the Congo (58.8%) had a high percentage of population living in urban centers, and in the majority of other countries the percentage was more than the sub-Saharan figure of 34.4 percent. Of eighteen urban centers in the region, eleven are in Zaire, with the largest city, Kinshasa, having a population of about 3 million in 1990.

Eastern Africa. Since the 1950s eastern Africa has had the lowest level of urbanization (21.7% in 1995), yet it has the highest rate of urban growth in sub-Saharan Africa (5.4% in 1990–1995). The highest level of urbanization is in Djibouti (82.8% in 1995), followed by Réunion (67.8% in 1995) and Zambia (43.1% in 1995). Low levels of urbanization are found in Rwanda, Malawi, Ethiopia, Eritrea, and Madagascar. They can be attributed to the fact that during the colonial period, Africans were forbidden to reside permanently in the urban areas. Besides, most eastern African countries are basically agricultural, with very few large-scale industrial or mining bases. In 1990–1995, the annual rate of urban growth for eastern Africa of 5.4 percent was one of the highest in sub-Saharan Africa. In that period the countries with the highest average annual rate of change of urban population were Mozambique, Burundi, and Tanzania; the countries with the lowest rate of change were Mauritius, Somalia, and Djibouti.

Except in Sudan, Uganda, and Ethiopia, most precolonial urban settlements in eastern Africa were concentrated in the coastal region, where trading centers emerged as a result of Arab and Portuguese activity along the coast. Urbanization is a contemporary issue in eastern Africa. In most parts of the precolonial interior, life was based on self-sufficiency and there was no need for specialized trade patterns because of the predominance of subsistence agriculture and stock herding. A major feature was the existence of periodic markets, which in some areas formed a hierarchy dealing with internal trade and rudimentary transportation and communication systems. Urbanization in eastern Africa in the twenty-first century can, therefore, be regarded as having emerged from the colonial regime. The major contemporary urban centers mainly had economic origins, and they remain industrial-mining complexes linked to the worldwide economy. Thus, they did not grow out of the need to serve the surrounding territory.

Southern Africa. A large proportion (48.1% in 1995) of the population in southern Africa is in urban centers with 20,000 or more inhabitants. The bulk of the urban population was, however, concentrated in the Republic of South Africa. The rest of the countries—Botswana, Lesotho, Namibia, and Swaziland—are over 20 percent urban. Of the fifteen urban centers in these countries with populations exceeding 100,000, eleven are in the Republic of South Africa. Johannesburg (1.9 million in 1995) is one of the ten African urban centers with more than 1 million inhabitants. In 1995 the Republic of South Africa had the four most populous urban centers in southern Africa—besides Johannesburg, Cape Town (1.9 million), Durban (1.1 million), and East Rand (1.2 million). Urbanization in southern Africa is high because of a large industrial base and mining activities in the region.

CONSEQUENCES OF URBANIZATION

The degree of urbanization and the rate of growth of the urban population in sub-Saharan Africa vary considerably from country to country and from region to region. Except for western Africa, urbanization is essentially a twentieth-century phenomenon and basically a product of Africa's colonial history. In sub-Saharan Africa, therefore, southern Africa has the highest rate of urbanization. Western Africa and parts of Central Africa have the longest trend of urbanization, and eastern Africa is the least urbanized, despite its long history of coastal urbanization.

URBAN PROBLEMS

Rapid Growth. Although the level of urbanization in Africa is still relatively low, the continued growth of the urban population poses serious planning problems. The high rate of urban growth is mainly due to rural-urban migration, high urban natural increase, arbitrary expansion of urban boundaries, and ethnic wars. In addition, nonspatial factors have had significant impacts on the form, rate, nature, and extent of urban growth. They include fiscal, industrial, defense, equalization, agricultural, and immigration policies.

Employment, Income, and the Increasing Role of the Informal Sector. In Africa real wages in the urban manufacturing sector have fallen dramatically since 1970. Real incomes in 1985 were about half those in 1970. This decline, which had started in the 1960s, has narrowed the urban-rural income gap. The informal sector is increasingly being accepted by African governments as having a dynamic potential for productivity and income generation. It is the most rapidly growing sector in Africa's urban economies, employing over 50 percent of the urban labor force. Lucrative activities are, however, often subject to monopolies through legislation, licensing, and control by political, ethnic, kin, and peer groups.

Public-Sector Jobs and Commercial Housing.

Two main trends can be discerned with regard to African urban centers: a decline in the provision of public-sector jobs and the increasing commercialization of low-income shelter. A policy of not demolishing slum and squatter settlements was partly responsible for the latter trend. As a consequence, the price of shelter and the proportion of income spent on shelter have increased considerably.

Urban Management.

Management problems resulting in dilapidated infrastructure and inadequate urban services have been noted in all African countries. These can be attributed partly to recession and partly to the tensions between central and local governments and between public and private sectors. Governmental institutions at the urban level are financially weak. Strengthening their financial position by pricing their services at market levels meets opposition from above (the central government) and from below (the citizens). The assumption that structural adjustment policies will increase institutional capacity is at least doubtful. Further reduction of the existing low salaries of government staff would further undermine the morale of local officials and lead to absenteeism, moonlighting, and other survival strategies.

Provision of Infrastructural Services.

Given that major urban centers in Africa have historically grown at the expense of small and intermediate urban centers, the increasing concentration of population has resulted in practical administrative difficulties related to the provision of communal and infrastructural services (such as education, water, and sewage treatment) to a rapidly growing population. There has been a failure to project and plan for urban growth. Local authorities have been unable to

grasp the implications of a population that doubles every nine years. Problems of accessibility to services are compounded by the fact that most urban residents earn low incomes and are not able to pay for the services they need. Despite the deficiencies in their basic infrastructure and social services, urban centers in Africa are the core of modern economic life and offer opportunities to migrants, as economic growth and economic activity rates are high, even against a background of poor infrastructure and inefficient urban management.

Decline in Gross National Product.

The rate of growth of the urban population of Africa has continued to increase even as the rate of growth of gross national product per capita declined from 1.3 percent in the 1960s to 0.7 percent in the 1970s and even further in the 1980s and 1990s. Migration has been fueled by planning policies that have favored urban dwellers.

Weak Interurban and Urban-Rural Linkages.

There are severe weaknesses in intraurban and urban-rural linkages, particularly in the lack of infrastructure that characterizes small and intermediate urban centers. This is a major inhibitor in the realization of urban-hinterland linkages such as trade. But in large urban centers, losses stem from flight to surrounding suburban centers.

Structural Adjustment Policy and the Urban Bias.

Most African economies are undergoing structural adjustment policies, which usually consist of "setting the prices right," better fiscal and monetary discipline, encouraging private savings and investment, and strengthening economic management. Part of structural adjustment policy is likely to change the terms of trade between urban and rural economic activities and households. Agriculture will tend to receive more attention than previously because one goal is to remove the "urban bias" in national and regional development planning by emphasizing bottom-up development aimed at rural populations.

Small and Intermediate Urban Centers and the Surrounding Hinterland Areas.

The development of Africa's small and intermediate urban centers will be the focus of urbanization in the twenty-first century because they link urbanization with rural development. The interdependence of urban and rural populations in Africa is striking. An estimated 70 percent of urban residents maintain strong links to the rural sector—and in some urban centers, the proportion may be as much as 90 percent. Small and intermediate urban centers have begun to grow very rapidly in Africa because the surrounding agricultural areas are prospering. More attention should be given to the role of these centers in agricultural processing, marketing, storage, bulking, and distribution. It is important to understand the nature of urban-rural linkages of small and intermediate urban centers by considering, inter alia, the demand by the rural population for nonfood goods, the inputs and services needed by the agricultural sector, and the demand for agricultural output, which is highly income-elastic. In fact, increasing the demand for the last two is necessary for an appropriate supply response by farmers to price increases for farm inputs. Increases in rural incomes brought about by improved accessibility to markets and rising agricultural productivity lead to higher levels of activity in small and intermediate urban centers. Low-income households consume products and services produced locally rather than in distant urban centers. Therefore, increased rural consumption due to increased income will tend to diversify the economic activities of nearby urban centers and create substantial off-farm employment opportunities.

African farms will come under the influence of urban markets. This spread of urban markets should greatly increase the disposable income of farmers. Such an increase will be more rapid than that anticipated for formal- or informal-sector activities in urban areas. The growth of urban centers and the linkages between them and rural areas will support improvements in agricultural productivity and thus help to improve macroeconomic performance. Barriers to the realization of effective urban-rural linkages in Africa include overvalued exchange rates and low administered food prices, reliance on parastatal companies, lack of access to credit, lack of transportation information, weak technological institutional strength, and an inability to generate sufficient local revenues.

Small and intermediate urban centers should be supported by investment in infrastructure on the basis of their own potential rather than by syphoning off capital to promote "territorial equity." Public expenditure should be geared toward those centers where rapid growth is already occurring or is very likely to occur as a result of structural adjustment policies and changes in macroeconomic and sectoral policies. The best measure of "need" is that economic activity levels are ahead of service provision by the public sector. However, the satisfaction of such needs will require all the public-sector resources likely to be available in the foreseeable future, given the very high urban population growth rates in many locations. Economic activity levels may be stimulated by public-sector investments, but in the end the local sector also has a contribution to make to human-resource development. Training programs are a key to successful decentralization efforts. These can include health care issues and family planning programs, facilitated by improved water supply and sanitation.

THE GROWTH OF MEGACITIES AND LARGE URBAN CENTERS

Africa will contain more megacities and large urban centers than any other continent in the twenty-first century. Although in 1990 only one of the thirty-three large urban centers was in Africa, urban centers there are growing faster than those in MDCs ever did.

The problems related to the high rates of urban growth in Africa are often accentuated by the concentration of population in the megacities and large urban centers. To the extent that these are the focus of development, they act as a magnet for migrants from both rural and other urban areas. The result is to increase the concentration of the urban population in one large metropolitan area to form what has been called a primate urban pattern. The growth of megacities and large urban centers and the prospects of their continued expansion rank among the most pressing urban problems of the twenty-first century. In addition, the size of megacities and large urban centers magnifies the problems of income and development discrepancies inherent in urbanization and suburbanization.

The megacities and large urban centers in Africa face increasing problems as population growth outruns investment in urban infrastructure. In most African megacities and the large urban centers, households spend over 40 percent of their income on food. Shelter is typically crowded, given generally high population densities. In Johannesburg and Lagos an average of five to six people per room has been reported. In Kinshasa and Johannesburg, at least two-thirds of the households lack water or electricity; for Lagos and Cape Town the figure is over 40 percent. In most African megacities and large urban centers there is less than one telephone for every ten persons. In Johannesburg and Lagos, at most one-third of residents aged fourteen to seventeen are in school; the percentages of school enrollment among that age group is higher in some other megacities. In terms of infant mortality, Cape Town and Johannesburg have reached relatively low levels (18 and 22 infant deaths per 1,000 live births, respectively). The two African megacities or large urban centers with the highest infant mortality (over 80 infant deaths per 1,000 live births) are Lagos and Kinshasa. Murder rates are high in Johannesburg.

CONCLUSION

Future policies should control urban growth, develop alternative methods of providing low-cost urban services, recover investment costs to permit financial replaceability, strengthen national and municipal institutions, stimulate community participation, develop economic and institutional links between the urban and rural sectors, and promote effective urban management strategies. To gain control of urban growth, it is necessary to reduce current levels of national subsidies to the capital and shift the financial burden to those who benefit from them. In order to develop alternative ways of providing urban services, their pricing and distribution must be reviewed and means of recovering an increasing share of the economic cost of the services provided must be devised, probably by eliminating the subsidies to urban consumers so that those using them pay according to their means. Implementation of an effective system of municipal taxation would help in recovering investment costs for services. Attention must be focused on major urban centers because they consume large amounts of national revenue, their income levels are relatively high (implying that their inhabitants are more able to pay for services than rural residents), and the efficient allocation of scarce national resources is essential if African countries are to improve national incomes in the future. African governments should reexamine the

standards and types of services provided to their growing urban populations. When services aim at maintaining relatively high standards, they are unlikely to reach the majority of urban residents, who are primarily low-income. African governments must experiment with privatization of services in order to improve administrative efficiency.

None of the aforementioned objectives can be achieved unless African governments make serious attempts to strengthen the institutions operating in the urban centers. In most African countries, the department concerned with urban planning has been understaffed and insufficiently financed to permit the execution of its legal responsibilities. There should be increased financial autonomy for the municipalities, training of staff, and a clearer definition of municipal jurisdictions. Programs must be designed to stimulate greater community participation in the financing and delivery of urban services. Self-help programs, incentives to the private sector, and the use of community-based organizations should be encouraged in order to generate increasing activity and interest by the urban population.

As part of the economic diversification of urban economies, efforts are needed to develop economic and institutional links between urban centers and rural areas. These links must include the urban production and provision of goods and services needed to support rural development, such as the manufacturing of farm implements, repair centers for agricultural machinery, and the processing of agricultural products. This approach requires that more resources be devoted to the development of small and intermediate urban centers so they can perform functions that will encourage the growth of economic, sociocultural, and administrative linkages. Economic linkages are very important aspects of not only local and regional development but also of national development, since the urban centers are where goods and services are exchanged. Urban centers are also important linkages with rural areas since the former are the centers of commercial, industrial, and cultural services.

There is an increasing recognition that the growth of urban centers is inevitable and that solutions to their problems depend heavily on their effective management. Urban management is best thought of as a holistic concept. It can strengthen the capacity of governmental and nongovernmental organizations to identify policy and program alternatives and to implement these with optimal results. The challenge of urban management is to respond effectively to the problems of particular urban centers so that they can perform their functions effectively.

The need for a clearly formulated national urban policy arises precisely because of the importance of ensuring an appropriate role for urban centers in regional and national development in Africa. It is against this background that productive investments must be placed in those urban centers that are most efficient and have already proved to have high economic potential, whatever their size. A crucial need is to develop links between the economic activities of the megacities, large urban centers, small and intermediate urban centers, and the national development strategies. The new planning strategy for African cities is to move beyond isolated projects that emphasize shelter and residential infrastructure, and toward integrated citywide efforts that promote urban productivity and reduce constraints on efficiency; increase the demand for labor, stressing the generation of jobs for the urban poor; improve access to basic infrastructure; and increase our understanding of urban issues through research. These efforts should promote the role of urban centers as engines of growth for rural areas, and hence for national economies as a whole.

See also **Accra; Benguela; Children and Childhood: Infancy and Early Development; Colonial Policies and Practices; Conakry; Economic History; Economic Systems; Ethnicity; Islam; Johannesburg; Kano; Kingship; Kinshasa; Kumasi; Lagos; Luanda; Lubumbashi; Réunion; Transportation; Women: Urbanism.**

BIBLIOGRAPHY

Amis, Philip, and Peter Lloyd, eds. *Housing Africa's Urban Poor*. New York: St. Martin's Press, 1990.

Baker, Jonathan, ed. *Small Town Africa: Studies in Rural-Urban Interaction*. Uppsala, Sweden: Scandinavian Institute of African Studies, 1990.

Baker, Jonathan, and Paul O. Pedersen, eds. *The Rural-Urban Interface in Africa: Expansion and Adaptation*. Uppsala, Sweden: Nordiska Afrikainstitutet in cooperation with Centre for Development Research, Copenhagen, 1992.

El-Shakhs, Salah, and Robert A. Obudho, eds. *Urbanization, National Development, and Regional Planning in Africa*. New York: Praeger, 1974.

Gugler, Josef, and William G. Flanagan. *Urbanization and Social Change in West Africa*. Cambridge, U.K.: Cambridge University Press, 1978.

Hance, William A. *Population, Migration, and Urbanization in Africa*. New York: Columbia University Press, 1970.

Howard, Allen. "Pre-colonial Centres and Regional Systems in Africa." *Pan African Journal* 8, no. 3 (1975): 247–270.

Hull, Richard W. *African Cities and Towns before the European Conquest*. New York: Norton, 1976.

Hutton, John, ed. *Urban Challenge in East Africa*. Nairobi, Kenya: East African Publishing House, 1972.

Kanyeihamba, George W., and J. Patrick W. B. McAuslan. *Urban Legal Problems in East Africa*. Uppsala, Sweden: Scandanavan Institute of African Studies, 1978.

Kuiper, Klaas. "Urbanization in Sub-Saharan Africa: Issues and Policies." *ITC Journal* 2 (1992).

Kuper, Hilda, ed. *Urbanization and Migration in West Africa*. Berkeley: University of California Press, 1965.

McNulty, Michael L. "West African Urbanization." In *Urbanization and Counterurbanization*, ed. Brian J. L. Berry. Beverly Hills, CA: Sage, 1976.

Miner, Horace. "The City and Modernisation: An Introduction." In *The City in Modern Africa*, ed. Horace Miner. New York: Praeger, 1967.

Obudho, Robert A. "National Urban Policy in East Africa." *Regional Development Dialogue* 4, no. 2 (1983).

Obudho, Robert A. "The Spatial Structure of Urbanization and Planning in East Africa." In *Urban Systems in Transition*, ed. J. G. Borchert, I. S. Bourne, and R. Sinclair. Amsterdam: Koninklijk Nederlands Aardrijkskundig Genootschap, 1986.

Obudho, Robert A. "Urbanization and Urban Policy in East Africa." In *Inequality and Development: Case Structures from the Third World*, ed. Kenneth Swindell, J. B. Baba, and M. J. Mortimore. London: Macmillan, 1989.

Obudho, Robert A. "Urbanization and Urban Development Strategies in East Africa." In *Urban Management: Policies and Innovations in Developing Countries*, ed. G. Shabbir Cheema. Westport, CT: Praeger, 1993.

Obudho, Robert A., and Constance C. Mhlanga, eds. *Slum and Squatter Settlements in Sub-Saharan Africa: Toward a Planning Strategy*. New York: Praeger, 1988.

Obudho, Robert A., and Salah El-Shakhs, eds. *Development of Urban Systems in Africa*. New York: Praeger, 1979.

O'Connor, Anthony M. *The African City*. New York: African Publishing Company, 1983.

Parker, D. J. *Town and Country in Central and Eastern Africa*. London: International African Institute, 1975.

Peel, J. D. Y. "Urbanization and Urban History in West Africa." *Journal of African History* 21, no. 1 (1980): 269–277.

Soja, Edward W., and C. E. Weaver. "Urbanization and Underdevelopment in East Africa." In *Urbanization and Counterurbanization*, ed. Brian J. L. Berry. Beverly Hills, CA: Sage, 1976.

Steel, Robert W. "The Towns of Tropical Africa." *In Essays on African Population*, ed. Kenneth M. Barbour and R. M. Prothero. New York: Praeger, 1961.

Stren, Richard E., and Rodney A. White, eds. *African Cities in Crisis: Managing Rapid Urban Growth.* Boulder, CO: Westview Press, 1989.

Tarver, James D., ed. *Urbanization in Africa: A Handbook.* Westport, CT: Greenwood Press, 1994.

R. A. OBUDHO

PREHISTORIC

Prehistoric African urbanism has formed only a peripheral part of larger discussions of global urbanism. This stems from a number of problems and assumptions: that African urban forms should conform to conceptual models developed in Mesopotamian and Mesoamerican contexts; that Africa's environmental context could not support urbanism; and that urban societies in Africa were foreign inspired.

Traditional models of urbanism excluded all potential cases in Africa by insisting that features such as literacy, writing, or monumental architecture were key features of urbanism. J. Desmond Clark concluded that "full urbanism was never achieved in southern Africa" (29) because settlements lacked these key traits. For Clark and other anthropologists of the mid-twentieth century, urbanism was unimaginable in sub-Saharan Africa because of the continent's favorable climate for agriculture, unlimited land, and the nature of its subsistence economies, a situation that removed incentive for the development of social complexity. These factors, they believed, meant that individuals in African societies were unable to accumulate wealth or capital, either through control over land or production, thus restricting the development of hierarchical societies.

A conventional wisdom thus emerged that those few large ancient centers that did appear on the continent—cities in the Inland Niger Delta, the Zimbabwe plateau, and the eastern African coast— did so at the instigation or through the inspiration of foreign agents. Cities of the western Sudan such as Jenné-jeno and Timbuktu were considered North African Arab trading colonies placed on the far side of the desert to help control the trans-Saharan trade. Europeans believed the stone-built capitals of the Zimbabwe plateau to be evidence of Mediterranean colonialism in southern Africa. Similarly, stone-built ruins of deserted Swahili towns were attributed to Arab colonizers who were pictured as coming to the coast to control Indian Ocean trade with the African interior. The assumptions behind these interpretations are clear: Africa was a place of inferior people, institutions, and accomplishment, ideas that resonated well with twentieth-century colonial thoughts of subject populations.

FROM URBANISM TO URBANIZATION

One way that the foreignness of urbanism has been challenged in African archaeology is through a shift in focus from urbanism itself—the political, social, and economic aspects of cities—to urbanization, a focus on cities and the territories and hinterlands to which they are connected. Susan McIntosh defined a city as follows: "Whatever else a city may be, it is a unit of settlement that performs specialized functions in relation to a broader hinterland.... Urbanism thus represents a novel kind of relationship among sites in a region and involves the emergence of specialization and functional interdependence" (1997, 463). This shift represents a movement outward, to the regions that surround cities, examining relationships between urban and rural areas, but it also indicates more concerted efforts to study the development of urban centers and regions through time. Both of these research trends have shown African cities to be parts of complex settlement systems that developed over the long-term rather than as the result of rapid colonization or external pressures.

AFRICAN URBANISMS

The massive stone ruins of Great Zimbabwe are now known as the central settlement of the Zimbabwe Tradition and the successor to the first Zimbabwe Tradition capital at Mapungubwe, 186 miles to the south. Both Mapungubwe (eleventh through thirteenth centuries) and Great Zimbabwe (thirteenth through fifteenth centuries) sat atop hierarchical settlement systems comprised of hundreds of smaller settlements that shared architectural features such as dry-laid granite walls and coursed earth structures. The specialized functions that these capital cities coordinated were as managers of the local productive and regional economies, linking cattle transhumance, agriculture, mining of stone and ores, and long-distance trade. The emergence of Mapungubwe and Great Zimbabwe are believed to be based on the successful efforts of leaders in managing the domestic production goods such as gold which was used in exchange for exotic, long-distance trade goods from the eastern African coast.

Similarly, the urban centers of eastern African, or Swahili coast, were places that negotiated the domestic regional economy with long-distance trade. Based on fishing and local trading villages founded in the eighth century CE, these towns emerged during the eleventh and twelfth centuries, reaching their apogee during the thirteenth to fifteenth centuries. Like Great Zimbabwe, long-distance trade was a crucial part of the economic foundation of Swahili cities. But unlike Zimbabwe Tradition sites, they were politically independent, even though they were linked through supra-local relationships, in commonalities of ritual and Islam. While status in Swahili cities was based partially on material accumulation, as can be seen by the display of long-distance trade goods in elite homes, mosques, and tombs, the abundance and independence of cities meant that status was also connected in large measure to people—the ability to draw and retain a population. For example, Shanga, a town on the Kenyan coast from the eighth to fifteenth centuries, was composed of different wards bound together with a corporate organization, rather than ruled coercively by a single individual. Though Swahili cities contained many traditional markers images of urban centers (monumental architecture, status ranking), other indicators suggest that crucial aspects of urban organization, such as craft production, were decentralized and household based.

The Swahili case is part of a growing body of evidence that suggests African urban forms diverge significantly from traditional models. Most well-known are the urban clusters of the inland Niger Delta, represented by research at Jenné-jeno and its surrounding region. Jenné-jeno (250 BCE to 1400 CE) marks the center of a cluster of more than forty mounds representing different settlements that were functionally integrated, with particular sites specializing in productive techniques such as iron-smithing and fishing. This urban cluster appears to have accomplished the functions of an urban center through a corporate organization rather than a hierarchical political authority. The organization explains the lack of more traditional markers of urban life at Jenné-jeno such as monumental public architecture, centralization of craft production, or visible stratification or ranking.

The variety of urban forms in Africa—from the hierarchical and centralized Zimbabwe Tradition to the corporate urban clusters of Jenné-jeno—suggest that African urbanisms may belie the normative understandings of what cities should be and how they should look. Recognizing the importance of corporate forms of sociopolitical organization as an alternative to highly centralized, hierarchical forms, forces historians and students alike to remember that in many African societies social wealth, "wealth-in-people," is a far more potent source of power than the accumulation of material goods. Understanding this concept is an important step toward recognizing the rich alternative urbanisms that Africa may have to offer.

See also **Jenné and Jenné-jeno; Prehistory; Timbuktu; Travel and Exploration; Zimbabwe, Great.**

BIBLIOGRAPHY

Childe, V. Gordon. "The Urban Revolution." *The Town Planning Review* 21, no. 3 (1950): 3–17.

Clark, J. Desmond. "Africa South of the Sahara." In *Courses toward Urban Life*, ed. Robert J. Braidwood and Gordon R. Willey. Chicago: Aldine, 1962.

Fleisher, Jeffrey. "Viewing Stonetowns from the Countryside: An Archaeological Approach to Swahili Regional Systems, AD 800–1500." Ph.D. diss. University of Virginia, 2003.

Haour, Anne. "Power and Permanence in Precolonial Africa: A Case Study from the Central Sahel." *World Archaeology* 37, no. 4 (2005): 552–565.

Horton, Mark. *Shanga: The Archaeology of a Muslim Trading Community on the Coast of East Africa.* London: British Institute in Eastern Africa, 1996.

Kusimba, Chapurukha M. *The Rise and Fall of Swahili States.* Walnut Creek, CA: AltaMira, 1999.

LaViolette, Adria, and Jeffrey Fleisher. "The Archaeology of Sub-Saharan Urbanism: Cities and their Countrysides." In *African Archaeology: A Critical Introduction*, ed. Ann Stahl. Oxford: Blackwell, 2005.

McIntosh, Susan Keech. "Urbanism in Sub-Saharan Africa." In *Encyclopedia of Precolonial Africa*, ed. Joseph O. Vogel. Walnut Creek, CA: AltaMira, 1997.

McIntosh, Susan Keech. "Pathways to Complexity: An African Perspective." In *Beyond Chiefdoms: Pathways to Complexity in Africa*, ed. Susan Keech McIntosh. Cambridge, U.K.: Cambridge University Press, 1999.

McIntosh, Susan Keech, and Roderick J. McIntosh "Cities without Citadels: Understanding Urban Origins along the Middle Niger." In *The Archaeology of Africa: Food, Metals and Towns*, ed. Thurston Shaw, Paul Sinclair, Bassey Andah, and Alex Okpako. London: Routlege, 1993.

Pikirayi, Innocent. *The Zimbabwe Culture: Origins and Decline of Southern Zambezian States.* Walnut Creek, CA: AltaMira, 2001.

Sinclair, Paul. *Space, Time, and Social Formation: A Territorial Approach to the Archaeology and Anthropology of Zimbabwe and Mozambique c. 0–1700 AD.* Uppsala, Sweden: Societas Archaeologica Upsaliensis, 1987.

JEFFREY FLEISHER

HISTORIC

Until the second half of the twentieth century, Africa was overwhelmingly rural. Even in the 1960s there were only a small number of large cities on the continent, notably Cairo, Ibadan, and Johannesburg. But if in the past the vast majority of Africans lived out their lives in small towns, in villages, and in the countryside, cities nevertheless played critical roles in the histories of most African regions from the very earliest periods for which historians have information. In this, of course, Africans shared the experience of most of the world's peoples.

Unfortunately, intellectual assumptions associated with imperialism and white supremacy have shaped the study of the history of urbanism in Africa. Colonial scholarship often focused on demonstrating that indigenous African urban sites did not somehow constitute true cities or if they did their origins could be traced beyond the continent. Most notoriously, the South African state, bent on protecting claims that the settlement of the future South Africa by Bantu-speaking people had not predated the arrival of whites, restricted research

that ultimately showed that Bantu-speaking peoples had built cities in the region long before the seventeenth century. In contrast, anticolonial scholars were similarly determined to demonstrate the historical existence of great African cities, although often implicitly using European urban development as the measure of greatness. Efforts to create typologies of African urbanism mire in analytical categories derived from European experience, while any attempt to define a characteristically African city runs up against the continent's enormous regional diversity.

Cities were distinct not only because of their size, but because of their structural complexity and cosmopolitanism. The accumulation of wealth, typically through control over elements of long-distance trade, sustained significant occupational differentiation, often including artisans, and supported the existence of political or religious classes—reflecting their positions as centers of temporal and spiritual power. Agricultural production was common within African cities, but cities could not sustain themselves without command over surplus food produced in surrounding hinterlands. Thus it is not so much the fact of the existence of cities that is of greatest interest historically, but rather the processes of urbanization, closely linked as cities were to the most powerful forces of change.

Dating from at least the fourth century BCE, Meroe and its successor centers in the upper Nile region had a powerful impact on the subsequent history of urban development in the horn of Africa and ultimately across the Sahelian region. Relatively isolated from the great cities of classical Egypt, Meroe emerged, in a pattern that would repeat itself across Africa, from an existing urban tradition, but was also highly influenced by outside contact. Meroe was apparently a substantial capital city located at the intersection of key trade routes; it boasted impressive palaces, public baths, temples, and cemeteries, whose remains indicate the existence of a commerce in precious metals and an artisan class. Meroe's influence reached east to Axum on the Red Sea coast, where by the first century CE the *Periplus of the Erythrean Sea* mentions the existence of port towns—the beginnings of a commercial power that would evolve over more than six centuries and provided the foundation for the later Christian kingdom of Ethiopia.

Unfortunately, a lack of archeological work limits historians' knowledge of the urban centers of Meroe and Aksum, and indeed much of early African history. As a consequence, not only are historians limited in what they know about sites that have been excavated, the existence of pockets of more detailed information, derived from particular archeological studies, may have the unintended effect of erasing the histories of cities whose remains have not been examined and whose existence may hardly be known.

In Ethiopia urban centers emerged, focused on political and religious power, and as a result were less determined by geography and the location of trade routes than cities in the Sahel, in West Africa, and along the Indian Ocean coast. By the seventeenth century Gondär had become the capital of Ethiopia, a position it held for two centuries. Gondär was a walled city as befitted its role as the center of political and military power, but in fact the urban locus of royal authority continued to migrate in temporary urban camps occupied by tens of thousands of people. At the same time, no site could have been more permanent than Lalibäla, whose ten churches carved in stone formed the center of a large religious community. The existence of these contrasting urban forms illustrates the diversity of impulses that drew people together in settlements and the similar diversity of spatial expressions of urbanism.

Mapungubwe, located on the Limpopo River and dating from the eleventh and twelfth centuries, is the oldest known urban settlement in southern Africa. In the surrounding region other smaller urban settlements developed around wealth in cattle and trade in gold. Farther to the north and developing slightly later is the most important urban center in southern and central Africa, Great Zimbabwe. This city was occupied from the eleventh to the sixteenth centuries and had a population of more than ten thousand people at its high point. Drawing its wealth from control over the gold trade to the Indian Ocean port of Kilwa, Great Zimbabwe was both a political and religious center for a large area.

In Great Zimbabwe, and in numerous, smaller settlements in the region, an elite lived within the walled stone enclosure, while ordinary people lived in less substantial dwellings in neighborhoods beyond the walls. This stark contrast underscores the fact that the development of cities also often involved the widening in the gaps between rich and poor, as well as the systematic reduction of the position and material conditions of ordinary people. Great Zimbabwe eventually fell victim to its own success. In Ethiopia "wandering" capitals permitted a distribution of the burden of maintaining the royal capital, but Great Zimbabwe's size and relentless need for food ultimately led to the environmental degradation of its hinterland. Without the technological capacity to transport food over longer distances, the city had to be abandoned.

Urban patterns in the intralacustrine region and across central Africa resembled the pattern of Great Zimbabwe, even if stone works were absent. Kibuga, the capital of the Buganda kingdom, was located at an exceptionally favored ecological niche of permanent productive cultivation. By the early nineteenth century, contact with the east coast had brought the exchange of slaves for cotton cloth and guns: this greatly centralized an already powerful state and concentrated fifty thousand to seventy-five thousand people in the capital. This capital was very strictly planned and constructed, though it was moved at least once every reign. The royal palace and great establishments of high officers all were related to one another in a symbolic arrangement of beautiful thatch-and-reed dwellings in enclosures fenced with elaborate woven elephant grass and shaded by the leaves of the ubiquitous banana.

Probably the best known of the cities of this vast region, however, was Mbanza Kongo, capital of the kings of Kongo. A Portuguese visitor estimated a population of 100,000, while others said it was only an extended village, as indeed it became after the Portuguese arrived. The divine king held some sway over a vast region of several million people, and the king and court elite received deliveries of foodstuffs from a wide area. Most important, however, were the deliveries of Nzimbu shells from the coast, especially Loanda Island. No one would sell anything, such as slaves, for silver or gold—only for Nzimbu.

The key theme in urban development across the continent from 1000 CE until the twentieth century was the emergence of entrepôt cities, located on or near the Atlantic or Indian coasts or on the southern edge of the Sahara Desert. These cities grew both in response to long-distance trade routes and as part of the effort to control and profit from them. The desiccation of the Sahara drove its peoples south and north, stretching but not breaking gold-trading routes from the Senegal-Niger headwaters. Local creative adaptation and external demand stimulated urban development in favorable conjunctures where human, social, economic, or external resources were conducive to settlement. Other factors stimulating urban development included rainfall, fertile soil, valuable minerals, complementary products from contrasting ecological zones, communications, and channels of supply and demand.

The kingdom of Ghana, with Kumbi-Saleh as its capital, was rich and powerful by 800 CE, possessing iron weapons and a large army. Kumbi-Saleh was a dual city: an earth-built indigenous town and royal palace, and a stone-built town of Muslim merchants six miles away, with the space in between also built up. It controlled the major gold-yielding areas, supplying the caravans in exchange for salt from Taghaza and other Saharan mines. Slaves, ivory, kola nuts, horses, textiles, and leather work swelled the trade. Increasing rivalry with Saharan Berbers led to the latter's conquest of Kumbi-Saleh in about 1076 CE, and then to its gradual decline. Timbuktu, founded on the Niger bend about 1000 CE, became a major caravan terminus and supreme center of Islamic learning in the fifteenth and sixteenth centuries.

The oldest city revealed by archaeology is Jenné-jeno, in the inner delta of the Niger close to gold- and copper-bearing areas. It was at an exceptionally favored site with abundant water, fertile soil, rich fisheries, and natural protection by impenetrable marshes. Iron users had occupied it by 250 BCE, and rapid growth ensued. By 800 CE it was a city in both size and complexity, a dense settlement of round brick houses surrounded by a wall, ruled by a king, and producing fine terra-cotta and pottery. Muslim pressure from the north increased, and Jenné-jeno gradually declined. It was superseded by the Islamic African city of Jenné two miles away, which with Timbuktu remained a major entrepôt of

the caravan trade. The expansion of Islam across the Sahara into West Africa and along the Indian Ocean coast played a critical role in shaping the evolution of urban forms in those areas. This was particularly evident in the gendered quality of the divide between public and private space. In local tradition, households were relatively open, but a Muslim-influenced Sahelian model of urban design that turned compounds away from the street to interior courtyards became increasingly prominent. Female seclusion was an urban phenomenon, but it was apparently not widely practiced except in the Swahili and Hausa cities.

Kano, Katsina, Zaria, and numerous other walled city-states of Hausa-speaking peoples were oriented more to trade than to empire. These cities created a remarkable exchange network supplying the caravan routes to Tripoli, Tunis, and Ghadames between the Mali-Songhay sphere to the west and Kanem-Bornu to the east. They fluctuated in links of domination and subordination, both with one another and with neighboring powers. They enriched the trade with swords and other weaponry, silks, spices, perfumes, leatherwork, and books. They had become Muslim by the fifth century.

Across the savanna margins further south to the rain forest, the Yoruba city-states arose, not from proximity to gold or other commodities of external demand, but rather from the potential of fertile soil and reliable rainfall. The Yoruba structure of knowledge and destiny, time and space, was symbolically based on multiples of four, eight, and sixteen. Sixteen corporate lineage-based sectors radiated out from the secluded divine king's central palace and market to the farms beyond the walls. Sixteen sons went out from Ife to found and rule other Yoruba city-states and Bénin as well. Most men cultivated their farms outside the walls while most women were traders, but all participated in the cycle of festivals that structured the urban year. Weavers, wood-carvers, drummers, metalworkers, and other craftspeople were organized into guilds. Around the thirteenth century, splendid heads and figures of rulers were made in brass and terracotta. The city of Oyo was in the savanna and able to develop cavalry, giving it political supremacy in the region from the seventeenth to nineteenth centuries.

As the Mediterranean world sought gold from the Sudan, Indian Ocean traders sought it down the east African coast, where gold sources ranged from Tanzania to the Transvaal, with copper found primarily in Katanga. The most remarkable site is Mapungabwe-Bambandyanalo on the Limpopo River, first settled in the eleventh century. The Mapungabwe gold hoard included a rhinoceros and bowl in beaten gold and gold anklets, a scepter, and beads. This was an extensive urban center, as evidenced by rough stone walls, pottery, metalwork, burials under stone mounds, and rain ponds and wells dug for livestock.

By 600 CE gold was traded to Sofala and Kilwa. By 700 the ancient city of Zimbabwe was occupied, but its spectacular stone structures were built later. Most of the gold, stone, and other art objects were later looted, but the remnants show that Zimbabwe had a ritualized divine kingship and a substantial population. Zimbabwe traded with the coastal ports, but when the Portuguese ousted the Arabs in the sixteenth century the gold trade declined, as did Zimbabwe.

From Somalia to Kilwa, the essentially urban-dwelling, Swahili-speaking population emerged from the fusion of Africans and immigrants, including Arabs. Kilwa was the greatest of these Swahili cities, with its magnificent thirteenth-century palaces, baths, and mosques, arcaded and vaulted in coral stone. At the end of the era, the city of Zanzibar dominated the coast and its trade; it was a larger and more populous but less splendid urban center than Kilwa.

The West African cities were more numerous, closer together, and more intensely interrelated, generating a stimulus of their own from within the African urban trading world, which kept West Africa the most urbanized sub-Saharan region. The European trade for gold, then slaves, on the western coast began with the Portuguese arrival and expanded with the entry of other Western nations. As a result, the dominant direction of trade was northward into the interior instead of southward from the Mediterranean. Innumerable cities grew to extend this trade in the next four hundred years—or to control and capitalize on its repercussions. Apart from the European trading posts on the coast, these were African cities in population, organization, and way of life.

In a parallel to the Sahelian cities, urban centers like those in Senegal and the Gold Coast developed in tandem with European quarters, although in this case these consisted in part of fortified outposts of European power. The slaving port of Ouidah grew, for example, in association with three European fortified trading posts in what is present-day Republic of Bénin. Although it eventually came under the suzerainty of Dahomey, that state's capital, Abomey, was located in the interior well beyond the reach of European authority. Similarly, the Asante capital Kumasi evolved in the nineteenth century as a consequence of its links to the Gold Coast trading towns like Cape Coast and Accra. But Kumasi was an imperial capital, turned as much to the north as to the coast. Closely tied to its hinterland, it was at the same time a highly distinctive urban center whose residents displayed the self-conscious cosmopolitanism that so often drew the boundary between the city and the countryside in Africa as elsewhere.

See also **Aksum; Bantu, Eastern, Southern, and Western, History of (1000 BCE to 1500); Cairo; Egypt, Early; Ethiopia and Vicinity, History of (600 to 1600 CE); Gondär; History of Africa; Ibadan; Ivory; Jenné and Jenné-jeno; Johannesburg; Kano; Lalibäla; Niger River; Nile River; Sahara Desert; Slave Trades; Timbuktu; Tripoli; Tunis.**

BIBLIOGRAPHY

Anderson, David, and Richard Rathbone, eds. *Africa's Urban Past*. Portsmouth, NH: Heinemann, 2000.

Connah, Graham. *African Civilizations: An Archaeological Perspective*, rev. edition. Cambridge, U.K.: Cambridge University Press, 2001.

Coquery-Vidrovitch, Catherine. *The History of African Cities South of the Sahara: From Origins to Colonization*, trans. Mary Baker. Princeton, NJ: Markus Wiener, 2005.

Hull, R. W. *African Cities and Towns before the European Conquest*. New York: Norton, 1976.

Law, Robin. *Ouidah: The Social History of a West African Slaving "Port," 1727–1892*. Athens: Ohio University Press, 2004.

Southall, Aidan W., ed. *Urban Anthropology: Cross-Cultural Studies of Urbanization*. New York: Oxford University Press, 1973.

Sutton, John. *A Thousand Years of East Africa*. Nairobi: British Institute in Eastern Africa, 1990.

AIDAN SOUTHALL
REVISED BY CHARLES AMBLER

INDEPENDENCE ERA

All over sub-Saharan Africa, the postcolonial period witnessed an explosive increase in the rate of urbanization. Especially in eastern and Central Africa, where the large European settler population had, in colonial times, denied Africans the right to urban residence, political independence meant tremendous liberation and the freedom to move into and live permanently in cities. In consequence, while in 1960 the urban population in sub-Saharan Africa was only 31 million out of a total of 215 million (14.4%), by 2002 the position had changed dramatically. The urban population jumped to 242 million out of a total of 688 million (35%).

What was even more remarkable was the pattern of agglomeration of this population. Whereas in 1960 there was only one city, Johannesburg, with a population of more than 1 million, accounting for 3 percent of the total urban population, by 2002 there were 35 such cities, accounting for over 44 percent of the total urban population.

The rural-urban migrations that political independence provoked throughout the region was partly the result of the close association of urbanism with modernism. For most migrants, who came from a largely precapitalist, rural subsistence background, urbanism entailed two major changes: wage employment in relatively large, nonagricultural establishments, and a new consumption pattern. The latter included living in better accommodations, having access to better health and educational facilities, being able to enjoy better clothing, food, drinks, entertainment, and recreation, and having opportunities for joint action and association.

The postcolonial period thus witnessed a significant differentiation among African cities. Five types of cities became distinguishable. First is the indigenous city, found especially in West Africa and coastal East Africa and precolonial in origin, which have preserved much of their traditional characteristics of winding, narrow roads and mud or stone buildings. Good examples are Timbuktu, Mali; Agadez, Niger; Hargeysa, Somalia; and Lamu, Kenya. Second is the colonial city, established by the colonial authorities at critical transport nodes or resource zones to house African workers. Such cities tend to be well laid out, with streets forming a grid pattern and houses built more substantially. Examples are Dakar, Senegal; Abidjan, Côte d'Ivoire; Port Harcourt and Kaduna, Nigeria; and Kinshasa, Zaire. Third is the dual city, which combines the characteristics of the two former types. Examples include Kano, Zaria, and Ibadan in Nigeria, and Khartoum in Sudan. Fourth is the European city, found largely in eastern, Central and southern Africa initially established exclusively for European habitation and hence have a European level of design and infrastructural facilities. Examples are Nairobi, Kenya; Harare, Zimbabwe; and Pretoria, South Africa. Fifth is the metropolitan industrial city, a hybrid usually combining features of all the preceding types but having invariably a substantial area of degraded squatter settlement established since independence to house the large number of rural-urban migrants who have been unable to realize the dreams that fired their migration into the city.

Regardless of the type of city, the period after 1960 witnessed a rapid growth in urban unemployment. Being very capital intensive, most of the modern establishments whether of factories, commercial houses, or offices, provided relatively limited employment opportunities. The migrants, however, continued to pour into the cities, hoping against hope that they would secure one of the very limited number of jobs. While they waited, those with any skills whatsoever began to exploit the opportunities to provide goods and services to the growing mass of underprivileged like themselves. The goods and services produced did not match the quality of those provided in the modern establishments, but they served the needs of the poor. In this manner, an informal economy blossomed and became a major feature of postcolonial urban centers.

AN INFORMAL ECONOMY

The term *informal economy* was first used by Keith Hart in the Nima district of Accra, Ghana, to describe urban economic activities characterized by ease of entry and exit, employing very few people (usually fewer than ten), without formal incorporation by state agencies, and therefore not subject to state regulatory surveillance. Its pattern of employment derives much from the preindustrial economic structure of master (or owner) served by skilled employee(s) or journeymen and apprentices.

Since the 1960s much has been learned about the nature, structure, and operations of this informal sector. The mission of the International Labor Organization (ILO) to Kenya in 1972 first drew international attention to the labor-absorptive capacity and income-generating opportunities provided by this sector. In recent years, reserchers have estimated that the informal economy workforce accounts for an extraordinary 78 percent of nonagricultural employment, 61 percent of total urban employment, and 93 percent of all new jobs created in sub-Saharan Africa. They also estimate that the contribution of the informal economy to the nonagricultural gross domestic product (GDP) in most years averages some 40 percent.

In the twenty-first century, in many developing countries including those of sub-Saharan Africa, a significant degree of integration has been achieved between the formal and informal sectors. In some subsectors, the dividing line between the two tends to be blurred. Especially in large metropolitan centers, the formal sector has become dependent on the informal market for the disposal of goods and services and the recruitment of cheap labor. On the other hand, the informal sector depends on the formal for some of its equipment, machinery, and raw material.

Improving urban economic performance thus entails promoting a deliberate linkage and inclusiveness of the informal sector and its poverty-reduction focus. This is why in 1999, under the inspiration of the World Bank and the UN-Habitat, an international organization known as the Cities Alliance was founded to bring together representatives of the world cities including those of Africa and bilateral and multilateral development agencies and financial institutions. The mandate of the organization was to improve the efficiency and scale up the impacts of urban development cooperation and urban investment worldwide. The operational program of the Cities Alliance has been to promote a two-prong global campaign of City Development Strategy and Cities Without Slums.

In this campaign a City Development Strategy involves developing a collective vision for the city that is responsive to its comparative strengths and advantages in the national and regional context, a vision that is owned by the city and all the stakeholders both in the formal and informal sectors, and provides an agreed strategic framework for growth and poverty reduction, and identified action areas with assigned roles for each stakeholder group. A City Development Strategy thus is pro-poor in focus and entails a participatory effort of all socioeconomic groups in the city. Already such strategies have been initiated in Bobo-Dioulasso, Mali; Maradi and Dosso, Niger; Karu, near Abuja, Nigeria; and Johannesburg, South Africa. Indeed, many cities in the Republic of South Africa are adopting this paradigm for enhancing their economic productivity and dealing with the challenging problem of urban poverty.

SHELTER

Shelter is an issue of paramount importance for migrants to the city. Lacking the resources to secure substantial rental accommodation or finding such accommodation unavailable at any cost, migrants are often forced to establish squatter settlements around or near existing urban centers. Initially, these settlements comprise buildings constructed from insubstantial material such as corrugated iron sheets, cardboard cartons, and containers of all types. Over time, most squatter settlements show patterns of development whereby occupiers of shacks gradually improve them by using bricks, concrete blocks, and corrugated iron roofing material to transform them into fairly respectable houses. This occurs only where the authorities are enlightened enough not to destroy the shanty settlement before the transformation has taken place. More usually, squatter settlements are regarded as degraded environments and are bulldozed out of existence. Yet so great is the need of the underprivileged for shelter that new squatter settlements quickly spring up in place of the ones destroyed. The cycle of construction and destruction begins again, this time with migrants using even more insubstantial materials.

The real problem with squatter settlements is, however, that very few arrangements are made to plan them and provide them with infrastructural facilities and services. The result is poor drainage, especially of waste water, and large piles of uncollected solid wastes, all of which soon form major environmental hazards. Squatter settlements are, however, neither unorganized nor unorganizable. Consequently, where the authorities are understanding and tolerant, as in Dakar, Senegal, or Lusaka, Zambia, the environmental situation in squatter settlements has been dramatically transformed.

Such transformation becomes even more impressive where squatter settlements have been integrated into the planning process of the city as a whole. Planning, through slum upgrading and sites and services programs, became the strategy for minimizing the seeming deleterious effects of these settlements. Throughout most of the 1970s, the World Bank became the champion of this strategy of urban planning and development in most countries of sub-Saharan Africa with emphasis on secure tenure for the poor. Partly for reason of this security, the poor for whom the programs were designed were often bought out by the wealthy. The resulting failure of the sites and services programs to resolve the shelter problem of the urban poor led in the 1980s to a retreat from their vociferous advocacy.

In the meantime, it was estimated by 2002 that some 56 percent of the city dwellers in sub-Saharan African cities lived in slums. Consequently, the other phase of the global campaign of the Cities Alliance concerned itself with the problem of eradicating slum conditions in cities. The City Without Slum campaign sets out to encourage cities and countries to adopt comprehensive, citywide slum upgrading policies and programs, setting development targets, undertaking reforms to prevent the growth of new slums, and leveraging public and private resources to improve the lives of slum dwellers. With the assistance of donor agencies, a Cities Without Slums Facility was established for sub-Saharan Africa in 2002 and has been providing assistance for slum upgrading in a number of African cities, notably Lagos, Nigeria; Addis Ababa, Ethiopia; Nairobi; Johannesburg; Mbabane, Swaziland; and Kumasi, Ghana.

URBAN GOVERNANCE

The existence of slums and the pervasiveness of poverty in African cities are increasingly being seen as two sides of the same coin of poor urban governance. As such, their effective resolution has to go hand-in-hand with reforms in the way African cities are governed. Consequently, the style and quality of urban governance are central focus of international attention. This focus emphasizes the primacy of municipal financial management in the resolution of urban problems and the relation between effective financial resource mobilization and the improved access of citizens to urban services of all kinds. The new focus also seeks an increasing involvement of the private sector, both formal and informal, in the provision of urban services, particularly mass transportation. After years of resenting the seeming intrusion of informal sector operators such as matatu drivers and their vehicles (usually minibuses or converted vans), municipal authorities are encouraged to legitimize their participation in urban mass transportation.

The effectiveness of urban governance in most countries of sub-Saharan Africa is, however, still largely a function of the power relation between the municipal authorities and both the central government on the one hand and the citizens of the cities themselves on the other. Especially in Anglophone Africa, the 1980s witnessed a noticeable movement away from centralized control of urban fiscal and budgetary policies and towards some support for various forms of decentralization and local initiative. The position, however, remains largely at the policymaking level and has not yet resulted in real empowerment of municipal authorities. As of 2006 most of them still cannot raise the funds they need for infrastructural and local economic development.

On the other hand, the relations of municipal authorities to their citizens is hardly empowering. The UN-Habitat global campaign for good urban governance emphasizes the increasing importance of participatory as distinct from purely representative democracy in the governance of municipalities if municipal government is to become more accountable to their citizens and be able effectively to mobilize them and their resources behind municipal developmental programs. Participatory budgeting, with its origin in the city of Porto Allegre, Brazil, is being canvassed as a vital complement to city development strategies to ensure that citizens help to determine priorities with respect to the development of the capital needs of their municipalities.

South Africa is one sub-Saharanan African country where resident participation isbeing reflected in city governance. The 1998 Municipal Systems Act spells out in some detail when and how municipalities must communicate and consult with residents and involve them in various structures and processes of local governance. Such participatory governance is meant to foster accountability, deal with issues of corruption and maladministration, promote improved quality of services to residents, and inform the development and implementation of integrated development plan for each city. The nine largest cities of the country, designated metropolitan municipalities, initiated in 2002 the establishment of a South African Cities Network to encourage the exchange of information, experience and best practices with this type of participatory governance and integrated development plans. Social scientists anticipate that the inauguration in 2004 of the United Cities and Local Government of Africa (UCLGA) with its first president from South Africa would facilitate the dissemination of this novel system of urban governance and planning to the rest of the continent.

WOMEN AND URBAN SOCIAL RELATIONS

Everywhere in sub-Saharan Africa, urban life has had a decisive impact on social relations. It has forced citizens of each African country to learn to adjust to the reality of ethnic diversity and heterogeneity in cities and promoted drastic changes in the relations between the sexes. Everywhere, the increasing rate of education for girls and women has freed more and more of them from the thrall of traditional existence. Their increasing professional qualifications and competence have meant that they are challenging their male counterparts at executive and policy levels of management. The resulting independence and individual self-reliance for women is, however, taking its toll on the pattern of family life. More and more, urban society in Africa is accepting the phenomenon of female-headed households and of respectable single mothers who do not see the compelling necessity to be married. All this takes place against the background of women rising capacity to control their own fertility through family planning programs.

However, this growing independence of women in the context of more permissive social and sexual norms has exposed them in most African cities to the HIV/AIDS pandemic especially as a result of the massive migrations and long absences of male workers away from their homes, a practice that dates back to colonial period. Consequently, in urban sub-Saharan Africa, HIV seroprevalence rates are estimated to be not only high but still on the increase. Recent studies of pregnant women indicate that over 31 percent of them in urban Botswana, and 32 percent in urban Rwanda, Malawi, and Zambia, are HIV-positive. Even in West Africa, where HIV prevalence has been estimated to be relatively low, it is on the increase in urban Nigeria and Cameroon. Seroprevalence rates in capital or major cities indicate that on average, almost one-quarter of the adult population has contracted the disease, a level much higher than that in rural areas.

Although precise estimates of the impact of HIV/AIDs on the economies of African cities are difficult to ascertain, there is no denying that the disease has been a major contributory factor to the economic crisis confronting most sub-Saharan countries since the 1990s. This has put the new-found empowerment of women under great stress, especially when they are the only breadwinner in a household. Galloping inflation and the declining value of national currencies have further undermined the well-being of most families, reduced health spending, and increased child malnutrition. The rise in the number of urban children orphaned due to the loss of both parents to the HIV/AIDs pandemic is also starting to emerge as a very serious problem in many urban centers on the continent.

THE FUTURE

For cities of sub-Saharan African countries, the new millennium promises to be the beginning of a new dispensation characterized by a greater emphasis on participatory democracy in urban governance and greater attention to the social and economic role of cities in the development of African countries. The Millenium Development Goals of the United Nations provide the bench mark against which to measure the achievements of African municipal and national governments over the succeeding years. In many ways these goals are mutually reinforcing and their achievements will require that African cities build up their capacity for effective, democratic, and accountable governance. This is the principal raison d'etre not only for UCLGA but also the New Partnership for African Development (NEPAD), an initiative of African governments, which supports UN-Habitat in facilitating the orderly growth and development of metropolitan cities through twining arrangements and in a manner that guarantees secure tenure, environmental sustainability, and effective poverty alleviation of the citizenry.

The prognosis is that by the year 2025, some 55 percent of African population will be living in cities and over 65 percent of these will live in large metropolitan areas, a number of which will have become megacities. In consequence, African governments are being enjoined to plan to confront the problems of their burgeoning cities through good participatory urban governance. There are initial indications that they are also increasingly being forced by circumstances to draw on the resources of their history and culture for popular participation to resolve some of these urban problems in the context of the enveloping globalization, the increasing developmental role of public-private partnership and especially the cascading streams of technological innovations in the communication and information fields that are changing urban social relationships in very dramatic ways.

See also **Abidjan; Addis Ababa; Dakar; Disease: HIV/ AIDS, Social and Political Aspects; Harare; Johannesburg; Khartoum; Kinshasa; Kumasi; Labor; Lagos; Lusaka; Mbabane; Nairobi; Port Harcourt; Poverty; Pretoria; Production Strategies; Senegal; Timbuktu; Transportation; Women: Urbanism; World Bank.**

BIBLIOGRAPHY

Charmes, J. *Estimation and Survey Methods for the Informal Sector.* Versailles: University of Versailles, 2002.

Montgomery, M. R.; Richard Stren; Barney Cohen; and Holly E. Reed; eds. *Cities Transformed: Demographic Change and its Implications in the Developing World.* Washington, DC: National Academies Press, 2003.

O'Connor, Anthony M. *The African City.* London: Hutchinson, 1983.

South African Cities Network. *State of the Cities Report 2004.* Pretoria: SACN, 2004.

Stren, Richard E., and Rodney R. White, eds. *African Cities in Crisis: Managing Rapid Urban Growth.* Boulder, CO: Westview Press. 1989.

United Nations Centre for Human Settlements (Habitat). *An Urbanizing World: Global Report on Human Settlements.* Oxford: Oxford University Press, 1996.

UN-Habitat. *The State of the World Cities 2004/2005: Globalization and Urban Culture.* London: UN-Habitat/ Earthscan, 2004.

AKIN L. MABOGUNJE

HOUSING

To understand the issue of urban housing in sub-Saharan Africa, specific attention must be paid to the historical development of urbanization, including the quantity and quality of shelter available, the provision of urban facilities in residential neighborhoods, and urban residents' access to housing. Cities in general in Africa have increasingly become sanctuaries for the poor, who determine a greater and greater proportion of the physical development. This is evident in the growth of settlements that have sprung up spontaneously, beyond the control of those authorities legally charged with regulating land use and building construction.

URBANIZATION IN PRECOLONIAL AND COLONIAL TIMES

In the precolonial era, before the nineteenth century, the population of the African continent was heavily rural. Though it would be inaccurate to say that urbanization was entirely a colonial importation, precolonial urbanization was restricted to certain regions. For example, there were stone-built urban centers in Southern Africa dating from 1000 CE, the most notable of which is Great Zimbabwe. There were also early, well-developed urban traditions in western Africa, on the Arab coast of eastern Africa, and in Ethiopia. By worldwide preindustrial standards, some of these towns were of significant size: the populations of Yoruba and Bénin towns ranged from 15,000 to 20,000; Timbuktu and Jenné ranged from 15,000 to 90,000 in the fifteenth and sixteenth centuries; Kumbi-Saleh may have been as large as 30,000 in the tenth century. As a benchmark of comparison, Cologne, the largest European city in the fifteenth century, had a population of 20,000.

Eyewitness accounts from these early periods provide some insights into population structure and housing provision in these cities. West African cities functioned as markets and feudal power centers economically supported by the agricultural production of their hinterlands. Towns were socially stratified. They were both the residences of the political elites and merchants, and the migration foci for rural poor making a living through prostitution and begging. The well-developed economies of these cities offered a wide range of unskilled occupations for the poor: petty trading, porterage, heavy manual labor, and such low-skill crafts as making rope and calabashes. Urban populations in this period were subject to striking seasonal and annual fluctuations that were responses to farming cycles, famines, and trading cycles. Urban residents were provisioned by taxation that was collected on consumption items or the production from elite urbanites and plantations. Housing in these precolonial West African towns consisted of well-built houses in the central zones within the walls of the towns. The peripheral zones typically comprised temporary, straw huts where recent immigrants and the poor residents involved in casual labor lived.

During the period of colonialization, urbanization occurred in all colonies. Colonial administrations needed urban centers for control, bureaucracy, taxation processes, trade, transport (at ports and railways), and servicing of mineral extraction and plantations.

By the end of the colonial period, sub-Saharan African towns could be classified into two types. Type A towns typically predated colonialism and were characterized by an indigenous population, ethnic homogeneity, diverse craft occupations, economic diversity, laissez-faire attitudes toward housing and landlordism, and a poor material standard of accommodation for the masses. Housing was locally built for owner occupation or rental.

By contrast, Type B towns (probably the majority of towns at the end of the colonial period) were new towns created by the colonial authorities either to service mines, plantations, and ports or to act as administrative centers. These were built as garden cities with strict planning controls. African in-migration was stringently controlled, especially in settler colonies, in terms of numbers and of where in-migrants were allowed to live. All residents in these purpose-built towns, whether European, Asian, or African, were by definition immigrants, but their legal rights differed widely. In current parlance, African urban immigrants were not defined as urban stakeholders, but only as transients. Africans were limited to unskilled labor or clerical work; little scope was permitted for African landlordism or entrepreneurship.

In many instances, migrant workers were provided strictly controlled housing by government or private employers (such as the railway authorities or the mine owners). In all the Type B towns, self-built African-style housing was rigorously controlled or considered illegal by the terms of urban planning legislation. The same was true in Type A towns, but it was harder to enforce. Control of housing was part of the colonial governments' overall policy of regulating population movements and dominating the economies of the colonies.

In European cities at this time, the housing stock expanded rapidly through the efforts of private developers. The housing policies in the colonies reflected the need to control African populations rather than a preference for the social production of housing.

Urban housing for Africans was not designed to accommodate families. Authorities preferred men to work in town for short periods of work and then return to their rural families. Urban regulations limited women's migration to town, although some women managed to gain access to urban areas. As a result of these policies, African men greatly outnumbered women in cities.

Cities, both old and new, remained relatively small until World War II. It is estimated that in 1920 only 2–3 percent of the sub-Saharan African populations lived in towns. Administrative towns were small; the fast-growing areas were port cities and mining towns. By 1940 only seven African cities had populations over 100,000: Ibadan, Kano, and Addis Ababa were Type A towns that took on new administrative functions; Lagos, Dakar, and Accra were Type B port towns; and Johannesburg was a mining center.

POSTCOLONIAL AFRICAN URBANIZATION

After independence, African cities grew quickly. A number of factors contributed to this rapid expansion: the abolition of direct controls on population movement, increased state investment funds, and the shift of African political activity from rural to urban associations. The time frame of these shifts varied. In Zambia, Malawi, and Kenya, they ended in the early 1960s; in South Africa controls increased in the 1940s and were only removed in 1994.

Also after independence, the policies of urban development and administration in the first twenty years were largely driven by political not economic agendas. Governments' elitist housing policies, combined with the massive internal migration, led to an inevitable expansion of informal housing.

The salient characteristics of sub-Saharan urbanization in the postindependence era are: (1) demographic changes that have included rapid and relatively uncontrolled growth of urban populations, a more equal sex ratio and a more youthful demographic; (2) a spatial organization of urban areas characterized by a well-built, modern, high-rise core surrounded by illegal, self-built housing; (3) the largely unsuccessful social production of housing by urban authorities, a vast expansion of the informal-sector market (self-built housing not conforming to the building codes), and recent combinations of government and private-sector initiatives; (4) a high demand for urban housing that makes self-built housing an attractive investment; (5) the collapse of the urban infrastructure; and (6) the dramatic growth of informal-sector employment as the survival strategy of the urban poor.

Demographic Structure of Urban Populations.

After independence, African urban populations grew rapidly. National population growth rates ranged from 2 to 4 percent after independence, but urban population growth rates were much higher than the rural population growth (6.2 to 9% per annum in the 1960s). Africa from 1965 to 1985 was the world's least urbanized and the most rapidly urbanizing continent, with an average urbanization rate of 13 percent. Due to high in-migration and natural growth rates, Africa's urban populations sometimes doubled every decade. In the year 2000 some countries, such as South Africa, achieved urbanization rates of over 50 percent.

From the mid-1990s, Africa's population growth rates have been slowing due to poverty and HIV/AIDS. Africa's significant cities continue to grow rapidly but more slowly than originally predicted in the early 1990s. For example, in 1994 Lagos was predicted to reach a population of 24.4 million inhabitants by 2015 (making it the world's third largest city), but by 2003 that prediction was revised downward to 16 million and eleventh place in world cities.

African urban populations became increasingly youthful in the last part of the twentieth century because in-migration was high. Immigrants typically leave their rural homes for the urban centers as young adults when they are between the ages of eighteen to forty.

Female migration to cities was also high, sometimes higher than male, and demographic imbalances still exist. In West Africa, for example, many cities have a 2:1 male to female ratio. In other cities, such

as Nairobi, the male to female ratio has gone from 2:1 to 1:1. This has been referred to as genderizing the urban space of Nairobi, a process replicated in other Type B towns.

Urban populations in postindependence Africa are also characterized by increasing poverty and disparity in incomes, and the continuation of circular migration.

Spatial Structure of Urban Areas.

In the decades following independence, the central urban cores have been overwhelmed by sprawls of self-built, uncontrolled housing, and minimal infrastructure.

The early colonial capital cities or major ports became important leaders of city development, the foci of power many times larger than the next largest cities, and absorbed disproportionate amounts of government and capital investment. At the end of the twentieth century the primary cities were balanced by the rapid growth of smaller towns. Estimates are that, by 2010, many small towns will be classified as large.

Another salient feature of postcolonial urbanization is an increase in overcrowding. The demand for housing has risen much faster than the public or private provision of houses or infrastructure.

Production of Low-Income Housing by Urban Authorities.

The social production of housing has been largely ineffective throughout the twentieth century and into the twenty-first. Even South Africa, with the most vibrant economy on the continent, has failed to achieve its ambitious housing production goals.

The history of African urban planning can be divided into three phases. In the 1950s and 1960s, governments operated on the assumption that the state should provide adequate housing and associated services (roads, electricity, water, and sewerage) for all citizens. In the 1970s and early 1980s, self-help became the solution favored by planners. By the late 1980s there was a retreat from the involving of governments in either building or assisting the construction of new housing. Almost all African countries have huge debts. According to World Bank's 2004 report on the progress of Heavily Indebted Poor Countries (HIPIC) initiative, thirty-two of the thirty-eight countries identified were African.

Due to the almost universal application of Structural Adjustment Programs, governments are increasingly unable to deliver basic urban services and are even privatizing water and sewerage and transport systems that were once run by the public sector.

During the period of the state provision of housing, urban authorities did not manage to build housing affordable by the majority. As well as a lack of political will, African governments lacked resources to meet even a quarter of the demand for low-cost housing. Structural adjustment has seriously eroded governments' capacity to upgrade existing self-built housing.

Between 1962 and 1980, the National Housing Corporation in Tanzania built 13,000 housing units, by any standards an inadequate number. In Cameroon during the 1980s, 5,800 of the 8,000 new units built by the National Housing Authority were too expensive even for higher-paid civil servants. In Nigeria, flush with promised high oil revenues, the 1980 Ten-Year Development Plan acknowledged a postindependence shortfall of state-provided urban housing of 867,000 units. After a decade of oil money income, the housing produced did not reach projected targets for one year. In South Africa in 1987, it was estimated that there was a shortfall of nearly a million dwellings for nonwhite urban dwellers.

Another problem is that the public-sector housing is too expensive for up to three-quarters of urbanites. For example, in Nigeria in the mid-1989s, a low-cost house (the minimum standard countenanced by the government) required monthly mortgage payments higher than the monthly salary of 70 percent of the population. In 1975, Nairobi planners made the same calculations for Kenyan National Housing Corporation low-income housing.

Why this disparity between the income and housing needs of urban residents and the social housing? First, there is a lack of political will. African leaders were determined to have city centers displaying the progressive symbols of wide streets, high-rise buildings, luxury hotels, and expensive, leafy suburbs. In the international prestige stakes, decent, low-income housing counts for less than a luxury hotel. But what is good for the prestige ranking of the state does not benefit the urban poor. In Africa, percentage of budgets for social development fell from 25 percent of annual budgets in 1972 to 15 percent in 1984. Compared with education and health, low-cost housing and urban ancillary services (water, sewers, and transport) have been greatly neglected.

Second, poor records in social housing can be attributed to municipal planning regulations inherited from the colonial era. These policies required unrealistically high standards of construction, materials, and services based on imported, high-cost materials, such as concrete blocks and galvanized steel roofing sheets. Little effort has been made to develop better local materials, such as stabilized mud bricks and compressed asbestos roofing materials. Efforts to create site and service schemes with lower building standards often were regarded negatively by officials. In Kenya in the late 1970s, low standards proposed for the Dandora low-income housing project were only accepted by the Nairobi Town Council after determined pressure from the World Bank.

Thus, private builders have largely been unable to legally use cheaper, locally produced materials common in the construction of rural housing. However, in the illegal informal sector such materials, as well as recycled urban waste products such as cardboard, tin cans, and plastic sheeting are regularly employed. These structures break housing regulations, create fire and health hazards, and risk demolition. All too often building regulations are enforced only after the fact when it is politically expedient. This is both economically wasteful and politically damaging.

In the second phase of urban development, government efforts to ensure housing for all citizens shifted to what has been called the aided self-help phase. Austerity measures were brought about by the worldwide recession and the demands of International Monetary Fund structural adjustment programs. International agencies made increased social-equity demands to instate reasonable appropriate technologies based on local materials.

The two alternative housing provision strategies emerging at the 1970s and 1980s were site and service schemes and informal-sector housing upgrading schemes. In Zambia, the World Bank provided 3,666 serviced plots and upgraded 20,000 existing houses in Zambia. In Kenya, it financed 6,000 serviced plots in Nairobi. In Tanzania the World Bank funded 20,000 serviced plots and 17,000 upgraded plots in Dar es Salaam alone.

The provision of low-income and self-help housing is important both to give people shelter and also to generate employment opportunities. The public sector, NGOs, and international donors have increasingly taken important roles to encourage maximum employment in the area of house building.

These projects undeniably met the needs of a large number of low-income households, although they did not redress wider inequalities in the urban housing system. Although women were largely responsible for the domestic production of rural, self-help housing, public sector production of self-help and state-produced housing became the province of men. Houses were allocated only to male heads of households. Toward the end of the twentieth century, drastically adjusting allocation procedures, building regulations, and funding structures challenged this bias.

The projects also did little to address class biases. Existing subsidies for housing were regressive, and because middle-class housing provision was inadequate, those who were financially better off often illegally obtained many of the serviced plots intended for lower-income families.

Upgrading of existing self-built, informal-sector housing proved less costly and complicated. Part of the strategy was to grant title to homeowners, thus encouraging owners to upgrade their houses closer to municipal building standards. Urban authorities installed roads, standpipes for water, and sewers. Owners were granted low-income loans to replace low-quality materials with more permanent equivalents (such as tin roofing for cardboard roofs, and stabilized mud bricks for plain mud walls) thus capitalizing on the industry of the owner/builders.

The long-term impact of these internationally funded projects on the housing policies and agencies of African countries is questionable. Externally funded alternatives demonstrated to local planning administration structures that alternative management styles were possible, and often left behind a cohort of trained staff at the end of the project. However, funds for these schemes were misappropriated, as elite interests often subverted allocation procedures. Replication was hampered by lack of

political support and infrastructural backup. Once external pressure and economic support were withdrawn, enthusiasm for this type of venture waned dramatically.

In the latter part of the twentieth century, the impact of structural adjustment policies that cut government social spending and pressure from donors to move social services into the private sector have had a depressive effect on the social production of housing.

The Rapid Growth of Informal-Sector Housing. From the beginning of the postcolonial period, one of the most salient characteristics of African urban development has been the rising percentage of urban residents living in uncontrolled or informal private-sector housing variously termed squatter housing (when built illegally on state or privately owned land) or shantytowns (referring to the poor materials, usually mud and wattle, cardboard, or tin sheets). Some have estimated that in the 1960s, 50–60 percent of urban populations lived in this type of housing.

The informal sector has met the public's demand for housing much more efficiently and effectively than the state sector has hitherto been able to do. The desperate need for urban housing has made the urban informal housing sector one of the safest and most buoyant forms of investment in Africa.

Changing Policies Toward Informal-Sector Housing. After independence, urban authorities continued to operate with outdated, high building standards left by outgoing colonial regimes, and also continued the practice of destroying uncontrolled, self-built housing. Politicians claimed this behavior would attract accusations of backwardness. In addition, politicians feared the poor as potential supporters of radicals, dissidents, marginals, and criminals

Informal-sector housing solves the shelter problem for owner-occupants and tenants. It is a form of housing that is a low-cost, structurally flexible, culturally sensitive form of housing; it also seems to be more gender equal.

Since the mid-1970s, local and national government policies on informal-sector housing have largely shifted away from the official destruction of

Typical shantytown, Mathare Valley, Nairobi, 1974. From the 1960s on increasing numbers of urban residents have lived in uncontrolled or informal private-sector housing variously termed "squatter housing" and "shantytowns." The housing is adequate by rural standards but fails to meet stringent urban housing regulations. PHOTOGRAPH BY NICI NELSON

low-income housing to more neutral, and in some cases more positive, attitudes. In South Africa these policies did not change until the election of the first black majority government in 1994. This change in attitude occasionally gives way to paranoia about the subversive political power of the poor who inhabit such areas, as was seen in 2005 when the government of Zimbabwe bulldozed whole shantytowns in Operation Murambatsvina (or Operation Drive Out Rubbish). Some estimates of the number of people who lost their homes and livelihoods in that operation were put as high as 700,000. For the most part, however, town planners and international development agencies applaud the more realistic and humane approach of most African governments.

Overcrowding. The more serious problems of informal-sector housing are social ones. All too often this housing is seen as overcrowded and of poor quality. Overcrowding and quality are closely related issues, as well as ambiguous and culturally relative concepts, but both notions represent attempts to measure the quality of life of the inhabitants. In the minds of politicians, some planners, and a few social scientists, overcrowding and poor housing quality in urban areas can be held directly responsible for immorality, delinquency, crime, broken homes, stress, and ill health. This connection is contentious enough. When one comes to define what overcrowding means, things become even more complicated. The concept is multifaceted as well as culturally determined.

For a start, various criteria are used to measure overcrowding. It may refer to the number of people per acre in a neighborhood, the number of people per dwelling, the number of residents per room, and even the square feet per occupant (difficult to calculate, because room sizes are rarely recorded in census data). It may also refer to space between housing units, such as the size of the plot in relation to that of the house or the space available for communal use in leisure activities or urban agriculture (small gardens, grazing goats, or free-ranging chickens). Finally, it may relate to the pressure on services (such as schools, meeting halls, drains, sewers, and water distribution systems).

Thus, overcrowding is a concept that is difficult to measure in absolute terms.

Overcrowding is more often defined by inhabitants themselves in terms of the inappropriate use of space rather than by fixed physical measurements. Many people originating in rural African cultures have norms of association and personal privacy different from those held by architects and planners trained in European traditions. Different norms of age-related and gender-related behavior and customs of segregation and privacy make different demands on housing structure. As a whole, designers of African domestic architecture have paid scant attention to urban African family structures or local customs of spatial use. Two young women with their four or five children may happily share a room in Mathare Valley in Nairobi. But a young woman and her mother sharing the same sized room may complain that they were too crowded. The crowding experienced here is psychological rather than physical.

In the 1960s, planning experts recommended housing densities of two people per room in tropical countries. This is considered an acceptable minimum occupancy rate for such countries, where many household activities (cooking, washing clothes, children playing) can be done outdoors. By comparison, the minimum recommended occupancy rate in temperate climates is 1.5 persons per room.

The literature on housing indicates that the majority of African urbanites effectively have less space than the minimum standards. In the 1980s most households had more than three people per room. In Accra, 42 percent of households were over this number; Kumasi, 75 percent; Nairobi, 52 percent; and Kampala, 28 percent.

Most rooms that constitute the household home are less than 86 square feet and few are larger than 140 square feet. Such household rooms have to hold the family furniture, provide a secure place for all household goods (perhaps even livestock), and double as a kitchen when it rains. If the head(s) of household is (are) engaged in informal-sector economic activity, it can also be a place of business. There is rarely room for more than two very small beds that during the day serve as seats.

Long-term research in Mathare Valley, a Nairobi squatter settlement, showed that almost all households here lived in one room. Average occupancy per

Site and service scheme started in 1973, New Mathare. One of the alternative housing-provision strategies emerging in the 1970s, this method provided a "wet core" on a site. Persons allocated these sites built their houses incrementally over time, as their own building skills and/or resources allowed. PHOTOGRAPH BY NICI NELSON

a one-room household was 3.5. All personal and livelihood activities took place in one room. A great deal of socializing, livelihood work, and housework was conducted out-of-doors. In the 1970s there were open spaces that were used for urban agriculture and children's play. By the 1990s this community had grown even more densely populated with the continuous in filling of houses in previously communal spaces, resulting in a decline of the quality of life. Despite recognizing that overcrowding is a culturally relative term, this density of occupation cannot be acceptable in terms of physical or psychological health or of quality of life.

Overcrowding has been increased in these unauthorized housing areas through subsequent redevelopment by richer urban residents for investment purposes. Again, using Nairobi as an example, from 1980 in the Dandora Site and Services Project there has been a gradual rebuilding of the standard project design: one-story buildings, four rooms around a courtyard that allowed air and light for the rooms, and relatively private outdoor leisure space. Since the mid-1980s, richer Nairobi residents have been buying these buildings, then tearing them down in order to construct narrow, five-story structures with an average of forty rooms (occupied by two to four people) with doors and windows opening onto long corridors with no source of light or air. Typically there is one shower and one toilet per floor, and no space for drying clothes or sitting outdoors.

Urban Infrastructure. In the 1990s African cities were entering their third phase of independent development. The major problems that faced politicians and planners were those of managing the infrastructure: the provision of water, sewers, electricity, refuse collection, and transportation. Systems created at the end of the colonial era have become inadequate to meet the pressures of the cities' growing populations and spreading suburbs. The machinery (such as buses and water treatment plants) needed upgrading and replacement. With structural adjustment and recession, there has been no money to do this. Increasingly, urban authorities have had to turn to the private sector to provide services such as piped water and electricity.

In the late 1970s, the numbers of people living without piped water ranged from 25 percent in Ethiopia to 75 percent in Zambia. World Health Organization figures for 2002 state that, overall for Africa, approximately 40 percent of people are living without easily accessed water and proper sanitation.

The Informal-Sector Economy as Support for the Urban Poor. One of the most salient characteristics of Africa's cities is that the majority of their residents live in informal-sector housing and support themselves by informal-sector economic activities. The inability of the formal sector to provide employment for Africa's rapidly expanding population has led to explosive growth in the continent's informal sector, as most new migrants become employed in it.

Informal-sector charcoal selle, Mathare Valley, Nairobi, 1971. The majority of residents living in shantytowns also support themselves by informal-sector economic activities, as this woman is doing outside her house. Women find this a useful way to gain a livelihood because conditions and locations are flexible enough to combine with child rearing. PHOTOGRAPH BY NICI NELSON

On the plus side, informal-sector employment is flexible, responsive to the market, and relatively dynamic. Because it is small-scale and requires low investment and relatively low levels of skill, it is easy for urban dwellers to gain a foothold in it. It is also especially attractive to women because its hours, conditions, and locations are flexible enough to allow for child rearing.

On the negative side, the informal-sector means harsh and insecure work conditions. Profits are generated by working long hours and the use of unpaid family labor under conditions that are at best uncomfortable and at worst dangerous. Employers often exploit workers. In Kenya this sector is called *jua kali* (hot sun), a name that acknowledges workers often toil outside, unprotected from the sun. Nevertheless, an increasing share of total employment of urban Africa is in the informal sector. In the 1980s the informal sector rates were typically between 25 and 50 percent, and higher in poorer localities. Into the twenty-first century this trend has continued. In 2004, approximately 72 percent of nonfarm employment in Africa was in the informal sector (78% if South Africa was included), accounting for a continental average of 42 percent of gross national income (GNI) across sub-Saharan Africa. In poorer countries such as Nigeria and Tanzania it accounted for 60 percent of the GNI.

In the early period of independence, the informal sector was the sector of the poor and uneducated. As the 1980s wore on, the inadequacy of wages and salaries in both public- and private sector white-collar jobs and increasing rates of retrenchment (due to structural adjustment wage restraints and high inflation) meant that, increasingly, people from a wider range of class backgrounds looked for economic opportunities in this sector. This trend continued as Structural Adjustment Policies bit deep in the 1990s. Many households may practice a form of income diversification as a long-term strategy, with different members engaged in both formal and informal economic activities.

The urban area provides the markets and informal economic possibilities for greater independent female participation in productive economic activity. Women's participation rates in the formal economy are rarely more than 15 percent. The division of labor in the informal sector is strongly gendered, as are the formal-sector division of labor and the domestic division of labor. Women are often restricted to the less lucrative forms of self-employment. Compared with men, they have lower levels of training, suffer sociocultural constraints, and have less access to capital. Food production, food hawking, pavement trading in small consumables, trading in vegetables and foodstuffs, beer brewing, tailoring, and commercialized sex are the province of women. Heavy production, metalwork, carpentry, motor vehicle repair, and taxi driving are typically the work of men.

Governments have been as unsympathetic to the informal-sector labor market as they have been to the informal housing market, despite the patent failure of African states to provide adequate formal sector employment. The rate and scale of the growth of cities have outstripped the capacity of modern-sector employment to absorb new workers. Just as the informal housing market has bridged the gap between provision and demand, so has the informal economy.

NEW CONCERNS AND THE FUTURE

Privatization of Urban Housing and Services.
Across Africa, international donors have driven the privatization agenda since the 1990s. It is important to make sure that governments are able to regulate properly and set appropriate agendas for private providers to make sure that consumer groups (most especially the low-income groups) are properly represented and their needs met.

NGOs and Social Movements.
Urban governments have increasingly been unable to provide appropriate housing. Into the vacuum have stepped nongovernmental organizations (NGOs) and social movements. NGOs such as Homeless International influence urban development through pragmatic advocacy and help to mobilize local NGOs and community-based organizations (CBOs) to build or to upgrade low-income housing.

Addressing Gender Bias.
In the past, most types of housing schemes have been gender biased. Throughout the 1990s and into the twenty-first century, increasing attention as been paid to the reasons and to the possible solutions to this bias. For example, initial selection criteria for most housing schemes, financial arrangements, and the sheer practicality of undertaking or organizing construction were biased against women, even though female participants frequently have a better repayment record. This gender bias related to all forms of formal sector housing. Women are systematically discriminated against in the following ways: land use planning inhibits women's economic activities; biases against local and improvised building materials limit women's ability to participate in shelter production; and land tenure rules limit women's access to land titles. Gender-neutral policies often

operate in men's favor. Care is needed to improve women's access to finance, tendering procedures, and property rights.

Sustainable Urbanization and Housing: Ecological Cities. In the 1990s, two paradigms converged: the growth and development model and the environmental movement. At the Earth Summit in Rio de Janeiro in 1992, the sustainability paradigm was elaborated. It called for new solutions and priorities in sustainable urban development and housing. Developed economies were to cease overproduction and overconsumption whereas poorer ones were to stabilize population growth and develop pro-poor economic growth. Urban authorities have been encouraged to develop Local Agenda 21s (environmental action plans) to ensure urban sustainability. Sustainability, as defined by the Brudtland Commission, means meeting the urban needs of present generations without ruining the chances of future generations to survive. Agenda 21s entail wide consultations and partnerships, stressing the importance of interconnections between sectors and various urban institutions. Sadly, as of the early twenty-first century, more effort has been expended on creating these Agenda 21 documents than on addressing the political and economic constraints on which they are attempting to operate.

Special issues of *Environment and Urbanization* explore all the ramifications of this concept. The themes explored are: (1) how to make cities perform better with regard to resource use and waste management; (2) the potentials and limitations of partnerships between local governments, the private sector, community organizations, and local or international nongovernmental organizations; (3) political issues that center on democracy and citizen participation; (4) improving transport; (5) ensuring the economic sustainability of settlements and cities with an accompanying equitable distribution of economic benefits; and (6) building ecological cities that will minimize the ecological footprint of settlements in terms of use of resources.

Increasingly, ecological urbanization or urban ecology in the twenty-first century has become the place where the physical and social sciences debate the complexities of integrating understandings of human behavior and the built environment with theories of ecosystem dynamics. The special issue

on "Ecological Urbanization" of *Environment and Urbanization* (2006) makes it clear that that "the very notion of urban ecology has become multiscalar, extending from individual urban systems to systems of cities and towns, and from ecosystems within urban settlements to urban settlements as ecosystems, to the ways in which cities and towns shape ecosystems beyond as well as within urban boundaries." Various important planning policy issues emerge from these debates: the need for compact, not sprawling cities; the importance of integrated planning; and ecologically sensitive architecture and planning

Integrated Urban Planning. The demands of ecological urbanization and poverty alleviation means that, from the points of view of politicians, planners, and development agencies, there is an increasing emphasis on integrated planning that stresses: (1) the importance of the spatial relationship of housing to transport networks, social services, and livelihood opportunities; (2) a coordinated spatially and programmatic delivery of services and supporting infrastructure so that neighborhoods function properly; (3) holistic planning that covers all facilities and amenities necessary for the proper functioning of city communities; (4) understanding how the market in urban land and housing really works; (5) the importance of cross-sectional coordination and inter-institutional connectivity, which is an important aspect of the Local Agenda 21; and (6) the creation of a more just society.

Whether this ambitious and difficult agenda can be achieved as Africa moves into the second decade of the twenty-first century remains to be seen.

See also **Accra; Addis Ababa; Aid and Development; Architecture; Dakar; Dar es Salaam; Gender; Household and Domestic Groups; Ibadan; International Monetary Fund; Johannesburg; Kampala; Kano; Kumasi; Labor; Lagos; Nairobi; Nongovernmental Organizations; Postcolonialism; Timbuktu; Town Planning; Transportation; Women: Urbanism; Women: Women and Trade; World Bank; Zimbabwe, Great.**

BIBLIOGRAPHY

Amis, Philip, and Peter Lloyd. *Housing Africa's Urban Poor.* New York: Manchester University Press for the International African Institute, 1990.

Becker, Charles M.; Andrew Hamer; and Andrew R. Morrison. *Beyond Urban Bias in Africa.* Portsmouth, NH: Heinemann, 1994.

"Ecological Urbanization I." *Environment and Urbanization* 18, no. 1 (2006).

Gilbert, Alan, and Josef Gugler. *Cities, Poverty, and Development: Urbanization in the Third World,* 2nd edition. Oxford: Oxford University Press, 1992.

Harrison, Philip; Marie Huchzermeyer; and Mzwanele Mayekiso; eds. *Confronting Fragmentation: Housing and Urban Development in a Democratising Society.* Cape Town, South Africa: University of Cape Town Press, 2003.

Iliffe, John. *The African Poor: A History.* Cambridge, U.K.: Cambridge University Press, 1987.

Jones, Sue, and Nici Nelson, eds. *Urban Poverty in Africa.* London: Intermediate Technology Publications, 1999.

Jones, Sue, and Nici Nelson, eds. *Practitioners and Poverty Alleviation: Influencing Urban Policy from the Ground Up.* London: ITDG, 2005.

King, Anthony D. *Urbanism, Colonialism, and the World Economy: Cultural and Spatial Foundations of the World Urban System.* London: Routledge, 1990.

Larsson, Anita; Matseliso Mapetla; and Ann Schlyter; eds. *Gender and Urban Housing in Southern Africa: Emerging Issues.* Roma: Institute of Southern African Studies, University of Lesotho, 2003.

McLeod, Ruth, et al. "Influencing Urban Development through 'Pragmatic Advocacy': The Case of Homeless International." In *Practitioners and Poverty Alleviation: Influencing Urban Policy from the Ground Up,* edited by Sue Jones and Nici Nelson. London: ITDG, 2005.

Moser, Caroline, and Linda Peake, eds. *Women, Human Settlements, and Housing.* London: Tavistock, 1987.

Nelson, Nici. "Women Must Help Each Other." In *Women United, Women Divided: Comparative Studies of Ten Contemporary Cultures,* edited by Patricia Caplan and Janet M. Bujra. Bloomington: Indiana University Press, 1979.

Nelson, Nici. "Genderizing Nairobi's Urban Space." In *L'Afrique Orientale Annuaire 2000,* edited by F. Grignon et al. Paris: l'Harmattan, 2000.

Njoh, Ambe. "Gender Based Discrimination in Housing and Urban Development Policies in Cameroon." In *Feminization of Development Processes in Africa,* edited by Valentine James and James Etin. Westport, CT: Praeger, 1999.

Perlman, Janice E. *The Myth of Marginality: Urban Poverty and Politics in Rio de Janeiro.* Berkeley: University of California Press, 1976.

Rakodi, Carol. "Some Issues in Urban Development and Planning in Tanzania, Zambia and Zimbabwe." In *Urban and Regional Change in Southern Africa,* edited by David Drakakis-Smith. London: Routledge, 1992.

Simon, David D. *Cities, Capital, and Development: African Cities in the World Economy.* London: Belhaven Press, 1992.

Smith, David M., ed. *The Apartheid City and Beyond: Urbanization and Social Change in South Africa.* London: Belhaven Press, 1992.

Stren, Richard. "Urban Housing in Africa: The Changing Role of Government Policy." In *Housing Africa's Urban Poor,* edited by Philip Amis and Peter Lloyd. New York: Manchester University Press for the International African Institute, 1990.

Stren, Richard E., and Rodney A. White, eds. *African Cities in Crisis: Managing Rapid Urban Growth.* Boulder, CO: Westview Press, 1989.

"Sustainable Cities Revisited II." *Environment and Urbanization* 11, no. 2 (1999).

"Sustainable Cities Revisited III." *Environment and Urbanization* 12, no. 2 (2000).

Tait, John. *From Self-Help Housing to Sustainable Settlement: Capitalist Development and Urban Planning in Lusaka, Zambia.* Aldershot, U.K.: Avebury, 1997.

Tipple, A. Graham. "The Need for New Urban Housing in Sub-Saharan Africa: Problem or Opportunity?" *African Affairs* 93, no. 373 (1994): 587–608.

United Nations Agenda 21. *The UN Programme of Action from Rio.* New York: United Nations, 1992.

United Nations Development Programme. *UN World Population Prospects.* New York: United Nations, 2003.

White, Luise. *The Comforts of Home: Prostitution in Colonial Nairobi.* Chicago: University of Chicago Press, 1990.

NICI NELSON

'UTHMAN DAN FODIO (1754–1817).

With a program of Islamic reform, 'Uthman dan Fodio created the largest independent state in nineteenth-century Africa. He was born 'Uthman ibn Muhammad Fudi ibn 'Uthman ibn Salih (later known in Hausa as Shehu dan Fodio) in Gobir at Maratta, in the district of Galmi. His family were Islamic scholars by profession; he grew up speaking Fulfulde, the language of the Fulani (Fulbe) pastoralists, but his education, in Arabic, included learning from Berber as well as Fulani scholars. He started preaching at the age of twenty (1774), first in rural areas and then at the court of the sultan of Gobir; he was more populist in his approach than many of his contemporaries, teaching the basics of Islam in simple language to herdsmen, farmers, and women.

By 1804 'Uthman's following had grown so large that he posed a threat to the authorities in Gobir. Threatened with attack, on February 21, 1804, he made the hegira (withdrew with followers) to Gudu, where he was elected imam and launched the jihad against Muslim states that refused his leadership and continued to harass him and his followers. Because of his advancing age, he did not participate in the fighting. In 1806 he sent his son Muhammad Bello to Birnin Gada to hand out flags of command to supporters from other areas of Hausaland and beyond. On December 31, 1808, the last of the great Hausa cities, Zaria, was captured; the jihad had been successful and an area of over 200,000 square miles was united under 'Uthman's imamship. In 1812 he divided the region into four quarters, the north and east under his son Muhammad Bello, and the south and west under his brother 'Abdullahi dan Fodio. By 1810 the shaikh had retired to Sifawa to teach; he then moved in 1815 to Sokoto, the capital of the new regime, where he died.

'Uthman wrote over a hundred works in Arabic and probably some fifty poems, mainly in Fulfulde. In the course of his life he had twelve wives and at least one concubine; he had thirty-seven children, of whom the most notable were the caliphs Muhammad Bello, Abubaker Atiku, and Ahmad Rufa'i; the poet Muhammad Bukhari; the Sufi Muhammad Sambo; and his scholarly daughters Asma'u (author of at least sixty poems), Hadija, and Mariam. His tomb is still today a place of pilgrimage (*ziyara*).

See also **Asma'u, Nana; Bello, Muhammad; Islam; Literatures in African Languages: Hausa; Pilgrimages, Islamic.**

BIBLIOGRAPHY

Boyd, Jean. *The Caliph's Sister: Nana Asma'u, 1793–1865, Teacher, Poet, and Islamic Leader.* London: Totowa, 1989.

Hiskett, Mervyn. *The Sword of Truth: The Life and Times of the Shehu Usuman dan Fodio.* New York: Oxford University Press, 1973.

Last, Murray. *The Sokoto Caliphate.* New York: Humanities Press, 1967.

Lovejoy, Paul E. *Slavery, Commerce and Production in the Sokoto Caliphate of West Africa.* Trenton, NJ: Africa World Press, 2005.

MURRAY LAST

VAN RIEBEECK, JAN (1619–1677).

The Dutch colonial administrator Jan Van Riebeeck was born in the Netherlands. His father worked for the Dutch East India Company, and Jan probably traveled with him from an early age. Although trained as a clerk, he may have been a ship's surgeon. He became wealthy while working for the Dutch East India Company in Asia, where he gained a deep and lasting respect for the Chinese.

The company found, however, that he had been trading on his own account and punished him by fining him two months and seven days' wages and forbidding him from working ever again in Asia. The punishment was light because many others in the company were doing the same. It was therefore as a punishment that he led the expedition that founded a settlement on the Cape of Good Hope in 1652, the first white settlement in the area that later became South Africa.

The original plan had been simply to create a replenishing station for ships on their way to the East Indies, but Van Riebeeck added a fort to the plans, to protect his people against both Africans and Europeans of other nations. The fort would soon prove vital to the survival of the settlement. Van Riebeeck thus decided to create a colony largely on his own initiative. The settlement he founded eventually became Cape Town. He imported slaves (he wanted Chinese but got west Africans instead) and began cultivating land and purchasing cattle from the locals. He bought so many animals that the local herdsmen could not

sell him more, and he had to trade with others farther and farther away. Whenever he could not buy cattle, he became violent.

Eventually, through intimidation and cunning, Van Riebeeck's settlers owned so many cattle that they required all of the local grazing land. Their appropriation of grazing land led to war in 1659 with the local Khoesan peoples. The settlers retreated to their fort, where they had provisions, and the Khoesan eventually abandoned their siege. When their leader protested to Van Riebeeck that the land was not his, Van Riebeeck replied that it had become his by right of conquest. He began to protect settlements with hedges of thornbushes from the Caribbean, a policy that he had wanted to implement since 1651 and that would have a lasting effect on South Africa; the thornbushes originally separating "settler" from "native" became the architecture of apartheid. From the very beginning, black and white people lived apart.

Van Riebeeck would have liked to conquer the Khoesan rather than trade with them, as became clear when a group of Khoesan raided the settlement to steal cattle they must have regarded as their own, and killed one Dutchman, David Janssen. Van Riebeeck wrote to Holland and the response was a letter allowing him to kill only the murderer. A nineteenth-century chronicler says Van Riebeeck:

> replied that it would be impossible to detect the real perpetrator of the murder ... the correct way of relieving the settlement of a horde of idle and useless robbers would be to reduce them to servitude. He maintained that the provocation received was ample to justify such a proceeding, while the

Dutch explorer Jan Van Riebeeck (1619–1677). Working with the Dutch East India Company, Van Riebeeck first claimed the land that became Cape Town, South Africa, for the Dutch. MANSELL/TIME & LIFE PICTURES/GETTY IMAGES

advantages of obtaining ten or twelve hundred head of cattle to breed from, and a large number of slaves for service on the islands and in Batavia, would be very great. (Theal, pp. 56–57)

Van Riebeeck was as intelligent as he was extremely avaricious. He worked for a company that promoted pious men, and his religion was never incompatible with his job. The council that made all rules in the colony opened its meetings with the "Prayer of Van Riebeeck," a verbose petition that begins thus:

O Merciful and Benignant God and Heavenly Father, since it hath pleased Thy Godlike Majesty to call us to the management of the affairs of the General United Chartered Dutch Company here at the Cape of Good Hope, and we are gathered together with our attendant Council to that end in Thy Holy Name, in order to take, on the advice of said Council, such resolutions as may the most advance the interests of the aforesaid Company, maintain justice, and in time possibly tend to the propagation and spread of Thy true Reformed

Christian Faith among those wild and brutal folk to the glorification and honor of Thy Holy Name and to the benefit of our Lords Principal [the directors of the company], the which we cannot do without Thy gracious help,...(Leipoldt, 101–102)

Van Riebeeck remained in charge of the settlement until May 5, 1662. From 1662 to 1665 he returned to Asia, evidently reprieved, as governor of Malacca. In 1665 he was allowed to live in the Dutch colony of Batavia, where he died a rich man.

See also **Cape Coast; Cape Colony and Hinterland, History of (1600 to 1910); Cape Town; Colonial Policies and Practices; Travel and Exploration: European (1500 to 1800).**

BIBLIOGRAPHY

Leipoldt, Christian Louis. *Jan Van Riebeeck, a Biographical Study.* London: Longmans, Green and Co., 1936.

Riebeeck, Jan Van. *The Secret Letters of Jan Van Riebeeck*, trans. and ed. Robert Kirby. New York: Penguin, 1992.

Theal, George McCall. *Chronicles of Cape Commanders.* Cape Town: W. A. Richards and Sons, 1882.

ALEXANDER GOLDMAN

VASSA, GUSTAVUS. *See* **Equiano, Olaudah.**

VERWOERD, HENDRIK FRENSCH (1901–1966). The South African politician and architect of apartheid Hendrik Frensch Verwoerd was born in Amsterdam in September 1901 and moved to Cape Town with his family at the age of two. His father ran a grocery store and worked as a missionary for the Dutch Reformed Church, notorious for its theology of the suppression of "savages." Verwoerd was educated at Wynberg High School in Cape Town, Milton Boys School in Bulawayo in Southern Rhodesia (present-day Zimbabwe), and Brandfort High School before he attended the Afrikaans-language University of Stellenbosch in Cape Province and then the universities of Hamburg, Leipzig, and Berlin.

Verwoerd returned to South Africa in 1927, married Elizabeth Schoombee, and began a career teaching at the University of Stellenbosch. He was

Hendrik Frensch Verwoerd (1901–1966). South Africa's former prime minister speaks at Milner Park, April 1, 1960, sixteen days prior to the first assassination attempt against him. He was eventually stabbed to death by Dimitri Tsafendas, a parliamentary clerk in the House of Assembly. © TERRENCE SPENCER//TIME LIFE PICTURES/GETTY IMAGES

professor of applied psychology until 1932 and then professor of sociology and social work until 1937. Verwoerd was among a group of Stellenbosch professors who vocally opposed the Union government's decision to grant asylum to German Jewish refugees. Verwoerd's interest in politics grew, and he became a member of the National Party as well as of a secret society of influential Afrikaners, the Broederbond. In 1936 he helped to organize a conference on the "Poor White Problem," referring to impoverished rural Afrikaners and distracting attention from the much larger and much poorer African populations of the country; and, in 1937, became editor in chief of the Afrikaans daily *Die Transvaaler*, where he was famous for his anti-British, antisemitic, and pro-Nazi sentiments. He brought a lawsuit against a rival newspaper, the Johannesburg *Star*,

when an article appeared in it denouncing his Nazi beliefs. The case was dismissed on grounds that he was, in fact, sympathetic to the Nazi cause.

In 1948, the year that the National Party won control of the Union government, Verwoerd was nominated to the Union Senate, where he led the National Party from 1950 to 1958 and served as minister of native affairs. During this period, Verwoerd masterminded the philosophy of apartheid, that is, that each race, principally the whites and blacks of South Africa, ought to develop independently of one another: a tragic misrepresentation of the real prospects of Africans under the political, economic, and social domination of whites in his country. Verwoerd devised the concept of Bantustans, substandard and remote lands reserved to which Africans would be restricted on the basis government definition of their blackness.

In 1958 Verwoerd was elected member of the Heidelberg constituency in Parliament and prime minister. As he selected only whites to represent African interests, tension mounted throughout the continent. The Pan-Africanist Congress (PAC) organized a protest against Afrikaner policies in March 1960, and some 5,000 Africans came to participate. Nervous police responded to the peaceful gathering at Sharpeville by firing into the crowd indiscriminately, killing 68 and wounding over 300. The African National Congress (ANC) called a day of stay-at-home mourning in honor of those who died. International media drew attention to the conflict, and both the PAC and the ANC were subsequently banned as the government feared further eruptions. David Pratt, a white, English-speaking farmer, failed in that same year in his attempt to shoot Verwoerd in the head at an agricultural show in Johannesburg. Pratt was declared mentally unstable, and eventually committed suicide.

Verwoerd, relatively unscathed and fully recovered in two months, interested himself in making South Africa a full-fledged republic. In a 1960 referendum in which only whites voted, a majority of 52 percent favored South Africa's departure from the British Commonwealth and the creation of a Republic. In 1961 Verwoerd attended a Commonwealth prime ministers' conference in London, where his requests to have South Africa thus recognized brought furious debate and led him to withdraw his application. Two months later, however, the Republic of South Africa was officially established, and elections in 1962 strengthened the National Party's majority.

In 1963, the first Bantustan of Transkei was established with a government nominally of its own. The white government, nevertheless, remained in complete control of defense, international security, post offices, public transportation, immigration, and most financial matters. The "separate" government of Transkei was obliged to submit its parliament's laws to the South African president (Verwoerd) for approval. As Verwoerd refused to budge in his white supremacist stance, asserting that the slightest compromise would lead to the ultimate undoing of white rule, South Africa became increasingly isolated in the global realm. Verwoerd was stabbed to death on September 6, 1966, by a white man who had gained entrance to parliament by posing as a messenger.

See also **Apartheid; Cape Town.**

BIBLIOGRAPHY

Kenney, Henry. *Architect of Apartheid: H. F. Verwoerd, an Appraisal.* Johannesburg: J Ball, 1980.

SARAH VALDEZ

VIOLENCE. *See* **Urbanism and Urbanization; Warfare.**

VOODOO. *See* **Vodún.**

VODÚN. Vodún (French: Vodoun, English: Voodoo), the traditional religion in the southern part of the Republic of Bénin (formerly Dahomey), is also popular among the coastal ethnic groups of Western Nigeria, Togo, and Ghana. Vodún is widely known largely because slaves carried it to the Americas, especially to Haiti and Brazil. The term "Vodún" may refer either to the religious practice as a whole or to the particular deities. Vodún is translated, although not undisputed, as uncovered mystery, derived from *vo* (mystery, secret) and *dún* (unveil, to remove).

Hundreds of different types of Vodún are known, though most of them are only regionally venerated, the most widespread being Sakpatá, Heviosò, Gun, and Dangbé. The deities' attributed responsibilities are directed toward innerworldly problems: they determine human reproduction, and, as personalized natural forces acting in consensus with the ancestors, they intervene in the world of the humans. Sickness, childlessness, and natural catastrophes are ascribed sanctions of the Vodún. In punishing theft, marital infidelity, or disregard of ancestor veneration, they perform social control at different societal levels. The cause of a particular misfortune is identified by a diviner (*bokono*) using the most prominent type of divination, the *fá* oracle. To avoid disasters and to maintain order, humans have to follow the rules associated with Vodún and must perform regular sacrifices, ceremonies, and secret initiations.

Two elements central to Vodún are the practice of initiation and the institution of the priesthood. The initiation occurs ideally every five to seven years and lasts two or three years, depending upon the Vodún involved. Only one-fifth of the population of a given village may become initiates, the majority of whom are women. Priestly status is generally inherited and limited to men. The initiation has a dual function: enabling the propagation of the cult and providing protection to the individual initiates.

There is no upward mobility within the cult hierarchy. An initiate (*Vodúnsi*) can never acquire the status of a priest. Access to knowledge, power, and wealth characterize the priestly office; submission, obedience, and devotion, the initiate. The central feature of the initiation is the trance. It does not occur spontaneously during the ceremonies; rather, its elements and application are learned. The trance should not be seen as a liberation of the initiate, as in other possession cults. To the contrary, it is the manifestation of the absolute command of the Vodún's will over the body of its slave, or wife, the Vodúnsi. Trance is performed only in a controlled ritual setting, during ceremonies intended to invoke Vodún. The trance is not meaningful for its actors but has a political function for the cult in that it proves the existence of Vodún. Only the Vodúnsi, never the priest, fall into trance. The initiation is expensive and forms one of the sources of priestly income, and it is also a cause of a household's indebtedness and

Bocio symbolizing the Vodún Gun. The chain and the headiron, the material of weapons and the wide open eyes, symbolize the power associated with Gun. PHOTOGRAPH BY KAROLA ELWERT-KRETSCHMER

village level. Vodún is a norm-giving and norm-controlling institution—a local authority that extends beyond the sphere of its adherents and beyond religious functions. The priests regulate both religious and civil deviance such as theft, violence, marriage disputes, and divorce.

It would be naive, however, to assume that Vodún exists in harmony with other such social and political institutions. Vodún in fact competes with other local political institutions, such as councils of elders and state assemblies. It was a major source of political debate in southern Bénin, with interdictions of religious practices during the Marxist-Leninist period of Bénin's political history after 1975. The struggle for the functionalization of the cults' political influence reaches as far back as the time of the Dahomean Kingdom in the eighteenth century.

As an institution vested with power, Vodún faces criticism not only from its competitors but also from its followers. These critiques are not merely a phenomenon of modernization, as is often assumed. Vodún's detractors base their criticisms on the controlling functions of the priests of the religion; the substance, its perceived ability to lessen the burdens of life, on the other hand, is widely appreciated. The high costs for initiations and the multiyear seclusion of initiates are major causes of complaints, as are the arbitrariness and corruption that accompany the priests' exercise of social control. Finally, the secrecy surrounding Vodún, a common element within possession cults, gives rise to fears not only of transcendental sanctions but also (although this fear is usually unspoken) of the use of poison.

At the end of the colonial period came the development of new, less hierarchical religions that claimed some elements of Vodún, such as promise of protection and trance, but rejected other aspects, such as seclusion for initiation and secrecy. Some of these newer movements are still considered to be part of Vodún (such as the Glo and Tro religious variants), whereas others portray themselves as Christian (such as Christianisme Céleste). The late twentieth and early twenty-first centuries have seen an explosion in the religious market. Esoteric cults and evangelical sects have been imported from the United States, Europe, India, Japan, and Korea. In southern Bénin, not everyone practices Vodún; other religions find an audience. Religious affiliation

impoverishment. In some cases, priests are the wealthiest men in the village.

Vodún has generally been described as a belief system. But more precisely, Vodún is also a means of social control that fulfills political functions exercised by the priests. As judges, the priests are embedded in the system of social control at the is not considered to be exclusivity—people may practice the rituals of several religions simultaneously. Thus, any statistics regarding religious practice should be read with caution.

In the cities, Vodún's power to explain misfortune has become less convincing. The reference to pacts between lineage elders and natural deities is less plausible in a setting where individual human action, especially economic action, appears to be more important than collective action and the forces of nature.

See also **Bénin; Diasporas; Divination and Oracles; Initiation; Myth and Cosmology; Political Systems; Religion and Ritual; Spirit Possession; Witchcraft.**

BIBLIOGRAPHY

Blier, Suzanne Preston. *African Vodun. Art, Psychology and Power.* Chicago: The University of Chicago Press, 1995.

Elwert-Kretschmer, Karola. *Religion und Angst. Soziologie der Voodoo-Kulte.* Frankfurt/Main: Campus Verlag, 1997.

Rouget, Gilbert. *La musique et la transe.* Paris: Gallimard, 1990.

Verger, Pierre. *Dieux d'Afrique. Cultes des orishas et vodouns à l'anciennne côte des esclaves en Afrique et à Bahia, la Baie de tous les Saints au Brésil.* Paris: Hartmann, 1954.

KAROLA ELWERT-KRETSCHMER

WALĀTA. Walāta is a town located on the southern edge of the Sahara in present-day eastern Mauritania. The town probably began as a Mandé farming village, but by the thirteenth century (and perhaps much earlier) it had become involved in regional and trans-Saharan trade. As a center of trade, Walāta attracted settlers from afar and became a multiethnic town with a reputation for Islamic scholarship. Because of a long history of immigration, Walāta has been dominated by three successive cultural groups, and accordingly has been known by three different names: Bīru, Iwalātan, and Walāta. In its earliest period the town was known primarily by the Mandé name Bīru, and may have been part of the kingdom of Old Ghana. Later it was drawn into the kingdoms of Mali and then Songhay, and began also to be known by the Berber name Iwalātan. By the end of the Songhay period in the late sixteenth century, West African scholars began to refer to the town as Walāta, the Arabized form of Iwalātan.

This sequence of cultural transformation was primarily the result of immigration, first of Berber and later of Arabic-speaking peoples into a town that was originally Mandé-speaking. But it was also partly the result of the politics of representation. Mandé-speaking people did not generally leave Walāta as it took on a primarily Berber identity, nor did Berbers abandon the town during the process of its Arabization. Indeed, the earliest Walātī sources suggest that both the chief and the judge (qāḍī) of the town in 1658 were men who belonged to Soninké lineages famous for their scholarship. Yet by about 1800 there seems to have been few if any prominent persons left in Walāta willing to claim a Mandé or Berber identity. When the French conquered the region in 1900, they found that many old women could still speak some Azer, a dying local language of mixed Mandé and Berber origin.

See also **Immigrants and Immigration Groups; Mauritania.**

BIBLIOGRAPHY

Cleaveland, Timothy. "Reproducing Culture and Society: Women and the Politics of Gender, Age and Social Rank in Walāta." *Canadian Journal of African Studies* 34, no. 2 (2000): 189–217.

Cleaveland, Timothy. *Becoming Walāta: A History of Saharan Social Formation and Transformation.* Portsmouth, New Hampshire: Heinemann, 2002.

TIMOTHY CLEAVELAND

WARFARE

This entry includes the following articles:
OVERVIEW
CIVIL WARS
COLONIAL
INTERNAL REVOLTS
LIBERATION
NATIONAL AND INTERNATIONAL

OVERVIEW

Warfare, defined as organized armed combat between distinct political units with the aim to militarily subdue, conquer, or incapacitate opponents, has been as common in Africa as in other continents, but is marked there by several specific features. One is the tenuous relation between warfare and state formation in Africa, still relevant in modern post-colonial order. While in Europe since circa 1500 state formation and empire building proceeded in tandem with armed combat and constant techno-logical innovation, and while Asia or the Middle East knew ancient and often more durable central-ized states and empires built upon organized vio-lence, conquest, and control, Africa has shown a more fragmented picture. It has indeed seen the emergence of well-organized states or empires, such as Aksum (first to tenth century), the Fulani states, Bénin, Kanem-Bornu, Baghirmi, Mali, and Kongo. Many of such states were buttressed by a clear leadership elite, an organized army, and an administrative structure, but as contestation over resources and people was a constant concern their borders were open and shifting, and institutionali-zation was weak. Many of these African states pre-ceded colonization, and thus cannot have been formed as a response to it.

However, most of Africa consisted of large zones of small-scale, segmentary polities, often cul-turally related but without strong overlords or cen-tralization (e.g., in southern Ethiopia, the Lake Chad area, the Yoruba and Ibo areas of Nigeria, or East Africa). Second, the ethnolinguistic and regional diversity of Africa, as evident in low-scale, relatively sparsely populated units in often ecolog-ically vulnerable regions, induced many local con-flicts between competing rulers, based on environ-mental scarcity, economic control (trade routes), and specialization, as well as personal bonds of loyalty guided by conceptions of unitary authority and ruler prestige. In some cases, religious identity (Islam in the West African empires, Christianity in highland Ethiopia and in some postcolonial states), contributed to state formation, as several wars were fought under a religious cover or ideology. In the colonial era, local ethnoregional differences were played upon by colonial powers and, sometimes intentionally, became fault lines for conflict.

Third, warfare in Africa was more concerned with establishing loyalty of people as subjects than with conquest, subjection or resource access per se, although these came into play as dominant rule by

the victorious group solidified. Authority and the conduct of war were usually inspired by superna-tural symbolism and ritual. Loyalty was expressed in tribute payment by subject units or leaders, and authority was exercised through claims on people (slavery, pawnship, corvée labor, assistance in war) and, to a lesser extent, to land and other resources. Growing trade with outsiders—from the Middle East and Asia since the formation of Muslim states there in the eighth and ninth centuries, and Europeans since the fifteenth century—led to new elites and patterns of power, partly reinforced by the slave trade.

The establishment of colonial rule marked a watershed in the practices and frequency of African warfare, with most of the local-level conflicts forcibly reduced by colonial powers. Nevertheless, violent contestation occurred frequently, based on united action of previously distinct groups vis-à-vis the col-onial power, which in a sense served to forge greater units from the smaller ones and changed native mili-tary practices and tactics. In addition, as colonial rule was usually maintained by force (although with sur-prisingly small armies), there were major revolts against its authority, although in many cases (as in Somalia, Nigeria, or East Africa) local groups were also internally divided or pitted against each other. In the colonies, African armed forces—such as the King's African Rifles in British East Africa or the Eritrean *askari*s in Italian Libya—became well-trained pillars of support of the colonial rulers. Throughout modern African history, the often-asserted causal link between warfare and linguistic or ethnic ("tribal") and cultural diversity is quite tenuous, because other variables of a political and socioeconomic nature usually intervene.

THE PRECOLONIAL PERIOD

In precolonial times, Africa's various political units ranged from "acephalous," segmentary societies to chiefdoms to proto-states and empires. This scale goes from absent central authority to highly devel-oped centralized power, and a corresponding decline in the power of kinship groups and of ethnic or "tribal" identities. The number of polit-ical units in precolonial Africa is estimated to have been about 7,000, but they were in constant flux as to size and exact number. The variety and nature of these units was too diverse to be really able to speak of centralized states versus noncentralized states as essentially different types, because both

Weapons inventory. African Union soldiers and Somali government forces make an inventory of weapons turned in by businessmen based in the strife-torn capital of Mogadishu, May 2007. Hundreds of weapons including heavy and small machine guns and rocket-propelled grenades were surrendered in support of a government disarmament plan. STRINGER/AFP/GETTY IMAGES

dimensions—of central power and of state organization in the sense of a governance support structure—moved on a continuum. Some "states" fell back into fragmented, decentralized units, and from various so-called acephalous societies or ritual chiefdoms powerful states emerged through the use of military force. While segmentary societies had no central rule or standing army, they had ordered relations of conflict and warfare, and indeed can be said to have allowed relatively peaceful relations among the various political units.

As warfare in precolonial Africa was much less focused on territorial gain and settlement of new lands than on the enforcing of loyalty of people and on booty, conquered groups were often incorporated and became full members of the dominant society. As in ancient Greece, warfare was also a means of acquiring adulthood or social mobility on the basis of prestige and status gained in battle, a feature that can be seen in age-grade societies with

a "warrior" class. Islam as a political ideology played a major role in warfare in West Africa, as in the Fulani expansion, and in several wars in Northeast Africa, like the sixteenth-century *jihad* of the Somali-Afar warrior Ahmed ibn Ibrahim against Christian Ethiopia, and the conquests of the nineteenth-century Ottoman-Egyptian ruler Mohammed 'Ali in Sudan. Islam provided the rationale for conquest and expansion in non-Muslim territories and was a divine "charter" for aspiring rulers.

The technology of warfare in precolonial Africa was fairly constant until the early nineteenth century when global trade started bringing in firearms and other modern equipment. Also in preparations for battle and in tactics there was less a fixation on applying new techniques and means to win than was the case in Europe. But also in Africa an important role was played by cavalry forces (both in Sudanic West Africa and eastern Africa), and the military organization and fighting skills of African populations and states were impressive.

In the precolonial period, slavery was an important and constant incentive to make war. Slave raiding and selling frequently pitted clan and ethnic groups against each other, and indigenous rulers used war captives or sold them to outsiders. This was continued and intensified after the contacts with Portuguese and other expanding European colonials who bought, captured, and transported African slaves to the Americas. Also in the relations with Muslim Arabs since the tenth century, slavery (to the Middle and Far East) played a very large role and rearranged politics and groups relations, notably in Eastern Africa. In North Africa, local Algerian Muslim slave traders attacked European ships and captured and sold tens of thousands of white Europeans as slaves. Other familiar motives for war were loot, raiding cattle or other possessions, revenging insults to honor or personal prestige, or elite competition.

In Africa, war codes existed, with restraining rules of engagement and of whom to attack, kill, or capture. Only in the nineteenth century devastating, arbitrary, all-out violence emerged as a mode of war (e.g., under Zulu king Shaka, who established a terror-like rule under which subjects were at the mercy of royal whims). During the establishment of colonial rule, indigenous African political units and armies ultimately succumbed to the better military, technological, and administrative skills of the invaders.

THE COLONIAL PERIOD

Warfare was part of the colonial expansion in Africa since the late nineteenth century, which covered the entire continent except the ancient state of Ethiopia, and meant in itself a qualitative change in local warfare patterns, both as to technology (massive use of new types of firearms) and responses evoked among local, indigenous populations. The establishment of colonial rule in Africa required considerable military effort. Major setbacks for Western powers were, for instance, the Zulu war against the British in 1879 and the battle of Adwa in 1896, where Ethiopians defeated the invading Italian colonial army.

Apart from the often, but not always, violent manner in which the new territories in Africa were carved out after the Berlin Conference of 1884–1885,

colonial rulers also engaged in regular punitive expeditions, for example, among the Turkana, the Ashanti, the Nuer, and in Madagascar, Guinea, and Niger. In Namibia, the Germans perpetrated a genocide-like mass-killing of revolting Herero people.

One important effect of colonial warfare and the establishment of colonies under Western hegemony was that incipient local processes of state formation, which often result from conflict and warfare, did not run their course, as they were cut short and redefined under colonial rule. The imposition of colonial order, resulting in a new geographical-administrative grid across the landscape and the demography, stopped local wars and brought disparate, conflicting groups together in new overarching units, often with unexpected borders that cut across old polities and ethnolinguistic groups. The colonial state claimed the monopoly of violence, and local wars and raiding were not tolerated. While precolonial patterns of small-scale warfare were thus largely halted, the new order did not eliminate the roots of deep-seated conflicts, several of which re-emerged in postcolonial times, for example, in Congo, Sudan, and Somalia. The political authoritarianism and often racist-discriminatory overtones of colonial rule, together with its economic policies, generated contestation and rebellion. This accelerated after the end of World War II and led to independence struggles under newly emerging local elites locked in competition for power.

THE POSTCOLONIAL PERIOD

Before African countries gained independence around 1960, some fought a war to realize or confirm it, as in Kenya (Mau Mau), Algeria, or the former Portuguese colonies. In other countries, internal divisions soon led to rebellions and civil war, as for instance in Sudan in 1956. Sudan has remained the most violent and divided country of Africa and a prime example of perpetual postcolonial warfare, with an ongoing war in Darfur, until 1915 an independent state. Latecomers were Namibia, gaining independence in 1990 after a protracted war with South Africa, and Eritrea, which after a long guerrilla war of varying intensity since 1961 seceded from Ethiopia in 1993, reproducing the borders of Italy's *Colonia Eritrea* (1890–1941).

At independence, the inherited machinery and institutions of the centralized, authoritarian colonial states, including the national army, became the prime loci of struggle. They were in essence maintained after independence and figured as resource machines and as control mechanisms over a very diverse population only partly incorporated in the state domain. Central authority exercised over the entire formal state territory was aimed at, but marginal areas, such as those inhabited by segmentary, pastoral peoples, were neglected and weakly policed.

The interference of outside forces in Africa has always been significant. Postcolonial political struggle and warfare soon became implicated in Cold War politics, with the West and the Soviet bloc (and to a lesser extent the Chinese) supporting either the incumbent regimes or insurgent movements in a proxy power contest, supplying their allies with arms and funds. Guerrilla wars that had a basis either in economics ("greed") or political-cultural motives ("grievances"), or both, grew into protracted armed combat, with ever-larger numbers of civilians as victims and increasing recruitment of child soldiers. Marxism long provided the ideology or idiom of insurgent and guerrilla movements. These wars led to regime change in Angola, Mozambique, Ethiopia, and Chad. Some wars were accompanied by social-revolutionary changes.

Mass killings as a result of domestic warfare occurred in Burundi since the early 1970s and in the genocide in Rwanda in 1994, prepared by the then incumbent regime and carried out by army units. Also the civil wars in Angola and Mozambique exacted heavy toll. Since 2003 Sudan has been involved in a state-supported "creeping genocide" in Darfur with an estimated 280,000 to 300,000 victims as of 2007.

Trends in postcolonial warfare have significantly changed since the mid-twentieth century, with few states able to effectively establish a monopoly over the use of violence or control the scale of killing. Victims result not only from the fighting but also increasingly from war-related disease and famine due to targeted destruction of livelihoods. Postcolonial wars have become entangled with economic competition and racketeering, both from the side of the governments and the insurgent movements: tendencies of criminalization of the state have occurred, with corruption and illegal trade led by sections of the ruling elite blooming.

Civil wars in Africa are frequent and cyclical, tending to offset development gains and state distributive capacity, thus perpetuating the reasons for disadvantaged regions or groups to continue to fight; Collier (2004) called this the "conflict trap." This situation, combined with the great dependency on primary resources and commodity exports as part of national GDP (e.g., oil), has led to higher (civil) conflict sensitivity of African countries in the postindependence era (see Collier 2003; Fearon & Laitin 2003).

Warfare in Africa shows a combination of technological innovation, via the use of modern weaponry (automatic weapons, rocket-propelled grenades, land mines, machine-gun mounted four-wheel drives, missiles) and air power (as in the Ethio-Eritrean war and in the Darfur war), with traditional patterns of warfare, such as raiding, ambushing, and looting by small, mobile bands of fighters who are loosely organized and operate rather independently from larger (state) armies. Examples are the Revolutionary United Front (RUF) in Sierra Leone in the 1990s, the rebellion of the Lord's Resistance Army in northern Uganda since the early 1990s, the militias in the Democratic Republic of the Congo (DRC) since the late 1990s, and the *Janjaweed* militias that scourge Darfur since 2003. This has resulted in massive abuse and killing of noncombatant civilians, a loss of ideological-political aims of combatants, and the emergence of a state of permanent "low-intensity" warfare that is not decided in battles or peace agreements because the fighting partners (states or movements) are diffuse and fragmented. The war in the DRC Congo is one example. Warfare in such cases has become an alternative, economically rooted way of life for socially uprooted youngsters and is usually accompanied by predatory accumulation of primary resources not controlled by the state. The rise of well-armed militias or vigilante groups that assume policing functions and claim political power (e.g., in Somalia, in the Niger Delta, and in urban areas of Nigeria) through extensive use of warlike violence is a related phenomenon.

These armed conflicts refer to an emerging economic logic of warfare; many of them become enmeshed in competition for resources, fuelled by the structural crisis of youth and by state failure (see Keen 2003).

A new conflict dynamic since the end of the Cold War and the accelerated demise of the postcolonial order is provided by Islamism: political Islam as an absolutist, unitary ideology of resistance against local divisions as well as foreign interference or even presence. While this is a movement that emerged in the Middle East, it has expanded to Africa, where the incumbent regime in Sudan since 1989 can be said to have followed an Islamist agenda. The war against non-Muslim southern Sudan (until 2005) was also a conversion war with elements of *jihad*. The evolution of certain Somali clan-based militias into a fighting force under the Islamic Courts Council, expanding over central Somalia, is another example. Various Islamist political and youth movements in East Africa and in Nigeria can also be seen in this light. Although the terrorist tactics of Middle Eastern, Al Qaeda–inspired branches of political Islam are not popular in Africa, these might spread with the arrival of non-African militants, as observed in Sudan, Somalia, and Kenya. In some aspects, Islamist violence signifies a return to early Muslim ideas of warfare against "unbelievers," and highlights again the vital, and often underestimated, role that religious, or more in general supernatural, beliefs play in African warfare.

PERSISTENCE AND CHANGE IN AFRICAN WARFARE IN THE TWENTY-FIRST CENTURY

While states in Africa still wage wars, like Sudan (in Darfur), Angola (in Cabinda), and Ethiopia-Eritrea, warfare in Africa is tending to become decentered, localized, and disorganized. Many conflicts are a fall-out of nonresolved, low-intensity war, and in the absence of effective state policies become imbricated in economic enterprise and survival struggles. Several armed conflicts, like Darfur since 2003, attract bandits and adventurers, who invest in violence to gain resources and enjoy themselves. These war opportunists come from a wide area and their activities may give rise to new local power formations competing with existing state structures. This indicates that armed conflicts in Africa have a tendency to cross borders. No modern African war is limited to just one country, either due to the populations involved being spread out over more than one country, or because the warring parties try to wage proxy wars and provoke regime change in the enemy country. In 2006 this was evident in Eritrea's activities in Somalia opposing pro-Ethiopia factions, and Sudan's in Chad, undermining the incumbent regime.

A notable feature of warfare in Africa in the early twenty-first century is its cyclical character. Wars end in one place—such as Sierra Leone, Angola, Burundi, Rwanda, Liberia, Ethiopia-Eritrea, Mozambique—but emerge in another: Somalia, Congo, Sudan, Chad, Côte d'Ivoire. Similar wars initiate in countries that have the same complex of problems, like persistent government deficit in service delivery or education, political repression, chronic poverty and youth unemployment, high population growth, ethnoregional tensions, or religious extremism. Wars can also return in different form in the same country (as in Congo, Somalia, Ethiopia-Eritrea, and Sudan). In addition, most current African wars are civil wars, provoked by government repression of insurgent groups, or by inter-regional, interethnic, or intercommunal disputes, which by themselves can also give rise to new subwars.

The social and psychological heritage of decades of warfare in Africa is important: most countries that saw war in the postcolonial era have a hard time to establish normality and regenerate the social fabric, especially when the needs of the defeated or affected people are neglected, or simply cannot be met due to lack of resources and poverty. In this sense, when people have been impoverished and victimized in a humiliating manner, war often returns after one or two generations if conditions do not allow them to "forget" and start life anew.

State capacity and legitimacy in Africa generally remain weak, and the social and political integration of many citizens is superficial. Almost fifty years of postcolonial rule have not allowed African states to effectively suppress warfare.

See also **Aid and Development: Humanitarian Assistance; Colonial Policies and Practices; Islam; Military Organizations; Postcolonialism; Shaka Zulu; Slave Trades; Slavery and Servile Institutions; Sudan: Wars.**

BIBLIOGRAPHY

Clayton, Anthony. *Frontiersmen: Warfare in Africa since 1950.* London: UCL Press, 1999.

Collier, Paul. "Natural Resources, Development and Conflict: Channels of Causation and Policy Interventions." Washington, DC: World Bank paper, 2003.

Collier, Paul. "Development and Conflict." Oxford: Centre for the Study of African Economies, 2004.

Davis, Robert C. *Christian Slaves, Muslim Masters: White Slavery in the Mediterranean, the Barbary Coast and Italy, 1500–1800.* Basingstoke, U.K. and New York: Palgrave-Macmillan, 2004.

Ellis, Stephen. "The Old Roots of Africa's New Wars." *Internationale Politik und Gesellschaft* 2 (2004): 29–43.

Evans-Pritchard, Edward E. "Zande Warfare." *Anthropos* 52, no. 2 (1957): 239–262.

Fadiman, Jeffrey A. *An Oral History of Tribal Warfare: The Meru of Mt. Kenya.* Athens: Ohio University Press, 1982.

Fearon, James, and David Laitin. "Ethnicity, Insurgency and Civil War." *American Political Science Review* 97, no. 1 (2003): 75–90.

Herbst, Jeffrey. *States and Power in Africa.* Princeton, NJ: Princeton University Press, 2000.

Keen, David. "Greedy Elites, Dwindling Resources, Alienated Youths: The Anatomy of Protracted Violence in Sierra Leone." *Internationale Politik und Gesellschaft*, vol. 2 (2003): 67–94.

Kurimoto, Eisei, and Simon Simonse, eds. *Conflict Age and Power in Northeast Africa.* Oxford: James Currey, 1998.

Lamphear, John. *The Scattering Time: Turkana Responses to Colonial Rule.* Oxford: Clarendon Press, 1992.

Spring, Christopher. *African Arms and Armor.* London: British Museum Press, 1993.

Thornton, John K. *Warfare in Atlantic Africa, 1500–1800.* London: UCL Press, 1999.

Walter, E. V. *Terror and Resistance.* New York: Oxford University Press, 1969.

JON ABBINK

CIVIL WARS

Since the end of World War II, most wars in Africa have involved armed combat between armed groups within the same country. This trend parallels global trends since the late 1940s and the beginning of the Cold War. African civil wars have changed over the past century, and they have been given many labels. They have been called wars of liberation, secessionist wars, and wars of attrition, insurgent conflicts, and resource wars. These names reflect the views of outsiders regarding conflicts as well as the strategies used in fighting these wars.

ANTICOLONIALISM AND CIVIL WARS

Beginning in the 1950s, most wars in Africa were anticolonial struggles of national liberation, which were fought to end what the international community came to view as the illegitimate rule of foreigners over a defined community. "Liberation insurgents" fought these conflicts and many Africans considered them national heroes. Other wars during this period were conflicts over national unification. These wars stressed the unity of groups inside the colony, and usually masked underlying ethnic and religious cleavages. During the 1960s and 1970s, at the height of the Cold War, many antigovernment groups adopted the ideology of their outside patron states. For example, during these years, Portugal fought Eastern bloc-backed communist rebels in its African colonies of Angola, Cape Verde, Guinea-Bissau, and Mozambique.

While many African fighters in these liberation wars were from rural areas, the leaders of these nationalist struggles were often university-educated urbanites. This may seem inconsistent to the unity of a liberation struggle, for the narrower the original social and cultural gaps between leaders and the cadres, the more likely they are to develop effective bases of legitimate leadership. Such leaders sought the safety of rural areas where they would be forced to communicate and live with peasant populations. During this process, incipient liberation leaders would come to understand the realities of peasant economies, social life, and the power of traditional myths and rituals.

In many of these struggles, the liberation organizations' strategies followed specific principles. The first task of the leadership was to travel through the rural areas and explain their political struggle to peasants. This tactic not only garnered support and mobilized locals to join movements; it created a relationship with local notables. The second step in the liberation movement strategy was to send in the military arm of the organization to establish a "liberated zone" and maintain a dominant presence in the villages. The dismantling of colonial infrastructure and the establishment of parallel hierarchies—rebel administrative and economic institutions that affirmed the insurgent presence and administered to the local population's needs—followed this process. The focus on out-administering and not on outfighting the enemy allowed the liberation insurgents to present locals with alternatives to repressive forms of rule and further highlighted to the cadres that the primary condition for mass support lay in the political realm, not the military arena. The use of violence against the masses was selective during early anti-colonial struggles in Africa. In a speech made to a local village in Portuguese-controlled Guinea-Bissau, revolutionary leader Amilcar Cabral, a Lisbon-trained agronomist, explained to villagers that "soldiers must never abuse the people. We must go on being united. Soldiers who turn their guns against the people are worse than the Portuguese" (Chaliand, 198).

Counterinsurgency strategies sought to undermine insurgents' social control in their liberated zones. Colonial authorities recruited informers, resettled rural people to isolate them from insurgents, and deployed commando units, often posing as insurgents to determine who in local communities supported the liberation struggle.

LATE AND POST–COLD WAR CONFLICTS

Many subsequent insurgent organizations exhibited much less hierarchy in their organization and appeared to exercise less discipline over their members. The causes of this change are found in the growing fractionalization of conflict and the numerous commercial activities of these groups. Some insurgents merged with organized crime networks and used terror and destabilization of local societies to build criminalized economies that they control. As one scholar describes, "[R]ather than highly organized armed forces based on a strict command hierarchy, wars are fought by loosely knit groups of regulars, irregulars, cells, and not infrequently by locally-based warlords under little or no central authority," who preyed upon local civilians (Holsti, 20). Vulnerable groups such as women, children, and refugees are often the primary targets as insurgents use rape and kidnapping as weapons of war.

Some explain this supposed nonideological tendency among insurgents in terms of changing local social structures, such as the rise of an urban "lumpen proletariat" that has little in common with the rural peasantry and uses violence as the only way to control them. For example, politicians in Sierra Leone were culpable in much of the violent behavior of "lumpenized youth" after recruiting thugs and criminals into national security apparatuses, detaching these new experts in violence from the social groups in whose name insurgents previously fought (Kandeh, 349). For these scholars, "new wars" are nonideological because they draw in the rural poor in ways that are much more difficult to mobilize and control with programmatic platforms. David Snow claims that these new wars are absent of a discernible political ideology altogether—something with which the group can justify its activities. While individual fighters are not bereft of ideas, they either have the wrong ones or they cannot coordinate among themselves. The problem then is one of poor leadership and faulty coordination.

Since the 1980s there has been a great deal of attention to the relationship between economic performance and the incidence and organization of internal conflict. The link between civil war and countries that have low incomes, poor growth rates, and reliance on natural resource exploitation for incomes has been tested with significant results. In his 2000 work, Paul Collier identified insurgent warfare as similar to organized crime. He and others link the scramble for natural resources to a perceived tendency for insurgents to abuse local community members in favor of exploiting opportunities in the global economy. Collier views the rational choices of insurgents in the context of individual incentives and the availability of lootable resources. In this context, insurgents fight for personal enrichment obtained through loot they seize in conflict. Material incentives are used to recruit participants in conflict; high levels of civilian abuse are exhibited. Several United Nations reports indicated that rebels and government soldiers in Sierra Leone and Liberia fought among themselves to seize diamonds and timber. This dynamic is the theme of much scholarship in which historians argue that these resources promote predatory conflict because insurgents do not have to mobilize local people to control and profit from these resources. It is sufficient to control a mine site or forest and organize commercial transactions with outsiders who supply guns and money in exchange.

Many scholars ignore the wider political context of this behavior. While a few such as Collier point to the presence of weak state institutions as contributing to the rise of predatory nonideological insurgents, most of the conflict literature discounts the ideological capacity of individual fighters. These two categories see a decline in ideological motivations and expression among insurgents, yet they differ on where they perceive the deficit. For the former, it is the problem of the society and leadership. For the latter, individual fighters do not seem to be capable of articulating ideologies.

CAUSES OF INTERNAL WARS IN AFRICA

Explanations that include ethnic diversity and the lack of political authority in rural areas compete with those that identify causes in personal calculations linked to the exploitation of economic opportunities. These explanations have some merit. One observes that at the same time as some insurgents fight as predatory looters in the 1990s (i.e., Charles Taylor's National Patriotic Front of Liberia), one finds at the same time insurgents like the Rwandan Patriotic Front, among the most disciplined and hierarchically organized insurgent groups in Africa's history.

Circumstances related to the ethnic diversity of African countries clearly contribute to the shape of conflicts. Colonial rule created these states out of many pre-existing polities and often mutually antagonistic communities. European colonizers created boundaries according to their own economic and political aims. Insurgencies of the late twentieth and early twenty-first centuries such as that found in Eritrea and the growth of ethnic-based vigilante movements in countries like Congo and Nigeria show dissatisfaction with the political arrangements of existing states and not just a desire to capture it.

A consistent theme throughout independent Africa's history has been that many African states lack the capacity for political control in rural areas. When a government's control does not extend far into outlying areas, it cannot monitor borders and arms traffickers, smugglers, and refugees can cross unchallenged. Some scholars, including Claire Metelits in her 2004 work, find that insurgents will reject the political and material resources of conforming to international norms of democracy if they believe they will lose power by doing so. While political control in areas where prior state control did not reach is better than no order at all, such dominance can promote predatory economies, or so-called warlordism.

These explanations for the prevalence of internal conflicts in Africa are not exhaustive. One major factor in the ubiquity of intrastate conflicts in Africa in the past and present is the nature of the international political system, especially since decolonization that occurred from 1960 onward and the associated norm of noninterference. During the 1960s wars of liberation, outside powers were quick to recognize anticolonial insurgents as rightful rulers of newly independent states. But these wars and military coups weakened these states, as they generated refugees, trans-border migration, and internally displaced people. Now armed groups contend for more fragmenting states. This means that even small groups can challenge Africa's weaker governments and make their own bid for power. Intrastate conflict is more violent and prevalent because the fragmentation of the ruling elite coalitions in states such as Somalia, the Congo, and Liberia. Political cliques in the regime fight each other and become more violent against local communities whose fighters are incorporated as tools of manipulation and support.

See also **Cabral, Amílcar Lopes; Cold War; Ethnicity; Military Organizations; Postcolonialism; Taylor, Charles Gahnhay.**

BIBLIOGRAPHY

Ahmad, Eqbal. "Revolutionary Warfare and Counterinsurgency." In *Guerrilla Strategies: An Historical Anthology from the Long March to Afghanistan*, ed. Gerard Chaliand. Berkeley: University of California Press, 1982.

Allen, Chris. "Warfare, Endemic Violence and State Collapse in Africa." *Review of African Political Economy* 81 (1999): 367–284.

Chaliand, Gerard. "With the Guerrillas in 'Portuguese' Guinea." In *Guerrilla Strategies: An Historical Anthology from the Long March to Afghanistan*, ed. Gerard Chaliand. Berkeley: University of California Press, 1982.

Clapham, Christopher. *Africa and the International System: The Politics of State Survival.* Cambridge, U.K.: Cambridge University Press, 1996.

Collier, Paul. "Rebellion as a Quasi-criminal Activity." *Journal of Conflict Resolution* 44, no. 6 (2000): 839–853.

Collier, Paul, and Anke Hoeffler. *Greed and Grievance in Civil War.* World Bank research paper, 2001.

Collier, Paul, and Anke Hoeffler. "On the Incidence of Civil War in Africa." *Journal of Conflict Resolution* 46, no. 1 (2002): 13–28.

Holsti, Kalevi J. *The State, War, and the State of War.* Cambridge, U.K.: Cambridge University Press, 1996.

Humphreys, Macartan, and Jeremy M. Weinstein. *Handling and Manhandling Civilians in Civil War: Determinants of the Strategies of Warring Factions*. Paper presented at the conference, Techniques of Violence in Civil War. PRIO, Oslo, Norway, 2004.

Kaldor, Mary. *New and Old Wars: Organized Violence in a Global Era*. Stanford, CA: Stanford University Press, 1999.

Kandeh, Jimmy D. "Ransoming the State: Elite Origins of Subaltern Terror in Sierra Leone. *Review of African Political Economy* 81 (1999): 349–366.

Keen, David. 1998. *The Economic Functions of Violence in Civil Wars*. New York: Oxford University Press, 1998.

Metelits, Claire. "Reformed Rebels? Democratization, Global Norms, and the Sudan People's Liberation Army." *Africa Today* 51, no. 1 (2004): 65–84.

Mkandawire, Thandika. "The Terrible Toll of Post-Colonial 'Rebel Movements' in Africa: Towards an Explanation of the Violence against the Peasantry." *Journal of Modern African Studies* 40, no. 2 (2002): 181–215.

Reno, William. *Warlord Politics and African States*. Boulder, CO: Lynne Rienner Publishers, 1998.

Ross, Michael L. "How Do Natural Resources Influence Civil War? Evidence from Thirteen Cases." *International Organization* 58 (Winter 2004): 35–67.

Snow, David. *Uncivil Wars: International Security and the New Internal Conflicts*. Boulder, CO: Lynne Rienner Publishers, 1996.

Van Creveld, Martin. *The Transformation of War*. New York: Free Press, 1991.

Weinstein, Jeremy. *Inside Rebellion: The Political Economy of Rebel Organization*. Cambridge, MA: Kennedy School of Government, Harvard University, 2003.

CLAIRE METELITS

COLONIAL

Until the nineteenth century, the interior of Africa remained largely in the hands of African peoples. Except for the colonies at the temperate extremities of the continent, Algeria and South Africa, the European presence in Africa was limited to a series of coastal trading enclaves. Indeed, as late as 1876, over 90 percent of the continent was still in indigenous hands. Over the next three decades, however, the situation would change radically. A scramble to seize African territory erupted in the late 1870s, and by 1914 only Ethiopia and Liberia would remain free of European control.

In his widely read primer on colonial warfare, *Small Wars: Their Principles and Practice* (1896), British Colonel Charles E. Callwell wrote that the small wars waged by the imperial powers in Africa fell into three main categories: (1) external campaigns of conquest or annexation; (2) expeditions to quell lawlessness or sedition or to protect settlers against aggression; and (3) campaigns abroad to avenge a wrong or to eliminate a dangerous enemy. From this account, the colonel obviously believed that some colonial wars were the result of *proactive* decisions made in European capitals, while others clearly constituted *reactions* to crises or provocations at the periphery.

Modern military historians tend to place much more emphasis on the reactive nature of European expansion. In this they follow the lead of the greatly influential study of British imperialism by Ronald Robinson and John Gallagher, *Africa and the Victorians: The Official Mind of Imperialism* (1961), which, by shifting the locus of initiative in the scramble for empire from metropolitan capitals to the global periphery, made the extra-European world an active and indispensable participant in the process. The two historians had argued that "peripheral flux," often the result of instability caused by the waxing and waning of indigenous "secondary empires," forced the hand of European powers that otherwise would have been reluctant to intervene in Africa.

"Flux" had to be stifled to prevent rival nations from taking advantage of it or to forestall the loss of markets or sources of raw materials. Not all the "flux" was the result of indigenous activity. Some imperial expansionism was the result of machinations by "men on the spot," ambitious army officers or colonial administrators who sought to achieve renown or promotions or to steal a march on an imperial rival. The latter phenomenon underscores the central role of the "secular religion" of the nineteenth century—nationalism—in imperial expansion. This was most obvious in the eagerness of the two new European nation-states, Germany and Italy, to obtain colonies and thus legitimacy as great powers. Italy, finally, sought colonies in Africa as an outlet for its surplus population, a hugely unsuccessful enterprise as most Italian emigrants opted to go to South America or the United States.

MOBILIZATION AND WEAPONRY

African military organization in the era of the colonial wars usually took one of four different forms. In some states, soldiers were raised locally and fought as bands from their home areas under territorial chiefs, in the fashion of feudal Europe. This was probably the most common kind of African armed force. Typical examples were the armies of Ethiopia and the Ashanti empire in present-day Ghana. In other states, soldiers were mobilized in age sets and then organized into regiments. This was the system adopted by the various Nguni peoples of southeastern Africa: the Zulus, of course, but also the Swazis of Swaziland, the Ndebele of Zimbabwe, and the Gaza Nguni of southern Mozambique. "Citizen armies" predominated in much of West Africa. All free adult males capable of bearing arms were subject to call-up in case of war. Finally, while there were units of full-time professional soldiers in Africa, they were rare and most of them emerged in the mid- to late nineteenth century, in emulation of the European armies they fought. They functioned as elite or specialist formations within traditional armies: musketeers early in the century, riflemen later on. Examples of this phenomenon include the battalion of musketeers raised for 'Abd al-Qādir's army fighting the French in Algeria in the 1840s and the rifle-equipped formations in the armies of Samori in West Africa and the Mahdi and his successors in the Sudan in the 1880s and 1890s.

In terms of organization, European armies operating in Africa fell into two main categories. Britain's troops in Africa were drawn from the regular army back home (or the Indian Army in the subcontinent) and dispatched as expeditionary forces. Italy's colonial army, the *Corpo Speciale*, followed a similar pattern. When troops were required in Africa, units were drafted for the purpose from the country's conscript army, fitted out in tropical kit at the colonial force's base in Naples, and shipped out. The other European powers involved in the African colonial wars tended to base their troops permanently in Africa. France's *Armée d'Afrique* and Foreign Legion made their home in Algeria, while the Marine Corps, whose African contingents did most of France's fighting in West Africa, had a permanent base in Senegal. Germany and Portugal, who fielded fewer European soldiers in Africa than the other colonial powers, maintained small contingents of volunteers from their regular armies in their various colonies but relied very heavily upon locally raised African troops to do the fighting. For the Germans, the exception to this pattern was South West Africa (the future Namibia), where its small military establishment consisted entirely of white mounted infantry, backed up by a settler militia.

The wars of colonial conquest in Africa coincided with a revolution in military weaponry in the West. Until the mid-nineteenth century, a rough parity in armaments had existed between Africans and European invaders. Most African armies were well acquainted with gunpowder weapons, the exceptions being those who, like the Zulus, abjured them for cultural reasons. Beginning in the 1840s and 1850s, however, technological innovations appeared in Europe that raised little or no echo among non-Western peoples: the submarine telegraph; steam-powered iron warships; breech-loading, rapid firing shoulder arms, handguns, and artillery; and, ultimately, the machine gun.

This has led some historians of the African colonial wars to the not surprising but nevertheless unwarranted conclusion that military technology was the determining factor in the subsequent European conquests. To begin with, there was a considerable lag between the availability of the new weapons and their actual appearance on African battlefields. In some cases, they never arrived at all. The French, for example, managed to absorb most of West and Equatorial Africa into their empire without use of the machine gun. Artillery was too cumbersome to be easily transported across the plains and deserts or through the rain forests of the African continent. Nor did the presence of the new weaponry on the battlefields of Africa necessarily guarantee European victory, as the British disaster at Isandlwana during the Anglo–Zulu War of 1879 amply demonstrates. A more satisfying, reliable, and historical explanation of European success in the African colonial wars than the thesis of triumphant technology is the ability of Europeans to recruit and deploy large armies of indigenous soldiers.

Nineteenth-century European armies, faced with growing commitments elsewhere and still wary of exposing their white soldiers to tropical diseases, bad water, and sunstroke, turned to mass recruitment of indigenous troops to wage war on their behalf in

Africa. France used the largest number of African troops. By the 1880s almost all of its gains in West Africa were the work of African light infantry (*Tirailleurs Sénégalais*) commanded by French officers. It was the Germans, however, who employed the largest percentage of African troops. In 1912 their colonial army, or *Schutztruppe*, outside South West Africa comprised 226 whites and 2,664 Africans. Britain also relied heavily on "native" soldiers in Africa. In 1902, the 11,500 troops following the Union Jack in Africa included just 300 white officers and NCOs (noncommissioned officers). As historian David Killingray argued, "European empires in Africa were gained principally by African mercenary armies, occasionally supported by white or other colonial troops" (1989).

STRATEGIES AND TACTICS

The armies of the European imperial powers chose to see their campaigns in Africa as "wars against nature"—disease, heat, distance, lack of food and water, inhospitable terrain—and only secondarily against human foes. Thus they saw no need to adopt a specific doctrine for fighting small wars. In line with the Napoleonic ethos that continued to inspire them, European commanders sought to maneuver indigenous enemies into pitched battles where their superior firepower and fire discipline would bring decisive victory. Their African opponents for the most part proved only too ready to oblige them, a major factor in the rapid conquest of the continent by the European powers. Few African insurgents in the nineteenth century responded to attack by going over to guerrilla warfare. A prominent exception was the army of 'Abd al-Qādir in Algeria in the 1840s. Algerian resistance provoked a vicious riposte from the French forces, a raiding strategy known as the *razzia* and featuring the systematic destruction of enemy villages and crops and the killing or carrying off of their livestock. Though this strategy brought victory for France in 1847, the widespread violence and destruction it entailed made reconciliation between the French and their new subjects impossible. In the twentieth century, mindful of the murderous outcomes of set-piece battles of the past, African insurgents would go over almost exclusively to the guerrilla warfare option.

As previously noted, African armies did not hesitate to accept pitched battle with their European foes. In some cases, this choice was culturally induced. The warrior ethos of the Nguni peoples of southeastern Africa, particularly the Zulus, would not permit the avoidance of direct confrontation with enemy armies. Jihadist motivations among some of the Muslim "secondary empires"—the Mahdist state in the Sudan, the Sokoto empire in Northern Nigeria, the Tukolor empire of al-Hajj 'Umar in West Africa—produced a similar penchant for pitched battle. The preferred tactic for African armies on the attack was to seek to envelop the enemy. To this end, the typical Nguni army employed a "cow horns" formation when attacking; its center had the mission of pinning enemy forces in place while its right and left wings raced out to enfold and destroy them. A "crescent" formation served the same purpose in the armies of the Mahdi and his successors. Those African armies that sought to emulate the European way of war in some cases developed a capacity for maneuver warfare. Perhaps the best example of this was the army of the Guinean *almamy*, Samori Touré, who managed to hold the field against the French from 1886 to 1898.

OUTCOME

For most Africans the nineteenth-century colonial wars marked the commencement of over half a century of alien rule. Aside from Liberia, the U.S. protectorate in West Africa, the only African polity still free to chart its own destiny at the beginning of World War I was Ethiopia. United behind its ancient Christian heritage, almost alone among African peoples in enjoying support against its enemies from European nations, well-armed with modern weapons, the Ethiopians managed to overwhelm a poorly led Italian army at Adowa in 1896. Although eventually defeated and conquered by the Italians in 1934, Ethiopia served for some time as a beacon of hope to Africans who wished to be free from European rule. In the meantime, a substantial number of them ended up serving their colonial masters as soldiers in the world wars of the twentieth century. These wars, though they brought death to African servicemen as far afield as Burma and the Balkans and wreaked havoc on the villages and towns of East Africa in World War I and North Africa in World War II, also opened the way for eventual African independence, through the weakening of the colonial powers and the rise to world domination of two superpowers committed for their own separate reasons to the end of European empire.

See also 'Abd al-Qādir; Colonial Policies and Practices; Colonialism and Imperialism; Military Organizations.

BIBLIOGRAPHY

Callwell, Charles E. *Small Wars: Their Principles and Practice* [1896]. Lincoln: University of Nebraska Press, 1996.

Kiernan, V. G. *From Conquest to Collapse: European Empires from 1815 to 1960.* New York: Pantheon, 1982.

Killingray, David, "Colonial Warfare in West Africa, 1870–1914." In *Imperialism and War: Essays on Colonial War in Asia and Africa,* ed. Jaap A. De Moor and Henk J. Wesseling. Leiden, Netherlands: Brill, 1989.

Pakenham, Thomas. *The Scramble for Africa: The White Man's Conquest of the Dark Continent from 1876 to 1912.* New York: Random House, 1991.

Porch, Douglas. *Colonial Warfare.* New York: Harper Collins, 2006.

Robinson, Ronald, and John Gallagher, with Alice Denny. *Africa and the Victorians: The Official Mind of Imperialism.* London: Weidenfeld and Nicolson, 1981.

Vandervort, Bruce. *Wars of Imperial Conquest in Africa, 1830–1915.* Bloomington: Indiana University Press, 1998.

Wesseling, H. L. *Divide and Rule: The Partition of Africa, 1880–1914.* Westport, CT: Praeger, 1996.

BRUCE VANDERVORT

INTERNAL REVOLTS

Internal revolts cannot always be readily distinguished from low intensity civil wars, but the former term is useful where rebel factions pursue a local agenda or are too weak to mount a serious challenge to the state. Some late-twentieth-century African occurrences reflect localized grievances; others are proxy conflicts on behalf of state factions or external interests (now including international militant Islamist groups). The number of low-level African internal conflicts appears to be increasing as major conflicts decline. Some scholars suggest this is because localized conflicts reflect greed, not grievance. Others point to the lingering destabilizing effects of the Cold War (including a flood of cheap small arms), and yet others to demographic factors. Africa is a continent with large numbers of unemployed youth. Internal revolts provide last-ditch self-employment, especially where the state has failed.

AFRICAN WARFARE BEYOND THE STATE

African internal revolts frequently deploy local (neotraditional) means. An early example of the African neotraditional internal revolt was the anticolonial settler Mau Mau revolt in Kenya in the 1950s. The Renamo insurgency in Mozambique in the 1980s is a major postcolonial case. West Africa (Liberia, Sierra Leone) provides examples from the late twentieth century. Neotraditional elements are strongly associated with localized revolts in the Democratic Republic of the Congo (DRC).

The practices of internal revolt vary on environmental grounds. Savanna and forest-based methods of warfare are quite distinct. The lightning cavalry raid on scattered, undefended villagers was a feature of savanna warfare. In desert conditions with few roads, the ability to swoop in without warning on defenseless settlements to raid, rape, and burn continues to be devastatingly effective. In Darfur, Janjaweed militia activities invoke a form of terror deeply etched in the local historical imagination, while hiding the extent of involvement of the Sudanese state in suppressing an internal revolt.

The horse or camel cannot survive in the wetter zones of Africa due to sleeping sickness. In the African forest cavalry (or armored vehicle) is replaced by small bands of fighters, or even lone operators, approaching stealthily on foot. Well-laid ambushes are among the basic tactics of forest warfare. The enemy is tracked and surrounded by stealth. Disguise and illusion prevail; nothing is quite what it seems. The fighter festooned in charms conveys an image of both power and insubstantial invulnerability in forest conditions.

Armed revolts tend to occur in regions where state rule is least present, for example, the boundary wilderness separating Liberia and Sierra Leone. Poverty and neglect often alienate these isolated rural populations from the state. Insurgents garner local support, but they may not be strong enough to build a national movement capable of toppling the state, or even of providing effective local administration. Rebel terrain rapidly reverts to statelessness.

If this condition is prolonged social, political, and economic arrangements found widely in earlier times tend to recur. Precolonial "stateless societies" were less regions of anarchy than complex trading alliances reaching from Atlantic coast into the savanna interior. In these network societies, power was diffuse and mainly exercised by alliances of merchants and warriors. Struggles took place among rival factions to control key nodes. A typical pattern was for a merchant to hire warriors and their apprentices ("warboys") to disrupt a rival's business. Merchants "bought war."

Professional warriors built base camps in forest tracts between competing trade routes. War combined well with hunting. Fighters knew how to move surreptitiously in the forest and set up ambushes, and (when required) they trapped humans much as they trapped other creatures. Esoteric means reinforced illusions of invulnerability and invisibility. Apprentices underwent initiation into "secret societies" (sodalities), weakening family bonds and ensuring silent loyalty to the armed band. The job of the warboy was as much to loot, fetch, carry, and spy, as to fight. Warriors steeped in the arts of magic, bluff, and boast might at times propose single-handed combat to decide the outcome of an attack.

These fighting bands lived off the land. A successful raid often resulted in the killing of the rival male fighters and abduction of village females. Many became wives of the successful group. Fighters regularly engaged by a particular merchant prince might settle locally, but the ruler was often careful enough to specify a separate location for the camp. Others would return to their forest fastness and await a new commission. An advantage in recruiting distant warriors was that the warboys had no local family linkages through which military activities might be betrayed. There was less compunction in killing local populations.

State failure and peripheral armed revolts in the last decade of the twentieth century returned several parts of the forested interior of the Upper Guinea coast (Liberia, Sierra Leone, and Côte d'Ivoire) to the conditions previously described. Hiring of specialists to protect or disrupt trade, socialization of fighters through initiation in warrior camps, and deployment of hunter craft as a tool of warfare feature in revolts from Casamance to Côte d'Ivoire. New warrior settlements have begun to emerge in the forests, set apart from mainstream society. Rebel leaders imagine themselves reincarnated as warrior chiefs, imbued with magic invulnerability. Counterinsurgency experts help

set up and train neotraditional "hunter" militia. Governments and rebels collude in reviving (or inventing) modalities of conflict resolution based on "classic" institutions of statelessness, for example the "joking relationship" (jocularity or abusiveness specially permitted between certain closely related groups or classes of persons marking out the special nature of the relationship) described by Ferdinand De Jong.

THREE EXPLANATIONS OF AFRICAN INTERNAL REVOLTS

Analysts offer three explanations of why contemporary African armed revolts assume neotraditional form. Some consider the methods highly functional, for example well-adapted to local environment and skills and resources. Others suggest they serve mainly to dissociate sponsors and practitioners of war in a continent in which fortunes are to be made (or lost) via intrigue over rich natural resources. A third view is that a durable African rural culture reasserts itself when modernity retreats. The arguments between these three positions—functionalist, constructivist, and essentialist—have yet to be resolved.

According to the functional argument neotraditional techniques are practically effective. Correct local knowledge explains military success. The Sierra Leone rebels titled their only document *Footpaths to Democracy* (Revolutionary United Front [RUF] of Sierra Leone, 1995). Unlike regular troops they were prepared to operate on foot, and knew the forest tracks better than government forces scrambling to find even a complete set of maps. Paul Richards (1996) argues that techniques of internal revolt, as deployed by the RUF, belong to a living tradition of local strategic knowledge.

The constructivist argument is supported by recent evidence that a number of internal revolts are closely linked to mining deals. South African Defence Force officers devised what J. Hooper termed an "immensely successful doctrine" (Hooper, 8) of counterinsurgency for Angola and Mozambique. Its basic aim was to disguise covert operations as apparently spontaneous revolt. Counterinsurgency was dressed in neotraditional clothes. After the end of apartheid in South Africa this military variant on the colonial "invention of tradition" (Hobsbawm and Ranger, 1983) spread from Angola and Mozambique to other parts of Africa via private security companies employing South African Defence Force veterans.

The third argument supposes that culture is causal. According to this argument ethnicity, religious beliefs, or social identity determine how people behave, not the other way around. Youth in Liberia, for example, mutilate their victims because they have absorbed a system of belief in which human sacrifice carries juridical force. When the modern state retreats, barbarism revives.

Deciding between the aforementioned explanations in particular cases requires a better grasp of why internal revolts are so numerous in Africa at the beginning of the twenty-first century. The major factors are economic and demographic. Instability is, for some, mainly linked to freebooting capitalism. Africa is rich in resources, especially oil and other readily extractable and highly valuable strategic minerals, demanded by a global post–Cold War economic boom. As at the end of the nineteenth century, a battle royal has been entered by competing international interests (including China and other emergent economies) to claim these resources. Local dissidents help secure resources for international business backers.

The Liberian revolt has been explained, for example, in terms of a business nexus centered on Charles Taylor, incorporating Eastern Europe and Asian business interests seeking timber and diamond deals. A Briton involved in Executive Outcomes, the company providing counterinsurgency advice in Sierra Leone, was arrested and jailed in 2004 for involvement in a plot to topple the government of oil-rich Equatorial Guinea. He had hired sixty-two veterans of covert South African operations in Angola and Mozambique, earlier associated with counterinsurgency in Sierra Leone, to topple the president of Equatorial Guinea and gain oil exploitation rights. The argument assumes that rebel movements (or counterinsurgency forces) are a cover for international mineral deals. No grievance is sincere. Africa internal revolts are economics by other means.

The second explanation draws attention to demographics. Africa is experiencing the world's fastest population growth. Too much attention has been paid to war and famine as the products of population outgrowing food supply. The truly destabilizing factor is how to socialize overwhelming numbers of impoverished young people.

Emile Durkheim's theory of social cohesion (1893) explains solidarity as an outcome of the division of labor. Young people become committed to community values through positive endorsement of the work they perform. An open, competitive opportunity structure is conducive to organic solidarity; a forced division of labor feeds revolt. Years of colonial rule through chiefs and mercantile elites, to which were added years of postcolonial redistribution of Cold War subsidies by military elites, kept alive old patrimonial values. African ruling elites assumed for far too long that African youths needed patrons more than they needed skills. Patrons supply jobs according to favoritism, not talent, perpetuating a forced division of labor historically rooted in domestic slavery. Mutinous feelings fester among the excluded.

Approximately 45 to 50 percent of the population of some African countries in the early twenty-first century are children and youth seeking education or a first job, compared to approximately 20 to 25 percent in the richest European countries. This huge growth in young people, combined with post–Cold War shrinkage of patrimonial funds, has resulted in an Africa-wide crisis. Increasingly, education and work no longer play their roles in equipping young people with skills to contribute to society and thus to gain feedback on their social worth. The worst-affected countries are those in which the state has become dysfunctional and can no longer run even a basic educational system. Revolt presents itself as an alternative. The skills are readily acquired. The gun secures instant gratification and respect. War spreads as the numbers of socially detached young people in the population increases.

THE LIKELIHOOD OF INTERNAL REVOLT

The choice between economic and demographic explanations remains hard to make. Some scholars have argued that if the division of labor model is correct then every African country would be at war, to which they sometimes respond "not yet." The capacity of revolt in West Africa to perpetuate itself across boundaries has alarmed commentators in the region. Analysts point to different sets of factors in fostering the conflicts in Liberia, Sierra Leone, and Côte d'Ivoire—ethnicity (and perhaps religion) in Liberia, diamonds in Sierra Leone, land and migration in Côte d'Ivoire. Yet neotraditional modalities of internal revolt are common to all three conflicts, spread by hypermobile youth crossing from country to country. The factions grow rapidly as economies collapse and fighting becomes the only kind of work available to poorly educated young people.

Greed-not-grievance seems to fit the facts in a number of cases, not least in three diamond-rich countries, Angola, Sierra Leone, and DRC, responsible for most of the world's output of so-called "conflict diamonds." But work with ex-combatants in Sierra Leone establishes that most came from impoverished rural backgrounds and were concerned about lack of education and jobs. Few if any said they had been induced to fight by promises of diamond wealth.

The spread of internal revolt from Liberia and Sierra Leone to Côte d'Ivoire (once considered to be the most stable country in the region, built on agrarian success) appears to confirm aspects of the demographic argument. Here, revolt has been fed, at least in part, by the inability of hyper-mobile youth to find a secure place in either urban or rural economies. At least some fighters see themselves as allied with and inspired by similarly marginalized groups of young people in Liberia and Sierra Leone, despite their different local aims. Armed revolt in the Niger Delta of Nigeria, however, returns to huge and inexplicable differences in access to mineral wealth as a cause of youth alienation. Here, in particular, it hardly seems possible to distinguish analytically between "greed" (for which read resentment at socially-shaming poverty amidst great wealth) and "grievance" (anger at the state and oil industry partners for their lack of commitment to the issue of youth unemployment).

It seems that the likelihood of internal revolt is best predicted by some kind of synthesis of the demographic and greed-not-grievance approaches. It is incontrovertible that international business interests have helped fund and supply wars in Africa, even if the story is not always straightforward. Charles Taylor and the rebels in Sierra Leone have been instanced as agents and beneficiaries of such support, but closer inspection suggests that other parties to the war in Sierra Leone were also supported by diamond mining and international private security inputs. The war against the rebels was presented as spontaneous, involving traditional hunter civil defense. But later evidence suggests

this owed as much to private sector counterinsurgency advice as local agency. At least one rural chief in Sierra Leone was explicit; he was told to form a "traditional" civil defense force by South African mine security experts.

At the same time, it seems incontrovertible that internal revolt provides employment opportunities for marginalized African youth, especially youth with low prospects from remote rural areas. When the first opportunities for peace approached in Sierra Leone in 1996, demobilization planning envisaged about 20,000 fighters. The eventual number demobilized in 2001—after five years of further chaos—was more than 70,000, with about 85 percent coming from impoverished rural backgrounds. The war was ended when serious offers concerning skills training in demobilization were made.

The idea that some African internal revolts at the beginning of the twenty-first century are products of deep alienation of youth is supported by the long catalog of bizarre and horrific atrocities they produce. At times fighters as far apart, as culturally distinct, and as differently motivated as Islamist insurgents in Algeria, Mai Mai warriors in DRC, and Taylor's bewigged "reggae" fighters in Liberia appear to be at war with society itself.

A reduction in the number of internal revolts in Africa is likely to require both scrutiny of international business practices and a radical overhaul of opportunity structures available to young people, especially in rural areas. The International Criminal Court announced in 2004 that it would henceforth scrutinize the activities of chief executives of international companies operating in African war zones. South Africa has moved to close down private security companies supplying mercenaries. In terms of binding African young people back into society, land issues have been suggested as a major focus for attention. Basic education, freedom of movement, land reform (including emphasis on the law of contract in regard to land renting), and support for agro-technical innovation will be needed if the danger of growing numbers of impoverished rural young people fueling an epidemic spread of internal revolt is to be avoided.

See also **Labor: Child; Military Organizations; Postcolonialism; Taylor, Charles Gahnhay; Youth: Rural.**

BIBLIOGRAPHY

Berdal, Mats, and David Malone, eds. *Greed and Grievance: Economic Agendas in Civil Wars.* Boulder, CO: Lynne Rienner, 2001.

Clapham, Christopher, ed. *African Guerrillas.* Oxford: James Currey, 1998.

Collier, Paul. *Economic Causes of Civil Conflict and Their Implications for Policy.* Washington, DC: World Bank, 2000.

De Jong, Ferdinand A. "Joking Nation: Conflict Resolution in Senegal." *Canadian Journal of African Studies* 39, no. 2 (2005): 389–413.

Durkheim, Emile. *The Division of Labor in Society* [1893], trans. G. Simpson. New York: Free Press, 1964.

Ellis, Stephen. *The Mask of Anarchy: The Destruction of Liberia and the Religious Dimension of an African Civil War.* London: Christopher Hurst, 1999.

Hobsbawm, Eric, and Terence Ranger, eds. *The Invention of Tradition.* Cambridge, U.K.: Cambridge University Press, 1983.

Hooper, J. "Appendix: Sierra Leone." In *Bloodsong! An Account of Executive Outcomes in Angola*, 2nd edition. London: HarperCollins, 2003.

Humphreys, Macartan, and Jeremy Weinstein. *What the Fighters Say: A Survey of Ex-Combatants in Sierra Leone, June–August 2003.* CGSD Working Paper No. 20. New York: Columbia University, 2004.

Jones, Adam. *From Slaves to Palm Kernels: A History of the Galinhas Country (West Africa) 1730–1890.* Wiesbaden, Germany: Steiner Verlag, 1983.

Kaplan, Robert D. *The Ends of the Earth: A Journey at the Dawn of the 21st Century.* New York: Random House, 1996.

Moyo, Sam, and Paris Yeros, eds. *Reclaiming the Land: The Resurgence of Rural Movements in Africa, Asia And Latin America.* London: Zed Press, 2006.

The Revolutionary United Front of Sierra Leone. *Footpaths to Democracy: Toward a New Sierra Leone.* The Revolutionary United Front of Sierra Leone, 1995.

Richards, Paul. *Fighting for the Rain Forest: War, Youth and Resources in Sierra Leone.* Oxford: James Currey, 1998.

Richards, Paul. "War as Smoke and Mirrors: Sierra Leone 1991–2, 1994–5, 1995–6." *Anthropological Quarterly* 28 (2005): 377–402.

Smillie, Ian; Lansana Gberie; and Ralph Hazleton. *The Heart of the Matter: Sierra Leone, Diamonds and Human Security.* Canada, Ottawa: Partnership Africa. 2000.

Vlassenroot, Coen, "A Societal View on Violence and War: Conflict and Militia Formation in Eastern Congo." In *Violence, Political Culture and Development in Africa*, ed. Preben Kaarsholm. Oxford: James Currey, pp. 49–65.

Wilson, Kenneth B. "Cults of Violence and Counter-Violence in Mozambique." *Journal of Southern African Studies* 18, no. 3 (1992): 527–582.

PAUL RICHARDS

LIBERATION

Africa's wars of liberation were fought primarily in the south, first against the Portuguese, and then both against the Marxist regimes that replaced them and the white regimes in neighboring Rhodesia and South Africa. With the end of the Cold War, these conflicts came to an end. Then the Tutsi struggle against the Hutu government in Rwanda resulted not only in the downfall of that French-backed government, but also in horrific genocide and the destabilization of neighboring states.

Portugal was not only Africa's first colonial power but also the last to depart. The African Independence Party of Guinea and the Cape Verde Islands (PAIGC), led by Amilcar Cabral, enjoyed the support of neighboring Guinée-Conakry and Senegal and received assistance from Algeria, Cuba, Ghana, and the Soviet Union. Its military wing, the Revolutionary Armed Forces of Povo (FARP) was formed in 1964. By 1968 it controlled much of Guinea.

With the arrival of Brigadier Antonio de Spinola, Portuguese fortunes improved, as he combined aggressive military leadership with a progressive civic action program designed to regain the support of the black population. His departure in 1972 coincided with the FARP's reorganization and receipt of more sophisticated Soviet weapons, to include surface-to-air missiles, which restored the initiative to the insurgents. Although the popular and successful Cabral was assassinated in 1973, the PAIGC claimed Guinea's independence as the Republic of Guinea-Bissau, which Portugal recognized the following year.

Upon his recall to Portugal, Spinola published the bestseller *Portugal and the Future*, which argued that the colonial wars were unwinnable, advocating a peaceful political solution to the conflicts. His dismissal by Premier Marcello Caetano led to a coup by the MFA (Armed Forces Movement), an association of professional officers, which was supported not only by the armed forces but by a war-weary public, in April 1974. The ruling junta negotiated independence treaties with Guinea-Bissau and Mozambique, where the PAIGC and the Front for the Liberation of Mozambique (FRE-LIMO) assumed power.

The Angolan situation was complicated by power struggles between competing liberation movements, which included the Popular Movement for the Liberation of Angola (MPLA), the National Front for the Liberation of Angola (FNLA), and the National Union for the Total Independence of Angola (UNITA). The MPLA was Marxist, and its membership included white intellectuals and mulattoes as well as black Africans. Support came primarily from the Soviet Union. The FNLA, led by Holden Roberto, received aid from Zaire (President Desire Mobuto was his brother-in-law), Algeria, China, and the United States. UNITA was formed by Jonas Savimbi when he split with Roberto in 1966.

Portuguese efforts to form a coalition government proved unsuccessful, and civil war erupted with the withdrawal of Portuguese troops in 1975. The MPLA prevailed thanks to extensive material support (including jet aircraft, artillery, and armored fighting vehicles) by the Soviet Union and direct intervention by thousands of Cuban troops. The FNLA and UNITA remained intact, however, the latter developing into a formidable opposition movement. Large-scale fighting raged throughout the 1980s, with significant American and South African aid going to UNITA in what became a major Cold War conflict. South African troops crossed into Angola on numerous occasions, joining with UNITA to inflict stinging defeats not only on the FPLA (the MPLA's army), but on their Cuban and Soviet allies as well.

Heavy losses and the collapse of the Soviet Union led to the withdrawal of Cuban troops and the cessation of Russian military aid, while diplomatic efforts by the United States and South Africa led to the temporary termination of hostilities. Despite its previously Marxist orientation, the MPLA profited from Western interests in Angolan oil. When the conflict resumed in 1992, the government defeated UNITA with Western assistance, including the South African professional military company Executive Outcomes.

FRELIMO had an insurgent force of 25,000 men that controlled almost 90 percent of Mozambique at the time of independence in 1974. The FPLM (FRELIMO's military arm) received sanctuary in

Tanzania and both Chinese and Soviet military assistance. Initially led by Eduardo Mondlane, FRELIMO's leadership passed to Samora Machal upon Mondlane's death in 1968. Machal advocated a people's struggle on the Maoist model, with the aim of establishing a revolutionary socialist state. More hegemonic in structure than its Angolan counterparts, FRELIMO established one-party rule upon Portugal's departure.

Efforts to restructure society on a radical socialist model met with opposition from both rural black traditionalists and urban white businessmen. Neighboring Rhodesia, recognizing the support the new government offered to Robert Mugabe's Zimbabwe African National Union (ZANU) created the National Resistance of Mozambique (RENAMO) as a counterweight. The movement developed into a serious challenge to FRELIMO and continued to receive South African support after Mugabe came to power in 1980.

Mozambique's bloody civil war raged until 1992. Although the FPLM originated as a lightly armed guerrilla force, it evolved into a mechanized army based on the Soviet model, which had trouble countering RENAMO insurgents. Ironically, the collapse of communism led not only to the cessation of Soviet influence but the restructuring of the FPLM with advice and support from the West. The new force was better suited for a counterinsurgency role, enabling the government to force RENAMO to negotiate, thus bringing a long and brutal conflict to an end.

Portugal's departure from Africa had a significant impact on the Rhodesian insurgency, since it led to the further isolation of the white regime. Two major groups competed for leadership of the liberation struggle: Robert Mugabe's ZANU and Joshua Nkomo's Zimbabwe African People's Union (ZAPU). While both combined as the Patriotic Front, they were rivals. ZAPU's military wing, the Zimbabwe People's Liberation Army (ZIPRA) was based in Zambia, received support from the Soviet Union (including armored vehicles and jet aircraft), and hoped to seize power by invading Rhodesia with conventional military forces. ZANU's Zimbabwe African National Liberation Army (ZANLA) operated from bases in Mozambique, was supported by China, and waged a guerrilla struggle based on Maoist principles. Its strategy was to infiltrate fighters into Rhodesia, building support among the black population while wearing down the white regime in a protracted struggle. In spite of repeated tactical victories by Rhodesian security forces, this strategy proved successful, since the white population was unable to sustain the fight over time and failed to maintain either support of the black population or make full use of black troops. Mugabe seized power with the establishment of majority rule in 1980, then turned on his former allies. The conflict assumed a tribal nature, since ZANU was largely Shona, while ZAPU was primarily Matablele. With military aid from North Korea, Mugabe's troops began a campaign of ethnic cleansing in Matabeleland to herald the beginning of his quarter century of misrule.

South Africa learned from Rhodesia's mistakes, conducting a highly successful counterinsurgency campaign against the Southwest Africa People's Organization (SWAPO) in Namibia. Large numbers of black troops served with the security forces, and great emphasis was placed on building support among the local population. SWAPO obtained support from the MPLA and largely operated out of bases in Angola. This led to South African support for UNITA, often in the form of mechanized columns with armor, artillery, and air support. Lighter forces conducting counterinsurgency operations in Namibia crossed the border as well, both in hot pursuit of fleeing SWAPO guerrillas and in strikes upon their Angolan bases.

The most effective unit operating in Namibia was composed of black Angolans opposed to the MPLA regime. Known as 32 ("Buffalo") Battalion, this formation was highly secretive and very successful in both counterinsurgency and conventional military operations. While led by white South Africans, junior officers had to gain the approval of their black subordinates, who had the right to reject candidates they deemed unsuitable.

Although SWAPO's leadership hoped to seize power in Namibia through an armed struggle, they were forced to seek it through the ballot box instead. The downfall of the Soviet Union led South Africa to initiate the political process through which the former German colony, administered as a mandate since its occupation in 1915, gained independence. The most successful transitions to majority rule were thus gained not through violent "liberation movements" but by successful efforts to suppress them until a political climate conducive to peaceful change emerged not only in Namibia, but in South Africa itself.

The conflict in Rwanda, often described as a civil war, was in many ways a war of liberation. Although the minority Tutsi population enjoyed a privileged status during the Belgian colonial regime, the Hutu majority gained power after independence. In 1990, the largely Tutsi Rwanda Patriotic Front (RPF) invaded form Uganda. French support, which included direct military intervention, enabled the Hutu government to withstand the invasion. Subsequent peace talks led to the Arusha accords, which established a framework for power sharing in the government. The assassination of President Juvenal Habyrimana in April 1994 led to the onset of genocide and the withdrawal of United Nations peacekeepers. The well trained and disciplined RPF, led by the able Major General Paul Kagame, defeated the Rwandan Armed Forces (FAR), but exodus of vast numbers of Hutu refugees into neighboring Zaire led to destabilization in the region with the spread of conflict into adjacent countries.

See also **Cabral, Amílcar Lopes; Cold War; Machel, Samora; Military Organizations; Mondlane, Eduardo Chivambo; Mugabe, Robert.**

BIBLIOGRAPHY

Abbott, Peter, and Philip Botham. *Modern African Wars*, Vol. 1: *Rhodesia, 1965–1980*. London: Osprey Publishing, 1986.

Abbott, Peter, and Manuel Ribeiro Rodrigues. *Modern African Wars*, Vol. 2: *Angola and Mocambique, 1961–1974*. London: Osprey Publishing, 1988.

Edgerton, Robert B. *Africa's Armies: From Shame to Infamy: A History from 1791 to the Present*. Boulder, CO: Westview Press, 2002.

Finnegan, William. *A Complicated War: The Harrowing of Mozambique*. Berkeley: University of California Press, 1992.

Heitman, Helmoed-Romer. *Modern African Wars*, Vol. 3: *South-West Africa*. London: Osprey Publishing, 1991.

Turner, John W. *Continent Ablaze: The Insurgency Wars in Africa, 1960 to the Present*. London: Arms and Armour Press, 1998.

FRANK KALESNIK

NATIONAL AND INTERNATIONAL

The nature of national and international warfare has changed considerably over the post–World War II period and can be placed into overlapping phases. In the immediate postwar period, wars of national liberation from colonial rule were the primary form, often containing internal settling of accounts among various national liberation movements as well. Although most colonies received their independence by legislation and negotiation, guerrilla warfare that often evolved into pitched battles occurred in Algeria (1954–1962), Angola (1963–1974), Mozambique (1964–1974), Portuguese Guinea (present-day Bissau, 1960–1974), South West Africa (present-day Namibia, 1964–1989), (Southern) Rhodesia (present-day Zimbabwe, 1972–1980), and Eritrea (1960–1991). Although the conflict was a war for nationalist independence, the nationalists often enjoyed support from the Eastern (Communist) bloc and the colonial powers from the West, of which they were a part.

The second phase involved internal conflicts, often from rivalries within the nationalist movement, and also a number of low-level interstate wars. The former include Congo (1960–1964, 1978, 1979), Rwanda (1963–1964, 1990–1994), Uganda (1966, 1981–1987), Nigeria (1967–1970), Burundi (1972, 1990–2006), Sudan (1955–1972, 1983–2005), Angola (1974–2005), Mozambique (1974–1994), Morocco (1974–1991), Chad (1980–1987, 1996), Congo (Brazzaville, 1994, 1997–1999), Liberia (1989–2003), Sierra Leone (1991–2000), Senegal (1974–2005), Congo (the War of the Zairean Succession, 1996–2006), and Somalia (1990–ongoing). Frequently these conflicts found support for one side or the other from the East and the West, although both Cold War parties also operated to keep the conflicts from escalating out of control. Interstate wars occurred between Morocco and Algeria (1963, 1979), Mali and Upper Volta (present-day Burkina Faso, 1963, 1974, 1982), Somalia and Ethiopia (1963, 1979), Nigeria and Cameroon (1972, 1981, 1996), Chad and Libya (1985–1987), Chad and Nigeria (1982), and Eritrea and Ethiopia (1998–2000), usually over contested boundaries and without producing any boundary changes. Indeed, such wars were part of the process, usually accomplished diplomatically, of "Africanizing" colonially inherited boundaries.

Internal consolidation and state collapse have outdistanced structural and territorial causes of conflict in the post–Cold War era, and have evolved into a rising category of intrastate conflicts with a source of their own, which can be termed cycles of need, creed, and greed. The cycle begins with greed, not as a motive for insurgency but as a characteristic of the governors. Privatizing and hoarding the usually meager (but sometimes full) resources of the state, the rulers take their time at the trough and deprive their populations of expected state benefits; Nigeria's Sani Abacha, Zaire's Mobutu Sese Seko, Togo's Gnassingbe Eyadema, Sierra Leone's Siaka Stevens and then Joseph Momoh, Liberia's Samuel Doe and then Charles Taylor, Congo-Brazzaville's Denis Sassou-Nguesso, Sudan's Hassan al-Bashir, Zimbabwe's Robert Mugabe, Somalia's Mohammed Siad Barre, Algeria's military junta, and Angola's Eduardo Dos Santos stand out as the most egregious examples. Unrest growing from generalized deprivation (need) is soon turned into a sense of targeted deprivation or discrimination (creed) by insurgency leaders seeking to consolidate their following. Typical and varied examples from the aforementioned states, respectively, in the 1990s and 2000s include the Ogoni protest, the Bayamulenge, southern and western Togolese opposition, the Revolutionary United Front (RUF), the National Peoples Liberation Front (NPFL) and then its assorted oppositions, opposition Congolese militias, Sudanese Peoples Liberation Movements and Fur and Beji insurgencies, the Zimbabwean Movement for Democratic Change (MDC), the Somali clan militias and then the Coucil of Islamic Courts, the Islamic Salvation Front (FIS) and Army (AIS), and the National Union for the Total Independence of Angola (UNITA).

At this stage—creed—the conflict is potentially manageable in a number of ways: victory of one side or the other, or negotiation between the two for a new political system. Rare examples of the first include Sassou-Nguesso's prevalence over his oppositions in 2000 and the National Liberation Front of Angola (FLNA) victory over Jonas Savimbi's UNITA in 2003. An even rarer example of a negotiated agreement is the gradually unfolding process of state rebuilding in Congo since the 1999 Lusaka Agreement and 2002 Pretoria Agreement, leading toward a new constitution and then national elections of 2006.

If an outcome proves elusive, however, because neither side is winning or losing, the insurgency digs in in its "liberated" area and turns its efforts to making money, initiating its own phase of greed. The militias in the Kivus in eastern Congo digging gold and coltan, the RUF in Sierra Leone mining diamonds, the NPFL during Taylor's war in Liberia exploiting diamonds and timber, the Armed Islamic Groups (GIA) in Algeria preying on neighborhoods, and UNITA in Angola living off diamonds provide examples of civil wars stuck in irresolution that have turned into moneymaking schemes for rebel leaders. This phase is even more difficult to bring to a conclusion short of a complete reversal of fortunes on one side and a victory on the other. Such prolonged wars debilitate the government side and undermine even the legitimate grievance aspect of the insurgencies; the country emerges from the conflict—when it does—ravaged and further impoverished. Research shows that such wars leave the country vulnerable to a return to conflict within half a decade.

Such cycles of civil war do not remain internal to the ravaged state, however; they tend to turn into regional conflicts, as the rapacious government and its civil war create a power vacuum that attracts neighbors' interference and intervention. Neighbors pursue their own geostrategic interests in the conflict, but also join in the pursuit of moneymaking on their own. Regional conflict arenas cover much of Africa. In West Africa, flowing out from the collapsed state of Liberia in the late 1980s, conflict flowed east into Côte d'Ivoire, and spread west to Sierra Leone, Guinea-Bissau, and Casamance in Senegal and hovered over Guinea in 2005 awaiting the death of its president. Outside the immediate conflict zone, Burkina Faso and Nigeria were predator states working the arena. In Central Africa the collapse of Rwanda and Burundi in 1994 attracted Zairean interest, and then the collapse of Zaire in 1996 brought Uganda and Rwanda into the Congolese eastern provinces, Burundi and Tanzania into the southeast, Angola into the west, and Zimbabwe into Shaba in the south in the ensuing ten-year War of the Zairean Succession. In the Horn of Africa, a long conflict within Ethiopia attracted interlocking attention from Sudan and Somalia as neighbors supported each others' subversive movements; the independence of Eritrea in 1993, the Eritrean-Ethiopian war of 1998–2000

(Africa's costliest border war ever), and the collapse of Somalia throughout the 1990s and early 2000s removed the southern part of the conflict arena and left Sudan as the main focus of conflict arena in the 2000s, with Libya, Chad, Central Africa, and Uganda as implicated neighbors.

Two other regional conflict arenas were in remission since the mid-1990s. Southern Africa, which had civil wars in Mozambique and Angola related to the civil conflict in South Africa, saw all three come to an end between 1994 (South Africa, Mozambique) and 2004 (Angola). North Africa, poised on the brink of a revival of the Saharan war, quiescent since 1982 and under formal United Nations (UN) ceasefire since 1991, kept the conflict between Morocco and Algerian, and their neighbors, at the diplomatic level.

COOPERATION IN CONFLICT

These wars have imposed an enormous waste of resources and productive capacity on the countries involved, and have destroyed the possibilities of regional economic cooperation. Regional cooperation organizations fostered in the 1970s and 1980s by the UN Economic Commission for Africa (ECA) have all had to turn to security first in order to create even the basic conditions for economic collaboration. The Economic Community of West African States (ECOWAS), after having been a major actor in the first Liberian civil war in an attempt to bring it to an end, played a role in ending the second civil war after Charles Taylor's election in 1997 and also in bringing the Sierra Leonean civil war under control before being incorporated into the finally successful UN efforts. ECOWAS also intervened in Guinea-Bissau and played a diplomatic role in bringing the Ivorian civil war to an end before ceding precedence to the African Union (AU).

The Inter-Governmental Agency on Development (IGAD) was the formal sponsor of the mediation that finally ended the second Sudanese Civil war in 2004, but was unable to handle the genocide in Darfur in 2004–2005. The Southern African Development Community (SADC) played a contradictory role in the War of the Zairean Succession, as three of its members (Zimbabwe, Angola, Namibia) gave military support to Congo and joined it is a military alliance, but the organization sponsored the negotiations that brought about the Lusaka and Pretoria Agreements. A regional peace process, first under Julius Nyerere and then under Nelson Mandela, gradually brought peace and a restoration of a working government to Burundi in the first half-decade of the 2000s. (The Arab Maghrib Union [UMA] was declared "frozen" by the Saharan conflict that it was unable to mediate, and so suspended its activities after 1994.)

Behind these efforts of regional organizations, the African Union (AU), a renewed version of the Organization of African Unity (OAU) after 2000, attempted to play a backup role. The AU allocated 7,000 troops to Darfur in 2005, with limited effectiveness. Other mediators withdrew in support of the efforts of South African president Thabo Mbeki to mediate the Ivorian conflict in 2005. Elsewhere it was the UN that played the backup role, supplying troops through the UN Armed Mission to Sierra Leone (UNAMSIL), UN Mission in Ivory Coast (MONICI), and UN Mission in Congo (MONUC).

As these activities show, regional organizations on the formal level can be effective in coordinating neighborhood pressures on a civil conflict toward the goal of bringing it under control; but they are not able to rein in local predation, often involving the same members who are part of the reconciliation efforts. The rebuilding of the conflicted state, its dysfunctional economy, and its traumatized society, has proven to be a task of huge proportions and long duration. The AU is a helpful mediator when conflicting interests among the neighbors in the conflict itself hamper their objectivity and effectiveness. The level of last resort, the UN, is also necessary to legitimize effective intervention by external security forces and then to provide technical and economic assistance to construct the state. Even if these efforts stay on track, the gaping wounds in the African landscape left by the collapsed states and civil conflicts in Ethiopia, Somalia, Sudan, Liberia, Sierra Leone, Côte d'Ivoire, Congo, Rwanda, Burundi, Angola, and Zimbabwe leave a legacy of retarded development and vulnerability to new civil conflict.

See also **Boundaries, Colonial and Modern; Cold War; Economic Community of West African States (ECOWAS); Ethnicity; Eyadema, Gnassingbe (Étienne); Mandela, Nelson; Mbeki, Thabo; Military Organizations: National Armies; Mobuto Sese Seko;**

Mugabe, Robert; Nyerere, Julius Kambarage; Organization of African Unity; Postcolonialism; Sassou-Nguesso, Denis; Savimbi, Jonas; Taylor, Charles Gahnhay; United Nations.

BIBLIOGRAPHY

Arnson, Cynthia, and I. William Zartman, eds. *Rethinking the Economics of War: The Intersection of Need, Creed, and Greed*. Baltimore: Johns Hopkins University Press, 2005.

Collier, Paul, et al. *Breaking the Conflict Trap: Civil War and Development Policy*. New York: Oxford University Press, 2003.

I. William Zartman

WATER AND IRRIGATION.

African people have used rivers and their associated wetlands as a source of water for drinking and agriculture, and/or hunting, fishing, grazing, and gathering for thousands of years. Most major rivers in Africa have floodplains associated with them, for example the Senegal and Niger in West Africa, the Zambezi, Rufiji, Tana, and Jubba Rivers in Southern and East Africa, and the Nile. Larger floodplain areas or internal deltas occur on the Niger in Mali, the Kafue in Zambia, and on the Chari-Logone system in Cameroon. These are often linked to permanent swamp systems, for example in the Sud on the White Nile, the Okavango Delta in Botswana, and on the Shire River draining Lake Malawi. Almost all of these environments have a long history of human occupation, and of economic production and trade based on agriculture, fishing, and livestock husbandry. In semiarid Africa, wetlands have a strategic importance well beyond their boundaries. The economic values of rivers are dependent on the interconnection of geomorphological, hydrological, and ecological processes. The aim of this entry is to describe the importance of African wetlands to local economies and the ways wetlands and their uses have been changed by modern development.

Most of Africa's rivers have strongly seasonal flooding patterns, with high flows in the wet season and extensive flooding, and low flows in the dry season. During the flood period, water overflows the river banks, causing widespread inundation in

Okavango Delta (Botswana), one of the great riverine wetlands of Africa. The delta is supplied by the Okavango River, which rises in the Angolan highlands and flows over 1,000 miles through Namibia to Botswana. It floods seasonally, starting around January in the north extension and July in the south. © JASON LAURÉ

the surrounding areas. The area flooded then falls until the dry season, during which some rivers can be reduced to pools of water. In the Senegal valley approximately 1,930 square miles is flooded at high flow, and about 193 square miles in the dry season. In the Kafue Flats in Zambia the area flooded varies from 10,810 square miles in the wet season to 5,019 square miles in the dry season. In the complex Logone-Chari floodplains south of Lake Chad (the Yaérés), flooding covers some 34,750 square miles, of which only 7 percent remains wet at low water.

RIVERINE WETLANDS AND AGRICULTURE
Floodplain farmers typically make use of both wetlands and adjacent drylands, exploiting the economic opportunities each provide. Dryland and wetland crops require labor at different times of the year, and by exploiting the two environments, farmers are able to minimize bottlenecks in labor supply, while at the same time spreading risks. Thus in the West African Sahel, floodplain agricultural

techniques include both farming on the rising flood (planting before the flood arrives), or on the falling flood, using residual soil moisture left by retreating waters. Floodplain farmers tend to have extensive knowledge of crop ecological requirements, flooding patterns, and variation in land types. Such agriculture is ancient—West African rice was domesticated 3,000 years ago in the Niger Inland Delta—and is still widespread.

In a number of areas of Africa, irrigation systems long predate the introduction of Western irrigation engineering and the formal government development schemes of the twentieth century. However, the extent and sophistication of indigenous irrigation were only recognized in the last decades of the twentieth century, particularly in the large wetland areas that lie within the extensive drylands of Africa, such as the Niger Inland Delta in Mali or the Senegal valley. These floodwater farming systems might be excluded by a strict definition of irrigation in engineering terms, but it is probably more useful to adopt a flexible definition that includes them with gravity irrigation systems (e.g., the hill furrow irrigation systems of the East African Rift and various forms of water harvesting) and systems dependent on the lifting of water (by bucket, shadoof, animal power, or pump).

The extent of small-scale informal irrigation in sub-Saharan Africa is not accurately known, but a study published in 1986 by the Investment Center of the Food and Agriculture Organization (FAO) suggested that it comprised 47 percent of the irrigated area in sub-Saharan Africa (9,266 square miles). In about half the countries in sub-Saharan Africa, more than 75 percent of the total irrigated area was classified as small-scale or informal. In many places African farmers have built new small irrigation systems since the 1980s. In some cases long-established methods are used, in others the technology is new (e.g., tubewells and gasoline-powered pumps in northern Nigeria). No large-scale surveys have been conducted in the twenty-first century, but the expansion of peri-urban irrigated market gardening in many countries suggests that the area of informal irrigation will have increased, not decreased.

River wetlands are not just important for farmers. Pastoralists also use wetlands seasonally, concentrating onto seasonally flooded land as surrounding rangelands dry out. A relatively small area of wetland that provides grazing at critical times of year and can thus support pastoralists through the rest of the year over a much larger area. In the central Senegal valley, Fulani pastoralists move away from the floodplain with their livestock in the wet season but come back to farm when the floodwaters recede from the valley in the dry season. Because of its floods the Niger Inland Delta is able to support over 1 million head of cattle and 2 million sheep and goats, 20 percent of the total numbers in Mali.

Fishing is also important in the economy of many African floodplains. The FAO estimates that there are over 60,000 fishermen on the Niger River and that together they produce 130,000 tons of fish per year, of which 75 percent comes from the Niger Inland Delta. The life cycle of many fish species is linked to seasonal flood regimes. Many fish species undertake a lateral migration in the flood season to breed in the warm, shallow nutrient-rich water of the floodplain. As floods recede, fish move back to the main river channel and eventually to standing pools, where they can be caught. If flood patterns change, breeding is disrupted.

RIVER BASIN PLANNING

Until the twentieth century the only large-scale hydrological developments in Africa were in the Nile Valley. Within sub-Saharan Africa only the Sudan had developed irrigation on any scale before the 1960s. Most of the development of Africa's rivers has taken place since the 1960s.

Major engineering works began on the Nile in the nineteenth century. Canals and barrages were built in the delta area and north of Cairo to allow perennial irrigated cropping in Egypt. The first Aswan Dam was built on the Nile in 1902, and heightened in 1912. Attention then turned to the upper Nile. Many schemes were proposed, and dams on the Blue Nile in 1925 and 1937; the Aswan Dam was heightened again in 1934. Meanwhile, Egypt and Sudan had concluded the Nile Waters Agreement, which allocated flows between the two countries. The first Nile Water Agreement, in 1929, allocated 48 billion cubic meters to Egypt and only 4 billion to Sudan. By the time of the second agreement, in 1959, it had been calculated that there was more water to be distributed, and 25.5 billion cubic yards was allocated to Sudan, while 72.6 billion cubic yards was allocated to Egypt.

Various attempts to plan water-resource development in the colonial period were made elsewhere in Africa (e.g., the Mission d'Aménagement du Sénégal in 1938), but international planning dates mostly from the 1960s and 1970s, when institutions such as the Senegal River Development Organization (Organisation pour la Mise en Valeur du Fleuve Sénégal, OMVS) were set up by Mali, Mauritania, and Senegal. Other international river basins subject to international planning included the Zambezi, where the Central African Power Corporation built dams at Kariba (between Zimbabwe and Zambia) and Cahora Bassa (Mozambique).

National river basin planning systems were also established, the most extensive in Nigeria. The Niger Delta Development Board was established in 1960 and the Niger Dams Authority in 1961. In 1973 the federal government of Nigeria established the first two River Basin Development Authorities (RBDAs) in the arid north of the country (in the Sokoto-Rima and Lake Chad Basins), and these were followed by a further seven RBDAs in 1976. There were eleven RBDAs by the end of the decade, a number that increased to eighteen in 1984. The Nigerian RBDAs were multifunctional parastatal agencies, whose functions ranged from dam construction and irrigation through water supply, pollution control, and fisheries to agricultural processing, seed multiplication, and dryland agriculture. Most focused their efforts initially on dams and irrigation schemes.

Dams, used for hydroelectric power generation and irrigation, are the most significant results of river basin planning in Africa. Almost all major African rivers have been dammed in at least one place, with a series of large schemes in the decade of the 1960s, as African states obtained independence. Both tributaries of the Nile are dammed, and the dam at Aswan controls flow of the combined river within Egypt. In the Zambezi basin there are dams on the Kafue at Kafue Gorge and Itezhitezhi and on the Zambezi itself at Kariba and Cabora Bassa. In West Africa, the Volta River is dammed at Akosombo, the Bandama at Kossou (Côte d'Ivoire) and the Senegal at Manantali and Diama. There are numerous dams in the Niger basin (e.g., Bakolori on the Sokoto and the Lagdo on the Benue, as well as Sélingué, Sotuba, Markala, Karamsasso, Kainji and Jebba on the Niger itself).

THE ENVIRONMENTAL IMPACTS OF DAMS

Dams are designed to transform the environment for human benefit. They hold back seasonal flood flows for later use (to generate power through the year, or to provide water for dry-season irrigation). The impacts of this restructuring of flooding patterns are complex in detail, but simple in principle. Upstream of the dam, a new reservoir is created. Land (often very productive floodplain land) is lost, and people's homes and economic infrastructure are flooded. Substantial numbers of people have to be resettled (e.g., 85,000 in the Akosombo Dam in Ghana and 57,000 from the Kainji Dam in Nigeria, both in the 1960s). The costs of resettlement include both actual financial costs (surveys, compensation reconstruction, and evacuation), and the less tangible human costs of the stress of resettlement. The ecology of such lakes is complex, but if conditions are right, economic benefits can sometimes result, for example the fishing industry and tourism of Lake Kariba.

Downstream impacts of dam construction are more complex and subtle. Many different aspects of floodplain economy are affected. Dams affect the magnitude and timing of downstream flows. Flood peaks are smaller although flood flows may be longer lasting. The exact effect depends on the size of the dam and reservoir and the purpose of the project. Dams to store irrigation water for dry-season use are often filled early in a wet season before water is released downstream. Such dams can change the regime of a river from one with a short flood season into a river with more moderate flows through the year. Dams tend to reduce the size and delay the peaks of floods. They also make the timing of floods at the whim of dam managers, which makes water flows hard for downstream farmers to predict or understand. Changes in natural river hydrology affect the ecology of floodplain environments, and hence the ability of farmers, pastoralists, and fishers to manage their land and resources effectively. Significant negative economic impacts on floodplain agriculture are recognized in many African rivers, particularly the major floodplain rivers of West Africa.

IRRIGATION IN AFRICA

The earliest large-scale irrigation development in sub-Saharan Africa was the Gezira irrigation scheme, begun in Sudan in 1925 using water from the Sennar Dam on the Blue Nile. The scheme more or less doubled in area between 1958 and 1962 when the Managil extension and the Roseires Dam were built. The scheme in the early twenty-first century covers about 3,088 square miles. Although critics have pointed to many problems of poor management at Gezira, the scheme was widely regarded by both British and French colonial governments as a success and served as a model for large-scale irrigation development elsewhere in Africa. For example, the French colonial government used the Gezira scheme as the model for the Office du Niger, developed in the 1940s in the Niger Inland Delta (in the territory that became Mali) which was intended to extended to 3,861 square miles of irrigated land.

Since independence, irrigation has been an important feature of agricultural development in many African countries. In Kenya, for example, the

World Bank funded construction of the Bura Project, Kenya's largest irrigation scheme, on the Tana River in 1975 for the National Irrigation Board. In Nigeria in the 1970s, massive investments were made in large-scale irrigation schemes through the River Basin Development Authorities. Irrigation was seen as an essential means to deal with the stagnation of agricultural productivity and rising food imports (particularly of wheat and rice), and as a way to use buoyant oil revenues. Plans were most ambitious. The fourth Development Plan (1981–1985) proposed that 5,405 square miles of land should be brought under irrigation in the future, and that a quarter of the 8.9 billion naira ($US5.24 billion) allocated to agriculture was to be invested in irrigation. There were similar stories elsewhere. Senegal allocated almost half its agricultural budget to irrigation in its Firth Plan (1977–1981).

However, actual rates of irrigation expansion were slower than planned in many countries. FAO data suggest that the total irrigated area in sub-Saharan Africa rose by about 671 square miles per year between 1965 and 1974 and by 157,000 hectares between 1974 and 1982. At the end of 1980 fewer than 606 square miles were actually irrigated in Nigeria. In the vast majority of countries, irrigation is carried out on a small proportion of the cropped land area; even in the Sudan only 15 percent of cropland is irrigated, in Mali it is 9 percent, in Mauritania it is 6 percent, and in Senegal and Nigeria it is 3 percent.

In retrospect, the large-scale government irrigation schemes of this era have a poor economic record. Projects like the Kenyan Bura scheme have been abandoned, and those in northern Nigeria failed to cover their operating (let alone construction) costs. Key problems included high capital cost, inappropriate and complex technology, poor project planning and management, lack of skilled people, and lack of basic research on the environment and local economies. Irrigation schemes also suffered from more widespread problems of poor national infrastructure and communications, poor performance of public-sector management (including corruption), and the ineffective "top-down" approach that predominated in African development planning. Furthermore, terrain, soil quality, and rainfall variability present significant technical constraints on irrigation in Africa. In 1994, a World Bank review of its experience with irrigation lending estimated that investment costs per square mile of irrigation in Africa were 15 times greater than in low-income countries in South Asia.

THE FUTURE OF AFRICAN IRRIGATION

Despite this poor record, rising urban and rural populations, shortfalls in food grains, the problems of drought, and seasonal rainfall suggest that irrigation will continue to have a place in Africa's agricultural planning. In many countries there is little potential for extending the area of farmland. Increased agricultural production must therefore be achieved by increasing yields from existing farmland. This can be done through crop breeding, improved cultivation techniques (e.g., manuring, mulching, agroforestry) greater use of agrochemicals (e.g. inorganic fertilizer and pesticides in fields and in storage), and irrigation where appropriate.

Although planners in national governments and aid agencies remain committed to irrigation development, it is not entirely clear how this irrigation should be achieved. There have been various experiments with farmer-managed irrigation systems (FMIS), attempting to "turn over" the management of inefficient government-run schemes to groups of farmers. Planners hope that putting farmers themselves in charge of water supply, irrigation scheduling, and service provisions, to harness farmers' skills and enterprise will create more economically efficient schemes at low cost to government. This strategy reflects the wider attempt to scale down government interventions in agricultural markets under the umbrella of structural adjustment.

In two agricultural sectors, irrigation has expanded over the turn of the millennium. The first is on large-scale commercial farms, usually providing high-value products for international markets. The classic example includes the production of cut flowers in countries like Kenya, where vast plastic greenhouses and extensive use of pesticides and fertilizers allow a completely controlled growing environment in which artificial watering forms part of a precision-farming system. One attraction of such farming systems is the availability of cheap labor from surrounding impoverished communities of rainfed-farming smallholders. The other growth sector has been in micro-scale irrigated farming

The Pongolapoort Dam on the perennial Pongola River in KwaZulu-Natal, South Africa. The floodplain of the river has long been used by Tembe-Thonga people for farming, fishing, and grazing. The river was dammed in the late 1960s for irrigation. However, the area, which is near the Mozambique border, never attracted white farmers as settlers, although a small irrigation scheme for African farmers was developed in the 1970s. © JASON LAURÉ

of vegetables and other high-value crops, often adjacent to or even within urban areas. Such "indigenous irrigation" represents part of the burgeoning informal sector within African economies.

THE FUTURE OF RIVER BASIN DEVELOPMENT

The grand sweep of river basin plans proposed in the past reflect the geography of the continent, the lack of good dam sites, and the long distances separating dams from potential users of water. They also reflect the expansive vision of expatriate planners (colonial government servants or contemporary engineering consultants) who have tended to see in Africa a blank drawing board on which they can build.

Schemes of vast scale are still being proposed for Africa with scant regard for the complexities of floodplain environments and economies. In 1978 construction began on the Jonglei Canal in the southern Sudan, designed to carry 26 million cubic yards of water per day around the swamps of the sudd to irrigate Egypt. Perhaps fortuitously, given the likely environmental impacts on the sudd wetlands and their people, work was halted in 1984 as a result of the renewal of civil war in southern Sudan. There are voices calling for it to be finished. There have also been proposals to transfer water from the Ubangui River (in the Zaire basin) northward into the headwaters of the Chari system and hence to Lake Chad and the dry Sahel using a series of dams, tunnels, pipelines, and canals. Such schemes reflect the megalomania that sometimes seems to afflict African development planners.

At the other end of the scale, there has been interest in the use of dams to release artificial floods for downstream users, restoring a version of natural flood regimes. The idea was suggested in the 1980s, and has been tried on the Pongolo River in Kawzulu Natal in South Africa, on the River

Senegal, and on the Waza-Logone in Cameroon. Such strategies are exciting, but technically and politically demanding.

Understanding of the potential environmental and social impacts of dams has grown immeasurably since the burst of major dam building in Africa in the 1960s. The World Commission on Dams, which reported in 2000, set out new approaches to the planning and design of dams to minimize harm and maximize benefits. River basin planning in Africa still faces formidable challenges. These relate to environmental complexity (particularly the problem of inter-annual rainfall variability and drought), the lack of African research and expertise (both lack of knowledge and lack of people within African institutions with that knowledge), and problems of governance and insecurity.

The large-scale projects for river basin development in Africa in the second half of the twentieth century had mixed success, creating as well as solving problems. Most observers have concluded the future should lie in smaller projects that are carefully developed in ways that are sensitive to local needs and environmental diversity. However, large-scale projects retain their allure for planners who are impatient to bring about change. The future is balanced between those who would wish river basin development to adapt to the environment, and those who wish to transform it.

See also **Agriculture; Desertification, Modern; Ecosystems; Energy; Niger River; Nile River; Production Strategies; World Bank.**

BIBLIOGRAPHY

Adams, W. M. *Wasting the Rain: Rivers, People, and Planning in Africa.* London: Earthscan, 1992.

Moris, J. R., and D. J. Thom. *Irrigation Development in Africa: Lessons of Experience.* Boulder, CO: Westview Press, 1990.

Scudder, T. *The Future of Large Dams: Dealing with the Social, Environmental, and Political Costs.* London: Earthscan, 2005.

Waterbury, J. *The Nile Basin: National Determinants of Collective Action.* New Haven, CT: Yale University Press, 2002.

World Commission on Dams. *Dams and Development: A New Framework for Decision-Making.* London: Earthscan, 2000.

WILLIAM M. ADAMS

WEAVING. *See* **Arts: Basketry and Mat Making; Textiles.**

WESTERN AFRICA, FOREST REGION, HISTORY OF (1000 TO 1880).

The rain forest of West Africa runs along the coast from Guinea Bissau to Cameroon with the exception of the Dahomey Gap, an area between eastern Ghana and western Nigeria where a drier woodland savanna reaches down to the coast. The limits of forest vegetation in the interior have varied historically with changing rainfall patterns, and to a lesser extent with the activities of humans. The boundary between forest and savanna is believed to have fluctuated as much as 124 miles over the past millennium. Beginning circa 1100 and continuing to circa 1500, the climate of West Africa was subject to a dry period that saw the retreat of the northern boundary of the forest to the south. A short wet period from 1500 to 1630 was followed by drier times that lasted to the late nineteenth century. These climate variations provided the setting for important changes in the relationships of forest to savanna peoples.

The relative wetness of the forest fostered a hostile disease environment that made human life difficult and resulted in pro-natalist values among the agricultural societies that developed there. Along with much of the savanna woodland that abutted it, the forest was home to malaria as well as the tsetse fly, a vector for trypanosomiasis (sleeping sickness), which infects humans and is deadly to horses, camels, donkeys, sheep, and all but one breed of cattle. Although a hindrance to local animal husbandry, the tsetse helped protect forest dwellers from domination by horse-mounted warrior societies of the savanna.

Because of the difficulty of clearing land in the forest areas, settlement tended to be later than the peopling of the savanna, and an increase in the human population in the forest of necessity was related to the dissemination of iron technology to clear the heavy vegetation, which occurred in the first millennium CE or before. Small settlements were created around cleared land and were only gradually enlarged; in some areas, these village polities remained the standard unit of government, even though peoples over a broad area might share cultural and linguistic habits. Trade with outsiders oriented these forest peoples initially toward the savanna and, with the arrival of sea links and European traders shortly before 1500, increasingly toward the coast. They produced kola, spices, gold, ivory, and slaves to trade both north and overseas. Communities and at times states developed both within the forest and at the boundaries that separated the forest from the savanna in the north and from the ocean in the south. But it was the boundary communities and states—as they straddled the physical and cultural differences between the forest peoples on the one hand and their trading partners in the savanna or in Europe on the other—that became important intermediaries between forest and savanna peoples. The history of the forest peoples is best understood through a consideration of three distinct sub-regions that now comprise portions of (1) Nigeria, (2) Ghana and to a lesser extent southeastern Côte d'Ivoire, and (3) Liberia, Sierra Leone and Guinea.

NIGERIAN FOREST

The watershed of the lower Niger River was home to major states even before 1000. East of the Niger, Igbo-speaking peoples developed the Nri civilization, which flourished in the ninth and tenth centuries CE and was on the decline by 1000, while the Yoruba-speaking city-state of Ife had been built west of the river by that date. Ife, the founding city-state of a series of urban-based polities scattered across the forest and the eastern Dahomey Gap, was the most powerful Yoruba state until the fifteenth century. Bénin, located between Ife and the Niger, grew up in the fourteenth and reached its zenith in the mid-fifteenth century.

The forest dwellers' preference for yams as staple crops, which grew best on virgin soil, required concentrations of population for clearing land and fostered long distance trade links within the region. Goods sent north through the middleman states of Igala and Nupe were exchanged in part for copper, which supported local brass casting technology. Remarkable brass castings and terra cotta works from these cultures have been famously incorporated into museum collections. The states of the Nigerian forest area were characterized by political systems that featured rulers with religious as well as secular authority who were balanced by chiefs representing major families. Women were important politically and are known to have been rulers, particularly in Yoruba states, though more commonly power was divided between male and female offices.

Portuguese mariners opened commercial contacts with the empire of Bénin in 1485. For more than a century cotton cloth, a women's enterprise, was Bénin's most common export to these Europeans, who exchanged it along the coast of modern-day Ghana for gold. This pattern of Europeans trading African goods up and down the coast persisted until the establishment of sugar plantations in the Caribbean in the mid-seventeenth century. After these developments in the Americas, there followed a massive expansion of the slave trade along the West African coast. The Atlantic trade over time depressed local manufacturing, affected the demographics of the region, and influenced the rise and fall of numerous states. New imports included cowrie shells used for currency, guns, alcohol, textiles, and tobacco, while important New World crops transformed agriculture, as maize and manioc joined yams as staple food crops. The impact of firearms on warfare was limited, for the most effective warring was through the use of cutlasses, spears, and clubs in hand-to-hand combat. It was only with the introduction of rifles and early repeating guns in the second half of the nineteenth century that European forces acquired the technology to achieve colonial conquest.

Each of the states and communities of the Nigerian forest reacted differently to the expansion of the Atlantic slave trade. The state of Bénin sold slaves intermittently well into the nineteenth century but also produced and exported a diverse set of goods in addition to slaves, who were largely war captives. In Igbo country east of the Niger, village-level polities dominated the political culture, but this did not prevent the communities there from participating actively in the slave trade. Through the manipulation of an oracle, Arochukwu, the Aro Igbo, for example, were able to funnel large numbers of individuals convicted rightly or wrongly of any number of crimes into the slave trade. Along the coast and in the Niger delta, warring middleman city-states in places like Bonny and Calabar emerged to control access to the interior and prospered from slave trading.

To the west and northwest of the Nigerian forest, the more open and accessible Dahomey Gap made slave raiding easier, and this, in turn, prompted consolidation of scattered settlements into states, even as slave trading routes developed through the area to coastal entrepôts. Allada, already in existence when Europeans arrived along the coast, became both a slave-trading kingdom and a major port for the export of slaves that flourished until its destruction by the inland kingdom of Dahomey in 1724. Dahomey appears to have formed sometime in the seventeenth century from the amalgamation of village-sized polities into a state that could prevent most raids from Allada and other neighbors. Dahomey, itself, then fell subject to Oyo in 1730, the most northerly of the Yoruba city-states, which was located between the forests and Muslim Hausa states in the savanna. Oyo's military successes were based, in part, on the fact that it was located in an area that permitted the use of horses. After developing a cavalry force by the early eighteenth century, Oyo made forays against adjoining regions to the southwest, set up tributary relationships with the peoples raided and conquered, and took advantage of its successful conquest of Dahomey to sell its war captives into the slave trade using trading routes that ran through the Dahomey Gap. In the late eighteenth century Oyo itself was destabilized by internal politics and the impact of the jihadist movement to the north, and civil war broke out. The resulting movement of people south disrupted both forest and woodland savanna peoples, leading to the founding of new Yoruba city-states such as Ibadan and to recurrent warfare among them in the nineteenth century. These struggles in turn resulted in enormous growth in slave exports, particularly to Cuba.

THE GOLD COAST AND NEIGHBORING AREAS

The exploitation of gold fields in the interior, which began sometime after 1000, expanded with the opening of overseas trade in the late fifteenth century along the beaches west of the Volta, which Europeans designated accordingly as the Gold Coast. Local coastal rulers kept the Europeans out of the interior but permitted them to build stone "castles" in exchange for the payment of rents and duties. Those castles, unique along the West African coast and important heritage sites in the early twenty-first century, were built in the sixteenth and seventeenth centuries by trading companies of the Portuguese, Dutch, English, Danes, and Germans.

In the heavily forested interior of southern Ghana, settlement was sparse in the 1000–1500 period. The gold sold to the Europeans paid for the purchase of slaves acquired both north of the forest and from the Portuguese that was needed to clear the forest areas for large-scale human settlement. The high-calorie New World crops maize and manioc fed these laborers brought in from elsewhere, who were then integrated into Akan matrilineages. A series of town-centered states developed as the population grew around the trading networks. As in the Nigerian forest, women were prominent politically and each state was headed by a male-female pair of rulers.

Political consolidation and the growth of larger states began in the seventeenth century. This often-violent process culminated in a powerful Asante state founded late in that century as a confederation headquartered in an inland capital, Kumasi. In less than 100 years Asante became an empire covering a good deal of present-day Ghana. In the eighteenth century, slave selling to Europeans and slave buying in the savannas to the north increased dramatically, while gold was kept internally as a mark of the success of the ruling classes. Coastal trading entrepôts, meanwhile, developed Creole cultures from the mixing of European traders and local women.

UPPER GUINEA FORESTS OF LIBERIA, SIERRA LEONE, AND GUINEA

Similar Creole communities, formed through the interaction of the early Portuguese with local women who had access to trading networks in the interior, were important from the fifteenth century on the coast of Guinea. However, ties to the interior, especially to the Mali empire and its sixteenth- and seventeenth-century successors in the savanna, shaped the forest cultures of Upper Guinea in important ways. Well before the era of European contact, peoples in the Guinea forest had developed techniques for cultivating wet rice, *Oryza glaberrima*, which had been domesticated in the Niger River inland delta to the north and which became their staple food. The Guinea forests also produced malaguetta pepper, ivory, iron, timber such as mahogany, and the cam from camwood that became an important dye.

The difficulty of clearing living spaces in these forests promoted village-sized settlements that persisted to the late nineteenth century, but regional cohesion emerged through the development of "secret societies" into which all young people were initiated in gender-separate schools. The Poro society for men and Sande/Bundu for women provided common cultural experiences, avenues for the exercise of political power, and limited means for safe travel in the region. These initiation societies were based on models from Mande peoples of the savanna. Like their neighbors to the north, the forest peoples practiced a form of social integration for outsiders in which (male) strangers were incorporated into lineages through being given women as wives by local patrons.

A mid-sixteenth century invasion of warriors known as *Mani*, and the movement into the area of smiths and traders who had been intermediaries between the forest and the Mande heartland in the savanna, followed the opening of trade links with European commercial interests and also helped integrate the Lower Guinea coast culturally. These invaders conquered and then were absorbed culturally in the areas of present-day Sierra Leone and Liberia. The constant lack of security in the area meant that the Guinea forest peoples developed important skills and strategies of defensive warfare unique to the area.

In the late eighteenth century, the British selected a site at the mouth of the Sierra Leone River for Freetown, designed as a colony for African peoples returning from the Western Hemisphere and later for victims of the slave trade re-captured and released there by the British navy. The American Colonization Society similarly established Monrovia in modern Liberia as a haven for freed slaves from the United States who wished to return to Africa. The Monrovia hinterland was recognized as the independent nation of Liberia by 1847, while Freetown's adjacent interior became the British protectorate of Sierra Leone at the end of the nineteenth century. Both of these colonies developed difficult relations with the peoples of their respective interiors that persisted into the twentieth century.

See also **Agriculture; Creoles; Niger River; Slave Trades: Atlantic, Western Africa; Slavery and Servile Institutions; Textiles; Western Desert and Margins, History of (1000 BCE to 600 CE).**

BIBLIOGRAPHY

Bay, Edna G. *Wives of the Leopard: Gender, Politics and Culture in the Kingdom of Dahomey*. Charlottesville: University of Virginia Press, 1998.

Brooks, George. *Landlords and Strangers: Ecology, Society, and Trade in Western Africa, 1000–1630*. Boulder, CO: Westview Press, 1993.

Ehret, Christopher. *The Civilizations of Africa: A History to 1800*. Charlottesville: University of Virginia Press, 2002.

Hawthorne, Walter. *Planting Rice and Harvesting Slaves: Transformations along the Guinea-Bissau Coast, 1400–1900*. Portsmouth, NH: Heinemann, 2003.

Iliffe, John. *Africans: The History of a Continent*. Cambridge, U.K.: Cambridge University Press, 1995.

EDNA G. BAY

WESTERN AND SAHARAN AFRICA, HISTORY OF (600 TO 1600 CE).

West Africa and the Sahara saw the rise and fall of several major empires from the mid-first millennium through first half of the second millennium. Archeology is beginning to understand that the region's history is much more than the sum of its imperial achievements. Though claiming grand swaths of land, these early states often failed to exercise direct control over the populations in their core territory. Empires were highly dependent on the largely autonomous communities in their lands, rather than vice versa. Most societies were small in scale, based on local agriculture and organized along ethnic and linguistic lines. Some had exaggerated political hierarchies, though most were fairly egalitarian. Postcolonial archaeological findings suggest that these populations were much more dynamic than historians previously thought, as revealed by the highly developed and interrelated networks of ideas, goods, and power flowing across the region. For example, Jenné-Jeno, lying along the Niger River in present-day Mali, was a major metropolitan cluster for more than two thousand years (1000 BCE–1400 CE), drawing in trade from near and far and exhibiting a high degree of socio-cultural sophistication.

The regional climate entered an 800-year-long wet phase around 300 CE, improving the conditions for farming. Ironworking was already a common practice throughout West Africa by 500 BCE.

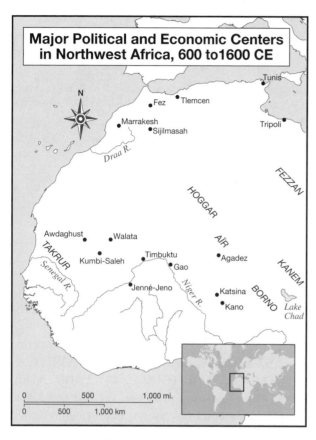

Major Political and Economic Centers in Northwest Africa, 600 to 1600 CE

COURTESY OF JACOB MUNDY

Nomadic and seminomadic groups in the Sahara and the predesert grasslands herded cattle and used camels for trade and transportation; their coastal counterparts often fished. In the much more lush climes further south, sedentary populations grew corn, millet, yams, nuts, African rice, cotton, and tobacco, while also hunting, fishing and herding. Since the first millennium BCE, interregional trade was already an important aspect of economic life. Caravans crisscrossing the Sahara sent out slaves, spices and ivory, bringing back copper, silver, and other goods. Among West Africa's exports, the region was best known for its gold, which dominated the markets of Europe and the Near East. It was the resource that made, and broke, local empires.

The first large West African power of the first millennium was Ghanaian empire of the Soninke people, emerging in the third century in Kumbi-Saleh. By the ninth century, Ghana controlled western Saharan trade, especially gold and salt. Its elite classes were a mix of warriors and traders, some claiming divine nature. Ghana's regional

political rivals were Takrur, to the west along the Senegal River, and Kanem, based around Lake Chad. The Empire of Ghana lasted until the eleventh century when it was challenged by a religious movement that stormed out of the Sahara.

ISLAM REACHES THE SAHARA

The Sahara Desert started developing some seven thousands years ago, attaining its current extent by 2000 BCE. As the environment became harsher and harsher, populations in the Sahara either adapted or migrated away. From the Atlantic to Lake Chad, the peoples of the region represent a mix of both West and North African influences, though genetic analyses suggest population continuity since the Paleolithic (30,000–40,000 years ago). The arrival of the camel two millennia later helped Saharans cope with the challenges of living in the great desert. It also helped facilitate trade between North and West Africa, the Sahara's signature enterprise. For many, the camel was—and still is—a way of life.

There were three major trans-Saharan trade routes during the first and second millennium. Their northern and southern ports often changed depending on which regional power could exert the most influence. In the northwest, there was Sijilmasa (Morocco); in the central north, Tlemcen (Algeria); and, in the east, Tunis (Tunisia) and Tripoli (Libya). An archipelago of southern ports stretched from the Atlantic to Lake Chad. The most prominent were Awdaghust, Tagdawst, Kumbi-Saleh and Walāta (Mauritania); Jenné, Timbuktu, and Gao (Mali); Kano and Katsina (Nigeria); Takkeda and Agdez (Niger); and Lake Chad. Some of these, such as Kumbi for Ghana and Gao-Timbuktu for Songhay, would become empires' seats of power, providing rulers with direct control over the flow of goods through the Sahara. Stretching from Mauritania to the Red Sea, the belt of grasslands separating the desert and the savanna below it earned the name *al-sahil* (Sahel), Arabic for littoral or shore.

The Islamic invasion of Northwest Africa reached the Atlantic by 700, and soon crossed into Spain. Saharan populations started adopting Islam a century later; in the Sahel, the ruler of Gao converted in 1010 and the Lake Chad region saw an early Islamic state around this time. As Muslim sociologists and historiographers started to study this region, they began making distinction between the "white" Arabs and native Berbers of North Africa, calling them both *al-bidan*, and the "black" peoples of south of the Sahara, *al-sudan*, from which the entire region below the desert would earn the name Sudan.

Islamic scholars also identified three main indigenous groups inhabiting the Sahara and the lands along the Mediterranean. The Zenagah (*al-sanhajah* in Arabic) were nomadic pastoralists in the western Sahara. Their homelands formed a triangle from present-day southern Morocco to the Aïr massif in Niger to the Senegal River. The Zenagah's neighbors to the north were the Masmudah, in present day Morocco, and the Zenata to the northeast, controlling Sijilmasa to Libya. The Zenagah had three major branches, the coastal Gudalah, the western-central Lamtunah and the northeastern Massufah. Where twentieth-century French and Spanish colonial ethnography insisted that Saharan societies were stratified into warrior, artisan and slave castes, more recent scholarship has revealed that these categories were regularly transgressed.

It was the Lamtunah Zenagah who would create one of the most spectacular—albeit short-lived—empires in all of Northwest African history. Around 1040, 'Abdullah Ibn Yasin al-Gazuli, a reportedly strict Islamic instructor, trained in southern Morocco, began proselytizing in the Sahara. Calling themselves *al-murabitun* (Almoravids), Ibn Yasin led a Lamtunah army out of the desert around 1050. By 1090, the Almoravid power was at its zenith, having seized Sijilmasa, established Marrakesh as their capital, occupied half of Spain and undermined the Ghanaian empire, mostly under the leadership of Ibn Yasin's successors, 'Abu Bakr Ibn 'Umar and Yusuf Tashfin. Controlling such a vast empire quickly became impossible. A Masmudah movement, *al-muwahhidun* (Almohads), emerged to claim the northern part of Almoravid lands; to the south, the Malian empire took the other half.

After the western Zenaga transitioned back to the margins of power, they found their lands increasingly under threat from Arabs of Yemeni origin. These were the Awlad Hassan, a massive contingent of Bedouin invaders grouped around the six sons of Hassan Ibn 'Aqil. Also known as the Banu Hassan or Ma'qil, this new regional

presence—what Islamic historian Ibn Khaldun likened to a swarm of locusts—had been unleashed by the Fatimid Caliphate in Egypt to North Africa circa 1050. Unable to break through the mountains of Morocco, these tribes headed south, taking control of Sijilmasa by the fourteenth century. Over the course of the next three hundred years, the Banu Hassan variously conquered, subordinated, assimilated and combined with the Zegana, resulting in the Arab-identifying and -speaking populations of modern Mauritania and Western Sahara. Further east, in lands untouched by Ma'qil influence, the mostly nomadic populations of the central Sahara, maintained their Berber language and social systems. In the twenty-first century, these populations are collectively known as Tuareg (*al-tawariq* in Arabic) or Kel Tamashaq.

THE GREAT WEST AFRICAN ISLAMIC EMPIRES

The crumbling Almoravid empire precipitated inter-regional conflicts among the Ghanaian communities in the twelfth century. One breakaway faction, the Malinke, formed their own kingdom in the upper Niger River and, a century later, created the Malian empire under the Keita dynasty (1230–1390), first led by Sundiata (or Sunjata) and then his son, Mansa Wali. Having taken control of key Saharan trade posts (Jenné, Gao, and Timbuktu) with their large army, Mali held immense influence over European and Middle Eastern gold markets. The height of Malian power was in the early fourteenth century during the reign of Mansa Musa, who doubled its land. Under him, Islam became the official religion, supported by efforts to develop Islamic knowledge and practices (architecture and scholarship) throughout West Africa. As a pious Muslim, Mansa Musa traveled to Mecca in 1324, bringing so much gold with him that he famously depressed global prices while visiting Cairo. In Timbuktu, Sankore University was founded as a center for international higher learning in 1327. Mansa Musa's successors, however, could not maintain the empire as more and more trading centers declared their independence.

The Malian empire disintegrated over the next two hundred years. The Hausa leader Yaji (1348–1385), their first to convert to Islam, challenged Malian hegemony from Kano. Other regional powers

Mosque of Sankore, Timbuktu, Mali. This mosque, built in the fifteenth century with mud and metal studs, was also used as a university. Within 100 years of its construction it held one of the largest schools of Arabic learning in the Islamic world. © SANDRO VANNINI/CORBIS

included Bénin, to the south of Mali, and Bornu, north of Lake Chad. However, the Kawkaw, along the Niger River south of Gao, began asserting the most influence. They eventually arose as the Songhay empire under Sunni 'Ali (1464–1492), taking Timbuktu (1468) and Jenné (1473). But it was under Askia Muhammed Turé (1493–1528) that the Songhay attained its greatest extent, encompassing all the lands of the defunct Malian empire. With Timbuktu as its major center of Islamic learning and trade, Songhay influence was felt from Europe to China. Like the empires of the Almoravids and Mali, the leaders of Songhay drew their legitimacy from Islam. Muhammed Turé, who had converted and made Islam the empire's religion, was later designated a *khalifah* (deputy) of the Sharif of Mecca. Following the death of Askia the Great, at the apex of its power, questions of succession destabilized the empire.

Sixteenth-century encroachment from the north also sapped Songhay power. In 1551, the Ottoman Empire seized Tunis and, twenty years later, pierced the Fezzan in the Libyan Sahara, giving them influence over the eastern Saharan trade routes outside of Songhay control. Then, in 1591, the Moroccan sultan Mulay al-Mansur, backed by European powers, crossed the Sahara and attacked the Songhay strongholds of Gao and Timbuktu, first looting them of their wealth and then leaving proxies to manage trade in Fez's interests. There were also more subtle interventions into West African and Saharan affairs at this time. Over the course of the 1400s and 1500s, Portuguese ships explored, raided, landed and traded all along Africa's Atlantic coast, a preview of the centuries to come.

See also **Fez; Gao; Ghana; Islam; Jenné and Jenné-jeno; Kano; Lake Chad Societies; Mali; Mansa Musa; Niger River; Sahara Desert; Sunni 'Ali; Timbuktu; Western Desert and Margins, History of (1000 BCE to 600 CE).**

BIBLIOGRAPHY

Cavalli-Sforza, L. Luca; Paolo Menozzi; and Alberto Piazza. *The History and Geography of Human Genes*. Princeton, NJ: Princeton University Press, 1994.

Cleaveland, Timothy. *Becoming Walāta: A History of Saharan Social Formation and Transformation*. Portsmouth, NH: Heinemann, 2002.

Falola, Toyin. *Key Events in African History: A Reference Guide*. Westport, CT: Greenwood, 2002.

Houtsma, Martijn Theodor, et al., eds. *The Encyclopaedia of Islam*, Vols. 3 and 6. Leiden and London: E.J. Brill and Luzac, 1991.

Lapidus, Ira M. *A History of Islamic Societies*. Cambridge, U.K.: Cambridge University Press, 1988.

MacEachern, Scott. "Two Thousand Years of West African History." In *African Archaeology: A Critical Introduction*, ed. Ann Stahl, pp. 441–466. London: Blackwell, 2004.

Norris, Harry T. *The Arab Conquest of the Western Sahara: Studies of the Historical Events, Religious Beliefs and Social Customs Which Made the Remotest Sahara a Part of the Arab World*. Burnt Mill, U.K.: Longman, 1986.

J. A. MUNDY

WESTERN DESERT AND MARGINS, HISTORY OF (1000 BCE TO 600 CE).

Climate and environment became significantly drier in the western Sahara and its margins after 4500–4000 Before the Present (BP), resulting in the progressive southward migration of the desert margin as rainfall declined. During the period 1000 BCE–600 CE (3000–1400 BP), the archaeological record of human occupation in Mali and Niger is concentrated between 15 degrees–17 degrees North, compared with a primary distribution from 18 degrees–22 degrees North in previous millennia. In Mauritania, people with livestock and domestic millet also moved south, but hunter/collectors persisted all along the coast and north to 20 degrees. Major arid crises occurred circa 3000 BP and circa 2000 BP, before climate ameliorated for several centuries beginning after 300 CE. Human responses to the challenges of climate change between 1000 BCE and 600 CE included changes in mobility patterns and schedules, colonization of new areas, adoption of new domestic animals, spread and further development of domesticated plants, increased sedentarization in favorable areas, and increasing importance of ecologically based exchange systems.

Between 3300 and 3000 BP (c. 1500–1000 BCE) agropastoralists who had occupied substantial villages in seasonally well-watered valleys and basins such as the Azawagh in Niger and the Hodh/Dhar Tichitt region of Mauritania moved southward with the sahel margin. They colonized regions such as the Middle Senegal Valley, the Méma along the Middle Niger, and the clay basins of a shrinking Lake Chad, for dry season pasture. Munson's classic work at Tichitt suggested that as seasonal lakes became less reliable after 3000 BP, sites were smaller, less numerous, and defensively positioned in nearly inaccessible areas. In the Lake Chad basin, defensive walls were built circa 500 BCE around several quite large (25-acre), recently discovered settlements. A widespread motif in Saharan rock art at this time is the bi-triangular-style, "libyan" warrior, carrying a spear and shield.

Increased mobility and conflict characterized the arid north during this period, while increased sedentarization characterized favored zones in the Sahel. In some cases of sedentarization and intensification, conflict may have been averted through the strategy of niche specialization and subsistence exchange, which linked producers in interdependent alliances. Archaeologists have suggested that this is the pattern seen in the first millennium BCE in the Mema and in the first millennium CE in the Inland Niger Delta. In both cases, the ecological interdependence (of fishers and agropastoralists) permitted the growth of larger settlements in a characteristic clustered pattern. By the mid-first millennium BCE in the Inland Niger Delta around Jenné-jeno, this pattern had assumed urban proportions. In areas unsuited for grazing or cultivation, hunting and collecting persisted, as in the case of the shellfish collectors of coastal Mauritania and along the estuary of the Senegal River.

In the Sahara, rock art of cattle from previous millennia was replaced by depictions of horses and riders and inscriptions in *tifinagh*, an alphabet related to Phoenician and used by Berbers into recent times. The introduction of horses provided distinct offensive advantages of speed and height that made raiding non-mounted groups highly successful. From 500 BCE to 400 CE, the Garamantes of the Fezzan (southwest Libya) used "Ethiopian" (i.e., black) slave-laborers kidnapped during raids using horse-drawn chariots to tap into the aquifers that made urban settlement in their desert kingdom possible. During this same period the horse may have begun to transform warfare and the political economy in the Sahel, but there is no evidence thus far for its presence before the sixth century CE.

With the introduction of the camel to the Sahara (the earliest archaeological evidence is second century CE), the horse, the chariot, and all wheeled vehicles disappear from rock art, replaced by camels. The ability of the camel to transport loads of 300 to 500 pounds across desert terrain without water for days transformed the desert economy, ultimately making large-scale, long-distance commodity trade possible. One of the earliest commodities traded surely was salt, which is required by camels, other livestock, and people, and is restricted in its West African distribution as rocksalt to a mere handful of localities in the desert. Control of salt sources and trade routes would emerge historically as a major source of political power in the first millennium CE. Whether the first millennium BCE salt trade was integrated into a true trans-Saharan trade carrying goods from North Africa to sub-Saharan regions has not yet been established.

Contacts between the Sahel and North Africa in the first millennium BCE are indisputable and implicated in the exploitation of copper sources in Mauritania (Akjoujt) and Niger (Agadez region) between 800 and 200 BCE. Mediterranean contact is demonstrated at Akjoujt by bronze jewelry in a North African style dated to the sixth century BCE. A distinctive style of copper earring has been found in graves from Morocco to southern Mauritania. Bronze jewelry has also been found in Niger. Years ago, it was suggested that Saharan Libyco-Berbers who worked the copper mines of southern Morocco for the Phoenicians, as Herodotus mentioned, may have introduced the technology to the south. The distribution of thousands of surface finds of copper in Mauritania along the seasonal grazing lands of interdunal depressions implicates mobile pastoralists in the movement of these objects from source areas such as Akjoujt.

Iron technology appears to be broadly co-eval with copper exploitation dating to 2600–2400 BP in the Agadez and Termit regions of Niger (smelting furnaces); 2600–2500 BP in the Lake Chad Basin; 2100 in the Inland Niger delta (Mali); and 2500 BP

in the Middle Senegal Valley. Scholarly debate about the indigenous versus exogenous origins of iron technology in West Africa centers on iron artifacts found on the eroded surface of some sites in the Termit region of Niger and the second millennium BCE dates on potsherds found on the same surfaces. Some archaeologists are skeptical that the iron and the pottery are contemporary; others argue that they are. Since iron contains carbon, it should be possible to radiocarbon date the iron objects directly and settle the question. Finer-grained chronological questions about the chronology of early metallurgy in various regions may be difficult to resolve with radiocarbon dating, however, due to the large date ranges (c. 300–400 years) that result when dates circa 2500 BP are calibrated. This is due to a plateau in the calibration curve at this point, created by the fact that tree-rings with known dates between 800 and 400 BCE have yielded radiocarbon dates circa 2500 BP. This phenomenon makes the chronological interpretation of a variety of events in the mid-first millennium BCE rather challenging.

In the western Sahara, the dry episode that occurred between 300 BCE and 300 CE was intense. The flow of the Senegal River was so reduced that freshwater did not reach the mouth, and salt water flowed 186 miles inland in the river channel circa 1900 BP. The abandonment of copper exploitation in both Mauritania and Niger by 2000 BP may reflect the disruptions to pastoral economies and the salt trade that accompanied this arid crisis. During this period, new settlers arrived in the Middle Senegal Valley, their pottery unlike that of the earlier agropastoralists, and Jenné-jeno in the Inland Niger Delta was settled as the flood level dropped. The development of camel herding in the first centuries CE was a strategy to cope with these environmental constraints.

Although it is unwise to generalize about climate change over large areas of Africa, since research has shown that at the scale of decades-long climate patterns adjacent regions can experience quite different patterns of wetter- and drier-than-usual climate, this dry period appears to have been quite widespread and severe. As it attenuated after 200 CE, Berber camel herders became more widely established. The appearance of black-and-white painted pottery in the Inland Niger Delta after 200 CE may testify to Berber contacts as far north as Germa in the Libyan Fezzan. Some historians are convinced that the trans-Saharan trade was established by this time, with the empire of Ghana emerging shortly thereafter. However, chemical studies of North African gold coinage indicate that the chemical signature of West African gold does not appear until the ninth century CE. Prior to that point, coins were struck from gold recycled from Byzantine coinage. While the empirical evidence for trans-Saharan exchange prior to the eighth century is weak, it is clear that climatic amelioration after 300 CE resulted in a new period of reinvigorated internal, long-distance trade for copper and salt, expansion of cattle pastoralism in the Sahel, and growth of communities in areas well positioned for agriculture and trade. On these foundations, the trading empires of the Western Sudan arose.

See also **Climate; Desertification, Reactions to, History of (c. 5000 to 1000 BCE); Ecosystems: Deserts and Semi-Deserts; Jenné-jeno; Sahara Desert; Transportation: Caravan; Western Africa, Forest Region, History of (1000 to 1880); Western and Saharan Africa, History of (600 to 1000 CE).**

BIBLIOGRAPHY

Bulliet, Richard W. *The Camel and the Wheel.* Cambridge, MA: Harvard University Press, 1975.

Keyes, David. "Kingdom of the Sands." *Archaeology* 57, no. 2 (March–April 2004).

Killick, D. "What Do We Know about African Iron Working?" *Journal of African Archaeology* 2, no. 1 (2004).

MacDonald, K. C. "Socio-Economic Diversity and the Origin of Cultural Complexity along the Middle Niger (2000 BC to AD 300)." Ph.D. diss. University of Cambridge, 1994.

McIntosh, Roderick. *Peoples of the Middle Niger.* London: Blackwell, 1999.

McIntosh, Susan. "Changing Perceptions of West Africa's Past: Archaeological Research since 1988." *Journal of Archaeological Research* 2, no. 2 (1994): 165–198.

Stahl, A., ed. *African Archaeology: A Critical Introduction.* London: Blackwell, 2004.

SUSAN KEECH MCINTOSH

WESTERN SAHARA. Also known as Sahara al-Gharbiyya and the Saharan Arab Democratic Republic (SADR), the Western Sahara is a sparsely populated desert territory in northwest Africa bordered by Morocco on the north, Algeria on the northeast, Mauritania on the east and south, and the Atlantic Ocean on the west. The Western Sahara covers 102,703 square miles and has a population of 273,000.

The first permanent inhabitants date back several thousand years to a period when the Western Sahara was part of a savanna zone covering much of the modern Sahara Desert. Rock paintings suggest that people lived by hunting and herding. Successive generations of mariners visited the coastal areas, including the Phoenicians in the fourth century BCE. The arrival of the camel in the first century CE brought a crucially important new way to travel across long distances and trade. Camels made new types of trading activities feasible and connected people across the Sahara. In the eighth century, intermarriage between Berbers and recently arrived Arabs and the spread of Islam worked together to create a new culture, with its own hybrid language, semi-nomadic lifestyle, and interpretations of Islam.

Beginning in the 1050s a group of holy warriors calling themselves *al-murabitun* originating from the Sahel moved north. The Almoravids (1073–1147) eventually ruled a territory that spanned the western portion of the Sahara, Morocco, and southern Spain, conquering the kingdom of Ghana. Successive Moroccan dynasties ignored their southern provinces, until the Saʿadian Sultan al-Mansur captured Timbuktu in 1591 in order to control the substantial trans-Saharan trade that went through it and defeat the Songhay Empire. The Moroccan invasion force drew on a large number of fighting men from south of the Atlas Mountains, including from the western desert.

Environmental shifts in the seventeenth and eighteenth centuries brought major changes to everyday life in the Western Sahara. Older trade patterns disintegrated and established long-distance routes slowly shifted from the Timbuktu corridor to the west, where trans- Saharan routes remained safer and water sources more assured. Growing long-distance trade and related services (guides, protection, supplies, and outfitting) also brought closer connections with Moroccan traders and holy men.

Long-distance trade waned after the 1830s, but by this time Europeans began to explore the area for possible ports. A series of European outposts were quickly abandoned, but in 1884 the Sociedad Española de Africanistas y Colonistas, led by Emilio Bonelli, signed a series of treaties with local leaders whereby the Spanish proclaimed a protectorate over the coastal zone. Rebel leaders such as Ma al-'Aynayn slowed Spanish colonization in the early twentieth century but could not stop it.

In 1957 Morocco claimed the Western Sahara but the Spanish army kept the disorganized Moroccan forces at bay. Spain merged Río de Oro and Saguia el Hamra into a single new province called the Spanish Sahara in 1958. Discoveries of valuable natural resources such as phosphates in the 1960s raised the interest of Mauritania as well as Morocco, but a new indigenous rebellion forced the Spanish to promise a referendum on independence.

On November 6, 1975, thousands of unarmed Moroccans crossed the border into the Western Sahara, an event known as the Green March. Spain immediately began to withdraw, although its official mandate ended February 26, 1976. Mauritania and Morocco subsequently split the territory, with Morocco claiming the phosphate-rich northern two-thirds and Mauritania taking the remaining third. A new insurgency called the Polisario Front (Popular Front for the Liberation of Saguia el Hamra and Río de Oro) emerged, supported by Algeria. The Polisario used the Algerian oasis of Tindouf as a base from which to attack both Moroccan and Mauritanian forces. Fierce fighting convinced Mauritania to pull out in 1979 and it now recognizes the Polisario's Saharan Arab Democratic Republic. Fighting with Morocco continued sporadically until a 1991 U.N. cease-fire, which hinged on a referendum over the future of the territory. The referendum has yet to take place, since neither side can agree on who should be allowed to vote. In the 1990s, the Polisario lost Algerian military support while the Moroccan government moved thousands of immigrants into the territory. Talks have since stalled with Morocco forcefully reasserting its claims and in 2005 renewed fighting seemed likely.

See also **Art, Genres and Periods: Rock Art, Saharan and North Africa; Ecosystems: Savannas; Morocco: History and Politics; Transportation: Caravan.**

BIBLIOGRAPHY

Hodges, Tony. *Western Sahara: The Roots of a Desert War.* Westport, CT: Lawrence Hill and Co., 1983.

Joffe, George. "Self-Determination and Uti Possidetis: The Western Sahara and the 'Lost Provinces.'" *The Journal of the Society for Moroccan Studies* 1 (1996): 97–115.

Keenan, Jeremy. *The Sahara: Past, Present and Future.* Spec. issue, *Journal of North African Studies* 10, nos. 3–4 (2005).

Pennell, C. R. *Morocco since 1830: A History.* London: C. Hurst and Co., 1997.

Zoubir, Yahia H., and Daniel Volman, eds. *International Dimensions of the Western Sahara Conflict.* Westport, CT: Praeger, 1993.

DAVID GUTELIUS

WIDOWS. *See* **Women: Widows.**

WILDLIFE

This entry includes the following articles:
PRESERVATION AND DESTRUCTION
NATIONAL PARKS
HUNTING, SPORT

PRESERVATION AND DESTRUCTION

Africa's wildlife is one of the earth's most unique and precious resources. Since time immemorial, Africans relied on many species as a food source. Early foreign travelers, hunters, explorers, and merchants returned to their homes with fantastic stories of magnificent and strange animals. As early as 166 CE, Roman merchants delivered ivory, rhinoceros horns, and tortoise shells to south China. Rome also imported many wild animals from North Africa for its games and circuses. In 1415, a giraffe arrived in China, much to the wonder and astonishment of court officials and the general population. Ivory, animal skins, and other curious or valuable trophies were prized throughout the Middle East, as well.

Preserving Africa's fauna historically has been a complex and frequently frustrating endeavor. As in other parts of the continent, North Africa had been home to a diverse array of fauna. Oral traditions and rock engravings throughout the region confirm the presence of a variety of wildlife, including Baboon, Barbary Lion, Barbary Red Deer, Barbary Sheep, Barbary Wild Boar, Cheetah, Elephant, Hippopotamus, Jackal, Gazelle (Addax, Atlas, Dama, and Dorcas), Leopard, Lion, Red Fox, Serval Cat, and Spotted Hyena.

The disappearance of most of these species has occurred primarily because of climatic change and desertification, deforestation, overgrazing, poor agricultural techniques, and unregulated hunting. Various North African and international conservation organizations are seeking to reintroduce at least some species to the region, however.

Between the mid-eighteenth and early nineteenth centuries, killing animals for profit became an increasingly lucrative industry in many parts of Africa. Robert Foran, one of the better-known British big-game hunters, estimated that, during the 1850–1890 period, at least 1,878,000 elephants had been killed to supply ivory to markets throughout the world. Other prized species included antelope, buffalo, cheetah, hippopotamus, leopard, and lion.

NINETEENTH-CENTURY CONSERVATION EFFORTS

The emergence of the European colonial powers (Britain, Belgium, France, Germany, Italy, Portugal, and Spain) marked a significant period of fundamental change in the nature of the human-fauna relationship. Big-game hunters flooded Africa seeking adventure and wealth, but many colonial governments took steps to protect Africa's rapidly diminishing fauna.

In 1886, for example, South Africa passed the Cape Act for the Preservation of Game and, in 1891, extended the legislation to all British South African territories. In 1892, the country established the Sabie Game Reserve in the Transvaal. In 1897, Herman von Wissman (1853–1905), governor of *Deutsch Ost Afrika* (present-day Tanzania), approved the establishment of a licensing system for hunting. In 1900, the colonial powers met in London and adopted the Convention for the Preservation of Animals, Birds and Fish in Africa. The Convention sought to standardize and enforce game laws throughout Africa; compile a list of endangered species; limit the sale of elephant tusks of less than eleven pounds; establish reserves and protect them from encroachment; and devise licenses that limited the numbers of each species that could be killed. However, the Convention never entered into force as most signatories failed to ratify it.

On December 11, 1903, Edward Buxton (1840–1924), a former British big-game hunter who became an ardent conservationist, established the Society for the Preservation of the Wild Fauna of the Empire (SPWFE) and served as its president. Within a year, the SPWFE had seventy ordinary and thirty honorary members, including Lord Kitchner of Khartoum; Alfred Lyttelton (1857–1913), Secretary of State for the Colonies; and President Theodore Roosevelt (1858–1919). The SPWFE also had five politically influential vice presidents (Lords Cromer, Grey, Milner, Curzon, and Minto). In later years, the SPWFE, which in 1950 changed its name to the Fauna Preservation Society, helped to facilitate the creation of the International Union for the Protection of Nature (1948), renamed the International Union for Conservation of Nature and Natural Resources in 1952, and the World Wildlife Fund (1961).

TWENTIETH-CENTURY CONSERVATION EFFORTS AND CHALLENGES

In the early twentieth century, conservationists advocated the creation of national parks throughout Africa. In 1925, King Albert Leopold I established a gorilla sanctuary in Congo called the *Parc National Albert* (later known as Virunga National Park); years later, three other national parks were created. In 1926, Colonel James Stevenson-Hamilton (1867–1957), who became the architect of South African game preservation, converted Sabie Game Reserve into Kruger National Park. The following year, Malagasy officials authorized the establishment of nature reserves in Madagascar.

On November 8, 1933, the London Conference for the Protection of African Fauna and Flora adopted the Convention Relative to Preservation of Fauna and Flora in Their Natural State. Two further technical meetings were held in London (1938) and Bukavu (1953), but little was accomplished, largely because of the outbreak of World War II and growing African demands for decolonization.

During the early postcolonial period, the Organization of African Unity (OAU; present-day

African Union), in collaboration with the World Conservation Union and several UN agencies, drafted the Algiers Convention that the OAU approved in 1968. In 1981, Cameroon and Nigeria urged the OAU to revise and update the Algiers Convention. On July 11, 2003, the African Union approved the Revised African Convention on the Conservation of Nature and Natural Resources. All these conventions, treaties, and agreements helped lay the foundation for the preservation of Africa's wildlife.

The history of African wildlife conservation varies from region to region. During the two world wars, hunters in Kenya, Tanzania, and, to a lesser extent, Uganda, killed untold numbers of wild animals to feed prisoners of war and Allied troops. In parts of these countries European settlers competed with wild animals for superiority over the land and its resources. An array of new threats also emerged, some more serious, including the advent of mass tourism that placed increasing pressure on fragile environments; lucrative big game hunting safaris, especially in Kenya and Tanzania; widespread large-scale poaching; and a rapidly growing human population that slowly established dominance over the land and its resources by killing wild animals or seeking to confine them to reserves or national parks.

In May 1947, the Conference on the Fauna of British Eastern and Central Africa was held in Nairobi. Conference resolutions called for scientific management, expert planning, and colonial governance in wildlife conservation. Game wardens who attended the meeting opposed the African hunting that had gone on for many centuries. Ironically, representatives from nearly all the territories reported that wildlife had been increasing. Nevertheless, Britain's Colonial Office accepted the report that African hunters had reduced fauna throughout the region.

By the early twenty-first century, many experts feared for the future of wildlife, despite the adoption of the 1977 Wildlife Conservation and Management Act that banned poaching and reckless killing of wild animals. In Kenya, for example, Lake Nakuru's pink flamingoes, which draw tourists from all over the world, have experienced a sharp decline because of receding water levels. Deforestation of the Mau mountain range, the region's largest remaining near-contiguous mountain forest, continues to deplete water levels in the Mara River that feeds the Maasai Mara National Reserve and the northwest corner of Tanzania's Serengeti. Developers are urging politicians to do away with Nairobi National Park, located on the city's southeast corner and now completely surrounded by the city and its suburbs.

In Uganda, the elephant population declined from some 30,000 in the 1960s to 1,350 in 1980 as a result of widespread ivory poaching and civil war. By the 1999–2003 period, the elephant population had increased to only 2,400. Other species also have suffered from the government's failure to protect the country's wildlife. According to a 2005 study titled *Wildlife Population Trends in Uganda, 1960–2005*, the Black Rhinoceros, White Rhinoceros, Oryx, and Derby's Eland are extinct. There also were significant declines in many other species between the 1960s and 1999–2003, including Burchell's Zebra (10,000 to 2,800), Eland (4,500 to 450), Elephant (30,000 to 2,400), Hartebeest (25,000 to 3,400), Hippopotamus (26,000 to 5,300), Uganda Kob (70,000 to 44,000), and Rothchild's Giraffe (2,500 to 240).

Tanzania's postindependence conservation record has been better than that of Kenya or Uganda. The number of national parks increased from eleven in 1989 to fourteen in 2005 and game reserves went from seventeen to thirty-four. The elephant population, which had been declining as a result of poaching, increased from 55,000 in 1989 to 141,646 in 2006. Tanzania and other African countries such as Botswana, Zambia, and Zimbabwe have embraced Community Based Conservation (CBC) that supposedly allows local communities to participate in the wildlife policy-making process. To facilitate grassroots involvement, Dar es Salaam devised a Wildlife Management Area whereby local people would have full mandate over conservation activities. However, some observers maintain that the governments that have adopted CBC still have the upper hand in devising and implementing wildlife policies.

South Africa, which maintains eighteen national parks, has one of Africa's better conservation records, especially with regard to its support of Trans-Frontier Parks. According to South African game officials and their counterparts throughout Southern Africa, Trans-Frontier Parks enhanced state-to-state cooperation and increased funding from implementing agencies, donors, and nongovernmental organizations (NGOs).

On May 12, 2000, South Africa and Botswana opened Southern Africa's first Trans-Frontier Park (Kgalagadi Trans-Frontier Park). On June 11, 2001, South Africa and Lesotho signed an agreement for the creation of the Maloti-Drakensberg Trans-Frontier Conservation and Development Area. On December 9, 2002, South Africa, Mozambique, and Zimbabwe opened the Great Limpopo Trans-Frontier Park.

CONSERVATION IN TWENTY-FIRST CENTURY AFRICA

In 2003, South Africa adopted The National Environment Management: Protected Areas Act No. 57. This legislation required the South African National Parks to produce conservation, protection, and management plans for all its national parks in consultation with local stakeholders. South Africa also acknowledged that wildlife and other natural resources had to contribute to the country's economic well-being.

In many respects, Zambia's postcolonial wildlife policies were in stark contrast to those of much richer South Africa. Kenneth Kaunda, Zambia's first president, wanted to preserve the country's wildlife but lacked the financial resources to fund large-scale conservation programs. Moreover, few Zambians shared his vision and wanted the country's limited resources to be devoted to social and economic development. Nevertheless, President Kaunda ensured the passage of the National Parks and Wildlife Act in 1968. However, it did not come into force until January 1, 1971 because of the need to add various amendments. Sadly, the ruling United National Independence Party used wildlife to reward its members, by virtue of their loyalty, with jobs, trophies, game meat, and concessions. There also was perpetual conflict between wildlife officials and the villagers whose ancestors had hunted fauna for food. As a result, poaching escalated and villagers found guilty of illegal hunting were fined or jailed. In the early twenty-first century, Zambia has nineteen national parks but many of them are not maintained, and contain no facilities and few animals.

Carcass of a black rhino mutilated by poachers, May 2006, Kenya's Tsavo east national park. Kenyan authorities killed three suspected poachers and recovered horns from rare black rhinos that were slain at the famed national park, which lies 300 kilometers southeast of Nairobi, during a massive hunt-down of poachers by security forces. STRINGER/AFP/GETTY IMAGES

West Africa's conservation record historically has also been substandard. Nigeria, West Africa's largest and most influential country, maintains eight national parks, nineteen game reserves/wildlife sanctuaries, and eight strict nature reserves. However, Nigeria lacks the resources to protect the conservation areas' biologically diverse environments.

Common problems throughout West Africa include environmental degradation, over-hunting, deforestation, unregulated poaching, logging, agricultural projects that pose dangers to fauna, growing urbanization, and widespread road construction. Despite enactment of wildlife regulations throughout the region, increasing international assistance for preserving the region's diminishing fauna, and some cooperation between states, public apathy, inadequate funding and game laws, and widespread corruption continue to threaten the conservation efforts.

One of the most serious threats to wildlife throughout Africa, particularly with regard to antelopes, chimpanzees, gorillas, and many other species, concerns bushmeat trafficking. According to the Washington, D.C.–based Bushmeat Crisis Task Force, more than one million tons of bushmeat is taken from Central Africa annually. Apart from the threat that bushmeat trafficking poses to wildlife, the Center for Disease Control and Prevention has reported that diseases that jump from wildlife to humans via the consumption of infected wild meat account for three-quarters of all emerging diseases.

Conservation of Africa's fauna faces an uncertain future despite widespread efforts to ensure its survival. Africa's great apes are diminishing at an increasingly alarming rate largely because of the insatiable demands of the industrialized world for cheap timber, agricultural products, and other natural resources. Africa's soaring human population and the relentless destruction of wildlife habitats are the most serious threats facing the continent. Additionally, land clearance, exploding human population, forest fires, and shrinking tropical forests not only reduces the survival rate of the great apes but also threatens many other wildlife species. Africans, particularly those who live in rural areas, frequently complain that wild animals eat crops and domestic livestock, destroy homes, and often injure or kill humans. In recent years, however, conservationists have sought to lessen human-animal conflict by creating new national parks and game reserves, building fences in areas populated by humans and fauna, and relocating species to more remote areas. Needless to say, many Africans who have suffered from the depredations of wild animals are not great supporters of conservation. Some countries share park fees and big game hunting revenues with local communities in hopes of lessening animosity toward wild animals. Tanzania and South Africa seem to have struck a balance between the needs of humans and wild animals, but this is unlikely to last because both are deeply committed to social and economic development.

See also **Colonial Policies and Practices; Dar es Salaam; Ecology; Heritage, Cultural: Management and Preservation; Ivory; Kaunda, Kenneth; Organization of African Unity; Tourism.**

BIBLIOGRAPHY

Anderson, David, and Richard H. Grove, eds. *Conservation in Africa: Peoples, Policies and Practice.* Cambridge, U.K.: Cambridge University Press, 1990.

Caldecott, Julian, and Lera Miles, eds. *World Atlas of Great Apes and Their Conservation.* Berkeley: University of California Press, 2005.

The International Union for the Conservation of Nature and Natural Resources—The World Conservation Union. *An Introduction to the African Convention on the Conservation of Nature and Natural Resources.* Cambridge, U.K.: The International Union for the Conservation of Nature and Natural Resources Publications Services Unit, 2004.

Morrison, Michael; Bruce G. Marcot; and R. William Mannan. *Wildlife-Habitat Relationships: Concepts and Applications.* Washington, DC: Island Press, 2006.

Neumann, Roderick P. *Imposing Wilderness: Struggles over Livelihood and Nature Preservation in Africa.* Berkeley: University of California Press, 2002.

Nienaber, Georgianne. *Gorilla Dreams: The Legacy of Dian Fossey.* Lincoln, NE: iUniverse, 2006.

Ofcansky, Thomas P. *Paradise Lost: A History of Game Preservation in East Africa.* Morgantown: West Virginia University Press, 2002.

Oldfield, Sara. *The Trade in Wildlife: Regulation for Conservation.* London: Earthscan, 2003.

THOMAS P. OFCANSKY

NATIONAL PARKS

Conservationists have long viewed national parks as the best way to protect wildlife in Africa south of the Sahara. In South Africa, the problem of wildlife diminution became a point of public concern in the early nineteenth century. Later in the century as European commerce and conquest expanded, observers noted a similar pattern of diminishing wildlife elsewhere. In response, big game hunters and conservationists in Europe and North America formed the Society for the Preservation of the Fauna of the Empire (SPFE) in 1903 to promote parks and conservation in the colonies. Using Yellowstone National Park in the United States as its model, London-based SPFE members began lobbying the British government to establish national parks in its new African colonies as early as 1905.

It was not until 1926, however, that the South African government established Kruger National Park (Kruger NP) as the first on the continent. Then in 1933 the London Convention, signed by all of the European colonial powers and their individual colonial governments, recommended the creation of national parks as the primary means of wildlife conservation. Colonial governments across Africa were slow to add new parks—Kenya and

Tanganyika established their first parks only in 1946 (Nairobi NP) and 1948 (Serengeti NP), respectively—and only in the postcolonial period did their numbers grow significantly.

The establishment of national parks was never simply and only about protecting wildlife. For instance, the growth of Afrikaner nationalism provided the political context for the creation of Kruger NP, which would serve to symbolically represent a white South African identity rooted in nature. National parks also served as the physical manifestation of a romantic European myth of Africa as an Edenic wilderness. Finally, and related to the myth of wild Africa, they came to serve as destinations for tourists from Europe and North America, especially after the establishment of international commercial air travel in the 1950s. As tourist destinations national parks can provide a major source of foreign exchange, a fact that helped convince postcolonial governments to greatly expand their number.

THE EFFECTS OF PARK ESTABLISHMENT ON INDIGENOUS AFRICAN COMMUNITIES

The establishment of national parks has historically generated conflicts with indigenous African communities, many of which remain unresolved in the early twenty-first century. By international agreement, a national park is a geographically expansive area where all human habitation and activities except tourism are prohibited. Thus parks were created in Africa through the linked processes of displacement of indigenous African populations and their relocation outside of park boundaries and the concentration of wildlife populations inside. Throughout Africa, parks have encompassed preexisting villages, cultivated fields, and grazing pastures, thereby altering rural settlement patterns, land use, and resource access. More often than not, those who claimed preexisting rights were compensated inadequately, if at all, and resettlement efforts were ill conceived or nonexistent.

The creation of national parks can affect customary land rights in several ways. First, governments may totally eliminate land rights through mass evacuations of people and their possessions from within the park's boundary. Second, governments typically have prohibited surrounding communities' access to critical resources (e.g., fuelwood, water, dry-season pasture, and building materials) or ceremonial sites within park boundaries. Access prohibitions have severely affected nomadic pastoralists since prime livestock pastures often overlap with important wildlife habitat, particularly in East Africa. Third, crop-raiding park wildlife can inhibit people's ability to fully utilize agricultural lands or pastures near boundaries. Governments often ban farmers and pastoralists from harming wild animals within the vicinity of national parks, even in the defense of crops.

It is important to view conflicts between people and parks within their larger social, legal, and political contexts. The origins of the park policy of exclusion can be traced to European colonization and an Anglo-American conservationist ideology that still prevails to a significant degree. Most of the conservation laws date from the colonial period and, although undergoing periodic revision, have not been substantively altered. Many of the national parks created by postcolonial governments have been based on existing colonial game and forest reserves. The SPFE and the big international conservation nongovernmental organizations (NGOs) that succeeded it—such as the World Conservation Union (IUCN; formerly the International Union for the Conservation of Nature and Natural Resources) and the Worldwide Fund for Nature (WWF; formerly the World Wildlife Fund)—have been instrumental in promoting and funding a "fortress" approach to conservation across the continent.

Moreover, colonial and postcolonial governments have incorporated park evictions and resettlement into larger national development schemes. Colonial governments created many of parks and reserves as part of an overall process of European land alienation. For example, some park evictions were integral to the Southern Rhodesian government's agenda of establishing exclusive European settlement zones in the 1950s and 1960s. Some postcolonial governments viewed evictions from parks as complementing their rural development agendas, such as in the case of Tanzania's *Ujamaa* (socialism and self-reliance) villagization scheme, which involved the forced abandonment of scattered homesteads and relocation of rural populations into concentrated settlements.

Compounding many of the people-park conflicts are the problems associated with identifying preexisting land rights. Identification of legitimate claims is difficult, partly because of the lack of title deeds or other written legal documentation of historic land occupation and in part because of the distortions of African tenure systems under colonialism. These two problems allow numerous and conflicting interpretations of the validity of land-rights claims within national parks.

PRESENT ISSUES AND TRENDS

The political and economic context for national parks has changed significantly since democratization and neoliberal economic reforms were implemented in the 1980s. Foreign investments are pouring into the tourist sector, creating new opportunities for and challenges to local community land claims. New Africa-based environmental, legal, and human rights NGOs have taken up the causes of populations displaced by national parks in the courts. African governments and big international NGOs have recognized that conflicts threaten wildlife protection and have initiated programs intended to redistribute the benefits of conservation locally and promote community participation. At the same time, concerns over declining elephant and rhino populations in the 1980s led toward further militarizing the parks. Another major new initiative is the creation of transboundary (also transnational or transfrontier) parks, most notably the Great Limpopo Transboundary Conservation Area that spans the boundaries of South Africa, Mozambique, and Zimbabwe. Such protected areas are intended to overcome the problems posed by political boundaries for ecological processes, such as long-distance wild animal migrations, and to promote regional integration. In the case of the Great Limpopo, the largest such endeavor, the establishment of transboundary protected areas has translated on the ground to new forms of enclosure, restrictions on human settlement and movement, and displacements of local communities. Thus, some of these new trends help relieve existing people-park conflicts, while others reproduce historic conflicts or create the conditions for new ones, thereby raising challenging questions about the future of national parks in Africa.

See also **Aid and Development; Colonial Policies and Practices; Human Rights; Nongovernmental Organizations;** **Production Strategies; Socialism and Postsocialisms; Tourism.**

BIBLIOGRAPHY

Adams, William. *Against Extinction: The Story of Conservation.* London: Earthscan, 2004.

Adams, William, and Martin Mulligan, eds. *Decolonizing Nature: Strategies for Conservation in a Post-colonial Era.* London: Earthscan, 2003.

Anderson, David, and Richard Grove, eds. *Conservation in Africa: People, Policies, and Practice.* Cambridge, U.K.: Cambridge University Press, 1987.

Brockington, Daniel. *Fortress Conservation: The Preservation of the Mkomazi Game Reserve, Tanzania.* Oxford: James Currey, 2002.

Carruthers, Jane. *The Kruger National Park: A Social and Political History.* Pietermaritzburg, South Africa: University of Natal Press, 1995.

Hughs, David McDermott. *From Enslavement to Environmentalism: Politics on a Southern African Frontier.* Seattle: University of Washington Press, 2006.

Igoe, Jim. *Conservation and Globalization: A Study of National Parks and Indigenous Communities from East Africa to South Dakota.* Belmont, CA: Wadsworth/ Thompson Learning, 2004.

Neumann, Roderick P. *Imposing Wilderness: Struggles over Nature and Livelihoods in Africa.* Berkeley: University of California Press, 1998.

Ranger, Terrence. *Voices from the Rocks: Nature, Culture and History in the Matopos Hills of Zimbabwe.* Oxford: James Currey, 1999.

RODERICK P. NEUMANN

HUNTING, SPORT

With the passage of a law in 1977 making all sport hunting in Kenya by residents and visitors illegal, a new era in African sport hunting began. Although hunting remains legal in Tanzania and many other African countries, including, most importantly, in Zimbabwe, Zambia, and Botswana, the response of the government of Kenya to the pressures and inducements of international conservation lobbies marked a watershed in the two-centuries-long history of sport hunting on the African continent.

If one excludes hunting for sport by Africans (a time-honored practice outside the usual understanding of sport or big game hunting), the beginnings of sport hunting in Africa are found among the early scientific and geographical observers and hunters on the South African frontier in the eighteenth and early nineteenth centuries. An avid readership was discovered for tales of frontier adventure by hunters such as Andrew Smith, William Harris, R. G. Cumming, and, later, Frederick Selous. South African sport hunting was tied closely to the expanding frontier of exploration and settlement. By the 1870s, the frontier and the variety and abundance of game animals in South Africa was declining. The frontier moved north through Zimbabwe (Rhodesia) and Mozambique and in the 1880s leaped northward as growing British influence on the Swahili coast and the well-publicized exploits of explorers such as Verney Cameron and Joseph Thomson drew attention to the hunting possibilities of the East African interior. Hunters with experience of Southern and Central Africa, such as Selous and Captain Charles Stigand, followed these new game trails.

The opening of the "sportsman's paradise" of the hunting grounds of Kenya, Uganda, and Tanganyika stimulated a flow of international visitors. Several factors beyond the shear abundance of game contributed to attracting the rich and famous of Europe and North America to East Africa: the relative ease of ocean transport after the opening of the Suez Canal in 1869; the existence of an established commercial caravan route; and the safari trade connecting the Swahili coastal ports to the distant interior of the East African Great Lakes. Later, the construction of the Uganda Railroad through some of the region's best hunting fields and the program of settlement of European men and women with capital and titles in what became the East African "white highlands" also contributed to the creation of a new kind of sport hunting: the big game safari, which reached its height between World War I and World War II.

Safari hunting emerged directly from the fusion of Arab-Swahili commercial caravans and the European, mostly British, tradition of "The Hunt" viewed as a suitable activity for gentlemen and nobles as well as many parvenus. The trading safari was a means of travel into the interior used by early explorers, soldiers, and administrators for whom hunting was a major preoccupation. Their interest led to European organization of their own safaris to the interior and to the exploitation of the abundant game shot en route as a "meat bonanza"

for their numerous porters and to subsidize their travel expenses.

Prompted by the decline of hunting in Europe and the American West as well as southern Africa, many wealthy and titled gentlemen came to East Africa on safari. Lords Delamere and Cranworth were among the first members of the English nobility to come to hunt and eventually settled in Kenya's white highlands to accommodate their hunting passion. Winston Churchill and Theodore Roosevelt both came to East Africa in the first decade of the twentieth century to hunt on safari using the pretext of imperial or scientific inquiries as justification. Roosevelt especially made a signal contribution to the fame of East Africa as a sportsmen's paradise and introduced the term *safari* to English speakers around the world. Moreover, these two distinguished visitors contributed directly to the other distinguishing feature of sport hunting in Africa: the emergence of the professional white hunter (PWH) as a class of entrepreneurs who used their local knowledge of African languages and terrains to create a market for their services as guides and hunting companions.

Because of their prominence, both Churchill and Roosevelt were accorded the hospitality of the British East African governments, which provided them with the services of local resident hunters as companions on their safaris. By the time of the outbreak of World War I, Nairobi had become the seat of an emerging industry of professional hunting guides, men of experience and skill as hunters, often well-educated and from the upper classes, who made their living doing what many of them had come to East Africa to do: hunt as sportsmen. Bror Blixen and Denys Fitch Hatton were the best known of these gentlemen professionals, or great white hunters, although ultimately both became better known for their marital and extramarital relations with the writer Karen Blixen (Isak Dinesen).

From early in the century until the end of legal hunting in Kenya, the presence on safari of such professional hunters became a distinguishing feature of sport hunting in Africa that was unparalleled elsewhere in hunting annals. Beneath the glare of celebrity of both the visitors and their professional white hunters, the big game safari's success depended always on the skills and labor of the hundreds of African hunters now turned trackers, gun bearers, scouts, porters, skinners, cooks, and laborers, without whom the safari could not have functioned. Indeed, the key skill required of the safari leader was his ability to recruit, organize, and communicate (generally in "kitchen" Swahili) with African staff, who knew where to find game and to locate their camp after dark.

Between 1919 and 1939 the reputation for glamour and status of the big game safari reached its peak of celebrity, not in small part due to the efforts of Dinesen, Ernest Hemingway, Beryl Markham, and other literary hunters. During this period, punctuated by a series of royal safari (e.g., the Dukes of York, Gloucester, and Norfolk, the Prince of Wales, and the Majarajah of Jodhpur), the safari practices of the early years were formalized. PWHs became a requirement for visiting hunters' safaris and created an association for their self-regulation. The trophy industry became regularized with careful recordkeeping and standards of measurement. The list of favored game animals was standardized as the "Big Five" (lion, leopard, elephant, rhino, and buffalo), and the well-established game department began to regulate the "bag" and permitted methods of hunting and taking game as well as publicizing the hunting opportunities for European and other sportsmen. In addition, photographic safaris grew in popularity and prominence as cameras became more portable and safari travel became specialized and easier with the development of the Land Rover and other overland vehicles for the transport of hunters, photographers, and their staffs, along with their equipment and supplies. Despite growing international attention and popularity, the big game safari remained the preserve of the wealthy elite of the world's sportsmen and sportswomen as the costs of international travel in time and money remained prohibitive for the world's growing middle classes.

After a hiatus in sport hunting caused by World War II, a new kind of safari hunter emerged as international air transportation and growing middle-class wealth in Europe and North America, and later in Latin America and Asia, made East Africa accessible to a larger class of travelers. The possibility of a two- or three-week African safari rather than one of as many months allowed the popularity in African tourism to increase the number of photographic safaris just as the emerging international conservation movement was bringing sport hunting into disrepute. Although hunter-writers like Robert Ruark continued to trumpet the virtues of big game hunting, the growth of national parks after 1946 soon overshadowed the shooting of game by game viewing and photographing. Similarly, the postwar introduction of more middle-class residents began to undermine resident sport hunting as the older generation of hunter aristocrats passed from the scene. The Mau Mau Emergency in the 1950s and the end of British colonial rule in the 1960s also accelerated the decline of big game hunting. In addition population growth since the 1950s and resulting land shortages, periodic droughts, and degradation of grazing lands has heightened competition between African farmers and herders and those who both hunt and preserve wildlife. But it was the combination of pressure from international wildlife conservation organizations such as the World Wildlife Fund (WWF) and the International Union for the Conservation of Nature (IUCN) and the growth of commercial poaching in the 1970s that drove sport hunters from the field and led Kenya to ban licensed hunting in 1977. The "end of the game" in Kenya in turn drove sport hunting back toward the southern cone of Africa (Botswana, South Africa, and Zimbabwe) where it had begun two centuries earlier.

See also **Ivory; Photography; Tourism; Transportation: Air.**

BIBLIOGRAPHY

Adamson, George. *Bwana Game.* London: Collins and Harvill, 1968.

Cameron, Kenneth M. *Into Africa: The Story of the East African Safari.* London: Constable, 1990.

Cranworth, Lord. *A Colony in the Making, or Sport and Profit in British East Africa.* London: Macmillan, 1912.

Holman, Dennis. *Inside Safari Hunting with Eric Rundgren.* New York: Putnam, 1970.

Mackenzie, John M. *The Empire of Nature: Hunting, Conservation and British Imperialism.* Manchester and New York: Manchester University Press, 1988.

Roosevelt, Theodore. *African Game Trails.* New York: Charles Scribner's Sons, 1910.

Selous, Frederick Courtney. *A Hunter's Wanderings in Africa.* London: Bentley, 1890.

Trzebinski, Errol. *The Kenya Pioneers.* New York: Norton, 1985.

EDWARD I. STEINHART

WINDHOEK. Windhoek is the capital of the Republic of Namibia. Settlements on the site of the present-day city date back at least to the Stone Age. Herero cattle pastoralists named the site Otjomuise ("steaming place") for its hot springs and seem to have settled there by the eighteenth century, along with the pastoralist Damara. In the early 1840s this highland area was inhabited by some 2,000 immigrants from the Cape Colony to the south under the leadership of Jonker Afrikaner, who gave the place the earliest version of its current name, Wind Hoock. Jonker Afrikaner built a church and recruited Rhenish missionaries. Although he departed in 1852, the settlement thrived for another twenty years, functioning primarily as a center of trade between the settlers and the indigenous Herero, Damara, and Nama. Windhoek was abandoned sometime in the 1870s and not resettled until 1890, when the Germans, then in the process of colonizing the area that came to be known as South-West Africa, built a fort and established their headquarters there.

Modern Windhoek evolved from the old German city, built between 1890 and 1915, when the Germans lost South-West Africa to the Union of South Africa. Until Namibia's independence in 1990, Windhoek served as the capital of the territory, a League of Nations mandate (later United Nations trust territory) that South Africa treated as a fifth province—or colony. Relatively few German-speaking settlers remain in Windhoek, though the heritage of German culture is obvious in the food, the beer, and an annual Oktoberfest. The population of the city is diverse, including Herero, Damara, Nama, as well as Ovambo from the north, Afrikaners who have remained, and Coloureds. This last group comprises South Africans of mixed-race heritage (mainly Khoi and European or Asian).

The segregated residential patterns of all these groups in contemporary Windhoek reflect the fact that the city, like the rest of Namibia, was subject for nearly forty years to most of the South African apartheid laws. In 1959 South African authorities moved all the black residents of Windhoek to a township just outside the city proper. The unwilling new residents of this new township named it Katutura, which means "we do not have a permanent dwelling place." Coloured residents were moved to another township, Khomasdal; Windhoek itself was reserved for whites. In the 2000s it is still mainly ethnic Germans and Afrikaners who live in the center of Windhoek (where major businesses are located), although some well-to-do Africans live there as well. Most residents of Namibian backgrounds still live in Katutura; it is the fastest-growing part of the metropolitan area, with a population of over 110,000 in 2004, fully 60 percent of the total population of Windhoek, Khomasdal, and Katatura combined.

Windhoek is the political center of Namibia, and not just because it is the capital city. All of the major political parties—from the governing South West Africa People's Organization (SWAPO) to the National Party (the oldest political institution in the country opposed to black majority rule)—have their headquarters there. Like most capitals, Windhoek is also a center for educational and cultural institutions: the University of Namibia is located in the city, as is the State Museum (housed in the old German fort, or Alte Feste). Local industries include the processing of karakul (Persian lamb) skins, as well as the production of food and clothing from sheep and cattle. Located at the center of the country, Windhoek is a key transshipment point by rail and road for goods to and from other parts of the country, the most important being Namibia's chief port at Walvis Bay. All the major links in the national transportation system (designed originally to meet South African needs) run through Windhoek; the sole international airport in the country lies twenty-nine miles from the city. Windhoek thus benefits from international tourism—the fastest-growing sector of the Namibian economy. Tourists are drawn there for the annual carnival at the end of April.

See also **Colonial Policies and Practices: German; Namibia.**

BIBLIOGRAPHY

Pendleton, Wade C. *Katutura, a Place Where We Stay: Life in a Post-apartheid Township in Namibia.* Athens: Ohio University Center for International Studies, 1996.

Simon, David. "Windhoek: Desegregation and Change in the Capital of South Africa's Erstwhile Colony." In *Homes Apart: South Africa's Segregated Cities,* ed. Anthony Lemon. Bloomington: Indiana University Press, 1991.

MARGARET ALISON SABIN

WITBOOI, HENDRIK (1830–1905).

The Nama chieftain, prophet, and guerrilla fighter Hendrik Witbooi was born in Pella, in what was known as Namaqualand, south of the Orange River in southern Africa. He was the son of Moses Witbooi, also a Nama chief. A carpenter by training and a church deacon by choice, Witbooi took up what he believed to be a divinely inspired mission following his near death at the hands of Herero in 1880, to lead his followers to a promised land in the north. In 1885 he led a trek of approximately six hundred Christian followers. Although they had been promised safe passage, the trekkers were ambushed by Herero under the command of Samuel Maherero. In the attack, Witbooi lost all his wagons, a large number of livestock, and twenty-four of his followers, including two of his sons. From then on he and his followers, operating out of a mountain stronghold at Hoornkrans, waged a successful guerrilla war against the Herero, whom he reviled for having agreed to a protection treaty with the Germans.

Witbooi was attacked by German soldiers at Hoornkrans, where eighty-five of his followers were killed. A year later he came to a negotiated settlement with the newly arrived German commander, Theodor Leutwein. For ten years Witbooi, confined by the Germans to the town of Gibeon, cooperated with the German colonial government, even to the extent of supplying troops to the colonial administration. In October 1904, ten months after the outbreak of the Herero-German war, Witbooi led his people into war against Germany. A year later he was fatally wounded in an attack on a German supply column near Vaalgras in southern German Southwest Africa (present-day Namibia).

See also **Colonial Policies and Practices; Maherero, Samuel.**

BIBLIOGRAPHY

Helbig, Ludwig. *The Witbooi.* Windhoek: Longman Namibia, 1992.

JAN BART GEWALD

WITCHCRAFT

This entry includes the following articles:
OVERVIEW
WITCHCRAFT AND CHRISTIANITY
WITCHCRAFT AND ISLAM
WITCHCRAFT AND POLITICS
WITCHCRAFT AND PROPHETISM
WITCHCRAFT AND WEALTH

OVERVIEW

Terms like "witchcraft," "sorcery," and "sorcellerie" are now generally used throughout Africa to indicate occult forms of aggression. The adoption of these Western terms has specific consequences. Especially important is the strong pejorative tenor of these terms, while the local terms that they are supposed to translate are often much more ambivalent: the latter refer to forces that in many situations are viewed as evil but that also may be used constructively. The general use of Western terms like "sorcery" and "witchcraft" therefore risks reducing a rich cosmology, in which the whole of the human environment is animated, to a negative, ugly core. Often a more neutral translation, such as "occult forces," would be preferable. However, terms like "sorcery" and "witchcraft" are so generally used—by *Radio Trottoir* ("sidewalk radio"; i.e., gossip) and in newspaper accounts and discussions of development and politics as much as in local affairs—that it is difficult for social scientists to avoid them.

Another disadvantage of these Western terms is that they gloss over all sorts of local variations. There are important differences between local discourses, for instance, on the description of witches and their abilities and on how "witchcraft" is transmitted. Sometimes it is believed to be inherited; sometimes it is thought to be acquired later in life. Yet, there is a common core to these representations. A basic theme is that misfortune—and often also spectacular success—are attributed to hidden human agency. Witches and sorcerers are believed to use secret forces to hurt other people or to enforce their own success.

Witchcraft and sorcery are therefore closely related to jealousy, inequality, and the illicit search for power. Such ideas are, of course, not special to African societies; rather, they seem to reflect a basic fear that may be universal. Indeed, the strong popular reactions triggered by rumors of sexual child abuse in the West, or the recourse to esoteric expertise—be it of astrologers or public-relations experts—in the politics of modern democracies, show intriguing parallels with the responses to and reliance upon witchcraft in present-day Africa. The same applies to the flowering of all sorts of spiritualist cults, for instance, in the newly industrialized countries of East Asia.

However, some traits seem to be particular to witchcraft in Africa. One is the heavy stress on the link between witchcraft and kinship in many African societies; another is the equation of witchcraft with eating. A basic image that haunts people in many parts of Africa is that of witches—both men and women—leaving their bodies at night and flying off to meet with others of their kind. At such meetings they deliver their kin, whose vital parts are often supposed to be consumed during cannibalistic banquets. In many African societies, the basic urge of witches is thought to be the eating of kin.

Since these discourses emphasize the use of hidden forces, there is always a close connection between witchcraft, sorcery, and divination. If one fears becoming the victim of a hidden attack, one has to look for the help of a specialist who is able to "see" what the witches have done and can force them to lift their spell. The diviner who "sees" and the counter-sorcerer who attacks the witches may be one and the same person or can be two different people. The conceptual triangle of bewitching/divination/countersorcery highlights the circular character of most witchcraft discourses. Only specialists can offer help, since they alone know their way in the world of the occult. The diviners must be able to "see" the witches, which means that they are themselves implicated. In many Bantu societies, acquiring "a second pair of eyes" is seen as the first step in one's initiation into the world of the witches.

Similarly, the power of the witch doctor to vanquish witches and force them to lift their spells is believed to derive from his or her own exceptionally developed witchcraft. Witch doctors are often described by the population as "superwitches." This makes them highly ambivalent figures. In the case of southern Cameroon, for instance, authors like Lluis Mallart and Elizabeth Copet-Rougier refer to a vague but widespread belief that one can become a *nganga* (healer, witch doctor) only by sacrificing a parent. *Nganga* themselves always emphasize that their "professor" has made them swear to use their power only in order to heal, never to kill. But the population is never sure of this: there is always the danger that the basic urge of the witch to kill his or her kin will break through. It is especially this circular reasoning characteristic of witchcraft discourses—the main protection against the witches is to be found in the world of witchcraft—that makes it so difficult to break out of these conceptions. This can also explain why these ideas seem to retain their relevance despite modern changes.

The inherent circularity of witchcraft discourses can also explain why the scientific distinctions that anthropologists and other social scientists have sought to apply in this field remain highly precarious. A good example is E. E. Evans-Pritchard's classic distinction between witchcraft, which he defined as an innate quality often unconsciously activated, and sorcery, which he understood to be the conscious use of an acquired technique. He deduced this distinction from his study among the Azande of the southern Sudan. Some later anthropologists have sought to generalize it, whereas others have insisted that this distinction simply does not fit their ethnographic data. One can doubt especially whether it is of much use to understand the modern transitions of these representations. It is, rather, the circularity of these discourses and the ease with which all sorts of possible conceptual distinctions are glossed over that make them so all-pervasive in present-day African society.

THE MODERNITY OF WITCHCRAFT

One of the most striking aspects of social interactions in contemporary Africa is the omnipresence of witchcraft and sorcery discourses in modern settings. Rumors about the use of these hidden forces abound in politics as much as in sport or in the churches; at school as well as in relation to modern forms of entrepreneurship; in urban contexts as much as (or even more than) in the village. An often implicit assumption of many Western observers was, and still is, that witchcraft would necessarily disappear under the impact of modernization. In the 1970s European priests in Cameroon stated that "there is no *sorcellerie* where there is electricity." Since then, Cameroon has witnessed an intensive campaign of electrification, but nobody would repeat this statement now.

On the contrary, one is struck—in Cameroon as in other African countries—by the dynamic and innovative character of the discourses on witchcraft. Rumors integrate, apparently without much difficulty, all sorts of borrowings: notions from other ethnic groups as easily as Christian or Islamic elements; "magical objects" sold by mail-order firms in Europe as well as medical knowledge or notions from books on Oriental wisdom. Witchcraft conspiracies are supposed to be reproduced on a truly global scale: the witches are thought to have their professors in Europe, or to be linked to the Mafia. This gives notions of the occult a fairly unsystematic character—inconsistencies seem to abound—but it is precisely this elasticity that makes them retain their relevance in the face of new developments. A growing fear of the proliferation of witchcraft—of witchcraft "running wild"—is expressed especially in new social settings, where people are confronted with new and baffling inequalities.

This is especially clear in the rumors about novel forms of witchcraft that are explicitly related to new forms of wealth. In many parts of Africa, the newly rich are presumed to accumulate wealth by exploiting the labor of their witchcraft victims. An explicit opposition is often made between old forms of witchcraft, in which the victims are eaten, and new forms, by which victims are transformed into zombies who are put to work on "invisible plantations." In western Africa, whites are still believed to play a mediating role in this. Other elements of these beliefs suggest that they reflect the traumas of the slave trade and forced labor during colonial times. But they are now closely linked with the emergence of new entrepreneurs among the African population. Eric de Rosny suggests that these beliefs have such a hold over

people's minds because they offer at least some explanation of the mysteries of the market: the spectacular successes of the few and the poverty and unemployment of the many. What is striking is that in some areas these beliefs seem to inspire determined attacks on the new rich, while elsewhere they seem to affirm or even legitimize their distance from the poor.

The role of these conceptions in politics and in relations to the state is equally filled with ambiguities. On the one hand, the representatives of the state seem determined to intervene against the proliferation of witchcraft. Postcolonial civil servants regularly admonish villagers to stop trying to sabotage government projects with their witchcraft. Indeed, in the official propaganda of many African regimes, witchcraft is branded as a particularly dangerous form of subversion. It is also seen as one of the major obstacles to realizing "development." At the end of the 1970s, such ideas inspired the Marxist-Leninist regime of Mathieu Kérékou in Bénin to instigate a true witch hunt through radio broadcasts. The results of such propaganda were, and are, often contradictory. It evokes an image, as Jean-François Bayart emphasized in his earlier publications, of witchcraft as some sort of "popular mode of political action" against the authoritarian state and its hegemonic pretensions. Yet, in practice, it is often not clear that people try to use these beliefs in such a sense. It is, rather, the government's insistence on witchcraft as an omnipresent form of subversion that serves to politicize it.

The civil servants' denouncement of witchcraft seems to reflect their private fears of leveling attacks to undermine their new and highly enviable position. In several parts of Africa, members of the national elite say they are afraid of being "eaten" by their former fellow villagers; in such expressions there is a clear reference to the threat of witchcraft. This is hardly surprising. Ever since the 1950s, anthropologists have emphasized that in many African societies, witchcraft conceptions have a strong leveling effect on relations within the local community. The new elites' accumulation of wealth and power dearly surpasses traditional boundaries: it is no wonder that they fear leveling attacks coming from inside their own community.

Yet here again, witchcraft appears to wear two faces. There are many examples of members of the new elite using the same witchcraft conceptions to protect and affirm the new inequalities. This is facilitated by the commodification of witchcraft and sorcery practices. In many settings, "medicaments," jujus, and other "charged objects" are literally for sale. Witch doctors offer their services to the highest bidder, who is generally a member of the new elite. Thus, witchcraft discourses, instead of having a leveling impact, can serve to affirm the new inequalities and make them seem self-evident. The continuing involvement of the elites with the occult makes the state offensive against witchcraft highly ambiguous in its effects.

A striking aspect of witchcraft rumors in new settings is the relative absence of women. In the older version of witchcraft, both women and men are thought to participate in hidden conspiracies. Indeed, many myths about the origin of witchcraft have women leading the way (although it is often added that the men soon followed). However, in speculations about the links between witchcraft and the new forms of wealth or the new power struggles, women are mostly absent. This may reflect the predominance of men in the new political and economic arenas. It may also relate to a tendency in many discourses on witchcraft to relegate women's activity primarily to the domestic sphere.

THE SEARCH FOR NEW PROTECTION: ANTI-WITCHCRAFT MOVEMENTS, THE CHURCH, AND THE STATE

The general fear of witchcraft running wild and the rumors about novel forms of occult aggression have encouraged an unremitting search for new forms of protection. The first reports on new, experimental anti-witchcraft movements date from before the colonial period. But the colonial period in particular saw a proliferation of such movements. They invoked a rich variety of forces and procedures in their struggle against witchcraft: poison ordeals, "traditional" jujus, Christian symbols. In the extensive literature on this topic, such anti-witchcraft "medicine" is often set apart from the occult forces of witchcraft itself. The supporters of such movements, of course, strongly emphasize this separation. However, if looked at over a period of time, such distinctions prove, again, to be quite unreliable. In a fascinating study on the northwestern Congo, Georges Dupré shows how an anti-witchcraft movement, initially directed against the

witchcraft of the elders, has been appropriated by the latter, who use its shrine to extort heavy fines from young men and wage laborers in the village.

In postcolonial times, the struggle against witchcraft has notably been waged by Christian movements: Independent Churches, Jehovah's Witnesses, more recently by Pentecostal movements, and also by the mainstream churches. Especially within the Roman Catholic Church, a lively discussion is going on about how far its priests can go in this. Several black priests and even bishops have run into difficulties with the Catholic Church because they went beyond orthodox exorcism rites and tried to follow too clearly in the footsteps of the *nganga*, as in the case of the Zambian archbishop Emmanuel Milingo.

Of special importance is the growing pressure on the state to intervene. Ever since the establishment of the colonial state, people have reproached the state for protecting the witches because it forbade the use of poison ordeals and the execution of witches by chiefs or witch doctors. The postcolonial state elites seem to be more inclined to intervene against the witches—or at least have more difficulty in withstanding popular pressure in this respect. Kérékou's witch-hunt in Bénin was certainly not an isolated example. Isak A. Niehaus shows, for instance, that the African National Congress (ANC) has considerable difficulty keeping its younger members from becoming involved in witch hunts in Lebowa as in other former "Bantustans."

An example of the state becoming directly involved comes from Cameroon. At the end of the 1970s, the state courts, especially in the Earl Province, suddenly started to convict witches, mainly on the basis of the expertise of witch doctors. This official recognition of the witch doctor constitutes a spectacular reversal of earlier jurisprudence. In colonial times and in the first decades after independence, witch doctors were always in danger of being prosecuted by the state courts (for defamation and breach of the peace). Now they appear as witnesses for the prosecution. This reversal is clearly related to the state's campaigns against witchcraft. But there also seems to be strong popular pressure in this region—where local societies have long been highly segmentary in character—for the state to intervene. In this respect, it is noteworthy that such processes seldom occur in other parts of the country, such as in the west, where the chiefs' authority still has strong roots in local societies, or in the Islamized parts of northern Cameroon.

Direct interventions by the state seem to go together with the emergence of a new, more modern type of *nganga*. The witch doctors who work with the state are often intent on seeking publicity. They make ostentatious use of all sorts of modern symbols: sunglasses, books on Oriental wisdom, Christian elements, and medical knowledge. And they boast of their membership in new organizations, such as the more or less official national associations of "traditional healers," as well as elite societies like the Rosicrucians. Most importantly, they have a highly aggressive style in recruiting clients and unmasking witches. Often they approach people on their own initiative, warning them about dangers in their close surroundings and insisting that they should have their courtyard "purified." Thus, they play an important role in reinforcing the popular fear of a proliferation of witchcraft, all the more so because by so doing they may gain official recognition.

ANALYTIC APPROACHES: WITCHCRAFT AND MORALITY

Even though witchcraft and sorcery have always been central themes in anthropological discourse, anthropologists have had surprisingly little to say—at least until very recently—about the modern transformations of these phenomena on the African continent. One reason for the long delay in confronting the modern dynamics of this old anthropological theme may have been the problems of the discipline's dominant paradigms.

In 1970 Mary Douglas noted some surprising shifts in the anthropological study of witchcraft and sorcery. Of course, she takes as her point of departure the undisputed classic in this field, Evans-Pritchard's *Witchcraft, Oracles, and Magic Among the Azande* (1937), which studied the witchcraft beliefs of this southern Sudanese people in relation to questions of cognition and the social restraints upon perception. This work had a profound influence on later anthropologists but, as Douglas notes, in "directions not foreseen or even blessed by its author." For instance, in the series of monographs on central Africa by British anthropologists of the 1950s and 1960s, which profoundly influenced the study of sorcery and witchcraft (especially those by Victor Turner,

James C. Mitchell, and Max G. Marwick, and the collection edited by John Middleton and E. H. Winter), Evans-Pritchard's problematic was refocused in a special sense. These authors concentrated not on issues of cognition but rather—in accordance with then-current functionalist theories—on the relation between witchcraft and the preservation of social order, and on micropolitics. They focused on witchcraft accusations, which were to be studied as a kind of "social strain gauge" (the term is Marwick's)—that is, as indicators of social tensions, especially in relations within the local kin groups where aggression could not be expressed in more direct ways.

Thus, witchcraft came to be seen as a "homeostatic control system": accusations of witchcraft were thought to be crucial to the reproduction of social order because they permitted hidden tensions to be expressed and dealt with, so that the local community could be reconstituted. This view of witchcraft, which dominated anthropological studies until the 1980s, had remarkable consequences. In her 1970 piece (an introduction to a set of conference papers by anthropologists and historians studying European societies), Douglas notes with some irony a striking difference:

> The anthropologists of the 1950s developed insights into the functioning of witch beliefs which seemed about as relevant to the European experience as if they came from another planet. Dangerous in Europe, the same beliefs in Melanesia and Africa appeared to be tame, even domesticated; they served useful functions and were not expected to run amuck. (p. xiii)

This anthropological view of witchcraft, as something "domesticated," seems to be of limited relevance for dealing with the increasing popular fears about its proliferation. In many parts of Africa, people in the early twenty-first century are convinced that witchcraft does indeed "run amuck."

Another problem with this micropolitical perspective is that the contents of the witchcraft accusations are neglected; the accusations are analyzed only as expressions of something else: hidden sociopolitical tensions. In his 1993 analysis of witch hunts in Lebowa, South Africa, Isak Niehaus emphasizes instead the need "to take the perceptions informants themselves have of witches seriously." His "Comrades"—young rebels vaguely related to the United Democratic Front or even the ANC—made a clear distinction in their witch hunts between witches and political opponents: the latter might be attacked but were not accused of witchcraft. In his view, the accusations had a specific aim: by denouncing witchcraft, the young men sought to affirm the legitimacy of their role in "the politics of public morality."

But the strong moralist tenor of the functionalist view on witchcraft also creates problems if one wants to understand the resilience of these notions in modern contexts. In the functionalist view, it was necessary to make a rigorous separation between the positive and negative expressions of occult forces. Often, this forced the anthropologist to impose a Manichaean distinction on more open local concepts. (A good example is Middleton's 1963 study of Lugbara witchcraft.) Only by isolating witchcraft as an unequivocally evil force could these beliefs be thought to function as a "homeostatic control system"—a kind of safety valve that permitted the expression of social tension without endangering the social order as such. But it is precisely the fundamental ambiguity of notions about the occult that allows them to remain relevant in modern contexts. Although witchcraft as such is certainly seen as evil, people often believe that the same forces can be used constructively, in order to accumulate wealth and power. It is the possibility of many interpretations that makes notions of witchcraft and sorcery such seductive tools for trying to understand the vicissitudes of life in the modern sectors. It is also why the use of a pejorative term such as *witchcraft* poses serious difficulties.

Instead of starting from seemingly fixed conceptual distinctions, it might be more clarifying to study the different ways and means by which societies try to impose conceptual demarcations on what are basically highly diffuse and volatile notions. The ongoing struggle for reproducing conceptual distinctions in this treacherous field might be a key to a better understanding of the remarkable dynamics of notions of witchcraft in present-day Africa. This is a common theme emerging from the recent and quite sudden wave of witchcraft studies on modern Africa, such as *Modernity and Its Malcontents* (1993), edited by Jean and John Comaroff; Niehaus's 1993 article in

Africa; and the 1988 article by Michael Rowlands and Jean-Pierre Warnier in *Man*.

An important point of departure for understanding the pervasiveness of notions of witchcraft in modern contexts is the close conceptual link between witchcraft and kinship. Even in highly urbanized contexts, witchcraft remains the dark side of kinship: when treating a patient, witch doctors always try to bring the family together; the sources of aggression are sought primarily within the sphere of kinship and intimacy. This link can help one to understand both the continuing strength of the witchcraft discourse and the uncertainty it evokes. In many parts of Africa, kinship and the family still seem to provide the basis for social security, even for the urban elites. However, it is clear that kinship relations are under a growing strain; they have to bridge ever-wider inequalities between rich and poor, between city and village; often they seem to be stretched to the breaking point. This configuration may explain both the omnipresence of witchcraft rumors, despite the modern changes, and the desperate search for new forms of protection from witches in many parts of Africa.

See also **Anthropology, Social, and the Study of Africa; Diasporas; Divination and Oracles; Kinship and Descent; Postcolonialism; Prophetic Movements; Religion and Ritual; Spirit Possession; Vodún.**

BIBLIOGRAPHY

Ashforth, Adam. *Witchcraft, Violence and Democracy in South Africa*. Chicago: Chicago University Press, 2005.

Bayart, Jean-François. *L'etat au Cameroun*, Paris: Presses de la Fondation Nationale des Sciences Politique, 1979.

Bayart, Jean-François. *The Illusion of Cultural Identity*, revised and updated edition., trans. Steven Rendall, Janet Roitman, and Jonathan Derrick. London: C. Hurst and Company, 2005.

Bernault, Florence, and Joseph Tonda, eds. "Pouvoirs sorciers." *Politique Africaine* 79 (2000).

Bond, George C., and Diane M.Ciekawy, eds. *Witchcraft Dialogues, Anthropological and Philosophical Exchanges*. Athens: Ohio University Press, 2001.

Ciekawy, Diane M., and Peter Geschiere, eds. "Containing Witchcraft: Conflicting Scenarios in Postcolonial Africa." *African Studies Review* 41, no. 3 (1998): 1–14.

Comaroff, Jean, and John Comaroff, eds. *Modernity and Its Malcontents*. Chicago: Chicago University Press, 1993.

Copet-Rougier, Elizabeth. "Catégories d'ordres et réponses aux déaasordres chez les Mkako du Cameroun." *Droit et cultures* 11 (1986): 79–88.

Douglas, Mary. "Introduction: Thirty Years after *Witchcraft, Oracles, and Magic*". In *Witchcraft Confessions and Accusations*, ed. Mary Douglas. London: Tavistock, 1970.

Dupré, Georges. *Un ordre et sa déstruction*. Paris: Editions de l'Office de la recherche scientifique et technique outre-mer, 1982.

Evans-Pritchard, Edward E. *Witchcraft, Oracles, and Magic Among the Azande*. Oxford: Clarendon Press, 1937.

Fields, Karen E. *Revival and Rebellion in Colonial Central Africa*. Princeton, NJ: Princeton University Press, 1985.

Fisiy, Cyprian F., and Peter Geschiere. "Judges and Witches, or How Is the State to Deal with Witchcraft? Examples from Southeast Cameroon." *Cahiers d'études africaines* 30, no. 2 (1990): 135–156.

Fisiy, Cyprian F., and Peter Geschiere. "Sorcery, Witchcraft, and Accumulation: Regional Variations in South and West Cameroon." *Critique of Anthropology* 11, no. 3 (1991): 251–278.

Geschiere, Peter. "Sorcery and the State in Cameroon." *Critique of Anthropology* 11, no. 3 (1990): 251–278.

Geschiere, Peter. *The Modernity of Witchcraft, Politics and the Occult in Postcolonial Africa*. Charlottesville: University Press of Virginia, 1997.

Geschiere, Peter. "Witchcraft and the Limits of the Law, Cameroun and South Africa." In *Law and Disorder in the Postcolony*, eds. Jean Comaroff and John Comaroff. Chicago: Chicago University Press, 2006.

Mallart Guimera, Lluis. *Ni dos ni ventre*. Paris: Société d'ethnographie, 1981.

Marwick, Max G. *Sorcery in Its Social Setting: A Study of the Northern Rhodesian Cewa*. Manchester, U.K.: Manchester University Press, 1965.

Meyer, Birgit. *Translating the Devil: Religion and Modernity among the Ewe in Ghana*. Edinburgh: Edinburgh University Press, 1999.

Middleton, John, and Edward Henry Winter, eds. *Witchcraft and Sorcery*. London: Routledge and Paul, 1963.

Niehaus, Isak A. *Witchcraft, Power and Politics: Exploring the Occult in the South African Lowveld*. London: Pluto, 2001.

Niehaus, Isak A., ed. Justice et Sorcellerie, Yaounde: Presses de l'Université catholique d'Afrique centrale, 2005.

Rosny, Eric de. *Les yeux de ma chèvre: Sur les pas des maîtres de la nuit en pays douala*. Paris: Plon, 1981.

Rowlands, Michael, and Jean-Pierre Warnier. "Sorcery, Power, and the Modern State in Cameroon." *Man* 23 (1988): 118–132.

Turner, Victor W. *Schism and Continuity in an African Society: A Study of Ndembu Village Life*. Manchester, U.K.: Manchester University Press, 1957.

Willis, Roy. "Instant Millennium: The Sociology of African Witch-Cleansing Cults." In *Witchcraft Confessions and Accusations*, ed. Mary Douglas. London: Tavistock Publications, 1970.

PETER GESCHIERE

WITCHCRAFT AND CHRISTIANITY

The relationship between Christianity and witchcraft has become a focus of Africanist research only since the 1990s. Instigated by Jean and John Comaroff's *Modernity and Its Malcontents* (1993) and Peter Geschiere's *The Modernity of Witchcraft* (1997), scholars started to conceptualize witchcraft no longer as a traditional phenomenon doomed to disappear with increasing modernization, but rather as a suitable entry point into people's ambivalent experiences vis-à-vis modern life. Even a quick search on the Internet reveals that the combination of the terms witchcraft and Christianity leads right into a minefield rife with misunderstandings, tensions, and conflicting interests. Representatives of Pentecostal Christianity have launched strong attacks on witchcraft, based on the idea that witches exist and operate in the world as the agents of Satan.

Those defending traditional values stress that witchcraft is a wrongful translation of a plethora of specific African forms of spiritual power that have nothing to do with the Christian figure of the devil. Others suggest a link between African witchcraft and the modern Wicca movement and New Age thinking at large, either stressing the need to eschew the hegemony of Christianity that sought to marginalize non-Christian religious forms, or, by contrast, incorporating African witchcraft into an ever more global diabolic scheme. These views, as research on the topic shows, stem from, as well as inform, actual practices in contemporary Africa: from violent attacks on alleged witches to self-confessions elicited in Pentecostal churches; from popular tracts and Ghanaian and Nigerian movies revealing the operations of witchcraft to the struggles of intellectuals and artists who dismiss the demonization of traditional religion by Pentecostal Christianity and view witchcraft as normal part and parcel of African belief systems.

The salience of the linkages between Christianity and witchcraft in contemporary Africa, however, should not be mistaken as indicative of the newness of the phenomenon per se. The point rather is that the recent approach to witchcraft as not opposed to, but rather intimately part of, modernity has engendered innovative historical and ethnographic research exploring the complex relationship between witchcraft and Christianity in the past and present.

MISSIONARY AND MAINSTREAM CHRISTIANITY AND WITCHCRAFT

It is often assumed that missionary Christianity alienated Africans from their cultural roots by launching attacks against certain elements of traditional culture and religion and propagating modern, enlightened attitudes. Research on missions shows that matters are far more complicated. A substantial number of nineteenth-century missionaries, especially those with Protestant-Pietist backgrounds, preached that witches—using both local terms and the English expression—were agents of Satan. More importantly, it appears also that a great number of African converts to Catholic, as well as Protestant missions, imagined witches as affiliated with the Christian devil. This imagination involved two dimensions: (1) originally ambivalent indigenous spiritual forces were recast as unambiguously evil demons; and (2) local terms referring to certain spiritual powers, employed either to achieve wealth or harm others by spiritual means, were conflated in the English term "witchcraft." The process of translation on which this imagination depended was not only imperfect in that it reduced a variety of spiritual forms to one term, but also excessive in that it created a link with European imaginations of witches as serving Satan, thereby extending the Great Witch Hunt across time unto the African soil.

Far from simply opposing witchcraft, local appropriations of Christianity reconfigured it as the dark side of the Christian universe, frequently to the dismay of European and African church leaders. In this way, witchcraft became part of Christian discourse, rather than being located outside of it (Meyer 1999, West 2005). The legacy of this translation process still shows in contemporary debates about witchcraft in Africa: in the same way as the claimed link between witches and Satan can be traced back to early African appropriations of Christianity, the attempt to create a positive link between African witchcraft and the modern Wicca movement may be viewed as a negation of the association of witchcraft with Satan.

Research has stressed the need to address the links between images of occult forces and overt socioeconomic relations, at least as modern social science construes the latter. Also in the context of Christianity, the synthesis of the devil and witchcraft was made to speak to broader socioeconomic concerns. Often to the disappointment of church leaders, many converts felt attracted to Christianity because they expected this new religion to offer effective protection against witchcraft, thereby drawing an analogy between antiwitchcraft movements in their own heritages and the missions. Christian ideas about witches as agents of Satan made it possible to continue taking seriously the danger of witchcraft as the dark side of kinship.

Christianity's appeal at the grassroots level can be attributed at least partly to its attitude toward the extended family and traditional patterns of distribution of material wealth. The individualist ethics offered by Christianity stood in sharp contrast to local modes of emphasizing obligations among blood relations, in the context of which witchcraft was called upon to level inequality and, conversely, dismiss excessive accumulation. For many local converts, conversion to Christianity entailed the ultimately unrealizable promise to enjoy the wealth expected from leading a civilized life, without having to fear that jealous relatives would attack or destroy them through witchcraft. The ongoing obsession with witchcraft as a destructive force operating along blood ties testifies to local converts' ambivalence regarding the new patterns of personal accumulation and limited distribution that emerged in the context of colonial modernity. In this sense, the modernity of witchcraft is not as recent as its current coinage suggests. What is new is scholars' awareness that the relationship between Christianity and witchcraft has been far more complex than common sense made it appear.

That common sense ideas about this relationship persisted for quite some time may be attributed to at least two factors: Africanist scholars' neglect of mission churches, which were considered to resemble their European mother churches and hence appeared as far less interesting than African Independent Churches; and contemporary mainstream churches' (Catholic, Methodist, Anglican, Presbyterian) stance that belief in witchcraft (and even the devil) is a superstition bound to disappear with the education they would provide. Certainly in the context of attempts, instigated by Vatican II and the World Council of Churches, to accommodate indigenous culture and beliefs in a more positive manner, many church leaders and theologians engaged in Africanizing Christianity from above. Although intellectual elites and enlightened Christians in Europe (who often felt embarrassed about earlier missions' disrespect of cultural and religious traditions) applauded such attempts, local believers often refused the Africanization thus proffered. Denial of witchcraft and failure to offer rituals for protection against and exorcism from witchcraft formed, and still forms, the Achilles' heal of mainstream churches that tend to lose members to other churches that take witchcraft seriously.

WITCHCRAFT IN AFRICAN INDEPENDENT AND PENTECOSTAL CHARISMATIC CHURCHES

African Independent Churches (AICs), Pentecostal Charismatic Churches (PCCs), as well as the Catholic Charismatic Renewal (CCR), display remarkably different attitudes toward witchcraft. These churches, though originating at different historical moments and stressing different concerns—the rootedness in the African context in the case of the AICs that gained prominence since the early twentieth century; the promise to provide entrance into global believers' networks in the case of the PCCs and CCR that became phenomenally popular in the last two decades of that century—observe a similarly strict dualism of God and Satan, in which witches are understood as an evil, satanic force to be fought and overcome by the Holy Spirit (Ashforth 2005, Green 2003, Meyer 1999, Ter Haar 1992). This deep opposition to witchcraft is rooted in popular grassroots Christianity. This evil force is often held to be located among poor kin in the village who seek to bring down successful family members—or prevent success at all—by means

of witchcraft. In a context in which people face serious problems in everyday life, and in which they encounter inexplicable instances of others' sudden wealth and loss, witchcraft is called upon to explain as well as condemn excessive success, and justify misfortune in a Christian frame. Whereas most churches mainly concentrate on fortifying and protecting members through prayer services, some also actively engage in elucidating self-confessions or pointing out witches who are to be exorcized.

Research on Pentecostal Charismatic theology shows that the emphasis placed by PCCs and similar churches on fighting witchcraft should not distract from the fact that witchcraft is at the center of a vast Christian fantasy space that sets apart the abject and immoral, yet continues to affirm it under the banner of the demonic. Although researchers disagree as to whether the Christian obsession with witchcraft expresses a moral critique in the registers of the fantastic or stands in the way of development and enlightenment, it is all the same clear that Pentecostal Charismatic Christianity not only fights against witchcraft but also actively affirms its dangers. The impossibility of keeping witchcraft out of Pentecostal Charismatic discourse also shows in rumors about pastors who are said to owe their power not to the Christian God but instead to a link with witchcraft and other occult forces. The image of the satanic pastor is a powerful testimony to the extent to which witchcraft is not simply opposed to contemporary Christianity but rather deeply enmeshed with it.

In contemporary popular culture, the images of the charismatic pastor who offers protection against witchcraft and that of the evil pastor who secretly depends on it have been taken up extensively. There is a host of tracts, paintings, popular plays, and video films addressing witchcraft from a Christian angle. Through the continent-wide popularity of Ghanaian and, above all, Nigerian videos that draw heavily on Christian repertoires and frame plots in terms of the war between God and Satan, these Christian imaginations of witchcraft have become visualized—and by the same token tend to be codified—all over Africa. These films, in turn, feed upon the Christian imagination, thereby affirming the danger of witchcraft as a real force and obliging theologians to react. Through this circularity that links the popular Christian

Hand-painted poster advertising the Ghanaian video-movie *Deliverance from the Powers of Darkness* (Sam Bea, Accra, 1992). This movie features a woman who is possessed by, and subsequently delivered from, the Spirit of witchcraft. The movie suggests that a spiritual fight is occurring between indigenous priests (depicted at the right-hand side of the poster) and Christianity (symbolized by the pastor). PHOTOGRAPH BY BIRGIT MEYER

imagination, modern mass entertainment, churches, and even politics, witchcraft appears as an ultimate reality that cannot be denied, only eschewed. Or, as one participant in the discussion about the BBC World News feature "Is Witchcraft Alive in Africa?" put it: "I don't believe in witchcraft, but I know that it exists" (2005).

That an increasing number of scholars has started to pay attention to the nexus of witchcraft and Christianity does not so much stem from a deliberate interest in studying witchcraft (or Christianity) per se, but rather from the salient as well as unsettling importance of witchcraft in people's everyday lives. Witchcraft has become an unavoidable challenge not only for Christianity—even mainstream churches increasingly allow for charismatic prayer groups that fight witchcraft—but also for contemporary researchers. How to develop adequate modes of writing about witchcraft without confirming its existence or writing it off as a mere superstition, and how to situate witchcraft discourses in relation to the broader social, political, and economic issues they address, is still subject to debate (Ashforth 2005, Geschiere 1997, West 2005). Genealogical approaches tracing how Christianity contributed to the introduction of witchcraft as a new concept that encompasses and at the same time rearticulates earlier local notions prove to be as pertinent as attempts to understand the moral subtexts of Christian witchcraft discourses, or to grasp the spread of popular Christian views about witchcraft into the realms of entertainment and politics.

The key point raised by research is that witchcraft and Christianity cannot be understood as being simply opposed to each other. The fact that contemporary debates present the dangers or virtues (whatever the case may be) of witchcraft as opposed to Christianity indicates the power of Christian discourses to define what is at stake in everyday life. Thriving on a logic of opposition and encompassment, the appeal of popular Christianity seems to depend to a very large extent on witchcraft, exactly because witches feature as God's most powerful counterparts.

See also **Christianity; Media: Cinema; Popular Culture.**

BIBLIOGRAPHY

Asamoa-Gyadu, Kwabena. *African Charismatics. Current Developments within Independent Indigenous Pentecostalism in Ghana*. Leiden, The Netherlands: Brill, 2004.

Ashforth, Adam. *Madumo. A Man Bewitched*. Chicago: University of Chicago Press, 2000.

Ashforth, Adam. *Witchcraft, Violence, and Democracy in South Africa*. Chicago and London: The University of Chicago Press, 2005.

Bastian. Misty L. "Vulture Men, Campus Cultists and Teenaged Witches: Modern Magic in Nigerian Popular Media." In *Magical Interpretations, Magical Realities. Modernity, Witchcraft and the Occult in Postcolonial Africa*, ed. Henrietta L. Moore and Todd Sanders. London: Routledge, 2001.

BBC News. "Is Witchcraft Alive in Africa?" July 27, 2005. Available from http://news.bbc.co.uk/2/hi/africa/4705201.stm.

Comaroff, Jean, and John Comaroff, eds. *Modernity and Its Malcontents. Ritual and Power in Postcolonial Africa.* Chicago: The University of Chicago Press, 1993.

De Boeck, Filip, and Marie-Françoise Plissart. *Kinshasa Tales of the Invisible City.* Tervuren, Belgium: Ludion, 2004.

Ellis, Stephen, and Gerrie Ter Haar. *Worlds of Power. Religious Thought and Political Practice in Africa.* New York: Oxford University Press, 2004.

Geschiere, Peter. *The Modernity of Witchcraft. Politics and the Occult in Postcolonial Africa.* Charlottesville: University Press of Virginia, 1997.

Gifford, Paul. *Ghana's New Christianity. Pentecostalism in a Globalising African Economy.* London: Hurst, 2004.

Green, Maia. *Priests, Witches and Power: Popular Christianity after Mission in Southern Tanzania.* Cambridge, U.K.: Cambridge University Press, 2003.

Meyer, Birgit. "The Power of Money. Politics, Sorcery and Pentecostalism in Ghana." *African Studies Review* 41, no. 3 (1998): 15–38.

Meyer, Birgit. *Translating the Devil. Religion and Modernity among the Ewe in Ghana.* Edinburgh: Edinburgh University Press, 1999.

Ter Haar, Gerrie. *Spirit of Africa. The Healing Ministry of Archbishop Milingo of Zambia.* Trenton, NJ: Africa World Press, 1992.

Van Dijk, Rijk. "Witchcraft and Specticism by Proxy: Pentecostalism and Laughter in Urban Malawi." In *Magical Interpretations, Magical Realities. Modernity, Witchcraft and the Occult in Postcolonial Africa*, ed. Henrietta L. Moore and Todd Sanders. London: Routledge, 2001.

West, Harry G. *Kupilikula. Governance and the Invisible Realm in Mozambique.* Chicago and London: University of Chicago Press 2005.

BIRGIT MEYER

WITCHCRAFT AND ISLAM

Witchcraft commonly refers to the intentional or unintended use of supernatural powers to gain control of that which is typically beyond access to humans. It may involve the use of magical or medicinal substances or tools, or consist of the psychic capacity to affect people's lives and health. It is often articulated in terms of wrongful consumption. Whether it is inherited, learned, or bought, witchcraft has traditionally been described by anthropologists as a representation of evil, an activity one engages in for nefarious ends, in addition to being an explanatory system that helps account for the unexplainable. In much of the anthropological literature, the term is used interchangeably with words such as magic, the occult, sorcery, and enchantment to characterize a wide variety of phenomena ranging from drought, disease, and murder to zombies and spirit possession to the destruction of one's career and the sale of body parts. Recent studies have shown that not all linguistic categories associated with the concept of witchcraft and power conjure negative experiences, however. In some cases, witchcraft is used for positive ends (to pass an exam successfully, and to protect oneself against harmful forces). As an ambiguous form of power, witchcraft may thus be harnessed to harm or to protect and empower.

Several decades ago, students of African societies took pains to distinguish witchcraft—a mystical power that one inherits—from sorcery, a malevolent magic one acquires with the conscious intention of harming others. In the early twenty-first century, such distinctions have been set aside. The signification of witchcraft, it is now recognized, remains linked to the European history from which it originated. As such, the term is nothing but a vague, catchall term that only imperfectly describes the complexity and diversity of African realities. Despite its problematic ontological status, it cannot be eschewed altogether. Africans themselves have adopted the words witchcraft and sorcery or the French term *sorcellerie* (as well as indigenous words borrowed from neighboring groups), a practice that further complicates anthropological efforts to measure the slippage that occurs in translation and to capture adequately contemporary social phenomena in all their changing expressions.

In part because Africa was historically singled out as the proverbial home of witchcraft, the occult became a central dimension of the anthropological focus on African societies. The history of anthropology's concentration on witchcraft may be broadly divided into a number of significant periods: Around the turn of the nineteenth century, French scholar Lévy-Bruhl (1857–1939) claimed that witchcraft was proof of the prelogical mentality of Africans. In 1937, British anthropologist E. E. Evans-Pritchard demonstrated in his landmark study on Azande witchcraft that Zande thinking was no less rational than European epistemologies. Witchcraft, he argued, was an idiom for explaining misfortune. After World War II, members of the Manchester School shifted the focus to the social implications of witchcraft. Through their exploration of the dynamics of witchcraft suspicions and accusations, they demonstrated how witchcraft led to the fission, and less often the fusion, of social groups. A generation later, concerted interest in the meanings that motivated human actions led anthropologists to examine witchcraft as an expression of people's confrontation with the problem of evil.

Since the 1990s, the study of witchcraft has experienced a revival as scholars have sought to demonstrate that, far from being a measure of primitiveness and an expression of tradition, witchcraft beliefs and practices are integral parts of contemporary modernities. Indeed, contrary to modernist predictions that religion would wane under the combined assault of science and development, beliefs in the magical have remained central to the way African people understand contemporary realities. In many places, these beliefs are on the rise, fueled by the uncertainties Africans have experienced in the wake of modernity's failure to deliver the progress that once seemed guaranteed to those who embraced development.

The intensification of witchcraft beliefs has routinely provoked the emergence of witch-cleansing movements during which self-appointed individuals would identify witches deemed responsible for the misfortune (drought, poverty, and epidemics) befalling communities. The notable incidence of such movements during the colonial period was seen as a result of the socioeconomic breakdown provoked by the imposition of colonial policies—and in some cases, the impact of missionary activity. From such a perspective, inequities and insecurities brought about by the emergence of new forms of production, consumption, and political power resulted in tensions that were often expressed through the idiom of witchcraft. In the 1930s, the Watchtower and *Mchape* movements in present-day Zambia aimed to create a radically new and harmonious society through the elimination of evil. Youthful leaders hoping to reinvigorate society exposed elders as witches. Concerns about fertility and production have elsewhere prompted accusations of witchcraft against elderly women who, as often wealthy but no longer fertile contributors to society, are seen as the prototypical witch. Among

the Sukuma of northwest Tanzania, such victims of witchcraft accusations are expelled or put to death. In Congo children have become the target of witchcraft accusations and have been subjected to family violence or abandoned altogether. Misfortune, a neighbor's death, and unexplained illness in the family are some reasons that prompt accusations of witchery against a child. There, as elsewhere on the continent, witches and the discourses they generate are often critiques of development and capitalism, that is, of a world in which the rich appear to generate their wealth through illicit means and often at the expense of the poor.

Whereas Christian missions originally condemned African attempts to seek protection against occult forces, Muslim clerics encouraged the use of protective charms, amulets, and other methods that they manufactured in exchange for a fee. Among other things, they shared with practitioners of indigenous religions a recognition of the existence of spirits—to them, *jinn*. They also prescribed Muslim prayers and amulets as preventive treatment against accusations of witchcraft. Most techniques devised for warding off the deleterious impact of spiritual forces on human lives made (and still make) use of Arabic texts such as the Qur'an from which they partly drew their efficacy. As the word of God, the Qur'an is regarded as containing divine potency. In fact, the holy book is often seen as a form of protection for the believer as well as a source of healing. Techniques such as prayers, blessings, geomancy (divination by reading scatters of sand or pebbles), astrology, and amulets draw their potency from the secret knowledge that Muslim clerics acquire through intense and specialized training.

Amulets (referred to as *gris-gris* in the French colonial lexicon) that may be worn on the body or suspended, inserted, or buried at specific locations generally contain verses of the Qur'an. The selection of Qur'anic verses for amulet making calls for specialized knowledge for different ailments, and specific threats require different chapters, verses, or combinations of verses. Although these protective devices are sometimes manufactured so that their contents may be rubbed into objects or used for bathing, another popular technique involves writing a verse of the Qur'an with ink on a wooden slate. The text is washed off with water that is then drunk by the cleric's client. Absorbing the potency of the Qur'an in such a way is generally seen as more efficient than carrying it on the body through the wearing of amulets. Amulets can be lost, and they are prone to ritual pollution and may lose their protective efficacy.

Given the power that Muslim specialists appear to wield over spirits, they are occasionally suspected of engaging in nefarious activities for primarily selfish ends. Some are even accused of engaging in immoral bargains with spirits to enrich themselves: in exchange for the wealth they receive from the work of the spirits, they must offer human victims to the supernatural workers.

Because of the ambivalent nature of the esoteric knowledge of Muslim specialists, some are also believed to manufacture harmful amulets at the bequest of clients wishing to harm a competitor or an enemy. Whereas many Africans rely on the expertise of Muslim specialists for protection against drought, automobile accidents, and a variety of other calamities, some Muslims believe that reliance on amulets, irrespective of the purpose for which they are used, is a corrupt interpretation of the Qur'an. Fourteenth-century North African scholar Ibn Khaldun called on Muslims to abandon such practices on the basis that it was a form of idolatry. More recently, reformist Muslims who have, throughout the continent, campaigned for the purification of Islamic practices have similarly condemned the making of amulets as a heretical activity.

See also **Famine; Ibn Khaldun, Abd al-Rahman; Islam; Linguistics and the Study of Africa; Religion and Ritual; Spirit Possession.**

BIBLIOGRAPHY

Masquelier, Adeline Marie. *Prayer Has Spoiled Everything: Possession, Power, and Identity in an Islamic Town of Niger.* Durham, NC: Duke University Press, 2001.

ADELINE MASQUELIER

WITCHCRAFT AND POLITICS

Witchcraft beliefs are encountered throughout African history, in virtually all parts of the continent, and continue to be an important feature of contemporary times.

Edward Evans-Pritchard's (1902–1973) classical study of the Azande in Sudan (1937) distinguished between witchcraft and sorcery by their differing techniques. He defined the former as the innate, inherited ability to cause misfortune or death. Witchcraft involved unconscious psychic powers, emanating from a black swelling located near the liver. By contrast, Azande referred to sorcery as the performance of rituals, the uttering of spells, and the manipulation of organic substances such as herbs with the conscious intent of causing harm. Although this distinction is widespread throughout East Africa, it is not made in other parts of Africa. Many contemporary authors therefore use the terms witch and witchcraft more broadly to denote both types of persons and modes of action.

Philip Mayer (1954) points to several common features of witchcraft beliefs:

1. Witches incorporate nonhuman power. Witches work with animals such as snakes, cats, baboons, and owls that they own as familiars; or witches themselves change into the shape of these animals.

2. Witches are nearly always adults.

3. Witchcraft tends to become socially important in times of crisis, when all sorts of misfortune are ascribed to them.

4. Witches harm their own kin and neighbors, rather than strangers.

5. Witchcraft is motivated by envy and malice, rather than by the pursuit of material gain.

6. Witches reverse usual expectations of behavior. They work at night, commit incest, practice cannibalism, go naked instead of clothed, or may stand backwards when they knock at doors.

7. Witchcraft is nearly always immoral.

Anthropological theories seek to unearth the ideological and social realities underlying these witchcraft beliefs and the cultural meanings they encode. Evans-Pritchard demonstrated how the belief in witchcraft among the Azande presented a logical explanation of unfortunate events. He insisted that the theory of witchcraft did not exclude empirical knowledge about cause and effect, but rather supplemented theories of natural causation and answered questions about the particularity of misfortunes. He cited the famous example of a granary that collapsed, injuring those sitting beneath it. The Azande explained this event in empirical terms: termites had eaten the supports. But they resorted to witchcraft to explain why particular individuals sat beneath the granary at the precise moment when it collapsed.

Another influential theory, by Max Marwick (1965), is that witchcraft accusations reformulate problematic social relations that are not susceptible to judicial processes. Among the Chewa of Zambia, accusations of witchcraft occurred when the matrilineage grew beyond the size that its resources could sustain. As tensions over inheritance became apparent, accusations of witchcraft served as an idiom for initiating processes of fission and enabled the accusers to break off redundant relationships.

More recent theorists postulate that witchcraft accusations are instrumental in political and economic struggles and that witchcraft discourses are avenues for interpreting modern changes. This association with power is because witchcraft involves constant transgression. Conceptions of power and political processes thus stand at the heart of witchcraft.

In precolonial Africa, political actors tapped an important source of political legitimacy by neutralizing witchcraft to manage misfortune. Among the Azande of Sudan, kings and princes owned prestigious poison oracles, to which commoners appealed for the final verdict in cases of witchcraft. Likewise, Nyakyusa chiefs in Malawi were considered leaders in the war by night against witchcraft. The chiefs were custodians of morality who used their python power to detect evil, defend villagers against witchcraft, and punish wrongdoers.

Colonial governments were committed to a civilizing mission and perceived witchcraft beliefs and practices as primitive, baseless, and even diabolical superstitions. They enacted a series of witchcraft suppression laws that prohibited accusations of witchcraft and attempts to practice witchcraft. However, in practice, colonial regimes constantly ignored witchcraft beliefs and allowed chiefs and headmen to continue trying witchcraft cases.

In colonial times, witch-cleansing cults readily crossed ethnic and national boundaries. The *kamcape* movement of the 1930s, for instance, spread from Nyasaland into Northern and Southern Rhodesia, the Congo, and Mozambique. The organizers used handheld mirrors as a form of divination and then administered medicines to render witchcraft ineffective and to protect the innocent against mystical attacks. Witches identified themselves by confessions and usually resumed their places in the community, and a morally regenerated life began for everyone. These cults nonetheless involved considerable ambiguity. Though they aimed to restore social order, they also fostered new unity. The cults temporarily invested power in the hands of younger men at the expense of elders. The younger men had a wider universe of interests and were often linked to African nationalist movements.

Witchcraft beliefs and accusations have remained important features of political processes in postcolonial societies. After independence, some governments, such as the Tanzanian, have vigorously pursued modernization schemes and continued the colonial suppression of witchcraft laws. Others, such as the Malawian and Cameroonian governments, have treated witchcraft as a reality and have allowed chiefly and state courts to convict witches. For example, regional courts in Cameroon's East Province even sentenced witches to imprisonment for periods of up to ten years on the basis of testimony provided by certified diviners (*nkong*). Similarly, the Ralushai Commission of Inquiry into witchcraft-related crimes in South Africa argued that accused witches should be judged by African standards of reasonableness and recommended that people who create reasonable suspicion of practicing witchcraft should be liable to punishment.

Postcolonial discourses of witchcraft are intimately related to new forms of inequality and address fears by youth that elders are blocking their paths to prosperity. Peter Geschiere (b. 1941; 1997) argued that, in countries such as Cameroon, witchcraft constitutes a popular mode of political action whereby village communities express dissent against the offensive behavior of elites. Cameroonian villagers see power, wealth, and success as reflecting possession of occult forces called *djambe*. Should villagers experience misfortune, they may accuse powerful and wealthy persons of witchcraft or may threaten to use witchcraft against them. Such accusations place members of the urban political elite under considerable pressure to redistribute resources.

See also **Colonial Policies and Practices; Kinship and Descent; Postcolonialism; Religion and Ritual.**

BIBLIOGRAPHY

Evans-Pritchard, Edward E. *Witchcraft, Oracles and Magic Among the Azande.* Oxford: Clarendon Press, 1937.

Geschiere, Peter. *The Modernity of Witchcraft: Politics and the Occult in Postcolonial Africa.* Charlottesville: University Press of Virginia, 1997.

Marwick, Max. *Sorcery and Its Social Setting: A Study of the Northern Rhodesian Cewa.* Manchester, U.K.: Manchester University Press, 1965.

Mayer, Philip. *Witches.* Inaugural Lecture. Grahamstown, South Africa: Rhodes University, 1954.

Wilson, Monica. *Good Company: A Study of Nyakyusa Age Villages.* Boston: Beacon Press, 1967.

ISAK NIEHAUS

WITCHCRAFT AND PROPHETISM

In the contemporary language of the social sciences and popular culture, the word *witchcraft* often refers to harm created as a result of human action undertaken with the assistance of special powers. The word witchcraft, derived from the Old English word *wiccan*, concerned human acts intended to affect nature in a wide variety of ways and was not exclusively associated with harm. It was similar to the twenty-first-century use of the word *magic*. Through the influence of some forms of Christian thought, the human beings who attempted to affect nature were assumed to rely on either harmful or helpful spirit entities, and their activities were categorically labeled harmful or helpful. During the Renaissance all forms of magic came to be associated with harm and the influence of the devil, and the term witchcraft largely came to stand for this hostile perspective on magic. Contemporary scholarship continues to reproduce the problem of identifying the different forms that magic takes. Some scholars use the term "harmful magic" in place of "witchcraft" in order to avoid some of its more narrow historical and geographic associations.

PROPHETISM

The English word *prophecy* is derived from the Greek word *propheteia* and shares the same root as the word *prophemi*, which means "to speak before or for someone." In ancient Greece the term *prophetes* referred to a religious specialist who both interpreted messages from the gods and other kinds of signs. These interpretations concerned the present and the future and could involve many different kinds of intermediaries. There is a long history in anthropological discourse, initiated by E. E. Evans-Pritchard, to elaborate the qualities of relatively benign "prophets" that place them in contrast to colonialist notions of harmful "witchdoctors."

In the twenty-first century most scholars use the term *prophet* to describe a religious specialist who has the ability to perceive, understand, and convey the communications of a supreme being, gods, or other nonhuman spirit entities. The term *diviner* often refers to a religious specialist who interprets the symbolic meaning of features of the natural world or the results of manipulative techniques. In some religious systems diviners communicate with divinity or a spirit in their attempt to discover meaning, as do prophets. In some religious systems diviners are distinguished from prophets because they seek out information on behalf of an individual client rather than for the good of the wider society. Most African societies maintain prophecy and divination in some form. As mediators between divinity and human beings, prophets and diviners have the potential to use their power to direct human thought and action.

Prophets often have unusual intellectual and spiritual talents. Some of them are also known to possess qualities of charismatic leadership. Those whose skills in prophecy are well developed are accorded high status in society. In some religious systems the prophet's ability is thought to be authorized by divinity or ancestor spirits, and in other systems, by the prophet's position in a line of succession from a former prophet. Most religious systems have particular rules that are used to determine the legitimacy of a prophet's work, or the particular words or interpretations prophets provide. During periods of rapid change prophetic leaders often blend different traditions of prophecy, and present novel ways of interpreting the world around them.

In the religious systems of some African societies there are people whose skills in prophecy include the ability to identify problems caused by harmful magic. In the Mijikenda society of coastal

Kenya, there are men and women prophets who work within a specialized guild or sodality. In the early twenty-first century the sodality is called the *kaya*. These prophets are senior Mijikenda who have prophets in their line of ancestry and are chosen by ancestral spirits to give guidance to members of their clan and other Mijikenda. They interpret the communications of ancestral spirits and the Supreme Being Mungu through dreams and during prayer. They warn Mijikenda about large-scale problems such as insect infestations, climactic change, communicable diseases, and harmful magic that affects rain and crop fertility.

It is possible for some religious specialists to combine the skills of prophecy and divination in order to identify sources of harmful magic as well as the practitioners of harmful magic. Claiming to be able to diminish or rid society of harmful magic, witch finders in Africa have led large-scale movements that reshape social and political life. Since the mid-twentieth century, several Mijikenda men claiming descent from a lineage of prophets as well as competence in divinatory skills have initiated such movements. The most well-known witch-finder was Kajiwe, who worked from 1966 to 1991. With the support of local elites and state administrative officials, he conducted rituals to both find alleged witches and cleanse society of the influence of harmful magic. Local and state political support allowed Kajiwe to assert his power to find witches over the power of prophets and other religious specialists with legitimate traditional claims to identify sources of social harm. The struggle among different religious specialists to identify and treat harmful magic, and to secure the political support of state officials, continues to characterize Mijikenda life.

In the history of religious movements and the creation of independent churches in Africa, prophetic leaders have often taken strong positions against the use of harmful magic and provided adherents with the means to avoid it. In the Kimbanguist movement that began in present-day Congo in 1921, there were a number of Kongo prophets who provided analyses of the moral failures of society in order to explain misfortune and other unacceptable life conditions. Among these failures was the practice of harmful magic. The greatest prophet, Simon Kimbangu, began the movement that later developed into one of the largest independent churches on the continent. He claimed to heal in the name of Jesus and taught people that the existence of evil in their hearts, largely identified as witchcraft, brought sickness and discomfort. His religious rituals and prayers offered his following new ways to reconceptualize and reform their lives.

See also **Death, Mourning, and Ancestors; Kimbangu, Simon; Kinship and Descent; Prophetic Movements.**

BIBLIOGRAPHY

Ciekawy, Diane. "Witchcraft and Statecraft: Five Technologies of Power in Colonial and Postcolonial Coastal Kenya." *African Studies Review* 41, no. 3 (1998): 119–141.

Johnson, Douglas, and David Anderson. "Revealing Prophets." In *Revealing Prophets: Prophecy in Eastern African History.* London: James Currey, 1995.

McGaffey, Wyatt. *Modern Kongo Prophets: Religion in a Plural Society.* Bloomington: Indiana University Press, 1983.

DIANE CIEKAWY

WITCHCRAFT AND WEALTH

Witchcraft, commonly defined as the use of supposed magical powers to achieve a particular goal, has always been part of the popular beliefs in many societies around the world, most notably in Africa, and varies from culture to culture and from time to time. In Africa, anthropological studies have shed light on the different significances of witchcraft beliefs and the ways in which they may have operated in this continent since the precolonial period. If earlier generations of anthropologists generally viewed African witchcraft as the expression of primitive mentality, early twenty-first-century scholarship considers this popular belief a product of the modernization process. In some cases, the belief in witchcraft is seen as a popular response to socioeconomic changes that many African societies have been experiencing since the early sixteenth century.

In relation to the accumulation of material wealth and political domination in Africa, the witchcraft frenzy witnessed in many African countries at the start of the twenty-first century has a long history that goes back to the sixteenth century, often seen as the early phases of globalization. Historically, the popular beliefs in what is known now as the sorcery of wealth were a result of the engagement of African societies in commercial exchanges with Europe and North America, notably the slave trade that primarily profited African coastal chiefs. Indeed, the slave business offered these customary leaders, who acted as middlemen, new economic opportunities for gaining wealth and acquiring dependents. As the commodification and enslavement of people increased throughout the continent, so too did witchcraft rumors that were directed against African slave brokers, who were suspected of capturing the spiritual and material vitality of their rivals and enemies and sending them to invisible forces located overseas. For example, many populations of the Gulf of Guinea and West Africa whose kings were prosperous in the slave trade strongly believed that their leaders owed their riches and power to their involvement in the sorcery of *nkong*, *djambe*, *evu* or *sem*, all of which emphasize the accumulative tendency of witchcraft in relation to power. As a result of this prevailing belief, any accumulation of imported European and North American commodities was viewed as suspicious because of their supposed connections with occult forces.

The colonial period witnessed a substantial recentering of witchcraft discourses in Africa around material accumulation. The witchcraft frenzy that arose at that period addressed the social and economic inequities exacerbated by the involvement of African societies in the expanding plantation economy. In many areas of the continent, notably in East, West, and Central Africa, the local populations generally expressed a certain apprehension of newly acquired riches. More important is that the witchcraft rumors triggered by these new forms of wealth accumulation were no longer leveled at the former customary leaders who had lost their economic and political prerogatives when the British and other colonial powers suppressed slave trading. The prime suspects were rather successful farmers and planters who took advantage of the new possibilities of enrichment provided by the growing business of commercial agriculture. The general opinion about these new financial elites, who were often untitled people and even former slaves, whose economic success, and consequently new status, contradicted their low positions in the traditional status system, was that they made their fortunes by turning their innocent victims into zombies who could then work invisibly on their behalf.

In regions where the accumulation of wealth was made at the expense of the autochthon populations, strangers and foreigners were the main targets of frenzied witchcraft rumors that generally depicted them as witches who enriched and empowered themselves by sucking the life forces of the natives. The Duala and Bakweri of the coastal regions of Cameroon regularly supposed that prosperous Bamileke and Bamenda planters from the mountain areas of the country had capitalized their wealth by enslaving them in the *nyongo* or *famla* sorcery. A *nyongo* or *famla* sorcerer was identified through his modern house with its zinc roof that, according to a general belief, could not have been constructed without the slave labor of invisible zombies.

Modern beliefs in witchcraft continue these ancient visions of wealth and power, fueling an unprecedented proliferation of alarming rumors about the nouveaux riches and their alleged magic money. These rumors hold that, in a context of generalization of poverty, only those who are members of some mystical organization can accumulate fabulous fortunes in times of economic crisis for most and a shrinking labor market. The rumors identify successful con men, corrupt bureaucrats and politicians, and dubious businessmen whose alleged association with occult forces enable them not only to accumulate huge fortunes in little time but also to secure political power and social prestige. In many African countries where marginalized groups are confronted with exuberant flows of luxurious imported commodities and fantastic but seemingly unobtainable wealth, many not so favored have been quick to give voice to their perplexity at the occult sources of these fabulous riches. Over time, some pervasive notions such as blood money, magic money, devil fortunes, or what the popular imagination in Cameroon calls *mokoagne moni* (money obtained through occult means), have become key concepts for explaining wealth acquired through sacrifices of innocent people to mystical organizations. These concepts also account for cursed money that never stays in its owner's pockets or allows itself to be spent wisely, because of a mystical power that compels the rich sorcerer to fritter away or waste his fortune on women and in lavish consumption.

The unique aspect of present witchcraft beliefs in Africa is that they are related to the present neoliberal capitalism and global proliferation of occult economies. Local populations interpret the novel forms of witchcraft in terms of global transactions of human goods and an international market of sorcery where rich sorcerers may buy and sell human flesh from and to one another. In Cameroon, for instance, the *mokoagne men* (rich sorcerers) are assumed to team up with the mafia, organizing a worldwide zombie traffic in which the country, as many African countries, is only a local relay of global occult transactions dominated by Europe and North America.

Since at least the early sixteenth century, witchcraft has been a powerful metaphor for interpreting social, economic, political, and other seemingly inhuman forms of domination in Africa.

See also **Colonial Policies and Practices; Divination and Oracles; Economics and the Study of Africa; Slave Trades.**

BIBLIOGRAPHY

Ardener, Edwin. "Witchcraft, Economics and the Continuity of Belief." In *Witchcraft Confessions and Accusations*, ed. Mary Douglas. London: Tavistock, 1970.

Comaroff, Jean, and John L. Comaroff. *Modernity and its Malcontents: Ritual and Power in Postcolonial Africa.* Chicago: University of Chicago Press, 1993.

Douglas, Mary, ed. *Witchcraft, Confessions and Accusations.* London: Tavistock, 1970.

Evans-Pritchard, Edward E. *Witchcraft, Oracles and Magic among the Azande.* Oxford: Oxford University Press, 1937.

Geschiere, Peter. The *Modernity of Witchcraft, Politics and the Occult in Postcolonial Africa.* Charlottesville: University of Virginia Press, 1997.

Latham, Anthony J. H. "Witchcraft Accusations and Economic Tension in Pre-Colonial Old Calabar." *Journal of African History*, 13, no. 2 (1972): 249–260.

Miller, Joseph. *Way of Death: Merchant Capitalism and the Angolan Slave Trade, 1730–1830.* Madison: University of Wisconsin Press, 1988.

Shaw, Rosalind. "The Production of Witchcraft/Witchcraft as Production: Memory, Modernity and the Slave Trade in Sierra Leone." *American Ethnologist*, 24, no. 4 (1997): 856–876.

White, Luise. *Speaking with Vampires. Rumor and History in Colonial Africa.* Berkeley: University of California Press, 2000.

BASILE NDJIO

WOMEN

This entry includes the following articles:
OVERVIEW
WOMEN AND ISLAM IN NORTHERN AFRICA
WOMEN AND ISLAM IN SUB-SAHARAN AFRICA
WOMEN AND NON-ISLAMIC RELIGION
WOMEN AND SLAVERY
WOMEN AND THE LAW
WOMEN AND THEATER
WOMEN AND TRADE
WOMEN AND URBANISM
WOMEN IN AFRICAN HISTORY
WIDOWS

OVERVIEW

In precolonial African societies, a woman's world was domestic, but her place was not just in the home, as it was in the late nineteenth through the mid-twentieth-centuries for bourgeois women in the West. Instead, it encompassed a more general responsibility for the reproduction and feeding of the household, so her place was in the fields as much as at home. Each wife was a unit of production and reproduction, given partial autonomy by her own granaries, kitchen, and sometimes even her own livestock but still in a state of quasi-servitude to the family head responsible for overseeing production. Of course at the same time women's reproductive roles—as child bearers and as cultural reproducers—were all the more important as fertility was very high, at the maximum limit of biological possibilities (birthrate close to 50 per 1,000, but with a very high infant death rate, according to statistics in Meillassoux 1981). Colonization brought significant changes, increasing women's burden of work but also bringing about opportunities for individual emancipation.

A number of women took advantage of these opportunities despite two obstacles: the reprobation linked to the Victorian style of colonialism and the traditional conservatism of African chiefs clinging to the last vestiges of their male privileges. Especially significant were those who left the harshness of life in the countryside, migrating in large numbers to the cities. In most late-twentieth-century African cities, women constituted the majority of the population, a fact that became particularly significant after independence. As a result, women are an explosive force, burdened with social and cultural handicaps but gifted with energy, creativity, and, most important, a crucial economic role in the subsistence sphere, giving them an important place in the future of sub-Saharan Africa.

DETERIORATION OF THE LIVING CONDITIONS OF RURAL WOMEN

In the case of most parts of Africa south of the Sahara, it is more fruitful to examine rural women than rural men. With some exceptions (among the Songhay of Mali, the Hausa and Yoruba of Nigeria, and to some degree the Fon of Dahomey), the hoe was reserved for women (to do the actual cultivation) while men used the ax (to cut trees and clear fields). Possibly women's burden, at least in western Africa, was increased by the impact of the Atlantic slave trade demanding more men than women (while the Arab and Muslim slave trade demanded more women than men). This might have had the consequence in certain societies (especially in Central/equatorial and Southern Africa) of assigning women to the most burdensome routine aspects of agriculture while men focused on defense, politics, and more prestigious—and often less critical for subsistence—activities such as hunting, fishing, and blacksmithing.

In most of the countryside and many urban settings, it was (and still is) common to see groups of women and children walking while carrying water and firewood on their heads. Rural women were beasts of burden, their lives harsh, their tasks many, even if they also found the ability to influence their own situations, to find some joy in life. That is why women accepted polygamy (possibly accentuated by the departure of male slaves that locally provoked, as it was shown in Loanda, a deficit of men), since it allowed them to divide the work among co-wives. The younger ones became servants (often, virtually slaves), of their elders, who earlier had served their mothers-in-law.

The condition of rural women grew worse with colonization, which disturbed the fragile internal balance of dependence and autonomy that might have existed beforehand between the sexes. There were two reasons for this. The first is that the cultivation of crops for export (peanuts, palm oil, coffee, cocoa) and of a surplus of subsistence crops (corn, yams, rice) destined for sale in local markets led to an increase in women's work, work that had to be performed in the interstices of the cycle of subsistence farming. While women continued to grow subsistence crops, they now also helped their husbands on the plantations, where they did much of the essential work. The men were the principal beneficiaries of the new system because it was they who conducted commerce with European merchants. Even when women were marketwomen (mainly in West Africa), they rarely saw actual money, because they found their old and reliable network of commerce and distribution in competition with, even ruined by, import-export firms and then the trucks bought by the men.

For marriage, the payment traditionally given by the husband's family to that of the wife in compensation for the loss of labor and children suffered by the wife's family—anthropologists call it "countergift"—gradually became an outright purchase of a woman. The process appeared in some societies—especially in West Africa—well before colonialism under the influence of greater commerce brought by trade contacts with the wider non-African world, but accelerated with the monetarization imposed by colonialism. The purchase—which had before been composed chiefly of a variety of gifts including livestock, ostentatious jewelry, copper pans, and loincloths—shifted to cash, a transformation of bridewealth into brideprice.

The chiefs, wealthy and old, practiced ostentatious polygamy. Their plantations of cash crops, such as cocoa and coffee in Cameroon, Uganda, and Northern Rhodesia (modern-day Zambia), ensured that they were protected by the colonial powers. These same plantations had a female labor force whose social status was closer to slavery than to marriage. Some chiefs had as many as thirty or even one hundred wives, who were in effect agricultural workers outside the money economy. Although the worst excesses disappeared after the 1930s, this system had profound and lasting consequences. Even in the 1980s the husbands of nurses at Salisbury Hospital in Harare, the capital of Zimbabwe, lined up at the end of the month to receive their wives' pay. They were encouraged to do so by laws supposedly based on tradition.

The colonial administration paid no attention to the needs of women. Instead, it focused on bringing men into the money economy by requiring from them taxes paid in cash, wage labor, and speculative farming. Women's lack of money trapped most of them in the old subsistence economy, further lengthening their work hours. The Gold Coast (present-day Ghana), which had a strong matrilineal tradition, began growing cocoa for export between 1891 and 1911. Between the world wars there was an evolution toward patrilineal heritage encouraged by the British authorities. The native authorities progressively had to ratify more or less willingly the process of change from matrilineal inheritance (from uncle to sister's son) to patrilineal (from father to son) as more likely to keep the plantations in the same hands.

Even if the impact made less difference than hoped by the colonizer on what happened on the ground, the results were still worse in Southern Rhodesia (present-day Zimbabwe), where colonial legal measures were more authoritarian and women's obedience more deeply rooted. Therefore this hostility to matrilineal practices quite often weakened women's rights. A colonial ideology molded by Christian morality and Roman or British common law was superimposed on ancient traditions of male supremacy. Private property, which was always in the name of the (male) head of the family, reduced women's access to land. As in France, this eviction of women became law with the adoption, in French colonies, of the Napoleonic Code. Part of the chiefs also participated, as they were consulted about customary laws. Like all elders, they had a tendency to distort the past, exaggerating the submissiveness of women, and thereby codified their dreams rather than reality.

Women quickly realized that rather than go before the customary chiefs, who always ruled against them, especially in land and divorce cases, it was better to bring legal complaints to the colonial authorities. They did so quite early, at the beginning of the twentieth century, as soon as there was a nearby administrative center. Some of them were more successful in the city to defend their land rights. This was the case in southern Tanganyika in 1901–1910. It was also true in the city of Lagos, Nigeria, where Yoruba women, who traditionally had strong family rights, defended their urban homes tooth and nail.

URBAN MIGRATIONS AND THE INDEPENDENCE OF WOMEN

The migration of women, especially of young women, to the cities was all the more important for being unexpected. Caused most fundamentally by harsh rural conditions for women, it was also spurred by political instability at the end of the nineteenth century. There were battered wives; widows obliged by custom to accept, against their will, their late husband's brother as spouse; women rejected because they were sterile; fugitive slaves; and women fleeing the exploitation of female production. Going to the city allowed them to marry whom and when they wanted, without waiting for their chosen man to amass enough wealth to pay the necessary brideprice. It allowed them to avoid marrying an older man, a polygamist, who would treat them like slaves.

This migration of young women was a social victory. They were encouraged neither by the colonizers nor by the traditional African world. The colonizers, in the Victorian spirit, did not accept the idea of female independence; to the missionaries, the idea of women working in the fields, their breasts bared, was the height of indecency. The administration hindered female migration as best it could, associating the migration of young girls to the city with prostitution. These independent women were unequivocally labeled "free women."

As for the Africans, they knew that women were needed to work in the fields. Not until just before the 1930s did arguments begin to appear, at first aimed at the daughters of the agrarian petite bourgeoisie, that the city was superior in terms of education and health. But at that time far fewer girls than boys were going to the city.

The sole exception, and it was an old and large exception, was in the cities of South Africa. The whites ignored women as a source of work, to the point of forgetting about them in legal terms. Women, therefore, were not regulated by the system of supervision and passbooks, that tragic imposition on black workers dating from the end of the nineteenth century. As a result, between the two world wars, women had far greater freedom of movement than men, and were able to migrate to the cities in large numbers. There they performed the essential functions that the single men, the majority of the labor forces required. The women took care of subsistence (as always): they purchased food in markets; made beer secretly; performed "informal" domestic chores of all kinds; and served as prostitutes for this mass of unmarried men. In the 1920s the most conservative state, the Orange Free State, attempted to impose the passbook on women. The women reacted so strongly—with demonstrations, delegations to the government in Pretoria, and other actions—that the Pretoria government was forced to back down. Only with apartheid was the passbook finally imposed on women; even then the law, passed in 1950, had to overcome fierce resistance. It was the women who organized the burnings of passbooks. Thus a path leading directly to their economic survival and their liberty brought them into politics, and once there, they fought, barefoot, to survive.

On the other hand, in tropical Africa more men than women were in the cities. When Zaire became independent in 1960, there was only one woman for every three men in Léopoldville (present-day Kinshasa). In the early twenty-first century there are more women than men in cities, except in Lagos, Nigeria, which is a major industrial port. In Senegal's Saint-Louis, the demography of which has been specially studied, the ratio is particularly marked at 877 men for every 1,000 women. Since the informal economy follows demographic trends, but the salaried economy lags behind it, women, who work in the informal economy, are more able than men to find employment.

A great deal of attention, perhaps too much, has been paid to prostitution. As in South Africa, women seized all available opportunities in the city. Lacking connections and means, they found occupations that required little or no capital and great flexibility in the local market, working in the "informal" economy and later in domestic work. On average, each white person working in the formal sector provided work for an average of six Africans, women working in the cheap informal sector (washing clothes, cooking, providing sex, and so on). Therefore prostitution was in the past, at least during the first part of colonial times, a job like another that allowed women to assert their economic independence. The fact is that before independence women had no choice but informal activities because they were absent in the schools; in 1960, at the time of independence, there was only one female entering college in all of Zaire, and she was the daughter of the mayor of Kinshasa.

WOMEN AND POLITICS

Although either officially ignored or vilified during the colonial period, women in the cities played an important role there, and they reacted sharply to attempts made to control them. In 1925 and again in 1929, in Igbo country (southern Nigeria), when the British administration attempted to impose licensing fees on female traders in markets, the women were united in their opposition. They organized the "women's war," involving mass demonstrations and the pillaging of administrative buildings, which led to the decision not to impose the fees. In 1933, in Lomé, Togo, the authorities attempted to tax fabric merchants; the women took to the streets, bringing everything to a standstill until they achieved their aims. The movement grew stronger around the time of World War II, especially in the Yoruba and Egba areas (western Nigeria).

In the west coast ports, from Saint-Louis, Freetown, and Accra to Portuguese Luanda, women had a long history of business activity going back to the sixteenth century. Ironically, though, in the colonial era the social conventions of the rising bourgeoisie tended to prevent the emergence of feminist movements. In one rare case, Freetown, women (such as Adelaide Smith Casely-Hayford, of Fante, English, Mandinka, and maroon parentage, who was the wife of a Creole lawyer), influenced by English suffragettes, won the right to vote in 1930. Between the world wars, the teaching profession produced some militant socialists, notably, at Abeokuta, Nigeria, Beere Anikulapo-Kuti-Ransome, the aunt of late-twentieth-century writer and Nobel Prize winner Wole Soyinka and the mother and grandmother of well-known musicians.

The pugnacity of the women worked wonders during the wars of national liberation. South Africa was only one of many nations where a female political conscience grew out of active resistance. Women played a significant role in the wars of independence in Kenya (the Mau Mau uprising), the Portuguese colonies, Zimbabwe, and Namibia. These were societies where the women had always been subservient to the men and attached to the land. The wars of independence were the first time they were allowed to participate in events. Even though few women were actually activists, they left an indelible mark.

In Mali a pioneer was Aoua Keita, a midwife who was born into the Sudanese aristocracy. Her father, who had fought in World War I, sent her in 1923 to Bamako's first school for girls. She was the only woman elected to Mali's Constitutional Assembly, and worked closely with Aissata Sow, president of the Sudanese teachers' association. But Aoua Keita was exceptional because she was divorced, independent, and had no children. Over time, women have found it less necessary to renounce marriage and children in order to obtain independence.

In 1991 Malians of all kinds took to the streets to overthrow the dictator, Moussa Traoré. In 1996 two women were ministers in the government of Alpha Umar Konaré; one was an ambassador, and some hold high positions in trade unions. Women in other African nations also occupy trade union posts.

In 2005, for the first time, a woman was elected president of Liberia, giving great hope to all African women that any woman might be recognized for her abilities and talents and no longer handicapped because of her gender.

WOMEN AND MODERNITY

Women may now be political actors, but daily survival rather than matters of state still occupy them. Having little education, most of them have no concept of a "social contract." In the early twenty-first century, women are fighting for an end to polygamy, the right to control fertility, and access to better education and health care. The traditional prejudice of men, however, is a major obstacle to change in the home, as is the position taken by international religious authorities, Catholic or Islamic.

The individualization of women was the outstanding development of the twentieth century. As a result of this change, at least in cities, it is often the woman who asks for a divorce; most of the time it is against a man's self-interest to get divorced because divorce may involve returning the brideprice, and also because in most cities, among poor people, women's informal economy may be more profitable than jobless husbands. Official or hidden polygamy often remains the rule, and the "ring wife" (a woman who believes in the monogamous marriage contract of the church, temple, or city hall) may fear that her

profits be used and misused by the husband. Of course this may vary by geographical area. For example, divorce and independent women are extremely frequent in Lusaka (Zambia) or Congo-Kinshasa; the rate of divorce also is very high in Lamu islands (Kenya), but Muslim women have to marry again quickly; in Senegal, the wife strongly believes that the husband's task remains to afford what they call *la dépense*, or covering the daily expenses for each of his wives (in a Muslim society). Therefore, according to where they live, women economically and socially adapt with regard to their children and their ability to get what they need in a world still dominated by men. As a rule, women's day-to-day independence, directly connected to women's economic autonomy (probably more developed in Africa than in the Western world, although on a very low general standard), very quickly increases, even if men's conservatism most of the time violently opposes it.

But is the modern woman truly emancipated? She is less and less willing to accept polygamous marriage. Nor is she willing to accept the semiofficial concubinage practiced by a large number of the male bourgeoisie, often called the "second (or third) office." What is surprising is the radical nature of women's reactions to modernity. In rural as well as urban areas, women are more and more the head of the family. In urban areas in particular, free unions have become more numerous since the 1980s. The modern woman is far better off than the traditional first wife, who would eventually be abandoned. Ironically, educated young women, seeing the misery of the "ring wife" or "indoor wife" are choosing to be the "outdoor wife."

Few data are available concerning contraception. Its use increases with education and urbanization. Those women who use it have abandoned ancient traditions and have both the knowledge and the means to employ effective techniques. They are also the women who have a profession (formal or informal) that enables them to hire domestic help. Therefore, those women who can use contraception are usually those whose pregnancies would not limit their independence. Even in the most modernized locations, the fertility of women has stabilized or even risen, with the average number of births per woman remaining as high as five to seven. However, since the early 1990s this number apparently has declined, a trend that will certainly accelerate.

Women empowerment in an AIDS-ridden society. These young women in the sprawling Kibera slum in Nairobi, Kenya, have little protection and less awareness of their rights as women. In these classes they teach each other about their bodies, their right to say no, how to avoid dangerous situations, AIDS, safe sex education, and financial empowerment. HIV rates for women in Kenya are five times the rate for men, indicating a strong feminization of the disease. © BRENT STIRTON/GETTY IMAGES

Finally, social scientists do not know what effect the rapid spread of AIDS will have on fertility. In Kigali, the capital of Rwanda, at the end of 1987 close to 40 percent of young pregnant women tested HIV-positive, and AIDS can be transmitted to children born of women who have it. Significantly, AIDS is especially high where machismo is most strongly developed (as in South Africa).

The independence of women not only changed morals, it also unleashed female creativity. Singers, dancers, artists, intellectuals, and especially authors appeared within a few years—women of originality, potential, and conscience. Modern businesswomen, women of power—ministers, ambassadors, and other important officers—were few but no less extraordinary in a worldwide context that remains unfavorable to the emancipation of women.

A fundamental fact is that the precondition of female emancipation has been the improvement of the preponderant economic position of women. In the early twenty-first century "informal" (popular) commerce, which is commerce outside the Western market economy, is undertaken by urban women. There were always women in the marketplace in Western Africa. In the cities of southern Ghana, for example, 90 percent of urban women performed some professional activity, generally commercial. In southern and Central Africa, women entered the market more slowly, and in large numbers only after independence. Their numbers increased as urbanization progressed and as the crisis of the capitalist sector spread. In Johannesburg and in Nairobi, women entered the market about the time of World War II. In Addis Ababa, Ethiopia, in the 1960s, 60 percent of street vendors were women. In Lusaka, Zambia, there were virtually no market women before independence.

In spite of their low level of literacy, 90 percent of women work in the popular economy. The growing scarcity of formal employment, the failure of salaries to keep up with the rising cost of living, and the devaluation of African currencies have made women's work essential to group survival. In the country as in the city women continue to perform the harsher tasks; they often assume total responsibility for group survival. This explains how, in the larger urban agglomerations such as Lagos and Kinshasa (in the the early twenty-first century there are over thirty cities in Africa with populations of over 1 million, whereas in 1960 there were only two), people manage to ensure that although life is certainly harsh, it is generally less subject to unpredictable disasters than is life in rural areas.

The role of women in development must be researched thoroughly. The large number of studies on this subject is deceptive. Certainly these studies reveal an awareness that a large part of nonindustrial production—outside the mines—is in the hands of women. It is therefore important to understand women. Despite repeated calls for consciousness raising, education, and mobilization, the official attitude remains that women are to be used rather than listened to.

One must not forget two facts. First, African women help themselves; especially in rural areas, the men and many women as well must (be made to) accept the right of women to participate in the process of decision making. In addition, and perhaps most important, working from dawn into the night, most women lack the time to learn new techniques that might help them. Women must be helped to help themselves. The only way is through education. Girls have always had less education than boys. In Islamic nations, the problem is of number—fewer girls are educated. In southern Africa, the problem is of quality. In the early twenty-first century three-quarters of adult African women are illiterate, and girls' schools are of lower quality than boys'. At most one-third, and perhaps as few as one-fourth, of girls attend school, as opposed to over one half of the boys. It is therefore essential that young women be educated, so that they can understand their role in the economy, the culture, and the nation.

See also **Colonial Policies and Practices; Demography: Fertility and Infertility; Diseases: HIV/AIDS; Economic History; Education, School; Kinship and Descent; Labor; Law; Literacy; Marriage Systems; Production Strategies; Soyinka, Wole; Urbanism and Urbanization.**

BIBLIOGRAPHY

Allman, Jean Marie, and Victoria Tashjian. *I Will Not Eat Stone: A Women's History of Colonial Asante.* Portsmouth, NH: Heinemann 2000.

Allman, Jean; Susan Geiger; and Nakanyike Musisi; eds. *Women in African Colonial Histories.* Bloomington: Indiana University Press, 2002.

Berger, Iris, and E. France White. *Women in Sub-Saharan Africa: Restoring Women to History.* Bloomington: Indiana University Press, 1999.

Boserup, Ester. *Woman's Role in Economic Development.* Brookfield, VT: Gower, 1986.

Coquery-Vidrovitch, Catherine. *African Women: A Modern History.* Boulder, CO: Westview Press, 1997.

Coquery-Vidrovitch, Catherine. *The History of African Cities South of the Sahara.* Princeton, NJ: Markus Wiener, 2005.

Cromwell, Adelaide M. *An African Victorian Feminist: The Life and Times of Adelaide Smith Caseley Hayford, 1868–1960.* London: Frank Cass, 1986.

Davies, Carol Boyce, and Anne Adams Graves, eds. *Ngambika: Studies of Women in African Literature.* Trenton, NJ: Africa World Press, 1986.

Hay, Margaret J., and Sharon Stichter, eds. *African Women South of the Sahara*, 2nd edition. London: Longman, 1995.

Hay, Margaret J., and Marcia Wright, eds. *African Women and the Law.* Boston: Boston University, 1982.

Jeater, Diana. *Marriage, Perversion, and Power: The Construction of Moral Discourse in Southern Rhodesia 1894–1930.* Oxford: Clarendon Press, 1993.

Keita, Aoua. *Femme d'Afrique: La vie d'Aoua Keita racontée par elle-même.* Paris: Présence africaine, 1975.

Mann, Kristin. "Women, Land, Property, and the Accumulation of Wealth in Early Colonial Lagos." *Signs* 14, no. 4 (1991): 682–705.

Mba, Nina. *Nigerian Women Mobilized: Women's Political Activity in Southern Nigeria, 1900—1965.* Berkeley: University of California Press, 1982.

Meillassoux, Claude. *Maidens, Meal, and Money: Capitalism and the Domestic Community.* Cambridge, U.K.: Cambridge University Press, 1981.

Mikell, Gwendolyn, ed. *African Feminism: The Politics of Survival in Sub-Saharan Africa.* Philadelphia: University of Philadelphia Press, 1997.

Obbo, Christine. *African Women: Their Struggle for Economic Independence.* London: Zed Press, 1980.

Parkin, David, and David Nyamwaya, eds. *Transformations of African Marriage.* Manchester, U.K.: Manchester University Press, 1987.

Roberts, Richard. *Litigants and Households: African Disputes and Colonial Courts in the French Soudan, 1895–1912.* Portsmouth, NH: Heinemann, 2005.

Wells, J. C. *We Now Demand! The History of Women's Resistance to Pass Laws in South Africa.* Johannesburg: Witwatersrand University Press, 1993.

Wright, Marcia. *Strategies of Slaves and Women: Life-Stories from East Central Africa.* London: James Currey, 1993.

CATHERINE COQUERY-VIDROVITCH

WOMEN AND ISLAM IN NORTHERN AFRICA

In their relation to Islam, women in North Africa are believing agents, participating in the construction of Islam through everyday religious practices, as well as persons subjected to Islamic laws and norms about femininity. Both positions are hotly debated and undergoing change.

WOMEN AND ISLAMIC AGENCY

As religious agents, women deal with the five central obligations of Islam according to their means and possibilities. The profession of faith is widely adhered to; even very secularized women consider themselves Muslim. The fast during Ramadan is widely kept—despite the temptations women have to withstand when cooking the elaborate Ramadan dinners—because women consider themselves a role model for their children in learning abstinence. The male provider usually gives the obligatory alms for the whole family, but women give money, help or food on their own. The pilgrimage to Mecca used to be reserved for more wealthy and elderly women, but economic developments and easy travel are now making it feasible for an increasing number of women. More common are visits to local saints, or participation in Sufi rituals.

Daily prayers are mostly said by older women. Young mothers feel that they are too often confronted by pollution caused by menstruation, childbirth, sexual acts, or caring for children and sick people to maintain the purity needed for regular praying. They often lack time, money, or permission to visit the bathhouse to perform the ablution and make oneself ritually pure. To show that they are nevertheless faithful believers, they promise to start praying when the children are older, and express their piety through modest, patient, and obedient behavior. Deficits in religiosity can be made up later by doing extra meritorious deeds, which elderly women actively do.

With the Islamic revival in the 1980s girls and young women started to express their Islamic identity by participating in teaching and praying sessions in the mosque and taking a serious interest in religion. Some used religious arguments to gain more say in the choice of a husband or to distance themselves from family control, which led to generational and affiliation conflicts within families. Many donned a modern veil plus foot-length long-sleeved overdress, the *hijāb*, which was compatible with their schooling or work activities but also was a strong, albeit contested, symbol of Islam. It replaced the traditional sheetlike body wrap, the *haik*, which was more a portable sign of seclusion and modesty that could not be worn when working. Women increasingly study and transmit Islamic knowledge and thus corrode the male dominance in religious matters from the inside and make unprecedented contributions to Islamic interpretations, which will undoubtedly affect women's positions in the future.

WOMEN UNDER ISLAMIC LAW

The Malikite Sunni Islam followed in North Africa is gendered in that men and women have unequal rights in marriage, divorce, children, sexuality, and inheritance. Men are allowed to marry up to four women. The percentage of polygynous men in North Africa is much lower than that in sub-Saharan Africa, however. Tunisia has legally restricted polygyny, and elsewhere it is inhibited by the high costs of marriage and of providing for another wife and her children, as most women are economically inactive.

The Islamic prerogative of men to divorce women at will is greatly feared. Most states have restricted this male privilege by requiring registration by a notary, or accepting only divorces in court as in Tunisia. Egypt and Morocco have in 2000 and 2004 respectively increased the possibilities of women to obtain a divorce. Feminist jurists advise women on how the marriage contract can be used to protect the right to study, work, not have a co-wife, or to keep the marital home after divorce. In practice, however, few brides have the power to do so. Women also have lesser rights over their children. Divorced mothers retain the right of care (*hadana*) of young children, but legal custody remains in the hands of the father, making the mother and the children subject to his whims.

Both men and women should be sexually modest according to Islam, but women are under much stricter social control and more heavily sanctioned when committing premarital sex, adultery, or prostitution. While boys and men enjoy relative freedom to experiment, girls and women are closely monitored, allowed only limited freedom to move in public space and kept segregated from unrelated males. Female genital mutilation is practiced only in East North Africa. In the Maghreb it is not practiced, nor seen as an Islamic form of purification.

Following Islamic law, women keep their own property and income in marriage, but are expected to contribute to the household when the husband cannot provide sufficiently for the family. The marriage payment (*mahr*) becomes the property of the bride, and not that of her father or male relatives as often happens in sub-Saharan Africa. It is usually converted into gold, like any salary the woman earns, to create a security fund. Given the threat of divorce, women closely guard this economic right to ownership accorded them by Islam, and frequently quarrel about it with their husband. For the same reason, inherited assets, reduced by the law that women's inheritance rights are half of those of a man, are often left in the hands of a woman's brothers who will take care of her when she is divorced or widowed. All North African states have signed the UN Convention on the Elimination of All Forms of Discrimination Against Women (1979), but all made the reservation that this should not contradict Islamic law (*shari'a*). Therefore none of these states has given women full equal rights as of the year 2006.

Since the early twentieth century, women's movements have tried to improve women's position. A continuous debate was whether this could be reconciled with Islamic tenets or not. Some secular feminists and nongovernmental organizations defend universalist values and see gender inequality as inherent in laws said to be Islamic, such as the global network Women Living under Muslim Laws, founded in 1984 by North African women with activists elsewhere. Others take the view that Islamic feminism is the only possible or viable road. Activism from within Islam ranges between strict Islamists who find that better adherence to Islam will provide many women with more rights than they actually have, to liberal Muslims who aim to interpret the Islamic sources in a more favorable way for women. Both groups actually managed to improve women's position in certain respects.

See also **Initiation: Clitoridectomy and Infibulation; Islam; Law: Islamic; Religion and Ritual; Religion and the Study of Africa.**

BIBLIOGRAPHY

Buitelaar, Marjo. *Fasting and Feasting in Morocco: Women's Participation in Ramadan.* London: Berg, 1993.

Charrad, Mounira. *States and Women's Rights: The Making of Post-colonial Tunisia, Algeria, and Morocco.* Berkeley: University of California Press, 2001.

Chérif-Chammari, Alya. *Le mariage: Guide des droits des femmes* [The marriage: Guide to the rights of women]. Tunis: Association des Femmes Tunisiennes pour la Recherche et le Development, 1995.

Cooke, Miriam. *Women Claim Islam: Creating Islamic Feminism through Literature.* New York: Routledge, 2001.

Jansen, Willy. *Women without Men: Gender and Marginality in an Algerian Town.* Leiden: E. J. Brill, 1987.

Jansen, Willy. "The Economy of Religious Merit. Women and *Ajr* in Algeria." *The Journal of North African Studies* 9, no. 4 (2004): 1–17.

Karam, Azza. *Women, Islamisms and the State: Contemporary Feminisms in Egypt.* New York: St. Martin's, 1998.

Mernissi, Fatima. *The Veil and the Male Elite: A Feminist Interpretation of Women's Rights in Islam.* New York: Addison-Wesley, 1991.

Mir-Hosseini, Ziba. *Marriage on Trial: A Study of Islamic Family Law in Iran and Morocco,* London: Tauris, 1993.

Moghadam, Valentine M. "Islamic Feminism and Its Discontents: Toward a Resolution of the Debate." In *Gender, Politics, and Islam,* ed. Therese Saliba, Carolyn Allen, and Judith A. Howard. Chicago: University of Chicago Press, 2002.

Women Living under Muslim Laws. Available from http://www.wluml.org.

Zuhur, Sherifa. *Revealing Reveiling: Islamist Gender Ideology in Contemporary Egypt.* New York: State University of New York, 1992.

WILLY JANSEN

WOMEN AND ISLAM IN SUB-SAHARAN AFRICA

It is difficult to identify the specific effects of Islamic normative principles on the regulation of gender relations in African Muslim societies, on women's position in the family, and on their status in society at large. This is so because many African Muslim societies are organized not only following their understandings of Islamic precepts, but also according to a highly complex status system stratified by occupation and genealogical descent. The repercussions of Islamic precepts on gender relations are further complicated, and often mitigated, by the ways historically and regionally specific political and religious authority structures and economic organization affect women's participation in public life and influence on family affairs. These various factors generate dissimilar, sometimes opposite, experiences for women, sometimes within the same society. Power inequalities and hierarchies thus exist not only between men and women, but among women of different age and social background.

It would be similarly problematic to assume the existence of a clearly circumscribed "Islamic" gender ideology in African Muslim societies. The view of women's and men's complementarity and interdependence, for instance, often considered a particular feature of societies under the influence of Islam, applies to African societies in general. Historically, Muslim social institutions and authorities have often exhibited considerable tolerance vis-à-vis local practices and gender norms, as long as central precepts of Islam were followed. For this reason, ideals of femininity (and of masculinity) vary from one Muslim society to the other, and sometimes even within a society, reflecting class-specific, rather than ethnically or culturally specific behavioral standards.

The differential life experiences of women in Muslim societies in Africa are also complicated by the particular ways in which regional discursive traditions of Islam have been interacting with intellectual trends from far away places within the Muslim world, among them Egypt, the *hejaz*, and areas of South Asia. The resulting dynamic mixture of foreign and local influences generates considerable controversy among Muslims, men and women, as to what are "genuinely Islamic" conventions and practices. For instance, the prominence of possession cults in Muslim societies has historically been strongly contested by male religious authorities whose denouncement of the practice as apostasy (Arabic, shirk) implies an invalidation of the central role played by women as medium and ritual leaders in these cults. Another bone of contention among Muslims that has emerged over the past decades is the question

as to what role women should play as leaders and educators in communal life.

Ideals of proper womanhood in African Muslim societies materialize in the legal regulation of marriage, divorce, and property. They transpire from the prevalent exclusion of women from formal office in the religious community, and in the practice of *purdah* that is, seclusion. Similar to veiling conventions, the adoption of purdah varies considerably across history, regions, and socioeconomic background. Lower-class women are bound by the rules of propriety required by purdah to a lesser extent than upper-class women. In some rural societies, in which women's work outside the domestic realm is indispensable, female seclusion is followed much less thoroughly. In some African societies, the adoption of purdah also varies according to a woman's age and status within the family. Women beyond the childbearing age may move more freely in the market and in other public spaces than at an earlier stage of their life cycle. Yet even younger women who practice seclusion may pursue their economic affairs, such as the trade that Hausa women in the Katsina Emirate, North Nigeria, conduct from their home with the help of sons and other dependents.

Thus many Muslim women do not perceive purdah primarily as a spatially restrictive convention, but as way of protecting and even increasing one's social standing. Depending on the sociopolitical context and a woman's life situation, living in seclusion may be an ideal that many strive for, yet only few manage to attain. Many low-status Swahili women on the East African coast, for example, adopted purdah as a status marker around the turn of the twentieth century to achieve greater social recognition. In the early twenty-first century, seclusion is practiced mostly among the more privileged strata of the urban population, whereas for poor women, seclusion is difficult or impossible to maintain. But there are also upper class women who opt for advanced Western school education, rather than a secluded life, as a marker of prestige and a modern orientation.

Wherever Muslim law is applied in African societies (without being limited or mitigated by state law), it ensures basic rights but not equality for women. In numerous Muslim societies, women need to obtain consent for marriage from a male

Competition for land fuels religious and ethnic violence. A woman from Yelwa holds her child as she waits in line at a clinic donated by a Muslim charity, May 2004, in the Lafia refugee camp in central Nigeria. Farmers with crops and those with cattle clashed across Africa as they competed for land. © JACOB SILBERBERG/GETTY IMAGES

relative, often an uncle, who acts as their legal representative. Once a woman is married, she can own and inherit property in her own name and is entitled to be maintained at a level she has been accustomed to in her own family. Formally, a husband's failure to provide maintenance may be a ground for divorce, to be obtained from a Muslim judge in some societies. But in practice, it depends importantly on a woman's material and social resources whether she is able to obtain a divorce. A husband, in contrast, is not obliged to present grounds for divorcing his wife to an external institution. He may simply pronounce three times the *talaq* or repudiation. Men also inherit twice the share of a woman unless otherwise specified in the will. Although these rules of inheritance, as well as

other legal regulations, treat women and men unequally, it is important to note that Islamic precepts grant more rights to women than in traditional, non-Islamic regulations of gender relations, for instance by establishing women as property owners, rather than treating them as part of an inheritance passed on to the next husband.

Within the same Muslim society, the status and rights accorded to a woman varies with her social origin, that is, her kinship affiliation and matrimonial alliances. Irrespective of a woman's socioeconomic position and social origin, a woman can accrue considerable prestige from the bearing and socialization of children. Seniority is accorded on the basis of differences in age and generation, and according to a woman's level of (secular or Islamic) education and her position of ritual power or religious authority. In numerous other Muslim societies, too, a woman's wealth, whether inherited or gained individually, importantly accrues her prestige and her capacity to control others, in particular junior men and women.

For instance, in northern Nigeria, prior to the early eighteenth century Fulani *jihad*, aristocratic Hausa women yielded high status and influenced public affairs either through direct involvement or, more frequently, by influencing male kin and affines. Their earlier roles as rulers and conquering warriors decreased after the establishment of the Sokoto Caliphate, and were further undermined as a result of British colonial administration and the concurrent gradual integration of the region into a global capitalist market economy. But there were also a few royal women who assumed an important function as educators in the consolidation of the Sokoto Caliphate. The ways royal wives conduct their affairs in the early 2000s reflects this loss in political standing. They continue to shape public affairs by exerting influence over affines inside and outside the palace, yet they do so through informal mechanisms of control and by leading a secluded life in the royal palace. Also, similar to women of privileged background in Muslim societies of East Africa, some aristocratic women exert considerable influence by acting as religious patrons and organizing and delivering Islamic education. Others sponsor community development services and act as role models for younger women.

Until the early decades of the twentieth century, some nonroyal Hausa women accrued considerable wealth by drawing on slave labor. They purposefully specialized in the acquisition of female slaves whose offspring was to increase the size of the household and of the manageable estate. Among them were widows who were entitled to keep and administer their husband's property in their children's interest. The abolition of slavery under British colonial rule seriously undermined these women's capacity to protect their and their children's interests.

These historical transformations illustrate the great variability of women's position of influence in Muslim Africa, across regions and historical periods, as well as within one and the same society.

See also **Gender; Islam; Kinship and Descent; Law: Islamic.**

BIBLIOGRAPHY

Boyd, Jean. "Distance Learning from Purdah in Nineteenth-Century Northern Nigeria: The Work of Asma'u Fodio." *Journal of African Cultural Studies* 14, no. 1 (2001): 7–22.

Coulon, Christian. "Women, Islam, and Baraka." In *Charisma and Brotherhood in African Islam*, ed. Donal B. Cruise O'Brien and Christian Coulon. Oxford: Clarendon Press, 1988.

Hutson, Alaine. "The Development of Women's Authority in the Kano Tijaniyya, 1894–1963." *Africa Today* 46, no. 3–4 (1999): 48–64.

Oppong, Christine, ed. *Female and Male in West Africa.* London: Allen and Unwin, 1983.

Strobel, Margaret. *Muslim Women in Mombasa, 1890–1975.* New Haven, CT: Yale University Press, 1979.

DOROTHEA E. SCHULZ

WOMEN AND NON-ISLAMIC RELIGION

Approximately half of the 800 million Africans practice religious traditions other than Islam, including over one thousand indigenous religions, various forms of Christianity, Judaism, Hinduism, and new religious movements. This entry examines the roles of women in indigenous religions and in Christianity, focusing on the ways in which gendered concepts of spiritual power and the leadership roles of women priests, prophets, and mediums remain important in indigenous religions and exert a profound influence in African Christianity.

Central to indigenous African religions is the idea of a supreme being, who is seen as the initial source of the life forces who created and populated the earth. This supreme being can be considered to be male, androgynous, or without gender. For example, the Fon of the Republic of Bénin regard the supreme being, Mawu-Lisa, as both male and female; Mawu is the senior and feminine aspect; Lisa is the masculine. For the Yoruba, the supreme being, Olorun, is the source of a masculine creative power, *ashe*, and a feminine creative power, *aje*. Lesser spirits created by the supreme being, are often gendered, though they may shift in gender depending on their role or the tradition that is being recalled. Usually, the earth is associated with the feminine powers of fertility. Thus, the Igbo of Nigeria worship an earth goddess known as Ala, the most powerful of the lesser deities (*agbara*). She is often seen as the more powerful spouse of male gods associated with the sky or thunder. She ensures the fertility of the land, of women, and of the Igbo's staple crops, while demanding ethical behavior from those who worship her. Asase Ya plays a similar role in Ashanti religious traditions.

Other female deities are associated with such natural phenomena as rivers or the ocean, or important aspects of community life. Among the Diola of Senegal, for example, married women who have given birth to a child are initiated into a women's fertility cult, known as *Ehugna*. The spirit associated with this shrine assists women in dealing with problems of infertility of women and the land, drought, disease, childbirth, and the proper treatment of women by men. Men who abuse women are seized by the *Ehugna* spirit and afflicted with a disease. Among the Yoruba, the goddess Oshun embodies the spiritual power of women, not only in areas of fertility and sexuality, but in the public market. Her devotees are helped to become fertile, confident, and economically secure.

Initiation societies also play an important role in women's lives. Such societies focus on the transition of girls to adulthood and parenthood. This is a time when women control the socialization of girls, instructing them on their religious responsibilities and what it means to be a woman in their societies. Among the Mande-speaking peoples of the Upper Guinea coast, the women's initiation society, Sande, has become the effective governing organization for women in a variety of societies. Many societies such as the Bemba of Zambia and the Diola of Senegal have important rites of passage for these transitions, which do not involve any form of bodily cutting. Other societies, like the Mande and Fufulde-speaking communities of West Africa and the Gikuyu of Kenya include various forms of female genital cutting as part of this transition. Likening the clitoris to the male part of a woman, as the foreskin is often regarded as the feminine part of a man, women's initiation societies remove either a part of or the entire clitoris, in order to eliminate the androgynous qualities of the uninitiated and prepare them for adulthood. The physical risks and long-standing consequences of such a procedure, however, are far more serious for women than for men. A number of countries, including Senegal, have outlawed the practice.

In many parts of Africa, women become possessed by various gods or spirits, becoming the vessel by which a divine force communicates with the human community. Among the Shona of Zimbabwe, the supreme being, Mwari, possesses women at various oracle sites. A possessed woman speaks in the voice of Mwari, which a male priest then interprets. Similar phenomena are found among women spirit mediums in the Interlacustrine area of East Central Africa where women become possessed by spirits associated with powerful spirits of ancestral rulers. In the mid nineteenth century, among the Xhosa of South Africa, a young woman named Nongqawuse had visions of her ancestors who commanded her to teach that the Xhosa had to kill all their cattle and destroy their grain, in order to purify their society of the taint of witchcraft and remove the Europeans who were conquering their lands. Among the Diola of Senegal, women have taken on prophetic roles, as people summoned by the supreme being, Emitai, to teach about the way to live in harmony with the supreme being, obtain sufficient rain for their crops, and preserve the autonomy of their institutions from European colonialism and various forms of neocolonialism.

In some African societies, such as the Yoruba, women's power is seen as dangerous and associated with witchcraft. The Gelede ritual, dedicated to maternal spirits, focuses on the cooling down of the destructive aspects of women's power (*aje*) and

enhancing its life supporting qualities. In most African societies, both women and men can be thought of as witches and there are some where only men are associated with the life destructive powers of witches.

Christianity has maintained a presence in Africa since the first century of the Common Era, but most of Africa did not come into contact with Christians until the age of European expansion beginning in the fifteenth century. Christianity enjoyed its most rapid growth in the twentieth century, when Europeans controlled most of Africa. In Catholic Churches, women have become active in social and charitable organizations, as well as assuming religious vocations. Women have also played central roles in charismatic Catholic groups like the Legio Maria in Kenya and the Jamaa movement in Congo. Of particular importance was a BaKongo Catholic, named Beatriz Kimpa Vita (c. 1686–1706), who believed that she died and that St. Anthony of Padua took over her body. Beginning in 1704, as the living vessel of St. Anthony, she rallied the BaKongo people to end a civil war and restore their capital city of Mbanza Kongo, before being captured by enemies and burnt at the stake as a witch.

Women played similar roles in Protestant churches, organizing women's prayer groups, charitable organizations, and social groups, but they also became active in new forms of Christianity, which are often identified as independent African churches. In these churches, women and men began to interpret biblical texts differently than European and American missionaries. In many instances, women decided to found their own churches, focused on African spiritual needs. One of the earliest of these churches, the Cherubim and Seraphim Society, was founded by Christina Abiodun, a young Yoruba woman who saw spiritual healing and the creation of communities of prayer (*aladura*) in ways that were not emphasized in the "mission" churches.

In 1954 in the British colony of Northern Rhodesia, a woman named Alice Mulenga claimed to have died four different times and encountered Jesus, and then rose from the dead. She took on the name Lenshina (regina or queen), broke away from the Presbyterian church and created a new church that viewed all involvement in politics as inevitably corrupting, and tried to create separatist communities of faith. The soon to be independent government of Zambia repressed the movement, arrested Lenshina and her husband, and killed hundreds of her followers.

Among the Luo of Kenya, women were active participants in spiritist (Roho) churches which have sustained an evangelical revival for nearly half a century. In neighboring Uganda, however, a woman named Alice Lakwena, had visions that her national rulers were witches. She raised an army, the Lord's Resistance Army, and marched toward the capital of Kampala. Defeated militarily, she renounced the struggle and settled in Kenya, but one of her aides, Joseph Kony, has continued the struggle, devastating the northern part of Uganda.

Indigenous African religions have stressed the importance of female spiritual power, religious leadership, and prophetic gifts. These religious concerns have become powerful influences in the development of distinct forms of African Christianity, which provide greater emphasis on women's prophetic voices, healing powers, and the concern that religious life address directly the spiritual concerns of women.

See also **Christianity; Initiation; Judaism in Africa; Kimpa Vita, Dona Beatriz; Lakwena, Alice; Lenshina, Alice; Nongqawuse; Religion and Ritual; Religion and the Study of Africa; Spirit Possession; Witchcraft.**

BIBLIOGRAPHY

Baum, Robert M. "Alinesitoué: A Diola Woman Prophet in West Africa." In *Unspoken Worlds: Women's Religious Lives*, ed. Nancy A. Falk and Rita M. Gross, 2nd edition. Belmont, CA: Wadsworth/Thomson Learning, 2001.

Drewal, Henry John, and Margaret Thompson Drewel. *Gelede: Art and Female Power among the Yoruba*. Bloomington: Indiana University Press, 1983.

Hoehler-Fatton, Cynthia. *Women of Fire and Spirit: History, Faith, and Gender in Roho Religion in Western Kenya*. New York: Oxford University Press, 1996.

Peel, J. D. Y. *Aladura: A Religious Movement among the Yoruba*. London: Oxford University Press, 1968.

Peires, J. B. *The Dead Will Arise: Nongqawuse and the Great Xhosa Cattle-Killing of 1856–1857*. Bloomington: Indiana University Press, 1989.

Richards, Audrey. *Chisungu: A Girl's Initiation Ceremony among the Bemba of Northern Rhodesia*. London: Faber and Faber, 1956.

Thornton, John. *The Kongolese Saint Anthony: Dona Beatriz Kimpa Vita and the Antonian Movement, 1684–1704*. Cambridge, U.K.: Cambridge University Press, 1998.

ROBERT M. BAUM

WOMEN AND SLAVERY

Slavery for women in Africa is both an ancient and a contemporary phenomenon, although it has seldom fit patterns common to the New World. Among slaves kept in Africa women and girls have been in the majority, the proportion of slaves who were female varying from society to society according to their uses. Most societies probably did not have enslaved persons, but many precolonial peoples did, especially where influenced by the trans-Saharan, Indian Ocean, and Atlantic slave trades. Slavery in Africa entailed a wide variety of statuses, from chattels with no rights held on plantations to a temporary status involving few disabilities and a wide variety of occupations. Women slaves, like free women, have been more often in disadvantaged statuses with fewer opportunities for emancipation or other means of improving their situations.

More women than men were kept as slaves because of their great utility first as agricultural or domestic laborers, and second as reproducers of kin relations. As producers women slaves more often than not replaced the labor of free women—in the fields and in the household. Therefore, in areas where seclusion was a desirable mark of the status of free women, or where women were heavily involved in market production, the demand for women slaves was high. Thus Islamic free women's seclusion was positively related to the availability of slave women's labor; in agriculture and cotton cloth or thread production, in particular. Precolonial and present-day sub-Saharan Africa has female farming systems in which women have performed upward of 70 percent of the routine labor-intensive farm labor. The acquisition of female slaves allowed free women to devote more time to other activities.

The strongly segregated gender division of labor placed most female slaves under the authority of senior women, who could therefore escape more onerous forms of agricultural and domestic labor and trade, organize craft production, use slave-produced goods as bridewealth for making advantageous marriages for their sons, carry on long-distance businesses, and otherwise improve their situation. Free women occasionally became slave traders themselves, one of the better known being Madame Tinubu of what is present-day Nigeria. Women called *signares* or *nharas* in Western coastal Africa were also traders on their own and on behalf of their European partners or husbands. The common West African practice of spouses' maintaining separate property facilitated such women's economic independence.

Females were also more often seen as being desirable slaves because of their reproductive functions, which allowed owners to maximize kin relationships. They could more easily be absorbed into lineages, whether matrilineal or patrilineal. If patrilineal, a slave woman could become a junior wife or concubine, producing offspring who could expand the labor force and who were usually free. In some Islamic societies a bondwoman who bore her master a son would be freed, while in most societies her children were free members of her owner's lineage, although some suffered disabilities in having lesser inheritance rights and from a certain stigma attached to slave descent. In matrilineal societies men sometimes found the acquisition of slave women to be a strategic move aimed at establishing de facto patrilineages; only in this way could they control their own children, who otherwise belonged to the lineages of the children's mothers.

The ownership of female slaves could also be used by free women to modify kin relations. In some societies the practice of "woman-marriage" allowed a prosperous woman to acquire female slaves as "wives," who could produce heirs for a deceased husband's lineage; remedy the status problems caused by the female husband's infertility; or create a de facto matrilineage headed by herself within a patrilineal system. Debtors also were more likely to pawn girls than boys for structural reasons; the girls' labor paid the interest on the debt and, if she married a member of the creditor's family, debt cancellation served as bridewealth. However, in times of want or out of greed, creditors sometimes sold pawns into the export slave trade.

Female slaves were also thought to be more docile and malleable, having been socialized into obedience. Thus for all these reasons in precolonial Africa female slaves were usually in greater demand, a factor demonstrated in their fetching higher prices than males and in slave trade statistics that show, for instance, that over the some 300 years of the trans-Atlantic slave trade more men were exported as African demand was the primary determinant of the sex ratio of approximately 3:2, with some temporal and regional variations. In the trans-Saharan trade the ratio was higher in response to Arab demand, sparked partly by the desire to replace secluded free women's labor and supply domestic and sex workers for harems. The East African coastal and Indian Ocean trade also reflected a strong demand for women and children, although in the nineteenth century Zanzibari clove plantation owners raised the demand for male slaves used in a system approximating chattel slavery. The South African Cape reflects Dutch preferences for male farm labor; more men were therefore kept as slaves than women by a ratio of about 3:2. In the Transvaal more women were captured by Boer commando raids for use as servant "apprentices," a form of forced labor. In such a situation the white settlers were trying to create a permanently enslaved class of useful labor.

When more females were wanted the type of slavery practiced more often had the ultimate goal of expanding the free population. Wealth in precolonial Africa was often counted in people, given that land ownership was usually collective by lineages, and the availability of labor was the primary constraint on expanding production. Therefore, women slaves were very valuable both for their own labor and their creation of new labor, as well as their ease of assimilation structurally as junior wives and the higher likelihood of their having been socialized into subordination.

Nonetheless, women slaves were by no means always devoid of agency and sometimes even power. Some nineteenth-century East African slaves fled to Christian missions to escape slavery. Some West African slave women rose within the trading hierarchy to become prosperous and others became queens or queen mothers in states like Dahomey. At less exalted levels of society ordinary women slaves could sometimes negotiate ways to free themselves

Slave women in Ghana. Slave women, called Trokosi, painted in kaolin, pose in Kilkor, Ghana. Ghana's slave castles attract tens of thousands of visitors every year as well as demands for an apology for centuries of oppression. ISSOUF SANOGO/AFP/GETTY IMAGES

and/or their offspring, and were less likely than U.S. chattel slaves to be confined, policed, and deprived of all rights. For instance, coastal East African culture was strongly influenced by women brought as slaves from the interior. In some societies one-generation slavery was practiced in which mostly women slaves were effectively assimilated as junior wives, their status shading into "free" and their children free.

Abolition of slavery for women in Africa more often came later than for men. Mid-nineteenth-century British naval efforts to discourage the trans-Atlantic slave trade were sometimes vitiated by, for instance, increased demand for West African palm oil for European industrial use, which in turn increased the demand for female plantation labor in southern Nigeria. In many cases legal abolition came with the imposition of colonial rule in the late nineteenth century, but male slaves were more likely to be freed at that point because women's slavery was hidden within households. The British in northern Nigeria purposely ignored the "domestic" slavery of women as part of a negotiation with local male rulers that exchanged noninterference with local domestic arrangements and Islam for submission to British rule.

Otherwise, colonial rule more often brought economic opportunities for men in nonsettler colonies (the majority). Men were more likely to get some formal education, learn European languages and skills, and qualify for low level clerical and domestic servant wage jobs before World War I. Women's work was more likely to remain highly labor intensive and nonwaged, meaning that the demand for slave women's labor remained high and, since it could be easily disguised, the trade in female slaves, especially girls, often endured. In a few areas it never stopped. Mauritanians continue to kidnap Senegalese women; some have taken advantage of weak policing and civil wars in postcolonial states to take Africans into the world sex traffic in women and sometimes boys. In Ewe shrine slavery in Ghana, girls are given to priests as slaves and may suffer abuse. While sex work was not a common use for African slave women precolonially, increased incorporation into the world capitalist economy, bringing poverty and displacement, has made it so in the twenty-first century.

See also **Labor: Domestic; Slave Trades; Slavery and Servile Institutions; Tinubu, Madame.**

BIBLIOGRAPHY

Campbell, Gwyn, Joseph C. Miller, and Suzanne Miers, eds. *Women and Slavery*, 2 vols. Athens: Ohio University Press, 2007.

Miers, Suzanne, and Igor Kopytoff, eds. *Slavery in Africa*. Madison: University of Wisconsin Press, 1979.

Robertson, Claire C., and Martin A. Klein, eds. *Women and Slavery in Africa*. Madison: University of Wisconsin Press, 1983.

CLAIRE ROBERTSON

WOMEN AND THE LAW

Women's relationship to the law in Africa is as diverse as the groups in which they live. Rural women living a traditional life are governed primarily by customary law, the precolonial law of the regional group to which they belong, most often originally codified by male colonial officers in collaboration with local male political leaders. "Customary" law is itself very diverse, varying by region, ethnic group or clan, and religion. By contrast, educated and urbanized women are likely to be governed by the legislation and case law of the independent African nations in which they live. Those laws also vary, according to the type of regime (secular, Muslim, democratic, or authoritarian) and by colonial heritage—legal systems based on a written code in former French colonies and on a common-law, or judge-made, system in former English colonies.

At independence the new African constitutions typically provided for the continued application of customary law. Although most of these constitutions contained guarantees of gender equality, customary law frequently gave unequal rights to men and women. Some countries, such as Ghana and Uganda, provided that gender-discriminatory provisions of customary law could be challenged under the constitution. Others, like Kenya and Zimbabwe, reserved certain topics for decision under customary law—typically, family law, land, and inheritance—the areas with most impact on women.

FAMILY LAW

Family law governs a large part of the life of women living in traditional African society, and customary family law typically discriminated against women—for example, with respect to custody of children and property distribution upon divorce. Upon marriage, a woman was regarded as leaving her family and becoming part of her husband's family. Because most immovable property was seen as belonging to the family or community rather than the individual, if divorced she might be left with only her household property and whatever she brought to the marriage, having to return to her family of origin for support. Customary law also endorsed practices many see as detrimental to women, such as child marriage and polygamy. While multiple wives could provide more children and labor within the rural family, with urbanization and the economic difficulties typical in modern-day Africa, a second wife can be economically threatening to the first wife and her children.

Modern African statutes typically prohibit child marriage, mandate that child custody be awarded according to the best interest of the child, and provide for some property distribution upon divorce. Yet statutory family law may have little effect upon women married under customary law (a ritual primarily involving the exchange of gifts between the two families), and these issues may be constitutionally reserved to custom. Even in countries with a "best interest" child custody standard, moreover, the persistence of traditional standards may result in automatically awarding child custody upon divorce to the father.

Finally, the statutory family law of most African nations often remains similar to that of the colonial power at the time of independence. Thus, for example, while the legal standard for property distribution upon divorce has changed in England to an equitable sharing system, in some former English colonies courts struggle with a standard awarding the home and other property to the person holding legal title, typically the husband.

Women's groups have worked hard to publicize these problems, and many reforms have been proposed or enacted. South Africa's post-apartheid regime passed legislation mandating equality within marriages, even those entered under customary law, and treating marital property as held equally by husband and wife. Moreover, in 1983 a Tanzanian court decreed that a wife's contribution to the acquisition of property through her services as a homemaker must be considered in allocating property upon divorce.

International conventions mandating equal treatment of men and women are increasingly used to challenge sex-discriminatory laws. Perhaps the most famous example was the 1992 Unity Dow case in Botswana. While traditional law provided that children take the citizenship of their father, the court drew upon international human rights treaties to overturn that law and provide that children's citizenship is also that of their mothers.

Another area in which the international human rights movement has made its mark is domestic violence. Although still a severe problem in Africa, African women lawyers have drafted domestic violence codes providing for simplified remedies, often using models from other countries; and these codes have been passed by the legislature in a number of nations. Activists have also established legal aid bureaus and shelters to assist battered women.

LAND AND INHERITANCE

Prior to the imposition of colonial law, in most areas of Africa land was considered to be "owned" by the community. Colonial law mandated individual ownership, however; and title was subsequently registered, usually by the male head of household. As women's right to use land is traditionally based upon their status as wives, they lose any right to it upon divorce or widowhood. Yet if women do not own title to land, they have difficulty accumulating capital or obtaining credit to start commercial enterprises.

African governments have only begun to confront these problems presented by land law. For example, the 1999 Tanzanian Land Act provided that whenever one spouse occupies land, his spouse (or spouses) will be presumed to have occupancy rights, and the land may not be sold without their consent.

Most women were unable to inherit land from either their fathers or their husbands under traditional African law. In most patrilineal societies, women inherit property only for their lifetime and cannot pass it on to their children as their brothers can. In areas with matrilineal descent, male children also inherit, but from their mother's uncle rather than their father's kin. Women subject to Islamic law, for example in Northern Nigeria, have more rights in this respect, as they can inherit land both as daughters and widows.

Although modern African statutes may make provision for widows, most people still follow customary law; and it is rare to make a will. Thus, when a woman's husband dies, either her male children or her husband's family may inherit the marital property, leaving the widow destitute. Under customary law in some communities, the widow herself was inherited by her dead husband's brother. While modern statutes forbid this practice, it may be the only way a rural widow can find a source of support.

See also **Dow, Unity; Kinship and Descent; Labor; Law; Marriage Systems.**

BIBLIOGRAPHY

Belembaogo, Akila. "The Best Interests of the Child—The Case of Burkina Faso." *International Journal of Law and Family* 8 (1994): 202–226.

Bowman, Cynthia Grant, and Akua Kuenyehia. *Women and Law in Sub-Saharan Africa*. Accra, Ghana: Sedco Publishing, 2003.

Butegwa, Florence. "Using the African Charter on Human and Peoples' Rights to Secure Women's Access to Land in Africa." In *Human Rights of Women: National and International Perspectives*, ed. Rebecca J. Cook. Philadelphia: University of Pennsylvania Press, 1994.

Gopal, Gita, and Maryam Salim, eds. *Eastern Africa Speaks*. Washington, DC: International Bank for Reconstruction and Development/The World Bank, 1998.

Kuenyehia, Akua, ed. *Women and Law in West Africa: Situational Analysis of Some Key Issues Affecting Women*. Legon, Ghana: Human Rights Study Center, Faculty of Law, University of Ghana, 1998.

Mikell, Gwendolyn, ed. *African Feminism: The Politics of Survival in Sub-Saharan Africa*. Philadelphia: University of Pennsylvania Press, 1997.

CYNTHIA GRANT BOWMAN

WOMEN AND THEATER

African women have always been performers. The often fragmentary information that exists from African societies in precolonial times shows that women performed traditionally in many societies as dancers, singers, and storytellers. Even in the early twenty-first century, in those societies that have maintained their heritage of popular performance forms, women continue in these roles.

The arrival of modern and commercial theater across the continent usually coincided with expanding colonial and missionary activities in the first half of the twentieth century. Western colonialism often denounced indigenous performance forms as uncivilized and sought to replace them with church performances of Bible stories and school productions of classic Western authors. Since colonialism occurred at a time of Western patriarchal dominance, opportunities in the new performance forms were usually only made available to males. Even in Ethiopia, African's only uncolonized nation, the Western-influenced theater that developed from around 1916 was performed only by men and boys up until the 1940s. Women performing on stage came to be seen as sexually promiscuous, and being an actress was often perceived as little better than being a prostitute. This equation of loose morals and social opprobrium with women and the stage has been pervasive across the continent and continues to be a major factor in limiting many women's contribution to African theater in the twenty-first century.

Husbands and fathers have often forbidden their daughters and wives from engaging in public performance. In the 1940s and 1950s the founder of Nigeria's first professional theater company, Hubert Ogunde, resorted to marrying many women as the only way to secure actresses for his immensely popular Ogunde Concert Party. Research on the 1980s Zimbabwe theater scene found no professional actresses who were married unless it was to actors; otherwise all were young single women or divorcees. Although the situation has gradually improved with the establishment of university drama departments across Africa from the 1960s, women still tend to be performers rather than occupy roles of executive control.

WOMEN WRITERS, DIRECTORS, AND PRODUCERS

Despite these difficulties African women have made, and are increasingly making, an impact on theater across the continent. The first significant women playwrights were probably the Ghanaians Ama Ata Aidoo and Efua Sutherland. In the 1960s both were concerned about developing theater that would bridge the gap between indigenous oral performance forms and Western theater. Their plays, such as Aidoo's *Anowa* and *Dilemma of a Ghost* and Sutherland's *Ananse*, were milestones in experimentation, developing syncretic theater forms that African playwrights have built on ever since.

Other important women playwrights from the late twentieth century include Tess Onwueme of Nigeria, Rose Mbowa of Uganda, Micere Mugo of Kenya, Amandina Lihamba and Penina Mlama of Tanzania, and the South Africans Gcina Mhlope, Fatima Dike, and Reza de Wet.

Many of these women have been university-based, and only their high status exempted them from the opprobrium so commonly visited on women in African theater. These same women have also often directed their own plays, as remains a common practice for playwrights in many parts of the continent. It is notable that women playwrights have been particularly concerned with social issues and have often addressed problems relating to the oppression of women, but also debates about politics and nation-building in such works as Rose Mbowa's *Mother Uganda and Her Children* or *The Trial of Dedan Kimathi*, co-authored by the Kenyan writer Micere Mugo and her male counterpart, Ngugi wa Thiong'o. Very few women have managed to run their own theater companies. The most famous is undoubtedly Werewere Liking, the actress/playwright/producer/founder of the Ivorian arts community, Village Ki-Yi, who has won international acclaim in the Francophone world. The Sudanese Nimrat Hammad also deserves mention in this category for her company, which operated in Khartoum in the 1980s until she was forced to flee the country in 1989.

In the 2000s women are challenging male dominance of some traditional performance forms. The southern African praise-singers, *imbongi* or *izibongi*, used to be all male but women such as the late Elizabeth Ncube of Zimbabwe have been taking them on at national competitions and winning major prizes. In community settings, many women's groups have established women-only part-time performance troupes, which provide a forum for women to discuss issues important to them and also serve as a source of income generation. There are also women superstars. In Tanzania the singers/performers of the indigenous form *taarab*, such as Siti binti Saad and Khadija Kopa, are famous and revered. Regrettably the commercial male-authored theater in many nations still far too often stereotypes women on stage as erotic dancers or temptresses when young, and as idealized mothers or domineering matriarchs when older.

Artist Gcina Mhlope Becker. Becker is a leading South African actress and playwright. Her most famous play, *Have You Seen Zandile?*, is a largely autobiographical account of her dislocated childhood. She has also led a movement to raise the profile of storytelling as a theatrical event. © ALEXANDER HASSENSTEIN/BONGARTS/GETTY IMAGES

See also **Aidoo, Ama Ata; Saad, Siti binti; Theater.**

BIBLIOGRAPHY

Banham, Martin, ed. *A History of Theater in Africa.* Cambridge, U.K.: Cambridge University Press, 2004.

Banham, Martin; Errol Hill; and George Woodyard; eds. *The Cambridge Guide to African and Caribbean Theater.* Cambridge, U.K.: Cambridge University Press, 1994.

Harding, Frances, ed. *The Performance Arts in Africa: A Reader.* New York: Routledge, 2002.

Plastow, Jane, ed. *African Theater: Women.* Oxford: James Currey, 2003.

JANE PLASTOW

WOMEN AND TRADE

African women's involvement in small-scale trade (as opposed to highly capitalized enterprises called "businesses") has a long and complex history. While it is widely known that women dominate small-scale African trade in many, perhaps most, areas, women's participation as traders in precolonial long-distance trade was also more pervasive than is commonly thought, as shown in studies of East African provisioning of caravans where local traders increased the scale of their businesses substantially to accommodate the demand, and as seen in the activities of West African women who traded in high-value commodities. Nevertheless, large business ownership has been strongly male dominated, whereas small business ownership has most often been a female specialty.

From ancient Egypt to contemporary South Africa, from the Atlas Mountains to Fernando Po, women have been important agents in the buying and selling of goods and services. They have been responsible not only for feeding their families, but also for provisioning Africa's growing cities by cultivating food crops, and collecting, wholesaling, and reselling them to the retail traders who form the majority of sellers in many African markets. This situation exists everywhere despite the seeming constraints placed on some women because of their religion. In a number of precolonial Muslim societies, for example, where seclusion was expected for free women, those confined largely to their homes used women slaves, who had no honor to protect, to conduct trade for them.

In the twenty-first century secluded women in northern Nigeria may send their daughters to conduct trade-related activities for them. Such activities are sanctioned because Islamic *shari'a* law has been interpreted to confirm women's property rights and therefore their right to trade. In fact, because women traders must have the power to conduct transactions independent of male approval, their involvement in trade appears to be foundational for women's property rights. In coastal West Africa, where women have traded for centuries in many areas, their rights to own and sell property were well established before colonial rule in the nineteenth century. In other areas, where women traders are a relatively new phenomenon, women have been able to establish full property rights as part of a newfound autonomy, despite colonial era laws to the contrary.

Colonial laws, in fact, especially in areas where women's trade is an old phenomenon, often diminished women's rights substantially and paved the way for increased male dominance in agriculture, and privileged their control of more valuable cash crops.

Successful women traders who had been involved in long distance trade working with the same commodities as men, including gold and slaves for instance, prior to colonial rule were reduced to the status of legal minors. This lessened their rights substantially, which they then had to defend in terms of local customary law. Unfortunately for these women, however, most customary law courts were presided over by local dignitaries or colonial-appointed officers, always male, who were often not concerned about protecting women's precolonial rights. Accordingly, customary laws—with support from European-controlled appeal courts—evolved to support male domination over women. In the few white settler colonies, where locals had less influence and European laws were often imposed more thoroughly, the situation was no better. Even after independence or the attainment of majority rule beginning in the mid-twentieth century, women still found themselves at a substantial disadvantage relative to men with regard to their rights.

Women who achieved a great deal of economic autonomy did so by selling their own produce, or retailing or wholesaling goods obtained from others, sometimes male relatives. Most sales usually involved women selling less lucrative women's food crops, however, because the prevailing notions about gender rights and responsibilities held that men should have primary control over the most lucrative cash crops. In most cases women did have full control over their own profits, albeit sometimes this was de facto not de jure. Women without secure control over their profits, as in parts of East Africa where women have been regarded as male property along with their earnings, have been particularly concerned to retain control over their take, necessarily withholding knowledge of their profits from related men in order to feed their children and maintain their businesses.

Such subterfuges have not been necessary for some of the large-scale, often single, successful women traders who import goods into the Congos, Nigeria, Côte d'Ivoire, and other countries. But they have not been free of their own difficulties. Regularly crossing borders with their goods by air or van, some have suffered attacks and other forms of persecution from governments intent on blaming them for shortages in "essential goods" so as to divert the public's attention away from their own mismanagement of the economy.

In Ghana in the late 1970s, for instance, soldiers and police shot some traders, regularly bulldozed markets, and otherwise terrorized ordinary market women. In Kenya the British colonial government's use of arson in the 1950s to burn out traders described as urban undesirables and possible insurgents continued under the Moi government in the 1990s and early 2000s, supplemented by the use of bulldozers. The Zimbabwean government has been carrying out similar policies.

Compared to most men traders, most women traders make lower profits; enter trades where less starting capital is required; have less access to capital in the form of loans or savings; have less trade infrastructure in terms of items such as market stalls, storage facilities, and processing machines like mills; have less time to devote to their businesses because of family obligations and an unequal gender division of labor; receive less formal education and training and therefore tend to rely more on others to keep accounts. They also receive less attention from government programs that provide loans, extension training, or other amenities. Therefore, women often cannot afford paid employees and tend to rely more on the labor of their children to help out, especially their daughters, who are often kept home from school or encouraged to leave school earlier than their sons.

Nonetheless, involvement in trade has offered many African women encouraging ways to overcome disabilities imposed by political, economic, and cultural constraints. Historically women traders were at the center of the 1929 Igbo Women's War, a tax revolt in which they used their networks to organize mass demonstrations that successfully ousted unpopular "warrant chiefs" appointed by the British. This, in turn, forced the colonial government to reconceptualize how it administered colonial rule in the area. In the 1922 Thuku demonstration against colonial rule in Nairobi, Kenya, traders taunted their men for being weak in their opposition to colonial rule and led a charge that turned into a massacre when the police fired upon the crowd. In 2004 hundreds of women, many of them traders, in eastern Nigeria's oil country occupied Chevron pumping stations, echoing the 1929 revolt, shutting them down and insisting that oil profits be devoted to local development.

More prosaically and in keeping with traders' dominantly economic goals, African women have led the world in the variety and pervasiveness of self-help groups aimed at everything from organizing traders by commodity in markets to paying funeral and roofing costs, and building schools and rental housing. One of the most famous forms of organization pioneered by Yoruba Nigerian traders is called *esusu*. Such groups, usually called rotating savings groups in the development literature, operate on a tontine principle by which all members contribute weekly or monthly to a pool that is distributed in turn to each member of the group on a regular schedule. This form of organization has spread widely within Africa and diasporic communities in the Americas and Europe (in St. Lucia in the Caribbean it is called *sousou*). While many Africans who are not traders also participate in such groups, traders usually have more intense participation, simultaneously belonging to more than one group.

Another function of such groups that is growing in popularity is the provision of micro-credit to women traders to remedy some of the previously mentioned discriminatory practices. In sub-Saharan Africa this strategy has proved to be very successful for women in particular, as they tend to repay loans more faithfully than men do and use the loans to increase their earnings. Because African women are widely expected to assume all or much of the responsibility for feeding their children, development projects aimed at improving children's nutrition have concentrated increasingly on inputs favoring women, which have been shown to have more efficacy in this regard than raising men's earnings. Women's cooperatives that produce and sell crafts are also popular in many areas.

African women's trade, then, has been pervasive, innovative, adapted to local and international conditions, strategic in meeting their own needs and those of their children, and sometimes dangerous to pursue. In the last category falls not only the incidents in which traders have been killed while pursuing political or economic goals, but also the instances in which they have become commodities themselves: the slave trade in which women were more commonly kept in Africa and men more commonly exported given the higher economic and social utility of women within African societies;

the contemporary sex trade in which they end up along with those of other nations as pawns and prostitutes; and the world trade in domestic servants, who often also become slaves, unable to leave their foreign employers, overworked and underfed, and confined so they cannot escape. As long as Africa as a continent is constrained by being incorporated into the world capitalist economy in a dependent, disadvantaged position, African women will, as traders and the traded, be limited in their agency, confined as well by indigenous and imposed male dominant ideology.

See also **Law; Slave Trades; Slavery and Servile Institutions; Trade, National and International Systems.**

BIBLIOGRAPHY

Clark, Gracia. *Onions Are My Husband: Survival and Accumulation by West African Market Women.* Chicago: University of Chicago Press, 1994.

Horn, Nancy E. *Cultivating Customers: Market Women in Harare, Zimbabwe.* Boulder, CO: Lynne Rienner, 1994.

Robertson, Claire C. *Sharing the Same Bowl: A Socioeconomic History of Women and Trade in Accra, Ghana.* Ann Arbor: University of Michigan Press, 1990.

Robertson, Claire C. *Trouble Showed the Way: Women, Men and Trade in the Nairobi Area, 1890–1990.* Bloomington: Indiana University Press, 1997.

Robertson, Claire C., and Martin A. Klein, eds. *Women and Slavery in Africa.* Madison: University of Wisconsin Press, 1983.

Spring, Anita, and Barbara E. McDade, eds. *African Entrepreneurship Theory and Reality.* Gainesville: University Press of Florida, 1998.

CLAIRE ROBERTSON

WOMEN AND URBANISM

Women have played a central role in the development of African cities. In West Africa there was a higher level of urban residence historically, and women were noted as active participants in the markets and other sectors. In eastern and southern Africa, cities more often emerged in connection with colonial settlements, and African women moved into urban areas in response to new work opportunities as well as to escape deteriorating rural conditions. Conventional studies have emphasized the male-dominant character of urbanization, as men found employment and women remained in rural areas engaged in agriculture, but many women also moved to the cities.

And although women did migrate with male family members, there were also women who traveled alone or with female kin when they sought a new and different life.

Women have influenced urban development and experienced a range of changes in their own lives as compared to rural African women. They have engaged in a wide variety of livelihoods to support themselves and their families. Whether living with men, married to them, or living alone, women have usually borne the primary responsibility for raising children. They have established households that showed continuity as well as change from rural family formations. In addition, they have participated in politics, religious organizations, and other community activities, all of which contributed to the development of distinctively African cities. While women's urban experiences have varied over time and place they have always been an essential component and sometimes the dynamizing factor in African urban life.

FAMILY

Urban African women and their families found a wide range of options available in the cities, choices that were in some cases unthinkable in the rural areas. Although most women still married and raised children within that marriage, city life included new arrangements of various kinds. Family life was under less scrutiny in the more impersonal conditions of urban life. More women remained single or lived in female-headed households, and urban women were more likely to use contraceptives and live in monogamous relationships than rural women. Unhappy marriages or early widowhood were frequent motives for women to seek a new way of life in urban areas. Women in southern Africa sometimes moved to cities to find work in order to repay bridewealth and finalize a divorce.

An issue related to family organization has been urban women's access to housing. Housing stock is generally limited in African cities, and women often have greater difficulty in gaining rights to rent or purchase housing. Urban housing is often marked by substandard dwellings on the periphery of burgeoning urban centers. Most such neighborhoods lack access to electricity and potable water, conditions which clearly have an impact on the daily household labor of women. Women

have sometimes had problems because they have not held title to property. In some cities only waged workers were allowed access to housing during colonial times, so that men were favored in seeking housing and women had to prove either employment or marriage to get shelter. Women found themselves in vulnerable conditions as renters, and research has shown that they often have a history of frequent moves from lodging to lodging. Their lack of education and regular employment means they are usually not able to get credit that would help them improve their housing situation. Scholars and policy workers have begun investigating gender and housing issues in greater depth, as with a research network based in Zimbabwe known as GRUPHEL (Gender Research on Urbanization, Planning, Housing and Everyday Life), and in work from the Mazingira Institute in Nairobi.

WORK

In the urban areas women have found a new range of employment and work opportunities. Their occupation as market vendors and in microenterprises has been the most observable, but women have also found positions in professional and clerical work, in factories, and as domestic workers. There has also been research focusing on prostitutes, a primarily urban work category.

Street or market vending of food is a central aspect of both women's work and of food distribution in the urban areas. Selling produce, snacks, or even full meals is not only an important source of income for women but provides a reliable source of food for urban residents. Although women in all regions of Africa are involved in market trading, those in West Africa are recognized as being exceptionally well organized. Women have also developed new areas of endeavor in the informal sector, often relying on gendered skills such as sewing and crocheting clothing or braiding hair, which they use to establish small businesses. Other women have continued rural activities such as farming and beer brewing as a way to support themselves and their families; such work indicated the permeable boundaries between urban and rural life. Farming in the cities contributes to urban food supply and has a noticeable impact on urban geography, as vacant lots and peripheral green zones are cultivated.

Women have been affected by extensive job segregation. When compared with men, women have many fewer options due to their lower level of education, the expectation by husbands that their wives will not work for a wage, and the responsibilities associated with motherhood. Yet in comparison with rural options, the urban employment situation offered many new possibilities for women.

COMMUNITY

Urban residence has also brought women into contact with a wide variety of organizations that were not available in rural locations, including neighborhood groups, religious affiliations, work-related associations, and political alliances. Although women have sometimes been underrepresented in formal political structures, their contributions to community organizations have been critical to developing urban neighborhoods and networks. Women have made fundamental contributions as well to the development of nationalism and to religious associations.

The issues women have dealt with have included improving educational opportunities for girls, trade union organizations, and protecting women's market rights. They have organized purchasing clubs, revolving credit associations, burial clubs, and Christian prayer groups, among many other formations. Their groups have played a vital role in linking rural and urban women and in providing a source of support for women dealing with adaptation to urban life.

In East Africa, urban women's dance societies have been an important site where new immigrants and long-term residents of varying ethnicities have met. Other less formal networks have been based on ethnicity and neighborhood residence. For instance, beer brewers in Nairobi have relied on good relations with neighborhood women to secure their own economic survival. Women in West African cities have worked together in dyeing fabric, an activity that illustrates the confluence of neighborhood, creative endeavor, and income earning.

Overall women have found new opportunities for work, family, and public involvement in the urban areas of Africa. These new choices have sometimes meant new difficulties, but have also brought greater personal independence and new possibilities for women to find their own way.

See also **Household and Domestic Groups; Urbanism and Urbanization.**

BIBLIOGRAPHY

Ishani, Zarina, and Davinder Lamba, eds. *Emerging African Perspectives on Gender in Urbanization: African Research on Gender, Urbanization and Environment.* Nairobi: Mazingira Institute, 2001.

Larsson, Anita; Matseliso Mapetla; and Ann Schlyter; eds. *Gender and Urban Housing in Southern Africa: Emerging Issues.* Roma, Lesotho: Institute of Southern African Studies, National University of Lesotho, 2003.

Nelson, Nici. "'Women Must Help Each Other': The Operation of Personal Networks among Buzaa Beer Brewers in Mathare Valley, Kenya." In *Women United, Women Divided: Comparative Studies of Ten Contemporary Cultures*, ed. Patricia Caplan and Janet Bujra. Bloomington: Indiana University Press, 1979.

Oruwari, Yomi. "Planners, Officials, and Low Income Women and Children in Nigerian Cities: Divergent Perspectives over Housing and Neighborhoods." *Canadian Journal of African Studies* 37, nos. 2–3 (2003): 396–410.

Robertson, Claire. *Sharing the Same Bowl: A Socioeconomic History of Women and Class in Accra, Ghana.* Bloomington: Indiana University Press, 1984.

Sheldon, Kathleen. "*Machambas* in the City: Urban Women and Agricultural Work in Mozambique." *Lusotopie* (1999): 121–140.

Sheldon, Kathleen, ed. *Courtyards, Markets, City Streets: Urban Women in Africa.* Boulder, CO: Westview Press, 1996.

Sithole-Fundire, Sylvia, Agnes Zhou, Anita Larsson, and Ann Schlyter, eds. *Gender Research on Urbanization, Planning, Housing and Everyday Life (GRUPHEL).* Harare: Zimbabwe Women's Resource Center and Network, 1995.

Strobel, Margaret. *Muslim Women in Mombasa, 1890–1975.* New Haven, CT: Yale University Press, 1979.

KATHLEEN SHELDON

WOMEN IN AFRICAN HISTORY

Women in African history represented a wide variety of societies with different geographies, social customs, religions, and historical situations. Despite the range of experiences, there were some common threads and shared occurrences. Africa was a predominantly agricultural continent, and a major factor in African agriculture was the central role of women as farmers. It has been estimated that between 65 and 80 percent of African women were engaged in cultivating food for their families at the end of the twentieth century, and in the past that percentage was likely even higher. In North Africa as well, women were commonly part of a rural agricultural family. Thus, one common thread across much of the continent was women's daily work tending their family plot. Women's work in agriculture was not static but evolved over the centuries. It was not identical in all regions of Africa, as different crops were grown depending on the geography and environment of each locality and there were arid zones and urban centers where women did not cultivate.

The centrality of agriculture, nevertheless, led to another important characteristic found in most African societies, which was the control of land and of labor by kin groups and clans. Land historically was not owned by individuals but a social group that held the rights of access to land. Use of specific plots of land was decided by leaders of the group, who were usually but not always senior men. Leadership was intertwined with control over women's labor, and the arrangement of families through marriage was a matter of significant interest to the senior clan leaders. One of the central markers of ethnicity was the method of descent, and that factor was directly linked to women through social ideas about marriage and kinship.

Africa has been the world region most noted for a high incidence of matrilineal descent systems, found in an extensive belt across the center of the continent, and including peoples in parts of West and southern Africa. Matrilineality referred to a social system that placed a woman and her female relations at the center of kinship and family, rather than a woman and her husband, or a man and his wife or wives and offspring. The method of reckoning kinship that centered on a man and his spouse and assigned offspring as belonging to the father's clan or family is patrilineality. Matrilineal societies embodied an idea of social organization that privileges the personal and social power of women. Mothers were revered, and frequently all senior female relations were considered to be "mothers" to the kin group. The role of a woman's brother was often of greater importance to her children than that of her husband (their father). Thus, there were examples of elder sisters holding central positions within the clan, and being considered as local chiefs because of their prominence within the kin group.

Societies in eastern and southern Africa, especially groups that depended to a greater extent on cattle or other livestock husbandry, and the predominantly Islamic groups of North Africa, often were patrilineal. It was common in southern African societies for cattle to be an integral part of the bridewealth exchanged as part of the marital process. The usual form was for the family of the husband-to-be to make an arrangement with the family of the woman he planned to marry regarding the number of cattle and other goods that would be given to her family. Although Western observers later described these transactions as commercial, and considered such exchanges to be the sale of a woman, for African communities it meant a tangible economic connection between clans that strengthened both the marital relationship and the bond between families that were now kin. In most cases livestock was controlled by men, and the amount of cattle a man accumulated reflected the social standing and strength of his household. Even in societies that were heavily dependent on cattle, women's agricultural labor was key, as grains and produce were the mainstay of people's daily diet.

POLITICAL AUTHORITY

Despite women's integral role in agricultural production and in the related issues of control over labor, access to land, and the formation of families in general, in most African societies women had only indirect access to power and authority. But there was evidence of a variety of routes to exercise authority, including through women's organizations. Women advanced to leadership positions through elaborate systems of rank and naming, and women's groups were viewed as complementary to men's within the community. In West Africa there were market women's groups that controlled marketplace activities. In many regions of Africa women had important religious roles, especially as they aged and became senior members of their societies. In others women had important roles as queen mothers, serving as essential advisers to male rulers who were usually their sons or other kin, and sometimes serving as co-rulers or regents.

Among the Yoruba in the region of present-day Nigeria, women's trading networks gained increasing importance in the fifteenth century. Existing markets in produce and crafts grew into long-distance systems of trade from their own coastal area into the northern hinterlands. Men dominated the trade in luxury items, but women controlled trade in cloth, food, and locally produced crafts such as woven mats. Women also organized their own local trading activities under a female authority known as the *iyalode*, a position that was earned through a life of prosperous trade and virtuous behavior. An *iyalode* mediated conflicts and determined the location of new markets, and women relied on her to protect their commercial and personal interests.

Although North Africa had been part of the Mediterranean world for many centuries, Europeans only arrived at coastal communities in sub-Saharan Africa at the end of the fifteenth century. Their written observations offer some of the earliest documentation concerning African women. Along the West African coast a number of successful female market traders played an important role as arbiters between local societies and European traders. Madam Tinubu (d. 1887) was an influential businesswoman in nineteenth-century Nigeria. Born in Abeokuta, she set up her own trade in tobacco and salt near Lagos, where she began dealing with European slave traders. She later reestablished her business in Abeokuta, where her prominence was such that she was named *iyalode* of Abeokuta in 1864. Other women developed relationships with European men and used that connection to further their own control over trade routes.

The experience of slavery is another area that has been documented in written sources, largely because of the involvement of Western traders. Slaves within Africa were more likely to be women, a reflection of their productive and reproductive contributions to their communities. Men were more often sold into the international market, or in cases where slaves were war captives women would be integrated into the new society while men were more likely to be killed as enemies. Women were also slave owners, especially in areas where they had the opportunity to accrue wealth through trading and market work. But the complicated issue of male control over women's labor meant that women were more vulnerable to capture, pawning, and enslavement, especially in areas where they were already dependent on men for access to land.

Women had been central in Islamic practices in North Africa, and they came to play a central role in the expansion of Islam in West Africa during the nineteenth century. A major event was the campaign by ʿUthman dan Fodio, as he brought extensive areas into the orbit of Islamic beliefs. His daughter, Nana Asmaʾu (1793–1864), was a prominent scholar and teacher who wrote many poems and religious tracts. She also organized a series of Qurʾanic schools for women, and devised teaching programs that allowed women to participate in the schools while honoring their seclusion.

COLONIALISM

Studies of women's work during the colonial period often show how they lost power and economic autonomy with the arrival of cash crops and their exclusion from the global marketplace, in contrast to men who were more likely to benefit from these economic changes. Even further, men and international commerce benefited because they were able to rely to some extent on women's unremunerated labor. The dynamic varied from place to place. In Egypt, women's household production of cotton textiles was taken over by factories in the early nineteenth century, and when the factories closed people turned to imported rather than local cloth, a decision that failed to revitalize household weaving. In Ghana when cocoa trees were introduced and it became clear that cultivating cocoa for export was a lucrative business, men bought land that they could devote to cocoa trees. In most cases they bought the land on credit using female kin as collateral, so that if the man could not repay the loan the women were pawned or transferred to the creditor. Women and children made up the major share of the labor force in the cocoa plantations, though when the cocoa was sold the male land (and tree) owner kept the proceeds.

In other places women typically continued their work growing food for their family's consumption while men entered the colonial economy and earned wages by working on tea and cotton plantations or, in Central and southern Africa, by going to work under contract at the gold, diamond, and copper mines. In the mining regions some women did move to the newly developing urban areas with their husbands or on their own in search of new opportunities, though the majority remained in the rural areas.

Women's formal political activity was generally ignored and denigrated by the colonial authorities, who turned exclusively to men when they established local political offices. Although much of the writing about African women under colonialism emphasizes the economic and political losses they suffered, women's specific experiences indicate that they found ways to progress and succeed in the face of blatant discrimination. Sometimes new forms of oppression spurred women to new kinds of activities. Women became politically active, as seen in Nigeria with the development of three different market women's associations in Lagos that mirrored ethnic and class divisions present in the city, or in Egypt where the 1920s saw the growth of a vibrant movement for women's rights.

Women also found new ways of working and initiated new family forms as urbanization accelerated. The development of mining compounds, though designed primarily as male workplaces, opened opportunities for women to move from their rural homes, establish new marital and kin relationships, and develop new ways of earning an income. Women who settled in urban areas began small businesses and became active in markets in areas of southern and Central Africa that did not have a history of market work such as in West Africa. Women found greater independence and were able to enter and leave marriages with more control over their own choices than was common in rural communities. They had more access to formal education, and though they continued to have a disadvantage in the job market when compared to men, in some cases they were able to train as teachers and nurses, and to work in offices and other urban workplaces.

RESISTANCE AND NATIONALISM

From the earliest years, Africans resisted the increasing control the Europeans were exerting over their societies. The modern nationalist movement gained strength in the early twentieth century, and women were involved in activities in every region. One of the best known political actions was the Igbo Women's War in 1929 in southeastern Nigeria, as Igbo women demonstrated against the extension of taxation to women. When local chiefs began counting women as part of a census, it was believed that counting would lead to taxing women as well as men. Women had a history of local authority through market organizations and trading networks, and the word spread rapidly throughout the region. Drawing on precolonial forms of protest that used insult and dancing, women destroyed British colonial buildings and attacked local and foreign personnel. The result was not promising for women's future role in politics, however, as fifty women were killed and the British did not incorporate women into their plans for colonial government.

In other parts of Africa women drew on their position as spirit mediums to lead their communities in anticolonial activities. Spirit mediums were responsible for guiding people's access to ancestors and for assisting in important decisions concerning social well-being. Because of that responsibility, some women played roles in anticolonial movements. Charwe (c. 1862–1898), who was involved in the anticolonial struggle among the Shona, was one example of how older practices reemerged with a new purpose in the face of oppression. Charwe was possessed by the Nehanda spirit, and while manifesting that spirit she emerged as a leader of the 1896–1897 resistance to British colonial activity in Zimbabwe (then Southern Rhodesia). Charwe was captured in 1897 and held responsible for the death of a British colonial official. Her reputation grew after she was hanged in 1898 and, as Nehanda, she came to be considered a legendary resistance leader in Zimbabwe.

African women were also at the forefront of overtly anticolonial protest activities, writing articles in local newspapers, working in organizations, and often arguing on two fronts as they fought for African political control and simultaneously for the inclusion of women at all levels of government. In South Africa women protested against the extension of pass laws. Charlotte Maxeke (1874–1939), drawing in part from her experience and education in the United States, took on a leadership role in and early successful protest, as passes were not issued to women until decades later. In West Africa, Olufunmilayo Ransome-Kuti (1900–1978) pioneered in women's political action and in promoting girls' education, and she also had a high profile on the international scene during and after the colonial period, when she attended meetings of the Women's International Democratic Federation and the Women's International League for Peace and Freedom.

Discovering the history of Muslim women in Dar es Salaam fundamentally changed the conventional historical view that the Tanzanian anticolonial movement was led solely by men who were products of Christian mission education. Bibi Titi Mohammed (1926–2000) used traditional women's dance groups and community organizations to recruit women who were outside the colonial educational system to join the Tanganyika African National Union. The support and activity of those women was essential to the success of the liberation movement.

In Kenya and the southern African nations of Angola, Mozambique, Rhodesia (present-day Zimbabwe), South West Africa (present-day Namibia), and South Africa, African nationalists encountered recalcitrant white settler populations. In those situations people turned to armed struggle to win independence and majority rule. Algeria, in North Africa, was also the site of armed resistance to French colonial rule. Women were centrally involved in all of those struggles, though generally not as actual combatants. In the 1950s Mau Mau struggle in Kenya the most noted leaders in the Land and Freedom Army were men, though they could not have survived in the forests without women supporting them by supplying food and other necessities, acting as spies and messengers, and performing other tasks. The British colonial authorities recognized the importance of women to the struggle, and incarcerated 13,000 female sympathizers in camps and holding areas, as well as fortifying villages to keep residents from leaving to join or aid the resistance. The colonial authorities used these locations to expand their training in Western-style domesticity, which was initially introduced by colonial women through the women's organization Maendeleo ya Wanawake, or Women's Progress.

In the 1960s and 1970s, as Portugal refused to relinquish its African territories of Angola, Mozambique, Guinea-Bissau, and Cape Verde, the local people initiated an armed struggle and again women were crucial to the success of the resistance effort through their work in supplying food, acting as couriers, and building an alternative social order in the liberated zones. Zimbabwe, Namibia, and South Africa also endured grueling armed revolts that eventually brought about majority rule. Women were active in all aspects of the struggle, including as

fighters, though they faced many more obstacles to full acceptance than did men. Women in these countries are recognized in the early twenty-first century as national heroines for the sacrifices and contributions they made to the freedom of their countries.

AFRICAN WOMEN IN THE LATE TWENTIETH AND EARLY TWENTY-FIRST CENTURIES

It sometimes seemed that women were stagnating in African societies, continuing as the family members primarily responsible for agricultural labor and facing ongoing hindrances to gaining education and employment equal to African men. Statistics suggested that for the continent as a whole women's literacy rates were improving, from 40 percent in 1995 to 50 percent in 2000. Women still had serious problems with unequal treatment in the areas of marriage, divorce, inheritance, and widowhood, as stories emerged about the families of deceased husbands arriving to claim the household goods as their own rather than belonging to the widow and her children. Since the 1980s the scourge of HIV/AIDS has inflicted untold hardships on women. The occurrence of so-called low-intensity wars in more than a dozen countries frequently made women the victims of war-related violence, sexual assault, dislocation, disease, and other traumas.

Yet the last half of the twentieth century also brought dramatic positive changes to the lives of many African women, as opportunities for formal education, new job possibilities, increased political involvement, and changing family expectations gained in importance. The United Nations Decade for Women, which included a 1985 meeting in Nairobi, Kenya, was an important catalyst for African women, as it increased international backing for their efforts to obtain legal changes in support of equality for women. A follow-up meeting in 1995 in Beijing was chaired by Tanzanian politician Gertrude Mongella.

In the 1990s, as democratization projects expanded, the numbers of women in national parliaments and in ministerial positions grew. In some countries special quota and electoral systems ensured that a core of female legislators would have seats. In 2003 women activists celebrated a victory when the African Union adopted a landmark Protocol on the Rights of Women that encouraged African nations to enact an impressive catalog of woman-friendly legislation. That was followed in 2004 by the recognition of Wangari Maathai with the Nobel Peace Prize for her work with Kenyan women in environmental issues as a route to increasing women's political activism and simultaneously protecting the earth. These events suggest the ways in which African women are building for the future, based on their own history and experience.

See also **Asma'u, Nana; Disease: HIV/AIDS, Social and Political Aspects; History and the Study of Africa; Islam; Maathai, Wangari; Mohammed, Bibi Titi; Mongella, Gertrude I.; Ransome-Kuti, Olfunmilayo; Slave Trades; Slavery and Servile Institutions; Spirit Possession: Mediumship; Tinubu, Madam; Warfare: Colonial.**

BIBLIOGRAPHY

Allman, Jean; Susan Geiger; and Nakanyike Musisi; eds. *Women in African Colonial Histories.* Bloomington: Indiana University Press, 2002.

Berger, Iris, and E. Frances White. *Women in Sub-Saharan Africa: Restoring Women to History.* Bloomington: Indiana University Press, 1999.

Coquery-Vidrovitch, Catherine. *African Women: A Modern History,* trans. Beth Gillian Raps. Boulder, CO: Westview Press, 1997.

Daymond, M. J., et al., eds. *Women Writing Africa: The Southern Region,* vol. 1. New York: Feminist Press at the City University of New York, 2003.

Diaw, Aminata, and Esi Sutherland, eds. *Women Writing Africa: West Africa and the Sahel,* vol. 2. New York: Feminist Press at the City University of New York, 2005.

Hafkin, Nancy J., and Edna G. Bay, eds. *Women in Africa: Studies in Social and Economic Change.* Stanford, CA: Stanford University Press, 1976.

Hodgson, Dorothy L., and Sheryl A. McCurdy, eds. *"Wicked" Women and the Reconfiguration of Gender in Africa.* Portsmouth, NH: Heinemann, 2001.

Imam, Ayesha M.; Amina Mama; and Fatou Sow; eds. *Engendering African Social Sciences.* Dakar, Senegal: Codesria, 1997.

Kethusegile, Bookie M., Alice Kwaramba, and Barbara Lopi, comps. *Beyond Inequalities: Women in Southern Africa.* Harare, Zimbabwe: Southern African Research and Documentation Center (SARDC), 2000. (SARDC also published individual volumes in the *Beyond Inequalities* series on Angola, Botswana, Lesotho, Malawi, Mauritius, Mozambique, Namibia, South Africa, Swaziland, Tanzania, Zambia, and Zimbabwe.)

Robertson, Claire, and Iris Berger, eds. *Women and Class in Africa.* New York: Africana Publishing Company, 1986.

Sheldon, Kathleen E., ed. *Courtyards, Markets, City Streets: Urban Women in Africa.* Boulder, CO: Westview Press, 1996.

Sheldon, Kathleen E. *Historical Dictionary of Women in Sub-Saharan Africa.* Lanham, MD: Scarecrow Press, 2005.

Tripp, Aili Mari, ed. *The Greenwood Encyclopedia of Women's Issues Worldwide: Sub-Saharan Africa.* Westport, CT: Greenwood Press, 2003.

KATHLEEN SHELDON

WIDOWS

Widows are often portrayed as one of the most disadvantaged groups of women in Africa. Due to local customs of male control of land, household goods, and offspring, women who are widowed may lose access to their children, their land, and their homes. Yet even within a particular society women have many options following the death of their husbands, and may choose to return to their community of origin, remain unmarried, or live with adult sons or daughters who have married. In some areas older women are considered to have entered into a stage of life where they enjoy respect and authority that is not accorded to younger women, and they may take on leadership roles.

A common assumption is that African widows must marry a brother of their late husband in a practice knows as levirate. The custom was prevalent in the past in many patrilineal African cultures, although the extent is difficult to ascertain, and was often considered an obligation as the clan was expected to care for widows who had no place to live. In some instances the father's family would claim any children from the marriage as part of their clan, and encourage the mother of those children to remarry within the clan as a strategy to maintain her link to her offspring. Widows in that situation would sometimes prefer to remarry within their deceased husband's family in order to keep contact with their children as well as to retain access to land they had cultivated. Yet many women would refuse such marriages and would feel free to make other choices. The impact of Christianity has also been significant, as Christian women would reject their brothers-in-law as a matter of religious belief.

Stories of widows in Zimbabwe, Nigeria, and elsewhere being stripped of all their belongings by their husbands' family members have circulated in the international news since the late twentieth century. Even women who worked and earned their own house and belongings have found their deceased husbands' families claiming all of the marital household goods after the funeral, as customary law in some areas considered the husband as owner of all household items, and sometimes even as "owner" of his wife. The impact of increased deaths from HIV/AIDS has seen a greater number of younger widows, and the problem of widows trying to support themselves and their children has expanded dramatically. Poverty has also led to greater difficulties for kin in caring for a widow and her children, while making the widow's belongings a more tempting target for relations to try to grab. Thus legal issues concerning inheritance have become a key arena for work to improve the conditions of widows.

Other studies indicate that not all widows suffer. Research among Kenyan widows found that their main concern in the 1940s and 1950s was not with inheritance and forced remarriage, but with securing a good husband for their daughters. They generally preferred not to remarry, and the choices they made within social constraints indicated their resourcefulness, as their daughters' success would enable the daughters to care for their aging mothers. Research in southern Mozambique has suggested that rural women may support each other in ways that permit widows to remain in their marital community and cultivate their land there following the loss of their husband. Thus there is no "typical" African widow.

See also Disease: HIV/AIDS, Social and Political Aspects; Law.

BIBLIOGRAPHY

Cattell, Maria G. "African Widows: Anthropological and Historical Perspectives." *Journal of Women and Aging* 15, no. 2–3 (2003): 49–66.

Ewelukwa, Uche U. "Post-Colonialism, Gender, Customary Injustice: Widows in African Societies." *Human Rights Quarterly* 24, no. 2 (2002): 424–486.

Mutongi, Kenda. "'Worries of the Heart': Widowed Mothers, Daughters and Masculinities in Maragoli, Western Kenya." *Journal of African History* 40, no. 1 (1999): 67–87.

Potash, Betty, ed. *Widows in African Societies: Choices and Constraints.* Stanford, CA: Stanford University Press, 1986.

Widows' Rights International. Available from http://www.widowsrights.org.

KATHLEEN SHELDON

WOMEN: WRITERS. *See* Literature: Women Writers, Northern Africa; Literature: Women Writers, Sub-Saharan Africa.

WORLD BANK. When British economist John Maynard Keynes and Harry Dexter White, the chief international economist at the United States Treasury, were asked by their respective governments to design a framework for stabilizing international financial relations and rebuilding Europe after World War II, they came up with two competing proposals that were adopted at the Bretton Woods Conference (officially called the United Nations Monetary and Financial Conference and held on July 1–22, 1944) in New Hampshire. White's idea lead to the creation of the International Monetary Fund (IMF), which was given the role of promoting global economic growth through international trade and financial stability. Keynes' proposal led to the creation of a sister institution, the World Bank.

The World Bank's main purposes were to assist in the reconstruction and development of territories of members by facilitating the investment of capital for productive purposes, including the restoration of economies destroyed or disrupted by war, the reconversion of productive facilities to peacetime needs, and the encouragement of the development of productive facilities and resources in less developed countries; to promote balanced growth of international trade and the maintenance of equilibrium in balances of payments by encouraging international investment for the development of the productive resources of members; promote private foreign investment by means of guarantees or participations in loans and other investments made by private investors; and when private capital is not available on reasonable terms, to supplement private investment by providing, on suitable conditions, finance for productive purposes. It was understood at the time that the primary mandate of the World Bank was basically to finance major infrastructure in European countries that had suffered the most from the war. France even received the first World Bank loan on May 9, 1947.

Its mission has evolved from that of a facilitator of postwar reconstruction and development imagined by Keynes to the present day mandate of worldwide poverty alleviation. While reconstruction remains an important focus of its work, given the natural disasters and post conflict rehabilitation needs that affect developing economies, the World Bank has broadened its portfolio's focus to include social sector lending projects, debt relief and good governance. In the early twenty-first century, the World Bank is an important source of financial and technical assistance to developing countries. As of January 1, 2006, it employs approximately 10,000 employees at its headquarters in Washington, D.C., and in more than 100 country offices around the world.

It is not a bank in the common sense. It has expanded from a single institution to a group of several development institutions. It is primarily made up of two development institutions owned by 184 member countries—the International Bank for Reconstruction and Development (IBRD) and the International Development Association (IDA). The IBRD deals with middle income and creditworthy poor countries, while IDA focuses on the poorest countries in the world. Together they provide low-interest loans, interest-free credit, and grants to developing countries for education, health, infrastructure, communications and many other purposes. The World Bank also has three other affiliates: the International Financial Corporation, the Multilateral Investment Guarantee Agency, and the International Centre for Settlement of Investment Disputes.

Since the early 1980s World Bank policies in Africa have been dominated by structural adjustment programs (SAPs) whose purpose was to address the two important issues: the negative evolution of terms of trade and the low productivity. Starting in the early 1960s, most of the newly independent Sub-Saharan countries benefited from a rapid rise in the value of their exports. This led to an increase in their foreign exchange revenues and Government revenues. This surge in income was stimulated by ambitious public policies aiming at increasing both investment and consumption. While often justified by the poor state of infrastructure and the huge social needs of the population (especially in the areas of education and health) who had suffered centuries of slavery and colonization, a lot of these investments were over-sized and ill-designed. Fueled by the nationalistic dream of the new political leaders, large projects and programs dominated government plans—often conceived on the model of Soviet Gosplan, regardless of the ideological background of the ruling elites.

These projects and programs also generated large current expenditures, as they required a large number of civil servants with salary levels often equivalent to ten times the average income per capita, or high levels of operation and maintenance spending. Furthermore, for ideological, political, and sometimes economic reasons, and also for reasons of pure greed, many countries opted for the nationalization of large fraction of the production apparatus. They were encouraged along this direction by the ease with which they could obtain foreign loans owing to abundant international liquidity.

In the 1970s many private American, European, and Japanese banks had at their disposal important deposits from members of the Organization of Petroleum Exporting Countries (OPEC) cartel—the so-called petrodollars. Acting under the assumption that even poor developing countries cannot go bankrupt, these banks started lending money to African countries with little rigorous analysis of their justification. Many African countries were provided large loans that, under normal circumstances, would have been considered unwise. They were considered financially viable, as the prices of commodities (coffee, cocoa, copper, diamonds) through which they obtained foreign exchange were relatively high.

These loans were used to finance huge investment projects with little or no economic rationale, imports of luxury goods, and personal bank accounts in European banks. Yet, by the early 1980s, the situation had changed considerably. OPEC had become less effective as a cartel, which drove down oil prices and substantially reduced petrodollars held as deposits in western banks. Also, the United States had elected Ronald Reagan as president, whose fiscal policy consisted mainly of large tax cuts and big buildup in military spending. The combination of these two factors (the limited availability of petrodollars on the international lending market and the need for funds to finance the large U.S. fiscal deficit) drove interest rates upward. To make matters worse, the world economy faced a major recession in the early 1980s and commodity prices on which African countries relied for foreign exchange decreased to historic lows.

Confronted with the rapid increase of interest rates on their variable-rate loan repayments, these countries were on the verge of default on their external debt. Since the loans they obtained in the 1970s were used to pay for politically motivated projects or expansive luxury goods—not productive investments—only one option was left to them: turn to multilateral financial institutions like the World Bank and the IMF for help.

The World Bank and the IMF designed SAPs as a remedy to these macroeconomic problems. These programs aimed at eliminating the imbalances of the economies and putting them back on the path to long-term sustainable growth. They combined two overlapping objectives: stabilization and adjustment. Stabilization as the reduction of national expenditure to bring it in line with national output or income, and structural adjustment as policies to increase national income/output through a more efficient use of resources. Stabilizing the economy implies adopting policies that lower the rate of inflation, reduce the current account deficit, restore external competitiveness, and limit the loss of international reserves. When this is achieved, there is the need for structural adjustment, that is, implementing policies to increase the productive capacity of the economy and to improve the efficiency with which the country's resources are utilized.

Many methodological difficulties (choosing the period of analysis and taking time lags into account, disentangling the effects of World Bank programs from other influences observed in African economies, measuring conditionality and the degree of implementation, constructing counterfactual scenarios to estimate what would have happened in the absence of SAPs in Africa) make the assessment of World Bank policies in Africa a difficult exercise. Still, critics have focused on their illegitimacy (they are externally imposed), their inability to take into account the political and institutional context, the macroeconomics underpinning the framework, their blind faith to virtues of market, and their high social cost.

See also **Aid and Development; International Monetary Fund.**

BIBLIOGRAPHY

Lipumba, Nguyuru H. I. *Africa beyond Adjustment.* Policy Essay no. 15. Washington, DC: Overseas Development Corporation, 1994.

Mkandawire, Thandika, and Charles Soludo, eds. *African Voices on Structural Adjustment.* Dakar: Codesria, 2003.

Monga, Célestin. "Commodities, Mercedes-Benz, and Structural Adjustment: An Episode in West African Economic History." In *Themes in West Africa's History,* ed. Emmanuel Akyeampong. Athens: Ohio University Press, 2005.

Mosley, Paul; Jane Harrigan; and John Toye. *Aid and Power: The World Bank and Policy-Based Lending.* London: Routledge, 1991.

Sahn, David E.; Paul A. Dorosh; and Stephen D. Younger. *Structural Adjustment Reconsidered: Economic Policy and Poverty in Africa.* Cambridge, U.K: Cambridge University Press, 1997.

CÉLESTIN MONGA

WORLD WAR I.

World War I spread surprisingly quickly into Africa. Following Britain's declaration of war on Germany on August 4, 1914, cabinet meetings held in London on the following two days authorized campaigns in four theaters of war in Germany's African colonies, namely in Togoland, German South-West Africa, Cameroon (Kamerun), and German East Africa. The immediate military aim of Britain and its Allies was to destroy German ports and wireless stations in Africa. The longer-term aim, shared by Britain and its Allies, was to put an end to the German colonial empire in Africa. The division of the former German colonies between Britain and its Allies in 1918 can thus be interpreted as the final phase of the European "scramble for Africa," in which Africa was partitioned in the interests of Europe, with little regard for the concerns of Africans themselves.

The Allied military campaign in Togoland (West Africa) came to a speedy conclusion. The German administration was removed in a matter of weeks when German forces surrendered on August 26, 1914, to a combined British-French military force. The British and French commanders on the ground immediately agreed to a partition of

Togoland, an arrangement that was subsequently confirmed by the Allies, with certain modifications, in 1918.

As far as German South-West Africa was concerned, the Britain requested that it should be white South African combatants who would carry out the invasion. Initially there was a reluctance on the part of the Union of South Africa to mount an invasion because of pro-German sentiments among the Boers leading to pro-German Boer risings in both the Orange Free State and the western Transvaal. The delayed invasion was eventually started by the Union of South Africa in 1915, bringing about German surrender six months later. With the end of hostilities in 1918 the former German South-West African colony passed to the Union of South Africa.

The Anglo-French campaign in Cameroon was a more complex and acrimonious venture among the Allies, lasting fifteen months from 1914 to 1916. In the north, German troops offered little resistance to the British forces. In the south and east of Cameroon where the French and Belgian troops were based, the Germans held on until 1916, when they retreated into the adjacent Spanish territory of Río Muni. In 1918 after much bargaining and debate, the partition of Cameroon between Britain and France was agreed, the precise border between the two being decided by a blue pencil line drawn in London on a War Office map.

Finally, there was the campaign in German East Africa that lasted from 1914 to 1918. This campaign most closely resembled the warfare taking place in Europe in that large numbers of troops, trucks, and airplanes came to be involved. The campaign was marked by an ill-conceived British attack on the port of Tanga, which the Germans successfully repulsed. The German commander was Paul von Lettow, who withdrew from the conflict in face of superior numbers, moving south and then into Mozambique. He managed to avoid surrender until three days after the November 11, 1918, armistice in Europe.

The main reason why the German East African campaign was so protracted was because Britain was reluctant to accept help from its European Allies in Africa because it did not wish to encourage them in territorial claims at the end of hostilities. The future of the former German East Africa eventually gave rise to extended debates and complicated maneuvers among the Allies in the peace negotiations after 1918. Britain eventually acquired most of the East African Colony under League of Nations mandate and the remainder was transferred to Belgium. Defeat in World War I therefore meant the end of the German empire in Africa. German markets and German shipping all but disappeared from Africa. This reversed the trend before 1914 when the economic influence of Germany in Africa had been growing in importance.

But what of the Africans themselves in World War I? To appreciate the impact of World War I on the indigenous people of Africa one needs to move beyond the policymakers in Europe's capitals, and study the consequences of the conflict on Africans participating directly as soldiers and porters, or indirectly as miners, farmers, missionaries, administrators, and as a host of other roles.

Africans were used as soldiers and porters in the Togoland, Cameroon and East African campaigns. The Union of South Africa also enlisted several thousand Africans for the campaign in South-West Africa, but refused to use them as combatants out of fear of arming the local population.

In Europe, there were large numbers of Africans from the French Colonies under arms. Estimates of the numbers of Africans on the Western Front and at Gallipoli must be interpreted with caution but the French historian Marc Michel believed that around 130,000 African troops were sent to Europe, of whom 30,000 were ultimately reported killed or missing. Seven Senegalese battalions fought for the French at Gallipoli, participating in the important diversionary landing at Koum-Kale. Though Britain did not use troops from Africa as combatants in Europe, one thousand Nigerians were employed as laborers by the British army in the Inland Water Service in Mesopotamia. Africans from the Gold Coast also served in the merchant marine alongside Africans from Liberia and Somalia.

How did Africans respond to the experience of the European war? For all nationalities that were combatants in the tragedy of World War I, many years were to elapse before historians began to appreciate the significance of interviewing the diminishing number of surviving veterans to assess the impact of war on the participants. The archival records in all countries nevertheless indicate an enormous scale of human suffering in World War I. African deaths in the various African and other campaigns of the war are estimated at around 250,000. This represents roughly 10 percent of those Africans who were recruited as noncombatants and laborers. Historians also estimate that for every soldier who was killed in the war, five suffered from wounds, disease, gas poisoning, or shell shock. The archival evidence shows that for Africans in particular the training offered to combatants was grossly deficient. As a body of recruits they also suffered disproportionately from ill heath and disability. For them too there was the added burden of racism. The Union of South Africa, which sent a noncombatant black labor force to work in France, kept it separate from other military and civilian units. Housed in compounds under the command of white South African officers, there were many instances of ill treatment. In 1917, 600 members of the SANLC (South African Native Labour Contingent) perished when the SS *Mendi* was sunk in the English Channel.

The impact of World War I on the economies of Africa also merits examination. Both imports and exports were severely affected by shipping shortages during the war. As a consequence most colonial economies introduced measures to increase local production of foodstuffs and raw materials. In East Africa remarkable increases in the local output of maize were recorded, much of which was destined for the military. In the settler economy of Kenya the local livestock industry also received a boost, again as a result of increased demand from the military. The colonial economies in Africa increased their circulation of currency during the war, and both public and private capital formation increased. The downside of all this for the local population was price inflation, brought about by increases in the supply of money and local shortages of food and other resources as domestic output was diverted towards military ends. Then, when hostilities ended, the ultimate blow was Spanish influenza, which struck Africa between 1919 and 1920. As many as 2 million Africans may have died from the virus, which was often carried back to Africa by returning soldiers and laborers.

On the credit side one of the unexpected gains to Africans from World War I, as a result of manpower shortages among Europeans, was the substitution of African for European labor in a variety of roles previously earmarked for whites. In settler economies, Africans took on the role of foremen-managers on estates. In colonial bureaucracies they took over administrative duties previously reserved for Europeans. When missionaries were called up (or interned in the case of the German colonies) African Christians shouldered new responsibilities. The gains tended to be short lived, however. When European soldiers and civilians returned to their peacetime occupations the old order was restored. Did this result in anger and resentment among Africans, particularly those with some education and ambition? It is by no means clear what effect the upheavals of the war had on the minds and outlook of those Africans involved. Many Europeans had feared that the war would lead to political radicalism, especially among returning soldiers. It could awaken "race consciousness" and a desire for independence from colonial rule. The evidence regarding this is unclear. Though radical groups led by African ex-soldiers did emerge from time to time after World War I, especially in France itself and in parts of the Caribbean, this scenario was by no means typical. As the French historian Marc Michel recorded, one African survivor of the Somme would later say, "Avant j'etais negre, maintenant je suis Français" ("Before, I was a Negro, now I am French").

See also **Colonialism and Imperialism; Warfare: National and International; World War II.**

BIBLIOGRAPHY

Crowder, Michael. "The Impact of Two World Wars on Africa." *History Today* 34 (January 1984): 11–18.

Farwell, Byron. *The Great War in Africa, 1914–1918.* New York: Viking Press, 1987.

Michel, Marc. *L'appel a l'afrique: Contributions et reactions a l'effort de guerre en AOF 1914–1919.* Paris: Publications de la Sorbonne, Serie Afrique No. 6, 1982.

Page, Melvin, ed. *Africa and the First World War.* London: Macmillan, 1987.

BARBARA INGHAM

WORLD WAR II.   With the exception of the liberation of Ethiopia from Italian control in 1941 and the minor skirmish of the Dakar Raid (the ill-fated attempt on September 23, 1940, by the British and Free French forces to seize Dakar from the control of the Vichy government), sub-Saharan Africa was not, as it had been in World War I, a major theater in World War II. Nonetheless, the significance of World War II for the twentieth-century history of Africa is considerable. At the level of geopolitics, the war finally ended the pretensions of the colonial powers to Great Power status. France had been defeated and then divided in the course of the war. Britain's war effort was to result in virtual bankruptcy. Belgium was occupied. Before the end of the European war, the Soviet Union and the United States had come to dominate world politics. Both superpowers were, for markedly different reasons, hostile to the maintenance of colonial empires. The newly created United Nations was, unlike its predecessor, the League of Nations, a forum in which colonialism was neither taken for granted nor was to remain uncriticized. When taken alongside the near certainty of the imminent independence of the Indian subcontinent and the heady libertarian language of the Atlantic Charter, this afforded African nationalists the most propitious international environment they had ever enjoyed.

Nationalism was, additionally, to gain broader support in the postwar period because of the widespread discontent and disenchantment that the era brought about. Economic and social change, some of which was painful, were expedited in wartime. The war enhanced the importance of African production; much of what Africans produced was strategically important and in short supply. While increased demand stimulated economic growth after the interwar depression and widened the job market, this was achieved at considerable political cost. Colonial governments took increasingly active roles in directing labor and controlling markets. Such interventions, most notably state oligopolies, which reserved to themselves the crucial functions of buying and selling the fruits of African agricultural production, were to characterize postwar colonial and even postcolonial economic policy. As a result the colonial state became more widely perceived by Africans as demanding, restrictive, confiscatory, and directive.

This was immediately visible in the labor market. Many Africans served in the armed forces of the colonial powers; over 400,000 served with the British alone in the North African and Southeast Asian theaters. About 160,000 of these were recruited in British West Africa. The majority of the 386,000 volunteers from South Africa were white,

and white anxieties about arming Africans technically restricted colored and black troops to noncombatant roles. Recruitment methods throughout Africa varied from volunteering to outright compulsion. Few former servicemen felt that they had been adequately rewarded, and some were to figure, sometimes quite prominently, in nationalist movements after the war. Many servicemen acquired literacy as well as skills like wireless telegraphy or heavy transport driving. Those who served in overseas theaters literally expanded their horizons; many learned firsthand that the invincibility of white men was no more than a myth. But even greater numbers of Africans than that were recruited as laborers and marshaled to increase colonial production in the fields and mines of Africa. Toward the end of the war, many labor recruits were discharged as war work wound down, and consequently urban unemployment and underemployment were added to the list of socioeconomic ills that were to be attributed by articulate nationalists to colonial rule.

Wartime demands for African production continued after the defeat of Germany and then Japan. Postwar reconstruction, especially in Europe, continued to put a high premium on African raw material production. But from 1943 on, the world prices for most commodities grown or produced in Africa began to dwarf the depressed price levels of the interwar period. This marked the inauguration of the longest secular rise in the value of African production, a boom that was not to cease until the end of the 1950s. This was not an unambiguous success. High producer prices were matched by a combination of increased demand for, and the widespread unavailability of, imported manufactured consumer goods; such goods continued to be necessities as, with the exception of South Africa, there was to be no significant increase in the scale of African manufacturing industry in this period. Accordingly, throughout Africa serious inflation began to make deep inroads into the value of the earnings and personal savings of Africans; this created yet another major grievance which nationalists were quick to ascribe to the maladministration of colonial powers. The reduction of wage values and other pressures upon labor further stimulated nascent labor organizations; despite restrictive emergency wartime regulations, extended and bitter strikes on the railroads and in the mines were a feature of this period.

Many African intellectuals supported the allied war effort. It was widely presented by the media as a struggle against fascism; the invasion of Ethiopia in 1935 by an expansionist Italian state was seen by Africans as a dreadful augury of things to come, long before Europeans and Americans recognized its importance. Accordingly, in support of the Allied effort, African nationalist agitation remained more muted until it was clear that the Allies would prevail.

Africans in the French West African territories endured further diminutions of the limited civil rights they had achieved under the Popular Front as these territories fell under the control of the collaborationist Vichy regime. French Equatorial Africa under its courageous Guyanese governor-general, Adolphe-Félix-Sylvestre Éboué; nonetheless remained a significant base for the Free French resistance movement. Portugal's wartime neutrality ensured that the country's highly authoritarian colonial states could continue to repress African aspirations for change.

But none of these restrictions could prevent the emergence of a palpable revolution of rising expectations within Africa. The successful termination of the war was widely assumed to be the signal for liberalization and amelioration on all fronts. Enhanced African production was enforced alongside an ideological proposition of temporary sacrifice; this increased expectation. The emphasis upon economic growth had altered employment patterns so that the war saw a vast increase in the size of colonial towns. Africans expected improvements in their often desperately poor housing conditions once the war ended. The greater numbers of Africans involved in the wage-earning sector led to a wider awareness of neglected issues, including trade union recognition, pensions, and sickness benefits. Larger numbers of educated Africans were being addressed by nationalist newspapers, which drew attention to the niggardly provision of public health facilities, state education, and general welfare provisions offered to most Africans in comparison with those enjoyed by, or at least promised to, nationals of the colonial powers.

These issues were brought to the surface by the practicalities of wartime and by the idiom of liberty from oppression which was exploited by the Allies. Anti-Nazi propaganda legitimated and stimulated debate among African intellectuals about colonial racism and authoritarianism. Nationalists were quick to use these experiences and feelings in their postwar campaigns to end colonial rule. This was apparent in the widespread demands for colonial liberation which were aired at the Pan-African Congress held in Manchester, England, from October 15 to 19, 1945. It was to be even more obvious in the foundation of nationalist parties throughout Africa in the immediate aftermath of World War II.

See also **Colonialism and Imperialism; Éboué, Adolphe-Félix-Sylvestre; Nationalism; Warfare; World War I.**

BIBLIOGRAPHY

Le Congo Belge durant la Second Guerre Mondiale. Brussels: Academie royale des Sciences d'Outre-Mer, 1983.

Cooper, Frederick. *Africa since 1940: The Past of the Present.* Cambridge, U.K.: Cambridge University Press, 2002.

Killingray, David, and Richard Rathbone, eds. *Africa and the Second World War.* London: Macmillan, 1986.

Louis, W. Roger. *Imperialism at Bay.* New York: Oxford University Press, 1977.

Olusanya, Gabriel O. *The Second World War and Politics in Nigeria, 1939–1945.* Lagos, Nigeria: University of Lagos Press, 1973.

Suret-Canale, Jean. *French Colonialism in Tropical Africa.* London: Universe, 1971.

RICHARD RATHBONE

WORLDVIEWS. *See* **Myth and Cosmology; Philosophy and the Study of Africa; Symbols and Symbolism.**

WRITING SYSTEMS

This entry includes the following articles:
AFRICAN SCRIPTS
AFRICAN LANGUAGES IN ARABIC SCRIPTS
AFRICAN LANGUAGES IN ROMAN SCRIPTS
EGYPTIAN
ETHIOPIC

AFRICAN SCRIPTS

Writing systems may be characterized as logographic (symbols represent words or morphemes) or phonetic (symbols representing sounds are combined to form words). Logographic systems are rare in Africa. Phonetic systems may be syllabaries (symbols represent syllables) or alphabets (symbols represent single consonants or vowels).

In some syllabaries, as in that used by the Vai of Liberia, there is little relationship among symbols representing syllables with the same initial consonant or with the same vowel. In others, as in the Ethiopic script, syllables with the same consonant show closely related shapes, and those with the same vowel show similar modifications of the consonant shape.

Most alphabets, like the Greek and Roman scripts, represent both vowels and consonants. Some represent vowels minimally or not at all; the Arabic script, for example, does not normally mark short vowels, though diacritic vowel markings are available. Wholly or primarily consonantal alphabets are sometimes seen as a special type of syllabary.

FIT

Although no phonetic writing system has yet been developed that records all that is significant in spoken language, syllabic and alphabetic systems normally mark the principal vocalic and consonantal contrasts of those languages for which they were originally developed. But most writing systems omit even important features of pronunciation. Few orthographies regularly mark tone. The Ethiopic script fails to note consonant gemination, although this is an important feature in the grammar of these languages. Many Nilotic languages distinguish nine or ten vowels, divided into two subsets with a rule of vowel harmony, which specifies that all of the vowels in a given word will normally belong to one subset. The orthographies, though, generally use only five symbols.

The redundancy in language allows inadequate scripts to be used, and writing systems are to a degree independent of the languages written. Kenyan Luo uses essentially the same orthography as Swahili, and Arabic script has been used for Fulani, despite great structural differences. In most cases, though, a phonetic script used for a language other than the one for which it was developed will be adapted, and linguists and policymakers keep working to improve the fit of script to language.

Common adaptations include additional symbols (in some cases borrowed from other scripts), modified symbols, assignment of unneeded symbols to new values, diacritics, and digraphs or trigraphs. In many cases adaptations made for other languages are transferred. Features taken from the Coptic adaptation of the Greek script remain in Nubian; diacritics used in writing Farsi or Hindi appear in some Arabic-script Swahili texts; and orthographic conventions of English, French, Spanish, Portuguese, German, Dutch, and Italian appear in African forms of the Roman script.

ORIGINS

Most writing systems used in sub-Saharan Africa were developed elsewhere. Sources include the Egyptian script, modified for use with Meroitic; the Greek alphabet, modified for Nubian; the Arabic script, used, for example, in Hausa and Swahili; and the Roman script, which is the system most commonly used.

Two other scripts have an ancestry outside Africa and a long history of development in Africa. One is Tifinagh, the Berber script still used for Tuareg, a distinctive offshoot of the Semitic script. The earliest records date from about the second century BCE in Numidia (present-day Algeria); the system currently used is clearly a descendant but shows great differences in some symbols. The other is the Ethiopian version of the South Semitic script. In its earliest form it was a consonantal alphabet minimally different from the scripts used for Sabaean and early Arabic dialects. In the fourth century CE it was reformed into a syllabary, with vowels represented by modifications in the shapes of the consonant symbols. Extra consonants were added, and in time modified shapes were devised to permit writing non-Semitic Ethiopian languages.

There are a small number of writing systems indigenous to sub-Saharan Africa. Among those documented are alphabets for Somali, Bassa, Fula, Wolof, and the artificial language Oberi Okaime; syllabaries for Vai, Kpelle, Loma, and Mende; and the Bamum script, which developed from a logographic system to a syllabary. Most of these seem to date from the late nineteenth and early twentieth centuries. The Vai and Bamum scripts are the best known and best documented. Both the respective inventors, Momolu Duwalu Bukele and Sultan Njoya, said they were inspired by a dream. In both cases it has frequently been pointed out that the inventors were

	BA	CO	FU	MA	OO	SO	WO
i		(ε)ı					
e							
ɛ							
ə							
a							
ɔ							
o							
u							
ü							
ö							
iu							
ā							
p							
ph							
b							
ɓ							
m							
mb							
β							
f							

	BA	ET	KP	LO	ME	VA
pi						
pī						
pe						
pē						
pɛ						
pa						
pā						
pɔ						
po						
pō						
pu						
pū						
pɯ						
pü						
puə						

Tables showing partial alphabets (left) and sample syllabaries (right) for selected languages. At left, Bassa (BA), Coptic (CO), Fula (FU), Manding (MA), Oberi Okaime (OO), Somali (SO), and Wolof (WO). At right, Barnum (BA), Ethiopic (ET), Kpelle (KP), Loma (LO), Menda (ME), and Vai (VA). International Phonetic Alphabet (IPA) equivalents are given in the first column of each table.

aware of the existence and value of writing systems, and in both cases the type of script and character shapes are clearly unrelated to the Arabic or Roman scripts. It has been suggested that both Bukele and Njoya made use of symbols already in use. In the Wolof script, by contrast, a number of the characters are very similar to Arabic, though the values differ.

CHOICES

Often, competing systems have been used for writing the same language. For example, Swahili at one point was written in Arabic script and in three modifications of Roman script (designed by Germans, French, and English). Choice of script is affected by religion, by colonial power, or by politics. There is a general tendency to use similar, if not identical, systems in groups of languages, especially if they are closely related or typologically similar. This makes for efficiency in printing and facilitates adjustment to more prestigious languages, that is, those for which a significant literature exists and those used by the elite at the highest levels of education.

Non-Roman scripts have generally declined where there has been competition from Roman-based orthographies. Administrators, educators, and publishers have in most cases preferred the Roman script. Roman-based orthographies have several real advantages. They use fewer and less complex symbols than logographic or syllabic systems. They represent vowels omitted in consonantal alphabets like Tifinagh, and their symbols do not show the positional variation characteristic of Arabic writing. Roman script is also the system most commonly used in the Western world.

Adaptations of the Arabic script have often survived where there is a substantial Muslim population, even though a Roman script may be better adapted to the language and preferred by policymakers. In Swahili, for example, Arabic script is used to write charms, poetry, and private letters; it is still sporadically proposed as a standard orthography.

Conflicts between orthographies have often been resolved by local or regional language committees, which have reached compromises on standard dialect, acceptable level of loanwords, and standard orthography. Similar committees also decide on changes in orthographic policy. The decisions of these committees usually affect education and presses under the control of the participants. However, where a language is spoken in two or more countries, decisions made in one may not apply across the border. Further, the writing of individual citizens may show wide variations. Individuals may mix systems, or fail to follow orthographic norms. Diacritics very frequently are omitted in informal usage.

TRANSCRIPTION SYSTEMS

In addition to standardized orthographic systems, designed for or adapted to individual languages, a number of standard writing systems designed for consistent notation of languages in general have been used in Africa. Karl Lepsius's alphabet (1855) was rich in diacritics. It was in widespread use well into the twentieth century. The International Phonetic Association's system (1886) was still much used in the late twentieth century; it employs special characters and avoids diacritics. The International African Institute's Africa alphabet (1928) influenced many orthographies; it reduces the International Phonetic Association's special characters to a minimum. All three have been used primarily by linguists, ethnographers, and others concerned to record phonetic detail. Of course, individual linguists have tended to use—or adapt—transcription systems in use in their homelands. An unusual example is Gerhard Lindblom's use of the Norwegian dialect alphabet for Kamba and other east African languages.

Like the various European orthographies, these transcription systems have often formed the basis for individual African orthographies, usually with adaptations aimed at reducing special characters and diacritics. Because of the conservative tendency of any orthography, systems proposed by linguists outside the community have rarely supplanted established orthographies.

NUMERAL SYSTEMS

Written number systems most commonly develop from strokes used in tallying (as in Roman numerals), or from the conventional order of symbols in an alphabetic or syllabic script (as in the Greek system). The so-called Arabic numerals (in fact of Indian origin) have shapes derived from tally strokes, but are no longer recognizable as such in either their Roman script or their Arabic script adaptations. The Roman variant of the Indo-Arabic numerals is the most commonly used in sub-Saharan Africa, as one might expect from the dominance of Roman-based writing systems.

Although numerals tend to be associated with particular writing systems and in some cases developed from symbols used in writing, there is a large degree of independence. The Greek system uses for *6* a symbol no longer used in writing. The Arabic system has two sets of symbols, the Indo-Arabic numerals and a system using letters of the Arabic alphabet, but with values reflecting an alphabetic order very different from that currently in use. The Ethiopian system uses Greek symbols transmitted through Coptic, though the syllabary is of different origin.

The Indo-Arabic system uses position to mark value, unlike, for example, the Ethiopian and older Arabic systems, which have special symbols for 10, 20, 100, 200, 1,000, and so on. The Indo-Arabic system can operate with only ten symbols; it is thus much more suited to calculation. This efficiency in part accounts for its predominance in the world; for most of Africa, it has come as part of a package with the Roman or Arabic script.

OTHER GRAPHIC SYSTEMS

In many parts of Africa there exist graphic systems with communicative value that are used neither to write the language nor for numeration. Parallels outside Africa include cattle brands, corporate logos, and traffic signs. Symbols may be associated with ownership, ethnic or religious identity, riddles or proverbs, or larger units such as stories or

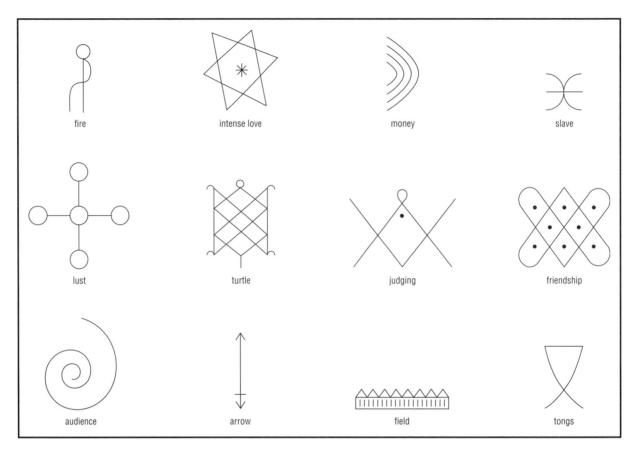

Some representative graphic systems for Nsibidi (Nigeria, top row), Tuconasona (Angola, middle), and Gicandi (Kenya, bottom).

oral traditions. Some such systems probably predate the introduction of writing to the cultures. Since they differ in function from writing, they often continue to exist side by side with written language. However, they do not form part of the Westernized culture often communicated in the schools. With the spread of formal education, it becomes harder to find people familiar with these graphic systems.

See also Language; Languages; Linguistics, Historical; Linguistics and the Study of Africa; Literacy; Literature; Number Systems; Symbols and Symbolism.

BIBLIOGRAPHY

Berry, Jack. "'The Making of Alphabets' Revisited." In *Advances in the Creation and Revision of Writing Systems*, ed. Joshua A. Fishman. The Hague: Mouton, 1977.

Dalby, David. *Africa and the Written Word*. Paris: Karthala, 1986.

Daniels, Peter T., and William Bright, eds. *The World's Writing Systems*. New York: Oxford University Press, 1996.

Diringer, David. *The Alphabet: A Key to the History of Mankind*. New York: Philosophical Library, 1948.

Kotei, S. I. A. "The West African Autochthonous Alphabets: An Exercise in Comparative Palaeography." In *Advances in the Creation and Revision of Writing Systems*, ed. Joshua A. Fishman. The Hague: Mouton, 1977.

Kubik, Gerard. "African Graphic Systems." *Muntu*, no. 4–5 (1986): 71–135.

Tucker, A. N. "Orthographic Systems and Conventions in Sub-Saharan Africa." In *Current Trends in Linguistics*, Vol. 7: *Linguistics in Sub-Saharan Africa*, ed. Thomas Albert Sebeok. The Hague: Mouton, 1974.

PATRICK R. BENNETT

AFRICAN LANGUAGES IN ARABIC SCRIPTS

Individual words from African languages, especially proper nouns and official titles, have been written in Arabic script almost from the first original literature in the Arabic language in sub-Saharan Africa, or from the first reports about sub-Saharan Africa written in North Africa or the Arabian peninsula.

Research on Arabic script vernacular languages in Africa is rare, and material is waiting to be discovered. No clearly datable literature in Hausa or Swahili has been found earlier than the seventeenth century. Much of the early literature in those languages was ephemeral and not dated, even at its origin. In addition to many uncataloged manuscripts in private hands, many undatable manuscripts are in public archives. Many more must have disappeared over time, as manuscripts written in languages other than Arabic were not considered valuable.

Although African languages could be written in Arabic script almost as soon as their speakers were exposed to Islam, several factors acted to inhibit adoption and adaptation of Arabic letters to African languages. Classical Arabic had important religious and ritual aspects, and international importance. The lack of correspondence between Arabic letters and African phonemes resulted in the necessity of creating additional letters and/or diacritical marks, but did not result in standard Arabic script orthographies of African languages.

In the absence of standard Arabic script orthographies for these languages, the use of additional letters can be idiosyncratic, often unique to an individual author. This does not hamper use of the script, because in the traditional community vernacular manuscripts in Arabic script were intended to circulate within a very small population, or simply be mnemonic devices for an individual author to remember a poem once written. It seems that only the Hausa extra character "tsa" has been codified in the Unicode standard computer encoding system, which is in wide, although far from universal, use in the twenty-first century.

Although the use of Arabic script to write African languages is most commonly identified with the largest sub-Saharan languages, Hausa and Swahili, in West Africa it probably began with others. In West Africa, the Tukolor (who speak a dialect of Fulfulde, the language of the Fulani), the Songhay, and the Kanuri were among the first to Islamize, with various Mande-speaking peoples coming later. These languages have been written in Arabic script for centuries. Other languages such as Somali and Wolof are still commonly written in Arabic script, although the Roman script now dominates. Nubian, Fur, and various other languages were written in Arabic to a greater or lesser

extent. With the Islamization of some Yoruba in the nineteenth century, poetry and other materials were soon written in that language.

Arabic itself was used for important works intended to reach an international audience, including letters and works of philosophy, theology, political science (siyasa), and so forth. Arabic script vernaculars were used primarily for poetry, which can never be adequately translated, and for such purposes as tafsir or Qur'anic exegisis.

The nineteenth-century revival of Islam served to encourage the production of literature in general, including vernacular literature, especially in West Africa. There, an extensive series of jihads began in the seventeenth century, accelerated in the eighteenth century, and became especially strong throughout the nineteenth century.

The tradition of Arabic script literacy continues in the early 2000s, most often privately. Newspapers have published in Arabic script Hausa, but none is known to be publishing. With independence in East Africa, the Swahili written on currency in Kenya and Tanzania was changed to Roman script instead of Arabic, but Arabic script Hausa continues to be the only African language on Nigerian currency notes. Arabic script Wolof continues to be published in Senegal, but generally seems in decline. Even Somalia chose to standardize its orthography in Roman characters rather than Arabic. Nonetheless, notices, billboards, and other public inscriptions written in Arabic script Hausa are not uncommon in Nigeria. African languages written in the Arabic alphabet also play a much more important role in private contexts.

The future of African languages in Arabic script is uncertain. The general tendency around the world is toward Romanization of almost every language. In addition, Arabic script literacy is a monopoly of Muslims, and thus serves to divide populations along religious grounds. Obtaining printing materials in Arabic script is difficult, especially when extra letters are required. Colonial governments standardized the Roman script versions of Swahili and Hausa, the largest languages traditionally written in Roman script, but no one has successfully standardized the Arabic script versions. (The different extra characters used to write them in different dialect areas would make this rather difficult.) Although Arabic script literacy will continue to be important, especially in private contexts, it is unlikely to become more important than Roman script literacy.

See also **Language: Choice in Writing; Literature; Literatures.**

BIBLIOGRAPHY

Allen, J. W. T. *Arabic Script for Students of Swahili.* Supp., *Tanganyika Notes and Records* (1945).

Hiskett, Mervyn. *A History of Hausa Islamic Verse.* London: School of Oriental and African Studies, 1975.

Philips, John. *Spurious Arabic: Hausa and Colonial Nigeria.* Madison: University of Wisconsin African Studies Center, 2000.

JOHN PHILIPS

AFRICAN LANGUAGES IN ROMAN SCRIPTS

In North Africa the Latin script was used in antiquity until the end of the seventh century, as well as Greek and Tifinagh. The second introduction of Roman or Latin script onto the African continent began in Ethiopia and south of the Sahara at the end of the eighteenth century and is still proceeding. It was only from this time on that missionaries went to Africa with the clear intention of teaching the population groups to read and write and introducing a culture of literacy in their own languages.

With regard to a number of African languages the introduction of the Roman script by missionaries caused the replacement of earlier scripts. For some of these languages there is now a competitive coexistence of the old and the new script with alternating "winners." In Ethiopia Ge'ez, Amharic, Tigrinya, and Oromo used to be written in the Ethiopic script. In 1991 Qubee, an adapted form of the Latin script, was officially recognized as a medium to write Oromo. The question which script to choose for the East Cushitic languages Kambatta and Hadiyya is still under discussion. Berber dialects were written first in Tifinagh and later mainly in Arabic. Swahili, Somali, Hausa, Kanuri, Manding, Wolof, and Fulfulde were written in adapted forms of the Arabic script, Ajami. In West Africa Ajami is still in use.

The foundation of the Fourah Bay Institute in Sierra Leone in 1812 marks the beginning of intensive research on African languages and the search of a maximally unified alphabet with Roman letters.

The graphization of African languages and the creation of standardized orthographies in Roman script as a prerequisite for a culture of literacy by Christian missionaries of various congregations constitutes the earliest language planning activities in Africa exerted by Europeans.

Aiming at unified systems of orthography, they had to cooperate with each other and also with the colonial administrations on an international level. Orthographical questions were discussed on three international conferences on education that convened in Uganda (1918), the Belgian Congo (1924), Rejaf/Sudan (1928), and Bamako (1966).

A major problem was to find an orthography that could be typed on standard typewriters as provided by the former mother countries and which at the same time reflected the linguistic structures of the languages. For a number of languages, for example Bambara and Sango, the search for a better orthography led to a series of modifications of given spelling systems.

NEW SCRIPTS

For a number of languages individual speakers themselves designed completely new scripts that are considered more appropriate than Roman script. For other languages new scripts were designed, because Roman script had not been provided.

The majority of the new scripts are syllabaries, but there are also two alphabets. Most of the autochthonous scripts were designed in Liberia, Sierra Leone, Guinea, and Cameroon, The most recent script was developed in the Democratic Republic of the Congo. Many of the modern African scripts suffered at the hands of colonial officials who did not support their usage or who took less subtle means to repress them. None of the new scripts had a chance to win recognition as a general medium of writing against the omnipresent Roman script.

1. The earliest of the new scripts, the Vai (Mande/Liberia) syllabary was designed by Dualu Bukele of Jondu in the 1820s. It is still used in the early twenty-first century.

2. The Bassa (Kru/Liberia) alphabet was developed in the late 1800s by Flo Darvin Lewis. Unlike Vai it is a phonemic alphabet, not a syllabary.

3. The Mende (Mande) script, which is syllabic, was created in 1921 by Mohammed Turay from Sierra Leone.

4. The Kpelle (Mande) syllabary was invented during the 1930s by Chief Gbili of Sanoyea, Liberia.

5. The Loma syllabary came into being during the 1930s by Wido Zobo of Boneketa, Liberia.

6. The most recent of modern scripts in West Africa is N'ko: It was created in 1949 by Sulemana Kante (Guinea). The script is popular in Guinea and Côte d'Ivoire, with smaller user communities in southern Mali.

7. Sultan Ibraham Njoya created an alphabet called Shumum for the Bamum language (Mbam-Nkam), around 1896.

8. In 1960, Asane Faye, president of the African Languages Teachers Movement created the Wolof alphabet.

9. In the early twentieth century the Bagam people of Cameroon employed a pre-modern alphabet for record keeping, correspondence, and farming calendars.

10. The Osmanya script, called *far Soomaali* (Somali writing) or *Cismaanya* in Somali, was devised in 1920–1922 by Cismaan Yuusuf Keenadiid to represent the Somali language. In the early twenty-first century, the orthography is only used symbolically by the Somali Youth Movement (SYL).

11. Mandombe, was designed in 1978 in RD Congo by Wabeladio Payi as a script for Kikongo, Lingala

INTERNET

The use of African languages on the Web increases albeit slowly. The majority of Web pages in African languages are edited by Christian missionary institutions. Swahili, Somali, Amharic, and Oromo are among the few languages intensively used on the Web by the speakers themselves. They provided above all political and religious (Islamic) information and poetry. Swahili is the only African language to be listed in position 40 in rankings of languages on the Web.

The use of African languages on the Internet largely reflects their use in the print media. Certain text-genres of print media cannot be found online or in a similar form, while others—in particular information by broadcasting stations and interactive communications as fora—are not easily available in print. In the 2000s international conferences dealing with problems relating to the production of literacy and knowledge in Africa discuss the design and application of special fonts for the production of digital texts rather than harmonization of orthographies.

See also **Communications: Electronics; Knowledge; Language: Choice in Writing; Literacy; Media.**

BIBLIOGRAPHY

Fishman, Joshua A. "Ethnocultural Issues in the Creation, Substitution, and Revision of Writing Systems." In *The Social Construction of Written Communication*, ed. Bennett A. Rafoth and Donald L. Rubin. Norwood, NJ: Ablex, 1988.

Haarmann, Harald. *Universalgeschichte der Schrift*. Frankfurt and New York: Campus Verlag, 2002.

Hutchinson, John P. "African Language Literature as a Weapon against African Language Marginalization." In *Selected Proceedings of the 35th Annual Conference on African Linguistics*, ed. John Mugane et al. Somerville, MA: Cascadilla Proceedings Project, 2006.

HELMA PASCH

EGYPTIAN

Ancient Egyptian, a branch of the Afro-Asiatic (Hamito-Semitic) language family, first appeared in written form c. 3200 BCE with the invention of the hieroglyphic script. The Egyptian hieroglyphic writing system employed both phonetic and ideographic pictographs, as well as determinative signs that marked a word's semantic class. Each phonographic sign represented one to three consonants; vowels were not overtly represented. Although more than 6,000 different hieroglyphs are known from inscriptions of the Greco-Roman period (323 BCE–300 CE), about 1,000 signs appeared frequently in earlier, pharaonic texts. Hieroglyphs were used predominantly for inscriptions on stone monuments and other formal contexts, whereas hieratic, a cursive adaptation of hieroglyphs, was suited for writing in ink on papyrus and other media; most literary texts, letters, administrative documents, and medical treatises were written in hieratic.

Around 2000 BCE, scribes attached to expeditions in Egypt's desert hinterlands developed hybrid signs adapted from hieroglyphs and hieratic for use in rock inscriptions; these signs provided the letters for the first alphabet, developed to write foreign (specifically Semitic) words and names. During the eighth century BCE, two additional cursive Egyptian scripts evolved: abnormal hieratic (in Upper Egypt) and demotic (in Lower Egypt). Demotic replaced hieratic for most documents and survived into the fifth century CE (hieratic survived as a priestly script, hence the Greek designation of the script). The Greek alphabet and five additional letters derived from demotic were used to write the Egyptian language from the late third century CE; originally employed to represent the vowel sounds in magical texts, the alphabetic script known as Coptic became the predominant writing system for the Egyptian language in Christian Egypt.

Developments in grammatical structures, vocabulary, and orthography allow for the division of the Egyptian language into five stages: Old Egyptian (c. 3000–2100 BCE), Middle Egyptian (c. 2100 BCE– 300 CE), Late Egyptian (c. 1570–715 BCE), Demotic (c. 715 BCE–470 CE), and Coptic (c. 300–1500 CE). Middle Egyptian was considered the classical form of the language and remained in use for elevated textual genres until the death of the hieroglyphic script. From the middle of the New Kingdom (c. 1350 BCE) onward, the classical Middle Egyptian language could be combined with later phases of the language to distinguish textual registers. The recognized stages of the Egyptian language may have concealed different dialects, not discernable prior to Coptic. Estimations of literacy rates in ancient Egypt range from one to ten percent, with the latter number including semiliterate status. Scribes initially learned the hieratic script, and knowledge of hieroglyphs was predominantly restricted to priests and high officials.

The ancient Egyptian word for hieroglyphic writing is *medu-netcher*, divine words, and the system, with its capacity for visual puns and cryptographic usages, is an essential aspect of Egyptian religious expression; as such, the hieroglyphic script was not finally abandoned until the fourth century CE and the adoption of Christianity in the Nile Valley. The visual nature of the hieroglyphic script facilitated a unity of artistic expression and writing, and the title scribe could encompass drawing and painting.

See also **Egypt, Early; Literacy.**

BIBLIOGRAPHY

Loprieno, Antonio. *Ancient Egyptian, A Linguistic Introduction.* Cambridge, U.K.: Cambridge University Press, 1995.

Parkinson, Richard. *Cracking Codes, The Rosetta Stone and Decipherment.* Berkeley: University of California Press, 1999.

COLLEEN MANASSA

ETHIOPIC

Ge'ez (also rendered with orthographic variants Giiz, Geez, and Gəʿəz) is the ancient classical language of Ethiopia and Eritrea. As a member of the south Semitic language group, Ge'ez is closely related to some of the major modern languages of the horn of Africa, namely Amharic, Tigrinya, and Tigre, and it has had an enormous influence on the culture and literature of the region for centuries. In this regard, the significance of Ge'ez compares with that of Greek and Latin in Europe, as the scholar Marvin L. Bender and colleagues have attested: "The effect of Giiz on the modern Ethiopian languages has been considerable. Just as modern European languages have borrowed heavily from Latin and Greek, the classical languages of Europe, Amharic and Tigrinya draw on lexical sources" (Bender et al. 1976, 100).

The Ge'ez alphabet is traditionally known as the *abugida*, but it is also increasingly referred to as *fidel.* It was devised in the early first millennium, and initially consisted of consonantal characters only, but was gradually perfected to become the first Semitic script to include vowels. One of the earliest Ge'ez inscriptions, written in unvocalized characters, is dated to the fifth century, and is found on the *Belew Kelew* monument of the ancient city of Metera, in Eritrea. Despite the damage by natural and humanmade disasters, the writing on the *Belew Kelew* has still remained intact. As the lines of the inscription reproduced below suggest, the text is, presumably, a tribute by a son named Agäzä to his forefathers for their victory over other forces.

ዘሐወለተ/ ዘአገበረ/
አገዘ/ለአበወህ/ወሰ
ሐበ/መሐዘተ/አወዐ/
አለፈነ/ወአበለነ/

The Ge'ez alphabet has twenty-six consonants and seven vowels. In this writing system, each regular, consonant character assumes seven different shapes. The basic shape of a character represents a *Consonant + ä* sound, which is then modified consistently to form syllables with the other vowel sounds: *u, i, a, e, ə, o.* In its complete form, the Ge'ez alphabet consists of 202 signs. The alphabet has also its own numerals. Unlike other Semitic languages such as Arabic and Hebrew, Ge'ez is written from left to right. Because the Ge'ez alphabet is used, with minor modifications, to write the other (south Semitic) languages of Ethiopia and Eritrea, especially Tigrinya, Amharic, and Tigre, these languages are similarly written in the same direction, from "left to right."

Ge'ez was brought to northern Ethiopia and Eritrea by Arabian immigrants who had crossed over the Red Sea to settle in the coastal areas of present day Eritrea, during the first millennium BCE. With the rise of the Axumite empire in the fourth through eleventh centuries, and the adoption and subsequent flourishing of Christianity in the fourth century, Ge'ez eventually became the language of the court, religion, literature, and other expressions of high culture. After the fall of Axum in the tenth century, Ge'ez lost its importance and died out as a spoken language.

However, Ge'ez retained its significance up till the present day as the liturgical language of the Tewahedo Orthodox Churches of Ethiopia and Eritrea, and was the sole written language of Ethiopia until the nineteenth century. The extant writings in Ge'ez are important for understanding the history and culture of the peoples of the area, and vital for scientific research on the region. They can be grouped into two categories: (1) translations of the Bible, the apochryphical books, and other religious works from Greek, Arabic, and other languages; and (2) original works, which include historical narratives, legal papers, ecclesiastical texts, and the *Qene* (traditional Ethiopian poetry), but also medical and mathematical documents.

See also **Ethiopia and Vicinity, History of (600 to 1600 CE); Ethiopia, Modern; Literatures in African Languages: Ethiopic.**

BIBLIOGRAPHY

Bender, Marvin Lionel, et al. *Language in Ethiopia.* New York: Oxford University Press, 1976.

Daniels, P. "Scripts of Semitic Languages." In *The Semitic Languages*, ed. Robert Hetzron. London and New York: Routledge, 1997.

Dillmann, August. *Ethiopic Grammar* [1857], trans. James Critchton. London: Williams & Norgate, [1907].

Ferenc, A. "Writing and Literature in Classical Ethiopic (Giiz)." In *Literatures in African Languages*, ed. B. W. Andrzejewski et al. Cambridge, U.K.: Cambridge University Press, 1985.

Ghebre-Iyesus, I.

ፈደል ናይ ደብተራ ታሪኻዊ ምህዞን ብልሓትን.

Asmara: Sabur, 2002.

Gragg, G. "Ge'ez (Ethiopic)." In *The Semitic Languages*, ed. Robert Hetzron. London and New York: Routledge, 1997.

Moges, A. "Geez and Amharic Study without Qene Is Incomplete." In *Proccedings of the Third International Conference of Ethiopian Studies*, Vol. 2. Addis Ababa: Institute of Ethiopian Studies, Haile Selassie I University, 1970.

Negash, Ghirmai. *A History of Tigrinya Literature in Eritrea: The Oral and the Written 1890–1991.* Leiden: CNWS Publications, Leiden University, 1999.

Ullendorff. Edward. *The Semitic Languages of Ethiopia.* London: Taylor's (Foreign) Press, 1955.

Weninger, Stefan. *Gəʿəz (Classical Ethiopic).* München-Newcastle: Lincom Europa, 1993.

GHIRMAI NEGASH

YAMOUSSOUKRO. Yamoussoukro, the village of late president Félix Houphouët-Boigny, was named the capital city of Côte d'Ivoire in 1983. It contains the largest Christian church in the world, the Basilica of Our Lady of Peace. Two questions cannot be ignored in any study of Yamoussoukro: (1) Why was the village the only choice for the capital of the country and what feasibility studies were done to select the village as the ideal site for locating the country's central seat of government?; and (2) Why did the Basilica of Our Lady of Peace have to be so large and extravagant and were the citizens of the country consulted before the edifice was constructed?

These questions will continue to be discussed since the emerging consensus among scholars seems to be that the village of Yamoussoukro was chosen and suddenly transformed into the second largest town in the country by fiat. More important, it reveals how most postcolonial independent African elite exploited their positions in the government in order to impose their will on the body polity of their respective countries and on their citizens. Planning in Yamoussoukro began as early as 1968 by the Tunisian-born architect, Olivier-Clément Cacoub, who was also the personal architect of the late Tunisian strongman, President Habib Bourguiba. Both Bourguiba and Houphouët-Boigny were good friends; the Tunisian president also undertook massive planning in his home village in Tunisia. The infrastructure—presidential palaces, the party headquarters, universities and polytechnic, and hotels and ministerial buildings—in the town of Yamoussoukro remains idle since the country is still effectively governed from Abidjan, the commercial hub of the nation.

See also **Abidjan; Côte d'Ivoire; Houphouët-Boigny, Félix.**

BIBLIOGRAPHY

The Basilica of Our Lady of Peace. Yamoussoukro, Cote d'Ivoire, 1988.

Cheynier, Pierre. *Yamoussoukro: Coeur de Côte d'Ivoire.* Abidjan: Fraternite-Hebdomadaire, 1978.

Elleh, Nnamdi. *Architecture and Power.* Westport, CT: Praeger, 2002.

NNAMDI ELLEH

YAOUNDÉ. The town of Yaoundé was founded in 1888 by the German explorer Georg August Zenker (1855–1922), who led a scientific exploration into the interior of the nascent colony of Kamerun, following initial occupation of the coast. Located in Ewondo territory, Yaoundé is known locally as Ngolla, a name reflecting the hilly nature of the terrain. A dense forest and difficult terrain separate the region from the coastal region. In 1909, the Germans located their administrative headquarters in Yaoundé, giving impetus to the town's expansion. The region was subsequently controlled by the French until Cameroon's independence in 1960.

Cameroon's second largest city, and the federal capital since 1961, Yaoundé became seat of the united republic in 1972. The city's importance has been enhanced by the establishment of the University of Yaoundé. As of 2004, the city's population was about 900,000, up more than 200,000 since the early 1990s. Extensive rail and road systems link Yaoundé to Douala (the nation's largest city and principal port) and to other important regional cities in the north. Yaoundé's industrial sector is small, but sugar refining, plywood manufacturing, breweries, and a quarry contribute to the provincial economy.

See also **Cameroon; Forestry.**

BIBLIOGRAPHY

d'Azevedo, Mario, ed. *Cameroon and Chad in Historical and Contemporary Perspectives.* Lewiston, Maine: E. Mellen Press, 1988.

Steel, William F. "Development of the Urban Artisanal Sector in Ghana and Cameroun," *Journal of Modern African Studies* 17, no. 2 (1979): 271–284.

KATHERINE CALDERA

YOUTH

This entry includes the following articles:

OVERVIEW

Youth in Africa has attracted considerable attention from across the disciplines most likely because the socially and culturally constructed population category to which the term youth refers is assuming crucial salience in the early twenty-first century. The special significance of youth has to do with demographic and socioeconomic changes that have turned young people into a disproportionately large segment of the overall population. What is more, Africa is becoming increasingly urban in terms of demographic projections. The massing of young people in Africa's rapidly growing cities places pressures on already limited employment and housing markets, straining fragile infrastructures,

and making public health issues, among them HIV/AIDS, into everyday concerns. The interval between childhood and the assumption of adult roles has increased in many African countries, prolonging the youth stage over many years. Shaping the experiences of young people as both actors and subjects, these processes challenge long-established hierarchical relations between the sexes and the generations, giving new meanings to Africa's youth in the twenty-first century. Because these processes take place in the context of globalization, youth experiences are influenced by complex dynamics, including new consumption desires, individual aspirations, and local appropriations of the international development language of rights and claims.

THE NOTION OF YOUTH

The notion of youth as a distinct stage between childhood and adulthood was not part of precolonial social organization in African societies but emerged in the wake of socioeconomic and political changes during the colonial period and independence through wage labor, formal schooling, urbanization, and family change. In a very general sense, youth are considered to be dependent, subject to hierarchical and authoritarian gender- and generation-based relationships with parents, guardians, and the larger society.

In precolonial Africa, age or generational categories served social organizational purposes and mediated access to power. Male age groups were characteristic of many East and southern African societies, and several West African societies had both male and female age groups. Such age groups were typically established around initiation, and age distinctions represented the cultural and social identity of specific age cohorts. Colonial recruitment for labor on farms, in mines, and in households pushed and pulled many young men away from their villages, complicating the succession of age groups as did attendance at school for both sexes both then and now. Young women's and men's participation in liberation wars and civil wars drew them away from their home societies voluntarily or by force as combatants and auxiliaries in political upheavals. Some observers suggest that labor migration, work, and war assume similar functions as age cohorts in the socialization of youth.

Long-standing cleavages between juniors and seniors that affected dependent labor practices

Young auto mechanics working on a reconditioned taxi. Not finding formal employment, young people are busy creating their livelihoods. Lusaka, 2004. PHOTOGRAPH BY KAREN TRANBERG HANSEN

through pawning and domestic slavery also shaped the age distribution of slaves exported to the Americas and the Islamic world across the Sahara, the Red Sea, and the Indian Ocean. Generational hierarchies play out in the early 2000s in the practice of fostering young children whose apprenticeship often amounts to unpaid labor rather than socialization. International organizations concerned with forced labor and trafficking have taken note of widespread household practices across the African continent where young persons of both sexes but especially girls perform unremunerated labor in return for their upkeep, of poor parents and guardians selling young persons' labor for work on plantations, fields, and mines, and of young women's involuntary work as prostitutes in Europe.

Although chronological age and generational categories are widespread in Africa, they are not always synchronized. Youth as a stage between childhood and adulthood is not a universally recognized category but a sociocultural construct, understood in diverse ways that vary by class, gender, and region, depending on time and place. In colonial settler Africa, men who performed domestic work in private households were commonly called "boys" regardless

of their chronological age. Some youth organizations and youth wings of ruling parties stretched the youth category well into their members' thirties or forties. Pressed on by external agencies today, many African countries have enacted national youth policies that follow the United Nations General Assembly's definition of youth (from the 1995 World Program of Action for Youth) as the age period between fifteen and twenty-four.

Socially and culturally constructed, youth is a relational notion, the meaning of which depends on context. Youth captures not only individual identities relative to others but also group experiences. These constructions are significantly gendered and shaped by class. In popular views in much of Africa, young people are typically considered to be male from fifteen to thirty or even thirty-five years of age. While some girls may experience youth only as a brief period from the onset of puberty to marriage and motherhood, many young urban women remain youth much longer, even if they bear children outside of marriage.

CONTEMPORARY DYNAMICS

Most scholarship on young people published since the 1980s has privileged publicly visible activities

Fabricating dreams. Charity at work on the sewing machine in a tailoring course. Because young women have fewer work options than young men, they view tailoring as an economic avenue they can pursue independently. Lusaka, 2001. PHOTOGRAPH BY KAREN TRANBERG HANSEN

and interaction from war and civil strife, to religion, and popular culture. Research on sexuality is more concerned with AIDS prevention than with young people's everyday life in the context of dramatic demographic shifts and ongoing socioeconomic and political transformations across the continent.

War and Political Upheaval.

In spite of numerous transitions to multiparty rule since the early 1990s, dominant parties in many African countries continue to exert control of state resources, giving rise to the "big man" syndrome, patronage, and personalized politics. In effect, the senior generation of African politicians has not been keen to retire. While this situation leaves youth with very few openings in formal party politics, they are active in

other ways. Almost emblematic of scholarship in Africa is a particular category of young people: the young soldiers, paramilitary, rebels, counterinsurgents from, for example, Sierra Leone and Liberia; and the African National Congress (ANC) youth, the *Inkata* militia, township gangs in South Africa, "area boys" in Nigeria, and the youth groups, and organizations who helped propel political shifts in Senegal and Mali. Some of these young people have been described as a "lost generation," who because of political and economic upheaval did or did not complete their education, are marginalized politically and economically, and have no wherewithal to set up independent households. Because their opportunities are circumscribed, they make do in a variety of ways, some of them illicit, and society tends to see them as a problem. Both of these groups are politicized but in different ways: first, as organized political movements aspiring to national power positions, and second, as what scholars working on Sierra Leone have termed "lumpen youth" (or subaltern youth) who are marginalized. They have been characterized by the normative term "New Barbarism" (Richards 1996) as perpetrators, driven by a disposition toward violence and greed without much attention to context.

Beyond the platforms of formal party politics are other spaces in which young people work to shape the political arena. Nongovernmental organizations (NGO) constitute a space for the promotion of a democratic political culture that with external funding seeks to strengthen local political capacity building, improve accountability, transparency, and democratic leadership. The NGO scene has created new career trajectories in political entrepreneurs for well-educated youth that the civil service and the formal employment sector cannot supply. This donor-facilitated professionalization with its access to skills (IT) and resources (networks) is an important angle of globalization.

Religion.

Both Islam and Christianity have contributed toward the creation of politicized space for young people because religious belief shapes both individual and group behavior. The nineteenth-century *jihad* in northern Nigeria, for example, created conditions that made it possible for a youth culture centering on Islamic studies to reduce the dominant influence of the older generation. In the

Young men hanging out in Solwezi, the provincial headquarters of Zambia's Northwestern Province. Out of school, they are looking for ways to establish themselves, mostly working in the informal economy. PHOTOGRAPH BY KAREN TRANBERG HANSEN

early 2000s the tradition of radical Islam among youth has reemerged as fundamentalism in a manner that clearly divides youth from elders in many places. Historically, the Christian church and its provision of education facilitated upward mobility, first for young men, then young women. The church was instrumental in shaping new notions of masculinity, femininity, and family/household structures that at times conflicted with normative cultural notions about gender and power, introducing tensions into relations between women and men as well as between students and their parents/ guardians.

Populist Islam and Pentecostal Christianity have attracted considerable media and scholarly attention as the single most important cultural response to

urban impoverishment and lack of opportunity resulting from World Bank– and International Monetary Fund–induced structural reforms and neoliberal market practices of the late twentieth century. To be sure, Islam and Christian churches of many denominations attract young people because of the appeal of their religious belief and because they introduce new notions of self-worth, status, and wealth. But statements about the rapid proliferation of Pentecostalism must be tempered with the recognition that it is religion in general that is growing, including Islam, and that religion, including many Christian denominations not only Pentecostals, is attracting growing numbers of adherents.

Regardless of specific denomination, all these churches are authoritative. They stress morality, responsibility, discipline, and hard work. Their organization is hierarchical and they tend to be male dominated. In most churches, women are auxiliaries except at the level of lay involvement and outreach. The Christian blueprint for family living stresses marriage as a precursor for sex and child bearing and puts husbands in charge of households as chief provider for the needs of wife and children. Comprising a nostalgic vision of how people ought to live, this blueprint is significantly at odds with the contemporary reality in the time of HIV/AIDS, namely a growing incidence of female-headed households, households headed by siblings, and households headed by children.

Late-twentieth-century scholarship on Pentecostal churches has showcased the break they introduce between their followers' preoccupation with "traditional" and "modern" ways of living. This rupture is held to enable young Pentecostal adherents to cast away witchcraft beliefs, question the authority of elders, and position themselves on an upwardly mobile trajectory. While witchcraft and demons may not play major roles in this break everywhere, many young people speak of their lives before and after they acquired faith in the Holy Spirit, constructing the break in terms of sin. Salvation puts these young believers in charge of their own lives, providing skills and strategies, opening a pathway for individual endeavors, a space for youth agency at a specific life stage to fashion a different trajectory toward adulthood. In sum, by offering a strategy for urban living, religious belief matters, having a special appeal to young people in their formative years.

Boys listening to boombox. Sunday in a rural area of Zambia, 2004. The radio brings them in touch with a global world, even if they live in remote areas. PHOTOGRAPH BY KAREN TRANBERG HANSEN

Popular Culture.   Different genres of popular culture have opened social, cultural, and economic space for young people to express their concerns and desires for better lives. Through consumption, especially fashion, sports, music, including songs, performance and dance, television and video, youth engage actively with local and global influences, including inspirations from across the African continent and India, as is evident in the popularity of Nigerian videos and Indian movies. Cable television and international programs like Cable News Network (CNN) and British Broadcasting Company (BBC) introduce young urban Africans to a global scene that only a few can expect to enter. Yet television's "Big Brother" production in South Africa, involving young people from across the continent, and M-net's search in different countries for women with "the face of Africa" put Africa squarely on the global map in terms of youth desires. Performance, in short, has interesting democratic properties and potentialities.

The music scene, for one, is extraordinarily vibrant in many African countries, creating not only economic openings and entrepreneurship for performers, writers, and composers but also good times for those who attend. Local, regional (Congolese, South African, Nigerian), and global styles (reggae, hip-hop, rap, and gospel) are appropriated, transformed, and turned into unique local sounds. "Afro-pop" is one of the continent's chief cultural exports, appealing to Africans in the diaspora and music lovers everywhere. At home in Africa, NGOs recruit well-known artists as ambassadors of public issues for live performances around election time. Networks of HIV/AIDS/ NGOs frequently hire musicians for special events, for example on World AIDS day. Beyond such organized events and above all, radio makes music available to all, and the music stations are eagerly listened to in cities and the countryside.

Popular music is intertwined with experiences of everyday life in ways that resonate with their time and place. The treacherous trajectory toward adulthood in the time of AIDS is an important theme in recent popular music with some lyrics admonishing young people against the dangers of indulgence, including both sex and consumption. Because of the economic pressures on everyday life and the challenges about the future, young women know that money and transactional sex can jeopardize their wish to improve their livelihoods. While in an ideal world the desire for the latest fashions and sexual relationships pertains to two distinct areas, in real life they easily get mixed up. The music scene tells young people to get on with their lives for the state is not going to help them out. This parallels the tenor of the political democracy project as well as the Pentecostal message, conveying an individualized politics of self-promotion that may or may not lessen the hierarchical hold of formal party politics and the institutional structures that underpin it.

CONCLUSION

The privileging of topics concerned with violence and political upheaval in research on African youth construes a partial understanding of today's youth problematic, hiding the more mundane dimensions and continuity of everyday life. Political trouble, Islamic and Christian religious practices, music and movies may engage parts of young people's lives on a temporary basis but they do not determine the entire unfolding of their trajectory toward adulthood. The steps toward successful adulthood depend also on the state and local institutional structures, external development support and economic revitalization, and above all on personal agency at a time when it is social adulthood rather than youth that may elude many young Africans.

See also **Disease: HIV/AIDS, Social and Political Aspects; Family; Initiation; International Monetary Fund; Labor: Child; Music, Modern Popular; Nongovernmental Organizations; Slave Trades; Slavery and Servile Institutions; Warfare: Civil Wars; Witchcraft; World Bank.**

BIBLIOGRAPHY

Baxter, Paul T. W., and Uri Almagor, eds. *Age, Generation and Time: Some Features of East African Age Organizations.* New York: St. Martin's Press, 1978.

Christiansen, Catrine; Mats Utas; and Henrik E. Vigh; eds. *Navigating Youth, Generating Adulthood: Social Becoming in an African Context.* Uppsala: Nordic Africa Institute, 2006.

Diouf, Mamadou. "Engaging Postcolonial Cultures: African Youth and Public Space." *African Studies Review* 46(2):1–12, 2003.

Honwana, Alcinda, and Filip de Boeck, eds. *Makers and Breakers: Children and Youth in Postcolonial Africa.* London: James Currey, 2005.

Last, Murray. "The Power of Youth: Youth of Power: Notes on the Religions of the Young in Northern Nigeria." In *Les jeunes en Afriques: La politique et la ville,* ed. Helene d'Almeida-Topor, O. Georg, Catherine Coquery-Vidrovitch, and F. Guitart. Paris: L'Harmattan, 1992.

Meyer, Birgit. *Translating the Devil: Religion and Modernity among the Ewe in Ghana.* Trenton, NJ: Africa World Press, 1999.

Richards, Paul. *Fighting for the Rain Forest: War, Youth and Resources in Sierra Leone.* Portsmouth, NH: Heinemann, 1996.

Simpson, Anthony. *"Half-London" in Zambia: Contested Identities in a Catholic Mission School.* Edinburgh: Edinburgh University Press, 2003.

Wilson, Monica. *Good Company: A Study of Nyakuysa Age Villages.* Boston: Beacon Press, 1951.

KAREN TRANBERG HANSEN

RURAL

The classic ethnographies represent youth as a biologically and temporally circumscribed period ritually marked as a phase in a person's life that presages the onset of full manhood or womanhood—in both the biological and legal/social senses. Many of these early studies focus upon eastern and southern African societies, the marked rites of passage and age-grades of which made a clear transition from one status to another relatively easy to observe and describe. E. E. Evans-Pritchard's studies of the Nuer of Sudan accordingly describe the time of youth as an idyllic period of free and easy associations between the sexes, but with marriage nonetheless "the purpose implicit in every romance" (1951, 56). In contrast to young women, whose status moves gradually from childhood to marriage without any sudden transformation, "the boy jumps at initiation from the grade of boyhood to the grade of manhood" (51). In Evans-Pritchard's analysis, the age-set system:

> segments the male population of a tribe into stratified groups which stand in a definite relationship to one-another and it cuts across territorial divisions, giving identity of status where there is political disparity and differentiating status where there is political identity (1974, 260).

Audrey Richards was able to balance the focus on men of such studies with her 1956 study of a women's initiation ceremony among the Bemba of Zambia. When it was published, there were few accounts of girls' initiation, few of single rites, and fewer still of women's initiation written on the basis of data gathered from female informants. The main body of the work is devoted to a detailed description of the twenty-three days of the *chisungu* rite of female initiation. The analysis attempts to move beyond informants' statements of the purpose of the rite to tentative psychoanalytic interpretations. This is a study carried out before the onset of feminist anthropology, however, and its analysis is uncritically limited to an elder's if not a man's point of view: In the rites, Richards argued, "The girl's proper conduct is expressed in the phrase 'be submissive, or make yourself soft and pliant before your elders'" (1982, 149).

In the conclusion to *Chisungu*, Richards mentioned Arnold Van Gennep's 1908 work *Les rites de passage*, but it was Victor Turner who would bring widespread recognition to the latter's model of social transformation by applying it to the initiation ceremonies of the Ndembu of the northwestern Zambia. In his 1967 work on *mukanda*, the boy's circumcision ceremony, Turner divided the rite into Van Gennep's three classic phases of *separation*, *transition* (or *limen*), and *incorporation*. In keeping with the liminal symbolism of the transitional phase, he saw the day of circumcision itself as "a complete reversal of the natural order... [in which] the status hierarchy of secular society is temporarily in abeyance" (1967, 192–193). The novices are accordingly represented as dead or dying, symbolic acts of homosexuality are engaged in, and the young initiates are permitted to heap insults upon the circumcisers. Distinguishing his approach from Max Gluckman's (1963), Turner explicitly warned against seeing this as a "rite of rebellion." Rather, he argued, it is predominantly a repressive ritual that brings together opposing factions, plays down conflicts, and restores the equilibrium that was threatened by the ambiguous status of pubescent boys in the society.

In his 1968 monograph on Ndembu religion, Turner turned his attention to *Nkang'a*, the Ndembu female initiation rite. In his analysis, Turner once again interpreted the three phases of the rite—*kwing'ija* or "causing to enter," *kunkunka* or seclusion in a grass hut, and *kwidisha* or "bringing out"—in terms of Van Genneps' tripartite model of rites of passage. The Ndembu are part of a matrilineal society that nevertheless practices virilocal marriage, and Turner saw in this the source of a structural contradiction at the heart of Ndembu social life. In his analysis, female initiation served

not only to transform girls into women, but further to overcome this contradiction. Once again, he warned against interpreting this women's rite in terms of Gluckman's model of rituals of rebellion, arguing that while the rite initially joins women together against men in the liminal phase, it reunites men and women together as joint producers of children in the final phase of incorporation or reaggregation. According to Turner, the rite dramatizes conflicts in the society—between girls and women, women and men—but only in order to overcome these and to restore an overarching "solidarity of the widest effective social group, of the whole Ndembu people" (1968, 268).

YOUTH AND SLAVERY

While early studies of complex age-grade systems and initiation ceremonies of eastern and southern Africa emphasized the effectiveness with which children could be unambiguously transformed into adults in one fell swoop, later studies of West and Central African societies have tended to highlight the systemic failures of many polities and social systems to effectively manage the transition of young men and women into manhood and womanhood, respectively. One of the explanations for the lack of classic studies of initiation in West and Central Africa is quite simply, as G. I. Jones pointed out in his 1962 article on age-grades among the Ibo of Eastern Nigeria, that many of them had no clear-cut rites of passage, but rather a protracted period of transition punctuated by several relatively minor rites and transactions. Another reason, however, clearly had to do with the Atlantic system of slavery. While studies such as those of Jones (1962) and Simon Ottenberg (1971, 1989) on the Ibo therefore parallel those from eastern and southern Africa in focusing on the functional aspects of age-grade systems, studies that focus on the impact of slavery in the region highlight the problems facing youth as an historically marginalized and oppressed group, and highlight the struggles, resistance, and periodic revolts of the young rather than their integration into society.

The concepts of rights in persons among the peoples of the Atlantic Coast of Africa and its hinterland were such that elders had rights over the children and youths in their lineages and could dispose of them according to the best interests of the lineage as a whole, including pawning and selling them. As the transatlantic slave trade intensified, this led to a gradual inversion of the terms of the category, so that it was no longer simply youths who were sold, but rather those sold who were youths. In other words, youth came to refer to a position in a social hierarchy more than it did to biological age. To be "a youth" signified disempowerment within the lineage hierarchy first and foremost; as a marker of servility it was therefore a moveable feast into which not only the young but biologically mature adults could also be subsumed.

THE IMPACT OF COLONIALISM

If youth were an oppressed and exploited category in the precolonial era, the advent of colonial rule was very much a double-edged sword for them: on the one hand, the introduction of forced labor often reproduced the conditions of slavery from which colonial authorities claimed to be emancipating the young and the dispossessed. In some cases, such as among the Ibo, it even had a deleterious effect on the age-grade system; in other cases, it led to the depopulation of entire areas, such as the Cameroon Grassfields—a well-known slaving ground that was never seriously threatened by depopulation until it was turned into a source of colonial labor for the Germans and then the British.

On the other hand, however, the colonial era has been said to have been the golden age of youth, even the inception of this category as a valued sector of society (which would explain why many African languages have no indigenous term for youth, or only derogatory ones). While the early colonial period was marked by the unrestricted use of forced labor, salaried labor later became the norm, and young men were thus able for the first time to find alternative avenues to wealth that did not depend upon servitude to one's elders. Some did so as plantation laborers and porters, while those who became literate moved to the cities to work for colonial administrations, forming a new generation of urban youth that would later become politically influential (see Martin 1995 for Brazzaville).

At the local level, chiefs and traditional authorities (some of them admittedly invented by the colonial authorities) still wielded power, but young people were able to use the literacy afforded by missionary education to enter into the lower echelons of colonial administration. For the elites and elders who had hitherto enjoyed a monopoly on political power, this came as a blow. As Jean-Francois Bayart put it, "the era of the Whites became the era of insolence, when 'children,' 'their mouths on fire,' came out of their silence" (1989, 151). However, only a minority of the emerging youth of Africa became overnight success stories. The great majority of young people who sought entry to the new order were not granted it and the postcolonial condition has been overarchingly described in terms of a crisis of youth. These young unemployed were deeply frustrated by the false promise of emancipation represented by mission-school educations that too often led to nothing. Since the 1990s economic crisis—compounded by International Monetary Fund and World Bank—imposed Structural Adjustment Plans and the 50 percent devaluation of the Franc CFA in 1994—cuts in the public sector have all combined to make school and university degrees otiose and the young rural population overeducated and underemployed. Overall, Africa's social cadets—most often bachelors without the wealth to marry and become "men"—began a huge but largely fruitless exodus from the rural areas to the cities that continues into the 2000s, increasingly blurring the distinction between rural and urban youth.

And while the continent's young men and women found it difficult to accede to power as represented by the modern state, they were also still marginalized in the gerontocracies that controlled so much of rural life. Dissatisfaction was manifest in millenarian movements and revolts, petty crime, and attacks against traditional elders. Some have argued that these revolts were driven primarily by the desire of the young to replace elders rather than to obliterate eldership, but this should not be taken to mean that these movements had no political rationale. In the colonial and the postcolonial eras, youth thus became a problem for both sets of authorities: a negative category that referred neither to children nor to adults. Not only for governmental and traditional authorities, but for many international policy-making bodies and academics, the term "youth" has come to denote an ambiguous category in which the liminality of an age-set uneasily poised between childhood and adulthood is juxtaposed with an ambivalent model that combines images of helplessness, dependency, and innocence on the one hand with images of waywardness, criminality, and radicalism on the other. As a result, contemporary studies of youth are "too often studies of deviance or of problems needing programmatic intervention" (Durham 2000, 116) and youth remains a shifting term reserved for those of all ages deemed a threat to the established order of political "elders."

YOUNG PEOPLE'S SEARCH FOR INFLUENCE IN THE POSTCOLONY

Young people in some parts of Africa have responded to the social and economic violence of their marginalization with political violence, taking up arms against their local and national governments or simply with the aim of plunder as a means of wealth accumulation. Despite emphasis on the more dramatic and alarming aspects of the so-called crisis of youth in much of the scholarly writing on the subject, however, the case has been argued that the majority of young people find ways of resisting their marginalization, of expressing their resentment, and of transcending their exclusion from the public sphere by overwhelmingly peaceful means. In some cases, rural youth achieve this by appropriating the traditional rites and performances that are meant to be the preserve of the elder, engaging them in a silent dialogue that often goes unnoticed in the literature. In other cases they invent "traditions" of their own with which to ridicule and to subvert the role of elders and government officers. In other cases still, youth self-help associations have sprung up modeled on the traditional savings associations (*njangi* in West African Pidgin, *tontines* in Francophone Africa). These enable young people to organize on a model that mixes modernist and local forms of political organization and to make savings with which to start businesses, to pay for buildings and marriages, and—increasingly in the age of HIV/AIDS—to bury their dead.

See also **Colonial Policies and Practices; Disease: HIV/AIDS, Social and Political Aspects; Initiation; International Monetary Fund; Labor: Conscript and Forced; Literacy; Political Systems: Chieftainships; Slavery and Servile Institutions; Urbanism and Urbanization; World Bank.**

BIBLIOGRAPHY

Argenti, Nicolas. "Air Youth: Performance, Violence and the State in Cameroon." *Journal of the Royal Anthropological Institute* 4, no. 4 (1998): 753–782.

Argenti, Nicolas. "People of the Chisel: Apprenticeship, Youth and Elites in Oku (Cameroon)." *American Ethnologist* 29, no. 3 (2002): 497–533.

Argenti, Nicolas. "Dancing in the Borderlands: The Forbidden Masquerades of Oku Youth and Women (Cameroon)." In *Makers and Breakers: Children and Youth as Emerging Categories in Postcolonial Africa*, ed. Alcinda Honwana and Filip de Boeck. Trenton, NJ: Africa World Press, 2005.

Argenti, Nicolas. *The Intestines of the State: Youth, Violence and Belated Histories in the Cameroon Grassfields.* Chicago: University of Chicago Press, 2007.

Banya, K., and Juliet Elu. "Implementing Basic Education: An African Experience." *International Review of Education* 43 (1997): 481–496.

Bayart, Jean-Francois. *L'etat au Cameroun* [1979]. Paris: Presses de la Fondation Nationale des Sciences Politiques, [1985].

Bayart, Jean-Francois. *L'etat en Afrique: La politique du ventre.* Paris: Fayard, 1989.

Bayart, Jean-Francois. "The Social Capital of the Felonious State, or the Ruses of Political Intelligence." In *The Criminalization of the State in Africa*, ed. Jean-François Bayart, Stephen Ellis, and Béatrice Hibou. Oxford: James Currey, 1999.

Bayart, Jean-Francois, et al. *Le politique par le bas en Afrique Noire.* Paris: Karthala, 1992.

Bazenguissa-Ganga, Rémy. "Milices politiques et bandes armées à Brazzaville: Enquête sur la violence politique et sociale des jeunes déclassés." *Les Etudes du CERI* 13 (April 1996).

Coquery-Vidrovitch, Catherine. "Des jeunes dans le passé et dans le future du Sahel." In *Les jeunes en Afrique: évolution et rôle (XIXe–XXe siècles)*, ed. Hélène d'Almeida-Topor et. al. Paris: L'Harmattan, 1992.

De Sardan, Olivier. *Les sociétés Songhay-Zarma (Niger-Mali): Chefs, Guerriers, Esclaves, Paysants.* Paris: Karthala, 1984.

Devisch, René. "Frenzy, Violence and Ethical Renewal in Kinshasa." *Public Culture* 7, no. 3 (1995): 593–629.

Durham, Deborah. "Youth and the Social Imagination in Africa." *Anthropological Quarterly* 73, no. 3 (2000): 113–120.

Durham, Deborah. "Disappearing Youth: Youth as a Social Shifter in Botswana." *American Ethnologist* 31, no. 4 (2004): 589–605.

Evans-Pritchard, E. E. *The Nuer* [1940]. New York: Oxford University Press, [1974.]

Evans-Pritchard, E. E. *Kinship and Marriage among the Nuer.* Oxford: the Clarendon Press, 1951.

Fortes, Meyer. *The Web of Kinship Among the Tallensi.* Oxford: Oxford University Press for the International African Institute, 1949.

Geschiere, Peter. *The Modernity of Witchcraft: Politics and the Occult in Postcolonial Africa.* Charlottesville: University Press of Virginia, 1997.

Gluckman, Max. "Rituals of Rebellion in South-East Africa." In *Order and Rebellion in Tribal Africa.* London: Cohen and West, 1963.

Jones, G. I. "Ibo Age Organization, with Special Reference to the Cross River and North-Eastern Ibo." *Journal of the Royal Anthropological Institute* 92, no. 2 (1962): 191–211.

Kopytoff, Igor, and Suzanne Miers. "African 'Slavery' as an Institution of Marginality." In *Slavery in Africa: Historical and Anthropological Perspectives*, ed. Suzanne Miers and Igor Kopytoff. Madison: University of Wisconsin Press, 1977.

Martin, Phyllis. *Leisure and Society in Colonial Brazzaville.* Cambridge, U.K.: Cambridge University Press, 1995.

Masquelier, Adeline. "The Scorpion's Sting: Youth, Marriage, and the Struggle for Social Maturity in Niger." *Journal of the Royal Anthropological Institute* 11, no. 1 (2005): 59–83.

O'Brien, Donal Cruise. "A Lost Generation? Youth Identity and State Decay in West Africa." In *Postcolonial Identities in Africa*, ed. Richard Werbner and Terence Ranger. London: Zed Books, 1996.

Ottenberg, Simon. *Leadership and Authority in an African Society: The Afikpo Village Group.* Seattle: University of Washington Press, 1971.

Ottenberg, Simon. *Boyhood Rituals in an African Society: An Interpretation.* Seattle: University of Washington Press, 1989.

Rasmussen, S. J. "Between Several Worlds: Images of Youth and Age in Tuareg Popular Performances." *Anthropological Quarterly* 73, no. 3 (2000): 133–144.

Richards, Audrey. *Chisungu: A Girl's Initiation Ceremony among the Bemba of Zambia* [1956]. London: Tavistock, [1982.]

Richards, Paul. *Fighting for the Rainforest: War, Youth and Resources in Sierra Leone.* Oxford: James Currey, 1996.

Richards, Paul. "To Fight or to Farm? Agrarian Dimensions of the Mano River Conflicts (Liberia and Sierra Leone)." *African Affairs* 104, no. 417 (2005): 571–590.

Seekings, Jeremy. *Heroes or Villains? Youth Politics in the 1980s.* Johannesburg: Raven Press, 1993.

Turner, Victor. "Three Symbols of Passage in Ndembu Circumcision Ritual." In *Essays in the Ritual of Social Relations*, ed. Max Gluckman. Manchester: Manchester University Press, 1962.

Turner, Victor. "*Mukanda*, the Rite of Circumcision." In *The Forest of Symbols: Aspects of Ndembu Ritual.* Ithaca, NY: Cornell University Press, 1967.

Turner, Victor. *The Drums of Affliction: A Study of Religious Processes among the Ndembu of Zambia.* London: International African Institute in Association with Hutchinson University Library for Africa, 1968.

Vidal, Claudine. "Les politiques de la haine: Rwanda, Burundi 1994–95." *Les Temps Modernes* 50, no. 583 (1995): 6–33.

Warnier, Jean-Pierre. *L'esprit de l'entreprise au Cameroun.* Paris: Karthala, 1993.

Warnier, Jean-Pierre. "Slave-Trading without Slave-Raiding in Cameroon." *Paideuma* 41 (1995): 251–272.

Warnier, Jean-Pierre. "Rebellion, Defection, and the Position of Male Cadets: A Neglected Category." In *African Crossroads: Intersections Between History and Anthropology in Cameroon*, ed. Ian Fowler and David Zeitlyn. Oxford: Berghahn, 1996.

NICOLAS ARGENTI

URBAN

The changes among and increasing prominence of urban youth in Africa, and the growth of scholarly interest in the category, reflect profound recent transformations in social life on the continent. The transformations typically represent attitudes toward the expansion in numbers of "youth" and the growth of "urban" populations: "youth" and "urban" are often cast as intense inflictions for the region to bear, and map an uncertain future for Africa that departs from global patterns in directionality, speed, and form. This entry sketches some trends in urbanization, migration, and demography that partially capture the scale and variation of the transformations; lays out four themes that cut across twenty- and twenty-first-century studies of urban youth in Africa; points to theoretical problems raised; and suggests future directions for research. One theme runs through the piece: Expansion of urban populations combined with the prominence of youth present tensions, offer possibilities, and alter expectations for productivity, vitality, and growth on the continent.

TRENDS

Data on migration, urbanization, and demography generally present African populations as becoming progressively younger and city based. Reasons for urban growth and the increased proportion of the young in African populations are linked to internal and international migration, shifting modes of production, employment and economic opportunity, access to social and state services, increased morbidity due to resource depletion and HIV/AIDS, and war. In 2005 the U.S. Population Reference Bureau projected that Africa's population will increase by 117 percent between 2005 to 2050 (906 million to 1.97 billion), compared to a world population increase of 43 percent (6.47 billion to 9.26 billion). The proportion of children and youth in Africa is expected to increase at a higher rate than any other age group during this period; in 2007 42 percent of Africa's population is aged under fifteen years, and 33 percent between ten and twenty-four years (world: 0–15 years 29%; 10–24 years 27%). Important details are eclipsed by gross continental figures: North Africa's population is projected to increase by 67 percent, compared to Middle and southern Africa at 175 percent and 0 percent respectively. Stark contrasts in population change at the country level include Swaziland (−34%), Botswana (−14%), Malawi (260%), and Niger (259%), though reasons for these changes differ.

In addition, the annual growth of African cities has ranged between 4 percent and 5 percent since 1990, ranking urban growth in Africa exponentially higher than elsewhere; Dar es Salaam grew by 1239 percent between 1970 and 2000 (inhabitants), and Lagos is predicted to become the third largest city in the world by 2010. The United Nations estimates that three-quarters of Southern Africans will live in urban areas by 2025, and half of all East Africans. The projections, however, gloss regionally specific detail and tend to work off assumptions that require interrogation (for example, that the prevalence of HIV/AIDS in Africa will stabilize and decrease from 2010 because it is assumed that antiretroviral therapies will be widely available by this time; that migration to South Africa will continue to rise). The changes have brought about new patterns of collective and family organization, and prompted alternative and creative survival strategies for African youth living in cities.

The City as a Site of Youthful Self-Expression.
Urban youth experiences are composite, multiple, and layered. Clashes between groups and ideas in cities such as Dakar and Dar es Salaam pave the ways for the young to reconsider their place in society as they negotiate a space and identity alongside others.

In his 1999 research Pieter Remes described how youth in Tanzanian cities perform rap compositions that blur North American, Jamaican, and African styles; comprise political expressions and social critique that aligns youth with new permutations of *ujamaa* socialism; and allow individuals means to distinguish themselves from their peers. Other studies have examined the making of art and music by youth in cities and the relationships between young people that are created and configured through urban performance, particularly in relation to how the activities foster group identity and peer alliances.

In Senegal, urban youth in Dakar played important roles in holding the Diouf government to account and demanding change in the period immediately following the 1987 student strikes and demonstrations. The *Set/Setal* youth movement, where young people took it upon themselves to clean and protect urban neighborhoods, allowed youth the means to exert claims of ownership and belonging in a city in which they had previously been alienated. Mamadou Diouf explained their actions as having done more than sweep the streets: "*Set/Setal* expresses a harsh critique of the world of adults and politicians by the vast majority of youth. It is an attempt to overcoming youth's dependent position and lack of attention from the adults who provide for them" (Diouf, 240).

"Urban Youth" and "Rural Elders."
Filip de Boeck and Marie-Françoise Plissart's 2005 stunning visual ethnography of Kinshasa explores some of the ways in which children and youth move between family, the street, and the Pentecostal urban church. They highlight one interesting phenomenon: the extent to which the acquisition by youth of resources can cause disturbance in society. Some Congolese youth became embroiled in the Angolan diamond and war economies and, in acquiring resources, came to be seen as a danger to society. The authors suggested a link between the fear of the resource-laden youth and accusations of witchcraft against the young. Rijk van Dijk's 1992 description of youth preachers in fundamentalist church organizations in Blantyre similarly forges connections to the common representation of urban youth as being in permanent conflict with older generations and cultural traditions. The theme of an urban-rural tension as

analogous to youth-elder conflict cuts across many research pieces, and contributes to long-standing depictions of the urban as a site of pathology, criminality, and immorality, and its youth as outcast.

Urban Youth as Economic and Sexual Agents.

AbdouMaliq Simone's 2004 analysis of the economic alliances forged among migrant youth in Johannesburg, and Chris Lockhart's 2002 study of heterosexual and *kunyunga* (homosexual) sexual relationships of urban street boys in Mwanza, Tanzania, highlight some of the economic strategies youth employ in urban contexts. Accounts such as these attempt to balance analysis between conceptualizing youth as powerless, exploited minors trying only to survive, and as "agents" imbued with strategies and capacities for negotiation. Lockhart's study, for example, demonstrates how intimacy and solidarity between urban youth can emerge through shared economic practices and marginal social positions. Sexual practices between boys in Mwanza can offer a relationship of protection between an older, experienced street youth and his junior newcomer: "It is clear that the boys depend on one another to survive in the often unforgiving and potentially dangerous environment of Mwanza's streets...*Kunyunga* is an important aspect of street life and maintaining the boys' interdependence that, in turn, is critical to their survival" (Lockhart, 296). The study connects to a larger body of research on sex work by girls and young women in the city, where cultivating relationships with older patrons through sexual activity is presented as a increasingly common strategy for economic survival and security.

Simone traces the relationships negotiated between groups of foreign youth in Johannesburg to reveal the degree of "economic collaboration among residents seemingly marginalized and immiserated by urban life," which remain contingent, adaptable, and improvised at all times (Simone, 407). The issues tackled in the studies raise questions concerning the importance of specific forms of behavior among youth in a lifetime trajectory and the means academics use to describe and evaluate them; and the immediate and long-term costs of using certain strategies—the relationship between cost and power, for example. The issues also demonstrate how the categories and meanings of gender for youth in African cities are being redrawn in relation to disparate access to resources and different forms of economic activity.

The Governance of the Urban Young.

Studies of young people's opposition to the apartheid state has contributed to an understanding of the ways young people organize themselves and act together in urban African settings, particularly in situations of violence and poverty. In her 2005 ethnographic paper on the "self-knowledge" and ethics activist youth acquired and acted in accordance with, Pamela Reynolds made explicit important relationships between state governance of youth and the means and morals youth use, in contrast, to bring about change (see Abdullah 2003 and Hoffman 2005 for comparable examples from West Africa). Reynolds' work can be taken further to underscore how categories and theories of "youth" and "urban" are consistently transposed from elsewhere in scholarship on Africa in unproblematic ways, for example, between the colony and metropole. The simple joining of youth studies and urban studies in the African context has not worked sufficiently well, largely because of underlying assumptions in models used that originate outside of Africa. In the early twenty-first century scholarship is beginning to show how connections between the governance of youth, the self-organization of young people, and everyday life in urban Africa may emerge on different grounds.

DIRECTIONS IN RESEARCH

Youth and urban themes tie together a number of scholarly and institutional interests in contemporary Africa. Innovative research that pays attention to the lives of youth in African cities has helped dislodge dominant frames of reference and to query the ways in which African worlds are persistently imagined. Data underscores the need for sustained research on the situation of African urban youth, brings to the fore the challenges such work entails, and calls for attention to be paid to rigorous research methods and innovative theoretical frames. Early twenty-first century scholarship also speaks of a broader challenge of finding a place for studies of urban youth within African studies—a challenge that, perhaps, parallels the struggle young people are experiencing in finding their place and voice within African cities.

It might be too early to predict how the forces within the two categories urban and youth will play off one another at the regional level, and it might be more helpful to ask whether urban youth constitutes only a fluid category of persons, or more clearly identifiable ways of being and forms of livelihood. That is to say, will urban youth be seen to negotiate identities that makes them more clearly and seriously a subject of knowledge or governance and gives them a more effective role in ethical, political, modern discourse? Despite claims to the contrary, it is already clear that the subjects youth and urban cannot serve as single halves of rigid dichotomies (urban/rural, youth/elder), nor, as maintained in much of the existing literature, as groups of persons divorced from extended networks of kin and other people, or as geographically unmoored from multiple places of affiliation. Following postcolonial criticism on the contested sign of Africa, attention to the topic of urban youth requires thought between categories.

See also **Apartheid; Dakar; Dar es Salaam; Disease: HIV/ AIDS, Social and Political Aspects; Labor: Child; Labor: Migration; Slavery and Servile Institutions; Socialism and Postsocialisms; Urbanism and Urbanization; Warfare: Civil Wars.**

BIBLIOGRAPHY

Abdullah, Ibrahim. "I Am a Rebel: Youth Culture and Violence in Sierra Leone." In *Readings in African Politics*, ed. Tom Young. Bloomington: Indiana University Press, 2003.

De Boeck, Filip, and Marie-Françoise Plissart. *Kinshasa: Tales of the Invisible City.* Ludion: Vlaams Architectuurinstituut Vai, 2005.

Diouf, Mamadou. "Urban Youth and Senegalese Politics." *Public Culture* 8, no. 2 (1996): 225–250.

Hoffman, Danny. "The Brookfields Hotel (Freetown, Sierra Leone)." *Public Culture* 17, no. 1 (2005): 55–74.

Lockhart, Chris. "Kunyenga, 'Real Sex,' and Survival: Assessing the Risk of HIV Infection among Urban Street Boys in Tanzania." *Medical Anthropology Quarterly* 16, no. 3 (2002): 294–311.

Population Reference Bureau. "The World's Youth 2006 Data Sheet" and "2005 World Population Data Sheet." Available from http://www.prb.org/.

Remes, Pieter. "Global Popular Musics and Changing Awareness of Urban Tanzanian Youth." *Yearbook for Traditional Music* (1999): 1–26.

Reynolds, Pamela. "The Ground of All Making: State Violence, the Family, and Political Activists." In *Violence and Subjectivity*, ed. Veena Das, Arthur Kleinman, Mamphela Ramphele, and Pamela Reynolds. Berkeley: University of California Press, 2000.

Reynolds, Pamela. "Imfobe: Self-Knowledge and the Search for Ethics among Former, Youth, Anti-Apartheid Activists." *Journal of Southern African Anthropology* 28, no. 3–4 (2005): 62–72.

Simone, AbdouMaliq. "People as Infrastructure: Intersecting Fragments in Johannesburg." *Public Culture* 16, no. 3 (2004): 407–429.

Sommers, Marc. "Urbanization, War, and Africa's Youth at Risk: Towards Understanding and Addressing Future Challenges." CARE, Inc. Available from http://www .beps.net/publications/BEPS-UrbanizationWarYouthat Risk-.pdf.

Straker, Gill. *Faces in the Revolution: The Psychological Effects of Violence on Township Youth in South Africa.* Cape Town: David Philip, 1992.

Van Dijk, Richard A. "Young Puritan Preachers in Post-Independence Malawi." *Africa* 62, no. 2 (1992): 159–181.

PAMELA REYNOLDS
JAMES WILLIAMS

MOVEMENTS

While African governments may tentatively sing the praises of youth as the "promise of the future," they equally often fear them as the source of twenty-first-century instability. Two stereotypes have thus simultaneously emerged, one portraying youth as heroes, the other as youth as villains.

YOUNG PEOPLE'S RELATIONSHIP TO TRADITIONAL SOCIAL ORDERS

Young men and women played markedly different social roles in precolonial societies than they do in the twenty-first century. While state and nongovernmental organizations (NGO) discourses of youth in Africa are often couched in Western terms that categorize youth strictly as a biological stage of maturity, the means whereby governments and political elites engage with young people in practice is strongly influenced by the social history of young people's roles in precolonial societies and in contemporary rural settings. These rural histories continue to influence the modern role, the expectations, the problems and the potential of young people (and others categorized as young) in Africa in the early 2000s. Indeed, because people's political power is indexed metaphorically in terms of their "age" in the predominantly gerontocratic social systems of the continent, many people who are not young can be classified as youths. The poor, the marginalized, bachelors, or the childless can thus all find themselves classified as life-long "youths" despite their biological age. The discussion of "youth" in Africa therefore needs to be understood to include not only the biologically young but also the politically, socially, and economically marginalized.

Colonialism wrought profound changes on youth throughout the continent, some advantageous to young men and women, others not. The main advantage of the onset of colonial authority for a minority of young men stemmed from the need of the new bureaucracy for skilled labor: literate clerks, secretaries, and low-ranking officials who could keep the machinery of government working at the national and local levels. Gaining an education (typically in a mission school) thus came to be seen as a ticket to freedom from the protracted subordination to one's elders. For the first time, young men did not need to wait half a lifetime to acquire status: they could take a shortcut through salaried employment, and even come to wield power over traditional elders. The moment when many African countries achieved independence—and many educated young men moved into positions of bureaucratic power, taking over the jobs of the departing colonial administrators—there came a major shift in domestic power relations. "Youth" had become a major political force. It is no accident that a number of nationalist movements identified themselves as "youth"—the Somali Youth League even incorporated the term into its name. Indeed, most African political leaders who fought for independence during colonial times were around thirty years old.

Some postcolonial regimes have reinvented traditional hierarchies in the political sphere under the guise of authenticity campaigns, with heads of state identifying themselves as traditional elders and the nation's youth defined as problem children needing strong paternal leadership. In this context, the notion of the Father of the Nation serves to reduce youth to the status of infants who owe allegiance, obedience, and gratitude to their "father." Opportunities for the political representation of young people, even in the multiparty political systems that have emerged since the 1990s, are thus often limited to the youth wing of the party in power.

STUDENT MOVEMENTS

Across the continent, while some advances have been made in the provision of education, the educational system prepares people for jobs that overwhelmingly do not exist. As Donal O'Brien has pointed out, students see themselves as an abandoned generation. The "high order of built-in frustration" (1996, 65) that results from this system has led to three distinct problems: a rural-urban imbalance, the educated unemployed, and the so-called brain drain. In addition to these problems, one should underline the fact that the high level of education of a small minority, while contributing to the development of a new class of elites, has not led to the devolution of opportunities for participation to the majority of the young. Furthermore, those university students who attempt to participate in the national debate by organizing in groups that do not come under the aegis of the party youth wing are often harassed by the paramilitary police (gendarmerie) and subjected to arbitrary acts of violence and incarceration without charge. Student uprisings and university closures and occupations by the military are consequently frequent. Some scholars have questioned the extent to which these uprisings represent struggles for the rights to free speech and to education or mere attempts to appropriate a slice of the "national cake" and entry to the circle of the new elite.

The ambiguity of some uprisings has been said to point to a pattern by which the persecution of a section of society (in this case the student body) leads to the disillusionment of its members, and then to their adoption of increasingly Machiavellian worldviews. Since their experience of the state is typically of a place in which democratic ideals are of no value save as a rhetorical device, they stop striving for such ideals, and become instead pragmatists who simply seek advancement within the status quo, adopting the "politics of the belly" of the ruling class as their only guiding principle, according to Jean-Francois Bayart. This miseducation of the student has been said to produce at best a class of passive and silenced academics and government functionaries, and at worst a faction of cynical pragmatists who reproduce the conditions of their own de-skilling.

Nevertheless, it must be acknowledged that since the democratization movements that swept the continent in the 1990s there has been a strong connection between student movements and genuine political revolt leading to political change and transformation. In some ways, these movements recall the student-led revolutionary anticolonial struggles of the 1930s, 1940s, and 1950s, and the fact that some movement leaders may seek entry into the government rather than its outright downfall therefore cannot always be interpreted cynically.

Moreover, while the Machiavellian interpretation could apply to autocratic regimes capable of absorbing a substantial proportion of their educated population, in the postrecession scenario of economic crisis that prevails in Africa in the twenty-first century, any apolitical pragmatism that the students might incorporate in secondary or higher education is insufficient to lead them straight into formal employment, either in the public or the private sector. Students therefore sometimes pass through a period of uprisings, protests, and insurrections that assume various degrees of violence. Intended as a form of control over the youth, the tactics of pacification and the ideal of cynical self-preservation promulgated by the state ironically often lead to further protests. It has been said that the state thus ultimately bears the fruits of its persecution of the student body in the consequent disenchantment and outright criminalization of the young. This is the reason why some do not think of young people straightforwardly as victims of state authoritarianism: when all other forms of agency are denied, some young victims tend in turn to become perpetrators themselves. This desperate form of self-preservation then leads to further violence against young people as it justifies further government oppression. The situation regarding students can thus be seen as a microcosm of the aggravated case regarding the militarization of youth.

YOUNG PEOPLE'S QUEST FOR ALTERNATIVES

Denied more open forms of participation in civil society, young people have exploited the invisibility, the creativity, and the humor of such movements to elude repressive manifestations of power. One of the points often overlooked is the degree to which overtly political activity is quite simply not practicable under authoritarian regimes. Often, young people's organizations and meetings are prohibited unless they explicitly represent the youth wing of the party in power (often the single party). In this context, young people and the disenfranchised in general seek participation in mundane practices that can pass for religious, theatrical, or folkloric when the need arises, thereby avoiding state censure. In his 1975 work on the Beni *ngoma* dance, Terence Ranger described a classic example of such a movement in colonial East Africa. These dances were modeled on the brass marching bands of the British military, complete with ranks and military-style uniforms. The Hauka movement of Niger—immortalized in its Ghanaian incarnation in Jean Rouch's film *Les maîtres fous*—emerged in response to French colonial rule. Jean-Pierre Olivier de Sardan and Paul Stoller's work emphasizes the subversive, political significance of this performance, during which the spirits of colonial administrators would possess the dancers.

After independence, the young men and women involved in such movements could become directly involved with the political cultures they represented. The young men who participated in the Ode-lay masquerades of Freetown, Sierra Leone, cultivate close links with the city's politicians at the same time as they implicitly satirize them by appropriating their titles and exaggerating their forms of attire and wealth. Many postcolonial youth movements remain unambiguously marginal phenomena, however, emphasizing rather than minimizing the exclusion of youth from power. The remarkable phenomenon of the young unemployed *sapeurs* of Brazzaville represents such a case. The *sapeurs* travel to Paris where they undergo extremes of penury in order to save the money with which to buy the necessary set of designer outfits with which to return to Brazzaville. There, they display their new *gamme*, the complete range of outfits that they hope will gain them entry (however illegitimate and fleeting) to the space of the elites. Its members are regularly referred to as delinquents by the elites whose exorbitant European designer style of clothing and general hedonism they mimic, but their adventures entail a subtle and trenchant political commentary as well as a set of practices that provide solidarity and support despite the alienating effects of postcolonial proletarianization.

In the same vein, the isicathamiya competitive song performances of Natal have been interpreted as a reflection of the introduction of capitalism to the Zulu world. At the turn of the nineteenth and twentieth centuries, choral competitions became a "compensatory strategy" for the loss of status and social capital associated with the proletarianization of young men in natal. This institutionalized friendly rivalry still informs the ideology of isicathamiya associations in the early twenty-first century, in which isicathamiya, along with stick fighting and *ingoma* dancing, can be seen as cultural responses to the alienation, dispossession, and poverty of contemporary South African migrant workers.

YOUNG PEOPLE'S PARTICIPATION IN NEW RELIGIOUS MOVEMENTS

Far from representing a means of opting out of society, Pentecostal churches (and equally Muslim brotherhoods) offer opportunities for participation in civil society that are so often denied to young people both in political life and the established churches alike. On the other hand, however, the emancipation from elders, the state, and the established clergy offered to young people often comes at the price of the "Satanization" of everyday life, and the pressure to reject one's kinship ties and cultural beliefs and practices.

Van Dijk's 1998 analysis of the Born-Agains, a Pentecostal movement that emerged in Malawi in the 1970s, highlights the youth of its participants. The preachers—themselves ranging in age from nine to thirty—emphasized to their followers the need to make a break with the traditions of their elders. The ultimate aim of the church was to attain a society in which power and authority would be resituated "beyond the clutches of tradition and its gerontocracy" (van Dijk 1998, 166). The "cultural amnesia" of the young Pentecostalists not only contrasted with the practices of their elders, but also with those of the state. The Banda regime of the day was actively reinventing a traditional Chewa past and putting it to work to legitimize its rule over all Malawians. Young people were thus made submissive to the regime in the same manner that they were to their traditional elders. Within such a political context, the Pentecostal rejection of everything the elders stood for simultaneously marked emancipation from gerontocratic structures and from subjection to a totalitarian regime. Throughout the continent, Pentecostal

churches evince an antinostalgic element that plays a role in protecting young followers from the perceived abuse of power by their elders and also acts as a critique of the state that so often models itself on precolonial cultural models of authority.

The Pentecostal cry to make a complete break with the past and to be *born again* also clashes directly with the current cultural policies of the Ghanaian state. There too, the state aims to instill in its ethnically diverse population a sense of national pride by celebrating certain traditional rites as aspects of Ghana's national heritage. A Ghanaian culture is thus created with which to oppose the globalizing cultural influence perceived to emanate from a neocolonial West. In contradiction with this project, the upwardly mobile young men and women who join the Pentecostal churches emphasize the global character of their religious practices and reject traditional practices as sinful. Despite however modernist the Pentecostal message is, the young Ghanaian members of these churches in fact evince an ambivalent relationship to modernity: Many of their beliefs, such as their very literal belief in the Satanic powers of traditional spirits, are directly inherited from their elders. By emphasizing the Satanic powers of traditional spirits, Pentecostals incorporate these spirits into their cosmology under a new guise. Pentecostal churches and Sufi Brotherhoods offer young men a distinct youth identity and a modicum of protection, representing a field of civil society capable of pressurizing the state by threatening a withdrawal of support.

Political parties in twenty-first century Africa often boast youth wings and party militants; some of them even erect whole parallel political structures at the youth level or associate themselves with semiofficial vigilante groups. Such measures should not be taken to evince the redundancy of youth as a mirror image of elite structures, however. Rather, these uneasy associations represent an ongoing struggle by political elites to co-opt the power and influence of young people, but such efforts only emphasize that youth movements may not in their inception be unambiguously aligned with specific political ideologies or established parties. More often than not, young people evade the straightjacket of party youth wings and orthodox ideologies and gather together under the guise of religious groups, performance troupes, possession cults, and new social organizations that do not represent party-political platforms but rather support independent agendas that meet specific, local needs. In the armed uprising in Cameroon in the 1950s and 1960s, for instance, the young Union des Populations du Cameroun (UPC) cadres in the Bamileke area of Cameroon fought for entirely different reasons from the UPC fighters in the Bassa part of the country. Research suggests that while it would be an error to view nonaligned youth groups in party-political terms, it would be a greater error to overlook their political significance altogether on the assumption that they are purely cultural.

See also **Brazzaville; Children and Childhood; Colonial Policies and Practices; Dance: Social Meaning; Education, University and College; Freetown; Literacy; Nongovernmental Organizations; Postcolonialism; Rouch, Jean.**

BIBLIOGRAPHY

Banya, K., and Juliet Elu. "Implementing Basic Education: An African Experience." *International Review of Education* 43 (1997): 481–496.

Bayart, Jean-Francois. *L'etat en Afrique: La politique du ventre.* Paris: Fayard, 1989.

Bayart, Jean-Francois; Stephen Ellis; and Beatrice Hibou; eds. *The Criminalization of the State in Africa.* Oxford: James Currey, 1999.

Comaroff, Jean. *Body of Power, Spirit of Resistance: The Culture and History of a South African People.* Chicago: University of Chicago Press, 1985.

De Boeck, Filip. "Domesticating Diamonds and Dollars: Identity, Expenditure and Sharing in Southwestern Zaire." In *Globalization and Identity: Dialectics of Flow and Closure*, ed. Birgit Meyer and Peter Geschiere. Oxford: Blackwell, 1999.

De Boeck, Filip, and Alcinda Honwana, eds. *Makers and Breakers: Children and Youth in Postcolonial Africa.* Trenton, NJ: Africa World Press, 2005.

Durham, Deborah. "Youth and the Social Imagination in Africa." *Anthropological Quarterly* 73, no. 3 (2000): 113–120.

Gandoulou, J-D. *Au Coeur de la Sape: Moeurs et Aventures de Congolais à Paris.* Paris: L'Harmattan, 1984.

Geschiere, Peter. *The Modernity of Witchcraft: Politics and the Occult in Postcolonial Africa.* Charlottesville: University Press of Virginia, 1997.

Gifford, Paul. "Democratization and the Churches." In *The Christian Churches and the Democratization of Africa.* New York: E.J. Brill, 1995.

Joseph, Richard. *Radical Nationalism in Cameroon: Social Origins of the UPC Rebellion.* Oxford: Clarendon Press, 1977.

MacGaffey, Janet, and Remy Bazenguissa-Ganga. *Congo-Paris: Transnational Traders on the Margins of the Law.* Oxford: James Currey, 2000.

Mbembe, Achille. *Les jeunes et l'ordre politique en Afrique noire.* Paris: L'Harmattan, 1985.

Meyer, Birgit. "'If You Are a Devil, You Are a Witch and If You Are a Witch, You Are a Devil': The Integration of 'Pagan' Ideas into the Conceptual Universe of Ewe Christians in Southeastern Ghana." *Journal of Religion in Africa* 22, no. 2 (1992): 98–132.

Meyer, Birgit. "Make a Complete Break with the Past: Memory and Postcolonial Modernity in Ghanaian Pentecostal Discourse." In *Memory and the Postcolony: African Anthropology and the Critique of Power*, ed. Richard Werbner. London: Zed Books, 1998.

Nunley, John W. *Moving with the Face of the Devil: Art and Politics in Urban West Africa.* Urbana: University of Illinois Press, 1987.

O'Brien, Donal Cruise. "A Lost Generation? Youth Identity and State Decay in West Africa." In *Postcolonial Identities in Africa*, ed. Richard Werbner and Terence Ranger. Atlantic Highlands, NJ: Zed Books, 1996.

Olivier de Sardan, Jean-Pierre. *Concepts et conceptions songhay-zarma: Histoire, culture, sociéte.* Paris: Nubia, 1982.

Olivier de Sardan, Jean-Pierre. "La surinterprétation politique: Les cultes de possession hauka du Niger." In *Religion et modernité politique en Afrique noire*, ed. Jean-Francois Bayart. Paris: Karthala, 1993.

Ranger, Terence. *Dance and Society in Eastern Africa 1890–1970: The Beni Ngoma.* London: Heinemann, 1975.

Seekings, Jeremy. *Heroes or Villains? Youth Politics in the 1980s.* Johannesburg: Raven Press, 1993.

Smith, Daniel Jordan. "The Bakassi Boys: Vigilantism, Violence, and Political Imagination in Nigeria." *Cultural Anthropology* 19, no. 3 (2004): 429–453.

Steiner, Christopher. "The Invisible Face: Masks, Ethnicity, and the State in Cote d'Ivoire." In *Perspectives on Africa: A Reader in Culture, History, and Representation*, ed. Roy Richard Grinker and Christopher B. Steiner. Cambridge, MA: Blackwell, 1997.

Stoller, Paul. *Fusion of the Worlds: An Ethnography of Possession Among the Songhay of Niger.* Chicago: University of Chicago Press, 1989.

Stoller, Paul. *Embodying Colonial Memories: Spirit Possession, Power, and the Hauka in West Africa.* London: Routledge, 1995.

Takougang, Joseph, and Milton Krieger. *African State and Society in the 1990s: Cameroon's Political Crossroads.* Boulder, CO: Westview Press, 1998.

Toulabor, Comi. "L'énonciation du pouvoir et de la richesse chez les jeunes "conjuncturés" de Lomé (Togo)." In *Le politique par le bas en Afrique Noire*, ed. Jean-Francois Bayart et. al., eds. Paris: Karthala, 1992.

Tozy, Mohamed. "Movements of Religious Renewal." In *Africa Now: People, Policies, Institutions*, ed. Stephen Ellis. Oxford: James Currey, 1996.

Van Dijk, Rik. "Pentecostalism, Cultural Memory, and the State: Contested Representation of Time in Postcolonial Malawi." In *Memory and the Postcolony: African Anthropology and the Critique of Power*, ed. Richard Werbner. London: Zed Books, 1998.

Van Dijk, Rijk. "Pentecostalism, Gerontocratic Rule and Democratization in Malawi: The Changing Position of the Young in Political Culture." In *Religion, Globalization, and Political Culture in the Third World*, ed. Jeff Haynes. New York: St. Martin's Press, 1999.

Van Dijk, Rijk. "Witchcraft and Skepticism by Proxy: Pentecostalism and Laughter in Urban Malawi." In *Magical Interpretations, Material Realities: Modernity, Witchcraft and the Occult in Postcolonial Africa*, ed. H. Moore and T. Sanders. London and New York: Routledge, 2001.

Young, C., and B. Kanté. "Governance, Democracy and the 1988 Elections (Senegal)." In *Governance and Politics in Africa*, ed. Goran Hyden and Michael Bratton. Boulder, CO: Lynne Rienner, 1992.

NICOLAS ARGENTI

GANGS

Accounts of delinquent urban youth began to appear in colonial records and newspapers in the early twentieth century. These reports describe gatherings of boys and young men who frequented city streets harassing passersby, committing petty crimes, and sometimes scuffling with rival groups. Although African residents often voiced outrage over the exploits of these unruly elements, youth gangs in colonial Africa, other than South Africa's notorious *tsotsis*, seem to have been viewed as more of a nuisance than a danger. In late 1920s Bulawayo, Zimbabwe, for example, youth gangs took the form of competitive associations that occasionally clashed with ethnic rivals, but they did not generally commit robberies or other street crimes. And, while criminal gangs became more visible and active in the 1930s and 1940s during periods of economic recession in Lagos and Ibadan, the majority of juvenile crime was against property, rather than muggings, armed robberies, or organized gang violence. The same pattern held in 1950s Dar es Salaam, Tanzania, despite the presence of an estimated 10,000 street children.

Politicized violence at the end of the colonial period sometimes drew urban youth into more aggressive forms of criminality. During the Mau Mau conflict in 1950s Kenya, youth in Nairobi engaged in activities that straddled the political-criminal divide and the predatory gangs that emerged in late colonial Kinshasa, Democratic Republic of the Congo, were associated with the militant youth wings of rival political parties. Notwithstanding these exceptions, it was only in South African cities, especially Johannesburg, that violent youth gangs established a consistent presence in the colonial period.

Johannesburg's gold industry required a massive African labor force and the black population increased from approximately 15,000 in 1896 to more than 200,000 by 1920. Ninety percent of these migrants were male and a large majority worked and lived on the mines with different ethnic groups housed separately in bleak, single-sex barracks. Adult criminal gangs, typically established along ethnic lines, assaulted, robbed, and murdered miners and neighboring township residents. Unless violence between Africans directly threatened workplace production or the security of white employees, mining officials and police rarely addressed this problem. The absence of regulation gave birth to a succession of migrant gangs. For example, in the late 1940s, migrants from colonial Lesotho formed the Marashea or Russians, the largest and most enduring migrant criminal society in Johannesburg. Although based in the mining compounds these Basotho migrants concentrated their campaigns of violence in the townships, exacting "protection" fees from residents and defending their territories against all comers, including the groups of young, fully urban thugs, known as *tsotsis*, which had risen to prominence in the 1930s.

The influx of substantial numbers of African women from the 1920s introduced a new dynamic to Johannesburg's criminal landscape, as their children formed the first wave of urban youth gangs. By the 1940s, *tsotsis* had eclipsed migrants as the greatest criminal menace in the townships. Like the migrant gang members who preceded them, *tsotsis* were almost exclusively male. Girls in the townships were subject to tighter parental control and were occupied by a range of domestic tasks from which boys were typically exempt. An aggressive masculine identity that valorized fearlessness, fighting skill, and the ability to dominate girls was central to the *tsotsi* subculture. The larger gangs controlled substantial territories, had dozens and sometimes hundreds of members, and were involved in an assortment of criminal activities including gang warfare, murder, rape, and robbery.

The escalation in youth violence and crime corresponded with the substantial increase in Johannesburg's African population and the severity with which pass laws, regulating African mobility and rights of residence, were enforced in the townships. Coming of age in a violent environment, male youth were attracted to gangs for status and security, but also because the pass laws made it difficult for them to obtain work. While the gangs spread terror throughout the townships, the police concentrated on arresting Africans for pass offenses. Every year South African prisons were filled with boys and men whose only crime was a passbook transgression. This development helped to sustain the gang phenomenon as otherwise law-abiding pass offenders were recruited into prison gangs. Virtually all colonial administrations implemented policies to limit and control African urbanization, but none imprisoned its subjects on anything approaching the same scale as South Africa. This criminalization of urban life contributed to the development of a youth gang culture in South African cities prior to elsewhere on the continent.

Massive urban migrations followed decolonization in many African countries, accelerating the deficiencies in housing, education, employment, and social services that colonial administrations had largely ignored. Substantial elements of urban youth populations, with poor access to education and formal sector employment, were increasingly perceived as a social menace. Gangs became more conspicuous and threatening and groups such as Lagos' ubiquitous Area Boys came to represent the face of postcolonial urban disorder. First achieving notoriety in the 1980s, these youth extort financial contributions from shoppers, shopkeepers, and

commuters through intimidation and violence and have become a daily hazard for Lagos residents. Along with youth who survive through street crime, urban gangs have been involved in violent electioneering in Kenya and Côte d'Ivoire, vigilantism in Nigeria, and turf wars over drug distribution in post-apartheid South Africa. The failure of police to provide adequate protection—indeed corrupt police are frequently seen as part of the problem—has resulted in the proliferation of vigilante movements. Nigeria's Bakassi Boys and Cape Town's People Against Gangsterism and Drugs (PAGAD) provide two twenty-first-century examples of vigilante outfits that have further undermined the rule of law and fuelled the cycle of violence.

Perhaps the most prominent role of marginalized urban youth in postcolonial Africa has been as combatants in various armed conflicts. Recruited and coerced into fighting for militias and rebel movements, from the civil wars in Sierra Leone and Liberia to the township battles that marked the dying years of apartheid, generations of youth have some sort of military experience. When these conflicts end, young veterans, who lived by the gun and have few employment options, often find it difficult to resist the short-term rewards of a criminal career. Many African cities are under enormous pressure as continuing urban migration, inadequate housing, and rising unemployment have resulted in large populations of youth who turn to criminal activities to carve out a living. Youth gangs, in all their manifestations, are both a product of this urban malaise and a key contributor to the insecurity of urban life.

See also **Bulawayo; Children and Childhood; Dar es Salaam; Johannesburg; Kinshasa; Lagos; Postcolonialism; Urbanism and Urbanization.**

BIBLIOGRAPHY

Abbink, Jon, and Ineke van Kessel, eds. *Vanguard or Vandals: Youth, Politics and Conflict in Africa.* Leiden, the Netherlands: Brill Academic Publishers, 2004.

Anderson, David. "Vigilantes, Violence and the Politics of Public Order in Kenya." *African Affairs* 101, 405 (2002): 531–555.

Burton, Andrew. *African Underclass: Urbanization, Crime and Colonial Order in Dar es Salaam.* Athens: Ohio University Press, 2005.

Glaser, Clive. *Bo-Tsotsi: The Youth Gangs of Soweto, 1935–1976.* Portsmouth, NH: Heinemann, 2000.

Harnischfeger, Johannes. "The Bakassi Boys: Fighting Crime in Nigeria." *Journal of Modern African Studies* 41, 1 (2003): 23–49.

Kynoch, Gary. *We Are Fighting the World: A History of the Marashea Gangs in South Africa, 1947–1999.* Athens: Ohio University Press, 2005.

GARY KYNOCH

SOLDIERS

Images of armed children and youth dressed in bizarre and makeshift uniforms and causing havoc in African cities have become one of the dominant media representations of the African continent since the late twentieth century. At a first glance the images seem to connote pure anarchy; societies gone mad with children and youth running amok, controlling public space by way of the gun. Yet, at a closer look many of the dynamics that underlie these instances of youth warfare are neither as uncommon nor as exotic as one might presume. Though many of the wars in question may be difficult to comprehend, when seen from Western societies of peace and plenty, they are not indicative of the intrinsic or meaningless violence of African youth but of the poverty and acute lack of life chances that color their existence. Rather than being expressions of social or personal barbarism or the particularly violent dispositions of Africans, they are directly related to global socioeconomic processes that negatively affect the lives and possibilities of the young people in question.

YOUTH AND VIOLENCE

There is in itself nothing novel about the fact that young men constitute the bulk of armies and militias in Africa or elsewhere. Encompassment into institutions built on violent possibilities or events has functioned as rites of passage into adulthood and citizenship for generations of young men around the world. Conscription has for centuries functioned as a mode of turn young men into "proper" citizens in many western countries, as well as the initiation rituals of groups of young men in Africa are often closely related to military structures, for example, among the hunter societies in Sierra Leone as well as the Masai and Kikuyu. In fact, there seems to exist a universally close relationship between youth and organized violence; a relationship that can be exemplified by the fact that young men are integrated into the very systematization and praxis of violence as military structures place seniority behind the front lines and juvenility in the very center of it, or even more bluntly by the fact that the lives that young people take or lose on the battlefield are seen as the legitimate waste product of the process of war (Vigh 2006a).

AFRICAN YOUTH

Within the African continent this relationship between young men, violence and military organizations has become especially clear. African youth constitute an increasingly growing percentage of the sub-Saharan population with more than 60% of the total population being under twenty-five years of age. Furthermore, many are being born into societies characterized by rampant poverty, generalized decline, and increasing inequality. Society is, as such, witnessing a situation in which state structures have withered and lost their capacity to provide jobs and futures for young people coupled with the fact that the intergenerational flow of resources has come to a halt in many areas of the continent, as parents and relatives are increasingly unable to fulfil their social obligation of passing on land and resources to their offspring due to, for example, unsuccessful migration, urbanization, and the HIV/AIDS pandemic.

What one sees is, in other words, the growth of a large superfluous population of youth who are finding it increasingly difficult to forge lives for themselves and make ends meet resulting in the emergence of what has, within the African literature, been termed "the lost generation," understood as a mass of "young people [who] have finished their schooling, are without employment in the formal sector, and are not in a position to set up an independent household" (O'Brien, 57). As such, there exists a large group of young people who are not just short of money to meet their immediate needs, but equally short of the social and economic foundation needed to meet their present and future social needs. They are stuck in the category of youth, with only a minimal space of possibilities and a complete truncation of social being, and the uncertainty and social frustration caused by the economy of survival forces many young men to make radical choices (Vigh 2006 a and b).

Child soldiers laugh outside UN compound, Bunia, Democratic Republic of Congo, May 2003. The northeastern town of Bunia was at the time a theater of violent clashes between the Hema and the Lendu militias. MONUC (UN Mission to Congo) compound was the main assembling point for the displaced from the region. MARCO LONGARI/AFP/GETTY IMAGES

FIGHTING FOR A POSSIBILITY

In this situation mobilization offers a means to possible futures and positions of social worth. What one is witnessing, in many of the wars on the continent that at a first glance may seem senseless, are conflict scenarios in which ideologies are not necessarily central to the fighting and the reward of fighting not necessarily related to immediate monetary gratification. Rather than fighting against an ideologically defined *enemy* or for concrete economic gain young people are, at a closer look, fighting for a *possibility*; that is, for the mere possibility of gaining a worthy life. In the conflict ridden parts of the continent being young means having to balance between social death and violent life chances.

One is accustomed to think of conflict participation as ideologically fueled and generally to perceive "legitimate conflict participation" to be tied to the political realm of statehood or nationhood, evolving around different perspectives on how a given society should be organized, resources distributed, and territoriality demarcated. Carl von Clausewitz' famous dictum, that "war is a continuation of politics by other means" (Clausewitz 1997: 22), has been the primary underlying perspective

informing Western theories and analyses of war and conflict since the mid-nineteenth century. Yet, tying warfare to ideology seems of little use here. Though conflict engagement outside the realm of ideology and politics may, from a Western perspective, be seen as objectionable, related to the anarchy of mercenaries or the archaism of fanatics, one needs to acknowledge that what one sees when focusing on youth warfare in Africa is a conflict scenario in which neither ideology, nor ideas of statehood, seem to be the primary points of departure for people's conflict participation. In other words, instead of looking for ideologies one needs to look at the situated rationalities that inform young people's turn to violence, and in doing so one is directed toward to the depressed state of affairs that young people have to live and envisage their lives in.

See also **Children and Childhood: Soldiers; Disease: HIV/ AIDS, Social and Political Aspects; Labor: Conscript and Forced; Urbanism and Urbanization.**

BIBLIOGRAPHY

Clausewitz, Carl von. *On War*. Ware: Wordsworth, 1997.

O'Brien, Donald B. C. "A Lost Generation? Youth, Identity and State Decay in West Africa." In *Postcolonial*

Identities in Africa, ed. Richard P. Werbner and Terrence O. Ranger. Atlantic Highlands, NJ: Zed Books, 1996.

Vigh, Henrik E. *Navigating Terrains of War: Youth and Soldiering in Guinea-Bissau*. Oxford: Berghahn Books, 2006a.

Vigh, Henrik E. "Social Death and Violent Life Chances: Youth Mobilization As Social Navigation in Bissau City." In *Navigating Youth, Generating Adulthood: Social Becoming in an African Context*, ed. Catrine Christiansen, Mats Utas, and Henrik E. Vigh. Uppsala: Nordic Africa Institute, 2006b.

HENRIK E. VIGH

YOUTH AND ISLAM

Youth are an increasingly compelling subject of study in sub-Saharan Africa, especially considering their demographic weight and their recent incursion into the public domain. Although the term youth has historically been constructed as a problematic generational category, the study of young sub-Saharan Africans has increasingly challenged generational constructions and concepts of agency. Interest in the question of youth and Islam was first stimulated by a wave of Islamic reformist movements that swept across sub-Saharan Africa from the late 1980s and onward. Early studies of youth and Islam tended to frame their analyses in relation to Sufism and religious authority. Such studies located questions of youth agency and social change in the context of intergenerational relations, with a focus on the dynamics of gerontocracy. Authors such as Donal Cruise O'Brien (b. 1917) went as far as suggesting that today's generation of African youths is a sacrificed generation, stripped of economic, political, and social power, and that young people are turning to religion, among other means, as a source of empowerment. To some extent, the focus on intergenerational features stems from the majority of Muslims in sub-Saharan Africa being young compared to a still much older religious and political leadership.

The growing attention to Islam and youth also stems from a shift in the study of sub-Saharan African Islam from the historical study of religious affiliations, especially Sufi lineages, and religious doctrines or texts, toward a social movement perspective that focuses on recent forms of political mobilization, agency, and practices. This perspective opened up the possibility for scholars to understand why and how young Muslims in the early twenty-first century are attempting to enhance their social status and to assert their sociopolitical objectives by adopting new strategies of self-representation and political contestation. When examining questions of youth and Islam in terms of sociopolitical dynamics, scholars have attempted to strike a balance between two sets of issues. Attention has been paid to both the impact of Islamic thought and Islamic movements on young people's status and identity, and the role of youths in altering Islamic practices and beliefs.

Questions of authority and charisma are central to processes of change within sub-Saharan African Muslim communities. Historically, sub-Saharan Muslims have followed a number of Sufi orders based on hereditary affiliation and charisma. Dynamics of change in Muslim societies have often been conceptualized in terms of reified doctrinal differences, with scholars opposing different branches of Sufism (Qadiri/Tijani/Hamallist), or alternatively opposing Sufi to Salafi, Wahhabi, or any other movement in Islam that could be regarded as foreign to local practices.

Although historically young people have not been the focus of studies centered on the transformations taking place within Muslim societies, the impetus for change within these societies has frequently stemmed from younger generations. For instance, in West Africa in the twentieth century, one can identify two generations of reformists. The first generation developed in the early 1950s in the context of the struggle against French colonialism. In the 1980s, a second generation of Islamic reformers attempted to transform religious and political practice. As a matter of fact, the democratization of secular schooling and the modernization of Islamic schools in West Africa since the late 1950s have had a tremendous impact upon Muslim youths. Both generations of reformist Muslims are characterized by their training in secular or religious schools, their push for the creation of a new religious leadership, and the formation of interest groups at local, national, and supranational levels. These waves of reformism suggest a relationship between the emergence of standardized mass schooling, the creation of voluntary associations by young educated Muslims, and efforts by religious leaders to transform religion into a political and an economic resource.

Reformist Islamic youth groups are often identified, especially by the popular media, with politicized forms of fundamentalism. In some instances radical Islamism orients social and political activism, as is the case in some states in northern Nigeria or in the Horn of Africa where groups of young Muslims stand against secularism and request the establishment of the *shariʻa*. In others, as the cases of Senegal, the *Izala* movement in Niger, and the Muslim Youth Movement in South Africa suggest, it is possible for Islamic reform movements to be integrated into the sociopolitical structure of society and thus develop in a rather peaceful way. As such, these movements may bring about new educational programs and organizational structures, as well as a sense of belonging for its members to a wider Muslim community embodied in the *ummah*, that is the "Community of the Believers," and thus the entire Muslim world.

Furthermore, the intricate relationship between youth and Islam cannot be understood outside of the momentous changes that have taken place since the 1980s across sub-Saharan Africa—namely the promotion of economic liberalization through structural adjustment programs; a partial process of political democratization; the weakening of the state and in some cases its collapse; the increase in global interconnections, including the growing influence of gulf countries on national economies since the 1970s; the spread of new media technologies; and the post-9/11 context. These processes have influenced Muslim societies in ways that are still not well understood. As a number of scholars have observed, social, political, and economic transformations that have taken place over the past several decades, compounded by the many challenges posed by colonization and secularization, have in fact stimulated new dynamics of Islamization on the continent, accounting for the emergence of new Muslim elites and the increased radicalization of secularly educated youths along Islamic lines. In a number of cases, Islamic radicalism has been tied to the bankruptcy of colonial and postcolonial projects of modernization, where youths have become increasingly disillusioned by existing inequities.

Such historical transformations suggest a refiguring of processes of socialization for young Muslims, including the place of the African diaspora and transnational processes in the definition of Islamic identities. In Muslim communities around the world in the early twenty-first century, young Muslims are being educated to think of themselves as members of the *ummah*, of a wider community that transcends national boundaries, promoting a possible redefinition of citizenship and democracy.

See also **Colonial Policies and Practices; Demography; Islam.**

BIBLIOGRAPHY

Brenner, Louis, ed. *Muslim Identity and Social Change in Sub-Saharan Africa.* Bloomington: Indiana University Press, 1993.

Diaw, T. "Les jeunes, la religion, la spiritualité. Formes d'encadrement habituelles, nouveaux groupements (sectes), le cas du Sénégal." In *Les jeunes en Afrique. La politique et la ville,* eds. Hélène d'Almeida-Topor, et. al. Paris: l'Harmattan, 1992.

Evers Rosander, Eva, and David Westerlund, eds. *African Islam and Islam in Africa: Encounters between Sufis and Islamists.* Athens: Ohio University Press, 1997.

Last, M. 1992. "The Power of Youth, Youth of Power: Notes on the Religions of the Young in Northern Nigeria." In *Les jeunes en Afrique. La politique et la ville,* eds. Hélène d'Almeida-Topor, et. al. Paris: l'Harmattan, 1992.

Magassouba, Moriba. *L'islam au Sénégal: demain les mollahs?* Paris: Editions Karthala, 1985.

Mbembe, Achille. *Les jeunes et l'ordre politique en Afrique noire.* Paris: Editions L'Harmattan, 1985.

Taoub, Abdulkader. *Islamic Resurgence in South Africa: The Muslim Youth Movement.* Cape Town, South Africa: UCT Press, 1995.

Wiktorowicz, Quintan, ed. *Islamic Activism: A Social Movement Theory Approach.* Bloomington: Indiana University Press, 2004.

MARIE NATHALIE LEBLANC

YUSUF IBN AL-HASAN. *See* **Chingulia, Dom Jerónimo.**

ZAIRE. *See* **Congo, Democratic Republic of the.**

ZAMBEZI RIVER. The Zambezi River is 1,678 miles long and therefore one of the four largest rivers in Africa along with the Nile, Congo, and the Niger. Rising in the northwestern corner of Zambia, it flows to the Indian Ocean through Zambia, Angola, Namibia, Botswana, Zimbabwe, and Mozambique. Its course runs through many different types of land formations. The chief features of its first 354 miles, also called the Upper Zambezi and stretching from the river's source to Victoria Falls, are its descent over an altitude of 886 feet, the floodplain of Bulozi, and the Caprivi swamps.

UPPER ZAMBEZI
Several peoples inhabit the Upper Zambezi region. The area of its source is the home of the Lunda who dominate northwestern Zambia, eastern Angola, and southern Democratic Republic of the Congo (DRC). In the past they formed part of the Mwata-Yamvwa's empire (the ancient kingdom of the Luba-Lunda of DRC) and lived mainly by hunting. But with the diminishing of wildlife due to unrestricted hunting, they have been forced to adopt fishing and farming in order to survive. In Namibia's Caprivi Region, authorities issued bans on fishing in 2006 when large numbers of dead fish began to surface. The fish were found to be carriers of coliform and salmonella, both potentially deadly bacteria forms to humans. Sewage leaking into the river from nearby settlements was believed to be the source of the pollution. In 2004, a new bridge over the Upper Zambezi was completed as part of the TransCaprivi Highway. One of just five bridges that cross the river over its entirety, the Katima Mulilo Bridge connects the town of the same name in Namibia to Sesheke, a settlement on the Zambian side.

Between the settlements of Chavuma and Zambezi are found the Luena (Lwena) and the Luvale. They have settled along the Zambezi, which they use to transport their goods in dugout canoes. Fishing and hunting provide them with their means of livelihood.

Just to the south of Lukulu, the Bulozi floodplain, home of the Lozi, starts and extends along the river for 155 miles up to Ngonye Falls. The Lozi originated in southern DRC and their kingdom is ruled by the *litunga* (king). One of their distinguishing characteristics is that the Lozi build their houses out of wooden frames that they cover with intricately woven reed matting. Because of the seasonal flooding of their plains, the Lozi are forced to practice seasonal migrations and live by subsistence crop cultivation, fishing, and cattle raising.

MIDDLE ZAMBEZI
The Middle Zambezi stretches from Victoria Falls to the confluence of the Zambezi and the Luangwa Rivers. Victoria Falls themselves are a world tourist attraction. They are 5,604 feet wide and have a

maximum depth of 338 feet. Immediately below the falls the river descends through four gorges before rushing through the sixty-two miles of the Batoka Gorge. Because of their harsh and rugged conditions, the gorges are uninhabited. After the Batoka Gorge the river enters Lake Kariba, created by one of the largest dams in the world. The lake stretches 137 miles and is as wide as nineteen miles in places. Besides supplying electricity to Zambia and Zimbabwe, the dam provides flourishing fishing and tourist industries and a favorable environment for wildlife. On leaving Lake Kariba, the Zambezi flows between Zambia and Zimbabwe for another 186 miles, hemmed in on both sides by inhospitable escarpments.

An important feature of the Middle Zambezi is the Mana Pools area, which, after being proclaimed a national park in 1963 developed into an excellent home for wildlife. It attracts tourists and safari lovers from all over the world. The status of the Mana Pools was enhanced considerably when the area was designated a World Heritage Site by UNESCO in 1984.

The sparse human habitation changes as one gets to the Zambezi-Luangwa junction. Here sizable settlements developed, which included Luangwa in Zambia, Kanyemba in Zimbabwe, and Zumbo in Mozambique Since the 1990s the national parks in this area—home to some of the world's richest and most diverse wildlife populations—have also become an important tourist destination.

LOWER ZAMBEZI
From the Luangwa confluence the Zambezi enters the Cahora Bassa dam, one of the largest artificial lakes in Africa. This is also the site of the Cahora Bassa Hydroelectric Generation Station. Construction began in 1977, and the dam was designed to provide hydroelectric power in the region and to South Africa. During much of the 1980s, however, the transmission towers were often targeted by guerrilla and rebel forces involved in Mozambique's civil war. Repairs began once the conflicts ended in 1992, and the system was working at full capacity by the end of the decade.

From the Cahora Bassa to the river's delta, the Zambezi Valley is habitable and, in some places, especially the delta itself, so fertile as to support densely settled communities. One of the Zambezi's branches in this area, the Quelimane River, has become increasingly constricted due to silting, a legacy of the Kariba and Cahora Bassa dams on the environment. The combined capacity of both the Kariba and Cahora Bassa dams has also resulted in occasional surges of water that force entire communities to flee to higher ground after heavy rains. Early in the twenty-first century, Mozambique had signed contracts with foreign companies such as Petronas, the Malaysian state-owned oil and gas company, permitting exploratory oil drilling in the Zambezi delta area.

With peaceful conditions in Mozambique, the people should be in a position to fully exploit the rich resources of the Lower Zambezi for the economic benefit not only of Mozambique but of the region as a whole.

See also **Congo River; Ecosystems: Coastal Environments; Energy; Niger River; Nile River; Wildlife: National Parks.**

BIBLIOGRAPHY

Bento, Carlos Manuel, and Richard David Beilfuss. "Wattled Cranes, Waterbirds, and Wetland Conservation in the Zambezi Delta." *Report for the Biodiversity Foundation for Africa for the International Union for the Conservation of Nature (IUCN).* Baraboo, Wisconsin: IUCN, 2000.

Edwards, Stephen J. *Zambezi Odyssey: A Record of Adventure on a Great River of Africa.* Cape Town, South Africa: T. V. Bulpin, 1974.

Hasler, Richard. *Agriculture, Foraging and Wildlife Resource Use in Africa: Cultural and Political Dynamics in the Zambezi Valley.* London: Keegan Paul International, 1996.

Ishemo, Shubi Lugemalila. *The Lower Zambezi Basin in Mozambique: A Study in Economy and Society, 1850–1920.* Aldershot, England: Ashgate Publishing, 1995.

Main, Michael. *Zambezi: Journey of a River.* Johannesburg, South Africa: Southern Book Publishers, 1990.

Teede, Jan, and Fiona Teede. *The Zambezi: River of the Gods.* London: Andre Deutsch, 1990.

NGWABI BHEBE
REVISED BY CAROL BRENNAN

ZAMBIA

This entry includes the following articles:
GEOGRAPHY AND ECONOMY
SOCIETY AND CULTURES
HISTORY AND POLITICS

GEOGRAPHY AND ECONOMY

GEOGRAPHY

Zambia is a landlocked country with an area of 290,586 square miles and a population of 11.4 million (2007). The country consists of an undulating plateau from 3,000 to 5,000 feet above sea level and is dominated by the Zambezi drainage system that flows east to the Indian Ocean. There are five distinct geographical areas. The Muchinga Mountains in the northeast rise to the Mbala Plateau with an altitude of 5,000 to 6,000 feet at the Tanzanian border; they form the Congo-Zambezi watershed. To the east lies the Rift Valley (the largest of the Zambian rifts), through which flows the 500-mile Luangwa River, meeting the Zambezi River at the border of Zimbabwe and Mozambique at the lowest point of the country (1,200 feet). The midland region covers the southern and central part of the Central Province and lies between 2,000 and 4,000 feet. The Western Province includes the Kalahari sand surface and is marked by the Zambezi and its tributaries. Finally, the northwestern part of the country includes the Luapula River drainage basin (flowing from Bangweulu Lake and swamp north into Lake Mweru and farther north to the Congo River in Democratic Republic of the Congo through the Luvua River).

Bangweulu Lake and Swamp is one of the largest inland lakes of the world. Other significant surface depressions include the Chambeshi and Kafue flats (the latter west of Lusaka, 149 miles from east to west) and the Lukanga Swamp. Close to Livingstone the Zambezi River flows through Victoria Falls, the largest waterfall in the world (with a 348-foot drop), where twenty million liters of water fall every second during the rainy season. To the east the river is dammed at the Kariba Gorge to form Kariba Lake.

Zambia's oldest rocks are 2.6 billion years old and are close to the town of Kapiri Mposhi, just south of the Copperbelt. In rocks 550 million to 620 million years old (the Katanga sediments) are found the copper deposits of such great economic importance to Zambia.

The most fertile of Zambia's soils lies in the river valley bottoms and lake basin soils. Also fertile are soils lying below the main plateau. But the sandy, clay soils of the plateau (the sandvelt) are difficult to farm, containing little humus with underlying laterite.

Zambia's temperatures are moderate, ranging on average from 30 to 100 degrees Fahrenheit. There are four seasons: hot (August to October), rainy (November to April), post-rainy (April to May), and cool (May to August).

Zambia's vegetation includes woody savanna, forests (8 percent is set aside as forest reserve or protected forest area), and grassland. There are seven hundred bird species and a notable variety of mammals, insects, and reptiles. The human population is small in relation to the area, with highest concentration in the Copperbelt, Lusaka, and Livingstone areas.

ECONOMY

Zambia, which achieved independence in 1964, has a one-commodity economy based on copper. The life stories of the country's first two presidents (Kenneth Kaunda, r. 1964–1991; and Frederick Chiluba, r. 1991–2002) illustrate the economic importance of copper. Kaunda was a youth organizer and welfare officer at the Chingola copper mine; Chiluba is the son of a copper miner. Until the mid-1990s mining and quarrying accounted for more than 90 percent of foreign exchange earnings and about 15 percent of Zambia's gross domestic product (GDP), with contribution to paid employment of about 15 percent. The percentage of export earnings from copper fell to 68 percent in 1994 and recovered to 72 percent in 1995.

At independence Zambia began to reap the benefits of its mineral wealth, hitherto controlled by the British South Africa Company. The mining companies enjoyed substantial autonomy when, in 1968, the government took majority shares. In 1969 it proclaimed that all mineral ownership would revert to the state. This was followed by nationalization of the mining companies. Because of rising copper prices, until 1969 Zambia's GDP grew by an average of 13 percent per year. In 1974–1975 a major collapse of the copper price precipitated a fall of per capita income by one-half. The year 1976 saw the beginning of structural adjustment programs based on economic packages negotiated with the International Monetary Fund (IMF) and the World Bank. In 1980 the government found it necessary to introduce an anticorruption law

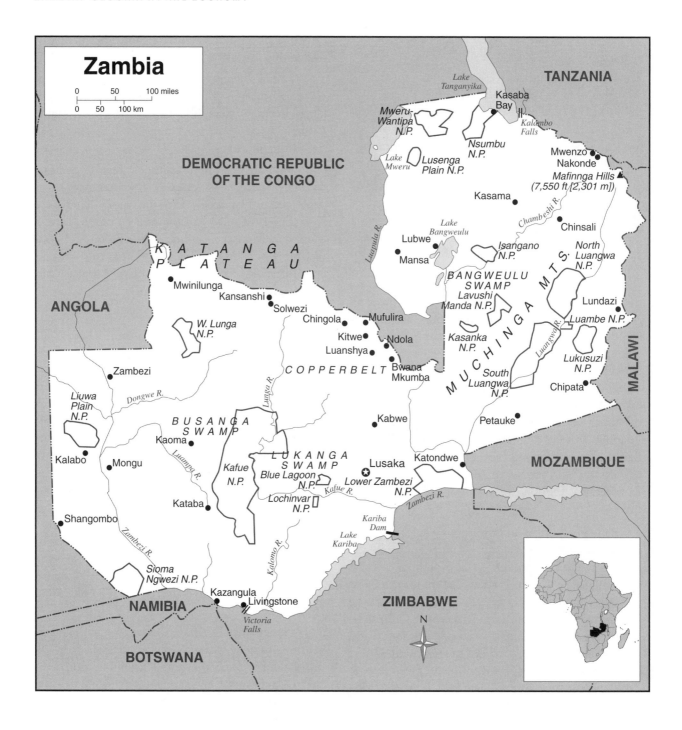

and in 1987 and 1988 arrested thousands of traders who were disregarding price controls.

By 1987 per capita income fell further by 20 percent. The principal cause was again the decline in terms of trade, especially for copper. The 1980s in Zambia were characterized by loan renegotiations, strikes, shortages of goods and food, and other hardships, with the state playing a major economic role and the government adjusting policies in response to the populace and lending sources. The IMF and World Bank requested devaluation of the kwacha, as well as wage limits and subsidy reductions on such staples as wheat, bread, flour, and maize meal. Popular response was reflected in wildcat strikes, riots, and unrest in the Copperbelt and other areas, particularly over reductions of maize-meal subsidies. In 1987 President Kaunda, with Zambia in arrears in loan repayments, severed negotiations with the IMF, holding that structural adjustment programs had not helped Zambia economically. But Kaunda's government continued economic policies similar to those agreed to with the international agencies. In September 1989 the government resumed relations with the IMF and World Bank; inflation was at 100 percent.

The 1990s saw more loan restructuring, lowered inflation, a major drought disaster, and stringency measures applied by President Chiluba, who was elected in 1991. The government reduced the civil service, and thousands of other jobs were cut. The Privatization Act was passed in July 1992, and foreign investors showed strong interest in Zambia. In 1992 inflation was 207 percent, but in 1994 it was only 35 percent and falling. President Chiluba asserted that the economy was benefiting from a strong recovery, but real gross national product per capita had fallen from US$610 in 1980 to US$370 in 1993. In December 1994 Kaunda returned to politics and criticized the government, affirming what was generally believed, that the vast majority of Zambians were living below the poverty line. Liquidation and privatization continued. The year 1995 saw a balanced budget at 854 billion kwacha.

In 1996 Zambia was US$6.3 billion in arrears on loan principal and interest payments. Loan repayments equaled two-thirds of export earnings. Despite its natural resources, it is one of the most heavily indebted countries in Africa.

An important sector of Zambia's economy is manufacturing, which contributed 26.2 percent to GDP in 1993. It is dominated by state-owned corporations and employs about 12 percent of the workforce.

Two-thirds of the Zambian population was still, in the late 1990s, engaged in traditional subsistence agriculture. The principal crops grown are maize, sugarcane, cassava, cotton, tomatoes, onions, sunflower seeds, yams, groundnuts, and tobacco. Secondary crops include peas, beans, potatoes, pumpkins, bananas, and rice. Cotton textiles, tobacco, and coffee are promising noncopper exports, produced largely by commercial farmers. Agriculture accounted for 28.6 percent of GDP in 1993.

In 1975 Kaunda made a major speech urging a focus on agriculture because of the critical economic situation, but spending focused on subsidies to producers and consumers rather than on expansion of the agricultural sector. It was estimated in 1991 that 50 percent of all people under fifteen and at least 30 percent of adults were malnourished. Zambian farmers are handicapped by lack of storage facilities, skilled staff in extension and marketing, and adequate infrastructure. Smuggling and corruption still exist. Foreign exchange expenditures for fertilizer and other items needed for commercial farms is high, and delays in transport of needed items occur.

Zambia was self-sufficient in maize production in 1985–1986 (953,800 metric tons). But droughts in 1982–1983, 1987–1988, 1991–1992, and the worst ever in 1994–1995 severely hampered production, and Zambia resorted to importing large amounts of maize during these periods. Government policies also affected maize production. In the national election of 1991, the newly founded political party, the Movement for Multiparty Democracy (MMD), under the leadership of President Chiluba, initiated the World Bank's neoliberal policies of structural adjustment and privatization. In the agricultural sector the adoption of these policies was a reaction to the fact that nearly 20 percent of the national budget went to agricultural subsidizes. The economic prosperity of small farmers was intimately connected to the Zambian national economy. With privatization, farmers had to buy their own hybrid maize seed, fertilizer, and bags at market prices and sell their produce on the open market. Since the mid-1990s, the agrarian sector has undergone severe adjustments affecting the capacity of small farmers to meet basic social obligations and provide sufficient maize to meet the demands of the urban centers.

Zambia's Copperbelt region is 68 miles long by 31 miles wide. Production of copper peaked in 1969 at 747,500 metric tons, falling to a low of 386,700 metric tons in 1991–1992. Extensive deep copper reserves exist. Early in 1996 an international consortium with the Anglo-American Corporation of South Africa in the lead was positioned through Zambia Consolidated Copper Mines (ZCCM) to develop the Konkola Deep Mining project. Zambia also mines coal, lead, zinc, tin, gold, emeralds, and amethysts.

Two dams (Kariba and Kafue) generate hydroelectricity. Seventy percent of nonhousehold power comes from these sources, with an additional 20 percent from oil and 10 percent from coal. Seventy-four percent of electricity produced is used by the copper mining industry. In its drought periods, Zambia imported power from Democratic Republic of the Congo.

See also **Aid and Development; Capitalism and Commercialization: Privatization; International Monetary Fund; Kaunda, Kenneth; Metals and Minerals; World Bank; Zambezi River.**

BIBLIOGRAPHY

Burdette, Marcia M. *Zambia: Between Two Worlds.* Boulder, CO: Westview Press, 1988.

Ferguson, James. *Expectations of Modernity.* Berkeley: University of California Press, 1999

Nag, Prithvish. *Population, Settlement, and Development in Zambia.* New Delhi, India: Concept Publishing Company, 1990.

Osei-Hwedie, Kwaku, and Muna Ndulo, eds. *Issues in Zambian Development.* Roxbury, MA: Omenana, 1985.

Sichinga, Austin. *Zambia: From Transition to Consolidation: Critical Policy, Review of the Liberalization of Maize and Agricultural Input Markets, 1993–1996.* Lusaka, Zambia: Ministry of Agriculture, Food, and Fisheries. No. 18, 1996.

Sklar, Richard L. *Corporate Power in an African State: The Political Impact of Multinational Mining Companies in Zambia.* Berkeley: University of California Press, 1975.

Tordoff, William, ed. *Politics in Zambia.* Manchester, U.K.: Manchester University Press, 1974.

NANCY C. WRIGHT
REVISED BY GEORGE CLEMENT BOND

SOCIETY AND CULTURES

In 1996 Zambia had a total population of about 11 million people, of which more than 98 percent were of indigenous African descent. The remaining fraction of Zambians were of Asian and European backgrounds. There was also a small population of mixed descent. During the period of British colonial rule, from 1924 to 1964, the British formed the ruling section, staffing the higher and middle rungs of the civil service, the mining and construction industries, and the major commercial and farming enterprises. The Asians were primarily in trade and commerce, while the bulk of Africans were small farmers or cultivators and unskilled and semiskilled workers. After independence in 1964 and the establishment of a one-party participatory democracy in 1972, the Zambian government and the ruling African party, the United National Independence Party (UNIP), pursued a policy of extensive Zambianization, through which Africans gradually assumed major government posts.

In the late twentieth century, Zambia had a high rate of annual population growth, increasing from 2.5 percent in the 1970s to 3.2 percent in the 1980s to an estimated 3.7 percent by the mid-1990s with a slight decline to 2.1 percent in 2006. The rate of increase from the 1970s through the 1990s caused Zambia's population to more than double between 1970 and 1995. As in most African countries, the population is young, with 49 percent under fifteen years of age. Zambia has been seriously affected by HIV/AIDS. In the 1980s it was primarily a disease found in the urban centers. In the first decade of the 2000s it is found throughout the country, with 17 percent of the population between 15 and 49 being infected; of those, 57 percent are women. The life expectancy has declined from fifty-five years in 2000 to forty years in 2006 and the infant mortality rate is 86 per 1,000 live births.

SOCIAL AND CULTURAL DIVERSITY

Historically, Zambians have been divided into seventy Bantu-speaking, ethnically distinguishable peoples, each located in a specific area and claiming its own language, history, and customs. The seventy ethnic groups may be differentiated according to the dominant group in the region, the main language spoken, and patterns of kinship. Ethnic and language clusters may include a main or dominant group as well as a number of other peoples who have become subject to and assimilated into the dominant group. The Bemba in the Northern Province, the Ngoni in the Eastern Province, and the Lozi in the Barotse Province of western Zambia are examples of dominant groups that have shaped the history and customs of other peoples of the area.

There is no single set of organizing principles common to the main language clusters of Zambia's ethnic groups. Varying kinship systems based upon tracing of descent through the female line (matrilineal), through the male line (patrilineal), and through both lines (bilateral) are found in each language cluster. The modes of tracing descent are present among peoples with highly centralized political systems as well as those that are acephalous. The most widely distributed pattern of descent is, however, matrilineal.

Zambians may be classified under seven major regional language clusters: the Bemba, Tonga, Nyanja, Tumbuka, Mambwe, Lunda-Luvale, and Barotse. The Bemba-speaking peoples consist of eighteen ethnic groups including the Bemba, Bisa, Lungu, and Lunda (Luapula) of northern Zambia. The Bemba state, under its ruler, or *citimukulu*, encompassed a broad territory that included various ethnic groupings. In the past, it was a strong military force, engaging in conquest and slaving. Once incorporated under the colonial government of Northern Rhodesia, its workers turned to agriculture and labor migration.

Many of the Bemba ethnic groups originated in Zaire and are matrilineal. Together they form about one-third of Zambia's population and have played an important role in national politics. During the struggle for independence they supported Kenneth David Kaunda (Zambia's president from 1964–1991) and UNIP.

The Tonga-speaking peoples of south-central Zambia include the Tonga, Ila, and Lenje. These acephalous, matrilineal peoples are thought to be some of the oldest residents of Zambia and form the second largest language cluster. They have been commercial farmers and were the mainstay of the African National Congress (ANC) and its founding president in 1951, Harry Nkumbula.

The Nyanja-speaking peoples of southeastern Zambia form a diverse agglomeration of ethnic groupings consisting of the Senga, Chewa, Kaonde, and Ngoni. Both the history and the customs of the region and those adjacent to it have been seriously affected by the northward movement of the Ngoni, a South African people who crossed the Zambezi River in the 1830s. In their drive northward, the Ngoni incorporated and imposed their customs on the people they conquered. The effect was to disseminate a patrilineal cattle-keeping complex among matrilineal cultivators, affecting their customs, practices, and beliefs. The Ngoni introduced the Zulu practice of *lobola*, the payment of cattle or

its equivalent as bride-price. The Ngoni and Bemba, both a military and conquering peoples, stand in a joking relationship. Individuals may engage in strong verbal abuse, jesting at one another's expense. The Tumbuka-speaking peoples in the northeast, though only a very small percentage of Zambia's population, were also affected by the Ngoni. Most keep cattle and are maize and millet cultivators. They are patrilineal and organized into small chiefdoms. They are often counted as Ngoni.

Many of these peoples were converted to Christianity at the turn of the twentieth century and went to the Livingstonia Presbyterian mission school at Kondowe in Malawi. At Livingstonia they were taught to read and write in Nyanja, Tumbuka, and English, and trained to be artisans, craftsmen, teachers, medical assistants, and of course evangelists. They formed the basis of a new Christian educated elite and were well equipped to become productive labor migrants in the developing urban industrial complexes of central and southern Africa. In the towns, they were often identified as Nyasa, persons from Malawi. Many were the founders of voluntary associations and religious movements that linked the countryside to the towns.

Northeastern Zambia has another small grouping of peoples who originate mainly from Tanzania and Malawi. These include the Mambwe language grouping consisting of the Mambwe, Lungu, Namwanga, Iwa, and Tambo, as well as some of the small enclaves of peoples in Isoka District. They are cultivators and keep livestock. They are primarily patrilineal and organized into small chiefdoms. Many of these ethnic groups, like the Namwanga and Nyika, straddle international borders. The men of these groups have a long-established pattern of labor migration, which may take them as far south as South Africa and as far north as Uganda. In the wider flame of Zambian ethnic relations, they may be counted as either Bemba or Ngoni, that is, as being from the Northern or Eastern Provinces. Many of the men and women of this cluster attended the Presbyterian mission at Mwenzo in Nakonde, a town on the border with Tanzania. They became part of the intellectual elite of the countryside and active in bringing about development and political change. They and their children were active in founding welfare associations during the 1930s and 1940s and branches of UNIP in the late 1950s and early 1960s.

The peoples of the northwestern region of Zambia form another language cluster. They include two major groupings, the Lunda-Luvale, including well-known peoples such as the Ndembu and the Kaonde. Together they make up about one-sixth of Zambia's population. Historically they are of Angolan and Zairian origin and at one point, most came under the sway of the Lozi. Their kinship systems are based on matrilineal descent. They engage in swidden agriculture, and there is active trade and commerce along the border regions with Zaire and Angola.

The Barotse language group of southwestern Zambia forms another large cluster. The Lozi are the dominant group and one of the best-known Zambian peoples because of their history of extensive conquest, their unique and complex system of floodplain cultivation, and the seasonal movement of the king and his court. At the height of their power, the Lozi rule extended to some twenty-five ethnic groups, including some three hundred thousand to four hundred thousand people and encompassing 80,000 square miles. Under British rule, their powers were reduced and they were incorporated into Barotse Province. They too have played a significant role in the political history of Northern Rhodesia and Zambia. Their kinship system is bilateral, and marriage requires the payment of a small bride-price.

RELIGION

The historical and social dimensions of religion are complicated in Zambia. Though 50 to 75 percent of the population is estimated to be Christian, a large percentage of those who are Christian may also believe in and practice their own indigenous religions. The most pervasive form of indigenous religious expression is the ancestor cult and a belief in witchcraft.

Mission Christianity played an important role in shaping Zambia's modern history. The early missionaries sought not only to convert Africans but to educate them, and until the mid-1930s African education was left in their hands. Their schools had a lasting effect on the making of Zambian elites and the political life of the nation. The influence of the Presbyterian Church in the

northeastern and northern regions of Zambia provides an example. The Livingstonia Presbyterian mission in Malawi founded missions at Mwenzo in Namwanga country near the Tanzanian border and at Lubwa in Chinsali in Bemba country. These two schools educated generations of northern Zambians and trained them to become urban wage earners. Educated Africans of the countryside were prepared to enter the new occupational structures of the towns as skilled and unskilled workers.

TOWNS

Zambia differs from most sub-Saharan African countries in its high rate of urbanization. Over 70 percent of Africa's population is rural and tied into its agricultural economy. Though the process of urbanization in Zambia began during British colonial rule, urbanization has grown steadily, increasing rapidly after independence. Twenty-three percent of Zambia's population was urban in 1965; by 1980, 43 percent lived in cities. In the late 1990s almost half of the population inhabited the main urban centers. In 1963, Lusaka, the capital of Zambia, had a population of about 123,000; in 2003 it was estimated to be over 1.2 million. Other main urban centers such as Mufulira, Kabwe, Ndola, and Kitwe range in size from 200,000 to 470,000 people.

With the exception of Lusaka, the major towns grew up next to mines. The demand for African labor to work in the mines was intense and the expansion of urban areas was rapid indeed. From 1944 to 1961 the population of Ndola grew from about 12,500 to 86,000; that of Kitwe from about 28,000 to 114,000; and that of Mufulira from about 21,000 to 75,000. Men came from all parts of Zambia to work in the mines and lived in these new towns. Thus since the 1920s there has been a great deal of movement as men have left the rural areas to find work in the urban industrial centers. Over the years some stayed in the towns, settled, and raised families, while others returned to the countryside to cultivate the land on small holdings, growing staple subsistence crops such as maize, millet, cassava, sorghum, and peanuts.

Since the 1920s Zambians have also sought wage employment in the developing urban areas of the neighboring countries of Tanzania to the north, Malawi to the east, Zaire to the west, and

ART AND ARCHITECTURE

Forum of Septimus Severus. At Leptis Magna, in Libya, the second-century Roman emperor Septimus Severus strove to elevate his birthplace, once a Phoenician trading outpost, to a stature rivaling that of Rome itself. © Nico Tondini/Robert Harding World Imagery/Corbis

LEFT: Great Zimbabwe. The "conical tower" at Great Zimbabwe is dramatically framed by trees growing in the ruins of this fourteenth-century structure. Its unknown builders took advantage of the rectangular shape of blocks chipped from local granite to build, without mortar, a stable array of curvilinear walls more than thirty feet high. © BETTMANN/CORBIS

TOP RIGHT: Preparing *adinkra* cloth. Africans have woven textiles from varied materials for many centuries, often creating elaborate designs to express the social standing of the wearer. In the Gold Coast region (modern Ghana) weavers picked threads from imported textiles to reweave them in elaborate and colorful representations of the *adinkra* system of symbolized Akan language and wisdom. © MARGARET COURTNEY-CLARKE/CORBIS

BELOW: Market and mosque at Jenné. The mosque at Jenné in Mali is a famous and grand example of the western African craft of building in adobe. The present structure, built on much older predecessors, was designed by a French architect along "neo-Sudanese" lines in 1908. © MICHAEL MARTIN

TOP RIGHT: Berber rug. The strong geometric patterning of Berber weavers has been celebrated for centuries and has powerfully influenced modern European art. This contemporary Moroccan example, with typical orange and saffron colors, reflects both the traditions of the tribe and the creativity of the individual weaver. © Walter Bibikow/JAI/Corbis

BOTTOM RIGHT: Soninke wall painting. The ubiquitous, warm brown surfaces of the adobe walls characteristic of architecture in the treeless western African plain invite decoration, sometimes sculpted, sometimes painted. Here Soninke women in Mauritania paint a house in colorful geometric designs. © Margaret Courtney-Clarke/Corbis

TOP RIGHT: Pyroengraved gourd with buffalo design, Kenya. While European scholars once regarded East Africa as being "without art," attention to the rich traditions of body painting and household object decoration tells another story. © WERNER FORMAN/CORBIS

BOTTOM LEFT: Drum with pedestal. The rhythmic variety of African drumming is complemented by the creative design of the instruments themselves. This nineteenth-century example from the western Congo region depicts a gin-drinking European trader. WERNER FORMAN/ART RESOURCE, NY

BOTTOM RIGHT: Dogon stool, Mali. The three parts of the stool reflect the Dogon concept of the cosmos: the seat (sky disc) is connected to the base (earth) by a central tree. The figure groups refer to cardinal points and include the bisexual ancestral Nommo couple with upraised arms. WERNER FORMAN/ART RESOURCE, NY

Akuaba fertility figure carvings, Ashanti people, Ghana; male twin figures, Yoruba people, Nigeria. West African sculpture emerged from a diversity of artistic traditions, all of which give artworks an important place in the daily life of the culture.
ALDO TUTINO/ART RESOURCE, NY

TOP RIGHT: Palace doors carved by Olowe of Ise. Societal creativity does not exclude recognition of individual artistry. This famous sculptor from Yorubaland (in modern Nigeria) was widely esteemed during his lifetime (c. 1875–c. 1938). Depicted here is the reception of a British captain by King Ogoga of Ikere in 1895. WERNER FORMAN/ART RESOURCE, NY

BELOW: Cheik Ledy, *Nelson Mandela*. The Congolese artist's (1962–1997) imaginative depiction of the South African leader pulling his people toward freedom is an example of growing pan-African sensibility. The artist's early death from AIDS testifies to the challenges facing African art and life. © CONTEMPORARY AFRICAN ART COLLECTION LIMITED/CORBIS

Republic of Zambia

Population:	11,477,447 (2007 est.)
Area:	752,614 sq. km (290,586 sq. mi.)
Official language:	English
Languages:	about 70 local languages and dialects, including Bemba, Lozi, Kaonde, Lunda, Luvale, Tonga, and Nyanja
National currency:	kwacha
Principal religions:	Christian 50–75%, Hindu and Muslim 24–49%, traditional 1%
Capital:	Lusaka (est. pop. 1,000,000 in 2006)
Other urban centers:	Kitwe, Ndola, Chingola, Mufulira, Luanshya, Kabwe, Livingstone, Chililabombwe, Kalalushi
Annual rainfall:	from 1,400 mm (50 in.) in the north to 510 mm (20 in.) in the south
Principal geographical features:	*Mountains:* Muchinga Mountains *Lakes:* Kariba (man-made), Bangweulu, Mweru, Tanganyika, Kampo-lombo *Rivers:* Zambezi, Kabompo, Kafue, Luangwa, Chambeshi, Luapula *Other:* Luangwa-Luano Trench of the Rift Valley, Victoria Falls
Economy:	*GDP per capita:* US$1,000 (2006)
Principal products and exports:	*Agricultural:* corn, sorghum, rice, peanuts, sunflower seed, vegetables, flowers, tobacco, cotton, sugarcane, cassava (tapioca), coffee, cattle, goats, pigs, poultry, milk, eggs, hides *Manufacturing:* construction, foodstuffs, beverages, chemicals, textiles, fertilizer, horticulture *Mining:* copper, coal, cobalt, lead, zinc, tin, gold, gemstones *Tourism:* 17 national parks and Victoria Falls contribute to the tourist sector of the economy.
Government:	Independence from Great Britain, 1964. Constitution approved in 1964, replaced in 1973. Constitution amended in 1991. New constitution adopted in 1996. Republic. President and 158-member National Assembly (150 elected, 8 appointed by president; 5-year terms). President appoints cabinet from among members of the National Assembly. For purposes of local government there are 9 provinces further divided into 72 districts.
Heads of state since independence:	1964–1991: President Kenneth David Kaunda 1991–2002: President Frederick Chiluba 2002–: President Levy Mwanawasa
Armed forces:	President is commander in chief. Voluntary enlistment. *Army:* 20,000 *Air force:* 1,600 *Paramilitary:* 1,400
Transportation:	*Rail:* 2,164 km (1,342 mi.), including 891 km (552 mi.) owned by the Tanzania-Zambia Railway Authority (TAZARA) *Port:* Mpulungu (on Lake Tanganyika) *Waterways:* 2,250 km (1,395 mi.) *Roads:* 91,440 km (56,819 mi.), 22% paved *National airline:* Aero-Zambia *Airports:* International facilities at Lusaka. Over 100 smaller airports and airstrips throughout the country.
Media:	Daily newspapers include the *Times of Zambia* and the *Zambia Daily Mail,* both government-owned. 3 weeklies, 10 biweeklies, several of which are published by the Zambian Informational Services. At least 7 book publishers, including Oxford University Press and the National Education Company. Zambia Broadcasting (state-owned) provides radio service in English and vernaculars. Television Zambia broadcasts in English. 24 radio stations, 9 television stations.
Literacy and education:	*Total literacy rate:* Men: 82%; Women: 61% (2003). Education is not compulsory but is free for 7 years. Technical training is administered by the Commission for Vocational and Technical Training. Postsecondary education provided by the University of Zambia, which in 1987 split to form the Copperbelt University in Kitwe and the University of Zambia in Lusaka. Other technical and professional schools.

Zimbabwe to the south. Though some Zambian ethnic groups straddle the borders with Angola and Mozambique, these Lusophone countries were not the main recipients of Zambian workers. However, large numbers of Zambians have been labor migrants in the urban industrial complexes of southern Africa, especially in the mines of South Africa. Thus Zambians have greatly contributed to the economic development and social life of central and southern Africa.

The new towns of Zambia became the main centers of wage employment. They brought together people from different ethnic backgrounds, provided the conditions for cross-ethnic associations, and laid the basis for a common national identity. They were the main centers for the rise of labor movements, nationalism, and political parties such as the African National Congress led by Harry Nkumbula, the United National Independence Party under Kenneth Kaunda, and the Movement for Multiparty Democracy led by Frederick Chiluba, who was elected president of Zambia in 1991.

In the towns, different types of cultural expression developed that both enunciated distinctive ethnic identities and established the transformative nature of the urban setting. An example is the Kalela dance studied by J. Clyde Mitchell in the 1950s, in which a group of unskilled working-class young men from the same ethnic background, Bisa, performed dances in front of multiethnic audiences in the Copperbelt town of Luanshya. The songs sung by the young men glorified their own ethnicity while demeaning that of others. They reconfigured ethnic categories in a manner such that regional origin became as significant as ethnicity. Though themselves African and unskilled laborers, they dressed as European professionals. Thus, new class identities were being forged within the context of occupational and status aspirations, and distinct ethnic categories collapsed into single regional designations. As Robert Molteno pointed out in his studies of Zambian national politics, many of the smaller distinct ethnic enclaves of the north became equated with the Bemba or the Ngoni, the two dominant ethnic groups of the Northern and Eastern Provinces.

The urban areas thus became crucibles for the reducing of ethnic distinctions. English, Bemba, and Nyanja were the three main languages spoken in towns. They were the languages of the civil service and secondary schools, the military, and the police and were in everyday use in social and commercial activities. Almost all adult Zambians have themselves experienced or have some knowledge of urban life and can communicate in one or more of these three languages. The towns broke down the provincial and parochial boundaries of rural life. Though Zambians born and raised in the towns have retained their ethnic identities and memories, increasingly they are oriented toward urban life and being "Zambian." In a number of different ways Zambians living in the main urban centers, small towns, and rural communities are linked together through historical, social, and political ties. With the collapse of the Zambian economy and the

limited possibilities for urban employment, new patterns of movement have been set in motion. Urban dwellers have returned to the countryside, bringing with them many of the circumstances of urban life. Thus, within the brief span of less than a century the people of Zambia have moved from small cultural and political units into an encompassing nation-state. Urban and rural areas are intimately interconnected, both affected by national and international economic policies.

See also **Christianity; Disease: HIV/AIDS; Ethnicity; Kaunda, Kenneth; Labor: Migration; Labor: Trades Unions and Associations; Languages; Lusaka; Political Systems: Chieftainships; Urbanism and Urbanization.**

BIBLIOGRAPHY

Berger, Elena L. *Labour, Race, and Colonial Rule: The Copperbelt from 1924 to Independence*. Oxford: Clarendon Press, 1974.

Bond, George C. *The Politics of Change in a Zambian Community*. Chicago: University of Chicago Press, 1976.

Colson, Elizabeth, and Max Gluckman, eds. *Seven Tribes of British Central Africa*. New York: Oxford University Press, 1959.

Crehan, Kate. *Fractured Community*. Berkeley: University of California Press, 1997.

Gluckman, Max. *The Judicial Process among the Barotse of Northern Rhodesia*. Glencoe, IL: Free Press, 1955.

Gould, Jeremy. *Luapula: Dependence or Development*. Zambia Geographical Association Regional Handbook 6. Helsinki: Finnish Society for Development Studies, 1989.

Hansen, Karen T. *Keeping House in Lusaka*. New York: Columbia University Press, 1997.

Hansen, Karen. *Salaula: The World of Secondhand Clothing and Lusaka*. Chicago: University of Chicago Press, 2000.

Ihonvbere, Julius O. *Economic Crisis, Civil Society, and Democratization: The Case of Zambia*. Trenton, NJ: Africa World Press, 1996.

Kaplan, Irving. *Area Handbook for Zambia*. Washington, DC: U.S. Government Printing Office, 1974.

Mitchell, J. Clyde. *The Kalela Dance: Aspects of Social Relationships among Urban Africans in Northern Rhodesia*. Manchester, U.K.: Manchester University Press, 1956.

Molteno, Robert. "Cleavages and Conflict in Zambian Politics: A Study in Sectionalism." In *Politics in Zambia*, ed. William Tordoff. Berkeley: University of California Press, 1974.

Pritchett, James. *The Lunda-Ndembu.* Madison: University of Wisconsin Press, 2001.

Turner, Victor W. *Schism and Continuity in an African Society: A Study of Ndembu Village Life.* Manchester, U.K.: Manchester University Press, 1957.

Watson, William. *Tribal Cohesion in a Money Economy: A Study of Mambwe People of Northern Rhodesia.* Manchester, U.K.: Manchester University Press, 1964.

World Bank. *Sub-Saharan Africa: From Crisis to Sustainable Growth.* Washington, DC: World Bank, 1989.

GEORGE CLEMENT BOND

HISTORY AND POLITICS

Zambia is a landlocked country in Central Africa, surrounded by eight neighbors: United Republic of Tanzania, The Democratic Republic of the Congo (DRC), Angola, Namibia, Botswana, Zimbabwe, Mozambique, and Malawi. The history of Zambia stretches back millions of years. The earliest inhabitants of the Zambian land mass were San groups living in isolated communities and using stone and wooden tools. They are remembered as *Akafula* in Eastern Province, *Mbolela Pano* in Mweru-Luapula or simply *Wamwenene kwi?* ("Where did you see me?"). Short in stature with copper-colored skins, they lived in caves and rock shelters, some of which were decorated with painting, and in simple structures that they built with grasses and branches of trees or shrubs. They hunted small and large game, and gathered fruits, roots, and other forest products for their food.

Archaeologists have excavated a number of sites in various parts of the country that have assisted in dating the country's prehistory. In the early twenty-first century, the oldest known archaeological sites are around Livingstone, the Victoria Falls, and Kalundu in Southern Province. Others are found at Kalambo Falls in Northern Province, and various places in Luapula and the Central and Eastern Provinces. Stone tools attributed to the San have been found in these sites, sometimes near lakes and rivers but often in caves and rock-shelters. They indicate the antiquity of human settlements. Among the tools used were hand axes and cleavers dating from the early Stone Age period. Other stone tools and weapons are spears, arrows, and grindstones.

During the first millennium CE, migrants from farther north and northwest who probably spoke Bantu languages occupied Zambia and settled in various parts of Zambia. These groups lived in isolated settlements and used stone tools. They were acephalous—they had no chiefs and no centralized authority. The earliest were the Tonga, an acephalous group that inhabited the southern part of the country from about 1000 CE. Leadership was in the hands of clan leaders who also acted as priests in propitiating ancestral spirits and in praying for the rain. The others were the Batwa, found in the northeastern and central parts of the country.

From the fourteenth through the sixteenth centuries, new migrants from the Luba areas of Katanga Region of the Democratic Republic of the Congo (DRC) arrived. Among the earliest were the Nsenga led by Kalindabwalo (later changed to Kalindawalo), who occupied the area east of the Luangwa up to the present Petauke District. The Chewa, led by Kalonga Mazura, settled further to the east to occupying areas that became Central Mozambique. Malawi and Zambia followed them. The other important chefs were Undi and Lundu. To the northeast came the Tumbuka speakers from northern and central Malawi led by Mlowaka, the one who crossed Lake Nyasa (now called Lake Malawi). Other chiefs included Mwase Mpangwe, Mwase-wa-Minga, and Kapichila. The Bemba-speaking groups followed and occupied northeastern and central parts of Zambia.

The Bemba-speakers comprised the largest group and had several leaders. Chitimukulu and his brother Nkole led one section. After wandering and coming in contact with the Chewa under Mwase-wa-Minga, they came to settle on the Lubemba Plateau with the Chambeshi River and its tributaries being the main drainage system The Bisa, led by Mwansabamba (later this title was changed to Kopa), came to settle on the areas adjacent to the shores of Lake Bangweulu in what have become the Luwingu, Chilubi, Mpika, and Chinsali districts in Northern Province. The Lala led by Kankomba settled in much of Central Province. The Ushi led by Chabala Muwe settled in Mansa area. The Bena Chishinga, Bena Mukulu, and Bena Kabende settled in the Kawambwa, Mwense, and Samfya Districts. The Lamba led by Chipimpi settled in the Ndola District and the areas forming the Pedicle area. The Lenje led by

Makuni, Chamuka, Chipepo, and other chiefs were probably the last group to arrive between the fourteenth and eighteenth centuries and settled in the Kabwe, Chibombo, and Livingstone Districts.

The latter Bantu groups lived in villages and developed a sophisticated social system of clans. At the political level, they created institutions of leadership: headmen, chiefs, and paramount chiefs to whom they paid obligatory tribute in the form of labor, salt, ivory, fish, meat, iron tools, and weapons, as well as agricultural products. They mined, smelted iron, and forged iron tools such as axes to cut down the forests; hoes to cultivate a variety of crops such as millet, sorghum, and cucurbits; hooks to catch fish; knives for cutting and for harvesting millet or sorghum varieties of beans and cucurbits; and weapons to defend their territory or to expand it. The same weapons were used to hunt and kill animals. Ironworking was an important occupation and some areas such as Lumbi and Ikabako in Western Province, Musomani in Serenje, Kamana Mpango near Chibote Mission in Kawambwa, Chofoshi in Mansa, Chief Chinakila's area, Isoka, and Lundazi became important iron mining areas. The Bantu hunted small and large game; fished in rivers, lakes, and swamps; and gathered forest products such as wild fruits, varieties of mushrooms and honey when they were in season, and also varieties of roots, edible leaves, and insects. They kept poultry and domestic stocks of goats, sheep, and cattle. Iron tools and weapons greatly increased mastery over both humans and nature and, together with food production, promoted population growth. They also mined copper and gold. Copper was used as a currency and to make insignias of power and decorative items. Gold was only found in smaller quantities and made into jewelry.

The next group of migrants came from the Lunda Empire in western Katanga, ruled by Mwatayamvu. These included the Luyana who settled in the Zambezi Plains; the Chokwe, Luvale, Lunda, and Kaonde, who settled in the northwestern part of the country; and the Lunda of Mwata Kazembe, who settled in the lower Luapula Valley. They probably arrived in the mid-eighteenth century.

During the nineteenth century, new migrants arrived from South Africa. They were fleeing a destabilized situation created by Shaka, King of the Zulus, who initiated wars to unite the Zulus and extend their territory (called Mfecane), starting around the 1820s. Zwengendaba led the first of these groups, called Ngoni. After leaving Zululand, he led the Ngoni into Mozambique and Zimbabwe and crossed the Zambezi in 1835, passed through Zambia and headed towards Lake Tanganyika where he died at a place called Mapupo. After his death, the Ngoni split into three groups. The first two went to occupy areas in northern and central Malawi among the Tumbuka. The third group led by Mpezeni came to Zambia and settled among the Chewa in present-day Eastern Province of Zambia and the central part of Malawi. Unlike the Kololo, the Ngoni did not compel their hosts to adopt and speak their language. Gradually, they adopted the language of their hosts, Nsenga and Chewa. Ngoni, a variant of Zulu, is only spoken during the N'chwala ceremony to celebrate the ripening of he first crops.

Around the year 1840 the Kololo, a Sotho group of warriors and herdsmen led by Sebitwane, entered the country. They were fleeing from their original area in present-day Lesotho to find sanctuary in the Central Zambezi Plains inhabited by the Luyana. After defeating the original inhabitants, they established their capital at Linyanti on the banks of the Chobe River in present-day Caprivi Strip, which is part of Namibia. During their rule that lasted into the 1870s, they decreed the use of Sesotho as a language of communication. In the process, a new language called Lozi, which was a fusion of Sesotho and Luyana, replaced the old one, Luyi, and has remained the language of the area.

EXTERNAL CONTACTS

Trade between Zambia and the Western world began with the Portuguese in Mozambique and Angola. Early in the seventeenth century, the Portuguese spread along the Zambezi and founded trading posts at Tate, Zumbo, and Feira, at the confluence of the Zambezi and Luangwa. By 1762, Portuguese caravans were regularly acquiring ivory and copper from Zambians among the Soli and Lenje in Central Zambia in exchange for cotton cloth. In the eighteenth century, slave-owning Goans and Portuguese mined gold, hunted elephants for ivory, and traded in European merchandise among the Chewa under Undi. In time, they came in contact with the Bisa traders who were exporting ivory, slaves, and copper to the Yao in Malawi. They were in touch with Kazembe III, the Lunda king on the Luapula who had indirect access to European goods from the west coast; he now hoped to cut out the African middlemen. A Goan visited Kazembe and was warmly received around 1796.

The Portuguese government, through the governor-general of Mozambique and the governor of Tete, dispatched expeditions in 1798 led by a renowned-scholar, Dr. de Laced, and another in 1831 led by Fr. Gamitto. These came to nothing, mainly because the Portuguese on the Zambezi were turning their attention to exporting slaves rather than ivory or gold. During the same period, Western Zambia was also beginning to be enmeshed in the Portuguese slave trade that extended to northern Namibia and Botswana in the south and Malebo Pool on the Congo in the north, directed to Luanda, the port of embarkation for slaves to Cape Verde and Brazil. From the early nineteenth century, African traders from Angola bought slaves to the north of the Lozi kingdom. The Lozi themselves kept slaves for labor at home but did not take part in this trade.

From about the 1830s, the Bemba and Kazembe's Lunda were selling ivory and slaves to Arabs and the Swahili and other Africans from the East Coast. At the same time, in central Zambia the Chikunda, a collection of disparate groups under Goan and Portuguese Prazo holders on the Zambezi, were moulded into an identifiable group. Armed with guns, they hunted for ivory and slaves. To the west, South African and a number of other European traders bought ivory from the Lozi in exchange for firearms, gunpowder and cloth.

Toward the second part of the eighteenth century, most of the states were involved in long distance trade in a variety of items that included slaves, ivory, rubber and copper. From the West Coast came the Luso-Africans, Mambari, Ovimbundu, and Mbundu to trade with the Lunda, Chokwe, Luchazi, Kaonde and Lozi. On the eastern side were the Arabs, Swahili, Yao, and Nyamwezi as well as the Portuguese and Chikunda trading with the Bemba, Chewa, and Bisa groups. Some states benefited from the trade in firearms, gunpowder, and cloth while others became victims of the destabilizing effects of this trade. Some rulers were dominant and able to extend their rule over a large area and subject inhabitants to a tribute system. A few rulers contrived to turn the trade to their own advantage. The general rise in demand for goods stimulated local production of ironwork, salt, tobacco, and food. Indeed, several crops of American origin were introduced from the West and East Coast, such as maize, cassava, peanuts, sugarcane, and a variety of fruits. Arab traders introduced rice. The slave traders and wars to capture slaves devastated much of Zambia.

Following in the steps of the traders were a number of European missionaries such as David Livingstone. Their goal was to win this part of Africa to Christianity, stop the trade in human beings, and report on the economic activities and prospects in the areas they visited. These reports created an immense interest in a number of European Powers in this part of Africa. Livingstone, the first to arouse British interest in the region, crossed Zambia in three famous expeditions between 1853 and his death, near Lake Bangweulu, in 1873. His reports on slave trade inspired other missionaries to come to Central Africa. After their meeting in Berlin from November 1884 to February 1885, a number of European countries sent emissaries to secure parts of this region through treaties and direct annexation.

COLONIAL PERIOD

In 1889 the British government granted Cecil Rhodes a charter, enabling him to form the British South African Company (BSAC) with powers to administer the area between the Limpopo River and the Zambezi–Congo watershed. In 1890, thanks to a series of "treaties" with such chiefs as Lewanika, Kazembe, and Mpezeni, the BSAC found few areas of resistance to their rule. Where this was the case, it was easy to isolate and break resistance by the force of arms, threats, and persuasion. The BSAC established company rule in a broad area admimnistered by two separate territories: North West Rhodesia with its headquarters at Kalomo (later moved to Livingstone), and North East Rhodesia with its headquarters at Fort Jameson. In 1911, to save money, the two territories were amalgamated into one territory called Northern Rhodesia. Company rule continued until

1924, when Northern Rhodesia became a British protectorate, a status that continued until 1964.

From 1895 to about 1902 a number of copper deposits in old mines were discovered, including those at Kansanshi and Bwana Mkubwa. A small number of deposits also were found in the Kafue Hook. In addition, a zinc and lead mine was pegged at Broken Hill (Kabwe) in 1902. During the first decade of the twentieth century a railroad was built between Livingstone and Katanga to transport machinery and smelted copper to the coast for export. The present Zambian Copperbelt was developed in the late 1920s, after the world economic depression that lasted from 1929 to 1934 and after World War II.

In 1953 Northern Rhodesia joined with Southern Rhodesia and Nyasaland to form the Federation of Rhodesia and Nyasaland, with its capital at Salisbury (present-day Harare). Much of Northern Rhodesia's earnings from the sale of copper went to develop Southern Rhodesia. Also during this period the Kariba Dam was built on the Zambezi.

Following strong opposition to the federation from African nationalists in Northern Rhodesia and Nyasaland, the British government dissolved it in December 1963. This paved the way for the independence of Nyasaland (Malawi) in July 1964 and of Northern Rhodesia (Zambia) in October 1964. Kenneth Kaunda, a son of a missionary from Nyasaland, became the first president; Reuben Kamanga was his vice president, and Simon Kapwepwe was the minister of foreign affairs.

GOVERNMENT

Zambia attained its independence on October 24, 1964. It established a multiparty constitution with the following characteristics: a president elected for a five-year term (and limited to two terms); a 125-member National Assembly elected for a five-year term, from which the vice president and cabinet were appointed; the House of Chiefs, consisting of twenty-seven chiefs representing all the provinces; and an independent judiciary.

On January 1, 1973, Zambia adopted a new constitution specifying a one-party government. The president was still elected for a five-year term, but there was no limit on the number of terms. The National Assembly grew to 135 members, from among whom the prime minister and cabinet were chosen. (It was later enlarged to 150 elected members, with eight nominated by the president.) The House of Chiefs and the judiciary were unchanged. All the political parties were combined into the ruling United National Independence Party (UNIP). Under this new dispensation, the party was supreme over the government; its Central Committee was placed higher than cabinet. President Kaunda, as president of UNIP and of the Republic of Zambia, appointed the members of the Central Committee of the ruling party, the cabinet, high ranking government and party officials, diplomats, and heads of parastatals (state-owned companies). Kenneth Kaunda continued as president from 1973 to 1991. His prime ministers were Mainza Chona (1973–1977), Daniel Lisulo (1977–1980), Nalumino Mundia (1981–1984), Kebby Musokotwane (1984–1988), and Major General Malimba Masheke (1988–1991).

During Kaunda's presidency, Zambia offered sanctuary to the freedom fighters from Angola and Mozambique, Southern Rhodesia, South West Africa and South Africa. Parts of the country were bombed and a lot of human lives were lost, and domestic animals and infrastructure destroyed. And in some parts, land mines were laid that have continued to maim and kill people and livestock. Peace gradually returned with Angola and Mozambique attaining their independence in 1975, Zimbabwe in 1980, and Namibia in 1990. In 1994 a new constitution, which allowed multiracial politics, was implemented, bringing to an end the military confrontation in southern Africa.

In 1990 a group called the Movement for Multiparty Democracy (MMD) was formed by young intellectuals to press for a multiparty government. On August 2, 1991, the National Assembly approved a new constitution that provided for such a government. The president and the National Assembly were to be elected at the same time, by popular vote. The president was again limited to two five-year terms but kept many of his appointive powers.

In the elections of October 31, 1993, Frederick T. J. Chiluba of the MMD was elected president with 79 percent of the vote; the MMD also won 125 of 150 seats in the National Assembly. As of 1995 the National Assembly consisted of 119 MMD members, 26 UNIP members, and 4 National

Party members. There are thirty-six parties in the country; besides the three mentioned above, the major ones are the Zambia Democratic Congress and the Labour Party. President Chiluba's vice presidents were Levy Mwanawasa (1991–1994) and Godfrey Miyanda (1994–2002) when he left office.

In 2001 Levy Patrick Mwanawasa, calling his government the "New Deal," was elected president. He retained Kavindele as vice president, but later dropped him and replaced him with Nevers Mumba, and subsequently with Lupando Mwape Katoloshi. The most significant achievements of this "New Deal" administration have been the fight against corruption, in which the second Republican president and a number of high ranking officials were charged of embezzling public funds; the opening of new mines at Kansanshi and Lumwana in north Western Province to mine copper, and the establishment of smaller mines in many parts of the country for the extraction of base metals such as copper as well as gold and semiprecious stones, creating much-needed employment; better performance in agriculture leading to increased food security and exports to neighboring countries; and better performance of the economy, including a much lower rate of inflation, the appreciation of the Kwacha against the U.S. dollar and other currencies, and lower prices for many retail goods. There is also a marked improvement in the road infrastructure, storage facilities, and telecommunications

On September 28, 2006, the country held a tripartite election to elect the president, members of parliament, and councillors. President Mwanawasa, one of five presidential candidates, was re-elected with a huge majority; the ruling MMD secured a majority of seats in parliament and in most of the councils but lost in the Copperbelt, Lusaka, Luapula, and Northern Provinces.

See also **Colonial Policies and Practices; Colonialism and Imperialism: Concessionary Companies; Harar; Harare; History of Africa; Kaunda, Kenneth; Livingstone, David; Political Systems; Rhodes, Cecil John; Shaka Zulu; Slave Trades.**

BIBLIOGRAPHY

Chiluba, Fredrick. J. T. *Democracy: The Challenge of Change.* Lusaka: Multimedia Publications, 1995.

Chipungu, S. N., ed. *The Elders in Their Time Social and Economic History of Colonial Zambia.* London: Macmillan, 1992.

Hill, Catherine B., and Malcolm F. McPherson, eds. *Promoting and Sustainable Economic Reform in Zambia.* Cambridge, MA: Harvard University Press, 2002.

Macmillan, Hugh, and Frank Shapiro. *Zion in Africa: The Jews of Zambia.* London and New York: I. B. Tauris Publishers, 1999.

Macola, Giacomo. *The Kingdom of Kazembe: History and Politics in North: Eastern Zambia and Katanga to 1950.* Hamburg: Li Verlag Munster, 2002.

Moore, Henrietta L., and Megan Vaughan. *Cutting Down Trees: Gender, Nutrition, and Agricultural Change in the Northern Province of Zambia, 1890–1990.* Portsmouth, N.H.: Heinneman, 1994.

Musambachime, Mwelwa. *Basic Facts on Zambia.* Indianapolis, IN: Authorhouse, 2005.

Mwanakatwe, John. *Teacher, Politician, Lawyer: My Autobiography.* Lusaka: Bookworld, 2003.

Roberts, Andrew D. *A History of Zambia.* London: Heinemann, 1976.

Sardanis, Andrew. *Africa: Another Side of the Coin: Northern Rhodesia's Final Years and Zambia's Nationhood.* London: I. B. Tauris, 2003.

Sichone, Owen, and Bornwell Chikulo, eds. *Democracy in Zambia: Challenge for the Third Republic.* Harare: Sapes Books, 1996.

Snelson, Peter. *To Independence and Beyond: Memoirs of a Colonial and Commonwealth Civil Servant.* London: Radcliffe Press, 1993.

Zukas, Simon. *Back into Exile.* Lusaka: Bookworld, 2002.

MWELWA MUSAMBACHIME

ZANZIBAR.

Lying about five degrees south of the equator and approximately thirty miles off the coast of mainland Tanzania, Zanzibar comprises two main islands—Unguja (994 square miles) and Pemba (630 square miles)—and adjacent islets. It receives 63–75 inches of rain, mostly falling in March through May and October to December. Pemba is wetter and has deeper soils than Unguja, and was known by Arab visitors as the Green Island.

HISTORICAL OVERVIEW

Archaeological and documentary evidence suggests that Zanzibar was settled by fishers, hunters, and gatherers well before 2,000 years BP and that these and later Bantu-speaking populations were part of Indian Ocean trade networks. A local form of Swahili culture developed in the archipelago as long-distance trade intensified after the tenth and eleventh centuries, by which time there was a significant Muslim and Swahili-speaking population on Pemba.

After Vasco da Gama first saw part of the Zanzibar archipelago in 1498, the islands became important provisioning points for the Portuguese. The Portuguese were a dominant power on the coast for several centuries before the Omanis finally seized control of Zanzibar at the seventeenth century's close.

By the mid-nineteenth century, the Omani sovereign Seyyid Said (1790–1856) had made Unguja his permanent home, whence he ruled Oman and Zanzibar, which then also encompassed a strip of the coast of present-day Kenya and Tanzania. Zanzibar Town, on Unguja, became the most important entrepôt in the region. Sending caravans into the mainland interior, Arabs based in Zanzibar Town exported slaves, ivory, and other mainland goods to ports along the Red Sea, the Persian Gulf, western India, and beyond. Products such as cloth, iron, and chinaware flowed into the port from India and the Gulf. To provide an outlet for unrest building up in Oman, Seyyid Said encouraged Omanis to move to Zanzibar and take up the production of cloves. Cloves became Zanzibar's most important homegrown export, followed by coconut products. Pemba was the world's foremost source of cloves, which were in high demand internationally as a flavouring and in hygienic and medicinal preparations on account of the antiseptic and anaesthetic properties of clove oil.

On Pemba, many Omani plantation owners resided in the countryside, integrating themselves into rural society through marriage and co-residence. By contrast, Omanis settling on Unguja generally remained town- or plantation-based and more aloof from the rural, indigenous society. Another important difference was that many more indigenous Pembans than Ungujans acquired their own clove tree holdings. The greater degree of sociocultural interpenetration and shared economic interests among Arab planters and indigenous people on Pemba, as opposed to Unguja, had ramifications that persist in the early twenty-first century, for example, in the islands' differing political alignments.

Following the signing of an 1890 treaty between Germany and Britain, which were both building competing presences in the region, Zanzibar became a British Protectorate. The northern part of the mainland coastal strip that had been under the control of the Sultans of Zanzibar was incorporated into British East Africa (later, Kenya). Germany took possession of the southern stretch of the mainland coast, in the hinterlands of which Zanzibar-based ivory- and slave-trading caravans had been most active; this territory became German East Africa (later, Tanganyika). The British abolished slavery on the islands in stages, emancipating what may have amounted to the majority of the islands' population. Though many of the freed slaves remained on the plantations as squatters, some moved to town or assimilated into rural communities. British authorities devoted considerable effort to compelling former slaves, as well as native islanders, to work on the clove plantations of the Arabs, with mixed results.

Labor difficulties, plantation owner indebtedness, dips in international prices, and other problems affecting the islands' clove-based economy plagued Zanzibar during the British period. With islanders increasingly involved in clove production either as growers or pickers and dependent on the cash this earned them for the purchase of imported foods, such as rice, and other goods, another challenge emerged: how to restore some measure of the food self-sufficiency that Zanzibaris had once enjoyed. The situation became particularly acute during World War II, when imports were curtailed.

After a decade of growing political unrest, Zanzibar was granted independence in December 1963. In January 1964, the Arab-dominated government whose election to power the British had carefully engineered was ousted in a popular, nominally leftist revolution. Thousands of Zanzibaris of Arab and Indian origin, perceived as a privileged class, are said to have been killed. In April 1964, President Karume of Zanzibar and Tanganyika's President Nyerere agreed to unite their two states to form the United Republic of Tanzania with Zanzibar retaining semiautonomous status within it. A period of relative isolation from the West followed, with China, the Soviet Union, East Germany, and Cuba serving as the main foreign

After a wedding in rural Zanzibar. A hired bus is loaded with a bed, mattress, cookware, and other household items contributed by the bride's kin as part of the exchanges strengthening the ties between the two newly joined families. The bus will transport members of the wedding party from the wife's village, where weddings customarily take place, to the husband's community, where the couple will reside in accordance with the norm of virilocality. PHOTOGRAPH BY HELLE V. GOLDMAN

influences to the autocratic regime of Karume and the Zanzibar Revolutionary Council. The postrevolutionary period was marked by the persecution of supposed supporters of the old order, including deportments, imprisonments and forcing Shirazis (see below) to formally renounce this ethnic identity. All land was nationalized, and large plantations were broken up and redistributed to those deemed needy; paid-up membership in the ruling party was a requirement for distribution.

This and other initiatives aimed at redressing past economic injustices were marred by mismanagement and corruption, exacerbating the islands' economic difficulties. Karume was assassinated in 1972. He was followed by President Jumbe, who held office until 1984. The ruling parties of Zanzibar (the Afro-Shirazi Party) and mainland Tanzania (the Tanganyika African National Union) merged into the Revolutionary Party (Chama cha Mapinduzi, CCM) in 1977, which remained the only legal political party until reforms in the 1990s. Government-sanctioned acts of persecution diminished in Zanzibar, but human rights abuses, such as the absence of freedom of the press, persisted. Zanzibar gradually opened up to the West during the 1980s, with economic liberalization.

CULTURE AND SOCIETY

Zanzibar's multifarious culture has developed from interactions between diverse groups of people over the course of the archipelago's history. Coastal people, slaves from different upcountry regions, and Arab and other settlers have all contributed heavily to the islands' dynamic culture. British authorities distinguished three ethnic groups among the indigenous islanders: the Wapemba (on Pemba), Wahadimu (Unguja), and Watumbatu (Tumbatu Island and the adjacent part of northern Unguja). Some indigenous Zanzibaris have claimed superior status by describing themselves as Shirazi, drawing on old stories, told in many parts of the coast, about prestigious immigrants from Persia.

There was some political centralization in Zanzibar before the nineteenth century. Early Portuguese accounts refer to "kings," some of whom were quite powerful, as well as to a ruling "queen." A fundamental principle of social organization was descent group membership, traced through both male and female lines. This gave individuals rights to arable and residential land. Kinship remains important, but its function in terms of land rights has eroded with the transition

Warming up spectators prior to a bullfight in Pemba. Traditional kirumbizi performers skillfully wield sticks in a fast-paced mock fight. In Zanzibar, bullfighting only occurs on the island of Pemba. It is generally presumed to have been introduced by the Portuguese. PHOTOGRAPH BY HELLE V. GOLDMAN

to a cash economy and the nationalization of land. Emphasis on the male descent line has increased with the influence of Arab patrilineal organization.

Zanzibaris are predominantly Muslim. The majority follows Sunni rites; those who claim descent from Omanis belong to the much smaller Ibadhi sect. The two denominations coexist largely without friction. Muslim orthodoxy is complemented by spirit propitiation and healing practices associated with spirit possession. Pemba has a reputation in the region as a center for witchcraft and sorcery. The Swahili language is the mother tongue of most Zanzibaris. There are several local dialects within the islands, including Kipemba, Ki tumbatu, and Kimakunduchi. In 1928, Kiunguja, the dominant dialect of Unguja, was selected by the British as the basis for standardized Swahili in East Africa. Arabic serves chiefly as the language of Islamic recitation.

ZANZIBAR IN THE EARLY 2000S

According to the 2002 census, the population of Zanzibar was 984,531. The population growth rate is 3 percent per year; the population density is 154 per square mile, more than ten times that of mainland Tanzania. Though urban centers are undergoing rapid growth as a result of an influx from the rural parts of the islands, most of Zanzibar's inhabitants still reside in the countryside.

Rural Zanzibaris support themselves through combinations of subsistence agriculture, cash cropping, seasonal clove picking for wages, fishing, sale of charcoal and firewood, and other small businesses. The rural economic situation is grim. Waning international demand for the islands' cloves and the pricing policies of the parastatal to which clove harvests must be sold have combined to cause the profits of clove growers to dwindle to almost nothing. Compounding Zanzibar's economic distress is mounting pressure on the islands' limited natural resources, caused by population growth and tourism, and land tenure insecurity, which the government has been attempting to address through a series of land reforms legislated in the 1990s, though their implementation has been delayed. Founded on the economic liberalization measures of the 1980s, tourism is a flourishing industry that brings in much-needed revenue, as well as consuming natural resources and causing land values to rise steeply in some areas, to the detriment of poorer Zanzibaris.

Part of united Tanzania's rocky transition to multiparty democracy, general elections held in Zanzibar at five-year intervals since 1995 have received international criticism for being seriously flawed. The chief opposition party, the Civic United Front (CUF), has its stronghold in Pemba. Tensions with the mainland, arising from the ill-defined union, have yet to be resolved. Zanzibar has its own flag, president, House of Representatives, and other autonomous government bodies. Some Zanzibaris are calling for the dissolution of the political union with the mainland.

See also **Archaeology and Prehistory; Colonial Policies and Practices; Gama, Vasco da; Kings and Kingdoms; Kinship and Descent; Land: Tenure; Nyerere, Julius Kambarage; Queens and Queen Mothers; Spirit Possession; Tanzania; Witchcraft; Zanzibar City; Zanzibar Sultanate.**

BIBLIOGRAPHY

Bennet, Norman R. *A History of the Arab State of Zanzibar.* London: Methuen, 1978.

Clayton, Anthony. *The Zanzibar Revolution and its Aftermath.* Hamden, CT: Archon Books, 1981.

Horton, Mark, and John Middleton. *The Swahili: The Social Landscape of a Mercantile Society.* Oxford: Blackwell, 2000.

Lofchie, Michael F. *Zanzibar: Background to Revolution.* Princeton, NJ: Princeton University Press, 1965.

Sheriff, Abdul. *Slaves, Spices and Ivory in Zanzibar: Integration of an East African Commercial Empire into the World Economy, 1770–1873.* London: James Currey, 1987.

HELLE V. GOLDMAN

ZANZIBAR CITY.

Zanzibar city (2002 population: 205,870) is located on the west coast of Zanzibar island, about twenty-three miles off the Tanzanian mainland. While the current site has been inhabited since at least the twelfth century, Zanzibar city is much more modern in genesis. Once known as the "metropolis of East Africa," it became the dynamic center of the expansive Omani sultanate in the nineteenth century, shaped in equal parts by Indian merchant capitalism and Omani colonialism. The city was built on wealth extracted from slaves, spices, and ivory: a plantation economy predicated on clove production coexisted with extensive trade networks linking Africa, Arabia,

Asia, Europe, and the United States. The British imposed a protectorate in 1890, seeking to counteract German expansion on the mainland opposite, in present-day Tanzania.

European colonialism sharply curtailed the political and economic prospects of the sultanate. Colonial urban Zanzibar was often described as a highly cosmopolitan space. Nonetheless, inequalities of race and class were inscribed in the built fabric of the city as colonial officials sought to distinguish elite stone areas—which they called "town proper"—from Ng'ambo, the "other side" where the vast majority, many of them former slaves, immigrants from the mainland, or members of the emerging working class, resided. The 1964 revolution overturned these colonial socio-spatial relations as elite dwellings were nationalized and poorer Zanzibaris moved into the city center. More recently, these experiments in constructing a socialist "new city" have been abandoned in favor of privatization and tourist promotion. As the colonial urban core has been marketed as an "exotic Arab casbah," the city as a whole has sprawled outward, resulting in burgeoning informal (and unserviced) settlements.

See also **Madagascar and Western Indian Ocean, History of (1500 to 1895); Tanzania; Zanzibar; Zanzibar Sultanate.**

BIBLIOGRAPHY

Bissell, William Cunningham. "Engaging Colonial Nostalgia." *Cultural Anthropology* 20, no. 2 (2005): 215–248.

Fair, Laura. *Pastimes and Politics: Culture, Community, and Identity in Post-Abolition Urban Zanzibar, 1890–1945.* Athens: Ohio University Press, 2001.

Sheriff, Abdul, ed. *The History and Conservation of Zanzibar Stone Town.* Athens: Ohio University Press, 1995.

WILLIAM CUNNINGHAM BISSELL

ZANZIBAR SULTANATE.

The islands of Unguja and Pemba, located off the East African coast and constituting geographical Zanzibar, along with a vaguely defined region on the African mainland, were part of the Omani state until 1862 when they were recognized by the British government as a separate Zanzibar sultanate. After the partition of Africa in 1884–1885, the two islands became a British protectorate in 1890.

Arab dhows in Zanzibar Harbor. These wooden sailing boats transport cargo between the mainland and the Indian Ocean islands. They are specially designed for the monsoon winds in the Indian Ocean. They are quick, have no keel or motor, and can be easily stranded on the beach during low tide. © Bojan Brecel/CORBIS

The eastern African coast has been in intimate contact with the northern rim of the Indian Ocean for centuries. Immigrants from the African mainland peopled the area. They mingled with visitors from Arabia, the Persian Gulf, and India and gave rise to a cosmopolitan coastal Swahili culture.

The most prominent among these visitors in more recent centuries were Omanis from the southeastern corner of Arabia, at the entrance to the Persian Gulf. They established their overrule on the eastern African coast after expelling the Portuguese in 1698. The al-Busaid dynasty, from its base at Zanzibar, extended its control over the whole coast from Cabo Delgado in the south to the Benadir in Somalia during the nineteenth century.

ECONOMIC TRANSFORMATION

Sultan Seyyid Saʿid (r. 1806–1856) laid the foundation of the Zanzibar sultanate. After his first visit as sultan to Zanzibar in 1828, he began to evolve his policies for the economic development of Zanzibar in the two sectors of agricultural production for export and commerce. The prohibition of the slave trade to the south of Cabo Delgado in 1822 had deprived Zanzibari traders of a valuable market for captives from the mainland in the former French islands of the southern Indian Ocean. This forced them to divert growing supplies of slave labor to produce commodities for export, especially cloves, on Zanzibar and Pemba. Realizing the great potential of such a transformation, Saʿid encouraged the planting of cloves on the islands. At its height in the 1860s, about 20,000 slaves entered Zanzibar, most of them absorbed on the plantations of the islands and on grain plantations on the adjacent East African mainland.

The commercial sector, on the other hand, was galvanized by the declining cost of the manufactured goods, notably textiles that were purchased with the proceeds of ivory and other exports, whereas the prices of these exports, especially ivory, rose with growing demand for luxuries in Europe and the United States. Such favorable terms of trade enriched the Zanzibar state and the merchant classes. To place Zanzibar's external trade on a regular footing, Sai'd negotiated most-favored-nation commercial treaties with the United States in 1833, with Britain in 1839, and with France in 1844, thus securing favorable tariff treatment in Zanzibar's principal markets in the West.

Growing demand for slaves in East Africa and for ivory, in India as well as in Europe and North America, led to a rapid expansion of Zanzibar's hinterland in the eastern half of equatorial Africa, and the creation of a vast commercial empire reaching well beyond the Great Lakes (Tanganyika, Victoria).

The population of Zanzibar Town grew from 10,000–12,000 in 1835 to 35,000 in 1910. It became the hub where the Indian Ocean and the world economies met, and progressively integrated a large part of the African interior, exchanging African ivory for *merekani* cloth from Massachusetts textile mills and beads. Burton, Livingstone, Stanley, and others used Zanzibar Town as a starting point for explorations of the African interior. Zanzibar Town was also the channel through which European and North American values, including Christianity and the antislavery impulse, made their entry into the region.

ADMINISTRATION

The sultan's direct political control rarely extended beyond the offshore islands and the narrow coastal belt. In all the principal towns along the coast, the sultan was represented by a *wali* (governor) and a customs agent. His influence in the interior was based more on his control over the trade outlets at the coast and on common commercial interests with coastal merchants and the trader chiefs, such as Mirambo in present-day western Tanzania, than on direct rule.

His administration at the coast was fairly simple. Many of the Omani tribes and clans (and even some of the other communities) continued to enjoy considerable autonomy over their internal affairs. Most of the decisions were handed down at the daily *majlis* (sittings), when he met members of the public. *Qadis* (Islamic judges), who belonged to the ruling Ibadi and the majority

Ancient ruins in Stone Town, Zanzibar, East Africa. The East African islands of Unguja and Pemba, along with a vaguely defined region on Africa's mainland, constitute Zanzibar, which was part of the Omani state until 1862. Stone Town is the cultural heart of Zanzibar and the only functioning historical town in East Africa. ADAM MCCONNACHIE/GETTY IMAGES

Sunni schools, handled judicial matters. Customs administration was farmed out to the most prominent Indian merchant, who appointed his own agents at various ports on the mainland.

Even on the islands of Zanzibar, Omani rule was superimposed over indigenous polities that retained considerable autonomy. On Unguja, the most prominent local ruler was the *mwinyi mkuu*, who ruled over the indigenous Shirazi population. He recognized the suzerainty of the Omani sultan, to whom he paid an annual tribute, over external affairs. In northern Unguja and Pemba, there were lesser chiefs (*shehas* or *diwanis*).

The loosely organized Omani state depended much on the personality of the ruler, and it was correspondingly fragile even during the life of Sai'd. In 1844, Sai'd tried to divide the sultanate between Oman and Zanzibar and guarantee succession to a son in each place. A dual succession was contrary to Omani constitutional practice, and he failed to gain the support of the British, who were jealous of their imperial interests along the sea routes to their possessions in India and who did not wish to be embroiled in a succession dispute. After Sai'd's death in 1856, the British in India decided it was more expedient for the two halves to be ruled separately under British hegemony and the sultanate was formally partitioned in 1862.

COLONIAL INTERVENTION

Zanzibar's reliance on the exports of slaves and on slaving as a source of labor for its plantations exposed it to British antislavery pressures over the same years. The trade south of Cabo Delgado was prohibited in 1822, and that north of Lamu (an island at the northern limit of Zanzibar's influence on the mainland coast) in 1845. All slave trade by sea was prohibited in 1873, and slavery itself was abolished in 1897.

This British interference was a prelude to more direct intervention by European powers in the 1880s. The struggle for markets, raw materials, and areas of expansion led to a scramble for territories claimed by the sultan. Eventually, a delimitation commission narrowed the sultan's area of effective control to the offshore islands and a ten-mile coastal strip. Inland from this narrow zone of Zanzibari influence, the Germans and the British divided the interior between them. They pressured the sultan to lease the coastal belt to them, to give these landlocked possessions outlets to the sea. In 1890 Zanzibar itself was declared a British protectorate.

Zanzibar's commercial empire, which had extended beyond the western limits of the German and British colonies, left a more lasting heritage. Based on the ethos of trade, it gave rise to a cosmopolitan society on Zanzibar and the coast, in which all the peoples of the Indian Ocean, and even Europeans and Americans, mingled, and religious tolerance was the norm. From there Swahili culture, including the language and Islam, spread throughout the interior to the Great Lakes and beyond.

See also **Barghash Ibn Sa'id; Eastern Africa and Indian Ocean, History of (1500 to 1800); Ivory; Madagascar and Western Indian Ocean, History of** (1500 to 1895); **Mombasa; Slave Trades: Indian Ocean; Tanzania; Tippu Tip; Zanzibar; Zanzibar City.**

BIBLIOGRAPHY

Bennett, Norman Robert. *A History of the Arab State of Zanzibar*. London: Methuen, 1978.

Bhacker, M. Reda. *Trade and Empire in Muscat and Zanzibar: Roots of British Domination*. London: Routledge, 1992.

Burton, Richard Francis. *Zanzibar, City, Island and Coast*. London: Tinsley Brothers, 1872.

Gilbert, Erik. *Dhows and the Colonial Economy of Zanzibar, 1860–1970*. Oxford: James Currey, 2004.

Gray, John Milner. *History of Zanzibar, from the Middle Ages to 1856*. London: Oxford University Press, 1962.

Nicholls, Christine Stephanie. *The Swahili Coast*. London: George Allen and Unwin, 1971.

Salme, Seyyida/Ruete, Emily. *An Arabian Princess between Two Worlds*, ed. Emeri van Donzel. Leiden, the Netherlands: Brill, 1993.

Sheriff, Abdul. *Slaves, Spices, and Ivory in Zanzibar*. London: James Currey, 1987.

ABDUL SHERIFF

ZARA YA'IQOB (1399–1468). Zara Ya'iqob was emperor of Ethiopia from 1434 to 1468. The son of Emperor Dawit (1380–1412), Zara Ya'iqob's education at his father's court was probably entrusted for a time to the noted theologian Giyorgis of Gascha. When his father died and his brother Téwodros became emperor, he was confined in the mountain prison of Amba Gishan, where he remained for more than twenty years until called to the throne.

Zara Ya'iqob was probably the most formidable of all Ethiopia's rulers: both militarily powerful and intellectually determined. It was he who imposed the celebration of the two Sabbaths (Sunday and Saturday) at the Council of Dabra Mitmaq in 1449. This reconciled the southern, Dabra Libanos monastic tradition of commitment to Sunday observance with the tradition of the monks of northern Ethiopia who followed Saint Ewostatewos in insisting upon the celebration of Saturday as the true biblical Sabbath. His principal writings, the *Mashafa Milad* and *Mashafa Berhan*, insist both upon this and upon a very high Mariology. On other matters he was far from tolerant, persecuting Stephanite monks, the Ethiopian Jews (Falasha), and all accused of non-Christian practices. He was unique among medieval emperors in building himself a stone palace, at Dabra Berhan, in which he lived his later years, almost invisibly. While his immediate successors did not follow him in this, resuming the peregrinatory lifestyle of earlier emperors, Zara Ya'iqob's theology remained an almost essential part of the Ethiopian tradition.

See also **Ethiopia and Vicinity, History of (600 to 1600 CE); Judaism in Africa.**

BIBLIOGRAPHY

Haile, Getachew. *The Mariology of Emperor Zar'a Ya'eqob of Ethiopia: Texts and Translations.* Rome: Pontificium Institutum Studiorum Orientalium, 1992.

Tamrat, Taddesse. *Church and State in Ethiopia, 1270–1527.* Oxford: Clarendon Press, 1972.

ADRIAN HASTINGS

ZAYANI, MOHA OU HAMMOU

(1863–1921). Moha ou Hammou Zayani was a Moroccan nationalist and military leader who fiercely resisted French colonial rule. At the age of twenty he became chief of the Zayyan tribes in the Middle Atlas, and was appointed *qa'id* (chief) of these tribes by Sultan Moulay Hasan I in 1886. In 1906 he opposed the treaty of Algesiras, which allowed the French to colonize Morocco. As a result, the French army, led by Hubert Lyautey, invaded the country and combated the Berbers in the name of "pacification." Moha ou Hammou organized a strong guerrilla movement against the French and managed to rally most of the Middle Atlas tribes against the colonizers. The Berber tribes in the region and other parts of Morocco opposed the invasion of their landed by *iroumiyn* (the Christians), and decided to join forces to liberate their country. After the occupation of the cities of Oujda and Casablanca in 1907, Moha ou Hammou ordered his troops to support the coastal Shawiya tribes in the battle of Mediouna in 1908 against the French colonel Mangin, nicknamed "the butcher."

Moha ou Hammou became famous for the 1914 battle of El Hri near Khenifra where the French troops were severely attacked and defeated. His charisma and skill in organizing resistance constituted an obstacle against the French expansion in Morocco. Forced to leave his *qasba* (fortress) in Khenifra, he fled to the mountains from where he continued violent attacks against the French. He refused to compromise with the colonizers and continued the resistance until he was killed in battle in 1921.

See also **Casablanca; Morocco: History and Politics.**

BIBLIOGRAPHY

Halstead, John P. *Rebirth of a Nation: The Origins and Rise of Moroccan Nationalism, 1912–1944.* Cambridge, MA: Harvard University Press, 1967.

Landau, Rom. *Moroccan Drama 1900–1955.* San Francisco, CA: American Academy of Asian Studies, 1956.

MOHA ENNAJI

ZIMBABWE

This entry includes the following articles:
GEOGRAPHY AND ECONOMY
SOCIETY AND CULTURES
HISTORY AND POLITICS

GEOGRAPHY AND ECONOMY

GEOGRAPHY

Zimbabwe is a landlocked country in the southeastern part of Africa, sharing borders with Zambia, Mozambique, South Africa, and Botswana. Most of the country is over 300 meters (1,000 ft.) above sea level. Its land surface (390,580 sq. km) comprises the so-called highveldt, middleveldt, and lowveldt. The highveldt (approximately 25 percent of the country's land surface) is a ridge that extends across the country in a southwest to northeast direction and consists of land above 1,200 meters (4,000 ft.), rising to the highest point in Zimbabwe at Mount Inyangani (2,592 m; 8,503 ft.). Sloping down from the highveldt toward the Zambezi River in the north and the Limpopo River in the south is the middleveldt (some 40 percent of the land surface) at 915 to 1,220 meters (3,000 to 4,000 ft.) high. This gives way to the lowveldt (23 percent of total area), of which the larger area is in the south. The lowest point of Zimbabwe (200 m; 660 ft.) is at Dumela, where the Limpopo flows into Mozambique. The eastern border of Zimbabwe is called the Eastern

Highlands, consisting of mountains, many of which exceed 1,800 meters (6,000 ft.). The rock underlying Zimbabwe is very old (up to 4.6 billion years).

Due to its altitude, Zimbabwe enjoys a moderate climate but has insufficient rainfall from November to March (from October to April in the Eastern Highlands). Temperatures in the Eastern Highlands range from a mean of 11°C (52°F) in July to 18°C (65°F) in October. Comparable figures for Harare are 14°C (57°F) to 21°C (70°F).

The predominantly light, sandy soil is characterized by low fertility. Cultivation is difficult because heavy, periodic downpours create leaching and drainage problems. Six different agricultural areas of the total 39 million hectares (96.5 million acres) have been identified. In about 1 percent of the country's acreage, the Eastern Highlands, diverse crops can be grown, and continuous cattle ranching, plantation cropping, and orchard growing is possible. On the other extreme, toward the Zambezi River, little agriculture or forestry is possible. Of the remaining land surface, about one-fifth may be intensively used for maize and tobacco farming and cattle raising, another one-fifth for mixed farming and semi-intensive livestock raising, a third for semi-extensive farming of maize, sorghum, millet and cotton, and another one-fifth only for ranching.

Zimbabwe is characterized by a forest savanna ecosystem. More than one-third of the country is forest and woodland. Primarily due to the use of trees for fuel by the rural population, the depletion of woodland is a serious problem. The country's diverse animal life is protected in the Hwange National Park and other parks but is disappearing elsewhere due to cultivation. Wildlife has been further depleted by the collapse of conservancies and the rise of poaching following the land invasions that began in 2000.

ECONOMY

Zimbabwe (formerly Southern Rhodesia) achieved independence in April 1980 following nearly one hundred years of occupation by white settlers backed by Cecil Rhodes's British South Africa Company and culminating in the white-supremacist rule of Ian Smith. At independence, land distribution was sharply skewed in favor of white landowners. Population density was twenty people per square kilometer, with over 50 percent of the population under the age of fifteen. The population was estimated at 12 million in 2007 with population growth rates declining from 3 percent to under 1 percent over the past decade due to AIDS-related mortality and out-migration.

Inequalities in land distribution were addressed to a limited degree in the first two decades following independence. Through laws enacted by the white-ruled government, the black population (96% of the total) was confined to the poorer lands, leading to land overuse and degradation; white settlers owned half the country's land and all the best farmland. The new black majority-ruled government's goal in the 1982–1985 Transitional

National Development Plan was to resettle 162,000 families on 9 million hectares of land, but by 1989 only about one-fourth of this population had been thus resettled. Critical to the government's subsequent efforts was a 1990 constitutional amendment that allowed it to purchase any land at government-set prices without any right of appeal; the government's stated intent was to buy half (about 6 million hectares) of the land farmed by whites by the year 2000. At this point there were 150,000 landless peasant families, and about 60 percent of Zimbabweans were crowded onto the poorer, and by then degraded, colonial-era tribal trust lands (subsequently renamed Communal Lands). In 1992 the Land Acquisition Act became law, providing for compulsory purchase of up to 11.5 million hectares. By 1997, 71,000 black farmers were resettled on 3.6 million hectares, and some 500 large-scale commercial farms had been purchased by blacks. The government's desire not to interfere with production and to retain white management expertise and investment along with the absence of adequate funds for compensating white farmers, account for the relatively slow pace of land redistribution. Beginning in 2000, however, a more radical program of land seizure (under the rubric of a "fast-track" land reform or *jambanja*) was authorized by the ruling ZANU (PF) regime in response to rising challenges from war veterans and an opposition movement initially based in the trade union movement. By 2004, only about 500 (out of 4,500) white farmers remained in possession of their farms, and a large majority of the 200,000 commercial farm workers had lost their jobs and livelihoods.

The land seizures precipitated the collapse of the commercial agriculture. Together with costly pension payouts to war veterans in 1997 and the deployment of the Zimbabwean army in the Democratic Republic of Congo thereafter, the formal economy went into freefall. The years following 2000 have been characterized by negative growth rates (at between -6 and -7% annually), hyperinflation (reaching 3,000% per annum in 2007), high formal sector unemployment (estimated at over 80% in 2007), severe shortages of fuel, food and foreign currency, and a burgeoning parallel market.

In 2003 agriculture represented 17.3 percent of the gross domestic product (GDP). Tobacco remains the largest single export commodity. Until the land seizures, Zimbabwe was generally self-sufficient in food production, in most years growing a surplus for export to the region. Maize and wheat are major food crops. Periodic droughts exacerbated the negative impact of structural adjustment in the early 1990s. The maize crop was almost totally destroyed by a catastrophic drought in 1991–1992, and another dry period followed in 1994–1995. Zimbabwe also produces and exports cotton (which is also sold to the local textile industry), raw sugar, coffee, and garden vegetables and flowers. Beef was once the third major export crop after tobacco and cotton, but Zimbabwe has lost its export quota to the European Union due to foot-and-mouth disease.

During the first decade of independence, the production of small farmholders showed impressive advances, reflecting improvements in the availability of inputs, marketing facilities, and credit. Between 1979 and 1988 the share of maize sold to the Grain Marketing Board by the smallholders grew from about 7 percent to 52 percent of total purchase. Increases in the productivity of smallholdings have not been sustained since 2000, with spiraling input costs and the collapse of government extension services and marketing infrastructure. Large areas of the country have become dependent upon food relief, access to which has become politicized.

Industry, including manufacturing, accounted for 22.6 percent of GDP in 2005. This had been a strong economic sector, supported by the white minority government in part to counterbalance worldwide economic sanctions imposed by 1965. Industries include production of construction and transport equipment, metal products, chemicals, and textiles, as well as tobacco and food and drink processing. However, much of the industrial infrastructure, already in need of modernization, has now fallen into disuse as the economic crisis has worsened.

The GDP share of the mining sector remains significant. Of forty minerals mined in Zimbabwe, gold and platinum are the most important. Both the manufacturing and mining sectors were traditionally dominated by multinational companies but have been targeted for nationalization.

Services accounted for 59.3 percent of the GDP in 2005. The government's expenditures after independence focused on education, defense, and land resettlement until the early 1990s, when public expenditure on education, health, and the civil service was compressed by International Monetary Fund-imposed structural adjustment policies.

Tourism was a fast-growing economic sector (reaching 1 million visitors in 1994) due to attractions including Victoria Falls, Great Zimbabwe, and national parks, but has fallen off dramatically with the political and economic turmoil following the land invasions.

Zimbabwe has an extensive road system. Railroads connect the country to ports (Beira and Maputo in Mozambique; Durban, East London, and Port Elizabeth in South Africa; Dar es Salaam in Tanzania). Energy is obtained locally from coal and hydroelectricity, but the deterioration of infrastructure and lack of spare parts has increased the energy import demand to 40 percent of national requirements by 2006.

South Africa is by far Zimbabwe's most significant trading partner (accounting for 43 percent of imports and 33 percent of exports in 2005), with China playing an increasingly important role. GNI per capita was estimated at US$350 in 2005; the estimated foreign debt was US$3.3 billion.

An increasing, if undetermined, proportion of national income is derived from remittances sent home by Zimbabweans living abroad. This pattern will likely coexist with very high levels of formal unemployment until inflation is brought under control and political conditions make the country more amenable to foreign and domestic investment.

See also **Climate; Dar es Salaam; Disease: HIV/AIDS, Social and Political Aspects; Ecosystems: Savannas; International Monetary Fund; Land: Tenure; Production Strategies: Mining, Modern; Rhodes, Cecil John; Tourism; Zambezi River.**

BIBLIOGRAPHY

Hammar, Amanda; Brian Raftopoulos; and Stig Jensen; eds. *Zimbabwe's Unfinished Business: Rethinking Land, State and Nation in the Context of Crisis.* Harare: Weaver, 2003.

Mosley, Paul. *The Settler Economies: Studies in the Economic History of Kenya and Southern Rhodesia, 1900–1963.* New York: Cambridge University Press, 1983.

Mutizwa-Mangize, N. D., and A. H. J. Helmsing. *Rural Development and Planning in Zimbabwe.* Brookfield, VT: Avebury, 1991.

Ncube, Mthuli. *Development Dynamics: Theories and Lessons from Zimbabwe.* Brookfield, VT: Avebury, 1991.

Raftopoulos, Brian, and Tyrone Savage, eds. *Zimbabwe: Injustice and Political Reconciliation.* Cape Town: Institute for Justice and Reconciliation. 2004.

Sylvester, Christine. *Zimbabwe: The Terrain of Contradictory Development.* Boulder, CO: Westview, 1991.

Worby, Eric, ed. "The New Agrarian Politics in Zimbabwe." Special Issue of *Journal of Agrarian Change* 1, no. 4.

NANCY G. WRIGHT
REVISED BY ERIC WORBY

SOCIETY AND CULTURES

About 73 percent of the population of Zimbabwe is rural, relying largely on small-scale agriculture, mostly for their own consumption. They try to supplement marginal cash earnings from this source with remittances of wages from family members employed in towns, or in mines or on commercial farms. These strategies sufficed through nearly a century of colonial rule but have collapsed since the late 1990s with the expulsion of the country's European population.

ETHNIC GROUPS

Roughly 80 percent of the population can be broadly classified as Shona. This group, whose ancestors have been present on the plateau since the first Bantu-speaking arrivals nearly two millennia ago, is now subdivided into six main linguistic categories: Korekore in the north, Manyika in the east, Zezuru in the center, Karanga in the south, Ndau in the southeast, and Kalanga in the west. The language and culture of the Ndau and Kalanga were strongly influenced by Nguni settlers from the south in the mid-nineteenth century. This broad grouping is largely accepted by the Shona themselves, although many people prefer to identify themselves with smaller local groups, often identical with chiefdoms extant at the time of colonial settlement in the 1890s. Such local identities are often politically significant in the urban centers.

The Shona are pastoralists as well as agriculturalists. They divide themselves into patrilineal clans, which they associate with particular chiefdoms and territories, although any population contains a mixture of several clans, within which marriages are not allowed. Marriage normally involves the transfer of community assets from the groom's family to the bride's. Traditionally, the payment was several cattle; in present-day Zimbabwe it is usually substantial cash payment by the groom to the bride's father, together with a variety of gifts to the bride's parents. The married couple traditionally lived at the home of the parents of the groom, with the result that village residential communities formed around male cores of dominant lineages. In areas such as the Zambezi Valley, where cattle are few as a result of tsetse fly, the transfer of assets is often largely replaced by brideservice, the groom's extended stay in the wife's home, where the new husband works for his father-in-law. In these areas, people live in scattered family hamlets.

The second largest ethnic group in the country is the Ndebele, who live in the dry southwest and comprise roughly 10 percent of the population. This group was an offshoot of the Zulu nation of modern KwaZulu Province in the Republic of South Africa. The Ndebele warrior leader, Mzilikazi, created a centralized political system and a standing army based in large regimental towns. The colonial settlers of Cecil Rhodes's British South Africa Company destroyed the kingship at the end of the nineteenth century, and the towns were largely abandoned. The Ndebele had large herds of cattle, some of which had to be grazed far from the main towns by herders who lived in smaller settlements. Prior to British colonization and pacification, the Ndebele also obtained cattle, food, and servants from periodic raids into Shona territory. They incorporated many subject Shona into their nation, together with other non-Zulu, but maintained a caste system designed to discourage intermarriage and ensure the elite status of those of Zulu descent. Ethnic tension between Shona and Ndebele continues to emerge occasionally; exacerbated conflict between the government, dominated by the Shona majority, and "dissidents" in Ndebele country broke out shortly after independence in 1980.

In the Zambezi Valley in the northwest of the country lives a significant population of matrilineal Tonga. These people, more closely related to the other matrilineal peoples of central Africa (Zambia, Angola, Democratic Republic of Congo), were largely left out of developments in the colonial era. Their historic association with the Tonga of southern Zambia was disrupted by the building of Kariba Dam across the Zambezi River in the 1950s and the formation of Lake Kariba.

Small pockets of other ethnic groups are found around the mountainous peripheries of the country: Sotho, Venda, and Hlengwe in the south; Ndau-Shangaan, Barwe-Tonga, Tavara, and Chikunda in the east and northeast. A significant number of mainly Chewa-speaking peoples from Mozambique and Malawi entered the country as labor migrants working on European farms during the colonial era. Immigrant minorities of whites have arrived from various nations, as well as Asians (i.e. from British India), both Hindu and Muslim. The past political dominance by the whites, and their control of much of the economy until the recent "reforms" of Zimbabwe President Robert Mugabe, was deeply resented by some of the black majority. Whites, who constituted as much as 5 percent of the population during the period of white minority rule and controlled most of the economy, declined to about 1 percent in the two decades after independence (1980–2000), and to about 0.5 percent following the expropriation of white-owned commercial farms from 2000 onwards.

RELIGION

Religious beliefs and practices among the indigenous peoples of Zimbabwe center around deceased ancestors, who are believed to care for the living members of lineage groups and are the focus of much ritual performed in the family homestead, often concerning healing of the ill. Neighborhood groups come together to honor more remote ancestors, usually of the royal family of the region; these territorial spirits are believed to provide rain and fertility to the land and to support political order within the community. Such spirits are usually honored at tree shrines in the forest. Other cults seek contact with the spirits of strangers, including animals that are believed to possess humans as hosts. Such cults are often associated with particular skills, such as healing and hunting.

In the south of the country is a cult of Mwari, the Shona high god, with a well organized priesthood and a number of central shrines. Priests at the shrines perform rituals in honor of Mwari, especially sacrifices of cattle to ensure good rains, and also consult its oracles. The Mwari cult transcend traditional political boundaries, recruiting children from various lineage groups who are dedicated to Mwari in their youth and become messengers of the cult in their home communities when they grow up. The Ndebele became involved in the cult's annual rituals for rain. Missionaries adopted "Mwari" as the Shona name for the Christian God and spread this designation to other parts of the country.

The dominant religious figures among the Shona are spirit mediums, who become hosts to particular spirits of varying degrees of importance. On appropriate ritual occasions, the host goes into a trance, during which he or she is said to be possessed and to speak the words of the spirit. Such communication with the spirit world is used for divination, particularly in times of trouble. The spirit mediums were accordingly very active in the guerrilla struggles against the Rhodesian regime (1965–1980) and have re-emerged since in times of ethnic conflict. There are indications of renewed local activity by the mediums since the economic distress stemming from Mugabe's "land reforms" of the early 2000s.

Many of the population (perhaps 25–50%) profess belief in the Christian faith. The Catholic and Anglican denominations are the largest of the established churches, although American Methodists are prominent in the far east. During the colonial period these and other missionary organizations provided schools, hospitals, and other resource and training centers, especially in the rural areas, and so became influential among the emerging elite in the 1950s. There are growing numbers of fundamentalist evangelical churches. Since the 1930s, there has been a rapid expansion of independent Christian churches, particularly those, like the spirit mediums, that emphasize gifts of prophecy and healing.

Many of those who have accepted Christianity continue to believe in the influence of the ancestors and other spirits. In the past, professed Christians frequently resorted to covert traditional practices, particularly to deal with illness and misfortune. Since independence (1980) many of the established

Republic of Zimbabwe

Population:	12,311,143 (2007 est.)
Area:	390,580 sq. km (150,803 sq. mi.)
Official languages:	English
Languages:	Shona, Sindebele, English
National currency:	Zimbabwe dollar
Principal religions:	Syncretic 50%, Christian 25%, animist, Christian sects, Muslim
Capital:	Harare (formerly Salisbury; est. pop. 1,500,000 in 2006)
Other urban centers:	Bulawayo, Gweru, Mutare, Kwekwe, Kadoma, Hwange, Masvingo, Zvishavane, Chinhoyi, Marondera
Annual rainfall:	varies from 1,020 mm (40 in.) in Eastern Highlands to 400 mm (115 in.) in Limpopo valley
Principal geographical features:	*Mountains:* Inyangani, Vumba Mountains, Umwukwe Range, Mount Binga *Rivers:* Sabi, Lundi, Kwekwe, Mufure, Zambezi, Umzingwane, Gwai, Shangani, Limpopo *Lakes:* Kariba
Economy:	*GDP per capita:* US$2,100 (2006)
Principal products and exports:	*Agricultural:* corn, cotton, tobacco, wheat, coffee, sugarcane, peanuts, sheep, goats, pigs *Manufacturing:* wood products, cement, chemicals, fertilizer, clothing and footwear, foodstuffs, beverages *Mining:* coal, gold, platinum, copper, nickel, tin, clay, numerous metallic and nonmetallic ores
Government:	Former British colony. Rhodesia declared itself independent from Great Britain in 1965 and declared itself a republic in 1970. Britain did not recognize its independence. The Republic of Zimbabwe-Rhodesia, in existence from 1979–1980, was under direct British control from December 1979 to April 1980. Independence granted in 1980. The Republic of Zimbabwe was proclaimed in 1980. Current constitution approved in 1979 amended in 2005 to establish a 66-member Senate. President nominated by the legislature and elected for 6-year term by universal suffrage. 150-member unicameral House of Assembly: 120 members elected for 5-year terms by universal adult suffrage, 8 seats held by provincial chiefs, 10 seats filled by customary, chiefs, and 12 members appointed by the president. President appoints the Cabinet, which is responsible to the House of Assembly. For purposes of local government there are 8 provinces and 2 cities with provincial status.
Heads of state since independence:	1980–1987: President Canaan Banana 1980–1987: Prime Minister Robert Mugabe 1987–: President Robert Mugabe
Armed forces:	The armed forces are completely integrated and are composed of an army (33,000 active duty) and an air force (4,000 men). President is commander in chief.
Transportation:	*Rail:* 3,077 km (1,912 mi.), controlled by National Railways of Zimbabwe *Roads:* 97,440 km (60,564 mi.), 19% paved *National airline:* Air Zimbabwe *Airports:* International facilities at Harare and Bulawayo. Over 400 other smaller airports and airstrips.
Media:	3 daily newspapers: *Herald, Chronicle,* and the *Daily Gazette.* About a dozen weeklies, including *Gweru Times, Sunday Mail, Sunday News.* There are several popular monthly magazines, including *Moto, Parade, Horizon.* 2 of the dailies and 3 of the weeklies are government owned; the rest are private. There are several book publishing houses, including the University of Zimbabwe Publications. The Zimbabwe Broadcasting Corporation (Radio and Television) is state-owned and -controlled. 27 radio stations, 16 television stations.
Literacy and education:	*Total literacy rate:* 90.7% (2003). Free and compulsory education introduced in 1980. Postsecondary education provided by University of Zimbabwe at Harare and National University of Science and Technology at Bulawayo. There are several religious, teacher-training, and polytechnic colleges.

churches have incorporated ancestor worship into their rituals. Independent churches recognize the influence of traditional spirits as causes of misfortune and illness, but seek to exorcise rather than appease such spirits.

See also **Christianity; Death, Mourning, and Ancestors; Ethnicity; Mugabe, Robert; Production Strategies; Prophetic Movements: Southern Africa; Religion and Ritual; Rhodes, Cecil John; Spirit Possession; Zambezi River.**

BIBLIOGRAPHY

Alexander, Jocelyn. *The Unsettled Land: State-Making and the Politics of Land in Zimbabwe, 1893–2003.* Oxford: James Currey; Harare, Zimbabwe: Weaver Press; Athens: Ohio University Press, 2006.

Bourdillon, M. F. C. *Shona Peoples: An Ethnography of the Contemporary Shona with Special Reference to Their Religion.* Gweru, Zimbabwe: Mambo Press, 1987.

Bozongwana, Wallace. *Ndebele Religion and Customs.* Gweru, Zimbabwe: Mambo Press, 1983.

Fontein, Joost. "Shared Legacies of the War: Spirit Mediums and War Veterans in Southern Zimbabwe." *Journal of Religion in Africa* 36, no. 2 (2006): 167–199.

Lan, David. *Guns & Rain: Guerrillas and Spirit Mediums in Zimbabwe*. London: James Currey, 1985.

Maxwell, David. *Christians and Chiefs in Zimbabwe: A Social History of the Hwesa People c. 1870s–1990s*. Edinburgh, Scotland: Edinburgh University Press for the International African Institute, London, 1999.

Ranger, Terence O. *Voices from the Rocks: Nature, Culture and History in the Matopos Hills of Zimbabwe*. Oxford: James Currey, 1999.

Reynolds, Pamela, and Colleen Cousins. *Lwaano Lwanyika: Tonga Book of the Earth*. Harare, Zimbabwe: Panos Publications, 1991.

M. F. C. BOURDILLON
REVISED BY ERIC WORBY

HISTORY AND POLITICS

Southern Rhodesia was ruled by a British chartered company from 1890 to 1923. Company rule was ended by the Constitution of 1923, which transformed the country into a self-governing British colony. It was run by a British governor through an executive council drawn from and responsible to a legislative assembly voted into power by an all-White electorate. Colonial Southern Rhodesia, like its neighbor, South Africa, subordinated and segregated its African population. The colony assumed a new political incarnation during 1953–1963, when it functioned as the dominant member of the Federation of Rhodesia and Nyasaland, also known as the Central African Federation (CAF). The affiliation—spearheaded by Southern Rhodesian politicians who sought access to the copper resources of Northern Rhodesia (present-day Zambia) and the labor of Nyasaland (present-day Malawi)—came to an end when the British, bowing to pressure from African nationalists, granted independence to Southern Rhodesia's two partners. The British concession fueled anxiety among the White elite in Southern Rhodesia and ultimately helped bring Ian Smith, an unabashed champion of White minority rule, to power.

In the election of 1962, Winston Field's newly formed Rhodesian Front (RF)—a coalition of White, right-wing organizations—won over the so-called liberals who had negotiated the 1961 constitution. During an RF party caucus in 1964, in an apparent power struggle over strategy, the RF's less cautious deputy Ian Smith rose to party leadership; subsequently he became prime minister. On 11 November 1965, Smith—driven by the widely held belief that Britain favored eventual Black majority rule in Southern Rhodesia, as it had in Northern Rhodesia and Nyasaland—announced the Unilateral Declaration of Independence (UDI), which severed Southern Rhodesia's constitutional links with Britain. The British government responded by imposing diplomatic and economic sanctions on the rebel colony, and it asked the international community to do the same. But the Smith regime held out for independence. The Constitution of 1969, which took effect in March 1970, declared Rhodesia a republic. It provided for a president as head of state (to take the place of the British Crown); it also provided for a prime minister with executive powers and a bicameral legislature, consisting of a House of Assembly and a Senate. Britain declared this constitution illegal; in the meantime Africans prepared for war.

AFRICAN NATIONALISM

Modern, organized African resistance to White minority rule began in 1957 when the African National Congress (ANC), based in Bulawayo, and the African National Youth League, based in Salisbury (present-day Harare), merged to form the Southern Rhodesian African National Congress (SRANC), under the leadership of Joshua Nkomo. SRANC's political activities led to its banning in 1959. It was succeeded by the National Democratic Party (NDP), which participated in the negotiations over the Constitution of 1961; in December 1961, however, the NDP was also banned. The successor to this organization, formed the same month, was the Zimbabwe African People's Union (ZAPU), which in September 1962 was, predictably, banned.

As white settler politics progressively drifted to the right in the 1960s, African nationalist methods and strategies became more militant. A major split occurred in the nationalist ranks in 1963 with the formation of the Zimbabwe African National Union (ZANU). Its leaders, Ndabaningi Sithole (president) and Robert Mugabe (secretary-general) announced a policy of "confrontation." Their declaration ultimately led to a full-scale liberation war during the 1970s, fought out of bases in Zambia and Mozambique. ZAPU and ZANU joined forces to form the Patriotic Front (PF) in 1976. (Subsequently they were known as ZAPU–PF and ZANU–PF.) The war continued till September 1979, when the British convened the all-party Lancaster House Conference to negotiate a cease-fire and yet another constitution. This meeting was the last in a series of attempts since the UDI to resolve the constitutional impasse between Britain and Rhodesia and bring about African majority rule. It was the prelude to Zimbabwean independence.

CONSTITUTIONAL NEGOTIATIONS, 1971–1980

After failed attempts at British led negotations in 1971 and 1976, Ian Smith took advantage of the infighting in the nationalist movement to evolve an "internal settlement" strategy that excluded the PF's mainstream liberation movements. The Constitution of 1979, the result of Smith's internal settlement approach, opened the franchise to all Africans eighteen years and older, and it required that 28 seats in the House of Assembly be reserved for Whites for a ten-year period. Bishop Abel Muzorewa's United African National Council (UANC) won the general election, which took place in February 1979. For six months Muzorewa held the position of prime minister of Zimbabwe-Rhodesia. Meantime, the Patriotic Front guerrilla war only intensified. It did not subside until September, when the British called the Lancaster House Conference. The Constitution of 1980, negotiated at Lancaster House, was a replica of the Constitution of 1979. It differed in its inclusion of a directive that provided for the special appointment of Africans into the civil service. The Lancaster House Constitution also protected White farmer's property rights for 10 years, making it difficult for the new government to implement a full-scale land reform policy during the 1980s.

INDEPENDENT ZIMBABWE

1980 Elections. The two wings of the PF-ZANU (led by Robert Mugabe) and ZAPU (led by Joshua Nkomo)—split for the purposes of the 1980 elections, each fielding its own candidates. Since ZANU was a predominantly Shona organization, with ZAPU mainly composed of Ndebele, the political contest between the two parties tended to divide the country along ethnic lines. ZANU-PF won the first election in February 1980, gaining 57 of the 80 seats open to Africans; ZAPU-PF won 20 seats; the UANC won just 3 seats. Mugabe then became prime minister, calling for reconciliation among the competing parties, including those who had previously been at war.

The 1980s was a period of much political tension in Zimbabwe, a great deal of it centering on the question of land redistribution—a major object of the guerrilla war of the 1970s. In 1982 a civil war broke out in Matabeleland (a ZAPU-PF stronghold), which lasted until December 1987, when Nkomo and Mugabe signed a "unity accord" that amalgamated ZAPU-PF and ZANU-PF into just one party called ZANU-PF. The war in Matabeland resulted in thousands of civilian deaths and increased the ethnic tensions between the ruling ZANU PF and the Ndebele former supporters of ZAPU. The unification of Nkomo's and Mugabe's organizations threatened to turn Zimbabwe into a one-party state right after the 1990 elections. This development was frustrated in 1989 when a former ZANU–PF secretary-general, Edgar Tekere, formed the Zimbabwe Unity Movement (ZUM), but the prospect of a one-party system was a source of considerable controversy in Zimbabwe. Tekere and others also charged the government with corruption during the 1980s. In 1985 Amnesty International accused the government of human rights violations in Matabeleland. In the late 1980s public-sector employees, as well as students, protested Zimbabwe's economic problems. The students' demonstrations, which continued into the early 1990s, often resulted in violent clashes with the police.

Political Forces in the 1990s. Parliament was reconstituted by constitutional amendment in 1989 as a 150-seat, single-chamber institution. A total of 120 members of parliament were to be elected on a constituency (winner-take-all) basis. (The proportional representation system had, in fact, been abandoned before the election of 1985.) Of the 120 elective seats in the parliament, ZANU-PF won 117 in 1990. ZANU-PF continued to retain its hold on power in the 1990s, though it has abandoned an earlier fixation on achieving a one-party state and on Marxist-Leninist ideology. The issue of land reform became increasingly recognized as the unfinished promise of the Liberation War. The Land Acquisition Act of

1992 made it easier for the government to acquire more land from white farmers, but little was actually done.

The early 1990s brought a devastating drought and the Economic Structural Adjustment Program (ESAP), a World Bank/International Monetary Fund sponsored program of economic reform. In the parliamentary elections held in April 1995 the party won 118 of the 120 publicly elected seats plus another 30 of the additional seats. Mugabe won the March 1996 presidential election with 92.7 percent of the vote. ZANU-PF is strongest in the rural areas of Zimbabwe, where the liberation struggle waged in the 1970s was mainly about land. (Land remained a contentious issue in the 1990s.) The harsh effects of the government's economic policies, detailed in the Economic Structural Adjustment Programme (ESAP), have been felt more in urban than in rural communities; as a result the urban population has tended to be alienated from ZANU-PF. Rather than sticking to the ESAP goals of shrinking government expenditures, ZANU-PF chose to print more Zimbabwean dollars in order to continue subsidizing food prices and to make payouts to disgruntled Liberation War Veterans.

In 1999, Mugabe and ZANU-PF lost their first election when a constitutional referendum giving Mugabe greater powers was defeated. Startled by the depth of opposition, Mugabe and ZANU-PF co-opted certain elements in the War Veterans movement who had begun illegally occupying white farm lands. Before the February 2000 elections, Mugabe's ZANU-PF gave support to the land occupations and encouraged ZANU-PF youth to attack and harass members of the Movement for Democratic Change (MDC) the coalition opposition group. The MDC's leader, Morgan Tsvangirai, still managed to obtain 46 percent of the vote in an election fraught with abuses. On July 15, 2000, ZANU-PF launched the Fast Track Land Reform Program. The result was the State's control of 99 percent of all agricultural land. The economic impact of the land occupations and the government's inequitable redistribution program has caused major problems for the economy. Food and tobacco exports plummeted and credit for the new farmers was all but non-existent.

The government's policy of printing money to meet budgetary requirements—including support of Zimbabwe's intervention into the war in the Democratic Republic of the Congo, and buying foreign exchange on the black market to repay IMF arrears—has led to the world's worst inflation rate in recent history, approaching 1200 percent in mid-2006. The ZANU-PF government avoided expulsion from the IMF by making payments in May 2006, and has since begun to use the nation's mineral resources to secure hard currency loans from France and China. A large number of Zimbabweans have been forced to seek employment in neighboring Botswana and South Africa, as well as around the world, in order to survive the current economic and political crisis. Their remittances have helped many others within Zimbabwe negotiate shortages of formal employment, petrol, and food. In June 2006, the United Nations recommended classifying Zimbabwe as a Less Developed Nation (LDC), but the Government of Zimbabwe has rejected the label, claiming instead that the current economic crisis is a temporary situation caused by droughts and Western economic sanctions.

The MDC leadership has split into two camps, however there were signs in 2006 of a resurgence of popular protest and political opposition involving trade unions, religious groups, and women's organizations. These protests have been met with arrests and, in the case of trade union leaders arrested in September 2006, beatings by police and security forces in the Mbare goal. Police beatings of opposition leaders continued, when on March 11, 2007, Morgan Tsvangirai and fifty others including 64-year-old Sekai Holland, were seriously injured while in police custody. On the same day that the leadership was taken into police custody from a Catholic Church meeting in Highfield, an opposition activist, Gift Tandare, was shot and killed by the police.

See also **Bulawayo; International Monetary Fund; Land: Reform; Mugabe, Robert; Nationalism; Postcolonialism; World Bank.**

BIBLIOGRAPHY

Alexander, Joyce; JoAnn McGregor; and Terence Ranger. *Violence and Memory: One hundred Years in the 'Dark Forest' of Matabeleland.* Oxford: James Currey, 2000.

Harold-Barry, David. *Zimbabwe: The Past Is the Future.* Avondale, Harare: Weaver Press, 2004.

Huddleston, Sara, and Dumisani Muleya. "Zimbabwe: Mugabe's Henchmen Unleash Torture Fury." *Business Day* (Johannesburg). March 15, 2007.

Kriger, Norma. "ZANU (PF) Strategies in General Elections, 1980–2000: Discourse and Coercion." *African Affairs* 104, no. 414 (2005): 1–34.

Mandaza, Ibbo, and Lloyd M. Sachikonye, eds. *The One-Party State and Democracy: The Zimbabwe Debate.* Harare: SAPES Books, 1991.

Martin, David, and Phyllis Johnson. *The Struggle for Zimbabwe: The Chimurenga War.* London; Boston: Faber and Faber, 1981.

Moyo, Jonathan N. *Voting for Democracy: Electoral Politics in Zimbabwe.* Harare: University of Zimbabwe Publications, 1992.

Moyo, Sam. *The Land Question in Zimbabwe.* Harare: SAPES Books, 1995.

Ranger, Terence. *The Historical Dimensions of Democracy and Human Rights in Zimbabwe.* Harare: Zimbabwe University Publications, 2003.

Sithole, Masipula. "Zimbabwe: Party and Ideological Transformation." In *Afro-Marxist Regimes: Ideology and Public Policy,* edited by Edmond J. Keller and Donald Rothchild. Boulder, CO: L. Rienner Publishers, 1987.

MASIPULA SITHOLE
Revised by TIMOTHY SCARNECCHIA

ZIMBABWE, GREAT. The Zimbabwe plateau lies between the Zambezi and Limpopo Rivers, the Kalahari grassland savanna to the west and the Nyanga and Chimanimani Mountains to the east. These mountains, over a mile above sea level, separate the plateau from the Mozambican Costal Plains. The Zambezi, Limpopo, and Save Rivers carve major lowland areas generally less than a mile above sea level. The geology, dominated by grano-diorites, gives rise to batholiths, whalebacks, and conical hills. Their rock has been exploited since the early second millennium CE, as stone that can easily be shaped into building materials and used in the construction of residences. These *dzimbabwe* ("houses of stone") became centers of political power and by the sixteenth century, whether constructed out of stone or not, had become synonymous with royalty.

The vegetation is primarily *miombo* woodland, with *Julbernardia* and *Brachystegia* occupying moist higher altitudes and *Colophosphermum* *mopane* growing in the lower and drier basins. These environments provide livestock grazing and teem with wild animals such as elephant and a variety of antelopes. The soils, ranging from iron-rich ferric luvisols to sandy loams, were cultivated for sorghum, finger millet, cowpeas and groundnuts. The plateau also has iron, copper and gold deposits, whose minerals were exploited and used to great advantage by traders, chiefs and kings. Together with ivory, gold opened the Zimbabwe plateau to the commercial world of the Indian Ocean, and from the early sixteenth century onward, Portuguese attempts to wrestle control of this gold trade negatively affected southern African societies.

Despite the environmental advantages, a major constraining factor is the uneven rainfall distribution, with lower altitude regions receiving less than fifteen inches per annum, compared with over sixty inches for the higher altitudes. In addition, this pattern is inconsistent, as drought is a recurring phenomenon. Significant episodes of aridity have occurred since 1000 CE, triggering large-scale abandonment of some regions. Chiefdoms and states arose as a collective response towards these constraints, and this was achieved through control of key resources such as salt, cattle, ivory, gold, and grain. Cattle played a significant role in the economy, and by 1000 CE those with the capacity to rear large herds attained social and political advantage over other people. Their wealth, enhanced by trade, was invested in monumental and public architecture. This reflected communal participation in projects initiated at the level above the village, and in demonstrated artistic skill and innovation.

Religion may not have been a prime mover in state formation, but an effective instrument for binding people into an interdependent political union. Leaders exercised the role of mediators, embodying the hopes and aspirations of their followers. The carved soapstone bird effigies at Great Zimbabwe probably symbolized this role.

THE RISE AND DEVELOPMENT OF GREAT ZIMBABWE AND ITS CULTURE

The story of Great Zimbabwe begins some 200 miles to the south, in the middle Shashe-Limpopo valley, following the demise of the state based at Mapungubwe (1220–1280). Mapungubwe, whose wealth was enhanced by trade in gold, ivory, animal skins, cloth, and glass beads with the Swahili on the Indian Ocean coast, declined following the abandonment of the region due to climate change. Iron Age farmers akin to early Karanga speakers then developed chiefdom-level societies at Chivowa and Gumanye hills in south-central Zimbabwe. They transformed from simple kin-warranted domestic corporations relying mainly on land and cattle, to long distance traders. With this newly acquired wealth, they financed the building of stonewalling. By about 1270, a wealthy elite emerged at Great Zimbabwe, which laid the foundations of an elaborate urban complex and the center of a state. From about 1300 stone buildings of a scale and magnitude unparalleled on the entire Zimbabwe plateau were constructed. For the next 150 years, Great Zimbabwe became the most dominant political authority south of the Zambezi.

Great Zimbabwe reached its peak during the fourteenth and fifteenth centuries when elaborate stonewalling was extended toward outlying areas. Stonewalls symbolized wealth, prestige, and status. With a population of about 18,000, Great Zimbabwe was more than an oversized African village. At its fluorescence it was the largest metropolis in southern Africa. Composed of elite residences, ritual centers, public forums, markets, houses of commoners and artisans, it covered more than 2.7 square miles.

The first stonewalls complex was raised on a whaleback hill. Here, two large enclosures and intervening smaller enclosures abut from the natural granite boulders and define the living spaces for royalty. A ritual spearhead, iron gongs and soapstone bird effigies attest to the presence of a ruling elite. Commoner settlements within a perimeter wall at the base of the hill soon became overcrowded, triggering further expansion beyond. Royalty also moved downhill to the more elaborate elliptical enclosure. The largest single stone-built structure in southern Africa, it has a girdle wall 800 feet long, 16 feet wide, and 32 feet high. It encloses subenclosures and parallel passages inside with a conical tower marking the focus of the settlement. This massive structure represents the peak of development of Great Zimbabwe. Five enclosure complexes to the northeast and east were built in the valley this time, but rose to prominence towards the terminal phases of the settlement. A

second perimeter wall attests to the continuously growing city. Stone enclosures in the periphery either housed members of the ruling family, or catered for increased administrative functions of the metropolis.

Historical process based on Karanga political succession and territorial control may explain the development of Great Zimbabwe as a city and center of state. It was organized around a principal lineage, associated with the city itself and sites beyond. A sacred leadership presided over a well-defined political and settlement hierarchy. Each *dzimbabwe* had impressive stone-built monumental architecture, specialized in domestic crafts, trade in gold, ivory, cloth, and glass beads with the Indian Ocean coast, and attached importance to cattle and grain farming.

Great Zimbabwe rulers exercised political control as far as the Save River to the east and the Shashe-Tuli Rivers in present-day Botswana to the west. Covering an area half the size of modern Zimbabwe, its influence was felt over much of the region including the Indian Ocean Swahili coast. The state was sustained by subsistence agriculture, livestock management, and through the domination of trade networks over a large portion of the plateau as an adjunct to its connection with the Swahili towns on the Indian Ocean coast. *Dzimbabwe* beyond the borders of the state in non-Karanga territory such as those located at the eastern edge of the Suwa Pan in eastern Botswana and Manyikeni on the Mozambican Coastal Plains represent further royal expansion taking advantage of lucrative regional trade, at the expense of Great Zimbabwe itself. This commerce involved gold, copper, iron, salt, wild game, cattle, and grain. Expansion into non-Karanga territory overshadowed the center, and sixteenth-century historical sources indicate that rival chiefdoms arose in the peripheral areas of the state following this development.

DECLINE, 1450–1550

The decline of Great Zimbabwe as a center of a powerful prehistoric state remains an unresolved archaeological problem. This is largely due to the unsystematic investigations of late-nineteenth-century European antiquarians and prospectors, who destroyed its stratigraphy and looted it in

The Great Enclosure at Great Zimbabwe. The Great Enclosure is the largest single structure in Africa south of the Sahara. Referred to by local people as "Imbahuru" (Queen's residence), it is thought to have been an enclosure occupied by the queen. REPRODUCED WITH PERMISSION OF ASHTON SINAMAI, MIDLANDS STATE UNIVERSITY, ZIMBABWE.

search of Near-Eastern artifacts and gold. Systematic research from the 1950s onward has resolved its chronology and the Karanga identity of its founders. Great Zimbabwe was abandoned by the middle of the fifteenth century. The shift in the gold trade from the south-central regions toward the northern Zimbabwe plateau is one possibility for this development. The emergence of Ingombe Ilede, a trading emporium on the Zambezi, posed serious challenges to Great Zimbabwe, which until then controlled the hinterland gold trade channeled into the interior through Sofala. After that, the Zambezi River became the preferred inland route. Great Zimbabwe's expansionary thrusts to control the gold trade undermined its political control over the plateau as this spawned new states elsewhere.

With the demise of Great Zimbabwe, two competing polities emerged in the northern and western areas of the plateau. Khami, Danangombe, Zinjanja, and Naletale are elaborately decorated stonewalled *dzimbabwe* of the Torwa-Changamire states (1450–1830), which dominated the southwestern acacia and mopane woodlands. The Changamire dynasty successfully stemmed Portuguese advance on the plateau during the eighteenth century, but was subdued by the Nguni during the 1830s. The Mutapa state controlled the fertile and auriferous northern plateau margins near Mount Fura, as indicated by stonewalled *dzimbabwe* at Zvongombe, Ngome, Chomagora, and Ruanga, and non-stonewalled centers such as Baranda. It lost the plateau to Portuguese conquistadores during the seventeenth century but continued the stone building canon farther north on the Zambezi Escarpment and adjacent basin. Mutapa was finally defeated by Portuguese *prazo* (estate) holders in the late nineteenth century.

See also **Ecosystems; Iron; Zambezi River.**

BIBLIOGRAPHY

Beach, D. N., et al. "Cognitive Archaeology and Imaginary History at Great Zimbabwe." *Current Anthropology* 39, no. 1 (1998): 47–72.

Garlake, Peter S. *Early Art and Architecture of Africa.* New York: Oxford University Press, 2002.

Huffman, Thomas N. *Snakes and Crocodiles: Power and Symbolism in Ancient Zimbabwe.* Johannesburg: Witwatersrand University Press, 1996.

Huffman, Thomas N. *Mapungubwe: Ancient Civilisation on the Limpopo.* Johannesburg: Witwatersrand University Press, 2005.

Pikirayi, Innocent. *The Zimbabwe Culture: Origins and Decline in Southern Zambezian States.* Walnut Creek, CA: AltaMira Press, 2001.

INNOCENT PIKIRAYI

ZINGA. *See* Njinga Mbandi Ana de Sousa.

ZIONIST CHURCHES. *See* Christianity: African Instituted Churches.

ZOMBA.
The capital of colonial Malawi (British Central African Protectorate then in 1907 Nyasaland Protectorate) from 1891 to 1964 and after independence until 1975, Zomba is, according to 2007 statistics, a town of roughly 60,000 people located in the shadow of Zomba Mountain. Zomba began as a Blantyre Mission substation that grew up among a number of African villages, peopled principally by Mang'anja and Yao speakers. In 1880 a mission retiree, John Buchanan, took up coffee and sugar farming and built the first consul's residence, which serves as a rest house in the twenty-first century. From the end of the nineteenth century, South Asian immigrants began to settle in Zomba and carved out a niche in wholesale and retail trade. As a colonial district and protectorate capital, Zomba became home to a large number of civil servants, African and European alike. It boasted three hospitals (including the country's only mental hospital), Zomba Central Prison, Cobbe Barracks, headquarters of the First Battalion of the Malawi Rifles (formerly Kings African Rifles), the police training camp and, from 1973, the Arts and Sciences campus of the University of Malawi at Chancellor College. It is also home to the Malawi National Examination Board, the National Statistical Office, and the Malawi National Archives, and has one of the country's best and largest permanent markets.

See also **Colonial Policies and Practices: British Central Africa; Malawi.**

BIBLIOGRAPHY

Kalinga, Owen J., and Cynthia Crosby, eds. *Historical Dictionary of Malawi*, 3rd edition. Lanham, MD: Scarecrow Press, 2001.

JOEY POWER

ZUBAYR, RAHMA MANSUR AL-
(1830–1913). The Sudanese trader, administrator, and military officer Rahma Mansur al-Zubayr was born near al-Jaili, north of Khartoum in the modern Republic of the Sudan. He was educated in Khartoum, and in 1856 he went to the Bahr al-Ghazal province in the south, where he traded in and raided for ivory, slaves, and other products. With the help of his army of slaves, Zubayr became the leading merchant in the region and established a commercial empire that included the Bahr al-Ghazal and the adjacent territories. In 1866 he made a treaty with the Rizeigat Baggara of southern Dar Fur by which he secured the trade routes through southern Dar Fur and Kordofan.

From his headquarters at Daim Zubayr, he subjugated such local groups as the Kreish, Binga, Kara, and Yulu. Following his defeat of the strong Azande principalities on the margins of the equatorial forest in 1872 Zubayr was recognized by the Turco-Egyptian government as the governor of the Bahr al-Ghazal. In 1874 he conquered Dar Fur and occupied Dar Masalit, Tama, Qimr, and Sula. A year later he visited Egypt and was prevented from returning to the Sudan by the Egyptian khedive. Suspecting him of dealing with the anti-Egyptian followers of the Mahdi Muhamad Ahmad, then taking control of the region, the British occupying power in Egypt exiled him to Gibraltar in 1885. He was allowed to return to the Sudan in 1899 and settled as a farmer in al-Jaili, where he spent the rest of his life.

See also **Jenné and Jenné-jeno; Rabih bin Fadlallah; Slave Trades.**

Rahma Mansur al-Zubayr (1830–1913). Zubayr was an Arab slave trader who British General Charles Gordon wished to appoint as governor of Sudan. HULTON ARCHIVE/GETTY IMAGES

BIBLIOGRAPHY

Hill, Richard. *A Biographical Dictionary of the Sudan*, 2nd edition. London: Cass, 1967.

Zubayr, Basha al-. *Black Ivory and White*, trans. Henry Cecil Jackson. Oxford: Blackwell, 1913.

AHMAD SIKAINGA

APPENDIX A: CHRONOLOGY

Paleontological evidence indicates that Africa is the continent where humankind was born, roughly within the last 100,000 years. The species transitional between other *hominidae* and the earliest hominids lived in northeastern Africa some five million years ago. Whether one looks to "Lucy" (3.2 mya) as our species' hominid precursors or uses modern genetic evidence converging on a hypothetical "African Eve" (mitochondrial DNA most recent common female ancestor) who lived in the same region some 150,000–200,000 years ago, the line to modern *Homo sapiens* begins and continues in Africa.

This means that the chronology of the African continent relevant to modern humans is far longer than for any other region of the world, long before anyone counted calendrical years. This chronology begins with very approximate dating—notional "dates" often spanning hundreds of thousands of years for a broad period—employed by prehistorians and archaeologists: "1.5 mya" thus means one and a half million years ago. Durations in the range of hundreds of thousands of years are designated "BP" (before the present) at an only slightly greater level of precision. Given the only very partial relevance of the Christian calendar to most of Africa, more recent and more precise yearly dates are designated as BCE (Before the Common Era); these years are exactly equivalent to the (modern) Christian calendar. The lunar Islamic calendar, dating from the prophet Muhammad's withdrawal from the mundane world to gather the first group of Muslim disciples (the *hijra*)—or, in English, "After the Hijra" (AH), or 16 July 622 CE—is the primary calendar in North Africa and for many other African Muslims, this chronology does not attempt to establish 354-day Muslim-year equivalents of the CE solar years of 365 (and a fraction) days.

Because the African continent is so vast—within its landmass the entire United States (including Alaska), all of western and eastern Europe, and Australia would comfortably fit, with a million square miles yet to spare—the chronology begins generally but then segments the events noted in the five regions into which scholars conventionally divide the continent: Northern, Western, Eastern, Central, and Southern Africa. These regional units are fundamentally arbitrary, as the shared criteria used to define them have changed over the millennia, and even within the last century. Ecological zones make sense in some contexts, and linguistic criteria or basic economic strategies make sense in others. Some of the subjects treated in the encyclopedia employ these geographical distinctions, while others, including all of the historical essays, follow other distinctions relevant to the topic under discussion.

JOSEPH C. MILLER

Era	Northern	Western	Eastern	Central	Southern
5 mya	Australopithecines (early hominids) in northern Rift Valley (Ethiopia, Kenya).				
2.5–1.5 mya	*Homo habilis* (tool-making hominids); Early Stone Age (Olduvai Gorge, Tanzania).				
1.5 mya–150,000 BCE	*Homo erectus* (hand-ax tools, Acheulian, increasing use of fire).				
1.2–1.0 mya	Colonization of Asia.				
280,000–140,000 BCE	"African Eve"?				
240,000–40,000 BCE	Middle Stone Age. New colonization of Asia.				
80,000– 20,000 BCE	Later Stone Age (microliths, bow and arrow, snares, specialized stone tools); emergence and proliferation of *homo sapiens* (modern humans); transition from imitative signaling to semantic language, and from instinctual synchronization to learned and calculated collaboration.				
20,000–10,000 BCE	Wet climate deteriorates; intensified gathering, digging sticks, seed grinding (Nile valley); Afro-Asiatic language speakers? Domestication of hunting dog (from SW Asia). Afro-Asiatic speakers introduce cultivation in lower Nile valley and SW Asia.	Other foragers concentrate around Lake Chad and Upper Niger River basin; development of languages ancestral to modern Niger-Congo and Nilo-Saharan macro-families of languages.	Khoesan-speaking hunter-gathers in eastern Zambian grasslands; refined microlithic tools adopted throughout Eastern highlands; increasingly specialized exploitation of broad environmental niches.		
10,000–6000 BCE	Return to wet climate. Ceramics adopted from Nilo-Saharans, borrowed also by southwest Asians. Cattle domesticated. Sheep, goats borrowed from southwest Asia.	Wild grain collection intensified. **9,000:** Ceramics, sedentary fishing camps (Niger, Lake Chad, upper Nile tributaries); speakers of Nilo-Saharan languages. Domestication of yam in forested regions; Niger-Congo language speakers. **7000 BCE:** Cultivation of millet, sorghum, gourds. "Aquatic" fishing civilization (upper Niger, Lake Chad, Upper Nile).			
6000–5000 BCE	Severe dry interval; specialized cattle herding. Intensification of temperate latitude agriculture in middle Nile valley; domestication of donkey. Tropical cultigens in upper Nile valley (sorghum, millet). Ideology of royalty ancestral to pharaonic Egypt.	Weaving, boat building. Yam growers (Niger-Congo language speakers) settle forests.			Khoesan hunters in southern Africa; rock painting.

(continued)

Era	Northern	Western	Eastern	Central	Southern
5000–3,000 BCE	Wetter conditions. "Saharan Neolithic" cattle keepers, rock paintings. **3500 BCE:** Centralized military polity in Lower Nile Valley (pyramids). Bronze worked in lower Egypt.	Intensified gathering of grains, agriculture; other cultigens. Niger-Congo languages differentiated along lines of environmental specialization?	Semitic-speakers of Ethiopian highlands develop agriculture. Kushitic-speaking cattle herders move south up Rift Valley.		
3000–1000 BCE	Desiccation of Sahara Desert. Consolidation of political unity in lower Nile valley under Pharaonic authority. "Libyans" (Berber-speaking?) introduce horses from Asia into Saharan regions. Lower Egypt trades up Nile valley, absorbs Nubia ("Kush"). Copper smelting in Maghreb.	Tropical grains (sorghum, millet, others) domesticated. Sheep, goats herded. Speakers of proto-Bantu language move east, south along tributaries of Congo River system.	Tropical grains cultivated in Lakes Plateau region (Central Sudanic speakers).	Banana agriculture in forest.	
1000–1 BCE	Berbers concentrate around desert oases. **1000:** Phoenicians bring iron-working to North Africa (Carthage). **730–660s:** Kushitic (Nubian) invasion of Egypt. **5th c.:** Meroë (iron-working) evident in upper Nile valley. **332:** Greeks occupy Egypt (Ptolemaic Dynasty, Alexandria). **200:** Romans in control in Carthage (first called "Africa"). **32:** Romans occupy Egypt. Meroë at height of wealth, extent.	**500:** Iron and copper in use south of the Sahara. Town settlements along desert edge. **5th–3rd c.:** Nok sculptures (modern central Nigeria).	Bantu-speakers in Lakes Plateau region, acquiring grain, crops, cattle; occupy highlands **800(?):** Iron smelting invented independently in Lakes Plateau region. **4th c.:** Sabeans establish trading colony in northern Ethiopian highlands (later Aksum).	Western Bantu-speaking settlers reach lower Zaire, occupy moist river valleys in dry woodlands to south. Forests settled (ceramics, oil palms), goats; symbiotic collaboration with forest-dwelling foragers.	**200:** Ceramics and cattle appear; herders on fringes of Kalahari adopt sheep.
1–600 CE	Roman control of Northern Africa in Decline by 4th c. Berbers adopt Christianity (Donatists–heretical from Roman point of view). Egyptians adopt Coptic Christianity. **325:** Meroë invaded by Aksum. **530s:** Byzantine empire takes Mediterranean ports.	Towns grow, particularly Jenné (inland Niger delta). Berbers adopt camel for desert transport. Soninke economic integration of gold trade between upper Senegal and Niger rivers.	Intensified Indian Ocean trading. Bantu-speaking settlers along northern coast. Aksum flourishes in Ethiopian highlands. **345:** King (Ezana) adopts Coptic (Monophysite) Christianity. **6th c.:** Aksum controls southwestern Arabia (Saba).	Bantu settlers occupy wider range of environments, intensify occupation, differentiate communities ethnically. Ethnic differentiation promotes trade, particularly along rivers of Congo system.	Bantu-speaking farmers rapidly settle rainfall agricultural areas. Khoe drive herds south to Cape of Good Hope. Indonesian mariners/traders settle Madagascar, bring Bantu-speaking slaves from mainland.
600–1000 CE	**640:** Muslim Arabs invade lower Nile valley. **Late 7th c.:** Arab armies occupy Mediterranean towns in Maghreb. **8th c.:** Berbers adopt Kharijite Islam. Tunisia, Algeria, Morocco take shape as Muslim polities. **8th c.:** Middle Nile states (Noba, Makurra, Alwa) preserve Christian culture. **966:** Fatimid caliphate in Egypt.	Takrur in lower Senegal valley. Early military consolidation (Kanem) on shores of Lake Chad. Trans-Saharan trade in gold intensifies. Soninke "Wagadu" (Ghana) controls Muslim merchants' access to gold. Igbo-Ukwu trading center along lower Niger.	Adaptation of sugarcane, coconuts, other southeast Asian crops. Arabs occupy Red Sea coast. Aksum isolated, declines. Arab and Persian trade along northern Indian Ocean coast. Early Swahili Muslim stone-built towns grow. "Zanj" (African slaves) revolt in Basra (Persian Gulf). Nilotic farmer-herders enter Lakes Plateau.	"Eastern Bantu" cereal crops adopted in southern grasslands as far west as modern Angola. Material culture and political systems ancestral to recent Bantu-speaking communities. **9th c.:** Copper mining along Zaire/Zambezi watershed; broad circulation of cross-shaped ingots.	Ivory exported through Muslim traders from southeastern coast, lower Limpopo River valley.
(continued)					

Era	Northern	Western	Eastern	Central	Southern
1000–1500 CE	**1050s–1117:** Western Saharan Berbers (Almoravids) take Morocco, Spain. **1140s–1250:** Mountain Berber Almohads take Maghreb, Spain. **1171:** Ayyubids (Salah al-Din, anti-Crusade leader) seize Egypt, create slave soldier (*mamluk*) regime. **13th–14th c.:** Arab immigrants suppress Christian regimes in middle Nile valley. **15th c.:** Portuguese begin voyages along northwest coast. Spaniards claim Canary Islands, defeat, capture native Guanches. Portuguese settle Madeira, cut wood for which they named the island, establish cultivation of sugar cane. **1444:** First recorded Portuguese purchases of slaves from mainland. **1440s:** Portuguese reach Jolof, Senegambia area. **1456:** Portuguese settle Cape Verde Islands. **1453:** Ottoman Turks capture Constantinople. **1492:** Columbus discovers Americas.	Shift to drier climate regime. "Ghana" disappears. Horses imported for military purposes, led by Soninke state of Soso. Soninke extend commercial networks southward. **13th c.:** "Sundiata" founds Mali kingdom (Mande-speaking peoples, upper Niger valley); warrior-rulers adopt Islam. Mande traders open Akan goldfields in forest. **1312–1337:** Mansa Musa (ruler in Mali) makes *hajj* through Egypt. **13th–15th c.:** Towns grow among Hausa, who extend trade networks south to Yoruba and Igbo. Gao trading center on middle Niger. Ife emerges as political center for Yoruba; sculpture flourishes. Kanem grows by raiding south of Lake Chad for slaves.	Southern Nilotes in Rift Valley, Kenya highlands. Swahili towns flourish; major construction at Kilwa, Zanzibar, Mogadishu, Malindi, Lamu, etc. **13th c.:** Zagwe dynasty in Tigre (Ethiopia); construction of monolithic stone churches at Lalibela. **1270:** "Solomonid" dynasty established in Amhara (Ethiopia). **13th–15th c.:** Bigo earthworks (modern Uganda); Chwezi in Lakes Plateau area. **15th c.:** Chinese voyages to Swahili trading towns. Amhara/Solomonid emperors flourish; wars with highland Muslim sultanates (Harar Adal). "Chwezi" state of Kitara?	Proto-Luba political system in valley of upper Lualaba River (Upemba). More sophisticated (Later Iron Age) metallurgy (eastern Zambia). Ivory exports from middle Zambezi, Shire River. Early Maravi states south of Lake Malawi. Proto-Kongo politics develop along lower Congo River. Phiri (Luba?) take over Maravi states. **15th c.:** *Ngola* warlords emerge along Kwanza River (modern Angola). **1472:** Portuguese reach São Tomé. **1482:** Portuguese (Diogo Cão) at the Congo River mouth contacts *mani* Kongo.	**11th c.:** Mapungubwe (extensive stone town) built on ivory exports in lower Limpopo valley. Shona on Zimbabwe plateau begin exporting gold, build in stone. **13th–14th c.:** Great Zimbabwe constructed. Sofala southernmost Swahili trading town (source of Zimbabwe gold). **15th c.:** Ingombe Ilede traders in Kafue-Zambezi valley (ivory, copper, gold, iron). Great Zimbabwe declines; rise of Mwene Mutapa nearer goldfields. **1492:** Portuguese round Cape of Good Hope.
16th c. Brazil discovered by Portuguese (**1500**); Spaniards conquer Aztecs (**1520s**), Incas (**1530s**), silver exports growing by **1560s**. Extensive slave raiding of Native Americans gradually outlawed; fails **1570s–1580s:** sugar industry in Brazil established on basis of enslaved workers from local native sources and from Upper Guinea. **1580–1640:** Portuguese crown united with monarchy in Spain; slave-delivery contract (asiento) for Spanish-American colonies to Portuguese merchants drawing slaves from Luanda.	**1517:** Ottoman conquest of Egypt. Ottomans take middle Nile, Red Sea ports, Mediterranean port towns (Tripoli, Tunis, Algiers); conflict with Christians ("Barbary Pirates"). **1549:** Sa'id dynasty preserves Moroccan independence. **1578:** Moroccans defeat Portuguese at Al-Ksar al-Kebir. **1578–1603:** Ahmad al-Mansur sultan in Morocco; buying slaves from south of desert to grow sugar. Islamic legal disputation over slaving. Funj sultanate asserts control of upper Nile. **1591:** Al-Mansur invades and defeats Songhai (battle of Tondibi).	Bornu (Bulala dynasty) succeeds Kanem, west of Lake Chad; captures slaves to sell to Ottomans in Tripoli. **1516:** Bénin stops slave trade to Portuguese. Songhai dominant along Niger Bend (Askia dynasty). Mossi military states at sources of Volta River. Hausa cities flourish (Kano, Katsina, Gobir). **1580s–1590:** Allada grows as military polity along Bight of Bénin. Portuguese buy Akan gold from base at Elmina fort. Fante states along Gold Coast flourish from gold trade.	Jo-Bito (Luo Nilotes) gain political influence in Lakes Plateau region (foundations of later state of Bunyoro). **1505:** Portuguese seize Swahili cities (Zanzibar, Mombasa, etc.). Swahili towns in decline. **1530s:** Muslim sultanate of Adal defeats armies of Christian dynasty in Amhara. **1585:** Swahili attack against Portuguese fails. **1580s–1590s:** Lundu warriors ("Zimba" from Zambezi valley Maravi) attack coastal towns. **1599:** Portuguese build Fort Jesus at Mombasa.	**1506:** *Mani* Kongo Afonso I converts to Christianity. **1520s:** Portuguese develop slave-worked sugar on São Tomé. Afonso in Kongo complains against slave traders. São Tomé planters buy slaves along lower Kwanza River; Ngola a Kiuanje builds military regime (Ndongo). **1560s:** Portuguese mission to Ngola a Kiluanje held captive. Severe drought. **1568:** "Jaga cannibals" allegedly invade Kongo. **1574:** Portuguese restore Christian authority in Kongo (Alvaro I). **1575:** Portuguese occupy bay at Luanda. **1580s:** Portuguese begin attacks against Ndongo. **1590s:** Exports of slaves from Luanda multiply ten-fold.	Torwa (at modern Bulawayo) breaks away from Mwene Mutapa. **1505:** Portuguese fortify Sofala. **1507:** Portuguese fortify Mozambique Island. Portuguese seize gold, ivory trade of Zambezi, explore Shona highlands. **1560s:** Mwene Mutapa conflict with Jesuits, Portuguese. Independent Portuguese settlers establish landed estates in Zambezi valley; trading posts at Sena and Tete.

(continued)

Era	Northern	Western	Eastern	Central	Southern
17th c. **1620s–1630s:** Dutch attacks against Portuguese fortifications along African coasts, seize sugar captain of Pernambuco in Brazil. **1640s:** Dutch and English introduce sugar into West Indies. **1660s–1670s:** English develop slave-worked plantations in Barbados, then Jamaica. French begin to develop sugar on Guadeloupe and Martinique.	Ottomans lose control of North African cities to local officials (*pashas*). "Barbary Pirates" raid Christian shores of Mediterranean, European shipping, take numerous captives as slaves. **1672–1727:** Mawlay Isma'il ruler in Morocco; builds sugar industry, buys slaves from south of desert.	Segu (Bambara) state succeeds Mali and Songhai on upper Niger. English, Dutch, French traders build informal trading posts along coasts, buying gold, other products, including slaves; European monarchies fortify positions along Gold Coast. **1637:** Dutch (West India Company) seize Elmina fort. British and French fortify positions in Senegambia. Akwamu (Akan) military state emerges and controls trade routes to interior. **1670s:** Akwamu military expansion; Gold Coast trade shifts to slaves. Oyo building cavalry forces. Trading towns in Niger Delta consolidate political authority around exports of slaves; English active as buyers. Ouidah (Whydah) major port in Bight of Bénin ("Slave Coast"). **1673–1674:** Nasr al-Din *jihad*, or "War of the Marabouts" (Senegal). **1690s:** Fulbe Muslim cleric (Malik Sy) takes power in Bundu (upper Senegal).	**1607:** Dutch (East India Company) seize Portuguese Indian Ocean trade. Bunyoro (Bito rulers) dominate Lakes Plateau. Solomonid kings in Ethiopia in retreat from Oromo (Galla) herders. Eastern Nilotes (Maasai, etc.) occupy Rift Valley. King Fasiladas (**1632–1657**) retreats north to Gondar and claims authority over remnant Ethiopian Christian polity. **1650s:** Oman expels Portuguese, extends influence into Swahili towns. **1664:** French (East India Company) claim island of Bourbon (later Réunion). **1698:** Omanis drive Portuguese out of Mombasa.	Imbangala mercenaries give military advantage to Portuguese in Ndongo wars. **1620s:** Queen Nzinga uses Imbangala backing to take power in Ndongo. **1630s:** Portuguese wars with Nzinga. Imbangala warrior bands establish slaving states east and south of Portuguese Angola conquista. **1641–1648:** Dutch seize Luanda; Nzinga consolidates power in Matamba, sells captives to Dutch. **1650s:** Brazilians restore Portuguese authority at Luanda, develop slave sources in east at Kasanje. **1656:** Nzinga peace treaty with Portuguese; dies in **1663**. Civil wars in Kongo, culminating in **1665** defeat by Portuguese at Mbwila. **1682:** Portuguese advance toward populous central plateau, build fortified post in south at Kakonda. Lunda military regime east of Kasai River growing on capture and sale of slaves. **1690s:** Kongo royalty locked in self-destructive conflicts.	Changamire builds military capacity of Torwa state (Rozvi). **1623:** Maravi invade Mwene Mutapa. **1629:** Portuguese estates in Zambezi valley given legal standing (as *prazos*). Portuguese *prazo*-holders build slave armies, weakening Mwene Mutapa. **1652:** Dutch East India Company establishes post at Cape of Good Hope (Cape Town). **1657:** First slaves reach Cape; Dutch establish wheat farms inland at Cape. Dutch wars against Khoe herders at the Cape. **1679:** Stellenbosch town founded. **1680s–1690s:** Changamire expels Portuguese from Shona plateau. **1688:** Huguenot settlers join Dutch in Cape Town.
1700–1749 English expand sugar production in Jamaica. French develop Saint-Domingue. **1706–1750:** Gold and diamond boom in south-central Brazil (Minas Gerais). **1720s–1760s:** Height of (very minor) slave importing in North America for tobacco (Chesapeake) and rice (Lowcountry Carolina). Africa population estimated ~100,000,000	"Barbary Pirates" (Algiers, Tunis, etc.) attract increasing attention of European monarchies.	**1700:** Osei Tutu and Asante control Akan goldfields. **1717–1750:** Asantehene Opuku Ware expands Asante control inland from Gold Coast; captives available at coast attract European slavers. **1720s:** Fulbe Muslim (Almany) rule consolidated in Futa Jalon in Upper Guinea; sell slaves. **1720s:** Dahomey emerges as military power behind Slave Coast, seizes Allada, Ouidah (1727). **1720s:** Oyo advances toward coast, subjects Dahomey to tribute payments; exports of slaves grow. **1738–1756:** Severe drought along upper Niger; Segu develops as militaristic slave-raiding state." Juula (merchant) revolution" creates Kong state (Kankan).	**1715:** French colonize Mauritius as Île de France; also hold Bourbon (now Réunion). Goan (Portuguese Indian) traders develop ivory trade at Kilwa, Mozambique Island. **1730s:** French develop sugar on Mascarenes (Bourbon and Île de France).	**1702–1704:** Beatriz Kimpa Vita leads millennial "Antonian" Christian movement in Kongo. Lunda chiefs expand west along slaving routes. British and French slavers develop sources along Loango Coast north of Zaire River mouth. **1720s:** Ovimbundu military rulers consolidate regimes on Angolan central highlands; Portuguese traders settle to buy captives. Benguela grows as slaving port for Brazilian shippers. Lozi consolidate control in upper Zambezi floodplain.	**1713:** Smallpox epidemic decimates Khoe. Dutch and French settlers occupy best lands to east of Cape Town; Cape grain and vineyard agriculture, worked by "Malay" and Malagasy slaves. Kora, Griqua, Nama frontier groups form north of Cape. **1746:** Swellendam town founded as gateway to eastern Cape.

(continued)

Era	Northern	Western	Eastern	Central	Southern
1750–1799 American Revolution (**1776–1783**), French Revolution (**1789**), Haitian revolt in Saint Domingue (**1791**), and French-British wars (**1793–1815**) leave British dominant power in Atlantic. Freed slave loyalists in North America and other American ex-slaves repatriated.	**1798:** Napoleon invades Egypt.	Increased slaving throughout Niger Delta supports prosperity in trading towns. Aro and others consolidate slave-trading networks inland among Igbo. **1780s:** Disintegration of Oyo. **1787:** British missionaries found Colony of Freedom (Sierra Leone) for American repatriates. Slaves from Hausa area appear at Slave Coast markets.	**1770s:** French buy slaves for sugar on Mascarenes at Kilwa and Mozambique. **1785:** Oman takes control at Kilwa from Zanzibar. **1787:** Andrianampoinimerina begins military conquests; Merina state in Madagascar.	**1750s:** Portugal attempts to wrest control of Angolan slave trade from Brazilians. **1770s:** Angolan merchant families assert control over trade routes in interior of colony; attack Mbailundu (central highlands). **1780s–1790s:** Drought widespread; slave exports peak. Portuguese expeditions east of Angola, also up Zambezi.	**1750s:** Western Cape imports Mozambican and Malagasy slaves to increase production of wheat, wine. **1770s–1780s:** Dutch settler conflicts with Xhosa in Eastern Cape. **1786:** Establishment of Graff Reinet town. **1790s:** Severe drought along Indian Ocean coast; slave exports rise; Brazilians enter Mozambique trade. **1795:** British seize Cape Colony from Dutch.
1800–1849 **1804:** Denmark illegalizes slave trade. **1807:** Britain and U.S. abolish slave trades. **1811:** Britain launches naval suppression of maritime slaving of continental powers (Portugal, France, Spain). Campaign against Atlantic slaving advances: Dutch ban trade. Spain (**1815**) and Portugal (**1817**) agree to confine slaving to south of equator.	**1805:** Muhammad 'Ali (*pasha*) in Egypt breaks free from Ottoman control. **1820s:** Egyptian military/commercial campaigns up Nile valley. **1824:** Egypt establishes Khartoum as capital on upper Nile. **1830:** Formal French rule proclaimed in Algeria. **1841–1847:** 'Abd al-Qādir fighting against French in Algeria. **1849:** Death of Muhammad 'Ali.	**1804:** 'Uthman dan Fodio proclaims "Fulani" *jihad* against Hausa kings. Sokoto capital of Muslim theocracy, proclaimed a caliphate. **1808:** Sierra Leone made British Crown colony. **1818:** Fulbe Muslim clerics create Masina on middle Niger. Slave exports continue in 1830s. **1821:** Freed slaves from U.S. settle on upper Guinea coast (Liberia). **1840s:** Al-Hajj 'Umar begins *jihad* on upper Senegal. Palm oil exports rise from forested regions; peanut exports established in Senegambia. **1847:** Republic of Liberia established.	**1806:** Seyyid Sa'id takes power in Oman. **1806:** Andrianampoinimerina consolidates power over highland Madagascar state. **1817:** Andrianampoinimerina ends slave exports. **1820s:** Oman takes other Swahili mainland towns, develops production of slave-grown cloves on Pemba and Zanzibar. **1828:** Queen Ranavalona takes throne in Imerina (Madagascar). **1830s:** Gikuyu and Nyamwezi trade links coast with Lakes Plateau region. **1840:** Seyyid Sa'id, sultan of Oman, relocates to Zanzibar. Ivory exports to India supplemented by slaves sent to Persian Gulf, Red Sea ports. Clove plantations worked by slaves thrive on Pemba and Zanzibar. **1847:** Zanzibar-Britain treaty prohibits exports of slaves.	**1802–1811:** *Pombeiro* slave traders cross continent from Angola to Zambezi valley. **1821:** Angolan administration in disarray when Brazil declares independence from Portugal. **1826:** Slave exports scheduled to end in 1830; colonial government seeks alternative exports. **1830s:** Slave shipments diverted from Luanda to other ports; continue illegally until 1850. **1838:** Nominal end of slavery in Angola. **1840s:** Wax and ivory exports spur Cokwe to expand between Kwango and Kasai; Bihe become leading Ovimbundu traders. Luanda Afro-Portuguese community prospers; Lunda military power at peak. **1840–1864:** Kololo (Nguni refugees) control Lozi area (upper Zambezi floodplain).	**1803:** Return of Cape Colony to Dutch. **1806:** British assume permanent authority at Cape. **1808:** Labor crisis at Cape as slave imports end at time of expanding European market for Cape wines. **1817:** Shaka emerges at head of growing Zulu kingdom. **1820:** British settlers arrive at Port Elizabeth, eastern Cape. **1820s:** Warfare widespread among Nguni; conflicts also in Sotho areas of highveld. **1830s:** Dutch settlers abandon eastern Cape and drive oxen and wagons into highveld to settle. **1834:** British abolish slavery in Cape Colony. **1835:** Main body of Dutch head north in "Great Trek." **1838:** Battle of Blood River (Dutch victory over Zulu). **1838–1840:** Ndebele driven from highveld north of Limpopo (Bulawayo). **1843:** British annex colony of Natal. Dutch establish highveld republics;

(continued)

Era: 1850–1899

- c. 1850: Africa population estimated ~110,000,000
- 1873–1879: World commodity prices fall, creating crisis for indebted African suppliers.
- 1884–1885: Berlin Congress legitimizes claims to colonies.
- 1890s: "Effective occupation" required by Berlin treaty spurs European governments to military conquest, treaty-making, and concessions to private commercial interests.

Northern

- 1854–1863: *Khedive* Sa'id (Egypt) pushes ivory trade to Nile headwaters. Egypt opened to British and French investors (railroads, military).
- 1859: Construction begins on Suez canal.
- 1863–1879: *Khedive* Isma'il (Egypt) promoting European technology; growing debt.
- 1869: Suez Canal opens.
- 1877: Ismail names Gordon governor of upper Nile (Sudan); accepts treaty banning slave trade.
- 1881: *Indigénat* (Native Code) drawn up in Algeria.
- 1881: *Mahdi* Muhammed Ahmad declares *jihad* in upper Nile region.
- 1881: France takes Tunisia.
- 1882: British-French protectorate in Egypt.
- 1885: *Mahdi* forces capture Khartoum (Gordon slain); Muhammed Ahmad dies.
- 1880s: French families settling in Algeria; wine industry established.
- 1890s: Private slave-raiding armies take control of upper Nile region.
- 1893: Morocco defeated by Spain.
- 1896: Anglo-Egyptian condominium established to rule Sudan
- 1898: British defeat Mahdist state on upper Nile.

Western

- 1850s: Umarians move east, absorb Segu.
- 1859: British annex Lagos as colony. Mission-educated Sierra Leoneans return to Yoruba homelands of enslaved parents (Lagos, Abeokuta).
- 1864: Death of al-Hajj 'Umar.
- 1865–1875: Samori Touré conquers Juula/Mande areas.
- 1872: British acquire Dutch possessions on Gold Coast.
- 1874: British protectorate declared over Fante; attack Asante capital (Kumasi), machine guns used.
- 1884: Germany occupies Togo, Kamerun.
- 1890s: French and British forces advance to secure territories claimed.
- 1890–1891: French defeat 'Umar's Tukulor state.
- 1892: French enter Abomey (capital of Dahomey).
- 1893: Rabeh (upper Nile slave raider) conquers Bornu.
- 1895: Baule drive back French (Côte d'Ivoire).
- 1896: British military expedition takes Kumasi (Asante).
- 1897: British Royal Niger Company advances north to Nupe.
- 1897: Aborigines Rights Protection Society formed.
- 1898: Samori defeated.

Eastern

- 1850s: Khartoum, Swahili traders reach Lakes Plateau.
- 1855–1868: Emperor Tewodros restores unity in Ethiopia.
- 1856–1884: *Kabaka* (king) Mutesa in Buganda negotiates with competing traders.
- 1860s: Mirambo uses Ngoni tactics to build political power in Unyamwezi.
- 1872: *Ras* Kassa (Tigre) emperor of Ethiopia, as Yohannes IV; Menilek king in Shoa.
- 1873: Sultan Barghash (1870–1888) accepts British treaty ending slave exports at Zanzibar.
- 1870s: Kabarega (1869–1899) uses muskets to establish Bunyoro in Lakes Plateau.
- 1870s: Kigeri (1865–1895) expands Tutsi power in Rwanda.
- 1879: Anglican, Catholic missionaries reach Buganda; politics shift to religious factions.
- 1884: *Kabaka* Mwanga consolidates power of Buganda in Lakes Plateau region.
- 1888–1899: German, British forces subdue widespread resistance to conquest in Kenya, German East Africa.
- 1889: Menilek unites Ethiopia.
- 1890s: Sustained Bunyoro and Buganda resistance against Lugard's forces.
- 1890s: *Rinderpest* (bovine epizootic), human epidemics devastate large areas.
- 1895: Uganda railroad construction begins at Mombasa, employing Indian laborers.
- 1896: Menilek defeats Italian army at Adowa; Ethiopian independence secured.
- 1899: Treaty confirms British authority in Lakes Plateau area.

Central

- 1850s–1860s: Cokwe expand as producers of wax, ivory. Ngoni (warrior communities from Zulu area) settle west and north of Lake Malawi.
- 1850s–1860s: Livingstone travels from Cape Colony to Angola, Mozambique, and (modern) Malawi.
- 1868–1891: Msiri extends Swahili-linked trading into Katanga and gains military control.
- 1869: Tippu Tip imposes Arab/Swahili military control along upper Lualaba.
- 1880s: Lunda rulers, under pressure from Cokwe, lose authority; Luba chiefs yield to Tippu Tip, Swahili, Msiri, Ngoni.
- 1880s: Portuguese exploit conflicts among Zambezi valley *prazo* warlords to expand area of control in Mozambique.
- 1880s: Stanley exploits Livingstone rescue, also "explores" on behalf of Belgian king Léopold II.
- 1889: Britain proclaims "Central African Protectorate."
- 1889–1899: Léopold II's Congo Independent State occupies central basin of Zaire River system.
- 1891: British ultimatum ends Portuguese hopes of trans-continental link of Mozambique to Angola.
- 1890–1899: Construction of railway to Stanley (Malebo) Pool.
- 1890s: Johnston subdues Nyasaland, northeastern Rhodesia.
- 1893–1895: Revolts against King Léopold's Congo.
- 1893–1898: Portuguese military campaigns secure occupation of Angola.

Southern

- 1850s: Moshoeshoe (c. 1786–1870) secures British recognition for Sotho.
- 1850s: British pressure Xhosa.
- 1852: British recognize Transvaal and Orange Free State (1854).
- 1856–1857: Xhosa cattle-killing.
- 1860s: British bring Indians as laborers on Natal sugar estates. Dutch-speaking settlers in highveld republics defining identity as "Afrikaners."
- 1869: Diamonds discovered at Kimberly (northern Cape).
- 1872: Cape Colony gains responsible government.
- 1875: Khama takes Tswana throne.
- 1877–1881: British occupy Afrikaner republics; conquer Pedi, Xhosa, Zulu.
- 1879: Zulu defeat British at Isandhlwana.
- 1880–1881: Afrikaners rebel (First Anglo-Boer War).
- 1885: Gold discovered on Witwatersrand (Transvaal).
- 1886: Johannesburg founded.
- 1888: Cecil Rhodes's British South Africa (BSA) Company wins treaty-ceding authority over Ndebele.
- 1889: British "protect" Lozi.
- 1890: BSA "Pioneer column" occupies Shona territories.
- 1893: BSA conquers Ndebele.
- 1895: Jameson leads BSA raid against Transvaal.
- 1896: Transvaal Chamber of Mines forms central labor-recruiting agency (Witwatersrand Native Labor Association = WNLA).
- 1896–1897: Rinderpest (bovine epizootic) devastates most areas of southern Africa. Chimurenga revolt in (BSA) Southern Rhodesia.
- 1899–1902: Second Anglo-Boer war (ends with Treaty of Vereeniging).

(continued)

Era	Northern	Western	Eastern	Central	Southern
1900–1920 **c.1900:** Africa population estimated ~133,000,000	**1900:** Italian control confirmed in Tripoli (Libya). **1906:** French and Spanish authority recognized in Morocco. **1911–1913:** Sanusiyya-led resistance to Italian invasion in Libya. **1912:** France declares protectorate over Morocco.	**1900–1903:** British military campaigns subdue Sokoto emirs. **1901:** Slavery illegal in southern Nigeria. *Indigénat* labor code imposed in French colonies. **1903–1905:** French laws against slave trading in colonies. **1900–1907:** Lugard in Northern Nigeria implements policy of "indirect rule."	**1899–1910:** M. Abdile Hasan mobilizes Somali resistance against Ethiopia, Italy. **1903–1906:** Gikuyu land given to settlers in Kenya "white highlands." **1905–1906:** *Majimaji* revolt in German East Africa.	**1902:** Bailundo revolt in Angola. **1908:** Belgium assumes control of Congo Independent State after revelation of brutality of Léopold's concessionary companies. **1910:** Slavery outlawed in Belgian Congo, and again in Portuguese colonies; end of transportation of *serviçais* (forced labor) to São Tomé cocoa plantations. **1913:** *Liga Angolana* recognized (*assimilado* organization) in Angola.	**1901:** WNLA recruiting monopoly in Mozambique. **1904:** Malagasy revolt against French rule in Madagascar. **1904:** *Indigénato* imposed in Mozambique (forced labor = *shibalo*). **1904:** Herero revolt in German South West Africa. **1906:** Bambata (Zulu) revolt. **1910:** Union of South Africa (constitution favoring Afrikaner electorate). **1912:** African National Congress founded (ANC). **1913:** Natives Land Act prevents African ownership outside designated "reserves."
1914–1918: World War I. Nascent colonial administrations depleted by manpower levies for war effort. Heavy recruiting for campaigns in Germany's colonies; c. 2,500,000 African soldiers, carriers.		**1914:** French revoke citizenship of Dakar residents. French, British capture German Togo. **1914–1918:** Blaise Diagne helps French recruit 170,000 *tirailleurs sénégalaises* for the war effort. **1916:** Gold Coast Legislative Council includes Africans. French, British capture German Kamerun.	**1913:** Emperor Menilek dies (Ethiopia). **1914–1918:** Kenyan settlers use war effort to secure political influence in colonial government. **1916:** Empress Zauditu on Ethiopian throne, under regent *Ras Tafari* (later Emperor Haile Selassie). "Carrier corps" drafts 700,000 porters in Kenya and Uganda.	**1915:** John Chilembwe leads revolt in Nyasaland. Era of harsh concessionary companies in French Equatorial Africa. **1917:** DIAMANG (diamond-mining concessionary company) established	**1914:** Afrikaner revolt against Union government decision to support Allies in WWI. **1915:** South African forces occupy German South West Africa.
1918–1919: Worldwide pandemic (Spanish influenza) deadly in Africa. **1919:** Treaty of Versailles establishes League of Nations. Paris Pan-African Congress, led by W. E. B. Du Bois (1919).		**1919:** Britain and France receive League of Nations mandate authority in Togo, Cameroon. **1920:** Formation of National Congress of British West Africa	**1919:** Britain receives mandate authority for Tanganyika. Gov. Northey asserts "paramountcy" of European interests in Kenya.	**1918:** Colonial minister Franck imposes administrative regime (*chefferie* forced labor) in Belgian Congo. **1919:** Portuguese complete military subjugation of Angola. **1920:** Land apportionment ("native reserves") completed in Southern Rhodesia.	**1918–1920:** Johannesburg workers strike. **1919:** Industrial and Commercial Workers (ICU) formed (Cape Town). Union of South Africa receives "mandate" authority for South West Africa (Namibia).

(continued)

Era	Northern	Western	Eastern	Central	Southern
1921–1950 **1923:** Pan-African Congresses (London, Lisbon). **1929:** Worldwide economic depression begins. **1939–1945:** World War II. **1941:** Atlantic Charter. **1942:** United Nations Declaration. **1947:** India independent. **1948:** United Nations convenes in San Francisco.	**1922:** Egypt independent as constitutional monarchy under King Fuad. **1923–1926:** Rif War (revolt against French in Morocco). **1925–1931:** Gezira cotton scheme established in Sudan. **1933:** League for Moroccan Action criticizes French protectorate. **1936–1937:** King Farouk succeeds. "Capitulations" phased out in Egypt, giving greater autonomy. **1940:** Italians attack Egypt from Libya. **1943:** Rommel's Afrika Corps defeated at El Alamein. De Gaulle's French Committee of National Liberation at Algiers. **1945:** Creation of Arab League (Cairo). Manchester Pan-African Congress. **1946:** Britain accorded responsibility for Somaliland and Eritrea. Eritrean struggle for independence. **1947:** Civil war also in Tigre. Eritrean Peoples Liberation Front moves into Ethiopia.	**1923:** Elections for 2 African seats on Nigerian Legislative Council. **1927:** Firestone Rubber Co. concession in Liberia. **1929:** Aba market women riot in Nigeria. **1938:** Gold Coast cocoa holdup (slowdown); railway workers strike at Thies (Senegal). **1939–1940:** Heavy conscription of Africans from French colonies for service on the European fronts, Indo-China. **1944:** William V. Tubman president in Liberia (until **1971**). **1945–1948:** Strikes in Gold Coast, Nigeria. Constitutions in British colonies create African majorities in legislative councils. Formation of first-generation nationalist parties. **1946:** Reforms in French colonies abolish *indigenat*, grant French citizenship; Rassemblement Democratique Africaine. **1947:** Kwame Nkruma returns to Gold Coast. **1947–1948:** Railway workers strike in Senegal. **1949:** Nkrumah forms Convention Peoples Party (CPP).	**1921:** Harry Thuku founds Young Kikuyu Association; arrested **1922.** **1923–1930:** Conflict in Kenya over female circumcision (Gikuyu). **1924:** Kikuyu Central Association formed. Ormsby-Gore Comm. endorses federation favoring white settlers. **1927:** Jomo Kenyatta general secretary of Kikuyu Central Association. **1930:** Haile Selassie crowned emperor of Ethiopia. **1935:** Italians invade Ethiopia (Fascist Ethiopia, **1936–1941**). Haile Selassie exiled in Britain. **1941:** Britain reconquers Ethiopia; Selassie returns. **1944:** Eliud Mathu joins Kenya Legislative Council. Kenya African Union formed. **1945:** Ethiopia independent. **1947:** Jomo Kenyatta president of Kenya African Union (KAU).	**1933–1934:** *Mchape* (Watchtower) witchcraft eradication movement. **1935:** African mineworkers on Northern Rhodesian Copperbelt organize strikes. **1940:** Free French regime at Brazzaville under Félix Éboué. **1944:** Nyasaland African Congress formed. **1944:** Brazzaville "French African Conference." **1945:** Railway strike and Douala riots in Cameroon. Settlement of Portuguese families accelerates in Angola and Mozambique. **1948:** Northern Rhodesian African Congress formed. **1949:** Belgians foresee formal *évolué* status for educated Africans in Congo.	**1922:** Nama revolt in South West Africa. Government suppresses white miners' Rand Revolt (Johannesburg). **1923:** Natives (Urban Areas) Act restricts African residence in Union. **1923–1927:** ICU coordinates millennial rural protest in South Africa. **1924:** Hertzog's National Party wins substantial vote. **1926:** Union wins dominion status within British empire. **1928:** Mozambique Convention for mine labor supply. **1930:** Membership of South African Communist Party peaks; influences ICU. **1934:** Tete Agreement for Mozambique laborers in Southern Rhodesia. Smuts/Hertzog Union Party wins election. **1936:** Union Party removes African voters from common roll in South Africa. Natives Registration Act establishes pass system in Southern Rhodesia. White population growing in Southern Rhodesia. **1947–1948:** Revolt in Madagascar. **1948:** National Party wins election in South Africa. **1949:** Seretse Khama (king, Bechuanaland) marries Ruth Williams, leading to exile. Prohibition of Mixed Marriages Act in South Africa. **1950:** Immorality Act; Suppression of Communism Act; Group Areas Act

(continued)

Era	Northern	Western	Eastern	Central	Southern
1951–1965 **c.1950**: Africa population estimated ~220,000,000 **1952**: Albert Schweitzer wins Nobel Peace Prize. **1954**: French lose battle at Dien Bien Phu, Vietnam. **1955**: Bandung conference of nonaligned nations. **1959**: Scientists identify HIV/AIDS virus **1963**: Organization of African Unity created.	**1956**: Tunisia becomes independent. **1958**: French generals revolt and bring de Gaulle to power in France; Fifth Republic. **1958**: Military coup in Sudan. **1960**: Somalia becomes independent. **1962**: Independence in Algeria. **1965**: King Hasan restores royal authority in Morocco.	**1958**: De Gaulle offers referendum to confirm "autonomy" in association with France. Guinea, under Sekou Touré, votes "*non,*" becomes independent. Nkrumah sponsors All-African Peoples Conference. **1960**: Independence for French colonies (Cameroun, Côte d'Ivoire, Dahomey, Haut Volta, Mauritania, Mali, Niger, Senegal, Togo). Independence in Nigeria. **1961**: Independence in Sierra Leone; British Cameroon joins Nigeria. **1963**: PAIGC begins guerrilla struggle in Portuguese Guinea. **1964**: Nkrumah proposes single-party state in Ghana. **1965**: Gambia becomes independent. Breakdown of law and order in Nigeria.	Tutsi monarchists in Rwanda provoke Hutu reprisals; flight of Tutsi into exile. **1960**: Independence in Congo. **1961**: Independence in Tanganyika (Julius Nyerere becomes president). **1962**: Uganda independent (Obote becomes president). Burundi becomes independent. **1963**: Kenya, Zanzibar independent; Kenyatta becomes president in Kenya; Kenya African National Union (KANU) established. **1964**: Tanganyika and Zanzibar join to form Tanzania. **1965**: Nyerere creates single-party (TANU) regime in Tanzania. Hutu coup with Tutsi army reprisals in Burundi.	**1953**: Central African Federation formed under Southern Rhodesian settler leadership. **1956**: Strike by workers on Northern Rhodesian Copperbelt mines. *Movimento Popular da Libertação de Angola* (MPLA) formed. **1957**: First elections in Belgian Congo. **1958**: Kenneth Kaunda forms United National Independence Party in Northern Rhodesia. **1959**: Hastings Banda leads defiance campaign in Nyasaland; detained after declaration of emergency. Riots in Léopoldville. Belgians publish gradualist plan for independence. **1960**: Government troops followed by secession of Katanga; UN intervention. Violence in cotton-growing regions of Angola. Independence in Chad, Congo (Brazzaville), Gabon, Oubangui-Chari. **1961**: Widespread revolt in Angola; declaration of emergency, MPLA-led launching of liberation struggle. Rwanda becomes independent. **1963**: End of Central African Federation. **1964**: Zambia and Malawi become independent. **1965**: Mobutu Sese Seko takes power in Congo; renames country Zaïre (**1971**).	**1951**: African "homelands" established. **1952**: ANC joins South African Indian Congress in "defiance campaign." **1953**: Bantu Education Act. **1955**: Freedom Charter proclaimed in South Africa. **1956**: Government arrests opponents and charges them with treason (trial drags on until **1961**). **1957**: Joshua Nkomo forms African National Congress in Southern Rhodesia. **1959**: Pan-Africanist Congress breaks away from ANC under Robert Sobukwe. **1960**: Government troops fire into crowd at Sharpeville; state of emergency declared. South Africa becomes republic. Madagascar becomes independent; renamed Malagasy Republic. **1960**: Albert John Luthuli wins Nobel Peace Prize. **1961**: Republic of South Africa leaves British Commonwealth. **1962**: Formation of *Frente de Libertação de Moçambique* (FRELIMO). **1962**: Nkomo reforms National Democratic Party as Zimbabwe African People's Union (ZAPU). **1963**: Robert Mugabe and others break away from ZAPU as Zimbabwe African National Union (ZANU), ANC turns to violence. **1964**: FRELIMO launches armed liberation struggle in Mozambique. **1964**: Nelson Mandela tried; jailed on Robben Island. **1965**: Rhodesia unilaterally declares independence (UDI) under Ian Smith.

(continued)

Era	Northern	Western	Eastern	Central	Southern
1966–1980 **c.1965:** Africa population estimated ~315,000,000 **1972– :** Long-term drought sets in, particularly in sahelinan regions. **1973:** Organization of Petroleum Exporting Countries formed (OPEC). **1973:** Council for the Development of Social Science Research in Africa (CODESRIA) established (Dakar). **1974:** Spinola-led coup ends Portuguese *Estado Novo.* **1974:** U.S., Soviet Union concentrate on cold war alignment of post-coup Angola and Mozambique. **1977:** United Nations embargoes arms shipments to South Africa. **c. 1980:** Africa population estimated ~470,000,000 (continued)	**1967:** Israel invades Egypt in "Six-day War." **1969:** Sa'id Barre takes power in Somalia. **1969:** Qadhdhafi seizes power in Libya. **1970:** Aswan dam completed at Egyptian-Sudan border; Nasser assassinated. **1975:** Morocco and Mauritania partition Western Sahara; war follows. **1976:** Ethiopia-Somali war in Ogaden. **1978:** Large petroleum reserves found in southern Sudan. **1978:** Anwar al-Sadat shares Nobel Peace Prize with Israeli Prime Minister Menachem Begin. **1980:** French paratroopers sent to Chad.	**1966:** Military coups depose nationalist governments in Ghana, Nigeria, Bénin, Togo, Upper Volta. **1967:** Biafra attempts to secede from Nigeria. Military coup in Sierra Leone. **1969:** General Spinola in command of anti-PAIGC army in Portuguese Guiné. **1970:** Oil production becomes significant in Nigeria. Biafra secession ends. **1971:** Tubman dies in Liberia; succeeded by William Tolbert. **1973:** PAIGC president Amilcar Cabral assassinated. **1974:** Guiné (Bissau) attains independence under PAIGC. **1975:** Economic Community of West African States (ECOWAS) formed. Cape Verde becomes independent. Dahomey becomes Republic of Bénin. Oil boom in Nigeria. **1977:** Attempted coup in Bénin lands French paratroops. **1979:** Lt. Jerry Rawlings leads coup against civilian government in Ghana. Restoration of civilian government in Nigeria ("Second Republic"). **1980:** Léopold Sédar Senghor retires as president in Senegal. Tolbert assassinated in Liberia; Sgt. Samuel K. Doe takes power.	**1966:** Obote civilian government overthrows in Uganda **1967:** Nyerere makes Arusha declaration in Tanzania. **1969:** Assassination of Tom Mboya in Kenya; KANU moving to one-party presidentialism. **1971:** Idi Amin expels Obote from Uganda. **1972:** Amin deports Asians from Uganda. **1974:** Military coup ends rule of Haile Selassie, Solomonid dynasty in Ethiopia; Marxist military council succeeds. **1977:** Kenyatta dies; succeeded by Daniel arap Moi as president of Kenya. **1979:** Amin expelled from Uganda.	**1966:** Bokassa takes power in Ouban-gui-Chari, declares Central African Republic. In exile, ANC regroups in Zambia. Oil drilling in Angola. **1968:** *União Nacional para a Independência Total de Angola* (UNITA) formed. **1969:** FRELIMO leader Eduardo Mondlane assassinated. Three-cornered guerrilla struggle intensifies in Angola (MPLA, UNITA, *Frente Nacional para a Libertação de Angola* [FNLA]) Cabora Bassa dam on Zambezi under construction to provide hydroelectric power for South Africa. **1974:** U.S., Soviet Union concentrate on cold war alignment of post-coup Angola and Mozambique. **1975:** Angola independent under MPLA. **1975:** Cubans arrive in Angola to defend MPLA; U.S.-backed invasion from Zaire; South Africans invade in support of UNITA; MPLA takes control of independent government. **1976:** Bokassa declares himself emperor of Central African Empire. **1977:** Assassination of President Ngouabi in Congo Democratic Republic, followed by military rule. **1979:** Angolan president Agostinho Neto dies; succeeded by João dos Santos	**1966:** Independence in Lesotho and Botswana.General Law Amendment Act. **1967:** South Africa Terrorism Act. **1968:** Swaziland becomes independent. **1971:** Violent protest in Namibia against South African control. **1971:** Armed struggle intensifies between ZAPU and ZANU in Rhodesia. South African Defense Force buildup in Southwest Africa against Southwest African Peoples Organization (SWAPO). **1975:** FRELIMO government independent in Mozambique. **1975:** Turnhalle Conference in Namibia excludes SWAPO; foresees negotiated independence. "Forced removals" of people living outside "group areas" in South Africa. **1976:** Residents in Soweto and other townships begin violent protests in South Africa against Bantu education. Transkei rendered "self-governing." **1977:** Venda declared "self-governing." Urban violence spreads throughout townships. Assassination of Steve Biko. **1978:** P.W. Botha prime minister; modest reform of apartheid (trade unions). **1979:** Tricameral uniracial parliament in South Africa. **1979:** RENAMO (Resistência Nacional Moçambicana) opposition to FRELIMO in Mozambique. South African military intervention increases in Angola. **1980:** Zimbabwe becomes independent under President Robert Mugabe.

Era 1981–2007	Northern	Western	Eastern	Central	Southern
c. **1980:** Africa population estimated ~480,000,000 **1981:** Scientific identification of Acquired Immune Deficiency Syndrome in U.S. **1982– :** World Bank, International Monetary Fund impose structural adjustment programs. **1984:** HIV/AIDS identified in Zaire, Rwanda. **1986:** World Health Organization develops Global AIDS strategy. **1986:** Wole Soyinka, Nigerian writer, wins Nobel Prize for Literature. **1989:** Fall of Berlin Wall. Democratic political reforms attempted in numerous nations. **1990:** WHO places Africa at head of list of populations afflicted with HIV/AIDS. **1992:** World Bank minimizes effects of HIV/AIDS in Africa. **1993:** European Union established; emigration (often illegal) from northern and western Africa increases. **1999:** World Bank identifies AIDS as major impediment to development.	**1980s:** Effects of drought afflict upper Nile **1982:** Civil war in Chad; Libya involved. **1983:** President Numeiri imposes Islamic law in Sudan and exacerbates rebellion in non-Muslim south. **1986:** U.S. air raid on Libya. War in Western Sahara (Polisario Front). **1988:** Rioting in Algeria, Islamic Salvation Front emerges. Sudan civil war continues. **1990:** Civil war breaks out among numerous factions in Somalia. **1992:** Chaos in Somalia brings UN peacekeeping force, culminating in U.S. intervention. Eritrea independent of Ethiopia. **1999:** King Hasan II (r. 1961–1999) dies in Morocco. **1999– :** Islamist movements challenge national governments, particularly in Algeria. Berber cultural self-assertion against Arabic national cultures.	**1983–1984:** Military coups in Nigeria; end of oil boom provokes strike, unrest. **1984:** Ahmed Sekou Touré (president of Guinea-Conakry) dies; military coup. Sankara military coup in Upper Volta; country name changed to Burkina Faso. **1987:** Assassination of Sankara in Burkina Faso. **1989:** Civil war in Chad eases. Charles Taylor leads insurgency against Doe regime in Liberia. Liberia dissolves into chaos. Structural adjustment improves servicing of foreign debt but destabilizes regimes. **1992:** Liberian rebels overthrow government in Sierra Leone. **1993:** Babanguida annuls election of Mashood Abiola in Nigeria. **1993:** Houphouët-Boigny dies (Côte d'Ivoire). **1994:** Abiola arrested in Nigeria. **1996:** Democratic election in Ghana returns Rawlings to power. Peace accord in Liberia: Ruth Sandra Perry takes presidency. **1998:** Gen. Sani Abacha (president, Nigeria) found dead; Olusegun Obasanjo elected president.	**1980–1985:** Obote returns to power in Uganda. **1984–1985:** Famine in Ethiopia. **1985:** Nyerere resigns in Tanzania. Civil war in Ethiopia, based in Eritrea, Ogaden, Tigray. **1986:** Moi regime suppresses civil rights in Kenya. Museveni takes power in Uganda. **1988:** Hutu-Tutsi violence erupts in Burundi. **1991:** Moi pressured by foreign donors to relax political controls in Kenya. Mengistu regime defeated in Ethiopia. **1993:** Ethnic strife breaks out in Burundi. **1994:** Hutu slaughter Tutsi in Rwanda. **1995:** Tutsi RDF reprisals drive Hutu refugees into neighboring Zaire and elsewhere. **1996:** Opposition parties in Kenya under renewed threat. **1998:** Al Qaeda bombings of U.S. embassies in Kenya and Tanzania. **1999:** Uganda begins screening for HIV/AIDS. Moi in Kenya declares HIV/AIDS "national disaster."	**1988:** Angolan government troops defeat South African Defense Force. **1990:** Food riots in Zambia, in wake of structural adjustment programs. **1991:** Kaunda loses democratic election in Zambia. Cuba withdraws troops from Angola; MPLA and UNITA sign pact. Elections in Angola fail to end civil war (MPLA/UNITA). **1996:** Disorders break out in eastern Zaire; Laurent Kabila forms army. **1997:** Kabila takes Zaire and renames country Democratic Republic of Congo; Mobutu dies in exile. **1998:** UNITA resumes war in Angola.	**1983:** United Democratic Front formed in South Africa. **1983:** Demond Mpilu Tutu wins Nobel Peace Prize. **1986:** State of emergency declared in South Africa. **1986:** Antiroyalist military coup in Lesotho. Growing violence in South Africa. **1989:** F.W. de Klerk becomes prime minister. **1990:** Nelson Mandela released from prison; takes control of ANC. Namibia becomes independent. Inkatha Freedom Party (IFP) of Mangosuthu Buthelezi engages in terrorism; violence wracks KwaZulu. **1993:** Nadine Gordimer wins Nobel Prize for Literature. **1993:** Apartheid ends in South Africa. Nelson Mandela and Frederick Willem de Klerk share Nobel Peace Prize. **1994:** Multiracial democratic election; Mandela president of "new South Africa." **1996:** National Party withdraws from Government of National Unity (GNU). **1997:** National Party dissolves in South Africa. **1999:** SWAPO returned to political power in Namibia.

(continued)

Era	Northern	Western	Eastern	Central	Southern
1981–2007 (continued) **c. 2000:** Africa population estimated ~795,000,000 **2001:** UN Secretary General wins Nobel Peace Prize. Annan urges major spending to combat AIDS at African Summit in Nigeria. Global AIDS and Health Fund expands efforts to include malaria and tuberculosis. **2002:** African Union created. **2002–2007:** WHO data identify Africa as location of significant majority of AIDS cases worldwide; political struggles intensify over means of transmission of the virus in Africa, ethics and efficacy of anti-retroviral drugs, and deception and corruption in government national health services, as estimates of deaths and rates of infection increase significantly. **c. 2007:** Africa population estimated 1,0000,000,000	**2003:** Fighting develops in Darfur region of Sudan; government militias intervene amidst widespread and continuing accusations of genocide. **2005:** Negotiated peace settlement in Sudan; Southern Sudan autonomous region leader John Garang killed in helicopter crash. **2005–2007:** Mediated negotiations between Algeria and Morocco over the future of Western Sahara deteriorate. **2006:** Divided portions of Somalia turn to open civil war; Ethiopian forces intervene against Islamists in Mogadishu.	**2000:** John Kufuor replaces Rawlings as president. **2000:** Rebels challenge President Taylor in Liberia, civil war follows financed by growing diamond trade ("blood diamonds"). Similar conflicts wrack Sierra Leone until UN intervention in **2002**. **2002:** Military mutiny in Côte d'Ivoire; regional violence grows. **2005:** UN-supervised elections in Liberia; Ellen Johnson-Sirleaf new president (first female head of state in Africa). **2007:** Taylor to be tried for "crimes against humanity." **2007:** Umaru Yar'Adua elected president of Nigeria.	**2002:** Mwai Kibaki succeeds Moi as president in Kenya. **2004:** Wangari Maathai wins Nobel Peace Prize. **2005–2006:** Ceasefire in Burundi between survivors of 1990s genocide. **2006–2007:** Disarming of Rwandan militias in eastern DRC.	**2001:** Kabila assassinated in Democratic Republic of Congo; son Joseph succeeds. Conflicts in eastern parts of country surpass WWII in numbers of deaths. **2002:** Cameroon national team advances to World Cup (football) play. **2002:** Banda dies in Malawi. **2002:** Drought, then floods afflict Malawi, Mozambique. **2002:** Jonas Savimbi dies in Angola; thirty-year civil war ends. **2006:** Multi-party elections return Kabila, but conflicts do not subside.	**2000:** Mbeki asserts "unique" character of HIV/AIDS in Africa; remarks widely misunderstood. **2000:** Mugabe announces redistribution of white-owned farms; health crisis, economic collapse, political violence, hyper-inflation follow. **2003:** John Maxwell Coetzee wins Nobel Prize for Literature. **2004:** Multiparty (FRELIMO/RENAMO) elections in Mozambique name Armando Guebuze president.

APPENDIX B: HISTORY COVERAGE IN THIS ENCYCLOPEDIA

The previous edition of this encyclopedia distributed references to selected high-points of Africa's past in short, specific articles—e.g. "Dahomey," the eighteenth-century kingdom famous for its rulers' dealings with European buyers of slaves at Ouidah and other ports on the part of the West African littoral that they knew as the "Slave Coast." This new edition places nearly all of these specific historical references in longer integrated historicized essays. This formatting of Africa's past is intended to contextualize prominent—at least to Europeans—monuments like "Dahomey" in the flows of human creativity in every sphere of life, as people in Africa developed solutions to the series of intellectual and organizational challenges that they faced. In broad terms, these form a dialectical sequence starting with their explorations of new and changing natural environments in order to appropriate local resources and to increase the size and coherence of the communities in which they lived. Success generated growing populations and denser settlements and left their descendants to seek accommodations with others around them as competition grew for space and for resources. Competition of that sort inclined those in touch with the commercial networks thriving on the seas and oceans surrounding the continent to turn to them for additional resources from outside, recurrently on terms of mercantile credit. Africans drew on their heritages of classical African strategies and concepts to manage growing indebtedness and eventually to preserve themselves, as they understood themselves, within the enveloping modern global contexts of imperial conquest, colonial-era constraints, and recent political independence and responsibility for continuing and draining debt.

The chronological and regional articles organized around this basic narrative are distributed alphabetically throughout the encyclopedia according to titles designating key strategies and/or the historically coherent regional scales on which people strategized. Each thus sketches a period and place in which the people who succeeded drew on an identifiable complex of resources to do so, using a coherent range of strategies that make it possible for historians to construct a narrative around the differences they were able to make. Historians, at base, tell such stories, according to the knowledge, intuition, and sense of human drama that they can bring to bear on times and places in the past relevant to what will intrigue readers in the present. History is decidedly not just "one damned thing after another," as a scattered set of isolated references to "facts" might leave one to suspect. It is rather the rich stories of human ingenuity challenged and—usually—succeeding. That is why history, as is often remarked, is the record of the winners, those who made a difference, and in particular differences of such utility that they provided the frameworks on which succeeding generations drew to confront the new dilemmas that their predecessors' solutions in earlier moments had left in the longer run for them. History, contrary to the illusions of the post-Enlightenment West, is not progressive, moving toward an ever-more-perfect world. Rather it is an ironic—and in Africa's recent past tragic, in the classical sense—series of imperfect trade-offs, accessible, short-term, and defensive stopgap measures taken in the face of much larger historical processes, costs displaced onto others for every gain by some, a "zero-sum" game when the full contexts are taken into account. Unlike the highly selective optimism of the modern West, Africans' historiographies are premised on this reality and totality of the human condition, and their metanarrative therefore is fundamentally restorative of an idealized primal state of balance, coherence, and integrity. Readers with cultural backgrounds premised on unconsidered validation of modernity, usually told as an idealized history of the "rise of the West," will note Africans' contrasting story of their own pasts as based on a more humble acceptance of the limits of the merely human enterprise that fully contextualized history in fact relates.

The following paragraphs outline the planned coherence of the contents of this encyclopedia's historicized mode of covering Africa's past . They are not the only essays in the work related to the past in Africa, as other academic disciplines have vital—though each distinctive—ways of understanding times gone by, or the evidence from those times that comes to hand in the present. Here other approaches appear primarily under the headings of "Prehistory" and "Archaeology." The encyclopedia also offers selected coverage of prominent historical topics such as the Slave Trades. The "History and Politics" sections of the sets of articles on each modern African nation include their colonial pasts, thus limiting the chronological range of the set of articles classed as "historical" to the centuries before the twentieth; in a few cases, the parameters of the modern nation have deeper roots in time, and so they are included in the country composites. In addition, the biographies highlight African personalities from the past as well as recent and contemporary women and men of note. The articles covering cities in Africa also include historical sites. Several topical composites include articles focused primarily on past aspects of the subjects at hand; among them are Arts, Christianity, Diasporas, Diseases, Economic History, Education, Eunuchs, Government, Islam, Languages, Linguistics, Literatures, Livestock (domestication), Plants (domestication), Political Systems, Trade, and Travel and Exploration. Otherwise, a primary purpose of the design of this encyclopedia has been to distinguish modern Africans from their ancestors as just that: modern Africans, fully engaged in the contemporary world, not in the least prisoners of some imaginary "traditional" past. Thus the "historical" articles are meant to move general understanding of Africa beyond the echoes of the myth, still reverberating even in the twenty-first century, as the continent where time stood still. No one in Africa somehow managed—preposterously, in view of the actual stories presented here—to survive into the present in pristine, prehistorical purity.

History, as the record of intentional human actions, begins with the transition from late hominids—still acting, in spite of enlarged cranial capacity and highly nuanced abilities to imitate—in relatively mechanical ways. Both of these capacities, however, provided the mental frameworks within which intentionality and sociability could appear, and these qualities defined the first fully historical humans, that is, people who had become dependent on one another for emotionally and intellectually meaningful lives, together. As it happens, the hominids that did this lived in the northeastern and Saharan latitudes of Africa. Syntactical language, distinct from earlier imitative signaling, however elaborated, in its ability to facilitate mutually creative thinking thus marks the very successful transition from late hominid herds to collaborative, intentional adaptations to changing circumstances: that is, to history. The essay covering these earliest eras of human history—perhaps as remote as the nominal era of approximately 50,000 BP [i.e. "before the present"] arbitrarily used here—covers the entire continent, since the systematic adaptations of much older stone and other technologies known through archaeology (and prehistorical studies of this evidence) demonstrate increasingly complex and community-distinguished orientations to specific environments throughout Africa. See Early Human Society, History of (c. 50,000 to 19,000 BCE).

Since historical strategies, not mechanical chronological periodization, define the coverages of the historical articles in the encyclopedia, the second essay—Technological Specialization Period, History of (c. 19.000 to 5000 BCE)—overlaps in time but tracks the successes attained by foragers forced by growing desiccation to intensify hunting to herding and fishing and to develop cultivated grains out of wild grasses that they formerly gathered, particularly in the paleo-Saharan latitudes. Desertification, Reactions to, History of (c. 5000 to 1000 BCE), again continental in scope but following other people's uses of these innovations developed on the fringes of the Sahara, picks up the development of strategies of integrating —politically, culturally, economically—the increasingly differentiated communities that people then were building around their growing specializations in particular environmental resources; in another extension of older innovations, they also dispersed the technologies they had worked out—riverain, leather-working, eventually metals—that they had devised to exploit them. The lower Nile Valley, both in this period and subsequently, receives coverage separately in the set of articles listed under Egypt, Early (Pharaonic, Greek, and Roman).

From the beginning of the first millennium before the Current Era environmental specializations had become sufficiently intense that people tended to define themselves, or rather to be defined by others, in terms of the distinctive products they developed from the areas they occupied or—later—the skills they controlled. Regionally distinct initiatives thus provide the organizing themes of the historical articles for the centuries from the beginning of the first millennium BCE until about the middle of the first millennium CE—both, of course, nominal dates of varying direct relevance to any particular local stream of events.

Indian Ocean, Africa, History of (1000 BCE to 600 CE)
Northeastern Africa, Classical Period, History of (1000 BCE to 600 CE)
Northwestern Africa, Classical Period, History of (1000 BCE to 600 CE)
Western Desert and Margins, History of (1000 BCE to 600 CE)

"Indian Ocean, Africa" includes the portions of the mainland and the western Indian Ocean islands—Seychelles, Comoros, Zanzibar, and Pemba, as well as Madagascar—where mariners from the southeast Asian archipelago began to introduce distinctively commercial strategies. Northeastern Africa in the same era came under similar commercial influences from the Red Sea Region and the Mediterranean. Northwestern Africa was similarly integrated increasingly into economic and political affairs centered on the northern shores of the Mediterranean and thus receives coverage here in those terms. Conceptualization of these articles in terms of Africans' contact with these external, maritime commercial networks places their focus not on the foreigners but rather on what people in Africa obtained from them and what they did with what they obtained. This important accent on the intentions and actions of Africans is clearest for the last of the set of articles covering this period, on the southern margins of the western Sahara, where archaeology has revealed a distinctive strategy of urban-like concentrations of the many specialized communities that thrived by then in that area; they, of course, provided the framework, the historical context, in which their descendants in the region reacted to more intensive contacts with the Mediterranean coasts of North Africa in the centuries following.

The dates of the set of articles tracking the next generation of historical strategies vary according to who moved in the directions that define each, and when. In general these were centuries during which the local communities elaborated in the preceding era developed strategies of political integration. Broadly, the eastern and southern regions of the continent, generally by then being settled in infinitely nuanced ways by heirs to the culture and languages known as "Bantu," drew mostly on this legacy to incorporate the intellectual and technological resources of others whom one or another group of them met in the areas they entered. Hence the earlier dates for the articles on these regions, marked below with an asterisk (*), reflect the more ancient roots of these dynamics; they are listed below in the approximate chronological sequence in which speakers of Bantu languages reached the regions distinguished. Madagascar had similarly continuous roots growing from its initial settlement by sailors and traders from Melanesia, particularly Borneo.

* Bantu, Eastern, Southern, and Western, History of (1000 BCE to 1500 CE)
* Interlacustrine Region, History of (1000 BCE to 1500 CE)
* Eastern African Coast, History of (Early to 1600) [Indian Ocean context]
* Southern Africa, History of (1000 BCE to 1600 CE)
Madagascar and Western Indian Ocean, History of (Early to 1500)
Muslim Northern Africa, History of (641 to 1500 CE)
Ethiopia and Vicinity, History of (600 to 1600 CE)
Western and Saharan Africa, History of (600 to 1600 CE)

Elsewhere Muslims, increasingly introducing horses suitable for military uses, brought commercial merchandise and credit and—in the Sudanic latitudes of western Africa—also military capabilities not previously integrated into the classical African political and economic strategies. The consequent escalations in the range and destructiveness of militarized power replaced political dynamics based on collaboration without centralization with a more centralized exercise of sheer force. This escalation of conflict in turn demanded more intense strategies of extracting the food, supplies, and people to support its high costs.

Christian Europeans probing along Africa's Atlantic coasts in the fifteenth century brought too few new resources to change Africans' strategies significantly, at least in the regions previously in contact with other commercial cultures centered on the Mediterranean and the Indian Ocean. The chronologies of the following set of, still more finely distinguished, regional essays on "early modern" Africa therefore vary even more than those defining previous epochs. Starting with Morocco and moving counter-clockwise around the continent, as the Europeans advanced:

Morocco, History of (1000 to 1900)
Sudan, Western and Central, History of (1500 to 1880 CE)
Western Africa, Forest Region, History of (1000 to 1880)
Kongo, Angola, and Western Forests, History of (1500 to 1880)
Cape Colony and Hinterland, History of (1600 to 1910)
Madagascar (1500 to 1895), History of
Southeastern Africa, History of (1600 to 1910)
Eastern Africa and Indian Ocean, History of (1500 to 1800)
Interlacustrine Region, History of (1500 to 1900)
Ethiopia and the Horn, History of (1600 to 1910)
Sudan, Eastern, History of (1500 to 1880 CE)
Ottoman Northern Africa, History of (1500 to 1850)

The chronology of these essays derives from the intensifying and diversifying engagements with commercial stimuli from the growing adjacent merchant economies and, in the case of the Ottomans, also military occupation in the regions delineated. Each contribution centers on a reasonably coherent regional strategy of assimilating, or failing to assimilate without significant violence, the rapid introduction of commercial goods, and credit. European armies at the end of the nineteenth century entered the ongoing course of Africans' histories that had brought many regions in the continent to critical moments of division and disruption. In every case, the terminating date marks military conquest by European powers; subsequent events are followed in the "history and politics" sections of the articles in this encyclopedia on the modern nations of the continent.

Additionally, the encyclopedia presents a separate sequence of essays written on broader continental scales defined more by Africa's external contacts (beginnings to seventh century CE [contact with Islam], seventh to sixteenth centuries [Europeans reach Atlantic Africa], sixteenth to eighteenth centuries [broadly "the slave trade" in the Atlantic], and nineteenth and twentieth centuries ["legitimate trade," imperialism, colonialism, and political independence]), as well as coverage of methodological issues and historiography, all alphabetized as History/Historiography. Perspectives on Africa's past are as numerous as the historians contemplating it, another aspect of "history" as an epistemology thus presented in the encyclopedia by the multiple coverages it offers of many of the specifics.

JOSEPH C. MILLER

APPENDIX C: ETHNIC AND IDENTITY GROUPS

The inhabitants of Africa divide themselves into several kinds and levels of what are usually known in English as ethnic or identity groups and in French as *ethnies;* in the colonial period they were usually known as "tribes," a term with no generally agreed significance other than a believed inferiority of political position. Some two thousand of these groups are known today, usually defined by location, language or dialect, history, believed ancestry, and sense of common membership and "custom." Their names are mostly chosen by themselves, others have been given them by neighbors or by colonial or postcolonial administrations. Each group is different from others. Many are kingdoms, but most are politically uncentralized units of immense variety: some are several million people in population, others have only a few hundred members; some are of long history and ancestry, others formed only recently; yet all are "African." New groups are formed continually, and others vanish, due to amalgamation, division, conquest, famine, epidemic sickness, or other factors. Eurocentric observers have often denied the importance or even existence of these groups on the grounds that most lack clearly definable boundaries and that many of their names were colonial inventions. On the other hand, African peoples themselves regard them as significant at the local, national, and regional levels, as either to be recognized and supported, weakened, amalgamated, divided, or abolished in efforts to form modern states, regions, and classes.

The following list includes the names of about half of these groups, whatever their attributes. Some on which there is most information are also mentioned in the fifty-three country entries but they cannot all be included there as they are too many, and in any case many live in more than a single country. A thousand groups are listed below. The list should be used as a type of index and not as reflecting groups' historical or political importance. They include virtually all those given for some eight hundred and fifty major groups by G. P. Murdock in his book *Africa: Its Peoples and Their Culture History,* as well as some two hundred others of less importance. A few are widely mentioned in histories of African peoples even though rarely in use today, but all others are in use and mentioned in anthropological and other accounts.

These ethnic groups are basically classified by country or territory and by language, and we show both. Each is also given a population figure, the most up-to-date we can find, but it should be stressed that census figures for Africa are notoriously unreliable and often little more than rough estimates. Finally each name is accompanied by a brief note on the group's main features.

The orthography of these names is confusing, each usually having several variants. Almost all African languages were first put into writing by missionaries and administrators from different European countries, each with its own language and orthography so that there are variant ways of spelling these names. Here we use what appear to be the most widely accepted forms.

There is a problem with names of those who speak Bantu languages. We give the root forms: all Bantu languages use prefixes to root forms to show singular, plural, language, and place. Examples are

Mkamba: a single Kamba person
Akamba: Kamba people in the plural
KiKamba: the Kamba language
Ukamba: Kamba country.

In the following list we show only the form Kamba. Other prefixes widely used include Wa-, Ba-, and Ama- for the plural, Mu-, and Omu- for the singular, Chi- and So- for languages, and Bu- for place.

JOHN MIDDLETON

A

Name	Alternate name	Location	Linguistic affiliation	Population estimate	Group or cluster	Subgroups	Notes
Ababda	Ababa	Sudan	Afro Asiatic, Northern Cushitic	>65,000	Beja cluster	Qireijab	Mainly sheep/cattle/goat pastoralists, Muslim, largely Arabicized
Abanziri	Banziri Gbanziri	Central African Republic	Niger-Congo, Adamawa-Ubangi	c. 15,000	Ubangi cluster	Buroka	Traditional mixed fishing/farming economy. Patrilineal. Formerly river traders.
Abarambo	Barambu	Dem Rep Congo	Niger-Congo, Adamawa-Ubangi	c. 60,000	Ubangi cluster	Amadi, Duga	Farming. Chiefdoms. Migrants from Sudan. At current location in 1600s.
Abe	Abbe, Abbey	Côte d'Ivoire	Niger-Congo, Kwa	c. 186,000	Akan group, Lagoon cluster		Village/commercial farmers. Uncentralized political system. Strong resistance to French colonization until early 1900s.
Abron	Abrong, Bono, Boron, Bron, Brong, Dom, Tchaman	Côte d'Ivoire, Bhana, Burkina Faso	Niger-Congo Kwa	>100,000	Akan group	Gyaman	Village/commercial farmers. Abron are legendarily credited with founding Boudoukou Empire c.16th century. Matrilineal.
Aburé	Abonwa, Abouré, Agoua, Compa	Côte d'Ivoire	Niger-Congo, Kwa	c. 53,000	Akan group, Lagoon cluster		
Acoli		Uganda, Sudan	Nilo-Saharan, Eastern Sudanic	>700,000 (Uganda), c. 25,000 (Sudan)	Western Niloctic cluster	Adilang, Pabala, Pacabol, Pacua, Paimol, Parumo	Mixed village farmers. Patrilineal descent. Stateless. Heavily involved in Holy Spirit prophetic movement.
Adangbe	Adampu, Adangme, Dangme	Ghana	Niger-Congo, Kwa	>500,000	Adangbe cluster		Linguistic and cultural association with Ga. Mostly small-hold farming and fishing. Indigenous towns, elaborate chiefships. Long Christianized.
Adarawa		Nigeria	Afro-Asiatic, Chadic	>300,000	Hausa	Azna, Gubei	Traders and settled farming. Muslim converts since 14th century.
Adja	Aja	Bénin, Togo	Niger-Congo, Kwa	>500,000	Ewe cluster		Origin: Oyo, Nigeria. Migrateed west c. 13th century. Split in two in 18th century: Ewe (Western Adja), Allada Kingdom in today's Benin.
Adjukru	Adjoukrou, Adioukrou, Aukru, Ojukru	Cote d'Ivoire	Niger-Congo, Kwa	c. 90,000	Akan group, Lagoon cluster	Dizi	Culturally similar to Abure. Principally com mercial farmers (palm oil) and traders.
Afar	Adal, Danakil, Dankali	Djibouti; Ethiopia	Afro-Asiatic, Eastern Cushitic	>850,000			Predominantly pastoralist (cattle, sheep, goats, camels). Formerly warlike raiders. Four traditional sultanates. Sunni Muslim.
Afawa	Pa'a	Nigeria	Afro-Asiatic, Chadic	c. 20,000	Warjawa		Central plateau. Mixed farming.
Afo	Elowi	Nigeria	Niger-Congo, Benue-Congo	c. 110,000	Idoma cluster		Mixed farming. Stateless. Patrilineal.

(continued)

Name	Alternate name	Location	Linguistic affiliation	Population estimate	Group or cluster	Subgroups	Notes
Afrikaner		Namibia	Oorlam, Koe	>2,200,000			Related to Oorlam. Once controlled cattle and arms trade with the Cape. Defeated by Witbooi (1889), lost independence. Distinct from European Africaners of S. Africa.
Afusari	Afusare, Izere, Jari, Fizere	Nigeria	Niger-Congo, Benue-Congo	>150,000		Anaguta	Traditional hunters. Now small-hold subsistence farmers. Also called "Hill Jarawa."
Agaw	Agau, Agew	Ethiopia, Eritrea	Afro-Asiatic, Central Cushitic	>220,000		Awi, Bilen, Falasha, Kemnant, Kwara	Among original inhabitants of Ethiopia. Linguistically assimilated with Amhara. Maintain independent identity. Mixed Christian, Sunni Muslim, Jewish (these called Falasha, who mostly migrated to Israel).
Ahanta		Ghana	Niger-Congo, Kwa	c. 150,000	Akan cluster		Peasant farmers, sea fishermen. Several chiefdoms.
Ajuran		Kenya, Ethiopia, Somalia	Afro-Asiatic; Eastern Cushitic	c. 60,000	Afar-Somali cluster		Mostly pastoralist. Some agriculture
Akan		Cote d'Ivoire, Ghana	Niger-Congo, Kwa	>9,000,000		Akuapem, Akyem, Kwahu, Ahafo, Asante, Abron, Assin, Denkyira, Nzima, Fante	Cluster of c. 12 linguistically and culturally related kingdoms, most founded between 1600–1850. Originally traders of gold, salt, slaves. Now cocoa farming, bauxite mining, timber. Matrilineal. The most powerful Akan Kingdom: Asante. Mostly Christian since 19th century.
Ake	Aike, Akye	Nigeria	Niger-Congo, Kwa	>5,000			Small-hold farming on Central Plateau. Stateless. Patrilineal.
Akposo	Akposso	Ghana, Togo	Niger-Congo, Kwa	>95,000 (Togo), c. 6,000 (Ghana)	Togo cluster		Predominantly commercial farming (cocoa, coffee). Patrilineal.
Akuapem	Akwapim	Ghana		c. 500,000	Akan cluster		Eastern Akan kingdom. Ethnically mixed Akan (matrilineal) and Guan (patrilineal). Cocoa and palm oil agriculture. Christian and literate since mid 19th century.
Akunakuna		Nigeria	Niger-Congo, Bantu	>350,000			Village farmers. SEE: Yakö.
Akwamu	Aquambo	Ghana	Niger-Congo: Kwa	>50,000	Akan cluster		Rulers of many eastern Akan kingdoms (17th c.), now small kingdom on Volta R. Matrilineal. Peasant farming. Christian.
Akyem	Akem	Ghana	Niger-Congo: Kwa: Volta-Comoe	>500,000	Akan cluster	Abuakwa, Bosume, Kotoku, et al.	Eastern Akan kingdom. Traded gold and slave in past, now cocoa farmers.
Alagaya	Nladja	Cote d'Ivoire	Benue-Congo	c. 25,000	Akan group, Lagoon cluster	Aware, Kovu, Akuri	Traditionally sea fishers, in 19th century became palm oil traders. Matrilineal.

(continued)

Name	Alternate name	Location	Linguistic affiliation	Population estimate	Group or cluster	Subgroups	Notes
Alagoa	Alago, Aragp	Nigeria	Benue-Congo	>50,000	Idoma cluster		Village farming. Patrilineal.
Alur		Uganda, Dem Rep Congo	Nilo-Saharan: Eastern Sudanic	>500,000	Western Nilotic cluster	Jonam	Peasant farming. Segmentary state. Wide renown as rainmakers.
Amarar		Sudan	Northern Cushitic	c. 65,000	Beja cluster		Seminomadic pastoralists (camels, sheep, goats, cattle). Muslim.
Americo-Liberian		Liberia	English	c. 60,000			Descended from approx. 16,000 freed slaves returned from U.S. in mid 19th century. Formerly Liberia's urban ruling elite.
Amhara	Abyssinian	Ethiopia	Afro-Asiatic: Semitic	>15,000,000			Ethiopia's dominant ethnic group, giving it the national language and most of its rulers.
Ana	Atakpame	Bénin, Togo	Niger-Congo: Kwa	c. 150,000	Yoruba cluster		Originally Ife (Nigeria). Became vassals of Dahomey Kingdom.
Anaguta		Nigeria	Niger-Congo: Adamawa	>8,000	Afware cluster		Central Plateau. Mixed farming. Stateless. Patrilineal.
Anang		Nigeria	Niger-Congo: Benue-Congo	c. 450,000	Ibibio cluster		Linguistically related to neighboring Efik and Ibibio. Farming (yams, palm oil).
Andoni		Nigeria		>400,000	Ibibio cluster		Village farmers, palm oil for export. Stateless. Patrilineal.
Angas	Kerang	Nigeria	Afro-Asiatic: Chadic	>200,000	Plateau	Ankwe, Goram, Gurka	Central Plateau. Village farmers. Stateless. Patrilineal.
Anlo	Anlo	Ghana, Togo	Niger-Congo: Kwa	>10,000	Ewe cluster		Allies of Asante in 1800s. Originated in Togo region.
Antaisaka	Taisaka, Tesaki	Madagascar	Malayo-Polynesian	c. 500,000	Malagasy	Antaifasy, Antaimoro, Antambahaoka, Sahafatra	SW coastal Madagascar. Migrant labor and rice farming. Patrilineal.
Antandroy	Tandroy	Madagascar	Malayo-Polynesian	>600,000	Malagasy	Antanosy	Southernmost Madagascar. Cattle keeping, farming, seasonal labor migration. Patrilineal.
Anuak	Anyuak	Ethiopia, Sudan	Nilo-Saharan: Eastern Sudanic	c. 100,000	Western Nilotic cluster		Mixed farming on Sudan-Ethiopia border. Politically weak ritual kingship.
Anyang		Nigeria	Niger-Congo: Benue-Congo	>92,000	Ibibio cluster	Banyang	Dense villages. Farming, trading. Stateless. Powerful title associations. Patrilineal.
Anyi	Agni, Bini, Kotoko, Ton	Cote d'Ivoire, Ghana	Niger-Congo: Kwa	>700,000	Akan cluster		Part of larger Anyi cluster with Nzima, Abure, Abron, Ehotile (Mekyibo). Fishing. Matrilineal.
Appollonians							SEE: Nzima.

(continued)

Name	Alternate name	Location	Linguistic affiliation	Population estimate	Group or cluster	Subgroups	Notes
Arabs		Northern Africa, Sahara region, many other countries	Afro-Asiatic: Semitic	Many millions			Descendants of Arab immigrants who have taken over land from indigenous peoples. Muslim.
Aro		Nigeria	Niger-Congo: Kwa	>700,000	Igbo		In past: oil, slave trade. Famed for oracle, consulted throughout SE Nigeria.
Arusha	Warusha	Tanzania	Nilo-Saharan: Eastern Sudanic	c. 150,000	Eastern Nilotic cluster		Linguistically and culturally related to Maasai. Traditional pastoralists, now settled commercial farmers (coffee)
Arusi	Arisi, Arsi	Ethiopia	Afro-Asiatic: Eastern Cushitic	c. 300,000	Oromo cluster		Mixed agriculture and cattle keeping. Muslim
Asante	Ashanti	Ghana	Niger-Congo: Kwa	>2.5 million	Akan cluster	Asokore, Assumigya, Bekwi, Bonwire, Effiduase, Ejiso, Juaben, Kokofu, Mampong, Nsuta, Senfi	Mostly village cocoa farming, urban traders. Gold and timber production. Matrilineal. King (asantehene) is most powerful ruler in Ghana. Christianized mid 19th century, except for Muslims in northern areas.
Assim		Cote d'Ivoire, Ghana	Niger-Congo: Kwa	c. 130,000	Akan group, Lagoon cluster		Mostly sea fishing. Matrilineal.
Atta		Algeria	Afro-Asiatic	no estimate			Pastoralists
Attié	Akié, Akyé	Cote d'Ivoire	Niger-Congo: Kwa	>330,000	Akan group, Lagoon cluster	Bodde, Kuroba	Culturally close to Anyi and Baule. Mostly coffee and cocoa farming. Matrilineal.
Atuot	Attuot	Sudan	Nilo-Saharan: Eastern Sudanic	c. 70,000		Apak, Luac, Jilek, Akot, Rorkec, Kuek	Closely related to Dinka. Cattle pastoralists, farmers. Greatly devastated by Sudanese government's genocidal actions.
Aushi	AUshi	Dem Rep Congo, Zambia	Niger-Congo: Central Bantu	>200,000	Bemba cluster	Chisinga	Small-hold farming, migrant labor. Stateless. Matrilineal.
Avatime	Afatime	Ghana, Togo	Niger-Congo: Kwa	c. 20,000	Central Togo cluster		Village hill farming. Patrilineal.
Avikam	Brignan, Gbanda	Cote d'Ivoire	Niger-Congo: Kwa	c. 15,000	Akan group, Lagoon cluster		Commercial farming/fishing, palm oil production, trade. Matrilineal.
Awiya	Awngi, Awawas	Ethiopia	Afro-Asiatic: Semitic	c. 80,000		Damot	Village farmers, cattle keepers. Patrilineal.
Aza		Chad, Niger	Daza	>22,000	Daza cluster		Chad: craft specialists (smithing, metalworking, leatherworking, pottery); Niger: Cattle and camel pastoralists.
Azande	Niam-Niam, Zande	Central African Republic, Sudan, Dem Rep Congo	Niger-Congo: Adamawa-Ubangi	c. 1.2 million	Ubangi cluster	Avungara, Bandya, Idio, Vungara	Village farmers. Several patrilineal kingdoms. Since 1800, spread widely and submerged neighboring peoples.

(continued)

Name	Alternate name	Location	Linguistic affiliation	Population estimate	Group or cluster	Subgroups	Notes
B							
Babukur		Dem Rep Congo, Central African Republic	Niger-Congo: Adamawa-Ubangi	est. 6,000	Ubangi cluster	Huma	Village farmers, subjects of Azande. Patrilineal
Bachama		Nigeria		c. 40,000	Plateau		Village farmers. Patrilineal.
Baga	Nalu	Guinea-Bissau	Niger-Congo: Western Atlantic	>80,000	Senegambian cluster		Mostly rice farming. Assimilating to neighboring Soso. Renowned blacksmiths and wood carvers
Baggara	Mesiriya, Seleim, Ta'aisha	Sudan	Semitic: Arabic	>1 million		Messiriya, Humr, Hawazma, Reizegat, Habbania	Cattle keeping, cotton growers. Sudanese governmentt has sponsored migration into Nuer, Nuba, and Dinka territory, with ensuing violence.
Bagirmi							SEE Barma
Baka		Central African Republic, Sudan	Nilo-Saharan: Central Sudanic	c. 130,000	Madi cluster		Small-hold farming. Patrilineal
Bako		Ethiopia	Afro-Asiatic: W. Cushitic	c. 50,000	Sidamo cluster	Amar	Intensive farming. Patrilineal.
Bakwé		Ghana, Guinea	Niger-Congo: Kwa	c. 50,000	Kru cluster		Traditional peasant farming, now coffee and cocoa cash cropping. Patrilineal.
Balanta	Balente	Guinea Bissau, Senegal	Nigre-Congo: W. Atlantic	>420,000	Senegambia	Kunante	Dominant ethnic group in area. Commercial rice farming, salt mining, palm wine producers.
Bamana							SEE Bambara
Bambara	Bamana, Banmanan, Bamanakan	Cote d'Ivoire, Gambia Mali, Senegal	Manding	>4 million		Somono	Dominant in Mali, language used as lingua franca. Mixed farming. Founded Segu and Kaarta kingdoms (17th c.). Traditional religion, with some Christians and a few Muslims. Renowned woodcarvers and oral poets. Somono fishermen on Niger River.
Bamiléké		Cameroon	Niger-Congo: Kwa	>1 million	Cameroon Highland cluster		Name refers to entire cluster of linguistically related, sometimes culturally distinct kingdoms of Western Grasslands. Traditional farmers, now strong in urban businesses and professions.
Banda		Cameroon, Central African Republic, Sudan	Niger-Congo: Adamawa-Ubangi	>1.2 million	Ubangi cluster	Dakpwa, Yangere	Largest ethnic group in Central African Republic. Mixed farming. Patrilineal.
Bangba	Bamgba	Dem Rep Congo	Nilo-Saharan: Central Sudanic	c. 11,000	Mangbetu cluster	Boki	Remnants of Mangbetu expansion. Farmers. Patrilineal.

(continued)

Name	Alternate name	Location	Linguistic affiliation	Population estimate	Group or cluster	Subgroups	Notes
Bangi	Bobangi	Congo, Dem Rep Congo	Niger-Congo: Benue-Congo	c. 200,000	Equatorial Bantu cluster	Furu, Loi, Ngiri	Once important traders on Congo River. Now village farmers. Patrilineal.
Bantu				>160 million			Refers to major language group, part of Niger-Congo family. Individual Bantu-speaking groups are referred to by their ethnic group names.
Banyun	Bainuk, Banun, Banhun	Gambia, Guinea Bissau, Senegal	Niger-Congo: W. Atlantic	c. 40,000	Senegambian Cluster		Rice farmers. Patrilineal.
Bara		Madagascar	Malayo-Polynesian: Malagasy	>400,000	Southern Highlands		Rice farming. Patrilineal.
Barabaig							SEE Tatoga
Barabra		Egypt, Sudan	Nilo-Saharan: E. Sudanic	>770,000	Nubian cluster	Danagla, Kenuze	Riverine farmers on the Nile. Stateless. Patrilineal.
Barea		Ethiopia, Sudan	Nilo-Saharan: E. Sudanic	c. 20,000	Barea cluster		Mixed farming, fishing. Stateless. Patrilineal
Bari		Sudan	Nilo-Saharan: E. Sudanic	c. 110,000	Eastren Nilotic		Mixed farmers, cattle herders.
Bariba	Bargu, Batomun	Benin, Burkina Faso, Nigeria, Togo	Niger-Congo: Voltaic	>650,000	Bargu cluster		Mostly farmers. Patrilineal.
Barma	Bagirmi	Chad	Afro-Asiatic: Berber	c. 39,500	Bagirmi cluster		Descendants of Bagirmi empire (18th c.) Predominantly Muslim. Village farmers, herders.
Basari	Bassari, Bassare	Ghana, Togo	Niger-Congo: Voltaic	c. 80,000	Gurma cluster		Tradition of metalworking, weapons makers, now sedentary farmers, cattle keepers. Patrilineal
Bassa	Basa, Gbasa	Liberia, Sierra Leone	Niger-Congo: Kwa	>500,000	Kru cluster	De, Klepo, Sikon	Several chiefdoms. Mostly small-hold farmers (cassava, yams, plantains). Patrilineal.
Bassa		Cameroon, Nigeria	Niger-Congo: Benue-Congo	>70,000	Plateau cluster		Village farmers. Patrilineal.
Bata		Cameroon, Nigeria	Afro-Asiatic: Chadic	c. 50,000	Plateau cluster		Peasant farming, animal husbandry. Some Muslims. Patrilineal
Baule	Baoule	Cote d'Ivoire	Niger-Congo: Kwa	>2 million	Akan cluster		Dominant ethnic group in country. Matrilineal social organization. Mostly peasant farmers (coffee, cocoa). Renowned for art.
Bede		Niger, Nigeria	Afro-Asiatic: Chadic	c. 120,000	Bornu cluster		Village farmers; patrilineal
Bedouin	Beduin	Sahara region	Afro-Asiatic: Semitic	no estimate	Arabic		Term used for mostly desert-dwelling Arabs
Beir							SEE Murle

(continued)

Name	Alternate name	Location	Linguistic affiliation	Population estimate	Group or cluster	Subgroups	Notes
Beja		Egypt, Eritrea, Ethiopia, Sudan	Afro-Asiatic: N. Cushitic	>2 million	Beja cluster	Ababda, Amarar, Amer, Ashraf, Beni, Bisharin, Hadendowa, Halenga, Hassenab	Northern Beja are pastoralists (camels, sheep); others are subsistence and commercial farmers. Predominantly Muslim
Bella	Bellah, Haratin	Burkina Faso, Niger	Afro-Asiatic: Berber	c. 50,000	Tuareg		Nomadic cattle pastoralists; traditional serfs of their Tuareg neighbors
Bemba	Awemba, Babemba	Tanzania, Dem Rep Congo, Zambia	Niger-Congo: Central Bantu	>2 million	Bemba cluster		Village farmers (millet, maize, cotton). Migrant labor for Copperbelt mines. Former powerful kingship. Matrilineal descent
Bena		Tanzania	Niger-Congo: Bantu	>100,000	Rafiji cluster	Sowe, Vemba	Mixed farmers. Patrilineal descent
Bende	Vende, Wabenda	Tanzania	Niger-Congo: Bantu	c. 30,000	Nyamwezi cluster	Tongwa	Mixed farmers and coffee growers. Patrilineal descent
Benga		Gabon	Niger-Congo: NW Bantu	>3,000			Offshoot of the Kota, splitting away in 19th century. Historically middlemen in ivory and wood trades, today farmers. Matrilineal descent
Beni Amer	Amer	Sudan	Afro-Asiatic: N. Cushiti	c. 100,000	Beja cluster		Pastoralists (cattle, camels). Highly stratified society. Arabic used as lingua franca, but some groups speak Cushitic languages; others speak Tigrinya (Semitic). Muslims
Beraber		Morocco	Afro-Asiatic: Berber	no estimate			Atlas Mountains. Agriculturalists.
Berbers		N. Africa, Sahara, Sahel	Afro-Asiatic: Berber	c. 15 million			Transhumant pastoralists. Self-named Imazighen ("free men"). Predominantly Muslim. 30 main groups with many subgroups. Egalitarian, patrilineal communities
Bergdama							SEE Damara
Beriberi		Nigeria	Nilo-Saharan: Saharan	c. 5.1 million	Bornu cluster	Dogara	Herders, farmers. Largely acculturated to Hausa, who also use this name for the Kanuri. Patrilineal.
Berti		Sudan	Nilo-Saharan: Saharan	>110,000	Darfur cluster		Original language replaced by Arabic. Mostly sedentary farmers, livestock keepers. Muslim. Patrilineal
Beta Israel							SEE Falasha
Bété		Cote d'Ivoire	Niger-Congo: Kwa	>720,000	Kru cluster		Village farmers, with cash-crop: cocoa, coffee. Patrilineal.
Beti		Cameroon	Niger-Congo: Bantu	c. 772,000			Rural Beti mostly farmers. Urban Beti: business, civil service, professions. Patrilineal.

(continued)

Name	Alternate name	Location	Linguistic affiliation	Population estimate	Group or cluster	Subgroups	Notes
Betsileo		Madagascar	Malayo-Polynesian: Malagasy	>1.5 million	Central Highlands	Arindrano, Ilalangina, Isandra, Manadriana	Mostly farmers. Also represented in politics, civil service, professions. Patrilineal.
Betsimisaraka		Madagascar	Malayo-Polynesian: Malagasy	>1.1 million	Eastern Coastal Lowlands	Betanmena	Commercial farming and farm laborers: coffee, cloves, vanilla. Graphite mining. Patrilineal
Biafada	Beafada	Guinea-Bissau, Senegal	Niger-Congo: W. Atlantic	>55,000	Senegambia cluster		A dominant ethnic group in the country. Historically, Atlantic slave traders.
Bijago	Bissago	Guinea-Bisseau	Niger-Congo: W. Atlantic	c. 30,000	Senegambia cluster		Live on Bijagos Islands off Guinea coast. Formerly slavers. Today, mostly fishing, palm oil production.
Bilen	Belen, Bogo	Eritrea, Ethiopia, Sudan	Central Cushitic	c. 160,000	Beja cluster		Largely scattered among refugee camps due to war. Muslim. Traditionally sedentary farmers, livestock keepers (cattle, goats, camels, donkeys).
Binga	Babinga	Central African Republic, Congo, Gabon, Dem Rep Congo	Niger-Congo: Equatorial Bantu	c. 35,000	Pygmy group	Belxa, Bongo, Kola	Hunter-gatherers. Rainforest dwellers.
Bini		Nigeria, Cote d'Ivoire					SEE Edo (Nigeria) and Anyi (Cote d'Ivoire)
Bira		Dem Rep Congo	Niger-Congo: Equatorial Bantu	c. 60,000		Pere	Marked cultural differences between plains and forest Bira. Mixed farming. Patrilineal
Birifor	Birifo, Malba	Burkina Faso, Cote d'Ivoire, Ghana	Niger-Congo: Voltaic	>200,000	Mole cluster		Close relation to Lobi. Mixed farming, cattle keeping. Patrilineal.
Birked		Chad, Sudan	Nilo-Saharan: E. Sudanic	c. 111,000	Nubian cluster		Pastoralists in Darfur. Patrilineal.
Birom	Berum, Borom, Kibo, Kibyen	Nigeria	Niger-Congo: Benue-Congo	>300,000	Plateau cluster		Traditional hunters, now mostly village farming, tin mining. Patrilineal.
Bisa		Zambia	Niger-Congo: Central Bantu	>200,000	Bemba cluster		Once separate from Bemba, absorbed in 19th c. via conquest. Pre-conquest ivory, slave, and copper traders. Today village farmers. Matrilineal.
Bisharin		Eritrea, Sudan	Afro-Asiatic: N. Cushitic	c. 110,000	Beja cluster	Atbaro, Athai	Livestock keepers (camels in north; also sheep, goats, cattle in south). Southerners also farm. Muslim.
Bobo		Burkina Faso, Mali	Niger-Congo: Voltaic	c. 90,000	Habe cluster	Bobo-Fing (Boua), Bobo Oule (Tara), Bobo Gbe (Kian, Tian)	Once a loose economic and political confederation. Today mostly village farming. Renowned for art.

(continued)

Name	Alternate name	Location	Linguistic affiliation	Population estimate	Group or cluster	Subgroups	Notes
Boki	Nki	Cameroon, Nigeria	Niger-Congo: Benue-Congo	c. 150,000	Ibibio cluster	Bete, Uge, Yakori	Rural: yam cultivation, palm oil production. Urban: business and professions. Patrilineal
Bolewa		Nigeria	Afro-Asiatic: Chadic	c. 50,000	Bornu cluster		Kindgom. Trade, manufacturing, service sector, farming, animal husbandry. Muslim.
Bondei		Tanzania	Niger-Congo: Bantu	c. 131,000	NE Coastal Bantu cluster		Cluster of chiefdoms. Mostly peasant farmers and plantation workers.
Bongo	Dor	Sudan	Nilo-Saharan: Central Sudanic	c. 12,000	Madi cluster		Mixed farming.
Boni	Ariangulu	Kenya, Somalia	Afro-Asiatic: Central Cushitic	c.4,900	Oromo cluster		Remnant Oromo group, once hunters. Now mixed farming, migrant labor.
Boran	Borana, Orma	Ethiopia, Kenya, Somalia	Afro-Asiatic: E. Cushitic	c. 200,000	Oromo cluster		Traditionally pastoralists (cattle, goats, sheep). Loss of grazing lands to desertification. Today raise camels.
Bororo	Wodaabe	Central African Republic, Niger, Nigeria	Niger-Congo: W. Atlantic	>1 million	Fulani cluster		Cattle pastoralists. Never successfully Islamicized.
Bozo		Mali, Niger	Niger-Congo: Mande	>250,000	Mande cluster		Groups living on Niger River. River fishing. Muslim.
Bubi		Equatorial Guinea	Niger-Congo: NW Bantu	c. 25,000			Probably from Cameroon, now live on Fernando Po. Matrilineal.
Budja		Dem Rep Congo	Niger-Congo: Equatorial Bantu	>250,000			Village farming. Patrilineal.
Budu		Dem Rep Congo	Niger-Congo: Equatorial Bantu	c. 278,000			Village farms, urban wage laborers in Kisangani. Patrilineal.
Buduma	Boudouma, Yedina	Chad, Niger, Nigeria	Afro-Asiatic: Chadic	c. 92,000	Bornu cluster	Kuri	Live on islands of Lake Chad. Chiefdoms.Cattle keeping and fishing. Mostly Muslim.
Buem	Boem	Ghana, Togo	Niger-Congo: Kwa	c. 50,000	Togo cluster	Ablo, Akpafu, Santrokofi	Village farms. Patrilineal.
Builsa	Builse, Bulse, Kanjaga	Burkina Faso, Ghana	Niger-Congo: Voltaic	>170,000	Grusi cluster		Mixed farms. Patrilineal.
Bulom	Bullom	Sierra Leone	Niger-Congo: W. Atlantic	c. 40,000	Temne cluster		Coastal farms. Patrilineal.
Bulu		Cameroon	Bantu	>150,000	Beti cluster		Mostly farmers (cassava, cocoa, yams). Formerly slave traders.
Bunu	Kabba	Nigeria	Niger-Congo: Kwa	>220,000	Yoruba cluster		Village farmers. Patrilineal.
Bura	Pabir	Nigeria	Afro-Asiatic: Chadic	c. 250,000	Plateau cluster		Mixed farms. Patrilineal.
Burungi	Burunge, Mbulunge	Tanzania	Afro-Asiatic: S. Cushitic	c. 40,000	Iraqw cluster	Alawa	Mixed hill farmers. Stateless. Patrilineal.

(continued)

Name	Alternate name	Location	Linguistic affiliation	Population estimate	Group or cluster	Subgroups	Notes
Busa	Busagwe, Busanse	Benin, Nigeria	Niger-Congo: Mande	c. 200,000			Mostly farmers. Cash-crops: rich, groundnuts, cotton, beans. Usually hire Fulani to raise their cattle. Patrilineal.
Busansi	Bisa, Bissa, Bousanou, Boussanse, Bouzantchi, Busanga	Burkina Faso, Togo	Mande	c. 150,000			Mostly small-hold farmers (millet, rice, groundnuts).
Bushmen							SEE San
Buye		Zambia, Dem Rep Congo	Niger-Congo: Central Bantuc	c. 12,000	Bemba cluster	Bwari, Goma, Hombo, Kalanga, Kundo	Village farmers. Matrilineal.
Bwaka	Gbwaka	Dem Rep Congo	Niger-Congo: Adamawa-Ubangi	c. 250,000	Ubangi cluster		Village farmers. Patrilineal.
C							
Chagga	C haga	Tanzania	Niger-Congo: Bantu	c. 200,000	NE Bantu	Kahe, Meru	Live on slopes of Mt. Kilimanjaro. Irrigated farming (coffee). Centralized political system. Mostly Christian. Patrilineal.
Chakossi	Anoufou, Anufo, Chokossi, Kyokosi, Tschokossi, Tyokossi	Ghana, Togo	Niger-Congo: Kwa	>120,000	Akan cluster		Descended from Akan mercenaries who came to area in 19th century. Partly Muslim. Matrilineal.
Chamba	Tchamba, Tsamba	Cameroon, Nigeria	Niger-Congo: Adomawa-Ubangi	>150,000	Plateau		Mixed farming, metalworking, sculpture pottery. Patrilineal.
Chawai	Atsam	Nigeria	Niger-Congo: Kwa: Benue	>100,000	Plateau	Irigwe	Mostly village farming. Patrilineal.
Chewa	Achewa, Cewa, Masheba	Malawi, Zambia	Niger-Congo: Central Bantu	>2 million	Maravi cluster	Nyanja, Maganja	Conquered by Nguni (1600s), but conquerors assimilated Chewa language, culture. Raded by Yao for slave trade. Among earliest Christians in central Africa. Matrilineal.
Chiga	Ciga, Kiga	Rwanda, Uganda	Niger-Congo: Bantu	>200,000	Interlacustrine Bantu		Mixed farming, fishing. Stateless. Many fled Rwanda udring 1994 civil war. Patrilineal.
Chokwe	Cokwe, Tschokwe	Angola, Dem Rep Congo, Zambia	Niger-Congo: Central Bantu	c. 1.7 million	Lunda cluster		Slaves, rubber, and ivory trade (1700s). Absorbed neighboring groups. Now village farming, industrial laborers, miners. Matrilineal.
Chopi	Vachopi	Mozambique, S. Africa	Niger-Congo: Bantu	c. 400,000	Shangane-Thonga cluster	Valenge	Village farmers. Renowned musicians. Patrilineal.

(continued)

Name	Alternate name	Location	Linguistic affiliation	Population estimate	Group or cluster	Subgroups	Notes
Chuabo	Chwabo, Maganja	Mozambique	Niger-Congo: Central Bantu	c. 700,000	Maravi cluster		Mostly peasant farming. Slave traders in 18th and 19th centuries. Matrilineal.
Comorians	Ngazija	Comoro Islands	Niger-Congo: Bantu	>475,000	NE Coastal Swahili cluster		Live on Comoro Islands. Mixed Bantu, Arab, Malagasy origins. Traditionally small kingdoms, today fishermen, farmers, traders. Mayotte Islanders are closely related to Malagasy. Some Comorians live in NW Madagascar. Also called Ngazija (local name for Grande Comore Island)
Copts			Egypt	no estimate	no estimate		Descend from original inhabitants of early Egypt. Christian. Closely linked with Ethiopian Christians.
Creoles	Crioulo (Portuguese Creole)	Cape Verde, Guinea-Bissau, Reunion, Mauritius, Senegal, Seychelles	Krio, Creole	no estimate			Various groups whose languages are mixtures of African and European languages that serve as lingua francas. Creoles often form local political and trading elites.
D							
Dafi	Dafing, Southern Marka	Mali, Burkina Faso	Niger-Congo: Mande	>200,000			Mainly pastoralist. Mostly Muslim. Patrilineal.
Dagari	Dagaba, Dagara, Dagati	Burkina Faso, Cote d'Ivoire, Ghana	Niger-Congo: Voltaic	>500,000	Grusi cluster		Mainly sedentary farmers. Patrilineal.
Dagomba	Dogamba	Ghana, Togo	Niger-Congo: Voltaic	c. 600,000	Mole-Dagbane		Kingdom established mid 1500s. Mixed farmeing. Export food to S. Ghana.
Dahalo		Kenya	C. Cushitic	c. 3,000			Oromo remnant. Mainly hunters, gatherers
Dahomean							SEE Fon
Daka	Dirim	Nigeria	Niger-Congo: Adamawa-Ubangi	c. 32,000	Plateau		Village farmers. Patrilineal
Dakakari		Nigeria	Niger-Congo: Benue-Congo	c. 70,000	Plateau	Bangawa, Liliwa	Village farmers. Patrilineal.
Damara	Dama, Bergdama	Namibia	Click	c. 100,000	Khoisan cluster		Formerly mountain herders, now mixed farmers, blacksmiths, potters.
Dan		Cote d'Ivoire, Guinea, Liberia	Niger-Congo: Mande	>2 million	Mende cluster	Gio, Tura, Yafuha	Mostly farmers (rice, kola nuts, peanuts, cotton, millet). Seasonal migrant labor. In Liberia, 4 clan-based chiefdoms. Famed for art. Patrilineal.
Danakil							SEE Afar
Darasa		Ethiopia	Afro-Asiatic: E. Cushitic	c. 30,000	Konso clustre	Gadji, Jamjam	Intensive irrigated farming. Governed by age-grade cycles. Patrilineal.

(continued)

Name	Alternate name	Location	Linguistic affiliation	Population estimate	Group or cluster	Subgroups	Notes
Dari		Cameroon, Chad	Niger-Congo: Adamawa-Ubangi	c. 25,000	Adamawa cluster		Mostly farmers (cotton, groundnuts). Patrilineal
Darod		Ethiopia, Kenya, Somalia	Afro-Asiatic: E. Cushitic	no estimate			One of 6 primary Somali clans. Mostly pastoralists (camels, sheep, cattle). In 1991, helped try to establish separatist state in former British Somaliland. Muslims.
Daza		Chad, Niger	Nilo-Saharan: Saharan	c. 50,000	Tebu	Djagada, Doza, Kokorda	Largest of Teda subgroups. Mainly pastoralists in Sahel. Muslim. Patrilineal clans
Deforo		Burkina Faso, Mali	Niger-Congo: Voltaic	c. 180,000	Habe cluster		Mostly farmers (groundnuts, millet, cotton, sorghum). Patrilineal
Degha	Deya	Cote d'Ivoire, Ghana	Niger-Congo: Voltaic	c. 20,000	Grusi cluster		Cattle keeping, peasant farming. Patrilineal
Delim		Mauritania	Afro-Asiatic: Semitic	no estimate			Pastoralists. Muslim. Patrilineal.
Dendi	Dandawa, Dandi	Benin, Nigre, Nigeria, Togo	Nilo-Saharan: Songhai	c. 150,000	Songhai cluster		Originally Mande, assimilated to Songhai Empire. Formerly merchants on trans-Saharan caravan routes. Muslim.
Dialonke	Dilonke, Djalonke, Jalonke, Jalunka, Yalunka	Guinea, Guinea Bissau, Mali, Sierra Leon	Mande	c. 200,000			Scattered cluster of migrants from Futa Jalon mountains. Farmers. Muslim. Patrilineal.
Dian	Dyan, Dianne, Janni	Burkina Faso	Niger-Congo-Voltaic	c. 25,000	Lobi cluster		Farmers (Millet, sorghum, groundnuts, cotton). Patrilineal.
Dida		Cote d'Ivoire	Niger-Congo: Kru	c. 150,000	Kru cluster		Mostly commercial farmers. Patrilineal.
Didinga	Birra, Karoko	Ethiopia, Kenya, Sudan	Afro-Asiatic: E. Sudanic	c. >80,000	Beir cluster		Mainly pastoralists. Patrilineal.
Digo		Kenya, Tanzania	Niger-Congo: NE Bantu	c. 300,000	NE Coastal Bandu, Mijikenda cluster		Mainly farmers. Matrilineal. Muslim.
Dilling		Sudan	Nilo-Saharan: E. Sudanic	>60,000	Nubian cluster	Gulfan, Kadero	Live in Nuba hills. Mixed farmers. Forcibly ousted from lands by Arab settlers.
Dinka		Sudan	Nilo-Saharan: E. Sudanic	>2.5 million	W. Nilotic cluster	Padang	Cattle pastoralists. Traditional patrilineal clan groups politically controlled by prophets. Today suffering wars by Sudan government.
Diola	Jola, Yola	Senegal	Niger-Congo: W. Atlantic	c. 300,000	Senegambia cluster		Rice farmers. Patrilineal.
Dir		Somalia	Afro-Asiatic: E. Cushitic	no estimate	Somali cluster		One of 6 primary Somali clans. Mostly nomadic pastoralists (camels, sheep, goats, cattle). Joined Aidid in 1991 to form Somali National Alliance.
Dodoth	Dodo, Dotho	Uganda	Nilo-Saharan: E. Sudanic	no estimate	Jie cluster		Pastoralism and agriculture (sorghum, maize). Patrilineal.

(continued)

Name	Alternate name	Location	Linguistic affiliation	Population estimate	Group or cluster	Subgroups	Notes
Dogon		Burkina Faso, Mali	Niger-Congo: Voltaic	>500,000	Habe cluster		Mostly farmers (millet, onion). Mountain villages. Ritual chiefs. Famed for complex religion and art. Patrilineal.
Dorobo							SEE Okiek
Drawa		Morocco	Afro-Asiatic: Berber	no estimate			Sedentary date farmers.
Duala	Douala	Cameroon	Niger-Congo: NW Bantu	>120,000			Origins in Dem Rep Congo, migrants to Cameroon (1500s). Middlemen in Atlantic slave trade. Long dominant in Cameroon culture, business, politics. Matrilineal.
Duruma		Kenya, Tanzania	Niger-Congo: NE Bantu	c. 200,000	Mijikenda cluster		Agriculture (maize, millet), some sheep and goats. Many work on plantations (sugar cane, sisal). Double descent.
Dyula	Diula, Joola, Jula, Juula, Wangara	Burkina Faso, Cote d'Ivoire, Ghana, Guinea Bissau, Mali, Senegal	Niger-Congo: Mande	>2 million			Once traders throughout W. Africa. Used trade contacts to spread Islam through the region. Patrilineal.
Dzing		Dem Rep Congo	Niger-Congo: C. Bantu	c. 180,000	Kasai cluster	Lori, Ngoli, Nzari	Village farmers. Matrilineal.
E							
Ebrié	Kyaman	Cote d'Ivoire	Niger-Congo: Kwa	c. 70,000	Akan group, Lagoon cluster	Mbato	Probable arrival in area via Anyi expansion (18th c.). Mainly sea fishing. Matrilineal.
Edo	Bini	Nigeria	Niger-Congo: Kwa	>1.2 million	Edo cluster	Ishan	Kingdom (15th, 16th c.) throughout midwestern Nigeria. Established kingdom of Benin. Famed for metal casting, other art forms, much of it looted during Benin War (1897).
Efe		Dem Rep Congo	Central Sudanic	31,000	Mbuti cluster		Pygmy subgroup. Hunter-gatherers in Ituri forest.
Efik		Cameroon, Nigeria	Niger-Congo: Benue Congo	c. 490,000	Ibibio cluster		Fishing on Cross River. Traders: palm oil, Atlantic slave trade. Governed by age associations, secret societies.
Efutu	Afutu, Awutu, Fetu	Ghana	Niger-Congo: Kwa	c. 150,000	Akan cluster		Originally Guan, assimilated into Fante of southern Ghana.
Egba		Benin, Nigeria	Niger-Congo: Kwa	>2 million	Yoruba cluster	Awori, Badagri, Egabo, Nago	First among Yoruba to be Christianized (19th c.). Now commercial farmers, merchants, some professions. Small towns.
Egede		Nigeria	Niger-Congo: Kwa	c. 300,000	Idoma cluster	Etulo	Mixed farmers. Patrilineal.
Ejagham							SEE Ekoi.

(continued)

Name	Alternate name	Location	Linguistic affiliation	Population estimate	Group or cluster	Subgroups	Notes
Eket		Nigeria	Niger-Congo: Benue Congo	>40,000	Ibibio cluster		Village farmers. Local government by powerful associations. Patrilineal.
Ekiti		Nigeria	Niger-Congo: Kwa	>1 million	Yoruba cluster	Akoko, Ondo, Owo-Ifori	Major Yoruba subgroup. Cocoa farmers. Small kingdoms.
Ekoi	Ejagham	Cameroon, Nigeria	Niger-Congo: Benue Congo	>300,000	Ekoi cluster	Akaju-Keaka, Nde, Oboang	Village and riverine farmers. Stateless. Indigenous writing system. Patrilineal.
Ekonda		Dem Rep Congo	Niger-Congo: Equatorial Bantu	>300,000	Mongo cluster		Village farmers. Patrilineal.
Embu		Kenya	Niger-Congo: Bantu	>350,000	NE Bantu, "Northern Kikuyu" cluster		Mixed farmers (millet, sorghum, cassava, maize, coffee, tea). Grow qat leaf for export.
Eton		Cameroon, Equatorial Guinea, Gabon	Niger-Congo: Adamawa-Ubangi	>80,000	Fang cluster		Mostly farmers (cassava, cocoa, yams) Mostly Christianized. Middlemen in Atlantic slave trade
Ewe	Krepe	Benin, Ghana, Togo	Niger-Congo: Kwa	c. 4.3 million	Ewe cluster	Anlo, Glidyi, Ho, Krepi, Maxe, Mina	Closely related to Fon. Origins in Oyo kingdom. Migrated in 13th century. Mixed farmers, sea fishing. Influential in politics, business, professions. Patrilineal.
F							
Fajulu	Pajulu	Sudan, Dem Rep Congo	Nilo-Saharan: E. Sudanic	no estimate	E. Nilotic cluster	Nyangbara	Mixed farmers. Stateless. Patrilineal.
Falasha	Beta Israel	Ethiopia	Afro-Asiatic: C. Cushitic	c. 111,000	Qemant cluster		Closely related to Agaw. Judaic. Most speak Amharic. Lost land (15th c.) by refusing to convert to Christianity. Crafts specialists. In 1980s, many emigrated to Israel.
Fali	Bana	Cameroon, Nigeria	Niger-Congo: Adamawa-Ubangi	c. 98,000	Adamawa cluster		Village farmers. Stateless. Called Bana in Cameroon. Patrilineal.
Fang	Fan, Fanwe, Mfang, Mpangwe, Pahouin	Cameroon, Gabon, Guinea	Niger-Congo: Equatorial Bantu	c. 100,000			"Fang-Pahouin" refers to larger group (Fang, Beti, Ewondo, Ntumu, Banen, Mvae, Fond, Eton, Maka, Bulu). Village farmers. Patrilineal.
Fanti	Fante	Ghana	Niger-Congo: Kwa	c. 1 million	Akan cluster		Dominant in coastal Ghana. Middlemen in palm oil and Atlantic slave trades. Large coastal towns. Early Christian converts.
Fezzan		Libya	Afro-Asiatic: Arabic	no estimate			Oasis farmers.
Filala		Morocco	Afro-Asiatic: Berber	no estimate			Date farmers. Walled towns.
Fipa	Wafipa	Tanzania, Zambia	Niger-Congo: Bantu	>220,000	E. Bantu, Rukwa cluster		Farming and fishing. Skilled metalworkers.

(continued)

Name	Alternate name	Location	Linguistic affiliation	Population estimate	Group or cluster	Subgroups	Notes
Fra-Fra							SEE Grusi
Fulani	Fufulde, Fula, Fulbe, Peul	Benin, Burkina Faso, Cameroon, Gambia, Guinea, Guinea Bissau, Mali, Niger, Nigeria, Senegal, Sierra Leone	Niger-Congo: W. Atlantic	>25 million		Bororo, Dorobe, Firdu, Ladde, Laube, Mbalu, Siire, Toroobe, Wodabe	Expanded by conquest east from Senegal R. Valley (12th c.), introducing Islam. Established Sokoto caliphate, other Hausa emirates. Cattle pastoralists, but some are mixed farmers. Urban Fulbe active in politics, business, professions.
Fulero		Rwanda, Dem Rep Congo	Niger-Congo: Bantu	c. 374,000	Interlacustrine cluster		Herders, village farmers. Patrilineal
Fulse		Burkina Faso, Mali	Nigre-Congo: Voltaic	c. 100,000	Grusi cluster		Traditional smiths, potters. Patrilineal.
Fur		Chad, Sudan	Nilo-Saharan: Furian	>750,000	Darfur cluster	Dalinga, Forenga, Kangara, Temurka	Fur Empire (fl. 17th and 18th c.) conquered by Egypt (late 19th c.) Semi-arid agriculture, herding. Muslim.
Fut	Bafut	Cameroon	Niger-Congo: Kwa	c. 78,000	Cameroon Highlands cluster	Babanki, Bafreng, Bamenda, Bandeng	Chiefdoms subordinate to Bafut king. Mostly village farmers (maize, cereals). Often grouped as Tikar. Patrilineal social organization.
G							
Ga		Ghana	Niger-Congo: Kwa	c. 665,000	Ga-Adangbe cluster		Coastal urban inhabitants of Accra. Several small kingdoms. Mainly Christian. Patrilineal
Gabri		Chad	Afro-Asiatic: Chadic	c. 70,000	Bagirmi cluster	Chiri, Nangiri	Small farmers, herders. Patrilineal.
Gagu	Gagon	Cote d'Ivoire	Niger-Congo: Mande	c. 60,000	Mende cluster		Village rice farmers. Patrilineal.
Gale	Hamej	Sudan	Nilo-Saharan: Koman	c. 15,000	Koman cluster	Kadalu	Once lived in Sennar Kingdom. Now mixed farmers.
Galla							SEE Oromo
Gamu	Gamo	Ethiopia	Afro-Asiatic: W. Cushitic	>850,000	Sidamo cluster		Highly stratified society. Terrace farming. Livestock. Patrilineal.
Ganda	Baganda	Uganda	Niger-Congo: Bantu	c. 5.4 million	Interlacustrine Bantu		Founded Buganda Kingdom (14th c.) Dominant in Uganda politics, business, education, professions. Rural Ganda are village farmers (plantains, coffee), patrilineal.
Gbande	Gbassi	Liberia	Niger-Congo: Mande	c. 100,000	Mende cluster		Village farmers. Patrilineal
Gbari	Gwari	Nigeria	Niger-Congo: Kwa	c. 500,000	Plateau		Mostly farmers. Related to Nupe. Patrilineal.
Gbaya	Baya	Cameroon, Central African Republic	Niger-Congo: Adamawa-Ubangi	>1.5 million	Ubangi cluster	Bogoto, Ikasa	Mixed farmers. Patrilineal
Gerawa	Gera	Nigeria	Afro-Asiatic: Chadic	c. 60,000	Plateau		Village farmers, livestock. Patrilineal.

(continued)

Name	Alternate name	Location	Linguistic affiliation	Population estimate	Group or cluster	Subgroups	Notes
Gesera		Burundi, Rwanda		>15,000	Pygmy	Zibaga	Pygmy group. Once hunters and gatherers. Now village farmers, potters.
Gibe		Ethiopia	Afro-Asiatic: W. Cushitic	no estimate	Sidamo cluster	Garo, Gera, Guma	Farmers. Conquered by Sidamo. Muslim.
Gikuyu	Akikuyu, Kikuyu	Kenya	Niger-Congo: Bantu	c. 8.5 million	NE Bantu		Dense settlements. Farming, labor migrants. Government by council. Many live as squatters on large farms in Rift Valley and Nairobi. Involved in Mau Mau movement. Patrilineal.
Gimira		Ethiopia	Afro-Asiatic: W. Cushitic	c. 80,000	Sidamo cluster	Benesho, Kaba, Shako, She	Once raided by Oromo and Amhara slavers. Mixed farmers. Patrilineal
Giryama	Giriama	Kenya	Niger-Congo: Bantu	c. 600,000	NE Coastal Bantu		Rice, maize, cassava, coconut farmers. Trade with coastal towns. Patrilineal.
Gisiga		Cameroon, Nigeria	Afro-Asiatic: Chadic	c. 100,000	Plateau		Village farmers. Patrilineal
Gisu	Gishu, Masaba, Sokwia	Uganda	Niger-Congo: Bantu	>850,000	Interlacustrine cluster	Masaba	Farming: millet, bananas, maize, coffee, cotton. Live on Mount Elgon. Stateless. Patrilineal.
Gogo		Tanzania	Niger-Congo: Bantu	>850,000	Central Bantu Rift cluster		Pastoralists, mixed farmers. Patrilineal
Gola		Liberia, Sierra Leone	Niger-Congo: W. Atlantic	c. 150,000	Temne cluster		Middlemen in Atlantic slave trade. Chiefdoms. Mostly peasant farmers. Acculturated to Mande
Gonja	Gongya	Ghana	Niger-Congo: Kwa	c. 150,000	Guan cluster		Migrants from Mali (17th c.) Conquered by Asante (18th c.). Northernmost Guan people. Large chiefdoms.
Gosha		Ethiopia, Kenya, Somalia	Niger-Congo: Bantu	no estimate	NE Coastal Bantu	Gobaweyn	Pastoralists, farmers. Descend from former slaves. Mostly moved to Tanzania.
Grebo		Liberia	Niger-Congo: Kwa	>330,000	Kru cluster		Clan-based chiefdoms. Farm plantains, bananas, sugarcane, rice. Patrilineal
Griqwa		Namibia, S. Africa	Click	no estimate	Khoisan		Scattered, mixed Khoi-European descent.Include Rehoboth Basters of Namibia (pop c. 20,000). Now urban dwellers.
Grusi	Grunsi	Burkina Faso, Ghana	Niger-Congo: Voltaic	c. 600,000	Grusi cluster	Awuna, Fera, Frafra, Isala, Kasena, Nagwa	Savanna village farmers. Stateless. Patrilineal
Guan	Guang	Ghana	Niger-Congo: Kwa	c. 600,000	Akan cluster	Anum, Atwode, Awutu, Bole, Bowiri, Buem, Efutu, Gonja, Kpesi, Krakye, Kyerepon, Larte, Likpe, Nkonya, Ntwumuru, Salaga, Santrofoki, Senya	Important Ghanaian language group. Subgroups organized as chiefdoms. Mixed farmers. Patrilineal.

(continued)

Name	Alternate name	Location	Linguistic affiliation	Population estimate	Group or cluster	Subgroups	Notes
Guanche		Canary Islands	Afro-Asiatic: Berber	no estimate			Extinct.
Gude	Cheke	Camreoon, Nigeria	Afro-Asiatic: Chadic	>100,000	Plateau		Village farmers. Matrilineal.
Gula	Goula	Central African Republic, Chad	Nilo-Saharan: C. Sudanic	c. 100,000	Sara cluster Mufa	Gele, Kudia, Kulfa,	Once major trading empire. Language was early lingua franca for northern trade routes. Village farmers. Patrilineal.
Gumuz		Ethiopia	Nilo-Saharan: Koman	c. 75,000	Koman cluster	Dach, Gubba	Pastoralists, farming, fishing. Patrilineal.
Guin		Cote d'Ivoire, Burkina Faso	Niger-Congo: Voltaic	c. 100,000	Senufo cluster	Turaka	Village farmers. Patrilineal.
Gun	Egun	Togo, Benin	Niger-Congo: Kwa	>850,000	Ewe cluster	Tofinu, Wemenu	Village farmers, sea fishing. Patrilineal.
Gurage		Ethiopia	Afro-Asiatic: Semitic	c. 2 million			Mixed farmers. Stratified. 1/3 Muslim, 1/3 Christian. Patrilineal.
Gurma	Gourmantche	Benin, Burkina Faso, Niger, Togo	Niger-Congo: Voltaic	>1 million	Gurma cluster		Mostly small farmers, pastoralists.
Guro	Koueni, Gouro	Cote d'Ivoire	Niger-Congo: Mande	>350,000	Mende cluster		Village farmers. Patrilineal.
Gusii	Kisii	Kenya	Niger-Congo: Bantu	c. 1.5 million	Interlacustrine Bantu		Village farmers. Patrilineal.
Gwandara	Gwandari	Nigeria	Afro-Asiatic: Chadic	>70,000	Plateau		Village farmers. Patrilineal. Today speak Hausa
H							
Ha		Tanzania	Niger-Congo: Bantu	>1.1 million	Interlacustrine Bantu	Jiji, Vinza	Cattle raising, tobacco growers. Kingdoms. Patrilineal
Hadarib		Eritrea	Afro-Asiatic: Semitic	no estimate	Beja cluster		Pastoralists. Muslim.
Hadendowa	Hendawa	Eritrea, Sudan	Afro-Asiatic: N. Cushitic	>100,000	Beja cluster	Halenga	Pastoralists, some settled farmers. Muslims. Emerged as ethnic group in 16th century. Patrilineal.
Hadimu	Shirazi	Tanzania (Zanzibar)	Niger-Congo: Bantu	>150,000	NE Coastal Bantu, Swahili cluster	Tumbatu	Indigenous to Zanzibar. Gardeners, fishing, casual labor. Last king in mid 19th century. Muslim
Hadza	Hadzapi, Kindiga, Tindiga	Tanzania	Click	c. 1,000	Hadza cluster		Hunter-gatherers on margins of Lake Eyasi
Hai//om	Heikom	Namibia	Click	c. 12,000	Khoisan cluster		Grouped with Damara as Bergdama (Mountain Dama). Once hunters, now scattered mixed farmers.
Hamama		Tunisia	Afro-Asiatic: Berber	no estimtae			Mountain farmers.
Harari	Hareri	Ethiopia	Afro-Asiatic: Semitic	c. 30,000			Lived in walled city of Harar (16th-19th c). Strongly endogamous. Muslim.

(continued)

Name	Alternate name	Location	Linguistic affiliation	Population estimate	Group or cluster	Subgroups	Notes
Hausa	Haoussa	Benin, Chad, Niger, Nigeria	Afro-Asiatic: Chadic	c. 28.75 million	Hausa cluster		Many subgroups. Traders, settled farmers. Converts to Islam c. 14th century. etc. Powerful emirs. Long tradition of literacy.
Hawiya	Hawiyeh	Somalia	Afro-Asiatic: E. Cushitic	c. 800,000	Somali cluster		One of 6 major Somali clans. Thousands of subclans. Rural pastoralists. Since civil war, Hawiye control Mogadishu. Patrilineal
Haya		Tanzania	Niger-Congo: Bantu	c. 1.5 million	Interlacustrine Bantu		A southern Lacustrine Bantu kingdom. Farmers. Patrilineal
Hehe		Tanzania	Niger-Congo: Bantu	c. 700,000	C. Bantu, Rufiji cluster Chungwe		Sedentary farmers, cattle keepers. United in mid-1800s by Muyugumba to conquer Ngoni.
Herero		Angola, Botswana, Namibia	Niger-Congo: Bantu	c. 80,000	SW Bantu cluster	Mbanderu, Himba	Cattle keeping, arid-land farmers. Survivors of German attempt at genocide fled to Botswana, Transvaal. Returned to form a renewed nation. Mostly Christian.
Hiechware		Botswana, Zambia	Click	c. 5,000	San cluster		Mostly serfs to Tswana cattle-owners.
Hima							SEE: Tutsi
Hlengwe	Bahlengue, Hlengue	Mozambique, S. Africa	Niger-Congo: Bantu	c. 800,000	Shona-Thonga cluster	Tswa, Nwanati	Village farmers. Patrilineal.
Holoholo	Guha	Tanzania, Dem Rep Congo	Niger-Congo: Central Bantu	c. 30,000	Bemba cluster	Tumbwe	Fishing, farming, cattle keeping. Matrilineal
Hona	Hwana	Nigeria	Afro-Asiatic: Chadic	c. 60,000	Plateau		Village farmers. Patrilineal.
Hora		Mali	Afro-Asiatic: Berber	no estimate	Tuareg cluster		Mixed pastoralists, farmers of southern Sahara.
Hova							SEE Merina
Hunde		Dem Rep Congo	Niger-Congo: Bantu	>250,000	Interlacustrine Bantu, Rwanda cluster, Kivu group		Farmers, cattle keepers. Overrun by refugees fleeing Rwanda civil war in 1994.
Hurutshe	Barutshe	Botswana, S. Africa	Niger-Congo: Bantu	no estimate	Tswana cluster		Chiefdoms. Herders. farmers. Patrilineal.
Hutu		Burundi, Rwanda, Uganda	Niger-Congo: Bantu	c. 17.5 million	Interlacustrine cluster cluster	Iru	Dominated by Tutsi from 15th century. Gained political control in 1950s. Hutu-Tutsi rivalries cross national borders. Civil war in 1960s through 1990s. Known as Iru in Uganda.
Ibibio		Nigeria	Niger-Congo: Kwa	c. 4 million	Ibibio cluster	Efik (riveraine) Enyong (northern), Eket (southern), Andoni, Ibeno (delta), Anang (western), Ibibio (eastern)	Mixed farmers, traders. Stateless. Many age and title assocations. Dense settlements, many migrating to cities. Seriously affected by oil industry, land pollution. Famed for wood carving, art. Patrilineal.

(continued)

Name	Alternate name	Linguistic affiliation	Population estimate	Location	Group or cluster	Subgroups	Notes
Idoma		Niger-Congo: Kwa	c. 800,000	Nigeria	Idoma cluster	Agala, Akpoto, Okwaga, Oturkpo	Mostly village dwellers, commercial farmers. Patrilineal.
Ife		Niger-Congo: Kwa	c. 1 million	Nigeria	Yoruba cluster	Ilesha, Illa	Major Yoruba subgroup. Powerful kingdom. Intensive farming. Patrilineal.
Igala	Igara	Niger-Congo: Kwa	c. 1 million	Nigeria	Idoma cluster		Village farmers. Patrilineal.
Igbira	Ebira	Niger-Congo: Kwa	c. 1 million	Nigeria	Nupe cluster	Igu, Okene	Village farmers. Part Muslim. Patrilineal.
Igbo	Ibo	Niger-Congo: Kwa	>18 million	Nigeria, Cameroon	Igbo cluster	Northern: Onitsha, Nri-Awka, Enugu; Southern: Owerri (Isu-Ama, Oratta-Ikwerri, Ohuhu-Ngwa, Isu-Item); Western: Ika, Ogwashi Uku; Eastern: Ada, Abam-Ohaffia, Okigwe, Zro; NE: Ogu Uku.	Traditional farmers, now participate throughout Nigerian economy. Stateless. Clan heads, councils, associations, title societies provide local government. Dense settlements. Mainly Christian. Known for carving, art. Severely affected by Biafran civil war. Patrilineal.
Ijebu		Niger-Congo: Kwa	c. 800,000	Nigeria	Yoruba cluster		Once middlemen in trade between Europeans and interior. Kingdoms. Intensive farming. Patrilineal.
Ijo	Ijaw	Niger-Congo: Kwa	c. 500,000	Nigeria	Ijaw cluster	Brass, Kalabari, Nemba, Okrika	Farms in Niger Delta. Salt mining, trade. Oil and natural gas in their territories.
Ik							SEE Teuso.
Ila	Baila, Mashuko-lumbwe	Niger-Congo: C. Bantu	c. 100,000	Zambia		Lumbu, Lundwo, Mbala, Sala	Cattle keeping, fishing, hunting. Some agriculture. Close to Tonga. Matrilineal
Ingessana	Tabi	Nilo-Saharan: E. Sudanic	c. 10,000	Ethiopia, Sudan	Ingessana cluster		Long raided for Arab slave trade. Mixed herders, farmers
Iramba	Amilamba	Niger-Congo: Bantu	>450,000	Tanzania	C. Bantu Eastern Rift cluster	Irambi, Izanzu	Rural farmers (sorghum, millet, maize) and cash cropping. Keep cattle, sheep, goats.
Iraqw	Mbulu	Afro-Asiatic: S. Cushitic	c. 500,000	Tanzania	Iraqw cluster		Isolated Cushitic group. Mostly mixed farmers.
Isoko		Niger-Congo: Kwa	c. 300,000	Nigeria	Edo cluster	Erakwa, Urhobo	16 clans. Intermarry with Edo, Ijo, Itsekiri.
Issa	Esa	Afro-Asiatic: E. Cushitic	c. 400,000	Somalia, Ethiopia, Djibout	Afar-Somali cluster	Gadabursi	Pastoralists. One of 2 major ethnic groups. Muslim.
Issaq	Ishaak	Afro-Asiatic: E. Cushitic	c. 700,000	Somalia	Afar-Somali	Awal, Gerhajis, Tojala	One of 6 major Somali groups. Herding (camels, sheep, cattle). Live mostly in North. Joined with Darod in 1991 to try to form separatist Somali state. Muslim.
Iteso	Teso, Wamia	Nilo-Saharan: E. Sudanic	c. 1.5 million	Uganda, Kenya	Eastern Nilotic	Itesyo, Kumam	Pastoralists, farmers. Stateless. Patrilineal

(continued)

Name	Alternate name	Location	Linguistic affiliation	Population estimate	Group or cluster	Subgroups	Notes
Itsekiri	Chekiri, Iwere, Shekiri, Warri	Nigeria	Niger-Congo: Kwa	c. 700,000	Edo cluster		Kingdom in 17th, 18th century. Palm oil and Atlantic slave trades. Town dwellers, farmers. Oil and gas deposits on territory.
Ittu	Ittu	Ethiopia	Afro-Asiatic: E. Cushitic	>1 million	Oromo cluster	Ania, Babile, Jarso	Live mostly around Harar. Mostly sedentary farmers. Mostly Muslim.
Iwa	Awiwa	Tanzania, Zambia	Niger-Congo: Central Bantu	c. 100,000	Rukwa cluster	Nyamwanga	Formerly cattle keepers. Today village farmers
J							
Janjero		Ethiopia	Afro-Asiatic: W. Cushitic	c. 10,000	Sidamo cluster		Kingdom. Hill farmers. Patrilineal.
Jarawa	Jangi	Nigeria	Niger-Congo: Benua-Congo	c. 200,000	Plateau		Village farmers. Partly Muslim. Patrilineal.
Jebala		Morocco	Afro-Asiatic: Arabic	c. 1.1 million			Mountain farmers. Inhabit cities of Tetuan and Ceuta.
Jerba		Tunisia	Afro-Asiatic: Berber	c. 100,000			Sedentary farmers, including on Djerba Island.
Jerid		Tunisia	Afro-Asiatic: Berber	no estimate			Oasis farmers.
Jie		Uganda	Nilo-Saharan: E. Sudanic	c. 60,000	Eastern Nilotic cluster	Dodoth	Pastoralists, mixed farmers. Local government by age-set councils. Patrilineal.
Jonam							SEE Alur
Jukun	Kororofa	Nigeria	Niger-Congo: Benue-Congo	c. 55,000	Plateau		Dominant until 19th century rise of Fulani. Now village farmers.
Jur		Sudan	Nilo-Saharan: E. Sudanic	c. 60,000	W. Nilotic cluster	Bor, Dembo	Once cattle pastoralists. Related to Dinka. Now mixed farmers.
K							
Kababish		Sudan	Afro-Asiatic: Arabic	c. 300,000	Baggara cluster		Camel herders. Opposed Mahdist movement (19th c). Muslim Patrilineal
Kabré	Kabure	Benin, Togo	Niger-Congo: Voltaic	c. 800,000	Kabre cluster	Lamba, Logba, Losso, Tamberma	Mostly mixed farmers. Patrilineal.
Kabyle		Algeria	Afro-Asiatic: Berber	c. 40,000			Sedentary farmers along coast.
Kadara	Adara	Nigeria	Niger-Congo: Benue-Congo	>85,000	Plateau		Historically dominated by Kanuri, Hausa, Fulani. Raided for Atlantic slave trade. Craft specialists (pottery, iron smelting) Patrilineal.
Kafa		Ethiopia	Afro-Asiatic: W. Cushitic	c. 730,000	Plateau		Once powerful kingdom. Mixed farmers, traders. Patrilineal.
Kagoro	Bagane	Mali	Niger-Congo: Mande	c. 30,000	Mande cluster		Origins in Jos Plateau. Raided by Hausa and Fulani for tribute, slaves.
Kaguru	Kagulu	Tanzania	Niger-Congo: C. Bantu	c. 250,000	Rufiji cluster		Mostly farmers (maize, beans, sorghum, cassava). Stateless. Matrilineal.

(continued)

Name	Alternate name	Location	Linguistic affiliation	Population estimate	Group or cluster	Subgroups	Notes
Kaka		Central African Republic	Niger-Congo: Equatorial Bantu	c. 30,000			Village farmers. Patrilineal.
Kakwa		Sudan, Uganda	Nilo-Saharan: E. Saharan	c. 150,000	Eastern Nilotic cluster		Related to Kuku, Mandari, Bari. Mixed farmers. Stateless. Patrilineal.
Kalabari							SEE: Ijo.
Kalai	Akele, Bakele	Gabon	Niger-Congo: Benue-Congo	c. 50,000	Equatorial Bantu cluster	Bangwe, Basission	Traditional elephant hunters. Subsistence farmers. Kept slaves.
Kalanga		Botswana, Zambia	Niger-Congo: Bantu	c. 150,000	Bemba cluster	Nanzwa, Lilima	Largest non-Tswana group in Botswana. Mainly herders.
Kalenjin		Kenya	Nilo-Saharan: E. Sudanic	c. 2.5 million	Eastern Nilotic cluster	Keyo, Kipsigis, Marakwet, Nandi, Okiek, Pokot, Sabaot, Sebei, Terik, Tugen	Cluster of settled non-Maasai Nilotes in Kenya highlands above Rift Valley. Do not form unified local or political group.
Kam		Nigeria	Niger-Congo: Adamawa-Ubangi	c. 6,300	Plateau		Village farmers. Matrilineal.
Kamba	Akamba	Kenya	Niger-Congo: Bantu	c. 3 million	NE Bantu cluster		Traditional farmers, ivory traders, caravaners. Mixed farmers living throughout Kenya. Known for wood carving.
Kambatta	Kembata	Ethiopia	Afro-Asiatic: E. Cushitic	c. 340,000	Konso cluster	Alaba, Hadya, Tamharo Patrilineal.	Intensive irrigation farming. Governed by age-grade cycles. Christian.
Kamberi	Kambari	Nigeria	Niger-Congo: Benue-Congo	c. 100,000	Plateau		Village farmers (maize, millet, rice, sorghum). Use Fulani to herd their cattle. Patrilineal.
Kamuku		Nigeria	Niger-Congo: Benue-Congo	c. 35,000	Plateau		Village farmers. Patrilineal.
Kanembu		Chad, Niger, Nigeria	Nilo-Saharan: Saharan	c. 630,000	Bornu cluster		Closely related to Kanuri. Farmers, herders. Muslim.
Kanuri		Cameroon, Chad, Nigeria	Nilo-Saharan: Saharan	c. 6.4 million	Bornu cluster	Magumi	Closely related to Kanembu. First conversion to Islam in 11th century via Sahara traders. Traders, manufacturing, farming. Powerful kingdom. Patrilineal.
Kaonde	Bakahonde, Bakaonde, Kaundi, Kunda	Dem Rep Congo, Zambia	Niger-Congo: C. Bantu	c. 250,000	Bemba cluster		Raided by Lunda for slave trade. Traditional farmers. Matrilineal.
Kapsiki		Cameroon, Nigeria	Afro-Asiatic: Chadic	c. 60,000	Plateau		Village farmers. Patrilineal.
Kara		Central African Republic, Chad	Nilo-Saharan: Central Sudanic	c. 17,000	Sara cluster		Population devastated by 19th c. slave raiding. Now village farmers.
Kara		Tanzania	Niger-Congo: Bantu	c. 140,000	Interlacustrine Bantu		Mixed irrigated farming. Live on small island in Lake Victoria.
Karaboro	Karakora	Burkina Faso, Cote d'Ivoire	Niger-Congo: Voltaic	c. 70,000	Senufo cluster	Tyefo	Mostly small farmers. Patrilineal.

(continued)

Name	Alternate name	Location	Linguistic affiliation	Population estimate	Group or cluster	Subgroups	Notes
Karamojon	Karamojong	Uganda	Nilo-Saharan: E. Sudanic	c. 500,000	Eastern Nilotic	Tepes	Arid-land pastoralists of NE Uganda. Local government by age-sets, councils.
Karanga		Zimbabwe	Niger-Congo: Bantu	c. 13,000	Shona-Thonga cluster	Duma, Govern, Kalenga, Matapo	Mixed farmers. Traditional states. Part of Shona nation. Patrilineal.
Karekare	Kerekere	Nigeria	Afro-Asiatic: Chadic	c. 50,000	Bornu cluster	Ngamo	Farming, manufacturing, trade, fishing (Lake Chad). Some cotton cash-cropping. Muslim.
Kasena	Kassena	Burkina Faso, Ghana	Niger-Congo: Boltaic	c. 200,000	Grusi cluster		Heavily raided by Zerma slave traders. Mostly small farmers. Patrilineal.
Katab		Nigeria	Niger-Congo: Benue-Congo	c. 60,000	Plateau		Conquered by Fulani (mid 19th c.), heavily raided for slaves. Village farmers. Patrilineal.
Katla		Sudan	Kordofanian	c. 15,000	Nuba cluster		Lived on Nuba mountains, but now supplanted by Arab settlers.
Kebu	Akebou	Togo	Niger-Congo: Kwa	c. 50,000	Togo cluster		Village farmers. Patrilineal.
Kela	Bakela	Dem Rep Congo	Niger-Congo: Equatorial Bantu	c. 200,000	Mongo cluster	Balang, Bambuli, Boyela	Village farmers. Patrilineal.
Kentu		Nigeria	Niger-Congo: Benue-Congo	c. 20,000	Plateau		Village farmers. Patrilineal.
Kerewe	Kerere	Tanzania	Niger-Congo: Bantu	c. 100,000	Interlacustrine Bantu		Farming, livestock herding on Ukerewe Island, Lake Victoria. Patrilineal.
Keyo	Elgeyo, Keiyo	Kenya	Nilo-Saharan: E. Sudanic	c. 150,000	Kalenjin cluster		Mixed farmers. Patrilineal.
Kgalagadi	Bakalahari	Botswana	Niger-Congo: Bantu	c. 40,000	Tswana cluster,		Chiefdoms. Traditional hunters for trans-Kalahari traders. Now cattle herders (often for Tswana). Patrilineal.
Kgatla		Botswana	Niger-Congo: Bantu	no estimate	Tswana cluster		Chiefdoms. Cattle herers. Patrilineal.
Khoi, Khoe, Khoikhoi							SEE Nama.
Khoesan	Khoisan	Botswana, Namibia, S. Africa	Click	no estimate			Generic name for both Khoe and San groups of southern Africa. Live in arid areas of SW Cape in S. Africa. Many groups extinct after White contact (17th, 18th centuries).
Kimbu		Tanzania	Niger-Congo: Bantu	c. 80,000	Central Bantu		Many enslaved in 19th century. Mixed mountain farmers. Patrilineal.
Kimbundu		Angola	Niger-Congo: C. Bantu	>3 million	Kimbundu cluster	Luanda, Mbaka, Ndongo, Tamba	Village farmers. Matrilineal.
Kindiga							SEE Hadza.
Kinga		Tanzania	Niger-Congo: C. Bantu	c. 140,000	Nyasa cluster		Rice farmers. Patrilineal.

(continued)

Name	Alternate name	Location	Linguistic affiliation	Population estimate	Group or cluster	Subgroups	Notes
Kipsigis	Lumbwa	Kenya	Nilo-Saharan: E. Sudanic	c. 700,000	Southern Nilotic cluster		Mixed farmers. Work on tea plantations, labor migrants. Today part of Kalenjin cluster. Patrilineal.
Kisama		Angola	Niger-Congo: C. Bantu	no estimtae	Kimbundu cluster		Village farmers. Patrilineal.
Kissi		Liberia, Sierra Leone	Niger-Congo: W. Atlantic	c. 475,000			Village farmers. Patrilineal.
Koalib		Sudan	Kordofanian	c. 50,000	Nuba cluster		Lived in Nuba Mountains, supplanted by Arab farmers.
Koko		Cameroon	Niger-Congo: NW Bantu	c. 320,000		Bimbi	Village farmers. Matrilineal.
Kom	Bikom, Nkom	Cameroon	Niger-Congo: Kwa	c. 150,000	Cameroon Highlands		Kingdoms. Village farming, fishing. Also called Tikar. Patrilineal.
Koma		Ethiopia, Sudan	Nilo-Saharan: Koman	c. 10,000	Koman cluster	Uduk	Pastoralists, mixed farmers. Stateless. Patrilineal.
Komono		Burkina Faso, Cote d'Ivoire	Niger-Congo: Boltaic	c. 10,000	Senufo cluster		Of the Mole-Dagbane peoples. Mostly settled farmers. Stateless. Patrilineal.
Kongo	Bakongo, Bandibu, Congo	Angola, Congo, Dem Rep Congo	Niger-Congo: C. Bantu	>5 million	Kongo cluster		Powerful kingdom (14th–16th c). Early converts to Christianity by Portuguese Decimated by slaving. Still powerful as ruling elite. Farmers, traders. as Matrilineal.
Konkomba		Ghana, Togo	Niger-Congo: Voltaic	c. 250,000	Gurma cluster		Mixed farmers, food suppliers to southern markets. Stateless. Patrilineal.
Kono		Cote d'Ivoire	Niger-Congo: Mande	c. 250,000	Mende cluster		Rice farmers. Losing territory (since 1955) to mining companies. Patrilineal.
Konongo	Kinongo	Tanzania	Niger-Congo: Bantu	c. 55,000	Central Bantu		Related to Nyamwezi. Mostly farmers. Patrilineal.
Konso		Ethiopia	Afro-Asiatic: E. Cushitic	c. 100,000	Konso cluster	Burji, Busso, Gidole, Gamole, Gardula, Gowaze	Intensive irrigation farming. Governed by age-grade cycles. Patrilineal.
Konyanka		Cote d'Ivoire, Guinea, Liberia, Mali, Sierra Leone	Niger-Congo: Mande	>2 million	Mande cluster		Origins in Mali Empire. Mostly peasant farmers. Patrilineal.
Koranko	Kuranko, Kouranko	Guinea, Liberia, Sierra Leone	Niger-Congo: Mande	>300,000	Mande cluster		Origins in Mali Empire. Mostly peasant farmers. Patrilineal.
Korekore	Northern Shona	Mozambique, Zimbabwe	Niger-Congo: Bantu	no estimate	Thonga cluster	Shangana, Tavara	Mixed farmers. Former state. Part of Shona nation. Patrilineal.
Koro		Nigeria	Niger-Congo: Kwa	c. 35,000	Plateau		Peasant farmers. Patrilineal.
Kossi	Bakosi	Cameroon	Niger-Congo: NW Bantu	c. 100,000			Village farmers (cereals, palm oil, coffee, cocoa). Patrilineal.

(continued)

Name	Alternate name	Location	Linguistic affiliation	Population estimate	Group or cluster	Subgroups	Notes
Kota	Bakota	Gabon, Congo, Cameroon	Niger-Congo: Benue-Congo	c. 125,000	Equatorial Bantu cluster	Chamai; Hungwa, Kiba	Major Gabon ethnic group. Migrated from NW, fleeing Fang expansion. Farmers, merchants. Historically active in European trade (Ivory, rubber in return for weapons, cloth).
Kotoko		Cameroon, Chad, Nigeria	Afro-Asiatic: Chadic	c. 150,000	Bornu cluster	Ngala	Fortified towns on Logone, Chari, other rivers. Islamic converts while subject to Borno Empire.
Kotopo	Korofo	Cameroon, Nigeria	Niger-Congo: Adamawa-Ubangi	c. 20,000	Adamawa cluster	Kutin	Mostly small-hold farmres. Patrilineal.
Koyam		Niger	Afro-Asiatic: Saharan	c. 25,000	Bornu cluster		Originated in Kanem (Chad). Herders, farmers. Patrilineal.
Kpe		Cameroon	Niger-Congo: NW Bantu	c. 100,000		Izuwu	Lost much land to colonial plantations. Matrilineal.
Kpelle	Guerze	Guinea, Liberia, Sierra Leone	Niger-Congo: Mande	c. 1 million	Mande cluster		Liberia's largest ethnic group. Rice farmers. Patrilineal.
Krachi	Kratye	Ghana	Niger-Congo: Kwa	c. 75,000	Togo cluster		Fishing, small farming on shore of Volta River and lake. Patrilineal.River and lake. Patrilineal.
Kreda		Chad	Nilo-Saharan: Saharan	c. 70,000			Farmers, herders. Patrilineal.
Kreish		Central African Republic, Sudan	Nilo-Saharan: Central Sudanic	c. 25,000		Aja, Veroge, Miu	Assimilating to Banda language, culture. Muslim.
Krobo	Krobou	Cote d'Ivoire, Ghana	Niger-Congo: Kwa	c. 330,000	Adangbe cluster		Commercial farmers, produce and trade palm oil. 2 small kingdoms. Patrilineal.
Kru	Crau, Krao, Krou, Krumen, Nana	Liberia, Sierra Leone	Niger-Congo: Kwa	c. 200,000	Kru cluster		Fishing, farming, renowned sailors on W. African coast.
Kuba	Bakuba	Dem Rep Congo	Niger-Congo: C. Bantu	c. 150,000	Kalai cluster	Bushong	Powrful state (17th c.) controlled trade from central Africa to Atlantic coast. Influential throughout Congo region. Famed for carving, other art.
Kuku		Sudan, Dem Rep Congo	Nilo-Saharan: E. Sudanic	c. 60,000	Eastern Nilotic	Nyepo	Mostly mixed farmers. Related to Kakwa, Mandari, Bari. Stateless. Patrilineal.
Kukuruku		Nigeria	Niger-Congo: Kwa	c. 200,000	Edo cluster	Akoko, Etsako, Ineme	Village farmers. Patrilineal.
Kulango	Kourlango, Kulamo	Burkina Faso, Cote d'Ivoire, Ghana	Niger-Congo: Voltaic	c. 100,000	Lobi cluster		Village farmers. Matrilineal.
Kunama	Kunema	Eritrea, Sudan	Nilo-Saharan: Kunama	c. 70,000	Kunama cluster		Cattle herders, mixed farmers. Stateless.Muslim.
Kundu		Cameroon	Niger-Congo: NW Bantu	c. 80,000			Village farmers. Matrilineal.

(continued)

Name	Alternate name	Location	Linguistic affiliation	Population estimate	Group or cluster	Subgroups	Notes
!Kung	Xhu, Zhu	Angola, Namibia	Click	>54,000	Khoisan cluster	Central (Namibia, Botswana); Northern (Angola); Southern (Ghanzi of Botswana)	Traditional nomad hunter gatherers of Kalahari. Now cattle herding, farming, largely ousted from traditional territory by modern governments.
Kurama	Akurumi, Bagwama, Rurama, Tikurimi	Mali, Nigeria	Niger-Congo: Kwa	c. 40,000	Plateau		Came to current location early 20th century from Zaria region. Farming, livestock herding. Patrilineal.
Kurfei	Kurfey, Soudie	Niger	Afro-Asiatic: Chadic	c. 60,000	Hausa cluster		Farming, cattlekeeping. Patrilineal.
Kuri		Chad	Afro-Asiatic: Chadic	c. 40,000	Bornu cluster		Mixed economy. Fishing, gardening, cattle keeping. Lost original language, now speak Buduma dialect.
Kuria	Kuriya, Tende	Kenya, Tanzania	Niger-Congo: Bantu	c. 400,000	Interlacustrine cluster		Farmers, some cattle raising. Urban Kuria active in politics, business, professions. Patrilineal.
Kusasi	Kusase, Kusai	Burkina Faso, Ghana	Niger-Congo: Voltaic	c. 200,000	Mole cluster		Mostly sedentary farmers. Patrilineal.
Kusu	Kutshu	Dem Rep Congo	Niger-Congo: C. Bantu	c. 75,000	Mongo cluster		Originally Tetela. Most speak Swahili. Muslim. Patrilineal.
Kwangare	Kwangali	Angola, Namibia	Niger-Congo: SW Bantu	c. 30,000			Village farmers, herders. Patrilineal.
Kwavi		Kenya, Tanzania	Nilo-Saharan: E. Sudanic	c. 8,000	Maasai cluster		Often used to refer to dispersed Maasi now practicing farming.
Kwena	Kuena	Botswana	Niger-Congo: Bantu	no estimate	Tswana cluster		Chiefdom. Herders, farmers. Patrilineal descent
Kwere		Tanzania	Niger-Congo: Bantu	c. 100,000	NE Coastal Bantu	Doe	Raided for E. African slave trade (19th c.). Mostly Muslim. Farmers, some livestock.
L							
Labwor		Uganda	Nilo-Saharan: E. Sudanic	10,000	W. Nilotic cluster		Pastoralists, traders. Close relation to Acoli. Patrilineal
Laka		Cameroon, Central African Republic, Chad, Dem Rep Congo	Niger-Congo: Adamawa-Ubangi	40,000			Village farmers, herders. Patrilineal.
Lala		Zambia	Niger-Congo: Central Bantu	c. 450,000	Bemba cluster		Village farmers. Matrilineal.
Lamba		Zambia, Dem Rep Congo	Niger-Congo: Central Bantu	c. 200,000	Bemba cluster		Village farmers. Migrant labor. Matrilineal.
Lambya		Malawi, Tanzania	Niger-Congo: Bantu	c. 70,000			Mixed farmers. Patrilineal.
Landuma	Landoma, Cocoli	Guinea	Niger-Congo: W. Atlantic	c. 25,000	Senegambia cluster		Rice farmers. Patrilineal.
Lango	Langi	Uganda	Nilo-Saharan: E. Sudanic	c. 1.5 million	W. Nilotic cluster		Traditional cattle keepers. Rinderpest forced into agriculture. Now mixed farmers. Stateless. Patrilineal.

(continued)

Name	Alternate name	Location	Linguistic affiliation	Population estimate	Group or cluster	Subgroups	Notes
Lega	Rega	Dem Rep Congo	Niger-Congo: Equatorial Bantu	c. 500,000			Small farmers. Ivory and wood carvers. Patrilineal.
Lele		Dem Rep Congo	Niger-Congo: Central Bantu	c. 50,000	Kasai cluster		Village farmers. Matrilineal.
Lendu	Bale	Uganda, Dem Rep Congo	Nilo-Saharan: C. Sudanic	c. 300,000	Madi cluster		Mixed hill farmers. Stateless. Patrilineal.
Lengola		Dem Rep Congo	Niger-Congo: Equatorial Bantu	c. 125,000			Fishing (Lualaba River), trading, farming. Patrilineal
Lenje		Zambia	Niger-Congo: Central Bantu	c. 150,000	Lozi cluster		Village farmers. Patrilineal
Lese		Dem Rep Congo	Nilo-Saharan: C. Sudanic	c. 75,000	Mangbetu cluster		Live in Ituri forest. Village farmers. Stateless. Patrilineal
Ligbi		Burkina Faso, Cote d'Ivoire, Ghana	Niger-Congo: Mande	c. 50,000			Former traders (kola nuts, gold) on Black Volta in Ghana. Now mixed farmers. Some Muslims. Patrilineal
Liilse	Lyelas	Burkina Faso	Niger-Congo: Voltaic	c. 200,000	Grusi cluster		Mostly farmers. Patrilineal
Limba		Guinea, Sierra Leone	Niger-Congo: W. Atlantic	c. 500,000	Temne cluster		Mixed farmers (rice, groundnuts, cassava). Enslaved during Samori Toure's conquest. Mostly Muslim.
Lisi		Chad	Nilo-Saharan: C. Sudanid	c. 55,000	Bagirmi cluster	Abusemen, Bulala, Kuka, Midogo	Pastoralists. Muslim. Patrilineal
Lobi		Burkina Faso, Cote d'Ivoire, Ghana	Niger-Congo: Voltaic	c. 500,000	Lobi cluster		Pastoralism (cattle, camels) and farming (millet, cotton, groundnuts). Matrilineal
Logo		Dem Rep Congo	Nilo-Saharan: c. Sudanic	c. 200,000	Madi cluster	Avukaya	Farmers, herders. Stateless. Patrilineal.
Lokele		Dem Rep Congo	Niger-Congo: Bantu	c. 200,000			Fishing, farming, trading. Patrilineal
Loko	Kokko	Sierra Leone	Niger-Congo: Mande	c. 250,000	Mende cluster		5 chiefdoms. Many Muslims. Farming (rice). Patrilineal.
Lovedu	Lobedu	South Africa	Niger-Congo: Bantu	c. 200,000	Sotho cluster		Mixed farmers. Queen widely known as rainmaker. Patrilineal.
Lozi	Balozi, Barotse, Rotse, Rozi	Botswana, Zambia	Niger-Congo: Central Bantu	c. 300,000			Fishing, farming, cattle herding. Several groups consolidated in 17th century. Kingdom. Patrilineal.
Luapula		Zambia, Dem Rep Congo	Niger-Congo: Central Bantu	c. 150,000	Bemba cluster	Londa	Village farmers, traders. Matrilineal.

(continued)

Name	Alternate name	Location	Linguistic affiliation	Population estimate	Group or cluster	Subgroups	Notes
Luba	Baluba	Dem Rep Congo	Niger-Congo: Central Bantu	>4 million	Luba cluster	Lulua, Mganbi, Songe, Yeke, et al.	Main group in Dem Rep Congo. Kingdom emerged in 15th century. Trade (ivory, slaves). Declined with rise of Chokwe in 19th century. Known for art. Patrilineal.
Lugbara	Logbara, Lugbwari	Sudan, Uganda, Dem Rep Congo	Nilo-Saharan: C. Sudanic	c. 300,000	Madi cluster		Mixed farmers, labor migrants. Stateless. Suffered genocide by Uganda government. Patrilineal.
Luhya	Bantu, Kavirondi; Luyia	Kenya	Niger-Congo: Bantu	>2.5 million	Interlacustrine Bantu	Kayo, Lagoli, Marach, Nyole, Samia, Tadjoni, Vugusu, Wanga, et al	20 subgroups in W. Kenya. Formerly called Bantu Kavirondo. Mixed farmers, labor migrants. Mostly stateless. Patrilineal.
Lunda	Alund, Arunde, Balonde, Luntu, Malhundo, Valunda	Angola, Dem Rep Congo, Zambia	Niger-Congo: Central Bantu	>4.3 million	Lunda cluster		Powerful 16th and 17th century state. Traded (salt, ivory, copper, slaves) through 18th century. Related to Luba. Kingdoms. Matrilineal.
Luo	Jaluo	Kenya, Uganda	Nilo-Saharan: E. Sudanic	c. 2.8 million	W. Nilotic cluster	Padhola	Origins in Sudan. Mixed farmers (maize, millet, cassava) and cattle herders. Cash crop (cotton) and labor migration. Stateless. Urban workers throughout Kenya. Patrilineal.
Lwoo		Kenya, Sudan, Uganda		no estimate			General name for all Nilotic speaking peoples.
M							
Maasai	Masai	Kenya, Tanzania	Nilo-Saharan: E. Sudanic	>800,000	E. Nilotic cluster	Arusha, Chamus, Kisongo, Kwavi, Loitokotok, Matapato, Purko, Samburu (with Ariaal) Uas Nkishu	Great Rift Valley pastoralists. Traditional warriors and cattle raiders on neighbors. Ruled by prophetic leaders. Age-set system. Patrilineal
Mada		Nigeria	Niger-Congo: Kwa: Genue	c. 80,000	Plateau		Village farmers. Patrilineal.
Madi		Uganda	Nilo-Saharan: C. Sudanic	c. 200,000	Madi cluster	Lulu'ba	Farmers, livestock.
Maguzawa		Niger, Nigeria	Afro-Asiatic: Chadic	c. 130,000	Hausa cluster		Herders, farmers. Primary non-Muslim Hausa group
Maha	Wadain	Chad, Sudan	Nilo-Saharan: Maban	c. 250,000	Wadai cluster	Karanga, Fala	Many subgroups, including economic specialists (hunters, potters, blacksmiths). Dominant in Wadai. Muslim. Patrilineal.
Mahafaly	Mehafaly	Madagascar	Malayo-Polynesian: Malagasy	c. 150,000	Southwest Lowlands		Mixed farmers. Probably related to Sakalava. Patrilineal
Maji		Ethiopia	Afro-Asiatic: W. Cushitic	>30,000	Sidamo cluster		Mixed farmers. Patrilineal.

(continued)

Name	Alternate name	Location	Linguistic affiliation	Population estimate	Group or cluster	Subgroups	Notes
Maka		Cameroon, Equatorial Guinea, Gabon	Niger-Congo: Equatorial Bantu	c. 100,000	Fang cluster		Related to Beti. Mainly farmers. Historical middlemen in slave trade. Patrilineal.
Makere		Dem Rep Congo	Nilo-Saharan: C. Sudanic		Mangbetu	Niapu	Mixed farmers.
Makonde		Malawi, Mozambique, Tanzania	Niger-Congo: C. Bantu	c. 1.5 million	Yao cluster	Matambwe, Mawia	Mixed farmers, labor migrants. Important in war for independence from Portugal (1960s-70s). Famed woodcarvers. Matrilineal.
Makua		Malawi, Mozambique, Tanzania	Niger-Congo: C. Bantu	c. 6 million	Yao cluster		Mixed farmers. Linked to Makonda. Matrilineal.
Mama		Nigeria	Niger-Congo: Kwa-Benue	c. 50,000	Plateau	Kalma	Village farmers. Patrilineal.
Mambila	Bang	Cameroon, Nigeria	Niger-Congo: Kwa-Benue	c. 160,000	Plateau	Ako, Daga, Kamkam, Magu	Village farmers. Patrilineal.
Mambwe		Tanzania, Zambia	Niger-Congo: C. Bantu	c. 350,000	Bemba cluster	Lungu	Village farmers, now labor migrants to Copperbelt.
Mamprusi		Burkina Faso, Ghana	Niger-Congo: Voltaic	c. 250,000	Mole cluster		Sedentary farmers. Kingdom emerged in 14th century, declined 18th c. Patrilineal.
Mamvu		Dem Rep Congo	Nilo-Saharan: C. Sudanic	c. 60,000	Mangbetu cluster	Mangutu	Small farmers, urban wage labor. Some commercial farming. Renowned for wood and metal art. Part of Mangbetu kingdom.
Mandara	Ndara, Wandala	Cameroon, Nigeria	Afro-Asiatic: Chadic	c. 70,000	Kirdi group	Gamergu, Maya	Mostly farmers (groundnuts, cotton). Muslim.
Mandari	Mondavi	Sudan	Nilo-Saharan: E. Sudanic	c. 40,000	E. Nilotic		Mixed farmers. Chiefdoms. Patrilineal.
Mande	Mandingo, Mandingue, Minding	Guinea, Mali, Senegal	Niger-Congo: Mande	c. 13.5 million		Main groups: Bambara, Mozo, Dialonke, Kagoro, Kasonke, Konyanke, Koranko, Malinke, Nono, Soninke, Susu	Origins in Upper Niger region, moved west and south. Farmers, traders, elaborate political authority. Most retain indigenous religion. Patrilineal.
Mandja	Mandjia	Central African Republic	Niger-Congo: Adamawa-Ubangi	c. 200,000	Ubangi cluster		Village farmers. Patrilineal.
Mandyako	Manjako	Gambia, Guinea-Bissau, Senegal	Niger-Congo: W. Atlantic	c. 200,000	Senegambia cluster		Related to Papel. Mostly small farmers, urban and plantation labor. Patrilineal.
Manga		Chad, Niger, Nigeria	Nilo-Saharan: Saharan	c. 600,000	Bornu cluster		Many identify ethnically with Kanuri. Herders, farmers, Muslim. Patrilineal.
Mangbetu		Dem Rep Congo	Nilo-Saharan: C. Sudanic	c. 500,000		Babelu, Mbae, Medja, Ngbelo, Popoi, Rumbi	Related kingdoms and subject peoples. Mixed farmers. Wood and metal arts. Patrilineal.
Manyika		Mozambique, Zimbabwe	Niger-Congo: Bantu	c. 200,000	Shona-Thonga cluster		Farmers (millet, maize, yams), herders. Part of Shona nation. Patrilineal.

(continued)

Name	Alternate name	Location	Linguistic affiliation	Population estimate	Group or cluster	Subgroups	Notes
Mao		Ethiopia	Nilo-Saharan: Koman	c. 10,000	Koman cluster		Mixed farmers, herders. Stateless.
Marakwet	Endo	Kenya	Nilo-Saharan: E. Sudanic	no estimate	Kalenjin cluster		Irrigation farmers. Patrilineal.
Maravi							SEE Chewa. Nyanja. Outdated term.
Margi		Nigeria	Afro-Asiatic: Chadic	c. 200,000	Plateau		Village farmers. Patrilineal
Masa	Massa, Banana	Cameroon, Chad	Niger-Congo: Adamawa-Ubangi	c. 220,000	Adamawa cluster	Budugam	Mostly farmers. Patrilineal.
Masalit		Chad, Sudan	Nilo-Saharan: Maban	c. 60,000	Wadai group		Mostly small farmers. Labor migrants.
Mashasha		Zambia	Niger-Congo: C. Bantu	no estimate	Lozi cluster		Village farmers. Patrilineal
Matakam		Cameroon, Nigeria	Afro-Asiatic: Chadic	c. 150,000	Plateau		Terrace farmers. Patrilineal
Matengo		Mozambique, Tanzania	Niger-Congo: Bantu	c. 250,000	Nyasa cluster		Hill farmers. Patrilineal.
Matumbi		Mozambique, Tanzania	Niger-Congo: Bantu	c. 100,000	Rufiji cluster	Ndendeuli	Rice farmers. Muslim. Patrilineal
Mbala		Dem Rep Congo	Niger Congo: C. Bantu	c. 220,000	Kwango cluster		Small farmers, urban labor. Matrilineal
Mbeere	Mbere	Kenya	Niger-Congo: NE Bantu	no estimate	Meru cluster		Mixed farming (cotton, tobacco, millet, cassava, maize) beekeeping. Patrilineal.
Mbembe		Nigeria	Niger-Congo: Benue-Congo	c. 110,000	Ibibio cluster	Adun, Oshopong	Small farmers on Cross River. Double descent.
Mbole		Dem Rep Congo	Niger-Congo: Equatorial Bantu	c. 150,000	Mongo cluster		Fishing, farming. Patrilineal.
Mbugu	Wumbugu	Tanzania	Afro-Asiatic: S. Cushitic	c. 50,000	Iraqw cluster		Mostly assimilated to Pare (Bantu). Mixed farmers. Stateless. Patrilineal.
Mbugwe		Tanzania	Niger-Congo: Bantu	c. 30,000	Central Bantu Rift cluster		Mixed farmers.
Mbukushu		Angola, Namibia	Niger-Congo: C. Bantu	c. 25,000			Village farmers. Matrilineal.
Mbula	Bula	Nigeria	Niger-Congo: Kwa	c. 50,000	Plateau	Bare	Village farmers. Patrilineal.
Mbum	Bum	Cameroon, Central African Republic, Chad	Niger-Congo: Adamawa-Ubangi	c. 60,000	Adamawa cluster	Kepere	Mixed village farmers. Patrilineal.
Mbunda		Angola, Zambia	Niger-Congo: Central Bantu	c. 75,000	Lunda cluster		Sometimes groups with neighbors as Balovale.
Mbundu	Ovimbundu	Angola	Niger-Congo: Bantu	c. 3 million	SW Bantu	Bailundu, Cenga, Cingalo, Citara, Eketete, Elende, Kakonda, Kasongi, Ngalonga, Sambu, Sange, Viye, et al.	About 1/4 of Angola population. Kingdoms in 16th century. Portuguese appropriated lands for plantations (c. 1650). Village farmers. Double descent.
Mbunga		Tanzania	Niger-Congo: NE Bantu	c. 30,000	Rufiji cluster		Rice farming. Patrilineal.
Mbuti	Bambuti	Dem Rep Congo	Niger Congo: Bantu	c. 40,000		Aka, Efe, Sua	Ituri forest. Pygmies.
Meban	Maban	Sudan, Ethiopia	Nilo-Saharan: E. Sudanic	c. 50,000	W. Nilotic cluster		Once a Fung kingdom. Mixed farmers.
Mende		Sierra Leone	Niger-Congo: Mande	c. 1.5 million		Ko, Kpa, Sewa	Largest group in Sierra Leone. >60 chiefdoms. Mostly small farmers. Labor migration to cities.

(continued)

Name	Alternate name	Location	Linguistic affiliation	Population estimate	Group or cluster	Subgroups	Notes
Merina	Antimerina, Hova, Imerina	Madagascar	Malayo-Polynesian: Malagasy	c. 3 million	Central Highland		2 groups: Fotsy (descended from free Merina) and Mainty (slave descent). Dominant ethnic group of Madagascar. Once ruled by Queens. Patrilineal.
Meru	Mweru	Kenya	Niger-Congo: NE Bantu	>700,000	Meru cluster		Live on Mt. Kenya (Northern Gikuyu). Mixed farmers, beekeepers. Ritual leader: mugwe.
Mfingo	Fingo, Mfengu	South Africa	Niger-Congo: S. Bantu	>1 million	Xhosa cluster		Mixed farmers, former refugees from Nguni wars. Now labor migrants, mixed farmers. Patrilineal.
Mijikenda	Nyika	Kenya	Niger-Congo: N.E. Bantu	>1 million		Chonyi, Digo, Duruma, Giriyama, Jibana, Kambe, Kauma, Rabai, Ribe	Farming and fishing peoples. Patrilineal. Muslim. Name means "Nine towns"
Mimi		Chad	Nilo-Saharan: Maban	c. 10,000	Wadai cluster		Semi-arid farmers, herders. Muslim. Patrilineal descent.
Minianka		Burkina Faso, Cote d'Ivoire, Mali	Niger-Congo: Voltaic	c. 400,000	Senufo cluster		Village farmers. Muslim. Patrilineal.
Moba		Ghana, Togo	Niger-Congo: Voltaic	c. 250,000	Gurma cluster		Village farmers. Patrilineal.
Mober		Chad, Niger, Nigeria	Afro-Asiatic: Chadic	c. 450,000	Bornu cluster		Farmers, herders. Muslim. Patrilineal.
Mongo		Dem Rep Congo	Niger-Congo: Equatorial Bantu	c. 4.2 million	Mongo cluster	Ekonda, Kela, Kutshu, Mongo, Mbole, Ngandu, Ngome, Nkundu, Songomeno, Tetela, et al	Mongo-dialect speakers. No single polity. Village farmers, traders. Patrilineal.
Moru		Sudan, Dem Rep Congo	Nilo-Saharan: C. Sudanic	c. 40,000	Madi cluster	Adi, Andri, Kedini	Related to Bongo, Baka. Mostly small farmers.
Mossi	Moose	Benin, Burkina Faso, Cote d'Ivoire	Niger-Congo: Voltaic	c. 5 million	Mole cluster		Kingdoms in 15th century. Mostly mixed farmers. Muslim. Patrilineal.
Mpongwe		Gabon	Niger-Congo: NW Bantu	c. 60,000		Galoa, Ininga, Jumba, Nkomi	Hunting, fishing, traditional middlemen between Europeans and interior peoples for trade. Matrilineal.
Mubi		Chad	Afro-Asiatic: Chadic	c. 50,000	Wadai cluster		Small farmers, laborers, pastoralists. Muslim.
Mumuye		Nigeria	Niger-Congo: Adamawa-Ubangi	c. 420,000	Plateau		Mixed farmers, many urban wage migrants. Patrilineal.
Mundang	Moundang	Cameroon, Chad, Nigeria	Niger-Congo: Adamawa-Ubangi	>110,000	Adamawa cluster	Kiziere, Mangbei, Yazme	Related to Sara. Linguistic ties to Mbum. Farmers. Cattle herded by Fulani. Kingships. Patrilineal.

(continued)

Name	Alternate name	Location	Linguistic affiliation	Population estimate	Group or cluster	Subgroups	Notes
Mundu		Sudan, Dem Rep Congo	Niger-Congo: Adamawa-Ubangi	>30,000	Ubangi cluster		Farming, herding. Patrilineal descent. Zande subgroup
Murle	Beir	Ethiopia, Sudan	Afro-Asiatic: E. Sudanic	c. 90,000	Beir cluster	Epeita, Longarim, Pibor	Mainly pastoralists. Patrilineal.
Musgu	Musgum	Cameroon, Chad	Afro-Asiatic: Chadic	>100,000	Bagirmi cluster		Mainly farmers (groundnuts, cotton). Muslim. Patrilineal.
Mwera		Malawi, Mozambique, Tanzania	Niger-Congo: C. Bantu	c. 420,000	Yao cluster		Farming (millet, sorghum). Matrilineal.
Mwimbe		Kenya	Niger-Congo: NE Bantu	c. 100,000	Meru cluster		Mixed farmers. Patrilineal.
Mzab		Algeria	Afro-Asiatic: Berber	c. 250,000			Oasis date farmers.
N							
Nafana		Burkina Faso, Cote d'Ivoire, Ghana, Mali	Niger-Congo: Voltaic	>50,000	Senufo cluster		Small-hold farmers. Patrilineal.
Nago		Benin	Niger-Congo: Kwa	>600,000	Yoruba cluster	Ketu, Chabe, Idacha	Western Yoruba group in Benin. Small kingdoms. Intensive farmers. Patrilineal.
Nama	Namaque	Namibia, S. Africa	Click	c. 90,000	Khoisan cluster		Sheep, cattle herding. Now also farmers.
Namshi		Central African Republic, Cameroon	Niger-Congo: Adamawa-Ubangi	>20,000	Adamawa cluster	Doyado, Kolbila	Mixed village farmers. Patrilineal
Nandi		Kenya	Nilo-Saharan: E. Sudanic	c. 500,000	S. Nilotic cluster	Terik	Cattle keepers, cash-cropping, urban labor. Traditional government by prophets. Patrilineal.
Nara		Eritrea	Afro-Asiatic: Semitic	c. 100,000	Beja cluster		Pastoralists. Muslim.
Naudeba		Burkina Faso	Niger-Congo: Voltaic	c. 100,000	Mole cluster		Cattle herding, farming. Patrilineal.
Ndaka		Dem Rep Congo	Niger-Congo: Equatorial Bantu	10,000			Farming (cassava, banana). Patrilineal.
Ndamba		Tanzania	Niger-Congo: C. Bantu	c. 70,000	Rufiji cluster		Rice farmers. Patrilineal.
Ndau	Vandau	Mozambique, Zimbabwe	Niger-Congo: Bantu	c. 110,000	Shona-Thonga cluster	Danda, Gova, Shanga	Mostly farmers. Part of Shona nation. Patrilineal.
Ndebele	Matabele	S. Africa, Zimbabwe	Niger-Congo: Bantu	c. 2.3 million	Ndebele cluster	Laka (Langa), Maune, Manala, Seleka	Unified by Mzilikazi (1820s), and incorporating Sotho and Tswana. Mixed farmers, cattle keepers, labor migrants. Kingdom. Patrilineal.
Ndembu	Mdembu	Angola, Dem Rep Congo, Zambia	Niger-Congo: Central Bantu	c. 80,000	Lunda cluster		Mixed farmers. From Lunda kingdoms. Matrilineal.
Ndogo		Sudan, Dem Rep Congo	Niger-Congo: Adamawa-Ubangi	c. 50,000	Ubangi cluster	Bai, Golo, Bviri, Sere, Tagbo	Village farmers. Remnants of Arab, Zande raids. Patrilineal.
Ndu	Okebu	Uganda, Dem Rep Congo	Nilo-Saharan: C. Sudanic	c. 300,000			Mixed farmers. Known for blacksmithing, use of magic.

(continued)

Name	Alternate name	Location	Linguistic affiliation	Population estimate	Group or cluster	Subgroups	Notes
Nduka		Chad, Central African Republic	Nilo-Saharan: C. Sudanic	c. 22,000	Sara cluster	Akunga, Awaka, Leto, Udiu	Small farms, livestock. Muslim. Patrilineal.
Nefusa		Libya	Afro-Asiatic: Berber	c. 400,000			Sedentary farmers.
Ngala	Bangala, Mangala	Congo, Dem Rep Congo	Niger-Congo: Benue-Congo	c. 20,000	Equatorial Bantu cluster	Boloki, Ngombe	Language used as lingua franca in region. Formerly river traders. Stateless. Patrilineal
Ngama		Chad	Nilo-Saharan: C. Sudanic	c. 230,000	Sara cluster	Daleba	Village farmers. Strong in business, professions.
Ngandu		Dem Rep Congo	Niger-Congo: Equatorial Bantu	c. 200,000	Mongo cluster	Bambale, Lalia	Traditional small farmers, now cash cropping, labor migrants in cities. Patrilineal.
Ngazija							SEE Comorians
Ngbandi		Central African Republic, Dem Rep Congo	Niger-Congo: Adamawa-Ubangi	c. 200,000	Ubangi cluster		Mixed farmers. Patrilineal.
Ngere	Guere	Sierra Leone		c. 400,000	Mende cluster		Rice farmers. Patrilineal.
Ngindo		Tanzania	Niger-Congo: C. Bantu	c. 250,000	Yao cluster		Mainly rice farmers, raise small livestock, beekeepers. Involved in Maji Maji rebellion against Germans (1905). Patrilineal.
Ngizim		Nigeria	Afro-Asiatic: Chadic	c. 50,000	Bornu cluster		Farmers, herders. Muslim. Patrilineal.
Ngombe		Dem Rep Congo		c. 200,000	Mongo cluster	Kutu, Linga, Ntomba, Mbesa	Village farmers. Patrilineal
Ngonde		Malawi, Tanzania, Zambia	Niger-Congo: Bantu	c. 200,000	Nyasa cluster		Age villages under central kingship. Mixed farmers. Patrilineal.
Ngongo		Angola, Dem Rep Congo	Niger-Congo: C. Bantu	c. 5,000	Kwango cluster		Village farmers. Matrilineal.
Ngoni	Angoru, Mangoni. Wangoni	Malawi, Tanzania, Mozambique	Niger-Congo: Bantu	> 1 million	Ngoni cluster	Gomani, Mangwangana, Mombera, Mpenzeni	Northernmost Nguni state. Took present territory after Mfecane. Patrilineal
Ngonyelo		Angola		no estimate			Village farmers. Patrilineal.
Ngumbi		Angola		c. 25,000		Hinga, Mulondo	Small kingdoms. Village farmers. Patrilineal.
Nguni		Southern Africa	Niger-Congo: Bantu	several million	Nguni cluster	Ndebele, Ngoni, Swazi, Tembu, Xhosa, Zulu	Cluster of patrilineal kingdoms formed early 19th century during Mfecane. Kingdoms still mostly exist.
Nguru	Ngulu, Wanguru	Tanzania	Niger-Congo: Bantu	c. 150,000	NE Coastal Bantu		Mostly mixed farmers
Ngwaketse		Botswana, S. Africa	Niger-Congo: Bantu	no estimate	Tswana cluster		Chiefdoms. Cattle herders. Patrilineal.
Ngwato		Botswana, S. Africa	Niger-Congo: Bantu	no estimate	Tswana cluster		Chiefdoms. Cattle herders. Patrilineal..

(continued)

Name	Alternate name	Location	Linguistic affiliation	Population estimate	Group or cluster	Subgroups	Notes
Njamusi	Njemp, Chamus	Kenya		c. 10,000	E. Nilotic cluster		Historically supplied caravans from Uganda to E. African Coast (19th c.). Livestock and fishing in Lake Baringo.
Nkole	Ankole, Banyankole	Uganda	Niger-Congo: Bantu	>1 million	Interlacustrine Bantu		One of Uganda's 4 kingdoms
Nkoya	Mankoya	Zambia	Niger-Congo: C. Bantu	c. 100,000			Village farmers. Patrilineal
Nono		Mali	Niger-Congo: Mande	c. 25,000	Mande cluster	Djennenke	Live in Jenné. Muslim.
Nuba	Anag	Sudan	Kordofanian	c. 100,000	Nuba cluster	Karla, Kaolib, Tagali, Talodi, Tumtum, Temein	Live in Nuba Mountains. Mixed farmers (non-Arab) being ousted by Arab militias.
Nubi		Sudan, Uganda		c. 50,000			Arabic speakers. Remnants of 19th century Egyptian army.
Nubians		Sudan		>800,000	Nubian cluster		From Aswan, Egypt. Raided for slaves. Muslim since 17th century.
Nuer		Sudan		c. 800,000	W. Nilotic cluster		Cattle herders on Upper Nile marshes. Related to Dinka. Stateless. Traditional prophetic leaders. Now suffering genocide by Sudan government forces. Patrilineal
Nunuma		Burkina Faso, Ghana	Niger-Congo: Voltaic	c. 500,000	Grusi cluster		Small farmers. Patrilineal.
Nupe		Nigeria	Niger-Congo: Kwa	c. 1 million	Nupe cluster	Nge	Powerful kingdom of midwestern Nigeria (est. 1800s). Mixed farmers, traders, weavers. Muslim.
Nyakyusa	Niabiussa, Sochile, Sokile	Tanzania	Niger-Congo: Bantu	c. 600,000	Nyasa cluster	Kukwe, Mwamba, Ngonde, Selya, Sukwa	Age villages. Farmers, wage labor. Patrilineal chiefdoms.
Nyamwezi	Banyamwezi	Tanzania	Niger-Congo: Bantu	c. 3 million	Nyamwezi cluster		Farming (maize, rice, yams, tobacco) livestock. Trading (ivory, slaves in 19th c.). Patrilineal chiefdoms.
Nyaneka		Angola	Niger-Congo: Bantu	c. 50,000	SW Bantu		Small-hold farmers, cattle herders. Small kingdom.
Nyanja	Anyanja, Nianja, Niassa, Wanyanja	Malawi, Mozambique, Zambia, Zimbabwe	Niger-Congo: C. Bantu	c. 2.5 million	Maravi cluster	Manganja	Mainly sedentary farmers, labor migrants. Christian. Matrilineal
Nyasa		Malawi	Niger-Congo: C. Bantu	c. 500,000	Maravi cluster		Farming, fishing. Matrilineal.
Nyiha							SEE Safwa.
Nyoro	Banyoro	Uganda	Niger-Congo: Bantu	c. 1.5 million	Interlacustrine Bantu		Kingdom. Traditional hunters (skins, ivory)
Nzakara		Central African Republic	Niger-Congo: Adamawa-Ubangi	c. 50,000	Ubangi cluster		Mixed village farms. Patrilineal.

(continued)

Name	Alternate name	Location	Linguistic affiliation	Population estimate	Group or cluster	Subgroups	Notes
Nzima	Nzema, Appollonians, Assoko, Amanya, Zema		Niger-Congo: Kwa	c. 500,000	Akan cluster, Lagoon group		Middlemen in trade between Europeans and interior groups. Now commercial farming, sea fishing. President Nkrumah was Nzima.
O							
Ododop	Erorup	Nigeria	Niger-Congo: Benue-Congo	c. 20,000	Ibibio cluster	Korop	Village farmers, traders. Stateless. Patrilineal.
Ogaden		Ethiopia, Kenya, Somalia	Afro-Asiatic: E. Cushitic	c. 100,000	Somali cluster		Pastoralists on Somali-Ethiopia border. Patrilineal.
Ogoni	Kana	Nigeria	Niger-Congo: Benue-Cnogo	c. 300,000	Ibibio cluster		Farming, fishing (Niger Delta). Economy disrupted by oil production
Okebu							SEE Ndu.
Okiek	Dorobo	Kenya	Nilo-Saharan: E. Sudanic	>40,000	Kalenjin cluster		Traditional forest hunting, gathering. Now small farmers.
Ometo		Ethiopia	Afro-Asiatic: W. Cushitic	c. 1 million	Sidamo cluster	Badiku, Dorge, Wallamo	Farming (tea, coffee, cotton, maize, barley). Stateless. Patrilineal.
Oorlam		Namibia	Afrikaans	no estimate	Khoisan cluster		Arrived from Cape in 18th, 19th centuries. Now small farmers, peripatetic craftspeople.
Oromo	Galla	Ethiopia, Kenya, Sudan, Somalia	Afro-Asiatic: S. Cushitic	>13 million	Oromo cluster	Arusi, Bararelta, Boran, Ittu, Rendille, Wallaga	Sedentary farmers, pastoralists. Expanded frmo Ethiopia c. 16th century. Patrilineal.
Oron		Nigeria	Niger-Congo: Kwa	>100,000	Ibibio cluster		Village farmers. Formerly traders with "secret" associations. Patrilineal.
Ovambo	Ambo	Angola, Namibia, Zambia	Niger-Congo: SW Bantu	>250,000		Eunda, Evale, Kuanyama, Okafima, Ombandji, etc.	Raided for slaves, traded in ivory, iron smelters. Today mostly migrant workers, small-hold farming. Traditional kingdoms.
Ovimbundu							SEE Mbundu.
P							
Papel	Pepei	Guinea, Guinea Bissau	Niger-Congo: W. Atlantic	c. 80,000	Senegambia cluster	Brame, Manjaco, Mankanya	Farmers (rice, cashews). Patrilineal.
Pare	Asu	Tanzania	Niger-Congo: Bantu	>320,000	NE Bantu cluster		Mainly mixed hill farmers. Patrilineal.
Pari	Beri, Feri	Sudan	Nilo-Saharan: E. Sudanic	c. 30,000	W. Nilotic cluster		Related to Anuak. Mixed farmers.
Pedi	Bapedi	South Africa	Niger-Congo: Bantu	>500,000	Sotho cluster		Militarily powerful in 19th century. Long-distance traders. Driven from original territory by Ndebele (19th c.). Now village farmers, urban workers. Patrilineal.

(continued)

Name	Alternate name	Location	Linguistic affiliation	Population estimate	Group or cluster	Subgroups	Notes
Pemba	Shirazi	Tanzania	Niger-Congo: Bantu	c. 100,000	Swahili cluster		Pemba Island. Fishing, rice and clove farming. Formerly small states. Muslim. Cognatic descent groups.
Pende	Bapende	Angola, Dem Rep Congo	Niger-Congo: C. Bantu	c. 500,000	Kwango cluster		Peasant farmers. Raided and sold slaves for Portuguese (18th, 19th c.) Renowned for art. Matrilineal.
Peul							SEE: Fulani.
Pimbwe		Tanzania	Niger-Congo: Bantu	c. 50,000	Rukwa cluster	Rungwa	Mixed farmers. Patrilineal.
Pogoro		Tanzania	Niger-Congo: Bantu	c. 200,000	Rufiji cluster		Mostly rice farmers. Patrilineal.
Pokomo		Kenya	Niger-Congo: Bantu	c. 60,000	NE Coastal Bantu		Mostly farmers, fishing on Tana River. 4 subgroups with different languages.
Pokot	Suk	Kenya, Uganda	Nilo-Saharan: E. Sudanic	c. 200,000	Southern Nilotic cluster	Endo, Kadam	Traditional pastoralists. Now village farming, urban employment.
Pondo	Mpondo, Amapondo	South Africa	Niger-Congo: S. Bantu	c. 2 million	Nguni cluster		One of the Cape Nguni groups. Mixed farmers, mine workers. Patrilineal.
Pono	Pounou	Congo, Gabon	Niger-Congo: NW Bantu	c. 50,000			Once active in rubber and slave trades. Now mostly farmers. Branch of Shogo. Matrilineal.
Popo		Togo, Benin	Niger-Congo: Kwa	c. 420,000	Ewe cluster	Ge, Hula, Peda	Village farmers, fishing. Patrilineal.
Pygmy		Burundi, Cameroon, Central African Republic, Congo, Gabon, Rwanda, Dem Rep Congo	Various	c. 200,000		Aka, Binga, Gelli, Gesera, Mbuti, Twa, Zigaba	European term: refers to numerous groups of C. Africa. Originally forest hunters. Savanna expansion has reduced their territory. Individual groups tend to use the languages of neighboring, non-Pygmy groups.
Q							
Qemant	Qimant, Kemant	Ethiopia	Afro-Asiatic: C. Cushitic	c. 35,000		Falasha, Quara	Related to Agaw. Live around Lake Tana.
R							
Rangi	Irangi	Tanzania	Niger-Congo: Bantu	c. 300,000	Central Bantu Rift cluster		Agriculturalists (sorghum, millet, maize), cattle, small livestock. Patrilineal.
Rashaida		Eritrea	Afro-Asiatic: Semitic	c. 120,000	Beja cluster		Pastoralists. Muslim.
Regeibat	Erguibat	Mali, Mauritania	Afro-Asiatic: Semitic	no estimate	Beduin cluster		Territory includes W. Sahara, Algeria, Morocco. Camel pastoralists. Fought French rule until 1934. Arabic speakers. Patrilineal.
Rendille		Kenya	Afro-Asiatic: E. Cushitic	c. 10,000	Oromo cluster		Mostly camel pastoralists. Patrilineal
Reshewa	Bareshe, Reshiat, Gungawa	Nigeria	Niger-Congo: Kwa	c. 130,000	Plateau cluster		Farming, fishing, patrilineal.
Reshiat	Darhanie	Ethiopia	Afro-Asiatic: E. Cushitic	no estimate	Konso cluster	Geleba, Marille, Arbore	Irrigation farmers. Governed by age-grade cycles. Patrilineal
Rif		Morocco	Afro-Asiatic: Berber	no estimate			Mountain grain farmers.

(continued)

Name	Alternate name	Population estimate	Linguistic affiliation	Location	Group or cluster	Subgroups	Notes
Rolong		no estimate	Niger-Congo: Bantu	Botswana	Tswana cluster		Chiefdoms. Cattle herders. Patriline
Ronga	Baronga	c. 500,000	Niger-Congo: Bantu	Mozambique	Shona-Thonga cluster		Farming, fishing. Patrilineal
Ruarha		no estimate	Afro-Asiatic: Arabic	Algeria			Oasis farmers.
Rukuba		c. 80,000	Niger-Congo: Benue-Congo	Nigeria	Plateau		24 village chiefdoms. Village farmers. Subgroup of Jerawa. Patrilineal
Rundi	Burundi	c. 6 million	Niger-Congo: Bantu	Burundi, Uganda, Tanzania	Interlacustrine Bantu	Hutu, Tutsi, Twa	Comprise Tutsi, Hutu and Twa. Pastoralists, farmers. Many died in Rwanda-Burundi war. Patrilineal.
Runga		c. 30,000	Nilo-Saharan: Maban	Chad	Wadai cluster		Oasis farmers
Rwanda	Ruanda	>6 million	Niger-Congo: Bantu	Rwanda, Tanzania, Uganda, Dem Rep Congo	Interlacustrine Bantu	Hutu, Tutsi	Composite group (Tutsi, Hutu, Twa) once dominated by minority Tutsi pastoralists. Civil war in 1990s ended Tutsi dominance.
S							
Sab		c. 500,000	Afro-Asiatic: E. Cushitic	Somalia	Afar-Somali cluster	Digil, Rahanwayn	Hunting, gathering, subsistence farming, craftwork. Many are low-caste remnants of Oromo and Bantu origin
Safwa		c. 300,000	Niger-Congo: Bantu	Tanzania	Rukwa cluster	Nyiha	Mostly mixed farmers. Patrilineal
Sagara	Saghala	c. 100,000	Niger-Congo: Bantu	Tanzania	Rufiji cluster		Raided in 19th c. for slave trade. Built fortified villages. Mostly farmers, some livestock. Patrilineal.
Saho	Sao	c. 250,000	Afro-Asiatic: Semitic	Eritrea	Beja cluster		Pastoralists. Muslim.
Sakalava		c. 1 million	Malayo-Polynesian: Malagasy	Madagascar	W. and N. Lowlands	Antiambongo, Antiboina, Antifiherenana, Antimailaka, Antimaraha, Antimenabe	Several states, some with queens. Farmers, fishing.
Sakata		c. 80,000	Niger-Congo: C. Bantu	Dem Rep Congo	Kasai cluster		Village farmers. Matrilineal.
Samburu		c. 100,000	Nilo-Saharan: E. Sudanic	Kenya	Eastern Nilotic		Northern Maasai groiup. Pastoralists, arid-land farming. Stateless. Local government by age-sets, councils. Patrilineal
Samo		c. 300,000	Niger-Congo: Mande	Burkina Faso, Mali			Origins in Mali Empire (13th c.) Mostly small farmers. Partly Muslim. Patrilineal.
San	Bushmen	c. 40,000	Click	Angola, Botswana, Namibia		/Auni, G/wi (Gikwe), !Kung (!Xu), !Xo (/Hoa), /Xam, //Xegwe	Originally hunters and gatherers, also herding and trading. !Kung is largest group. Many groups now extinct.

(continued)

Name	Alternate name	Location	Linguistic affiliation	Population estimate	Group or cluster	Subgroups	Notes
Sandawe		Tanzania	Click	c. 45,000			Livestock herders. Language related to Kxoe. Patrilineal.
Sanga	Bosango	Central African Republic, Chad, Congo, Dem Rep Congo	Niger-Congo: Equatorial Bantu	c. 60,000			Sanga was trade language throughout Ubangi R. region. Many subgroups. Village farmers. Patrilineal.
Sangu		Tanzania	Niger-Congo: Bantu	c. 75,000	Central Bantu	Poroto	Farmers, cattle keepers.
Sanye		Kenya	Afro-Asiatic: S. Cushitic	c. 5,000			Hunter-gatherers. Subjects of Oromo.
Sara	Kaba, Ngambai, Sar	Chad	Nilo-Saharan: Central Sudanic	c. 1 million	Sara cluster	Barma, Dindje, Joko, Kaba, Mbai, Tie	Raided for Arab slave trade. Largest ethnic group in Chad. Village farmers, traders. Patrilineal.
Sarakole							SEE Soninké.
Sarwa		Botswana	Click	c. 5,000			Herders. Serfs for Twsana landlords.
Sebei	Sabaot	Uganda	Nilo-Saharan: E. Sucanic	c. 100,000	Southern Nilotic	Kipsorai, Kony, Pok, Sipi	Traditional cattle keepers. Commercial farming (tobacco, maize) and urban labor.
Segeju		Kenya	Niger-Congo: Bantu	c. 34,000	Swahili cluster		Mostly farming, fishing. Muslim.
Seke		Cameroon, Equatorial Guinea, Gabon	Niger-Congo: Bantu	c. 5,000			Once traders (ivory, wood, copal, slaves). Now mostly farmers, laborers, craftspersons. Patrilineal.
Sena		Mozambique, Malawi	Niger-Congo: Central Bantu	c. 1.5 million	Maravi cluster		Riverine farmers, fishing, trade. Matrilineal.
Senga	Nsenga	Mozambique, Zambia, Zimbabwe	Niger-Congo: C. Bantu	c. 300,000	Bemba cluster		Mixed farmers, labor migrants. Often raided for Arab slave trade. Patrilineal.
Senufo	Sene, Siena	Burkina Faso, Cote d'Ivoire, Mali	Niger-Congo: Voltaic	c. 3 million	Senufo cluster		Mostly peasant farmers. Integrating to commercial economy, migrating to cities. Famous for art. Patrilineal.
Serer	Sarer	Gambia, Senegal	Niger-Congo: W. Atlantic	c. 1 million	Senegambia cluster		Agriculture (millet, groundnuts). Some groups assimilating to Wolof. Mostly Muslim.
Shai		Ghana	Niger-Congo: Kwa	c. 50,000	Adangbe cluster		Related to Ada and Krobo. Small farmers. Patrilineal
Shambaa	Sambaa, Shambala	Tanzania	Niger-Congo: Bantu	c. 500,000	NE Bantu		Fortified villages against slave raiders. Mostly farmers. Once powerful kingdom. Patrilineal.
Shangaan	Shangana	Mozambique, S. Africa, Swaziland	Niger-Congo: Bantu	c. 1.5 million	Tsonga cluster		Origins in Nguni. Mostly peasant farmers. Patrilineal.
Shashi		Tanzania	Niger-Congo: Bantu	c. 100,000	Interlacustrine Bantu		Close relation to Sukuma. Village farmers. Patrilineal.

(continued)

Name	Alternate name	Location	Linguistic affiliation	Population estimate	Group or cluster	Subgroups	Notes
Shawia		Algeria	Afro-Asiatic: Berber	no estimate			Mountain farmers.
Shebelle		Somalia	Niger-Congo: Bantu	c. 200,000	NE Coastal Bantu		Predate Somali arrival. Farming, hunting. Muslim.
Sherbro		Sierra Leone	Niger-Congo: W. Atlantic	c. 200,000	Temne cluster	Krim	Chiefdoms. Village farmers. Patrilineal
Shila		Zambia	Niger-Congo: C. Bantu	c. 30,000	Bemba cluster		Fishing in Luapula River and Lake Mweru.
Shilluk	Collo	Sudan	Nilo-Saharan: E. Sudanic	c. 150,000	Western Nilotic cluster		Sedentary farmers. Centralized political organization. Divine king.
Shirazi		Kenya, Tanzania	Niger-Congo: Bantu	c. 300,000	Swahili cluster	Hadimu, Mbwera, Pemba, Tumbatu	Name used by southern Swahili groups claiming Persian origins. Actual origins were in northern Kenya coastal regions
Shluh		Morocco	Afro-Asiatic: Berber	no estimate			Grain farmers.
Shona	Mashona, Vashona	Botswana, Mozambique, Zambia, Zimbabwe	Niger-Congo: Bantu	>7 million	Shona-Thonga cluster	Karanga, Korekore, Manyika, Ndau, Tawara, Zezuru	Main group in Zimbabwe. Origins in early Zimbabwe kingdom. Mixed farmers, labor migrants. Traditional chiefs and prophets. Played major role in Zimbabwean fight for independence.
Shukriya		Sudan	Afro-Asiatic: Semitic	c. 150,000	Baggara		Camel pastoralists. Patrilineal.
Shuwa		Cameroon, Chad, Nigeria	Afro-Asiatic: Semitic	c. 2 million	Baggara		Lake Chad pastoralists. Patrilineal.
Sia		Burkina Faso, Mali	Niger-Congo: Mande	c. 150,000			Origins in Mali empire. Pastoral nomads. Many now farm (millet, sorghum) and raise cattle. Muslim. Patrilineal.
Sidamo		Ethiopia	Afro-Asiatic: C. Cushitic	c. 3 million	Sidamo cluster	Bako, Gibe, Bimira, Janjero, Kafa, Ometo	SW Ethiopia farmers and herders. Stratified. Tradition of powerful divine kingship.
Sihanaka		Madagascar	Malayo-Polynesian: Malagasy	c. 200,000	Central Highlands		Mostly rice farmers, cattle herders, fishing. Patrilineal.
Sisala	Sasala, Pisala, Isala	Burkina Faso, Ghana	Niger-Congo: Voltaic	c. 100,000	Grusi cluster		Sedentary farmers. Many work in cities. Patrilineal.
Soga	Basoga	Uganda	Niger-Congo: Bantu	>1.5 million	Interlacustrine Bantu		Mostly small farmers, including cash-crops. Several powerful chiefdoms. Patrilineal.
Sokoro		Chad	Afro-Asiatic: Chadic	c. 7,500	Bagirmi cluster		Herders, farmers. Patrilineal.
Soli	Asoli	Zambia	Niger-Congo: C. Bantu	c. 60,000	Tonga cluster		Small farmers. Matrilineal.
Somali	Somal	Djibouti, Ethiopia, Kenya, Somalia	Afro-Asiatic: Cushitic	c. 9 million			Traditional patoralists (cattle, camels). Now many in cities. Subgroups based on clan confederations. Clan rivalries frequently violent. Muslim.
Somba	Bataba, Batammaraba	Benin, Togo	Niger-Congo: Voltaic	c. 300,000	Barga cluster		Peasant farmers. Patrilineal.
Somrai		Chad	Afro-Asiatic: Chadic	c. 10,000	Bagirmi cluster		Herding and small-hold farming. Patrilineal.

(continued)

Name	Alternate name	Location	Linguistic affiliation	Population estimate	Group or cluster	Subgroups	Notes
Songe	Songye	Dem Rep Congo	Niger-Congo: C. Bantu	c. 1 million	Luba cluster	Zimba	Village farmers, traders. Famed for art. Patrilineal.
Songhai	Songhay, Songrai	Burkina Faso, Mali, Niger	Nilo-Saharan: Songhai	c. 2 million	Songhai cluster	Dendi, Zerma	Generic term for W. African groups derived from Songhai empire. Primarily Muslim. Traditional pastoralists. Also farmers. Many work in cities.
Songo	Basongo, Nsongo	Angola	Niger-Congo: C. Bantu	c. 50,000	Lunda cluster		Village farmers. Matrilineal.
Songola		Dem Rep Congo	Niger-Congo: Equatorial Bantu	c. 30,000			Fishing, small-hold farming. Patrilineal.
Soninké	Sarakole, Serahuli	Burkina Faso, Mali, Mauritania, Senegal	Niger-Congo: Mande	c. 1.1 million			Origins in Berbers of N. Africa. Traditionally traders, today mostly farmers, labor migrants to France. Descend from rulers of medieval Ghana. Muslim. Patrilineal.
Sonjo		Tanzania	Niger-Congo: Bantu	c. 12,000	Interlacustrine Bantu		Irrigated farming. Live among Maasai.
Sotho	Basuto	Botswana, Lesotho, S. Africa	Niger-Congo: Bantu	c. 7 million	Sotho cluster	Suto	Mainly language cluster. Groups include S. Sotho, Tswana, Pedi, Venda. Many are commercial farmers. Also miners, plantation workers, work in cities.
Suafa		Algeria	Afro-Asiatic: Arabic				Oasis farmers.
Subiya		Botswana, Zambia	Niger-Congo: Bantu	c. 15,000	Lozi cluster	Leya	Village farmers. Patrilineal.
Suk							SEE Pokot.
Suku		Dem Rep Congo	Niger-Congo: C. Bantu	c. 60,000	Kwango cluster		Village farmers. Matrilineal.
Sukuma		Tanzania	Niger-Congo: Bantu	c. 3 million	Nyamwezi cluster	Rongo, Shashi	Related to Nyamwezi. Traditional subsistence farmers, now cash-cropping (cotton, tobacco) is common.
Sumbwa		Tanzania	Niger-Congo: Bantu	c. 200,000	Nyamwezi cluster	Msalala	Primarily farmers. Patrilineal.
Sundi	Basundi	Angola, Congo, Dem Rep Congo	Niger-Congo: C. Bantu	c. 200,000	Kongo cluster	Bemba, Bwende, Dondo	Village farmers. Stratified. Matrilineal.
Suri		Ethiopia, Sudan	Nilo-Saharan: E. Sudanic	c. 35,000	Beir cluster	Surma	Cattle herders, farmers. Patrilineal.
Susu	Soso	Guinea, Guinea Bissau, Sierra Leone	Niger-Congo: Mande	c. 1.3 million	Mande cluster		Influential in politics, commerce in Guinea. Farmers. Muslim.
Suto	S. Sotho	Lesotho, S. Africa	Niger-Congo: Bantu	c. 2 million	Sotho cluster		One of 3 major Sotho language groups. Present population of Lesotho under ruling king. Labor migrants to S. Africa mines and farms.
Swahili		Kenya, Mozambique, Somalia, Tanzania	Niger-Congo: Bantu	c. >1.3 million	Coastal Bantu cluster		E. African coast dwellers. Middlemen between inland peoples and Indian Ocean trade (slaves, ivory, gold). Urbanized. Language is lingua franca throughout East Africa. Muslim.

(continued)

Name	Alternate name	Population estimate	Linguistic affiliation	Location	Group or cluster	Subgroups	Notes
Swazi	Swati	>2 million	Niger-Congo: S. Bantu	S. Africa, Swaziland	Nguni cluster		Swazi kingdom. Traditionally cattle herders. Many now farm (maize, millet, rice, groundnuts) and work in minds of S. Africa, also timber and sugar plantations. Driven here by Zulu expansion. Patrilineal
T							
Tabwa		c. 200,000	Niger-Congo: C. Bantu	Tanzania, Dem Rep Congo, Zambia	Bemba cluster		Farming, cattle keeping. Matrilineal.
Tallensi		c. 300,000	Niger-Congo: Voltaic	Ghana	Mole cluster		Mostly settled farmers (sorghum, millet). Patrilineal.
Tama		c. 200,000	Nilo-Saharan: E. Sudanic	Chad, Sudan	Darfur cluster		Peoples of the Chad/Sudan region. Village farmers, herders. Patrilineal.
Tanala		c. 420,000	Malayo-Polynesian: Malagasy	Madagascar	Central Highlands		Traditionally hunters. Now commercial farmers (rice, coffee) Patrilineal.
Tangale	Biliri	c. 200,000	Afro-Asiatic: Chadic	Nigeria	Plateau		Village farmers. Patrilineal.
Tatoga		c. 40,000	Nilo-Saharan: E. Sudanic	Tanzania	Kalenjin cluster	Barabaig	Cattle herders. Patrilineal.
Tavara		c. 14,000	Niger-Congo: Bantu	Zimbabwe	Shona cluster		Subgroup of Korekore. Village farmers. Patrilineal.
Taveta		c. 12,000	Niger-Congo: NE Bantu	Kenya			Mixed farmers. Originally traders for interior-coastal trade.
Tawana	Batawana	c. 116,000	Niger-Congo: Bantu	Botswana	Tswana cluster		Traditionally cattle herders. Many work mines and at wage labor. Patrilineal.
Tazarawa		c. 1 million	Afro-Asiatic: Chadic	Niger	Hausa cluster		Remnant groups of Northern Hausa. Muslims.
Teda	Tebu, Tibbu, Tubu	c. 40,000	Nilo-Saharan: Saharan	Chad, Libya, Niger	Tibesti cluster		Live primarily in Tibesti Mountains. Camel, goat herding. Clan-based subgroups. Muslims.
Teita	Taita	c. 250,000	Niger-Congo: Bantu	Kenya	NE Bantu		Mostly farmers. Stateless. Patrilineal.
Tekna		no etsimate	Afro-Asiatic: Berber	Morocco, W. Sahara			Mixed farmers, pastoralists.
Tem	Kotokoli, Temba	c. 350,000	Niger-Congo: Voltaic	Benin, Ghana, Togo	Kabu cluster		Village farmers. Mostly Muslim. Patrilineal.
Tembu	Thembu	c. 310,000	Niger-Congo: Bantu	S. Africa	Nguni cluster	Bomvana, Mpondomisi, Ngabe.	One of Nguni's societies. Farming, herding people of the Transkei.
Temne	Timne	c. 1.5 million	Niger-Congo: W. Atlantic	Guinea, Sierra Leone	Temne cluster		Migrated to region prior to 15th century. Mostly rice farmers, also groundnuts, palm oil, tobacco, kola, ginger. Patrilineal.
Tenda	Tanda	c. 30,000	Niger-Congo: W. Atlantic	Guinea, Senegal	Senegambia cluster	Bassari, Boeni, Koniagi	Rice farmers. Only the Boeni are Muslim. Patrilineal.

(continued)

Name	Alternate name	Location	Linguistic affiliation	Population estimate	Group or cluster	Subgroups	Notes
Tera		Nigeria	Afro-Asiatic: Chadic	c. 60,000	Bornu cluster		Trade, services, manufacturing, farming. Partly Muslim.
Teso							SEE: Iteso.
Tetela		Dem Rep Congo	Niger-Congo: Equatorial Bantu	c. 750,000	Mongo cluster		Fishing, trading, farming. Patrilineal.
Teuso	Ik	Uganda	Nilo-Saharan: E. Sudanic	c. 5,000			Remnant elephant hunters. Now refugees after Uganda government removed them from their territory to create a tourist park.
Tharaka		Kenya	Niger-Congo: NE Bantu	c. 100,000	Meru cluster		Mostly farmers. Live on Mt. Kenya. Patrilineal.
Thonga	Tsonga	Mozambique, S. Africa, Zimbabwe	Niger-Congo: Bantu	c. 4 million	Shona-Thonga cluster	Chopi, Hengwe, Lenge, Ronga	Herding and farming peoples to North and West of Zululand. Include many Nguni immigrants (Shangaan).
Tienga		Burkina Faso	Niger-Congo: Mande	c. 40,000			Origins in Mali Empire. Pastoralists, peasant farmers. Part Muslim. Patrilineal.
Tigre		Eritrea, Ethiopia	Afro-Asiatic: Semitic	c. 2 million			Main group of Eritrea. Pastoralists and farmers. Muslims and Christians. Speak Tigrinya.
Tikar	Fut, Bafut	Cameroon	Niger-Congo: Kwa	c. 40,000	Cameroon Highlands cluster		Several independent kingdoms, distinct languages. Mostly farmers. Known for crafts: metalworking, pottery, sculpture. Patrilineal.
Tindiga							SEE Hadza.
Tio	Teke	Congo Dem. Rep. Congo	Niger-Congo: NW Bantu	c. 60,000			15th century kingdom based on Dem Rep Congo River trade. Matrilineal.
Tiv	Munshi	Nigeria	Niger-Congo: Kwa	c. 2.5 million	Plateau		Farmers. Stateless. Patrilineal.
Tlokwa	Batlokwa	Botswana	Niger-Congo: Bantu	no estimate	Tswana cluster	Birwa, Malate, Molepa	Tswana chiefdom. Mostly farmers, herders. Patrilineal
Toma	Loma	Liberia, Sierra Leone	Niger-Congo: Mande	c. 200,000	Mende cluster		Rice farmers. Patrilineal.
Tonga	Batonga	Malawi, Zambia, Zimbabwe	Niger-Congo: C. Bantu	>800,000	Tonga cluster	Ronga, Shangana, Tswa	Maize farmers. Plateau and Lakeside groups. Stateless. Patrilineal.
Topotha	Toposa	Sudan	Nilo-Saharan: Eastern Sudanic	c. 100,000	Eastern Nilotic	Conyiro, Nyanjatom	Pastoralists. Stateless. Patrilineal.
Toro		Uganda	Niger-Congo: Bantu	c. 700,000	Interlacustrine cluster		Kingdom. Mixed farmers. Patrilineal.
Trarza		Mauritania	Afro-Asiatic: Berber	no estimate			Farmers. Main group of Mauritania.
Tsimihety		Madagascar	Malayo-Polynesian: Malagasy	>700,000	Northern Highlands		Rice farmers, cattle herders. Patrilineal.
Tsonga							SEE Thonga.

(continued)

Name	Alternate name	Location	Linguistic affiliation	Population estimate	Group or cluster	Subgroups	Notes
Tswana		Botswana, Namibia, S. Africa	Niger-Congo: Bantu	>5 million	Tswana cluster		Indigenes of Botswana. Mixed farmers, herders. Several powerful chiefdoms, now united under one king (Botswana president). Much labor migration to S. Africa.
Tuareg	Asben, Aulliminden	Burkina Faso, Mali, Niger, N. Africa	Afro-Asiatic: Berber	c. 1 million		Ahaggaren, Antessar, Asben, Aulliminden, Azjer, Ifora, Udalan	Traditional desert pastoralists. Complex stratification, with slaves. Muslim. Patrilineal.
Tuburi	Tupur	Cameroon, Chad, Nigeria	Afro-Asiatic: Chadoc	c. 400,000	Plateau		Fishing, cattle herding, terrace farming. Patrilineal.
Tugen	Kamasya, Tuken	Kenya	Nilo-Saharan: E. Sudanic	c. 200,000	Kalenjin cluster		Terrace farmers. Patrilineal.
Tukulor	Toucouleur	Mauritania, Senegal	Niger-Congo: W. Atlantic	C. 1 million	Fulani cluster		Commercial farmers. Muslim. Patrilineal.
Tulama	Galla, Shoa, Tulema	Ethiopia	Afro-Asiatic: E. Cushitic	no estimate	Oromo cluster		Mostly sedentary farmers. Patrilineal.
Tumbuka	Butumbuka, Matumbuka	Malawi, Zambia	Niger-Congo: C. Bantu	c. 2 million	Maravi cluster	Fungwe, Henga, Kamanga, Kandawire, Sisya	Loose confederation (18th c.). Mostly village farmers. Patrilineal.
Tunjur		Chad, Sudan	Afro-Asiatic: Semitic	c. 163,000	Baggara cluster		Mainly pastoralists. Tunjur kingdom flourished in 16th century. Muslim. Patrilineal.
Turkana		Kenya	Nilo-Saharan: E. Sudanic	c. 300,000	Karamojong cluster		Desert pastoralists, related to Maasai. Stateless. Local government by age-sets and councils.
Turu	Nyaturu	Tanzania	Niger-Congo: Bantu	c. 500,000	Central Bantu Rift cluster		Mostly mixed farmers. Patrilineal.
Tusyan	Toussain	Burkina Faso, Cote d'Ivoire	Niger-Congo: Voltaic	c. 60,000	Lobi cluster		Mostly farmers. Patrilineal.
Tutsi	Batutsi, Tussi, Watutsi	Burundi, Rwanda, Uganda	Niger-Congo: Bantu	c. 3.1 million	Interlacustrine Bantu		Historically dominant in Rwanda. Hutu/Tutsi rivalries of 1990s led to civil war. Called Hima in Uganda.
Twa	Cwa, Chwa	Burundi, Rwanda, Dem Rep Congo	Niger-Congo: Bantu	c. 100,000	Pygmy cluster		Pygmy related groups of Rwanda and Burundi. Traditional hunters and gatherers, have served as troops for former Tutsi rulers.
U							
Udalan		Mali	Afro-Asiatic: Berber	no estimate			Mixed farmers.
Uduk	Udok	Sudan	Nilo-Saharan: Koman	c. 15,000	Koman cluster		Mixed farmers. Raided for Arab slave trade. Matrilineal.
Unga		Zambia	Niger-Congo: Central Bantu	c. 25,000	Bemba cluster		Live in swamp region of Lake Bangweulu. Fishing. Matrilineal.
Urhobo							SEE Isoko.

(continued)

Name	Alternate name	Location	Linguistic affiliation	Population estimate	Group or cluster	Subgroups	Notes
V							
Vagala	Vigala, Vagele	Burkina Faso, Ghana	Niger-Congo: Voltaic	c. 50,000	Grusi cluster		Village farmers. Patrilineal.
Vai		Liberia, Sierra Leone	Niger-Congo: Mande	c. 150,000	Mende cluster		Origins in Mali. Migrated c. 16th century. Village agriculturalists. Mostly Muslim. Have own script, literature
Venda	Bavenda	South Africa	Niger-Congo: Bantu	c. 720,000	Sotho cluster	Lemba	Chiefdoms. Farmers. Patrilineal.
Vere	Werre	Cameroon, Nigeria	Niger-Congo: Adamawa-Ubangi	c. 25,000	Plateau		Village farmers. Patrilineal.
Vili		Angola, Congo, Gabon, Dem Rep Congo	Niger-Congo: Central Bantu	c. 20,000	Kongo cluster	Kakongo	Traditionally farmers, fishing, hunting, trade (salt, palmcloth, ivory, slaves). Matrilineal
W							
Wala	Oule, Walba, Walo	Burkina Faso, Cote d'Ivoire	Niger Congo	c. 120,000	Mole cluster		Village farming. Patrilineal.
Walaga	Walega	Ethiopia	Afro-Asiatic: E. Cushitic	c. 1 million	Oromo cluster	Macha (Merja)	Village farming, herding. Muslims and Christians.
Wallo		Ethiopia	Afro-Asiatic: E. Cushitic	c. 1 million	Oromo cluster	Tulama	Mixed with Amhara. Village farmers, herders. Muslims and Christians.
Wanga		Kenya	Niger-Congo: Bantu	c. 100,000	Interlacustrine cluster		Small kingdom based on trade. One of the modern Luhya groiup.
Warain		Morocco, W. Sahara	Afro-Asiatic: Berber	no estimate			Mixed farmers. Pastoralists.
Widekum		Cameroon	Niger-Congo: Kwa	c. 230,000	Cameroon Highland cluster	Bofang, Esimbi, Menka, Meta, Ngemba, Ngwo	Village farmers (maize, millet, coffee). Stateless. Patrilineal.
Witbooi		Namibia	Afrikaans	no estimate	Khoisan cluster, Oorlam group		Mostly merged with Nama. Led by Hendrik Witbooi and family. The group no longer exists.
Wobé	Ouobe	Cote d'Ivoire, Liberia	Niger-Congo: Kwa	c. 100,000	Kru cluster		Village farmers. Patrilineal.
Wodaabe							SEE Bororo
Wolof	Jolof, Oulof	Gambia, Senegal	Niger-Congo: W. Atlantic	c. 3 million	Senegambia cluster	Lebu	Came to Senegambia c. 15th century. Language serves as regional lingua franca. Dominate in politics, business, professions. Rice farming. Muslim.
Wum	Aghem	Cameroon	Niger-Congo: Kwa	c. 30,000	Cameroon Highland cluster		Farming, fishing. Kingdoms. Matrilineal descent.
X							
Xam		South Africa	Click	no estimate			Also called "Cape Bushmen." Extinct.
Xhosa	Xosa	South Africa	Niger-Conto: Bantu	>6 million	Nguni cluster		Largest of Cape Nguni cluster. Mixed farmers, herders. Dispersed across S. Africa. Each group has own king/ruler. Patrilineal.

(continued)

Name	Alternate name	Location	Linguistic affiliation	Population estimate	Group or cluster	Subgroups	Notes
Y							
Yaka		Angola, Dem Rep Congo	Niger-Congo: Central Bantu	c. 1 million	Kwango cluster		Village farmers. Famed for art. Matrilineal.
Yakō			Niger-Congo: Benue Congo	c. 150,000	Ibibio cluster	Abayong, Agoi, Akunakuan	Village farmers, traders. Stateless. Double descent.
Yakoma		Central African Republic	Niger-Congo: Adamawa-Ubangi	c. 80,000	Ubangi cluster		Farming, fishing. Patrilineal.
Yanzi		Dem Rep Congo	Niger-Congo: Central Bantu	no estimate	Kasai cluster	Ampur	Village farmers. Matrilineal.
Yao	Wayao	Malawi, Tanzania	Niger-Congo: Bantu	>1.6 million	Yao cluster		Ethnolinguistic group. Served as go-betweens in trade (ivory, slaves, tobacco, cloth, guns) with Swahili and interior groups. Stateless. Mostly Muslim. Matrilineal.
Yeke		Dem Rep Congo	Niger-Congo: Central Bantu	no estimate	Luba cluster		Descend from independent Nyamwezi traders who settled in region.
Yeskwa	Yasgua	Nigeria	Niger-Congo: Kwa	c. 25,000	Plateau		Village farmers. Patrilineal.
Yombe	Mayombe	Angola, Congo, Dem Rep Congo	Niger-Congo: Central Bantu	c. 150,000	Kongo cluster		Most live in Yombe Mountain region. Mostly farmers. Matrilineal.
Yoruba	Nago	Benin, Ghana, Niger, Nigeria, Sierra Leone, Togo	Niger-Congo: Kwa	>20 million	Yoruba cluster	Ibadan, Igbolo, Igbara, Ilorin, Oyo	Generic name for people of several Yoruba kingdoms. Mixed farming, urban trading. Traditional religion powerful. Mostly Christian and Muslim converts.
Yungur	Binna	Nigeria	Niger-Congo: Adamawa-Ubangi	c. 100,000	Plateau		Village farming. Patrilineal.
Z							
Zaghawa		Chad, Sudan	Nilo-Saharan: Saharan	>200,000	Darfur cluster		Closely related to Berti. Sedentary farmers, some livestock. Seasonal migrants to Libya for wage work. Sunni Muslim. Patrilineal.
Zanaki		Tanzania		c. 72,000			Subgroups: Bira, Bahari. Primarily farmers, cattlekeepers.
Zaramo		Tanzania	Niger-Congo: Central Bantu	c. 400,000			Predominantly agriculturalists. Heavily raided during E. African slave trade. Mostly Muslim.
Zekara		Morocco, Algeria	Afro-Asiatic: Berber	no estimate			Grain farming.
Zenaga		Mauritania	Afro-Asiatic: Berber	no estimate			Mixed farming.
Zerma		Benin, Burkina Faso, Mali, Niger, Nigeria	Nilo-Saharan: Songhai	c. 3.5 million			Primarily subsistence farming, some cattlekeeping. Muslim

(continued)

Name	Alternate name	Location	Linguistic affiliation	Population estimate	Group or cluster	Subgroups	Notes
Zezuru		Mozambique, Zimbabwe	Niger-Congo: Bantu	no estimate			Primarily subsistance farming, cattlekeepers. Part of Shona nation.
Zigua		Tanzania	Niger-Congo: NE Bantu	c. 350,000			Predominantly farmers. Mostly Muslim.
Zimba		Malawi	Niger-Congo: Central Bantu	no estimate			Village farmers. Matrilineal descent.
Zinza		Tanzania	Niger-Congo: Bantu	150,000			Cattlekeeping and agriculture, skilled ironworkers. Chiefdoms. Patrilineal.
Zombo		Angola, Dem Rep Congo	Bantu: Kongo	no estimate			Originally part of Kongo Kingdom. Specialized in trade (17th to 20th c.). Village farmers. Matrilineal.
Zulu	AmaZulu	Lesotho, Malawi, S. Africa, Swaziland	Niger-Congo: Bantu	>8.5 million (S. Africa), 300,000 elsewhere	S. Bantu group, Nguni cluster	Bhaca, Bhele, Hlubii, Zizi	Mainly in KwaZulu and Natal, S. Africa. Agriculture and pastoralism (cattle, sheep, goats/millet, maize, legumes). High labor migration. Fnded by Shaka in early 19th c.
Zumper	Kuted, Kutev	Nigeria, Cameroon	Niger-Congo: Benue-Congo	c. 50,000	Plateau		Village farmers. Patrilineal descent.

DIRECTORY OF CONTRIBUTORS

† = DECEASED

JON ABBINK
Leiden University, African Studies Centre
Senior Researcher
    Warfare: Overview

ISMAIL H. ABDALLA
College of William and Mary, Department of History
Professor
    Healing and Health Care: Islamic Medicine
    Islam: Overview
    Pilgrimages, Islamic

GARIBA ABDUL-KORAH
The College of Saint Rose, Department of History and Political Science
Assistant Professor
    Ghana: Geography and Economy

WILLIAM M. ADAMS
University of Cambridge, Department of Geography
Professor
    Water and Irrigation

WILLIAM Y. ADAMS
University of Kentucky, Department of Anthropology
Professor Emeritus
    Nubia

AGBENYEGA TONY ADEDZE
Illinois State University, Department of History
Associate Professor
    Museums: Memory

MORADEWUN ADEJUNMOBI
University of California, Davis, Department of African American and African Studies
Associate Professor and Director
    Literatures in African Languages: Malagasy

OLUTAYO ADESINA
University of Ibadan, Nigeria, Department of History
Professor
    Adama, Modibbo
    Du Bois, W. E. B.
    Ibadan
    Nigeria: Society and Cultures, Northwest Nigeria

CLEMENT EMENIKE ADIBE
DePaul University, Department of Political Science
Associate Professor
    United Nations: Africa in the United Nations

ALI JIMALE AHMED
Queens College and the Graduate Center of the City University of New York, Department of Comparative Literature
Professor
    Literatures in African Languages: Somali

ALI AHMIDA
University of New England, Department of Political Science
Chair and Professor
    Libya: History and Politics

J. F. ADE AJAYI
University of Ibadan, Nigeria, Department of History
Professor Emeritus
    Crowther, Samuel Ajayi
    Johnson, Samuel
    Kano, Alhaji Aminu
    Macaulay, Zachary

S. ADEMOLA AJAYI
University of Ibadan, Nigeria, Department of History
Senior Lecturer
    'Ali, Mohammed Duse
    Freetown
    Harris, William Wadé
    Kano

G. A. AKINOLA
University of Ibadan, Department of History
Professor
Colonialism and Imperialism: The African Experience

AKÍNTÚNDÉ AKÍNYEMÍ
University of Florida, Department of African and Asian Languages and Literatures
Associate Professor
Literatures in African Languages: Yorùbá

HEATHER MARIE AKOU
Indiana University, Department of Apparel Merchandising and Interior Design
Assistant Professor
Body Adornment and Clothing: Trade

E. J. ALAGOA
University of Port Harcourt, Department of History
Professor Emeritus
Historiography: Oral

ERDMUTE ALBER
University of Bayreuth, Department of Ethnology
Professor
Bénin: Society and Cultures

PETER ALEGI
Michigan State University, Department of History
Assistant Professor
Sports: Overview

RICHARD ALLEN
Worcester, MA
Research Consultant
Mauritius: Geography and Economy
Mauritius: Society and Cultures
Réunion
Seychelles: Geography and Economy

Seychelles: History and Politics
Seychelles: Society and Cultures

TIM ALLEN
London School of Economics, Development Studies Institute
University Reader
Aid and Development: Humanitarian Assistance

CLAUDE ALLIBERT
Centre d'Etude et de Recherches sur l'Ocean Indien occidental
Director
Indian Ocean, Africa, History of (1000 BCE to 600 CE)

EDWARD A. ALPERS
University of California, Los Angeles, Department of History
Professor
Ivory

HOYT ALVERSON
Dartmouth College, Department of Anthropology
Professor
Names and Naming

IFI AMADIUME
Dartmouth College, Department of Religion
Professor
Diop, Cheikh Anta

CHARLES H. AMBLER
University of Texas at El Paso, Department of History
Professor
Stimulants and Intoxicants: Alcohol
Urbanism and Urbanization: Historic

DAVID AMBROSE
National University of Lesotho
Associate Professor
Maseru

SAMIR AMIN
Third World Forum
Director
Neocolonialism

KHALID AMINE
Abdelmalek Essaâ University, Department of English
Senior Professor
Theater: Northern Africa

KWASI AMPENE
University of Colorado-Boulder, College of Music, Department of Musicology
Associate Professor
Mensah, E. T.

KWAME ANTHONY APPIAH
Princeton University, Department of Philosophy
Professor
Philosophy and the Study of Africa

ANDREW APTER
University of California, Los Angeles, Departments of History and Anthropology
Professor
Festivals and Carnivals

CLAUDE ARDOUIN
British Museum, Department of Africa, Oceania, and the Americas, Africa Section
Curator
Museums: History

NICOLAS ARGENTI
Brunel University, School of Social Sciences
Research Lecturer
Youth: Movements
Youth: Rural

JOHN ARGYLE
University of Natal, Department of Social Anthropology
Professor Emeritus
Dance: Social Meaning

MARY JO ARNOLDI
National Museum of Natural History, Smithsonian Institution, Department of Anthropology
Curator
    Masks and Masquerades: Sub-Saharan Africa

KELLY M. ASKEW
University of Michigan, Department of Anthropology and Center for Afroamerican and African Studies
Associate Professor
    Mongella, Gertrude I.
    Socialism and Postsocialisms

RALPH A. AUSTEN
University of Chicago, Department of History
Professor Emeritus
    Economic History
    Slave Trades: Northeastern Africa and Red Sea

TOKUNBO AYOOLA
Tulane University, Department of History
Assistant Professor
    Transportation: Railways

MARIO AZEVEDO
Jackson State University, Department of Epidemiology and Biostatistics
Professor
    Bokassa, Jean-Bédel
    Central African Republic: History and Politics
    Chad: Geography and Economy

CHUKWUMA AZUONYE
University of Massachusetts at Boston, Department of Africana Studies
Professor
    Literature: Modern Poetry

O. BABALOLA
University of Ibadan, Nigeria, Department of Agronomy
Professor
    Soils

TESSY D. BAKARY
Laval University, Department of Political Science
Professor
    Houphouët-Boigny, Félix

AIDA BAMIA
University of Florida, Department of African and Asian Languages and Literatures
Professor Emeritus
    Literatures in African Languages: Arabic

MWESIGA BAREGU
University of Dar es Salaam, Department of Political Science
Professor
    Nyerere, Julius Kambarage
    Tanzania: History and Politics

LAWRENCE S. BARHAM
University of Liverpool, School of Archaeology, Classics, and Egyptology
Professor
    Archaeology and Prehistory: Stone Age Societies

BAWURO M. BARKINDO
National Boundary Commission, Lagos
    Kanemi, Muhammad al-Amin al-

NIGEL BARLEY
British Museum, Department of Ethnography
Assistant Keeper
    Ceramics

ALAN BARNARD
University of Edinburgh, Scotland, School of Social and Political Studies
Professor
    Botswana: Society and Cultures
    Kinship and Descent

SANDRA T. BARNES
University of Pennsylvania, Department of Anthropology
Professor
    Lagos
    Nigeria: Society and Cultures, Southwest Nigeria

TERESA BARNES
University of the Western Cape, Department of History
Associate Professor
    Harare

JOHNATHAN B. BASCOM
Calvin College, Department of Geography
Professor
    Sudan: Geography and Economy

IAN BAUCOM
Duke University, Department of English
Chair
    Gordimer, Nadine
    Nwapa, Flora
    Schreiner, Olive
    Sekhukhune I
    Tutuola, Amos

ROBERT M. BAUM
University of Missouri, Columbia, Department of Religious Studies
Associate Professor
    Women: Women and Non-Islamic Religion

EDNA G. BAY
Emory University, Graduate Institute of the Liberal Arts

Professor
> Ouidah
> Western Africa, Forest
>> Region, History of (1000
>> to 1880)

CYNTHIA BECKER
*Boston University, Department of
Art History*
Assistant Professor
> Masks and Masquerades:
>> Northern Africa

HEIKE BEHREND
*University of Cologne, Institute of
African Studies*
Professor
> Lakwena, Alice
> Photography: Aesthetics and
>> Social Significance

T. O. BEIDELMAN
*New York University, Department
of Anthropology*
Professor
> Anthropology, Social, and
>> the Study of Africa
> Kings and Kingdoms

MHAMMAD BENABOUD
*Abdelmalek Essaadi University,
Tetouan, Morocco, Faculty of
Letters, Department of History*
Professor
> Tétouan

WOLFGANG BENDER
*Johannes Gütenberg-Universität,
Mainz, Institut für Ethnologie
und Afrika-Studien*
Professor
> Music, Modern Popular:
>> Overview

F. JOHN BENNETT
Primary Health Care
Consultant
> Disease: Sexually Transmitted
> Healing and Health Care:
>> Hospitals and Clinics

PATRICK BENNETT
*University of Wisconsin,
Department of African Studies*
Professor Emeritus
> Writing Systems: African
>> Scripts
> Writing Systems: Overview

MARLA C. BERNS
*University of California, Los
Angeles, Fowler Museum*
Director
> Odundo, Magdalene

STEPHANIE F. BESWICK
*Ball State University, Department
of History*
Associate Professor
> Sudan, Eastern, History of
>> (1500 to 1880 CE)

J. JOOST BEUVING
*Free University Amsterdam,
Faculty of Social Sciences,
Department of Social Research
Methodology*
University Lecturer
> Immigration and Immigrant
>> Groups: Lebanese

SURENDRA BHANA
*University of Kansas, Department
of History*
Professor Emeritus
> Immigration and Immigrant
>> Groups: Indian

ANN BIERSTEKER
*Yale University, Departments of
African Studies and Linguistics*
Associate Professor
> Farah, Nuruddin
> Languages: Malayo-
>> Polynesian
> Literature: Translation
> Literatures in European
>> Languages: Anglophone
>> Eastern Africa
> Lopes, Henri
> Maathai, Wangari

DAVID BIRMINGHAM
*University of Kent at
Canterbury, Department of
History*
Professor Emeritus
> Colonial Policies and
>> Practices: Portuguese

WILLIAM BISSELL
*Lafayette College, Department of
Anthropology and Sociology*
Assistant Professor
> Architecture: Town Planning
> Zanzibar City

HELMUT BLEY
*University of Hannover,
Department of History*
Professor Emeritus
> Colonial Policies and
>> Practices: German

HARVEY BLUME
Independent Scholar
> Benga, Ota

NEMATA BLYDEN
*George Washington University,
Department of History*
Associate Professor
> Garvey, Marcus Mosiah
> Immigration and Immigrant
>> Groups: African
>> American

ALEX BOATENG
*Gateway Community College,
Department of Humanities*
Instructor
> Theater: Anglophone
>> Western Africa

BOUBACAR BOCOUM
*World Bank, Department of Oil,
Gas, Mining, and Chemicals*
Project Officer
> Production Strategies:
>> Mining, Modern

MICHAEL BOLLIG
Institut für Völkerkunde, Universität zu Köln, Department of Philosophy
Professor
Production Strategies:
Peripatetic Production

GEORGE CLEMENT BOND
Columbia University, Teachers College, Program in Anthropology and Education
Professor
Lenshina, Alice
Prophetic Movements:
Central Africa
Zambia: Geography and
Economy
Zambia: Society and Cultures

MICHAEL E. BONINE
University of Arizona, Tucson, Department of Geography
Professor
Tripoli

CHARLES BONN
University of Lyon, Department of Comparative Literatures
Professeur Emérite
Kateb, Yacine

ALAN R. BOOTH
Ohio University, Department of History
Professor
Sobhuza I and II

CHRISTO BOTHA
University of Namibia, Department of History
Professor
Namibia: Geography and
Economy

JANE BOULDEN
Royal Military College of Canada, Department of Politics and Economics
Canada Research Chair

United Nations: United
Nations in Africa

MICHAEL BOURDILLON
University of Zimbabwe, Department of Sociology
Professor Emeritus
Labor: Child

LOUISE M. BOURGAULT
Northern Michigan University, Department of Communication and Performance Studies
Professor
Media: Overview

ARTHUR BOURGEOIS
Governors State University, Illinois, Department of Art
Professor
Art, Regional Styles: Central
Africa

CYNTHIA GRANT BOWMAN
Cornell University, School of Law
Professor
Women: Women and the
Law

STEVEN BRANDT
University of Florida, Department of Anthropology
Associate Professor
Plants: Domestication

MICHAEL BRATTON
Michigan State University, Department of Political Science
Professor
Kaunda, Kenneth

DEBORAH BRAUTIGAM
American University, School of International Service
Associate Professor
Immigration and Immigrant
Groups: Chinese

COLIN BREEN
University of Ulster, Centre for Maritime Archaeology

Lecturer
Archaeology and Prehistory:
Marine

NANA ARHIN BREMPONG
National Commission on Culture, Ghana
Director
Osei Tutu
Prempeh, Agyeman

CAROL BRENNAN
Freelance Writer
Zambezi River

LOUIS BRENNER
University of London, School of Oriental and Asian Studies, Department of History
Professor Emeritus
Hamallah of Nioro
Mukhtar, Sidi al-

MICHAEL BRETT
University of London, School of Oriental and African Studies, Department of History
Emeritus Reader
Egypt, Early: Islamic
Immigration and Immigrant
Groups: Arab

ROY C. BRIDGES
Aberdeen University, Department of History
Professor Emeritus
Livingstone, David

DAVID WARWICK BROKENSHA
University of Cape Town, Department of Social Anthropology
Honorary Professor
Energy: Domestic

GEORGE E. BROOKS
Indiana University at Bloomington, Department of History
Professor Emeritus
Correia, Mãe Aurélia

KENNETH L. BROWN
Mediterraneans /
Méditerranéennes
Founding Editor
    Rabat and Salé

L. CARL BROWN
Princeton University,
Department of Near
Eastern Studies
Professor Emeritus
    Colonial Policies and
        Practices: French North
        Africa
    Northern Africa: Historical
        Links with
        Mediterranean

DEBORAH FAHY BRYCESON
Oxford University, African
Studies Centre
Research Associate
    Peasants: Eastern Africa

LYNNE BRYDON
Centre of West African Studies,
University of Birmingham
Senior Lecturer
    Education, School:
        Anglophone Western
        Africa

PHILIP BURNHAM
University College London,
Department of Anthropology
Professor
    Cameroon: Society and
        Cultures

EDOUARD BUSTIN
Boston University, African Studies
Center
Professor
    Colonial Policies and
        Practices: Belgian

ANDREW BYERLEY
Stockholm University, Sweden,
Department of Human Geography
Researcher

Uganda: Geography and
    Economy

KATHARYN CALDERA
University of California at
Berkeley, Department of
Anthropology
    Luanda
    Yaoundé

JOHN C. CALDWELL
Australian National University,
Canberra, Research School of
Social Science, Demography and
Sociology Program
Professor Emeritus
    Demography: Population
        Data and Surveys

JEFFREY CALLEN
University of California at Los
Angeles, Department of
Ethnomusicology
Postdoctoral Fellow
    Music, Modern Popular:
        Northern Africa

BRUCE CAMPBELL
Charles Darwin University, School
for Environmental Research
Director
    Plants: Varieties and Uses

GWYN CAMPBELL
McGill University, Indian Ocean
World Centre, Department of
History
Canada Research Chair
    Madagascar and Western
        Indian Ocean, History of
        (Early to 1500)
    Slave Trades: Indian Ocean

MARIA CARDEIRA DA SILVA
Universidade Nova de Lisboa,
Department of Anthropology
Professor
    Mauritania: Geography and
        Economy

MARGRET CAREY
Independent scholar
    Arts: Beads
    Arts: Sculpture

VINCENT CARRETTA
University of Maryland,
Department of English
Professor
    Equiano, Olaudah

NEIL CARRIER
St Antony's College, Centre for
African Studies
Postdoctoral Fellow
    Stimulants and Intoxicants:
        Overview

REBECCA CASSIDY
Goldsmiths College, University of
London, Department of
Anthropology
Senior Lecturer
    Symbols and Symbolism:
        Animal

A. PETER CASTRO
Syracuse University, Maxwell
School, Department of
Anthropology
Associate Professor
    Energy: Domestic
    Forestry: Eastern Africa

ELIZABETH CHALLINOR
CRIA-Network Centre for
Anthropological Research, Lisbon,
Portugal
Researcher
    Cape Verde: Geography and
        Economy

ERIC CHARRY
Wesleyan University, Department
of Music
Associate Professor
    Ethnomusicology and the
        Study of Africa
    Keita, Fodeba
    Keita, Salif
    N'Dour, Youssou

DAVID CHIDESTER
University of Cape Town,
Department of Religious Studies
Professor
> Religion and the Study of
> Africa

LUCY CHIPETA
University of Malawi,
Department of Geography and
Earth Sciences
Lecturer
> Blantyre

DIANE CIEKAWY
Ohio University, Department of
Sociology and Anthropology
Associate Professor
> Witchcraft: Witchcraft and
> Prophetism

JULIA CLANCY-SMITH
University of Arizona,
Department of History
Associate Professor
> Bin Shaykh, Tawhida
> Bouhired, Djamila
> Djebar, Assia

GILLIAN CLARK
University of Bristol, Department
of Classics and Ancient History
Professor
> Augustine of Hippo, Saint

JOHN F. CLARK
Florida International University,
Department of International
Relations
Associate Professor
> Congo, Republic of: History
> and Politics

DUNCAN CLARKE
Independent Scholar
> Textiles

TIMOTHY DALE
CLEAVELAND
University of Georgia,
Department of History

Associate Professor
> Walāta

REGINALD A. CLINE-COLE
University of Birmingham, Centre
of West African Studies
Senior Lecturer
> Forestry: Western Africa

JULIET CLUTTON-BROCK
Natural History Museum,
London, Department of Zoology
> Livestock: Domestication

JAMES R. COCHRANE
University of Cape Town,
Department of Religious Studies
Professor
> Huddleston, Trevor

MICHELLE COCHRANE
University of California, Berkeley,
Department of Public Health
Postdoctoral Fellow
> Disease: HIV/AIDS,
> Medical Aspects

RONALD COHEN
University of Florida, Department
of Anthropology
Professor Emeritus
> Government: Historical
> Political Systems

E. JOHN COLLINS
University of Ghana at Legon,
School of Performing Arts,
Department of Music
Professor
> Music, Modern Popular:
> Western Africa

ROBERT O. COLLINS
University of California, Santa
Barbara, Department of History
Professor Emeritus
> Nile River
> Transportation: River

BARBARA COOPER
Rutgers University, Department
of History
Director
> Niger: Society and Cultures

FREDERICK COOPER
New York University, Department
of History
Professor
> Colonialism and Imperialism:
> Overview
> Decolonization

JEREMY COOTE
University of Oxford, Pitt Rivers
Museum
Joint Head of Collections
> Art, Regional Styles: Eastern
> Africa

R. L. COPE
University of the Witwatersrand,
Department of History
Professor Emeritus
> Cetshwayo

ELISABETH COPET-
ROUGIER†
Collège de France
Professor Emeritus
> Marriage Systems

DAVID B. COPLAN
University of the Witwatersrand,
Johannesburg, Department of
Anthropology
Professor
> Popular Culture: Southern
> Africa

CATHERINE COQUERY-
VIDROVITCH
Université Diderot-Paris-7,
Laboratoire SEDET/CNRS
(Sociétés en Développement dans
l'Espace et le Temps)
Professor Emerita
> Colonial Policies and
> Practices: French West
> and Equatorial Africa

Gender: Overview
Production Strategies:
Overview
Women: Overview

RAYMOND CORBEY
Leiden University, Department of Archaeology
Professor
Heritage, Cultural: Trade

DENNIS D. CORDELL
Southern Methodist University, Clements Department of History
Professor
Demography: Overview

ANTONIO CORREIA E SILVA
University of Cape Verde
Director
Cape Verde: Society and Cultures

LOUISE CRANE†
Durham, NC
Games

EVE L. CROWLEY
Rural Institutions and Participation Service, Department of Sustainable Development
Senior Officer
Cape Verde: Society and Cultures
Guinea-Bissau: Society and Cultures

DONALD CRUMMEY
University of Illinois at Urbana-Champaign, Department of History
Professor Emeritus
Production Strategies: Plow Farming
Téwodros

JAMES CURREY
James Currey Publishers
Chair
Media: Book Publishing

NORBERT CYFFER
University of Vienna, Institute for African Studies
Professor
Languages: Nilo-Saharan

M. E. KROPP DAKUBU
University of Ghana, Institute of African Studies
Professor
Ghana: Society and Cultures

PAUL DARBY
University of Ulster at Jordanstown, School of Sports Studies, Faculty of Life and Health Sciences
Senior Lecturer
Sports: Football

BASIL DAVIDSON
Bristol University
Independent Scholar
Cabral, Amílcar Lopes
Machel, Samora Moises
Mondlane, Eduardo Chivambo
Nationalism
Neto, Agostinho
Pereira, Aristides Maria

DIANA K. DAVIS
University of Texas at Austin, Department of Geography and the Environment
Assistant Professor
Morocco: Geography and Economy

NATALIE ZEMON DAVIS
Princeton University, Department of History
Professor Emerita
Leo Africanus

FILIP DE BOECK
Catholic University of Leuven, Africa Research Centre, Department of Social and Cultural Anthropology
Professor
Kinshasa

EMILIE DE BRIGARD
FilmResearch, Higganum, CT
Independent Scholar
Film and Cinema

WILLY DE CRAEMER†
University of Pennsylvania
Associate Professor Emeritus
Tempels, Placied

JOHN W. DE GRUCHY
University of Cape Town, Department of Religious Studies
Senior Research Associate
Tutu, Desmond Mpilo

LUC DE HEUSCH
Université Libre de Bruxelles, Center for Cultural Anthropology
Professor Emeritus
Kingship

PIERRE DE MARET
Université Libre de Bruxelles, Department of Archaeology and Anthropology
Professor
Prehistory: Central Africa

ALEX DE WAAL
Social Science Research Council
Program Director
Disease: HIV/AIDS, Social and Political Aspects
Famine

CHRIS DE WET
Rhodes University, Department of Anthropology
Professor
Peasants: Southern Africa

HILARY JOHN DEACON
University of Stellenbosch, Cape Town, Department of Archaeology
Professor
Prehistory: Southern Africa

CHRISTOPHER DECORSE
Syracuse University, Department of Anthropology
Chair and Professor
    Prehistory: Western Africa

MARK W. DELANCEY
University of South Carolina, Department of Government and International Studies
Professor Emeritus
    Ahidjo, El Hajj Ahmadou

MARIE-BÉNÉDICTE DEMBOUR
University of Sussex, School of Law
Professor
    Congo Independent State

FASSIL DEMISSIE
DePaul University, Department of Public Policy Studies
Associate Professor
    Urbanism and Urbanization:
        Colonial

ADEL P. DEN HARTOG
Wageningen University, The Netherlands, Division of Human Nutrition
Professor Emeritus
    Food: Nutrition

FRANCIS M. DENG
Sudan Peace Support Project
Director
    Slavery and Servile
        Institutions: Sudan

LARAY DENZER
Independent Scholar
    Cummings-John, Constance
        Agatha
    Ransome-Kuti,
        Olufunmilayo
    Stevens, Siaka

BILL DERMAN
Michigan State University, Department of Anthropology and African Studies Center
Professor
    Peasants: Western Africa

RENÉ DEVISCH
Katholieke Universiteit Leuven, Africa Research Center
Professor Special Emeritus
    Divination and Oracles

ROBERT DEWAR
University of Cambridge, McDonald Institute for Archaeological Research
Fellow
    Madagascar: Early Settlement

MIALA DIAMBOMBA
Université Laval, Faculty of Education Sciences
Professor
    Education, School:
        Francophone Central
        Africa

GERRIT J. DIMMENDAAL
University of Cologne, Institute of African Studies
Professor
    Linguistics, Historical

JESSE A. DIZARD
Southwest Oregon Community College
    Bangui
    Harar
    Port-Louis

JACQUELINE COGDELL DJEDJE
University of California, Los Angeles, Department of Ethnomusicology
Professor
    Nketia, J. H. Kwabena

AIDAN DODSON
University of Bristol, Department of Archaeology and Archaeology
Research Fellow
    Egypt, Early: New Kingdom

EMMANUEL DONGALA
Simon's Rock College of Bard, Natural Sciences Program
Chair
    Pointe-Noire

MARY DOUGLAS†
University of London, Department of Anthropology
Professor
    Taboo and Sin

SUSAN DRUCKER-BROWN
Cambridge University, Department of Sociology and Anthropology
Professor
    Food: Preparation and
        Cuisines

BRIAN M. DU TOIT
University of Florida, Department of Anthropology
Professor
    Immigration and Immigrant
        Groups: European

MYRON ECHENBERG
McGill University, Department of History
Professor
    Burkina Faso: Geography and
        Economy
    Burkina Faso: History and
        Politics

ROBERT EDGAR
Howard University, Department of African Studies
Professor
    Lesotho: Geography and
        Economy
    Lesotho: History and Politics

CHRISTOPHER EHRET
University of California, Los Angeles, Department of History
Professor
> Early Human Society, History of (c. 50,000 BP to 19,000 BCE)
> Technological Specialization Period, History of (c. 19.000 to 5000 BCE)

SIMEON EHUI
World Bank Africa Region, Sustainable Development Department
Sector Leader
> Agriculture: World Markets

DALE F. EICKELMAN
Dartmouth College, Department of Anthropology
Professor
> 'Ali, Muhammad
> Ben Barka, Mehdi
> Bin Ali, Zine el-Abidine
> Casablanca
> Education, University and College: Northern Africa
> Fez
> Hasan II of Morocco
> Ibn Khaldun, Abd al-Rahman
> Morocco: History and Politics
> Morocco: Society and Cultures
> Mubarak, Husni
> Muhammad VI
> Nasser, Gamal Abdel
> Political Systems: Islamic

ANDREW EISENBERG
Northwestern University, Department of Music
> Music, Modern Popular: Eastern Africa

MAUREEN N. EKE
Central Michigan University, Department of English
Professor
> Soyinka, Wole

ABOULKACEM AFULAY EL KHATIR
Institut Royal de la Culture Amizighe, Center for Anthropological and Sociological Studies
Researcher
> Popular Culture: Northern Africa

MOHAMED EL MANSOUR
Mohammed V University, Rabat, Department of History
Professor
> Marrakesh
> Morocco and Sub-Saharan Africa

IVANA ELBL
Trent University, Department of History
Associate Professor
> Travel and Exploration: European (Pre-1500)

MANSOUR O. EL-KIKHIA
University of Texas at San Antonio, Department of Political Science and Geography
Chair
> Qadhdhafi, Muammar

NNAMDI ELLEH
University of Cincinnati, College of Design, Architecture, Art, and Planning
Associate Professor
> Architecture: Contemporary
> Architecture: Monumental
> Yamoussoukro

KAROLA ELWERT-KRETSCHMER
Graduate Institute of Development Studies, Geneva, Switzerland
> Bénin: Geography and Economy
> Vodún

MOHA ENNAJI
University of Fez, Morocco, Department of English
Professor
> Allal al-Fassi
> Bouabid, Abderrahim
> Mekki, Aicha
> Mohammed V
> Zayani, Moha ou Hammou

VEIT ERLMANN
University of Texas at Austin, School of Music
Professor
> Ladysmith Black Mambazo
> Music, Modern Popular: Southern Africa

MANASSÉ ESOAVELOMANDROSO
University of Antananarivo, Madagascar, Department of History
> Madagascar and Western Indian Ocean, History of (1500 to 1895)

MARTIN EVANS
University of Leicester, Department of Geography
Research Associate
> Military Organizations: Guerrilla Forces

PABLO B. EYZAGUIRRE
International Plant Genetic Resources Institute (IPGRI), Rome
Senior Scientist
> Plantation Economies and Societies

MARCEL FAFCHAMPS
Oxford University, Department of Economics
Professor
> Economics and the Study of Africa

J. D. FAGE†
University of Birmingham,
Institute of West African Studies
Professor Emeritus
Dike, Kenneth Onwuka

LAURA FAIR
Michigan State University,
Department of History
Associate Professor
Mohammed, Bibi Titi
Saad, Siti binti

FRANCIS FALCETO
French Center of Ethiopian
Studies, Addis Ababa
Associate Searcher
Music, Modern Popular:
Ethiopia

TOYIN FALOLA
University of Texas at Austin,
Department of History
Professor
Awolowo, Obafemi
Tinubu, Madame

RICHARD FARDON
University of London, School of
Oriental and African Studies,
Department of Anthropology and
Sociology
Professor
Knowledge: Traditional

FRANK FARQUHARSON
Centre for Ecology and Hydrology,
Wallingford, Water Resources
Group
Fellow
Hydrology

RODOLFO FATTOVICH
University of Naples L'Orientale,
Department of African and
Arabian Studies
Professor
Prehistory: Ethiopia and the
Horn

FRANCOIS-XAVIER
FAUVELLE-AYMAR
National Center for Scientific
Research, France, French Center
for Ethiopian Studies, Addis
Ababa
Director
Ibn Battuta, Muhammad ibn
Abdullah

DERICK FAY
Union College, Department of
Anthropology
Visiting Assistant Professor
Land: Reform

GILLIAN FEELEY-HARNIK
University of Michigan,
Department of Anthropology
Professor
Death, Mourning, and
Ancestors
Madagascar: Religion in

ROQUINALDO FERREIRA
University of Virginia,
Department of History
Assistant Professor
Benguela

EDDA L. FIELDS-BLACK
Carnegie Mellon University,
Department of History
Assistant Professor
Guinea: Society and Cultures

RUTH FINNEGAN
Open University, Faculty of Social
Sciences
Professor
Literature: Oral

NIALL FINNERAN
School of Oriental and African
Studies, Department of Art
History and Archaeology
Honorary Research Associate
Aksum
Archaeology and Prehistory:
Christian

Northeastern Africa, Classical
Period, History of (1000
BCE to 600 CE)
Travel and Exploration:
Chinese

KATHERINE FISHBURN
Michigan State University,
Department of English
Professor Emeritus
Emecheta, Buchi

C. F. FISIY
World Bank, Department of Social
Development in East Asia
Sector Manager
Research: Scholarly Ethics

JEFFREY FLEISHER
Rice University, Department of
Anthropology
Assistant Professor
Urbanism and Urbanization:
Prehistoric

WILLIAM J. FOLTZ
Yale University, Department of
Political Science
Professor Emeritus
Chad: History and Politics
Government: Military
Senegal: History and Politics

JOSHUA BERNARD FORREST
University of Pittsburgh,
Graduate School of Public and
International Affairs
Adjunct Faculty
Nujoma, Samuel Shafiishuna

ODILE FRANK
International Labour
Organization, Geneva, Research
and Policy Analysis Unit
Senior Research and Policy Adviser
Demography: Fertility and
Infertility
Demography: Mortality

ROSALIND FREDERICKS
University of California, Berkeley,
Department of Geography

Doctoral Candidate
    Niger River

G. S. P. FREEMAN-GRENVILLE†
Independent Scholar
    Azania
    Bushiri ibn Salim
    Chingulia, Dom Jerónimo
    Gama, Vasco da

MICHAEL FRISHKOPF
University of Alberta, Canada, Department of Music, Faculty of Arts
Associate Professor
    Music: Islamic

CHRISTOPHER FYFE
University of Edinburgh
    Blyden, Edward Wilmot
    Horton, James Africanus
      Beale

C. MAGBAILY FYLE
Ohio State University, Department of African American and African Studies
Professor
    Sierra Leone: Geography and
      Economy

SAMBA GADJIGO
Mount Holyoke College, Department of French
Professor
    Sembène, Ousmane

GARY GAILE
University of Colorado-Boulder, Department of Geography
Professor
    Boundaries, Colonial and
      Modern

CHRISTRAUD M. GEARY
Museum of Fine Arts, Boston, African and Oceanic Art
Curator
    Art: Markets
    Njoya, Ibrahim Mbombo
    Photography: History

PAULUS GERDES
Research Center for Mathematics, Culture and Education, Maputo, Mozambique
Professor
    Arts: Basketry and Mat
      Making
    Geometries
    Mathematics
    Number Systems

PETER GESCHIERE
University of Amsterdam, Amsterdam School for Social Science Research
Professor
    Witchcraft: Overview

TREVOR R. GETZ
San Francisco State University, Department of History
Associate Professor
    Eunuchs

JAN-BART GEWALD
Leiden University, African Studies Centre
Senior Researcher
    Energy: Internal Combustion
      Engine
    Maherero, Samuel
    Witbooi, Hendrik

DAVID GIBBS
University of Arizona, Department of History
Associate Professor
    Cold War

PAUL GIFFORD
University of London, School of Oriental and African Studies, Department for the Study of Religions
Professor
    Christianity: Africa and
      World Christianity

SIMON GIKANDI
Princeton University, Department of English
Professor
    Literature: Overview

MICHELLE GILBERT
Sarah Lawrence College, Department of Art History
Professor
    Douglas Camp, Sokari
    Queens and Queen Mothers

TAMARA GILES-VERNICK
University of Minnesota, Department of History
Associate Professor
    Forestry: Central Africa

MICHAEL H. GLANTZ
National Center for Atmospheric Research, Center for Capacitiy Building
Senior Scientist
    Desertification, Modern

KENT GLENZER
Emory University, Center for the Study of Public Scholarship
Research Associate
    Mali: History and Politics

ODILE GOERG
University of Paris, Department of History
Professor
    Colonialism and Imperialism:
      Concessionary
      Companies
    Guinea: Geography and
      Economy
    Guinea: History and Politics
    Touré, Sékou

ALEXANDER GOLDMAN
Freelance Researcher
    Éboué, Adolphe-Félix-
      Sylvestre
    Mugabe, Robert
    Olympio, Sylvanus Epiphanio
    Van Riebeeck, Jan

HELLE V. GOLDMAN
Norwegian Polar Institute, Polar Environmental Centre, Tromsø, Norway
Chief Editor
    Zanzibar

LAMECK K. H. GOMA†
University of Zambia
Chancellor
    Education, University and College: Central Africa

CH. DIDIER GONDOLA
Indiana University-Purdue University Indianapolis, Department of History
Associate Professor
    Congo, Republic of: Society and Cultures

YVES GONZALEZ-QUIJANO
University of Lumière Lyon, Maison de l'Orient et de la Méditerranée, Department of Arabic Studies
    Mahfouz, Naguib
    Salih, Tayeb

JACK GOODY
St. John's College, Cambridge, Department of Anthropology
Professor Emeritus
    Kinship and Affinity

ROBERT J. GORDON
University of Vermont, Department of Anthropology
Professor
    Namibia: Society and Cultures

CHARLES GORE
University of London, School of Oriental and African Studies
Lecturer
    Popular Culture: Western Africa

CANDICE GOUCHER
Washington State University, Vancouver, Department of History
Professor
    Metals and Minerals: Iron

JOHN A. J. GOWLETT
University of Liverpool, Department of Anthropology
Professor
    Archaeology and Prehistory: Tools and Technologies

APOLLOS GOYOL
North Carolina Central University, School of Education, Curriculum Instruction and Professional Studies
Assistant Professor
    Education, School: Francophone Western and Indian Ocean Africa

DAVID GRAEBER
University of London, Goldsmiths College
Reader
    Madagascar: Society and Cultures

BRIAN GRAHAM
University of Ulster, School of Environmental Sciences
Professor
    Transportation: Air

RAOUL GRANQVIST
Umeå University, Department of Modern Languages
Professor
    Literature: Popular Literature

MIRIAM GRANT
University of Calgary, Department of Geography
Associate Professor
    Bulawayo

NANCY E. GRATTON
New Haven, CT
Independent Editorial Consultant
    Annan, Kofi
    Asmara
    Bourguiba, Habib bin 'Ali
    Buthelezi, Mangosuthu
    Fugard, Athol
    Johnson-Sirleaf, Ellen
    Masekela, Hugh
    Mutebi II
    Taylor, Charles Gahnhay
    Taytu, Empress

RICHARD GRAY†
University College London, School of Oriental and African Studies
Professor Emeritus
    Gordon, Charles George
    Mvemba Nzinga

STEPHEN GRAY
University of Johannesburg, Department of English
Professor
    Literatures in European Languages: Anglophone Central and Southern Africa

BEVERLY GRIER
Clark University, Department of Government and International Relations
Associate Professor
    Children and Childhood: Status and Roles

JOHN GRIMSHAW
Royal Botanic Gardens, Kew
Honorary Research Associate
    Ecosystems: Montane Environments

MARK GRUBER
St. Vincent College, Department of Anthropology
Professor
    Christianity: Coptic Church and Society

ELLEN GRUENBAUM
*California State University,
Fresno, Department of
Anthropology
Professor*
   Initiation: Clitoridectomy
      and Infibulation

PAULINE GUEDJ
*Université Paris X Nanterre/
Laboratoire d'Ethnologie et de
Sociologie Comparative (CNRS)
Doctor in Anthropology*
   Diasporas: Re-Africanization

CATHERINE GUIMOND
*University of California, Berkeley,
Department of Geography
Graduate Student*
   Liberia: Geography and
      Economy

DAVID GUTELIUS
*Stanford University, Department
of History
Visiting Scholar*
   Western Sahara

JEFF GUY
*University of Kwazulu-Natal,
Department of History
Professor*
   Colenso, John William

JANE I. GUYER
*Johns Hopkins University,
Department of Anthropology
Professor Emerita*
   Food: Supplies and
      Distribution
   Household and Domestic
      Groups
   Money: Commodity
      Currencies
   Peasants: Overview

GETATCHEW HAILE
*Saint John's University, Hill
Museum and Manuscript Library
Professor*

Christianity: Ethiopian
   Church
Ezana
Gondär
Lalibäla
Literatures in African
   Languages: Ethiopic
Massawa
Menelik II

BRUCE S. HALL
*Johns Hopkins University,
Department of History
Postdoctoral Fellow*
   Historiography: Islamic

C. R. HALLPIKE
*McMaster University, Department
of Anthropology
Professor Emeritus*
   Time Reckoning and
      Calendars

PETER HALLWARD
Yale University
   Beti, Mongo
   Kourouma, Ahmadou

CAROLYN HAMILTON
*University of the Witwatersrand,
Department of Anthropology
Researcher*
   Shaka Zulu

RUSSELL HAMILTON
*Vanderbilt University,
Department of Spanish and
Portuguese
Professor Emeritus*
   Literatures in European
      Languages: Lusophone

KAREN TRANBERG HANSEN
*Northwestern University,
Department of Anthropology
Professor*
   Labor: Domestic
   Youth: Overview

HOLLY HANSON
*Mount Holyoke College,
Department of History
Associate Professor*
   Mwanga, Kabaka

JOHN W. HARBESON
*City University of New York,
Department of Political Science
Professor*
   Government: Presidential

REBECCA HARDIN
*University of Michigan,
Department of Anthropology
Assistant Professor*
   Central African Republic:
      Society and Cultures

JOHN D. HARGREAVES
*University of Aberdeen,
Department of History
Professor Emeritus*
   Colonial Policies and
      Practices: British West
      Africa
   Lewis, Samuel K.

ROBERT HARMS
*Yale University, Department of
History
Professor*
   Congo River

ELIZABETH HARNEY
*University of Toronto,
Department of Art
Assistant Professor*
   Art, Genres and Periods:
      Contemporary
   Diasporas: Arts

BARBARA HARRELL-BOND
*American University in Cairo,
Department of Forced Migration
and Refugee Studies
Distinguished Adjunct Professor*
   Refugees

JOSEPH E. HARRIS
Howard University, Department of History
Professor Emeritus
Diasporas: Overview

KELSEY HARRISON
Ahmadu Bello University, Zaria, Nigeria, Department of Obstetrics
Head
Childbearing

ADAM HASSAN
University of Cologne, Institute for African Studies
Lecturer
Shaaban Robert

FEKRI A. HASSAN
University College, London, Institute of Archaeology
Professor
Egypt, Early: Predynastic

ADRIAN HASTINGS†
University of Leeds, Department of Theology
Professor Emeritus
Fasiladas
Galawdewos
Kimbangu, Simon
Kiwanuka, Joseph
Susenyos
Zara Ya'iqob

MARTHA HANNAN
International Development Exchange
Djibouti City
Monrovia

TEMPLE HAUPTFLEISCH
University of Stellenbosch, Centre for Theatre and Performance Studies
Director
Theater: Southern Africa

PHILIP HAVIK
Instituto de Investigação Científico Tropical (IICT),
Centro de Estudos Africanos e Asiaticos (CEAA)
Researcher
Bissau

CHRISTOPHER HAYDEN
Northwestern University, Department of History
Ph.D. Candidate
Conakry

PRISCILLA HAYNER
International Center for Transitional Justice, International Policymakers Unit
Director
Truth Commissions

JONATHAN HAYNES
Long Island University, Brooklyn Campus, Department of English
Professor
Media: Cinema

EDWIN HEES
University of Stelllenbosch, Department of Drama
Theater: Southern Africa

BEATRIX HEINTZE
Johann Wolfgang Goethe-Universität, Frobenius Institut
Ethnologist
Njinga Mbandi Ana de Sousa

DAVID HENIGE
University of Wisconsin-Madison, Memorial Library
Bibliographer
Historiography: European
King Lists and Chronologies
Research: Historical
Resources

EUGENIA HERBERT
Mount Holyoke College, Department of History
Professor Emerita
Metals and Minerals: Copper and Alloys

STEFANIE HERRMANN
National Center for Atmospheric Research
Postdoctoral Research Fellow
Desertification, Modern

ANDREW HILL
Yale University, Department of Anthropology
Professor
Human Evolution: Patterns of Evolution
Leakey, Louis and Mary

DANNY HOFFMAN
University of Washington, Department of Anthropology
Assistant Professor
Military Organizations: Militias

JARITA HOLBROOK
University of Arizona, Bureau of Applied Research in Anthropology
Assistant Research Scientist
Astronomies

ALCINDA HONWANA
Open University, International Development Centre
Chair
Children and Childhood: Soldiers

NICHOLAS S. HOPKINS
American University in Cairo, Department of Sociology, Anthropology, Psychology, and Egyptology
Professor Emeritus
Cairo
Egypt, Modern: Geography and Economy
Egypt, Modern: History and Politics
Tunisia: Geography and Economy
Tunisia: History and Politics

MARK HORTON
University of Bristol, Department of Archaeology and Anthropology
Reader
 Archaeology and Prehistory:
  Islamic
 Archaeology and Prehistory:
  Overview
 Egypt, Early: Roman and
  Byzantine
 Islam: Eastern and Central
  Africa

JAMES HOUSEFIELD
Texas State University,
Department of Art and Design
Distinguished Teaching Professor
 Art, Regional Styles:
  Northern Africa

RHODA E. HOWARD-HASSMANN
Wilfrid Laurier University,
Canada, Department of Global
Studies and Political Science
Canada Research Chair in
International Human Rights
 Human Rights

JOHN HUNWICK
Northwestern University,
Department of History
Professor Emeritus
 Abu Bakr, Muhammed ibn
 Baba, Ahmad
 Bello, Muhammad
 Ilori, Adam Abdullahi al-
 Maghili, Muhammad ibn
  ʿAbd al-Karim al-
 Sunni ʿAli
 Tijani, Ahmad

GORAN HYDEN
University of Florida, Department
of Political Science
Distinguished Professor
 Civil Society: Forms of Civil
  Society
 Political Science and the
  Study of Africa
 Research: Research Funding

MOHAMED HYDER
University of Nairobi, College of
Biological and Physical Sciences
Professor Emeritus
 Ecology: Human Roles
 Research: Biological Sciences

JACQUES LOUIS HYMANS
University of San Francisco
 Senghor, Léopold Sédar

DYMITR IBRISZIMOW
Bayreuth University, Department
of Languages and Literatures
Chair, Professor
 Languages: Afro-Asiatic

BARBARA INGHAM
University of Salford, School of
Management
Lecturer
 World War I

KENNETH INGHAM
University of Bristol, Department
of History
Professor Emeritus
 Smuts, Jan Christiaan

JOSEPH E. INIKORI
University of Rochester, Frederick
Douglass Institute, Department of
History
Professor
 Slave Trades: Atlantic,
  Western Africa

SEAN JACOBS
University of Michigan,
Department of Communication
Studies
Assistant Professor
 Media: Politics

PHILIP J. JAGGAR
University of London, School of
Oriental and African Studies,
Department of Africa
Professor
 Languages: Overview

WENDY JAMES
Oxford University, Institute of
Social and Cultural Anthropology
Professor
 Sudan: Society and Cultures

JONATHAN JANSEN
University of Pretoria, Faculty of
Education
Professor
 Education, University and
  College: Southern Africa

WILLY JANSEN
Radboud University Nijmegen,
Institute for Gender Studies
Professor
 Women: Women and Islam
  in Northern Africa

JOHN M. JANZEN
University of Kansas-Lawrence,
Department of Anthropology
Professor
 Healing and Health Care:
  African Theories and
  Therapies

RACHEL JEAN-BAPTISTE
University of Chicago,
Department of History
Assistant Professor
 Domitien, Elizabeth

M. C. JEDREJ
University of Edinburgh, School of
Social and Political Studies
Associate Dean
 Secret Societies

RICHARD JEFFRIES
University of London, School of
Oriental and African Studies
Teaching Fellow
 Rawlings, Jerry

VILLIA MARIA JEFREMOVAS
Queen's University, Department
of Global Development Studies
Canada Research Chair

Rwanda: Geography and
Economy
Rwanda: History and Politics

SHAMIL JEPPIE
University of Cape Town,
Department of Historical Studies
Senior Lecturer
Colonial Policies and
Practices: Egyptian

BOGUMIL JEWSIEWICKI
Université Laval, Department of
History
Canada Research Chair
Mami Wata
Popular Culture: Political
Ideology
Samba, Chéri

D. M. JOHN
Natural History Museum,
London, Department of Botany
Ecosystems: Coastal
Environments

ADAM JONES
Universität Leipzig, Institut für
Afrikanistik
Professor
Travel and Exploration:
European (1500 to
1800)
Travel and Exploration:
European (Since 1800)

HILARY JONES
University of Maryland, College
Park, Department of History
Assistant Professor
Dakar
Saint-Louis

JOHN N. JONES
Yale University
Biko, Steve

CÉDRIC JOURDE
University of Ottawa, School of
Political Studies
Assistant Professor

Mauritania: History and
Politics

NANTANG JUA
South Carolina State University,
Department of Social Sciences
Assistant Professor
Cameroon: Geography and
Economy
Cameroon: History and
Politics

BENNETTA JULES-ROSETTE
University of California, San
Diego, Department of Sociology
Professor
Maranke, John

JOHN O. KAKONGE
Yale University, School of Forestry
and Environmental Studies
Associate Research Scholar
Aid and Development:
Environmental Impact
Forestry: Overview

FRANK KALESNIK
Orange County Community
College, Department of Global
Studies
Assistant Professor
Military Organizations:
National Armies
Warfare: Liberation

PETER KALLAWAY
University of the Western Cape,
Faculty of Education
Senior Professor
Education, School:
Anglophone Central and
Southern Africa

DANIEL M. KAMMEN
University of California, Berkeley,
Energy and Resources Group and
Goldman School of Public Policy
Professor
Energy: Electrification

TABITHA KANOGO
University of California, Berkeley,
Department of History
Professor
Kenyatta, Jomo

STEVEN KAPLAN
Hebrew University of Jerusalem,
Faculty of Humanities
Professor
Judaism in Africa

LIDWIEN KAPTEIJNS
Wellesley College, Department of
History
Professor
Hasan, Muhammad
'Abdallah

NELSON KASFIR
Dartmouth College, Department
of Government
Professor
Museveni, Yoweri

SIDNEY L. KASFIR
Emory University, Department of
Art History
Professor
Art, Genres and Periods:
Tourist

ELAINE NATALIE KATZ
University of the Witwatersrand,
Johannesburg, School of Social
Sciences, Department of History
Senior Research Fellow
Johannesburg

PETA KATZ
University of North Carolina at
Charlotte, Department of
Sociology and Anthropology
South Africa, Republic of:
Society and Cultures

MICHAEL KEVANE
Santa Clara University,
Department of Economics
Associate Professor
Economic Systems

EDMOND J. KELLER
University of California at Los Angeles, Department of Political Science
Professor
Mengistu, Haile Mariam

SINDANI KIANGU
University of Kinshasa, Faculty of Letters and Human Sciences, Department of History
Associate Professor and Head
Congo, Democratic Republic of the: Geography and Economy

JAMES P. KIERNAN
University of Natal, Department of Social Anthropology
Professor Emeritus
Prophetic Movements: Southern Africa
Shembe, Isaiah

DAVID KILLINGRAY
University of London, Goldsmiths College, Department of History
Professor Emeritus
Military Organizations: Colonial Armies

JOHN KING†
BBC Arabic Service
Program Executive
'Abd al-Qādir

CHARLES KIRUBI
University of California, Berkeley, Energy and Resources Group
Graduate Student
Energy: Electrification

ANTHONY KIRK-GREENE
University of Oxford, Saint Anthony's College
Emeritus Fellow
Barth, Heinrich
Bello, Ahmadu
Gowon, Yakubu
Tafawa Balewa, Abubakar

MARTIN KLEIN
University of Toronto, Department of History
Professor Emeritus
Gorée
History of Africa: Nineteenth and Twentieth Centuries
History of Africa: Sixteenth to Nineteenth Century
Slavery and Servile Institutions: Colonial
Sudan, Western and Central, History of (1500 to 1880 CE)

PERI KLEMM
California State University, Northridge, Department of Art
Assistant Professor
Body Adornment and Clothing: Cosmetics and Body Painting

KAIRN KLIEMAN
University of Houston, Department of History
Associate Professor
Kongo, Angola, and Western Forests, History of (1500 to 1880)

INES KOHL
Austrian Academy of Sciences, Centre for Studies in Asian Cultures and Social Anthropology
University Lecturer
Libya: Society and Cultures

IGOR KOPYTOFF
University of Pennsylvania, Department of Anthropology
Professor Emeritus
Frontiers
Slavery and Servile Institutions: Anthropological Perspectives

SUE KOSSEW
University of New South Wales, School of English, Media, and Performing Arts
Associate Professor
Coetzee, J. M.

DIRK KOTZE
University of South Africa (UNISA), Department of Political Sciences
Associate Professor
Mbeki, Thabo

BERTIN KOUADIO
Florida International University, Department of International Relations
Lecturer
Côte d'Ivoire: Society and Cultures

CORINNE A. KRATZ
Emory University, Center for the Study of Public Scholarship
Co-director
Initiation: Overview

KAI KRESSE
University of St. Andrews, Department of Anthropology
Lecturer
Knowledge: Overview

MARGARET KROMA
Cornell University, Department of Education
Assistant Professor
Education, University and College: Western Africa

GERHARD KUBIK
University of Vienna, Department of Anthropology
Professor
Music: Overview
Music: Structures

CHAPURUKHA M. KUSIMBA
Field Museum of Natural History, Chicago, Department of Anthropology

Associate Curator
  Heritage, Cultural:
    Management and
    Preservation
  Metals and Minerals:
    Metallurgy

MATTHEW KUSTENBAUDER
*Yale University Graduate School,
Council on African Studies
Graduate Student*
  Islam: Western Africa
  Prophetic Movements:
    Eastern Africa
  Prophetic Movements:
    Western Africa

STEVEN KYLE
*Cornell University, Department of
Applied Economics and
Management
International Professor*
  Energy: Petroleum and
    Derivatives

GARY KYNOCH
*Dalhousie University, Department
of History
Associate Professor*
  Youth: Gangs

JAMES LA FLEUR
*College of William & Mary,
Department of History
Assistant Professor*
  Plants: Imported Species

GEORGE M. LA RUE
*Clarion University, Department
of History
Professor*
  Slave Trades: Northern Africa
    and Sahara

PAUL LANE
*University of York, Historical
Ecologies of East African
Landscapes
Director*
  Archaeology and Prehistory:
    Historical

J. AYODELE LANGLEY
*Howard University, Department
of African Studies
Professor*
  Organization of African
    Unity

LORNE LARSON
Independent Scholar
  Kinjikitile

PIER M. LARSON
*Johns Hopkins University,
Department of History
Associate Professor*
  Andrianampoinimerina
  Radama I

MURRAY LAST
*University College London,
Department of Social
Anthropology
Professor Emeritus*
  'Uthman dan Fodio

ROBERT LAUNAY
*Northwestern University,
Department of Anthropology
Professor*
  Education, School: Muslim
    Africa

ADRIA LAVIOLETTE
*University of Virginia,
Department of Anthropology
Associate Professor*
  Eastern African Coast,
    History of (Early to
    1600)

BABATUNDE LAWAL
*Virginia Commonwealth
University, Department of Art
History
Professor*
  Azikiwe, Benjamin Nnamdi
  Ife (Ile-Ife)

BENJAMIN LAWRANCE
*University of California, Davis,
Department of History*

Assistant Professor
  Togo: Geography and
    Economy
  Togo: History and Politics
  Togo: Society and Cultures

ÉTIENNE LE ROY
*Université de Paris I, Centre
d'études des mondes africains,
Laboratoire
Professor*
  Land: Tenure

MARIE-NATALIE LEBLANC
*Concordia University,
Department of Sociology &
Anthropology
Associate Professor*
  Youth: Youth and Islam

**MATHILDE LEDUC-
GRIMALDI**
*Royal Museum for Central
Africa, Belgium, Department of
History
Scientific Attaché*
  Schnitzer, Eduard

SONIA LEE
*Trinity College, Department of
Modern Languages
Professor*
  Hampâté Bâ, Amadou
  Literature: Women Writers,
    Sub-Saharan Africa
  Saadawi, Nawal el-

SUSANNA LEE
*Georgetown University,
Department of French
Associate Professor*
  La Guma, Alex

RENÉ LEMARCHAND
*University of Florida, Department
of Political Science
Professor Emeritus*
  Tombalbaye, François-
    Ngarta

CAROLA LENTZ
Johannes Gutenberg University, Mainz, Germany, Department of Anthropology and African Studies
Professor
>Colonial Traditions and Inventions
>Ethnicity: Overview

LORI LEONARD
Johns Hopkins School of Public Health, Department of Health, Behavior, and Society
Associate Professor
>Chad: Society and Cultures

MARK LEOPOLD
University of Sussex, Department of Anthropology
Lecturer
>Refugees

DEBORAH K. LETOURNEAU
University of California, Santa Cruz, Department of Environmental Studies
Professor
>Agriculture: Pests and Pest Control

MICHAEL L. LEVINE
New York City
Freelance Writer and Editor
>Aggrey, James
>Alexandria
>Bâ, Mariama
>Bashir, Omar Ahmed el-
>Bouteflika, Abdelaziz
>Déby Itno, Idriss
>Gbagbo, Laurent Koudou
>Gidada, Negasso
>Kibaki, Mwai
>Lesotho: Society and Cultures
>Mkapa, Benjamin
>Pohamba, Hifikepunye
>Ravalomanana, Marc
>Saro-Wiwa, Ken
>Sassou-Nguesso, Denis
>Touré, Amadou Toumani

ROBERT A. LEVINE
Harvard University, Graduate School of Education
Professor Emeritus
>Children and Childhood: Infancy and Early Development
>Education, School: Overview

IOAN M. LEWIS
London School of Economics, Department of Anthropology
Professor Emeritus
>Somalia: History and Politics
>Somalia: Society and Cultures

SIMON KEITH LEWIS
College of Charleston, Department of English
Associate Professor
>Paton, Alan
>Serote, Mongane

DAVID LEWIS-WILLIAMS
University of the Witwatersrand, Rock Art Research Institute, South Africa
Professor Emeritus
>Art, Genres and Periods: Rock Art, Southern Africa

VICTOR MORALES LEZCANO
Open University, Madrid, Research Institute
Professor
>Canary Islands

OLGA F. LINARES
Smithsonian Tropical Research Institute
Senior Research Staff
>Production Strategies: Agriculture
>Senegal: Geography and Economy

STAFFAN I. LINDBERG
University of Florida, Department of Political Science and Center for African Studies
Assistant Professor
>Government: Parliamentary

MAX LINIGER-GOUMAZ
Commercial High School, Switzerland, School of Economics and Business Administration
Professor Emeritus
>Equatorial Guinea: Geography and Economy
>Equatorial Guinea: History and Politics

RICHARD LOBBAN
Rhode Island College, Department of Anthropology
Chair
>Kerma

THOMAS LODGE
University of the Witwatersrand, Department of Political Science
Professor
>Luthuli, Albert John
>Mavumbi

PAUL E. LOVEJOY
York University, Ontario, Department of History
Distinguished Research Professor
>Lugard, Frederick John Dealtry
>Slavery and Servile Institutions: Overview

JON LOVETT
University of York, Centre for Ecology, Law and Policy, Environment Department
Senior Lecturer
>Ecosystems: Tropical and Humid Forests

KENYETTA LOVINGS
University of Chicago, Department of Anthropology

Graduate Student
  Media: Comic Art

UTE LUIG
Institut für Ethnologie, Berlin
Professor
  Spirit Possession: Modernity

CHRISTIAN LUND
Roskilde University, Denmark,
Department of Society and
Globalisation
Professor
  Niger: Geography and
    Economy

CLEMENS LUTZ
University of Groningen, The
Netherlands, Department of
Strategy and Business
Environment
Coordinator
  Food: Marketing

GHISLAINE LYDON
University of California, Los
Angeles, Department of History
Assistant Professor
  Sahara Desert: Caravan Routes

DAVID MABEY
London School of Hygiene and
Tropical Medicine, Department of
Infectious and Tropical Diseases
Professor
  Disease: Viral and Infectious

WILLIAM MABEY
University of Leeds, Department of
History
  Disease: Viral and Infectious

AKIN L. MABOGUNJE
Development Policy Centre,
Ibadan, Nigeria, Development
Policy Centre
Professor Emeritus
  Nigeria: Geography and
    Economy
  Obasanjo, Olusegun
  Urbanism and Urbanization:
    Independence Era

WYATT MACGAFFEY
Haverford College, Department of
Anthropology
Professor Emeritus
  Art: Overview
  Fetish and Fetishism

ELIZABETH MACGONAGLE
University of Kansas, Department
of History
Assistant Professor
  Mozambique: History and
    Politics
  Southeastern Africa, History
    of (1600 to 1910)

BEVERLY MACK
University of Kansas, Department
of African and African American
Studies
Professor
  Asma'u, Nana
  Literacy
  Literature: Islamic
  Literatures in African
    Languages: Hausa

GREGORY H. MADDOX
Texas Southern University,
Department of History,
Geography, and Economics
Professor
  Tanzania: Society and
    Cultures

DRISS MAGHRAOUI
Al Akhawayn University, Ifrane,
Morocco, School of Humanities
and Social Sciences
Assistant Professor
  Northern Africa: Historical
    Links with Sub-Saharan
    Africa

ZINE MAGUBANE
Boston College, Department of
Sociology
Associate Professor
  Postcolonialism

SLOAN MAHONE
University of Oxford, Department
of History/History of Medicine
University Lecturer
  Healing and Health Care:
    Medicine and Drugs

DONNA MAIER
University of Northern Iowa,
Department of History
Professor
  Kumasi

DANIEL MAINS
Washington University, African
and African American Studies
Program
Postdoctoral Research Fellow
  Ethiopia, Modern: Society
    and Cultures

CHRISTIAN JOHNS MAKGALA
University of Botswana,
Department of History
Senior Lecturer
  Khama, Seretse
  Khama III

FOUAD MAKKI
Cornell University, Department of
Development Sociology
Assistant Professor
  Eritrea: History and Politics

DOMINIQUE MALAQUAIS
Centre National de la Recherche
Scientifique (CNRS), Centre
d'Etudes des Mondes Africains
(CEMAf)
Senior Research Fellow
  Douala

COLLEEN MANASSA
Yale University, Department of
Near Eastern Languages and
Civilizations
Assistant Professor
  Writing Systems: Egyptian

TAKYIWAA MANUH
University of Ghana, Institute of African Studies
Director
Afua Kobi
Ghana: History and Politics

HAROLD G. MARCUS†
Michigan State University, Department of History
Professor
Haile Selassie I

RICHARD R. MARCUS
University of California, Long Beach, International Studies Program
Assistant Professor
Babangida, Ibrahim
Gbadamosi
Margai, Milton Augustus
Striery

PETER MARK
Wesleyan University, Department of History of Art
Professor
Architecture: Colonial

JONATHAN MARKS
University of North Carolina at Charlotte, Department of Anthropology
Professor
Human Evolution: Human
Biological Diversity

SHULA MARKS
University of London, School of Oriental and African Studies, Department of History
Professor Emerita
Healing and Health Care:
Medical Practitioners

DENIS-CONSTANT MARTIN
Centre for International Research and Studies (CERI-FNSP, Paris)
Senior Research Fellow
Diasporas: Music

BARBARO MARTINEZ-RUIZ
Stanford University, Center for African Studies

Professor
Cartography

FIDELIS T. MASAO
Open University of Tanzania
Professor
Art, Genres and Periods:
Rock Art, Eastern Africa

ADELINE MASQUELIER
Tulane University, Department of Anthropology
Associate Professor
Rouch, Jean
Spirit Possession:
Mediumship
Witchcraft: Witchcraft and
Islam

JOSEP LLUÍS MATEO DIESTE
Universitat Autònoma de Barcelona, Spain, Department of Social and Cultural Anthropology
Professor
Colonial Policies and
Practices: Spanish

J. LORAND MATORY
Harvard University, Departments of Anthropology and African and African American Studies
Professor
Diasporas: Religions

BÉNÉDICTE MAUGUIÈRE
University of Louisiana at Lafayette, Department of Modern Languages
Professor
Literatures in European
Languages: Francophone
Indian Ocean Africa

DAVID MAXWELL
Keele University, Department of History
Professor
Christianity: African
Instituted Churches
Christianity: Overview

ALAMIN MAZRUI
Rutgers University, Department of Africana Studies
Professor
Literatures in African
Languages: Islamic
Media: Language

ALI A. MAZRUI
State University of New York, Binghamton, Institute of Global Cultural Studies
Director
Slavery and Servile
Institutions: Reparations

JOSEPH MBELE
St. Olaf College, Department of English
Professor
Literature: Epics and Epic
Poetry

PATRICK MCALLISTER
University of Canterbury, New Zealand, Department of Sociology and Anthropology
Associate Professor
Ethnicity: Southern Africa

E. ANN MCDOUGALL
University of Alberta, Department of History and Classics
Professor
Mauritania: History and Politics
Salt

JAMES MCDOUGALL
Princeton University, Department of History
Assistant Professor
Algeria: Society and
Cultures

THOMAS F. MCDOW
Yale University, Department of History
Dean
Addis Ababa
Amin Dada, idi

Antananarivo
Dar es Salaam
Kadalie, Clements
Khartoum
Kigali
Lilongwe
Lobengula
Lusaka
Mirambo
Mogadishu
Mombasa
Mzilikazi
Nairobi
Nkrumah, Francis Nwia Kofi
Obote, Milton

MONTGOMERY MCFATE
U.S. Institute of Peace,
Jennings Randolph Fellowship
Program
Senior Fellow
Military Organizations:
Mercenaries

RODERICK J. MCINTOSH
Yale University, Department of
Anthropology
Professor
Desertification, Reactions to,
History of (c. 5000 to
1000 BCE)

SUSAN KEECH MCINTOSH
Rice University, Department of
Anthropology
Professor
Jenné and Jenné-jeno
Koumbi-Saleh
Niani
Western Desert and Margins,
History of (1000 BCE to
600 CE)

FATIMA MEER
University of Natal, Institute for
Black Research
Director
Nelson Mandela

SHEILA MEINTJES
University of the Witwatersrand,
Department of Political Studies
Associate Professor
Joseph, Helen
Mandela, Winnie

PETER KARIBE MENDY
Rhode Island College, Department
of History
Associate Professor
Guinea-Bissau: Geography
and Economy
Guinea-Bissau: History and
Politics
Law: Lusophone Africa

RONALD MESSIER
Vanderbilt University,
Department of History
Senior Lecturer
Sijilmasa

CLAIRE METELITS
Washington State University,
Department of Political Science
and Criminal
Assistant Professor
Warfare: Civil Wars

BIRGIT MEYER
Vrije Universiteit, Amsterdam,
Department of Social and
Cultural Anthropology
Professor
Witchcraft: Witchcraft and
Christianity

DOROTHY MIDDLETON†
Royal Geographical Society
Stanley, Henry Morton

JOHN MIDDLETON
Yale University, Departments
of Anthropology and Religious
Studies
Professor Emeritus
Anthropology, Social, and
the Study of Africa
Benin City
Religion and Ritual

Research: Overview
Saint Helena
Tippu Tip
Tourism
Tribe and Tribalism

CHRISTOPHER L. MILLER
Yale University, Department of
French
Professor
Camara Laye
Diop, Alioune

JOSEPH C. MILLER
University of Virginia,
Department of History
Professor
Angola: History and Politics
Capitalism and
Commercialization:
Overview
Congo, Democratic Republic
of the: Society and
Cultures
Gaborone
Historiography: Western and
African Concepts
History, World: Africa in
Slave Trades: Atlantic,
Central Africa

DAVID MILLS
University of Oxford, Department
of Education
Lecturer
Education, University and
College: Eastern Africa

CÉLESTIN MONGA
World Bank, Office of the Senior
Vice President and Chief
Economist
Lead Economist
Aid and Development:
Balance of Payments
Aid and Development:
Overview
Civil Society: Political
Accountability

Debt and Credit:
    International Trade
Family: Economics
International Monetary Fund
Law: Francophone Western,
    Equatorial, and Indian
    Ocean Africa
World Bank

JAMIE MONSON
*Carleton College, Department of
History
Associate Professor*
    China in African History

JOÃO MONTEIRO
*Eastern University, Department of
Sociology
Associate Professor*
    Évora, Cesária

SALLY FALK MOORE
*Harvard University, Department
of Anthropology
Professor Emerita*
    Law: Overview
    Research: Social Sciences

MARISSA MOORMAN
*Indiana University, Department
of History
Assistant Professor*
    Angola: Society and Cultures
    Cabinda, Angola

MARY H. MORAN
*Colgate University, Department of
Sociology and Anthropology
Professor*
    Liberia: Society and Cultures
    Perry, Ruth Sando

ELISABETH MUDIMBE-BOYI
*Stanford University, Departments
of French/Italian and
Comparative Literature
Professor*
    Literatures in European
        Languages: Francophone
        Central Africa

SALIKOKO S. MUFWENE
*University of Chicago,
Department of Linguistics
Professor*
    Languages: Creoles and
        Pidgins

CAROL MULLER
*University of Pennsylvania,
Department of Music
Associate Professor*
    Makeba, Miriam

JACOB MUNDY
*University of Exeter, Institute of
Arab and Islamic Studies
Ph.D. Candidate*
    Western and Saharan Africa,
        History of (600 to 1600
        CE)

MWELWA MUSAMBACHIME
*University of Zambia, Lusaka,
School of Humanities and
Social Sciences, Department
of History
Professor*
    Zambia: History and Politics

P. MUSILA MUTISYA
*North Carolina Central
University, School of Education,
Curriculum Instruction, and
Professional Studies
Professor*
    Education, School:
        Francophone Western
        and Indian Ocean Africa

EVAN MWANGI
*Northwestern University,
Department of English
Assistant Professor*
    Achebe, Chinua
    Ngũgĩ wa Thiong'o

E. WAYNE NAFZIGER
*Kansas State University,
Department of Economics
Distinguished Professor*

Capitalism and
    Commercialization:
    Privatization

SYLVESTRE NDAYIRUKIYE
*University of Burundi, Faculty of
Letters and Human Sciences,
Department of Geography
Professor*
    Burundi: Geography and
        Economy

BASILE NDJIO
*University of Buea, Cameroon,
Department of Social Sciences and
Management
Associate Professor*
    Witchcraft: Witchcraft and
        Wealth

ELAVIE NDURA
*George Mason University,
Initiatives in Educational
Program
Associate Professor*
    Burundi: History and Politics

GHIRMAI NEGASH
*Ohio University, Department of
English/African Studies
Assistant Professor*
    Writing Systems: Ethiopic

NICI NELSON
*University of London, Goldsmiths
College, Department of
Anthropology
Professor Emerita*
    Urbanism and Urbanization:
        Housing

**ANITRA CATHERINE
ELIZABETH NETTLETON**
*University of the Witwatersrand,
South Africa, Wits School of Arts
Professor*
    Art, Regional Styles:
        Southern Africa

RODERICK P. NEUMANN
Florida International University, Department of International Relations
Professor
Tanzania: Geography and Economy
Wildlife: National Parks

DAVID NEWBURY
Smith College, Department of History
Professor
Rwabugiri

SASHA NEWELL
University of Illinois Urbana-Champaign, Department of Anthropology
Postdoctoral Fellow
Person, Concepts of
Popular Culture: Central Africa

DJIBRIL TAMSIR NIANE
Société Africaine d'Édition
Founder
Mansa Musa
Sundjata Keïta

ISAK NIEHAUS
University of Natal, School of Anthropology and Psychology
Lecturer
Dreams and Dream Interpretation
Globalization
Witchcraft: Witchcraft and Politics

KIMANI NJOGU
Twaweza Communications, Nairobi, Kenya
Director
Communications: Oral
Language: Slang
Language: Sociolinguistics
Popular Culture: Eastern Africa
Theater: Anglophone Central and Eastern Africa

INSA NOLTE
University of Birmingham, Centre of West African Studies
Lecturer
Political Systems: Chieftainships

WILL NORMAN
ESRO (Ethnographic Social Research), London
Director
Mozambique: Geography and Economy
Mozambique: Society and Cultures

APOLO R. NSIBAMBI
Government of Uganda
Prime Minister
Kagwa, Apolo

BALAM NYEKO
University of Swaziland, Department of History
Associate Professor
Labor: Industrial and Mining
Swaziland: Geography and Economy
Swaziland: History and Politics
Swaziland: Society and Cultures

ANTHONY NYONG
International Development Research Centre, Climate Change Adaptation in Africa Program
Senior Program Specialist
Disease: Climate and Disease

R. S. O'FAHEY
University of Bergen, Centre for Middle Eastern and Islamic Studies
Professor
Idris, Ahmad ibn
Turabi, Hasan 'Abd Allah al-

IBRAHIM OGACHI OANDA
Kenyatta University, Nairobi, School of Education
Lecturer

Education, School: Anglophone Eastern Africa

CHRISTINE OBBO
Independent Anthropologist
HIV and Gender Education and Policy Consultant
Entebbe
Kampala
Uganda: Society and Cultures

R. A. OBUDHO
University of Nairobi, Center for Urban Research
Professor Emeritus
Urbanism and Urbanization: Overview

MOSES E. OCHONU
Vanderbilt University, Department of History
Assistant Professor
Nigeria: Society and Cultures, Central Nigeria

DAVID ODDEN
Ohio State University, Department of Linguistics
Professor
Linguistics and the Study of Africa

E. S. ATIENO ODHIAMBO
Rice University, Department of History
Professor
Ogot, Grace

THOMAS P. OFCANSKY
Private Researcher
Wildlife: Preservation and Destruction

C. OGBOGBO
University of Ibadan, Nigeria, Department of History
Lecturer I
Bamako
Calabar

Ja Ja, King
Libreville
Ogunde, Hubert Adedeji
Sarbah, John Mensah

OLATUNJI OJO
*Syracuse University,
Maxwell School, Department
of History
Assistant Professor*
Abeokuta
Macaulay, Herbert Samuel
Heelas
Macaulay, Thomas
Babington
N'Djamena
Niamey
Porto Novo

GODFREY OKOTH
*Maseno University, Kenya,
Department of History
Professor*
Kabarega

RASHEED OLANIYI
*University of Ibadan, Nigeria,
Department of History
Lecturer*
Livestock: Species

ROLAND OLIVER
*University of London, School
of Oriental and African Studies
Professor Emeritus*
History and the Study of
Africa

BAMIDELE OLOWU
*Obafemi Awolowo University,
Department of Public
Administration
Professor Emeritus*
Government: Local

KENNETH OLSON
*SIL International, Department of
International Linguistics
Associate Coordinator*
Languages: Niger-Congo

AYODEJI OLUKOJU
*University of Lagos, Nigeria,
Department of History and
Strategic Studies
Professor*
Labor: Transport
Transportation: Shipping and
Ports

VALÉRIE ORLANDO
*University of Maryland, College
Park, School of Languages,
Literatures and Cultures,
Department of French and Italian
Associate Professor*
Literatures in European
Languages: Francophone
Northern Africa

IZABELA ORLOWSKA
*University of Edinburgh, School of
History and Classics
Postdoctoral Fellow*
Ethiopia, Modern:
Geography and Economy
Ethiopia, Modern: History
and Politics

**HARRIET JOSEPH
OTTENHEIMER**
*Kansas State University,
Department of Anthropology
Professor*
Comoro Islands: Geography
and Economy
Comoro Islands: History and
Politics
Comoro Islands: Society and
Cultures

MARTIN OTTENHEIMER
*Kansas State University,
Department of Sociology,
Anthropology, and Social Work
Professor Emeritus*
Comoro Islands: Geography
and Economy
Comoro Islands: History and
Politics
Comoro Islands: Society and
Cultures

**ABDEL WEDOUD OULD
CHEIKH**
*University of Metz, Department of
Philosophy, Sociology, Social
Anthropology*
Mauritania: Society and
Cultures

OYEKAN OWOMOYELA
*University of Nebraska,
Department of English
Professor*
Language: Choice in Writing
Literature: Proverbs and
Riddles

DAVID OWUSU-ANSAH
*James Madison University,
Department of History
Professor*
Asantewa, Yaa
Cape Coast
Osei Bonsu

ADEBAYO OYEBADE
*Tennessee State University,
Department of History
Professor*
Liberia: History and Politics
Nigeria: History and Politics,
Southern Nigeria

RANDALL PACKARD
*Johns Hopkins University, School of
Medicine, Department of History
of Medicine
Professor*
Disease: Industrial

STEPHAN PALMIÉ
*University of Chicago,
Department of Anthropology
Associate Professor*
Diasporas: Institutions

DAVID PARKIN
*University of Oxford, Institute of
Social and Cultural Anthropology
Professor*
Ethnicity: Eastern Africa

JACK PARSON
College of Charleston, Department of Political Science
Professor
    Botswana: History and
       Politics

HELMA PASCH
Institut für Afrikanistik, Universität zu Köln
Research Fellow
    Languages: Surrogates
    Writing Systems: African
       Languages in Roman
       Scripts

DAVID PEACOCK
University of Southampton, Department of Archaeology
Professor Emeritus
    Adulis

J. D. Y. PEEL
University of London, School of Oriental and African Studies, Department of Anthropology and Sociology
Professor
    Oshitelu, Josiah Olunowo

JEFF PEIRES
University of Transkei, Department of History
Professor Emeritus
    Nongqawuse
    Soga, John Henderson

DEBORAH PELLOW
Syracuse University, Maxwell School, Department of Anthropology
Professor
    Gender: Gender Roles
    Sexual Behavior

PAULINE E. PETERS
Harvard University, John F. Kennedy School of Government, Department of Anthropology
Lecturer
    Family: Organization

DEREK PETERSON
University of Cambridge, Faculty of History
Lecturer
    Language: Government and
       Mission Policies

JOHN PHILIPS
Hirosaki University, Japan, College of Humanities, International Society
Professor
    Writing Systems: African
       Languages in Arabic
       Scripts

JOHN PICTON
University of London, School of Oriental and African Studies, Department of Art and Archaeology
Professor Emeritus
    Art History and the Study of
       Africa

JIMMY PIETERSE
University of Pretoria, Centre for the Study of AIDS
Researcher
    Philip, John

INNOCENT PIKIRAYI
University of Pretoria, Department of Anthropology and Archaeology
Senior Lecturer
    History of Africa: To Seventh
       Century
    Southern Africa, History of
       (1000 BCE to 1600 CE)
    Zimbabwe, Great

EMMANUEL PINTO MOREIRA
World Bank Headquarters, Africa Region and Latin America and Caribbean Region
Senior Economist

Economic Community of
    West African States
    (ECOWAS)

CHARLES PIOT
Duke University, Department of African and African-American Studies
Associate Professor
    Ethnicity: Western Africa

GORDON H. PIRIE
University of the Western Cape, Department of Geography
Professor
    Transportation: Overview

JANE PLASTOW
University of Leeds, School of English, Workshop Theatre
Professor
    Women: Women and
       Theater

EDITHA PLATTE
University of Frankfurt am Main, Frobenius-Institut
Senior Researcher
    Lake Chad Societies
    Maiduguri
    Nigeria: Society and
       Cultures, Northeast
       Nigeria

OLIVIER PLIEZ
CNRS (National Center of Scientific Research, France)
Researcher
    Libya: Geography and
       Economy

JOHAN POTTIER
University of London, School of Oriental and African Studies, Department of Anthropology and Sociology
Professor
    Rwanda: Society and
       Cultures

JOEY POWER
Ryerson University, Department of History
Professor
> Malawi: Society and Cultures
> Zomba

LABELLE PRUSSIN
Independent Scholar
> Architecture: Domestic
> Metals and Minerals: Gold
> and Silver

JEAN-AIMÉ RAKOTOARISOA
Institut de Civilisations, Antananarivo
Director
> Madagascar: Geography and
> Economy

SOLOFO RANDRIANJA
University of Toamasina, Department of History
Professor
> Madagascar: History and
> Politics (1895-2006)

SUSAN J. RASMUSSEN
University of Houston, Department of Anthropology
Professor
> Myth and Cosmology

RICHARD RATHBONE
University of London, School of Oriental and African Studies, Department of History
Professor Emeritus
> Busia, Kofi A.
> World War II

EVA RATHGEBER
Carleton University, Institute of Women's Studies
Adjunct Research Professor
> Communications: Electronic

JAMES READ
University of London, School of Oriental and African Studies, Department of Law
Professor Emeritus
> Law: Anglophone Eastern
> Africa
> Law: Anglophone Western
> Africa
> Law: Southern Africa

RICHARD REID
University of Durham, Department of History
Lecturer
> Colonial Policies and
> Practices: British Central
> Africa
> Eritrea: Society and Cultures
> Interlacustrine Region,
> History of (1500 to
> 1900)
> Malawi: History and Politics

ELISHA P. RENNE
University of Michigan, Department of Anthropology and Center for Afroamerican and African Studies
Associate Professor
> Body Adornment and
> Clothing: Fashion
> Symbols and Symbolism:
> Overview

PAMELA REYNOLDS
Johns Hopkins University, Department of Anthropology
Professor
> Youth: Urban

JESSE C. RIBOT
World Resources Institute, Institutions and Governance Program
Senior Associate
> Forestry: Western Africa

JEREMY RICH
Middle Tennessee State University, Department of History
Associate Professor
> Central African Republic:
> Geography and Economy
> Gabon: History and Politics

PAUL RICHARDS
Wageningen University and Research Centre, Department of Social Sciences
Professor
> Ecology: Modern Issues
> Warfare: Internal Revolts

UTE RITZ-MÜLLER
Independent Scholar
> Burkina Faso: Society and
> Cultures

RICHARD ROBERTS
Stanford University, Department of History
Professor
> Touré, Samori

CLAIRE ROBERTSON
Ohio State University, Departments of History and Women's Studies
Professor
> Women: Women and Slavery
> Women: Women and Trade

MELINDA B. ROBINS
Emerson College, Department of Journalism
Associate Professor
> Media: Journalism

DAVID ROBINSON
Michigan State University, Department of History
Distinguished Professor
> 'Umar ibn Sa'id Tal (al-Hajj)

STEVEN J. ROCKEL
University of Toronto, Department of History
Associate Professor
> Transportation: Caravan

JON ROHDE
EQUITY Project

Senior Health Advisor
> Healing and Health Care:
> Hospitals and Clinics

ERIC ROSS
Al Akhawayn University, Ifrane, Morocco, School of Humanities and Social Sciences
Associate Professor
> Africa, History of the Name
> Afrocentrism
> Algiers
> Carthage
> Gao
> Moors in African History
> Nouakchott
> Tangier
> Timbuktu
> Travel and Exploration: Arab
> Tunis

ROBERT ROSS
Leiden University, Department of African Languages and Cultures
Professor
> Cape Colony and Hinterland,
> History of (1600 to 1910)
> Kok, Adam, III

ROBERT I. ROTBERG
Harvard University, John F. Kennedy School of Government
Adjunct Professor
> Rhodes, Cecil John

JOHN A. ROWE
Northwestern University, Department of History
Visiting Professor Emeritus
> Mutesa I

CHRISTOPHER ROY
University of Iowa, School of Art and Art History
Professor
> Art, Regional Styles: Western
> Africa

YAKUBU SAAKA
Oberlin College, African-American Studies Department

Chair
> Kufuor, John

LISA SABBAHY
American University in Cairo, Department of Sociology, Anthropology, and Egyptology
Assistant Professor
> Egypt, Early: Old and Middle
> Kingdoms

HANAN SABEA
University of Virginia, Department of Anthropology
Assistant Professor
> Labor: Plantation

MARGARET ALISON SABIN
Freelance Researcher
> Brazzaville
> Pretoria

FATIMA SADIQI
University of Fez, Morocco, Department of English
Professor
> Abouzeid, Leila
> Kahena
> Literature: Women Writers,
> Northern Africa
> Literatures in African
> Languages: Berber
> Mernissi, Fatima
> N'Ait Atiq, Mririda

ABDOULAYE SAINE
Miami University, Ohio, Department of Political Science
Associate Professor
> Gambia, The: History and
> Politics

ABDI ISMAIL SAMATAR
University of Minnesota, Department of Geography
Professor
> Botswana: Geography and
> Economy
> Somalia: Geography and
> Economy

SALOMON SAMEN
World Bank, Sector and Thematic Programs-Trade Group
Senior Economist
> Money: Colonial Currencies
> Trade, National and
> International Systems

MAXINE SAMPLE
Virginia State University, Department of Languages and Literature
Associate Professor
> Head, Bessie Emery

BONNY SANDS
Northern Arizona University, Department of English
Adjunct Assistant Professor
> Languages: Khoesan and
> Click

S. N. SANGMPAM†
Syracuse University, Department of Political Science
Associate Professor
> Lumumba, Patrice
> Tshombe, Moïse Kapenda

LAMIN SANNEH
Yale University, School of Divinity
Professor
> Braide, Garrick Sokari
> Christianity: Missionary
> Enterprise
> Quaque, Philip

SANDRA SANNEH
Yale University, African Program in African Languages
Senior Lector II
> Literatures in African
> Languages: South
> African Languages

JAMES N. SATER
Al Akhawayn University, Ifrane, Morocco, School of Humanities and Social Sciences
Assistant Professor

Algeria: Geography and
Economy
Algeria: History and Politics
Morocco, History of (1000
to 1900)

PAUL KHALIL SAUCIER
Northeastern University,
Department of Sociology
Lecturer
Cape Verde: History and Politics

CHRISTOPHER SAUNDERS
University of Cape Town,
Department of Historical Studies
Professor
Cape Town
South Africa, Republic of:
Geography and Economy
South Africa, Republic of:
History and Politics
(1850-2006)

TIMOTHY SCARNECCHIA
Kent State University,
Department of History
Assistant Professor
Zimbabwe: History and
Politics

HAROLD SCHEUB
University of Wisconsin-Madison,
Department of African
Languages and Literature
Professor
Literature and the Study of
Africa
Literatures in European
Languages: Afrikaans
Literatures in European
Languages: Anglophone
Western Africa

DAVID SCHOENBRUN
Northwestern University,
Department of History
Associate Professor
Interlacustrine Region,
History of (1000 BCE to
1500 CE)

R. J. SCHOLES
Council for Scientific and
Industrial Research, Department
of Natural Resources and
Environment
Fellow
Ecosystems: Savannas

MAREIKE SCHOMERUS
London School of Economics,
Development Studies Institute
(DESTIN)
Doctoral Candidate
Sudan: Wars

DOROTHEA SCHULZ
Indiana University, Department
of Religious Studies
Assistant Professor
Mali: Society and Cultures
Media: Religion
Women: Women and Islam
in Sub-Saharan Africa

PAMELA SCULLY
Emory University, Department of
Women's Studies and Institute of
African Studies
Associate Professor
Baartman, Sara

GERHARD SEIBERT
Tropical Research Institute
(IICT), Lisbon, Portugal,
Department of Human Sciences
Researcher
Equatorial Guinea: Society
and Cultures
São Tomé e Príncipe:
Geography and Economy
São Tomé e Príncipe: History
and Politics
São Tomé e Príncipe: Society
and Cultures

EMAD EL-DIN SHAHIN
American University in Cairo,
Department of Political Science
Associate Professor
Sadat, Anwar al-

ROSALIND SHAW
Tufts University, Department of
Anthropology
Associate Professor
Sierra Leone: Society and
Cultures

KATHLEEN SHELDON
University of California, Los
Angeles, Center for the Study of
Women
Research Scholar
Amina
Diogo, Luísa Dias
Kimpa Vita, Dona Beatriz
Machel, Graça
Maputo
Ramphele, Mamphela
Suzman, Helen
Women: Widows
Women: Women and
Urbanism
Women: Women in African
History

GEORGE SHEPPERSON
University of Edinburgh,
Department of History
Professor
Chilembwe, John

ABDUL SHERIFF
Zanzibar Indian Ocean Research
Institute
Executive Director
Barghash Ibn Sa'id
Eastern Africa and Indian
Ocean, History of (1500
to 1800)
Zanzibar Sultanate

PARKER SHIPTON
Boston University, Department of
Anthropology
Associate Professor
Debt and Credit:
Entrustment
Money: Overview

ANDRÉ N. SIAMUNDELE
Wells College, Department of Foreign Languange and Literatures
Assistant Professor
　　Theater: Francophone Africa

OWEN SICHONE
Jawaharlal Nehru University, New Delhi, Centre for West Asian and African Studies
　　Peasants: Central Africa

DANIEL SIFUNA
Kenyatta University, Department of Education Foundation
Professor
　　Education, School:
　　　　Anglophone Eastern
　　　　Africa

AHMAD ALAWAD SIKAINGA
Ohio State University, Department of History
Professor
　　Ahmad, Mahdi Muhammad
　　Labor: Trades Unions and
　　　　Associations
　　Rabih bin Fadlallah
　　Sudan: History and Politics
　　Zubayr, Rahma Mansur al-

ZELINDA MARIA SILVA COHEN CORREIA E SILVA
Ministry of Culture, Institute of Cultural Investigation and Patrimony, Cape Verde
Researcher
　　Cape Verde: Society and
　　　　Cultures

RAYMOND A. SILVERMAN
University of Michigan, Department of the History of Art
Professor
　　Art, Regional Styles: Ethiopia

PAUL SILVERSTEIN
Reed College, Department of Anthropology

Associate Professor
　　Ethnicity: Northern Africa

ALICE NICOLE SINDZINGRE
National Centre for Scientific Research (CNRS), Paris, and University Paris-10
Research Fellow
　　Aid and Development:
　　　　Consequences

DAVID SMETHURST
University of California, Berkeley, Department of Geography
Visiting Scholar
　　Climate
　　Metals and Minerals:
　　　　Resources
　　Nongovernmental
　　　　Organizations

FRED T. SMITH
Kent State University, School of Art
Professor
　　Body Adornment and
　　　　Clothing: Overview

NEAL SOBANIA
Pacific Lutheran University, Department of History
Professor
　　Candace
　　Kenya: Geography and
　　　　Economy
　　Kenya: History and Politics
　　Kenya: Society and Cultures

GENESE SODIKOFF
Rutgers-Newark, State University of New Jersey, Department of Sociology and Anthropology
Assistant Professor
　　Labor: Conscript and Forced

ALIKO SONGOLO
University of Wisconsin, Madison, Department of African Languages and Literature
Professor
　　Armah, Ayi Kwei

Césaire, Aimé
Rabemananjara, Jacques

ELISEE SOUMONNI
National University of Bénin, Abomey-Calavi, Department of History and Archaeology
Assistant Professor
　　Bénin: History and Politics

AIDAN SOUTHALL
University of Wisconsin–Madison, Department of Anthropology
Professor Emeritus
　　Stratification, Social

PAUL SPENCER
University of London, School of Oriental and African Studies, Department of Anthropology and Sociology
Professor Emeritus
　　Age and Age Organization

DEBRA SPITULNIK
Emory University, Department of Anthropology
Associate Professor
　　Media: Radio and TV

GUY STANDING
University of Bath, Department of Social Policy
Professor
　　Capitalism and
　　　　Commercialization:
　　　　Employment and
　　　　Unemployment

ANDREW ELLIAS STATE
Makerere University, Department of Sociology
Lecturer
　　Uganda: History and Politics

GEORG STAUTH
Bielefeld University, Department of Transnationalisation and Development
Professor and Reader
　　Egypt, Modern: Society and
　　　　Cultures

NANCY RHEA STEEDLE
Yale University, Program of African Studies
Graduate Student
> Djibouti, Republic of
> Niger: History and Politics
> Nigeria: History and Politics, Northern Nigeria
> Nigeria: Society and Cultures, Southeast Nigeria
> Sierra Leone: History and Politics

EDWARD STEINHART
Texas Tech University, Department of History
Professor
> Wildlife: Hunting, Sport

ROBERT STOCK
University of Saskatchewan, International Programs Unit, College of Arts and Science
Internationalization Coordinator
> Production Strategies: Artisan Production

DAVID STONE
Florida State University, Department of Classics
Assistant Professor
> Northwestern Africa, Classical Period, History of (1000 BCE to 600 CE)

KARL STRIEDTER
Johann Wolfgang Goethe-Universität, Frankfurt, Frobenius-Institut
Researcher
> Art, Genres and Periods: Rock Art, Saharan and Northern Africa

CHRIS STRINGER
Natural History Museum, London, Department of Palaeontology
Professor
> Human Evolution: Origins of Modern Humans

JOHN E. G. SUTTON
British Institute in Eastern Africa
Honorary Research Fellow
> Agriculture: Beginnings and Development

PATRICE TALLA TAKOUKAM
World Bank, Environment and International Law Unit (LEGEN)
Counsel
> Law: Anglophone Central Africa

JEAN-CLAUDE TCHATCHOUANG
World Bank, Office of the Executive Director
Senior Advisor
> Money: Exchange Rate Systems

VIJAYA TEELOCK
University of Mauritius, Department of History and Political Science
Senior Lecturer
> Mauritius: History and Politics

MUSSIE TESFAGIORGIS
University of Hamburg, Department of History
Independent Researcher
> Eritrea: Geography and Economy

MOSES KANGMIEVE TESI
Middle Tennessee State University, Department of Political Science
Professor
> Côte d'Ivoire: Geography and Economy

MOTLATSI THABANE
National University of Lesotho, Department of History
Professor Emeritus
> Moshoeshoe I

JÖRN THIELMANN
Kompetenzzentrum Orient-Okzident Mainz KOOM, Johannes Gutenberg-University Mainz
Managing Director
> Farouk, King of Egypt
> Fuad, King of Egypt
> Islam: Northern Africa
> Law: Islamic
> Muslim Northern Africa, History of (641 to 1500 CE)
> Ottoman Northern Africa, History of (1500 to 1850)

ANNE ELISE THOMAS
Jefferson Center
Educational Program Coordinator
> Music, Modern Popular: Egypt

DOMINIC THOMAS
University of California at Los Angeles, Department of French and Francophone Studies
Chair
> Sony Labou Tansi

STEVEN THOMSON
Pacific Lutheran University, Department of Anthropology
Assistant Professor
> Gambia, The: Society and Cultures

ALEC C. THORNTON
University of Otago, New Zealand, Division of Humanities, Department of Geography
Postdoctoral Research Fellow
> Angola: Geography and Economy
> Congo, Republic of: Geography and Economy

JOHN K. THORNTON
Boston University, African American Studies Program
Professor
    Military Organizations: History of Military Organizations

GARY THOULOUIS
Brooklyn, NY
    Brazza, Pierre François Camille Savorgnan de
    Casely-Hayford, Joseph Ephraim
    Chitapankwa, Mutale Mutaka
    Danquah, Joseph Kwame Kyeretwi Boakye
    Eyadema, Gnassingbe (Étienne)

DIANE THRAM
Rhodes University, International Library of African Music
Director
    Tracey, Hugh

DAVID W. THROUP
Center for Strategic and International Studies, Washington, DC, Africa Program
Senior Associate
    Colonial Policies and Practices: British East Africa

FAROUK TOPAN
University of London, School of Oriental and African Studies, Department of Africa
Professor Emeritus
    Literatures in African Languages: Swahili
    Saʿid bin Sultan

ANDREW TRACEY
Rhodes University, International Library of African Music
Founder
    Musical Instruments

ALESSANDRO TRIULZI
Oriental University, Naples, Department of African and Arab Studies
Professor
    Colonial Policies and Practices: Italian

CHARLES TSHIMANGA-KASHAMA
University of Nevada, Reno, Department of History
Assistant Professor
    Music, Modern Popular: Central Africa

MATTHEW TURNER
University of Wisconsin-Madison, Department of Geography
Professor
    Ecosystems: Deserts and Semi-Deserts

THOMAS TURNER
Virginia Commonwealth University, School of Government and Public Affairs
Adjunct Professor
    Congo, Democratic Republic of the: History and Politics
    Kisangani

MICHAEL TWADDLE
University of London, Institute of Commonwealth Studies
Emeritus Reader
    Kakungulu, Semei Lwakirenzi

ROBERT UTTARO
University of Florida, Department of Political Science
    Banda, Ngwazi Hastings Kamuzu
    Fanon, Frantz
    Tubman, William Vacanarat Shadrach

GOOLAM VAHED
University of KwaZulu-Natal, Department of Historical Studies
Associate Professor
    Islam: Southern Africa

SARAH VALDEZ
Freelance Researcher
    Abidjan
    Accra
    Agaja
    Ahmad ibn Ibrahim al-Ghazi (Ahmad Grañ)
    Banjul
    Dingiswayo
    Gungunyana
    Kruger, Paul
    Mapondera, Paitando Kadungure
    Moi, Daniel arap
    Mswati II
    Plaatje, Sol
    Savimbi, Jonas
    Shyaam aMbul aNgoong
    Thuku, Harry
    Verwoerd, Hendrik Frensch

JUDITH IMEL VAN ALLEN
Cornell University, Institute for African Development
Research Fellow
    Dow, Unity
    Khama, Tshekedi

WIM M. J. VAN BINSBERGEN
University of Leiden, Netherlands, Faculty of Social and Behavioral Sciences
Professor
    Ethnicity: Central Africa

AAD VAN TILBURG
Wageningen University, Netherlands, Marketing and Consumer Behaviour Group
Associate Professor
    Food: Marketing

JACQUES VANDERLINDEN
Université de Moncton, New Brunswick, Faculty of Law
Professor Emeritus
    Law: Burundi, Congo, and
        Rwanda

BRUCE VANDERVORT
Virginia Military Institute, Department of History
Professor
    Warfare: Colonial

JAN VANSINA
University of Wisconsin–Madison, Departments of History and Anthropology
Professor Emeritus
    Bantu, Eastern, Southern, and
        Western, History of
        (1000 BCE to 1500 CE)
    History of Africa: Seventh to
        Sixteenth Century
    Kagame, Alexis
    Political Systems: States

MICHAEL VEAL
Yale University, Department of Music
Associate Professor
    Adé, Sunny
    Kuti, Fela

DENIS VENTER
Africa Consultancy and Research, Pretoria
Independent Researcher
    De Klerk, Frederik Willem

FRANÇOISE VERGÈS
Goldsmiths College, London, Centre for Cultural Studies
Reader
    Creoles

KEES VERSTEEGH
University of Nijmegen, Institute of the Middle East
Professor
    Languages: Arabic

ULF VIERKE
Bayreuth University, Afrikanistik
    Photography:
        Photojournalism

HENRIK VIGH
Research and Rehabilitation Centre for Torture Victims, Copenhagen
Senior Researcher
    Youth: Soldiers

KNUT VIKØR
University of Bergen, Department of History
Professor
    Islam: Sufi Orders
    Sahara Desert: Geography
        and History
    Sanusi, Muhammad ibn
        ʿAli al-

LEONARDO VILLALÓN
University of Florida, Center for African Studies
Director
    Diouf, Abdou
    Senegal: Society and Cultures

MARY VOGL
Colorado State University, Department of Foreign Languages and Literatures
Associate Professor
    Art, Regional Styles: Egypt

MICHELE WAGNER
University of Minnesota, Department of History
Assistant Professor
    Burundi: Society and Cultures

PETER WALKER
University of Oregon, Department of Geography
Associate Professor
    Aid and Development:
        Structural Adjustment
    Forestry: Southern Africa
    Malawi: Geography and
        Economy

MARION WALLACE
British Library, African Collections
Curator
    Namibia: History and
        Politics

RICHARD WALLER
Bucknell University, Department of History
Associate Professor
    Production Strategies:
        Pastoralism

GRETCHEN WALSH†
Boston University, African Studies Library
Head
    Libraries

KEITH WALTERS
University of Texas at Austin, Department of Linguistics
Professor
    Tunisia: Society and
        Cultures

IAN WATTS
University of Cape Town, Department of Archaeology
Professor
    Bujumbura

MICHAEL J. WATTS
University of California, Berkeley, Department of Geography
Professor
    Geography and the Study of
        Africa
    Lubumbashi
    Port Harcourt

JENNIFER WEIR
Murdoch University, Australia, Teaching Learning Centre
Senior Lecturer
    Nandi

BRAD WEISS
College of William & Mary, Department of Anthropology

Professor
   Modernity and
     Modernization:
     Antimodern and
     Postmodern Movements

DAVID JOHN WELSH
*University of Cape Town,
Department of Political Science
Professor Emeritus*
   Apartheid

TOBIAS WENDL
*University of Bayreuth, Institute
for Africa Studies
Director*
   Photography: Aesthetics and
     Social Significance

FRED WENDORF
*Southern Methodist University,
Department of Anthropology
Professor*
   Prehistory: Sahara and
     Northern Africa

LUISE WHITE
*University of Florida, Department
of History
Professor*
   Prostitution

BENSON FUNK WILDER
*University of Colorado-Boulder,
Department of Geography
Doctoral Candidate*
   Boundaries, Colonial and
     Modern

GAY WILENTZ†
*East Carolina University,
Department of English
Professor*
   Aidoo, Ama Ata

DRID WILLIAMS
Journal for the Anthropological
Study of Human Movement
*(JASHM)
Co-editor*
   Dance: Aesthetics

JAMES WILLIAMS
*Johns Hopkins University,
Department of Anthropology
Graduate Student*
   Youth: Urban

MIRYAM EHRLICH WILLIAMSON
Independent Scholar
   Gabon: Geography and
     Economy
   Gabon: Society and Cultures

EDWIN N. WILMSEN
*University of Texas at Austin,
Department of Anthropology
Senior Lecturer*
   Kalahari Desert
   Production Strategies:
     Hunting and Gathering

PENELOPE WILSON
*Durham University, Department
of Archaeology
Doctor*
   Cleopatra VII
   Egypt, Early: Late and
     Ptolemaic

KWASI WIREDU
*University of South Florida,
Department of Philosophy
Distinguished University Professor*
   Philosophy

JOSEPH MALLORY WOBER
*Michigan State University,
Department of
Telecommunication, Information
Studies, and Media
Adjunct Professor*
   Psychology and the Study of
     Africa

DWAYNE WOODS
*Purdue University, Department of
Political Science
Associate Professor*
   Côte d'Ivoire: History and
     Politics

DOROTHY WOODSON
*Yale University Library, African
Collection
Curator*
   Mbabane

STEPHEN WOOTEN
*University of Oregon, Department
of Anthropology and
International Studies Program
Assistant Professor*
   Mali: Geography and
     Economy

ERIC WORBY
*University of the Witwatersrand,
School of Social Sciences
Head*
   Zimbabwe: Geography and
     Economy
   Zimbabwe: Society and
     Cultures

DAVID WORTH
*University of Cape Town, Centre
for Higher Education
Development
Faculty Finance Manager*
   Archaeology and Prehistory:
     Industrial

CAROLINE WRIGHT
*University of Warwick,
Department of Sociology
Senior Lecturer*
   Labor: Migration

DAVID K. WRIGHT
*University of Illinois at Urbana-
Champaign, Department of
Anthropology
Postdoctoral Research Associate*
   Prehistory: Eastern Africa

DONALD R. WRIGHT
*SUNY, Cortland, Department of
History
Distinguished Teaching Professor*
   Gambia, The: Geography and
     Economy

NANCY G. WRIGHT
New York City
Independent Researcher
> Ranavalona, Mada

JAMES WUNSCH
Creighton University, Department
of Political Science and
International Relations
Professor
> Government: Local

LARRY YARAK
Texas A&M University,
Department of History
Associate Professor
> Elmina

CRAWFORD YOUNG
University of Wisconsin-Madison,
Department of Political Science

Professor Emeritus
> Mobutu Sese Seko

PHILIP ZACHERNUK
Dalhousie University, Department
of History
Associate Professor
> Independence and Freedom,
> Early African Writers

I. WILLIAM ZARTMAN
Johns Hopkins University, School of
Advanced International Studies,
Conflict Management Program
Director
> Warfare: National and
> International

MALIKA ZEGHAL
University of Chicago, Divinity
School

Associate Professor
> Islam: Islamism
> Islam: Modernism

PAUL TIYAMBE ZELEZA
University of Illinois at Chicago,
Department of African-American
Studies
Professor
> Education, University and
> College: Overview

BAHRU ZEWDE
Addis Ababa University,
Department of History
Professor Emeritus
> Ethiopia and the Horn,
> History of (1600 to 1910)
> Ethiopia and Vicinity,
> History of (600 to
> 1600 CE)

THEMATIC OUTLINE OF CONTENTS

Entries may appear under one or more of the following headings. Beneath each heading, entries are listed in order of appearance in the encyclopedia, that is, alphabetical order modified by certain geographic and chronological considerations. The list attempts to classify biographical subjects according to their roles or occupations or principal claims to fame. Many persons appear under multiple headings. "Religion" and "Philosophy" are interpreted broadly, in accordance with the diversity of African cultures. Frequently, as in the Islamic world, there is little separation between religion and government. Hence, many African leaders appear in both categories.

The outline is divided into fifteen parts: 1. Africa in World Tradition and Knowledge; 2. Environment, Geography, and Human Origins; 3. Prehistory and Archaeology; 4. History and the Past; 5. Modernity and Modernization; 6. Society and Social Structures; 7. Religion and Philosophy; 8. Economics, Infrastructure, and Development; 9. Law, Government, Politics, Diplomacy, and War; 10. Health and Education; 11. Language and Literature; 12. The Arts; 13. Countries; 14. Cities; 15. Biographies (15.1 European Explorers, Missionaries, and Colonial Leaders; 15.2 African Rulers and Leaders: Historical; 15.3 African Rulers and Leaders: Colonial; 15.4 African Rulers and Leaders: Independence; 15.5 Religious Figures and Intellectuals; 15.6 Authors; 15.7 Artists, Musicians, and Filmmakers; 15.8 Other).

1. AFRICA IN WORLD TRADITION AND KNOWLEDGE

Africa, History of the Name
Afrocentrism
Anthropology, Social, and the Study of Africa
Christianity: Africa and World Christianity
Diasporas: Institutions
Diasporas: Re-Africanization
Ethnomusicology and the Study of Africa
Festivals and Carnivals
Geography and the Study of Africa
Globalization
Historiography: European
History, World: Africa in
Human Rights
Knowledge: Overview

Linguistics and the Study of Africa
Literature and the Study of Africa
Modernity and Modernization: Antimodern and Postmodern Movements
Museums: History
Museums: Memory
Person, Concepts of
Philosophy
Philosophy and the Study of Africa
Political Science and the Study of Africa
Psychology and the Study of Africa
Religion and the Study of Africa
Research: Overview
Research: Biological Sciences
Research: Social Sciences
Research: Historical Resources
Research: Research Funding

5. MODERNITY AND MODERNIZATION

6. SOCIETY AND SOCIAL STRUCTURES

9. LAW, GOVERNMENT, POLITICS, DIPLOMACY, AND WAR

10. HEALTH AND EDUCATION

11. LANGUAGE AND LITERATURE

14. CITIES

15. BIOGRAPHIES

15.1 EUROPEAN EXPLORERS, MISSIONARIES, AND COLONIAL LEADERS

15.2 AFRICAN RULERS AND LEADERS: HISTORICAL

Colenso, John William
Crowther, Samuel Ajayi
Dike, Kenneth Onwuka
Hamallah of Nioro
Harris, William Wadé
Hasan, Muhammad 'Abdallah
Huddleston, Trevor
Ibn Khaldun, Abd al-Rahman
Idris, Ahmad ibn
Johnson, Samuel
Kagame, Alexis
Kahena
Kimbangu, Simon
Kimpa Vita, Dona Beatriz
Kinjikitile
Kiwanuka, Joseph
Lakwena, Alice
Lenshina, Alice
Maathai, Wangari
Maghili, Muhammad ibn 'Abd al-Karim al-
Maranke, John
Mukhtar, Sidi al-
Nongqawuse
Oshitelu, Josiah
Quaque, Philip
Shembe, Isaiah
Tijani, Ahmad
Touré, Amadou Toumani
Turabi, Hasan 'Abd Allah al-
Tutu, Desmond Mpilo
'Uthman dan Fodio

15.6 AUTHORS

Abouzeid, Leila
Achebe, Chinua
Aidoo, Ama Ata
'Ali, Mohammed Duse
Armah, Ayi Kwei
Asma'u, Nana
Bâ, Mariama
Baba, Ahmad
Beti, Mongo
Blyden, Edward Wilmot
Cabral, Amílcar Lopes
Camara Laye
Césaire, Aimé
Coetzee, J. M.
Diop, Alioune
Diop, Cheikh Anta
Djebar, Assia

Dow, Unity
Du Bois, W. E. B.
Emecheta, Buchi
Equiano, Olaudah
Fanon, Frantz
Farah, Nuruddin
Fugard, Athol
Gordimer, Nadine
Hampâté Bâ, Amadou
Head, Bessie Emery
Ibn Battuta, Muhammad ibn Abdullah
Ibn Khaldun, Abd al-Rahman
Idris, Ahmad ibn
Ilori, Adam Abdullahi al-
Johnson, Samuel
Kateb, Yacine
Kourouma, Ahmadou
La Guma, Alex
Leo Africanus
Lopes, Henri
Mahfouz, Naguib
Mekki, Aicha
Mernissi, Fatima
N'Ait Atiq, Mririda
Ngũgĩ wa Thiong'o
Nwapa, Flora
Ogot, Grace
Paton, Alan
Plaatje, Sol
Rabemananjara, Jacques
Ramphele, Mamphela
Saadawi, Nawal el-
Salih, Tayeb
Saro-Wiwa, Ken
Schreiner, Olive
Sembène, Ousmane
Senghor, Léopold Sédar
Serote, Mongane
Shaaban Robert
Soga, John Henderson
Sony Labou Tansi
Soyinka, Wole
Tracey, Hugh
Tutuola, Amos
'Uthman dan Fodio

15.7 ARTISTS, MUSICIANS, AND FILMMAKERS

Adé, Sunny
Djebar, Assia
Douglas Camp, Sokari

INDEX

Page numbers in boldface refer to the main entry on a subject. Page numbers in italics refer to illustrations, figures, and tables. Number preceding colon (:) indicates volume in which entry appears. Overviews of subjects and peoples and profiles of countries are listed as the first subhead below the main headings.

Anyi language, number system in, **4**:80

Anyidoho, Kofi, **3**:333

Anyuak. *See* Anuak

Aouloube, peripatetic production by, **4**:255

apartheid, **1**:88–92; **2**:14; **4**:492–494. *See also* anti-apartheid movement
  aid supporting, **1**:44
  art on, **1**:173
  Bantu Education Act (1953), **3**:277, 474
  and caste system, **4**:520–521, 524
  chiefdoms and, **4**:175–176
  costs of, **2**:602–603
  de Klerk, F. W., and, **2**:11–12
  education under, **2**:205, 206
    higher, **2**:226, 228, 237–238
  effect on literature, **3**:378
  ethnicity and, **2**:336–341
  Group Areas Act (South Africa, 1950), **1**:310, 311; **3**:277, 474
  Huddleston on, **2**:609
  human rights and, **2**:627
  influence on music, **3**:663–664
  Joseph, Helen, opposition to, **3**:80
  land rights and, **4**:110–113
  legal system of, **3**:277
  in Namibia, **4**:6, 7, 9, 10
  neocolonialism and, **4**:22
  pass laws, **4**:486, 492
  Paton, Alan, on, **4**:101–102
  peasants under, **4**:110–113
  Philip, John, on, **4**:123–124
  Ramphele, Mamphela, on, **4**:297
  reconciliation after, **2**:569–570
  refugees from, **4**:302
  relations of Malawi with, **3**:460
  rise of, **2**:601
  system of pass controls, **4**:484
  Tafawa Balewa and, **5**:5
  testimony of Miriam Makeba before the U.N., **3**:452
  theater and, **5**:46–47, 49
  thornbushes as architecture of early, **5**:167
  in town planning, **1**:125
  Tutu on, **5**:116
  United Nations and, **5**:129–130
  and use of Afrikaans in schools, **3**:318
  Verwoerd, Hendrick, and, **5**:168, 169
  Windhoek under, **5**:219
  women under, **5**:240

Apaya, Philip Kwame, **4**:140

Apithy, Sourou Migan, **1**:235; **4**:205

Apollo II Cave rock art (Namibia), **2**:585

Apologia ad Constantium (Athanasius), **2**:349

Apostolic churches
  Christ Apostolic Church, **1**:385; **4**:275
  Christian Catholic Apostolic Church in Zion, **1**:393
  New Apostolic Church in São Tomé e Príncipe, **4**:370
  in South Africa, **1**:393; **4**:488
  Zimbabwean Apostolic movements, **1**:392

Appadurai, Arjun, **1**:141; **4**:339

Appiah, Joseph William Egyanka, **4**:273

Appiah, Kwame Anthony, **3**:160
  ethnography and, **1**:86
  on postcolonialism, **4**:206

Appollonians. *See* Nzima

Apter, Andrew, **4**:327

Apter, David, **4**:169

Aptidon, Hassan Gouled, **1**:361, 362; **2**:135

Apuleius of Madaura, **3**:496

Aquambo. *See* Akwamu

Arab Democratic Republic, **5**:210

Arab Human Development Report, **2**:236

Arab League, Somalia and, **4**:477

Arab Maghrib Union, **5**:194

Arab Revolt (1888) in German East Africa, **1**:457

Arab Socialist Union (Libya), **3**:310

Arab Women's Solidarity Association, **4**:355

Arabic, **3**:224–226
  comic art in, **3**:520
  creolization, **3**:225–226
  in Djibouti, **2**:134
  in Eritrea, **2**:294
  historiography, **2**:564–565
  in Islamic education, **2**:202, 220, 222
  in Libya, **3**:308
  in Madagascar, **3**:430
  in Morocco, **1**:3; **2**:595; **3**:596
  popular culture and, **4**:193
  script, **5**:273
    African languages in, **5**:275, 276–278
  in Tunisia, **5**:112–113
  vernacular, as language of majority of North Africans, **3**:7
  women's literature in, **3**:346
  writing system for, **1**:92; **5**:275
    art and, **1**:168, 185
    in rock art, **2**:586

Arabic numerals, **5**:275

Arabs. *See also* Omani Arabs
  overview, **5**:370
  Berbers distinguished from, **1**:62

in Buganda, **3**:36

in Burundi, **1**:281

in Chad, **1**:359–360

conquests
  of Egypt, **1**:409–410
  of northern Africa, **4**:70

Creoles, **1**:529

and divination, **2**:129–130

in Djibouti, **2**:135

in Fez, **2**:370

immigration of, **3**:6–8

in Kampala, **3**:91

in Kenya, **3**:99

in Morocco, **3**:596

in Nigeria, **4**:31, 42

in Nubia, **4**:77

in the Sahara, **4**:357

in slave trade, **4**:301

in Sudan, **4**:530–531

Swahili Arabs
  in Malawi, **3**:456
  Mogadishu in trading system, **3**:570

Aragp. *See* Alagoa

Arawa, **4**:44

archaeology and prehistory, **1**:91–113
  overview, **1**:91–98
  agriculture and, **1**:25; **4**:155–157
  at Aksum, **1**:55–56
  astronomy in, **1**:204–205
  Christian, **1**:111–113
  cultural heritage and, **2**:550–552
  desertification data in, **2**:63–64
  in eastern Africa, **2**:149
  Egypt
    Byzantine, **2**:253, *253*
    Kom el Dikka site, **4**:*69*
    late and Ptolemaic, **2**:*249*, 249–250, *250*
    predynastic, **2**:241
    Roman and Byzantine, **2**:252, *252, 253*
  historical, **1**:104–106; **4**:334–335
  historiography and, **2**:557
  industrial, **1**:106–108
  Islamic, **1**:109–111
  marine, **1**:108–109
  museums and preservation of, **2**:550–552
  at Niani, **4**:28–29
  in Nigeria, **4**:47
  in northwestern Africa, **4**:74, *75*
  in Nubia, **4**:77
  pillaged sites in, **1**:135
  in Rabat and Salé, **4**:295
  research on, **4**:317
  rock art, **2**:584–586
  shamanism and, **2**:144–145

Beauvoir, Simone de, **2**:440
Bebey, Francis, **3**:667
Bechuanaland. *See also* Botswana
  currency, **3**:587
  railways in, **5**:86
  Roman-Dutch law in, **3**:276
Becker, Gary, **2**:179–180, 354
Becker, Gcina Mhlope, **5**:*256*
Becket, Samuel, **5**:38
Bede, **5**:372
Bedford, Emma, **4**:147
Bédié, Henri Konan, **1**:520, 524,
    526, 527
Bedik, **4**:385
Bedouin (Beduin)
  overview, **5**:372
  and Arab immigration into Africa,
    3:6
  ethnicity and, **2**:334
  in the Sahara, **4**:357; **5**:205
  segmentary political systems,
    2:486
  in western Africa, **5**:205
Beecher Report on language policy,
    3:211
beehive storage, **1**:164–165
Beek, Walter E. A. van, **3**:155
beekeeping in Central African
    Republic, **1**:343
beer, **2**:382. *See also* breweries
  brewing, **2**:271
    in Angola, **1**:74
    baskets in, **1**:196
    in Ghana, **1**:4
  early, **4**:518
  and exchange, **2**:394
  Ghana, **2**:389
  in Uganda, **5**:121
  women and production, **2**:394;
    5:259–260
beeswax, **4**:162, 163
  in Angola, **1**:79
  export from Benguela, **1**:227
  in Tanzania, **4**:166
Begho ivory trade, **3**:67
Begin, Menachim, **4**:357
Behanzin, king, **1**:235
Behind the Mask (Dawood), **4**:192
Behr, Mark, **3**:382
Beidelman, Thomas O.,
    4:122, 556
Beier, Georgina, **1**:137
Beier, Ulli, **1**:137
Being and Nothingness (Sartre),
    4:132
Beir. *See* Murle
Beja
  overview, **5**:373
  in Eritrea, **2**:292

Islam and, **3**:54
  in Sudan, **4**:531
bejel, **2**:101, 112–113
Beji insurgency, **5**:192
Bekela. *See* Kela
Bekolo, Jean-Pierre, **2**:375
Bel, Mbilia, **3**:652
Belafonte, Harry, **3**:452, 488
Belandier, Georges, **4**:319
Belen. *See* Bilen
Belew Kelew monument (Eritrea),
    5:280–281
Belgian Centre d'Information and
    Documentation, **4**:143
Belgium. *See also* Brussels
  and broadcasting, **3**:511
  and Central African Republic, **1**:346
  colonial policies and practices,
    1:431–435, 499
    administration, **1**:476
    colonial army, **3**:554
    Burundi, **1**:282–283
    Ruanda, **1**:283
  decolonization by, **1**:472; **2**:37
  and Lumumba, **1**:502
  and mining, **3**:538
  railway constructions, **3**:190
  research in, **4**:319
  Rwanda and, **4**:352
  trade with Chad, **1**:357
Belgo-Congolese Union, **3**:418
Belhadj, Ali, **3**:45
Belkahia, Farid, **1**:168
Belkhodja, Abdelaziz, **3**:402
Bell, Andrew, **3**:425
Bell, Deborah, **1**:173
Bell, Hesketh, **2**:103
Bella, **1**:155
  overview, **5**:373
  activism of, **2**:335–336
  in northern Africa, **2**:334
Bellah. *See* Bella
Belle (Kuwaa), **3**:297
Bello, Ahmadu, **1**:*224*, **224**, **224–225**
  Islamization campaign of, **4**:49
  Tafawa Balewa and, **5**:5
Bello, Muhammad, **1**:225
  al-Hájj and, **4**:278
  biography by, **2**:564
  as physician, **2**:540
Bellow, Bella, **3**:667
belly politics, **4**:340–341
Bemba
  overview, **5**:373
  beadwork, **1**:*200*
  influence extended by Mutale Mutaka
    Chitapankwa, **1**:379
  initiation, **2**:445; **3**:26, 156
  marriage, **3**:484

matrilineal clans, **3**:132, 143
  as mega-ethnic group, **2**:326
  rites of passage among, **5**:249
  in Zambia, **5**:312
Bemba, Jean-Pierre, **1**:504
Bemba, Sylvain, **3**:394
Bemba language, **3**:220; **5**:313, 316,
    317–318
Bembe
  masks, **1**:153
  sculpture, **1**:152
Bembeya Jazz, **3**:648, 666, 669
Bemebe sculpture, **1**:152
Ben Barka, Mehdi, **1**:225–226
  remembrance march for, **1**:*226*
Ben Bella, Ahmed, **1**:64; **4**:*462*
  overthrow of, **4**:461
Ben Jelloun, Tahar, **3**:360–361, 365, 402
Ben Youssef, Salah, **5**:113
Bena, **5**:373
Benadou, Albert, **3**:*550*
Benchekroun, Siham, **3**:402
Benchrerifa, Abdellatif, **2**:460
Benda-Beckmann, Keebet von, **3**:199
Bende, **5**:373
Bender, M. Lionel, **3**:234
Bendor-Samuel, John, **3**:231–232
Beng
  beliefs about babies, **4**:122
  in Côte d'Ivoire, **1**:522
  myths, **3**:688
  symbolism of kapok trees, **3**:687–688
Benga, **5**:373
Benga, Ota, **1**:226–227
Benga language, **2**:423
Benghazi (Libya), **3**:306
Benguela (Angola), **1**:227–228
  and slave trade, **1**:79; **4**:422
  urbanization of, **5**:136
Benguela Current, **1**:71–72, 425, 426
Benhadouga, Abdelhamid, **1**:62
Beni Amer
  overview, **5**:373
  in Eritrea, **2**:292
  in Sudan, **4**:531
Bénin, Republic of, **1**:228–237. *See
    also* Cotonou (Bénin); Porto-Novo
  profile, **1**:*233*
  agriculture, **2**:119
  art, **2**:90
  and CFA franc, **3**:577, 585
  Christianity in, **4**:312
  community radio stations, **3**:526
  in Economic Community of West
    African States, **2**:161–163
  education, **2**:217
  emigration to Côte d'Ivoire, **1**:522
  geography and economy,
    1:228–230

state formation in, **4**:173
truth commission in, **5**:105
urbanization, **5**:139, 140
warfare in, **5**:177
Burungi (Burunge)
  overview, **5**:375
  in Tanzania, **5**:9
Busa
  overview, **5**:376
  in Nigeria, **4**:44
Busagwe. *See* Busa
Busaid, al-, dynasty, **5**:326
Busaidi dynasty, **3**:55
Busanga. *See* Busansi
Busanse. *See* Busa
Busansi
  overview, **5**:376
  in Ghana, **2**:470
Bush, George W., **2**:279, *280*
bush schools, **2**:204
Bushiri ibn Salim, **1**:289–290
bushmeat
  trade, ecological impact of, **2**:153
  wildlife preservation and, **5**:213–214
Bushmeat Crisis Task Force, **5**:213
Bushmen. *See* San
Bushoong, **1**:190
The Bushtrackers (Mwangi), **4**:191
Busia, Kofi A., **1**:290, *290*
Busia, Kofi Abrefa, **2**:475
Busiri, Sharaf al-Din al-, **3**:644
Busoga, in Uganda, **5**:125
Butake, Bule, **5**:34
Butana Group, **4**:213
Butfunast, The Cow Man (film),
    4:194
Buthelezi, Mangosuthu, **1**:291, *291*;
    4:494
  ethnicity under, **2**:338
Butler, Guy, **5**:47
Butrso Ghali, Butros, **1**:409
buttons as money, **3**:576
Butumbuka. *See* Tumbuka
Buxton, Edward, **5**:211
Buye, **5**:376
Buyoya, Pierre, **1**:270, 287, 288
Bvenda. *See* Venda
Bwa
  art, **1**:175
  in Burkina Faso, **1**:273, 274
  masquerades, **3**:491
Bwaka, **5**:376
Bwami initiation association, **1**:154;
    3:492
Bwende sculpture, **1**:152
Bwiti religion, **1**:454
  death and mourning in, **2**:14–15
  in Equatorial Guinea, **2**:282

in Gabon, **2**:424
  use of iboga, **4**:517
byeri figures, **2**:553
byssinosis, **2**:119
Byzantine Empire
  archaeological evidence of
    Christianity, **1**:111
  art, **1**:185, 187
  Egypt and, **2**:252–253; **4**:68–69
  Egypt under, in Northwestern Africa,
    4:76
  Tangier in, **5**:6
  Tripoli under, **5**:104

C

C-Group, **2**:245
Cabinda, Angola, **1**:293–294
cabinets of curiosities, **1**:136
Cable News Network, **3**:522, 526
Cabo Verde. *See* Cape Verde
Cabral, Amílcar Lopes, **1**:294,
    294–295, 316; **2**:512, 514;
    3:332; **4**:16
  assassination, **1**:316–317
  on civil war, **5**:180
  Marxism of, **4**:132
  in Partido Africano da Independência
    da Guiné e Cabo Verde,
    4:117–118
  peasants under, **4**:114
  support for, **5**:189
Cabral, Luís, **1**:317; **2**:514
Cabral, Vasco, **3**:405
Cabrera, Lydia, **2**:91
Cacoub, Olivier, Clément, **5**:283
Cadastre (Césaire), **1**:352
Cadbury, William, **4**:368
cadmium, **1**:494
Caecilian, **4**:76
De Caelo (Aristotle), **4**:129–130
Caesar, Augustus, **2**:251; **4**:74
Caesar, Julius, **1**:424; **4**:74
Caetano, Marcello, **5**:189
Les Cahiers d'outre-mer (journal),
    2:455
Cahiers d'un retour au pays natal
    (Césaire), **1**:352
Cahora Bassa dam, **5**:196, 308
Cairo (Egypt), **1**:295–297
  air transportation in, **5**:82
  eunuchs in, **2**:347
  Khan el-Khalili bazaar, **1**:136
  Mansa Musa in, **3**:477
  map, **1**:296
  trade in, **2**:591
  University, **2**:227, 236

Cairo International Biennale, **1**:186
Cairo Summit (1993), **4**:92
Cairo Trilogy (Mahfouz), **3**:451
Caitaani Mutharaba-ini (Ngũgĩ),
    3:388
Calabar (Nigeria), **1**:297; **4**:41
Calasow, Maxamuud Cali, **3**:375
Calata, James Arthur, **2**:22
Caldwell, Jack, **2**:42
calendars. *See* time reckoning and
    calendars
Calender, Ebenezer, **3**:666
Caliph's Sister (Boyd), **3**:50
Callaghy, Thomas, **4**:170
Callaway, Henry, **3**:376
Callet, Father, **3**:373
calligraphy, **1**:168, 185; **4**:201
Callwell, Charles E., **5**:182
Caluza, Reuben T., **3**:662
Camara Laye, **1**:297–298; **3**:323, 362
*The Cambridge History of English
    Literature* (Warren), **3**:383
Cambridge University Press,
    2:579–580, 581
Cambyses (king of Persia),
    2:249; **4**:68
camels, **3**:407, 412
  Berber herders of, **5**:208–209
  and caravan trade, **4**:358, 360
  in Kenya, **3**:98
  in modern Egypt, **2**:255
  pastoralists and, **4**:244
  plow farming and, **4**:239
  in rock art, **1**:147
  in Saharan trade, **2**:27; **4**:439; **5**:204,
    208
  in Somalia, **4**:471
  trade, **1**:356
  in warfare, **5**:185
  in Western Sahara, **5**:209
Cameron, Donald, **1**:440
Cameron, Verney Lovett, **1**:263;
    2:308; **5**:102, 217
Cameroon, **1**:298–307
  profile, **1**:304
  agriculture, **1**:24
    plantations, **1**:481; **4**:152
  under Ahidjo, **1**:29–30
  antiquities legislation, **1**:135
  Arabic in, **3**:225
  art taken from, **1**:135
  beadwork, **1**:200
  broadcasting, **3**:527
  ceramics, **1**:349
  and CFA franc, **3**:577, 585
  colonial slavery in, **4**:454
  copper sculptures, **3**:547
  currency under Britain, **3**:587

Centre National des Recherches
    Scientifiques (Paris), **4:**319, 344
Cepeda, William, **2:**83
ceramics, **1:**349–352
  in Adulis, **1:**8
  agriculture and, **2:**588
  in Aksum, **1:**57
  archaeological classifications of,
    1:94–95
  in architecture, **1:**115
  artisan production in, **4:**250
  in Bamako, **1:**215
  central African, **1:**151, 154
  Chinese, **2:**597
  Christian pilgrimage, **1:**111–112
  dead remembered in, **4:**138–139
  early, **2:**583, 593
  in Egypt, predynastic, **2:**241, *242*
  in Equatorial Guinea, **2:**282
  in Ethiopia, **2:**303
  in Madagascar, **3:**440
  northern Africa, **1:**167, 168
  Odundo, Magdalene, and, **4:**87
  prehistoric, **4:**208
    Sahara and northern Africa,
      4:217–218
    in western Africa, **4:**223
  in the Sahel, **5:**208–209
  southern African, **1:**169–170;
    4:499–500
  Swahili, **2:**149
  technological specialization period, **5:**22
  trade
    early, **2:**593
    imports of Chinese porcelain, **3:**447
    trans-Saharan, **4:**360
Le Cercle des représailles (Kateb), **3:**93
Cercles des Amitiés Françaises, **5:**62, 66
Certenza (journal), **3:**403
Cerulli, Enrico, **4:**254
Cervantès, Ignacio, **2:**83
Césaire, Aimé, **1:***352,* **352–353;** **3:**21;
  5:37
  in Afrocentrism, **1:**10
  influence on Frantz Fanon, **2:**361
  in Négritude, **4:**132–133
  postcolonialism and, **4:**207
Cesars, Hendrik, **1:**212
Cesars, Pieter, **1:**211–212
C'est le soleil qui m'a brûlée (Beyala), **3:**351
Cetshwayo kaMpande, **1:***353,*
  353–354, 431
Cewa. *See* Chewa
CFA franc, **3:**577–578, 582, 585–586
  devaluation, **1:**520; **3:**587
  meaning of name, **3:**577
cha'abi music, **3:**661
Chaamba, **4:**357

Chad, **1:354–363.** *See also* French
    Equatorial Africa
  profile, **1:**360
  Arabic in, **3:**225
  army, **3:**553
  censuses, **2:**54
  and CFA franc, **3:**577, 585
  Darfur war and, **4:**529
  under Déby Itno, **2:**35
  Douala in trade of, **2:**138
  education, **2:**217
  Frolinat movement, **2:**496
  geography and economy, **1:354–358**
  history and politics, **1:361–363**
  human evolution in, **2:**583–584
  internal conflicts, **5:**192
  interstate wars, **5:**192
  Islamism in, **3:**62
  language policy, **3:**212
  Libyan military defeat in war with,
    3:310
  map, **1:***355*
  as member of the Monrovia Group,
    4:91
  Nigeria and, **4:**45
  oil industry, **2:**176–177
  plow farming in, **4:**240
  refugees in, **4:**305, *305*
  rural population in, **5:**138–139
  society and cultures, **1:358–361**
  spread of Arabic to, **3:**225
  Sudanese intervention in, **5:**178
  under Tombalbaye, **5:**67–68
Chad, Lake, **4:**541
  desertification and, **2:**65, 66
  flooding around, **5:**195
  management plan for, **2:**631–632
  pastoralism around, **5:**207
  shrinkage of, **2:**586
  as trade port, **5:**204
Chad Basin, **4:**42
Chadic languages, **3:**218, 219–220,
  223
Chaga. *See* Chagga
Chagga
  overview, **5:**376
  chiefs and colonial authority, **1:**465
  divination among, **2:**130
  storage buildings, **1:**165
  in Tanzania, **2:**332; **5:**10
chaikhas, **3:**660
Chaka (Mofolo), **3:**360, 384
Chakali, **2:**470
Chakossi
  overview, **5:**376
  in Ghana, **2:**470
Chakuamba, Gwanda, **3:**460
Chala, **2:**470

Chalbi Desert, **2:**188
chalk in Central African Republic,
  1:346
Challenge Cup '67 (Adé), **1:**7
The Challenge of Africa (Busia),
  1:290
Chama Cha Mapinduzi (Tanzania),
  2:11; **3:**247, 589; **5:**14
Chamba
  overview, **5:**376
  in Nigeria, **4:**43, 49
  secret cult among, **4:**380
Chamberlain, Joseph, **1:**443; **4:**54
Chambeshi flats, **5:**309
Chami, Felix, **1:**93; **3:**23, 447
Champion, A. W. G., **3:**86
Champollion, Jacques-Joseph, **1:**95
Chamus. *See* Njamusi
Changamire, **2:**598
Changamire state, **4:**495
Changana basketry, **1:**197
Changes (Aidoo), **1:**54
Channel Africa, **3:**527
chant, **1:**486
Un chant écarlate (Bâ), **1:**211;
  3:356
Chantal Radimilahy, Marie de,
  3:442
Chao Ju-Kua, **5:**97–98
charcoal, **2:**263; **4:**160
  and deforestation, **2:**406
  reliance on, **2:**266
  seller in Mathare Valley, **5:***162*
  sustainable production, **2:**270
  urbanization and, **2:**265
  use in western Africa, **2:**409
Chargeurs Reunis shipping line, **5:**91
Charismatic Singers, **3:**668
Charley, Dele, **5:**34
chartered companies, **1:**481–482
Charton, Albert, **5:**37
Charwe, **5:**263
chat (drug), **2:**296–297
Chattering Wagtails of Mikuyu Prison
  (Mapanje), **3:**334
Chaudhuri, K. N., **3:**446
Chawai, **5:**376
Chaza, Mai, **2:**450
Chazal, Malcolm de, **3:**398
Chazan, Naomi, **4:**170
Che Guevara, Ernesto
  in Congo-Kinshasa, **3:**556
  Kabila, Laurent Désiré, and,
    3:84–85
Chebaa, Mohamed, **1:**168
Chedid, Andree, **3:**333
Chege, Michael, **4:**170
Cheke. *See* Gude
Chekiri. *See* Itsekiri

colonial policies and practices
(*continued*)
profile, **1**:500
aid to, **1**:39
architecture in, **1**:120–121
art in, **1**:128
censuses in, **2**:54
children soldiers, **1**:374
civil war in, **2**:532, 603; **5**:192
ethnic-based, **5**:181
clothing in, **4**:185
cobalt, **3**:538
Cold War and Congo Crisis (1960),
1:429
constitutional law, **3**:258
copper, **3**:538
corruption, **1**:44
currency, **3**:588
diamonds in, **3**:537
diasporas from, **2**:77
economic history of, **2**:169
education, higher, **2**:231–232
emigration of European settlers,
3:11–12
ethnicity in, **2**:326
famine, **2**:359
female genital mutilation, **3**:29
fifty-zaire bill in, **4**:180–181
forests
effect of civil war on, **2**:402
equatorial rain forests conservation,
2:401
geography and economy, **1**:494–496
guerrilla forces, **3**:556
history and politics, **1**:501–505
human rights in, **2**:625, 626
humanitarian aid to, **1**:51–52
IMF technical assistance to, **3**:38
income, **2**:169
infertility, **2**:47
informal sector, **1**:333
Islam in, **3**:57
language policy, **3**:212
law, **3**:256–259, 262
Loi Fondamentale, **3**:261
Mami Wata imagery, **3**:469–474
map, **1**:*495*
Maranke's Church in, **3**:480
Marxist-Leninist military government, **4**:461
mercenaries in, **3**:559
militias in, **5**:177
mining, **4**:248
Moroccan troops under U.N. flag in,
3:606
Morocco and, **3**:607
nationalization of mines, **3**:538
neocolonialism in, **4**:24
neotraditional internal revolt in, **5**:185

oil industry in, **2**:*274, 275*
rain forests in, **2**:199
refugees from, **4**:305
refugees in, **4**:303
renaming as Zaire, **3**:565
rural population in, **5**:138–139
sapeurs, **4**:187–189, *188*
society and cultures, **1**:496–501
textiles, **5**:27
timber industry, **2**:200
truth commission in, **5**:105
Tshombe and, **5**:106–107
United Nations and, **5**:130–131,
132, *133*
urbanization in, **5**:139, 140
war of 1996–1997, **1**:503–504
war of 1998–2002, **1**:503–504
Zimbabwe intervention in, **5**:338
Congo, French. *See also* Congo,
People's Republic of; Congo,
Republic of
Chinese in, **3**:9
establishment of, **1**:268
Congo, My Country (Lumumba), **3**:418
Congo, People's Republic of. *See also*
Congo, Republic of
establishment of, **3**:148
forests nationalization, **2**:400–401
French settlers in, **3**:12
neocolonialism in, **4**:25
Congo, Republic of, **1**:505–510. *See
also* Brazzaville; Congo, French;
Pointe-Noire
profile, **1**:509
and CFA franc, **3**:577, 585
civil war, **2**:174
under Denis Sassou-Nguesso,
4:374–375
diasporas from, **2**:77
economic history of, **2**:171
education, **2**:217
elite fragmentation in, **5**:181
equatorial rain forests conservation,
2:401
geography and economy, **1**:505–506
history and politics, **1**:510–512
infertility, **2**:47
informal sector, **1**:333
internal conflicts in, **5**:192
language policy, **3**:212
literature, **3**:394–395
map, **1**:*506*
as member of the Monrovia Group,
4:91
Pointe-Noire, **4**:168
society and cultures, **1**:507–510
wild foods in, **4**:161–162
witchcraft in, **5**:231

Congo (Brazzaville). *See* Congo,
Republic of
Congo Basin
desertification in, **2**:65
European conflict over, **1**:475
Congo Free State. *See* Congo
Independent State
Congo Independent State, **1**:325, 482,
494, 499, **512–513**
slavery replaced by servitude, **4**:454
taken over by Belgium, **1**:431
Congo-Kinshasa. *See* Congo,
Democratic Republic of the
Congo Liberation Movement, **1**:504
Congo-Ocean railway, **1**:269, 453,
510
and forced labor, **2**:400; **3**:175–176
from Central African Republic,
1:342
Congo Reform Association, **1**:482
Congo River, **1**:514–515
in Angola, **1**:73
management plan for, **2**:631–632
transportation on, **5**:89
Congolese National Liberation Front,
1:503
Congolese Rally for Democracy,
1:504; **3**:85
Congregation of the God of Ntsikana,
1:381
Congress of Democrats (Namibia),
4:10
Congress of Non-European Trade
Unions (CNETU, South Africa),
3:188
Congress of South African Trade
Unions (COSATU), **3**:178, 188;
4:486, 493
anti-privatization strike, **1**:329
Congress of South African Writers,
3:385
Congress of the People (Kliptown,
South Africa, 1955), **3**:474
Coniaguis, **4**:385
Conley, Tom, **1**:335–336
*Connections between the Nyakyusa and
the Nkonde from the Viewpoint of
Dance and Trade: with Video
Data of Dances* (Kurita), **2**:6
Conrad, Joseph, **2**:453
Conscience africaine (review), **1**:433
consciencism, **4**:461
*Consciencism: Philosophy and Ideology for
DeColonization* (Nkrumah), **4**:135
conservation, **1**:264–265
community approach to, **2**:159–161
early thinking, **2**:453
human role in, **2**:155–159
industrial archaeology and, **1**:107

Gallais, Jean, **2**:458

Gallieni, Joseph-Simon, **2**:343; **3**:432, 435
  in Madagascar, **1**:84
  Touré, Samori, and, **5**:71

Gallipoli, World War I in, **5**:269

Gallo (recording company), **3**:664

Gallo, Thierry Jacques, **3**:392

Gallus, Gaius Cornelius, **2**:251

Gama, Cristovão da, **1**:414; **2**:428
  Ahmad ibn Ibrahim al-Ghazi and, **1**:31

Gama, Vasco da, **2**:*428,* **428–429**; **3**:447
  Dias and, **5**:99
  explorations before, **5**:96
  ivory trumpet presented to, **1**:136
  and Mombasa, **3**:574
  on Moors, **3**:592
  and Mozambique, **3**:610
  on trade, **2**:68
  in Zanzibar, **5**:322

Gambia, the, **2**:**429–436**. *See also*
    Banjul; British West Africa
  profile, **2**:433
  censuses, **2**:53
  currency, colonial, **3**:587
  disease in
    dengue, **2**:108
    meningococcal meningitis, **2**:104
  in Economic Community of West
      African States, **2**:162–163
  education, **2**:211–213
  female genital mutilation, **4**:399
  financial institutions in, **2**:32
  forest management, **2**:414
  geography and economy, **2**:429–430
  history and politics, **2**:**434–436**
  language policy, **3**:212
  map, **2**:*430*
  market-gardening, **4**:234
  music, modern popular, **3**:666
  prostitution, **2**:114
  society and cultures, **2**:**431–433**

Gambia National Army, **2**:434

Gambia River
  peasants and, **4**:115
  transportation on, **5**:89

game reserves. *See* wildlife parks

games, **2**:**436–437**
  mankala board games, **2**:130

Gamk. *See* Ingessana

Gamo. *See* Gamu

Gamu
  overview, **5**:381
  textiles, **1**:188

Gan. *See* Ga

Gan Ying, **5**:97

Ganda
  overview, **5**:381
  administrative system, **3**:35

and Christianity, **1**:383
  kingship, **3**:129
  peasants, **4**:103
  royal women, **4**:292
  scarification, **1**:242
  time reckoning, **5**:55
  in Uganda, **2**:329–330; **5**:125

Ganda, Oumarou, **2**:374

Gandhi, Mohandas K., **3**:14, *15;*
    4:487, 492

Gandoulou, Justin-Daniel, **4**:189

Ganwa (Baganwa), **1**:282, 284, 286

Gao, **5**:206

Gao (Mali), **2**:**437–438**; **5**:206
  Islamic education center, **3**:42, 465
  as trade port, **5**:204
  and trans-Saharan trade, **4**:360

Garamantes, **4**:360; **5**:**207–208**
  horses and, **1**:147

Garang, John, **4**:537, 539

Garcia V (Kongo king), **1**:381

"Garden of Eden" model of evolution,
    2:619

gardens, home, **4**:235–236

Garoua (Cameroon), **1**:303

Garuba, Harry, **3**:333

Garvey, Marcus Mosiah, **2**:438, *438;*
    3:21
  'Ali, Mohammed Duse, and, **1**:67
  Du Bois, W. E. B., on, **2**:142
  and Pan-Africanism, **4**:90

Gash Group, **4**:213

Gates, Henry Louis, **3**:302

Gates (Bill and Melinda) Foundation
  AIDS research funding by, **4**:338
  schistosomiasis program of, **2**:102

*Gathering Seaweed: African Prison
    Writing* (Mapanje), **3**:334

Gauguin, Paul, **1**:129

Gauteng province (South Africa), **3**:74

Gauvin, Axel, **3**:398

Gayflor, Fatu, **3**:666

Gaza Nguni, **4**:495, 496; **5**:183

Gazargamu Islamic education center,
    3:50

Gbagbo, Laurent Koudou, **1**:521,
    524, 527; **2**:**439,** *439*

Gbagyi, **4**:49

Gban, **1**:522

Gbanda. *See* Avikam

Gbande, **5**:381

Gbandi, **3**:297

Gbari, **5**:381

Gbasa. *See* Bassa

Gbassi. *See* Gbande

Gbaya
  overview, **5**:381
  in Cameroon, **1**:303

in Central African Republic, **1**:343, 347
  marriage, **3**:486

Gbee, **3**:297

Gbich! (cyber-magazine), **3**:519

Gbili (chief of Sanoyea), **5**:279

Gbwaka. *See* Bwaka

Gciriku, **4**:7

Gciriku language, **3**:229

Gcui, **1**:257

Gcumisa, M. S. S., **3**:377

Gebré, Telaye, **3**:659

Gebre-Medhin, Tsegaye, **3**:387

Gebrekidan, Assefa, **1**:188

Gèbrèyès, Seyoum, **3**:659

GECAMINES, **1**:496, 503; **3**:416, 548

Gede (Kenya), **2**:151

Ge'ez language
  demise of, **3**:322
  literature in, **3**:367
  manuscript collections in, **3**:302
  poetry, **3**:329
  writing system for, **5**:278, 280–281
  in art, **1**:141

Gelede ritual
  masks, **1**:*178*
  women in, **5**:249

Gemian complex, **4**:216–217

gender, **2**:**440–452**. *See also* men;
    women
  overview, **2**:**440–444**
  age organization and, **1**:13–14
  agriculture and, **1**:28
    in Republic of Congo, **1**:506–507
  art and, **1**:131, 174
    western Africa, **1**:179–180
  ceramics and, **1**:349
  and child labor, **3**:173
  dance and, **2**:6–7
  in death and mourning, **2**:19–20
  death due to famine and, **2**:356
  Diop, Cheikh Anta, on, **2**:98
  division of labor by, **3**:176;
      5:250–251
  equity, mortality and, **2**:52
  ethnicity and, **2**:338–339
  in Gabon, **2**:423
  gender roles, **2**:**445–452**
  Head, Bessie, on, **2**:522–523
  in healing, **2**:529–530
  higher education and, **2**:229
  HIV/AIDS and, **2**:125
  home gardens and, **4**:236
  housing and, **5**:161, 163–164
  imbalance in Kinshasa, **3**:132
  and initiation, **3**:26
  Islam and, **5**:149, 246
    healing and health care and, **2**:540
  kingship and, **3**:118

Glebo, democratic organization of,
3:251
Glo religion, 5:171
Global Fund, HIV/AIDS and, 2:126
Global Shadows (Ferguson), 4:327
Global Witness on Equatorial Guinea,
2:284
globalization, 2:477–481
African irrelevance in, 4:341
art commodification and, 1:138,
140
consumerism and, 2:575
education and, 2:230
mining and, 4:249
names and naming and, 4:3
political science on, 4:169–170
popular culture and, 4:182
religion and, 4:315
remittances from abroad in,
2:178–179
trade and, 5:77–78
Tunisia and, 5:111
Gluckman, Max, 2:366; 3:122, 197,
243; 5:290
apartheid and, 1:86
on ethnicity and urbanism, 2:325
influence of, 1:85
on legal systems, 1:86–87
research by, 4:319
Gnabziri. *See* Abanziri
Gnaoua and world music festival of
Essaouira (2006), 4:*438*
Gnassingbé, Faure, 5:67
Gnawa, 2:334
Gnawa Diffusion (band), 3:661
Gnostics, 2:251
Goans, 3:14
goats. *See* livestock
Gobedra (Ethiopia), 4:157
The Gods Are Not to Blame (Rotimi),
5:33
The Gods Must Be Crazy (Uys),
2:371–372
Goes, Damião de, 4:496
Gogo
overview, 5:382
in Tanzania, 5:9, 10
Going Down River Road (Mwangi),
4:191
Gola
overview, 5:382
education, 2:201
masquerades, 3:492
in Sierra Leone, 4:412
Gola Forest, 2:156
Gola language, 3:297
gold, 3:537, 538, 549–550. *See also*
gold mining; gold trade
American, 2:572, 573

art and, 1:190
beads, 1:198, 199
coinage, 5:209
early trade in, 2:592, 593
in eastern Africa, 2:151
economic history of, 2:166–167, 168
in Egypt, 2:255
predynastic, 2:242
in Equatorial Guinea, 2:279
fibula, 3:*550*
in forest regions, 5:201
in Ghana, 5:204
Accra, 1:4
Elmina, 2:261–262, 262
goldfields, 3:537
in historiography, 2:560
Indian Ocean trade in, 2:147
in Malian empire, 5:205
reserves of, 4:247
in Somalia, 4:472
in South Africa, 2:600
in South America, 2:71
in Swaziland, 4:550
techniques of smithing, 3:549
travel accounts on, 5:95
undeveloped deposits, 3:537, 539
western and Saharan, 5:204
Gold Coast. *See also* British West
Africa; Ghana
anticolonial rebellion, 3:556
architecture, 1:119
armies, 3:551
British colony, 2:467
censuses, 2:56
Chinese in, 3:9
cocoa production, 1:470
concessions to European timber
merchants, 2:410
currency, 3:587
early European immigration, 3:9
early newspaper, 3:524
fight against colonialism, 4:372
Harris Church in, 2:520–521
impact of slave trade on, 4:431
National Research Center, 1:340
railways in, 5:86
slavery in, 4:453
Gold Coast Aborigines Rights
Protection Society, 3:20
Gold Coast Echo (periodical), 1:339
Gold Coast Institutions (Casely-
Hayford), 4:19
Gold Coast Leader (periodical), 1:339
*The Gold Coast Nation and National
Consciousness* (Attoh Ahuma),
4:13
Gold Coast Native Institutions (Casely-
Hayford), 1:340; 3:19

The Gold Coast People (newspaper),
4:373
Gold Coast Weekly (newspaper), 4:373
gold mining, 4:*248*
in British central Africa, 1:435
in Burkina Faso, 1:273
in Cameroon, 1:305
in Central African Republic, 1:346
in Congo Independent State, 1:499
in Côte d'Ivoire, 1:520
in Democratic Republic of the
Congo, 1:494, 502
and destruction of forest environments, 2:401
in Ghana, 2:467, 469
in Guinea, 2:502, 508
Kumasi, 3:169
in Liberia, 3:292
in Mali, 3:463, 469
Maputo and, 3:478
and migrant labor, 3:183
occupational health in, 2:118
peasants and, 4:105
profitability, 1:325
sexually transmitted diseases and,
2:112
in Sierra Leone, 4:411, 412
in South Africa, 4:484
and founding of Johannesburg,
3:73
Kalahari as labor reserve, 3:90
Witwatersrand, 1:324; 3:537, 538
urbanization and, 5:150
and wage-labor force, 3:179
women and, 5:262
in Zimbabwe, 5:332
in Zimbabwe, Great, 5:339, 341
gold trade, 1:322, 356; 3:549
Aksum and, 1:56
in Bamako, 1:215
China and, 5:97
early, 1:321; 2:591
in Indian Ocean, 3:447
and Mali empire, 2:504
Mogadishu in, 3:570
Muslim merchants and, 3:49
salt and, 4:365
smuggling in Central African
Republic, 1:342
trans-Saharan, 3:603; 4:358, 360,
440
Goldblatt, David, 4:144
The Golden Bough (Frazer), 3:118
Golden Mercury of Africa (band),
1:7
Golden Stool, 4:94
Golden Trade of the Moors, 3:72
Goldie, George Taubman, 1:475, 481,
531; 4:36

I

revivalism in, **3:**41; **4:**201
revolutionary, **3:**42–43
in Rwanda, **4:**346
in the Sahara, **4:**358
Salafiyya movement, **3:**65, 601
 in Algeria, **1:**62
 Sufism and, **3:**61
scholarship in
 'Abd al-Qādir in, **1:**2
 Allal al-Fassi in, **1:**68
 Harar, **2:**519
 Timbuktu, **5:**51, 205, *206*
 Walata, **5:**173
schools of law, **3:**265–267
in Senegal, **4:**388–389, 390
and slavery, **4:**427, 433
in Somalia, **4:**473
as source of law, **3:**263
in southern Africa, **3:**57–59
spread of
 caravan trade and, **4:**360
 and law, **3:**252
 and literacy, **3:**328
 production of manuscripts, **3:**302
 'Umar ibn Sa'id Tal and, **5:**127–128
 in West Africa, **4:**545
 to West and Central Africa, **3:**602
in sub-Saharan Africa, **4:**72–73
Swahili literature and, **3:**379
symbolism and, **4:**559–560
in Tanzania, **5:**10, 11
time reckoning and, **5:**55, 56
in Togo, **5:**64
Touré, Samori, and, **5:**70–71
tradition in, **4:**315
and trans-Saharan trade, **4:**440
tribal armies of, **3:**6
in Tunisia, **5:**110–114
in Uganda, **5:**123, 125
 Amin Dada and, **1:**70
urbanization and, **5:**136, 145, 146,
 149
warfare and, **5:**178
western Africa, **3:**48–53
Western and Saharan, **5:**204–205,
 209
witchcraft and, **5:**222, 230–232
women and, **5:**244–248
 anticolonialism and, **5:**264
 healing and, **2:**529–530
 influence of, **5:**262
 seclusion of, **5:**246, 256
 slavery and, **5:**250
as world religion, **4:**314
on Yoruba twin carvings, **4:**203
youth and, **5:**286–287, 299,
 305–306
in Zanzibar, **5:**324

Islam and Democracy (Mernissi),
 3:536
Islam and Human Rights (Ilori), **3:**4
*Islam and the Challenges of the
 Fifteenth Islamic Century* (Ilori),
 3:4
Islam wataqalid al-jahiliyya, al- (Ilori),
 3:4
Islamic associations
 in Mali, **3:**465
 popular culture and, **4:**199
Islamic brotherhoods. *See* Sufism
Islamic Conference, **5:**114
Islamic empires in Niger, **4:**36
Islamic Jihad Community, **3:**45
Islamic law, **3:**265–272. *See also* shari'a
 in eastern and central Africa, **3:**53
 reform, **3:**65
 in Sudan, **4:**537
 in Zanzibar, **3:**249
Islamic Party of Kenya, **3:**574
Islamic Salvation Front (Algeria). *See*
 Front Islamique du Salut
Islamic Writers' workshop, **3:**63
Islamism, **3:**44–45, **62–64**
 in northern Sudan, **4:**529
 in Senegal, **4:**389
 Sufism as tool against, **3:**47
 youth and, **5:**305, 306
Islamiya schools, **2:**202
 Tangier under, **5:**6
Ismail, Khedive, **1:**446; **2:**309
Isma'il, Moulay, **3:**601, 605; **4:**71,
 Gordon, Charles, and, **2:**483
Ismailis, **3:**14, 58
Ismant el-Kharab (Egypt), **2:**253
Isoko, **5:**385
Ìsòlá, Akínwùmí, **3:**380
Israel
 Egyptian war with, **2:**261
 Sadat, Anwar al-, and, **4:**357
Issa
 overview, **5:**385
 in Djibouti, **2:**134–135
 in Djibouti City, **2:**137
Issakaba films, **4:**202–203
Issaq, **5:**385
Issoufou, Mahamadou, **4:**34
Istiqlal party (Morocco)
 Allal al-Fassi in, **1:**68, *68*
 Ben Barka, Mehdi, and, **1:**225
Ita, Eyo, **4:**15
Italo-Ethiopian War (1935), **1:**203;
 2:305
Italy
 and Central African Republic, **1:**346
 colonial policies and practices,
 1:460–461
 colonial army, **3:**554

control of Massawa, **3:**495
Corpo Speciale, **5:**183
Eritrea and, **2:**294
 Taytu and, **5:**17
Ethiopia and, **1:**6–7; **2:**37, 304, 305,
 309–310
 Harar, **2:**519
immigration to, **2:**70
 from Burkina Faso, **1:**275
and Libya, **3:**309
Menilek II and, **3:**533
Mogadishu and, **3:**570–571
nationalism and imperialism in,
 5:182
research in, **4:**319
and Sahara, **4:**359
and Somalia, **4:**477
strong anticolonial lobby in, **1:**460
Iteso
 overview, **5:**385
 in Kenya, **2:**330
 person concept of, **4:**119, 120
 spirit possession, **4:**122
 in Uganda, **5:**122
Itezhitezhi dam, **5:**197
Itja-tawy (Egypt), **2:**244
Itsekiri, **5:**386
Ittu, **5:**386
Itu. *See* Ittu
Ituri Forest (Zaire), **2:**199
Ivorian Popular Movement for the
 Greater West (MPIGO), **1:**521
ivory, **3:**67–69
 in Angola, **1:**79
 art, **1:**128, 129
 trade in, **1:**137
 beads, **1:**198, 200
 in Congo Independent State, **1:**499,
 501
 economic history of, **2:**166–167
 in forest regions, **5:**201
 in French Equatorial Africa,
 1:452–453
 in Guinea forests, **5:**202
 industrialization and, **2:**573
 Kalahari as source of, **3:**89
 in Namibia, **4:**4
 sculpture, **1:**201–202
 smuggling, **1:**342
 trade, **1:**190; **2:**410
 Adulis, **1:**8
 Aksum, **1:**56
 from Benguela, **1:**227
 Cameroon, **1:**305
 caravans, **5:**83–84
 China and, **5:**97
 early, **1:**321
 East Africa, **4:**211–212
 eighteenth-century, **2:**598

M

Makiwane, Cecilia, **2**:546
Makombe Hanga, **3**:478
Makonde
  overview, **5**:394
  art, **1**:138
  body art, **1**:157
  Dias, Antonio Jorge, on, **3**:611–612
  emergence of, **3**:613
  masks and masquerades, **1**:163;
    3:492
  in Mozambique, **3**:611
  number systems of, **4**:80
  sculpture, **1**:201
Makua
  overview, **5**:394
  chieftancies, **3**:613
Makua-Lomwe, **3**:611
Makumu, W. M., **3**:377
Makuria, kingdom of, **4**:77
Mal, Baba, **3**:669
Malabo (Equatorial Guinea), **2**:282
La maladie de l'islam (Meddeb),
  3:402–403
Malagasy Broadcasting System, **4**:*299*
Malagasy language, **3**:24, 220, 230,
  430, 439
  comic art in, **3**:520
  as official language, **3**:213
  poetry, **3**:330
Malagasy Republic. *See* Madagascar
malaguetta pepper, **5**:202
Malan, Daniel F., **4**:101, 492
malaria
  bed nets and, **2**:100
  in Burkina Faso, **1**:273
  and childbearing, **1**:365–366
  climate and, **2**:106–107, 107, *107t*
  colonialism and, **2**:542
  drug-resistant, **2**:548
    children and, **1**:373
    and infant mortality, **1**:370
  endemic zone of, **2**:*108*
  forest regions and, **5**:200
  in Gabon, **2**:423
  Global Fund for, **2**:126
  HIV/AIDS and, **2**:121
  human rights and, **2**:627
  irrigation agriculture and, **2**:119
  and mortality, **2**:50, 356
    childhood, **2**:99–100
  plant introductions and, **4**:159
  production strategies and, **4**:228
  Rawlings' campaign against, **4**:300
  structural adjustment programs and,
    1:44
  traditional medicines for, **2**:548
Malawi, **3**:453–461. *See also* British
  Central Africa; Nyasaland
  profile, **3**:457

agriculture
  maize, **4**:237
  pest control, **1**:26
  plantations, **4**:153
  women and, **2**:446
alternative energy, **2**:265, 270
balance of payments in, **1**:47
contraception, **2**:47–48
corruption, **1**:44
education, **2**:206, 208
  higher, **2**:231–232, 237–238
famine, **2**:*357,* 359
on firewood, **4**:160
forestry, **2**:407, 408; **4**:166
geography and economy, **3**:453–455
history and politics, **3**:458–461
HIV/AIDS in, **5**:154
income, **2**:169
independence, **1**:438
Indians in, **3**:14, 16
Islamic law, **3**:271–272
land tenure, **3**:204
language policy, **3**:212
literature, **3**:385
map, **3**:*454*
Maranke's Church in, **3**:480
migrant labor from, **3**:183
mushrooms, **4**:162
peasants in, **4**:104–105
population, **5**:294
  rural, **5**:138
  vital registration, **2**:56
prophetic movements in, **4**:259
religion in
  Born-Agains, **5**:299
  Christian-Muslim violence, **3**:58
  Christianity, **4**:261
  Islam, **3**:57
rock art, **4**:499
society and cultures, **3**:455–458
theater, **5**:45
traditional medicines, **4**:164
urbanization, **5**:139, 140
witch hunts, **5**:233
Zomba in, **5**:342
Malawi, Lake, **3**:455
Malawi (Marave), **3**:612
Malawi (Marawi), **3**:611
Malawi Congress Party (MCP), **1**:438;
  3:456, 459
Malawi Freedom Movement, **3**:460
Malawian Congress Party, **1**:215
Malba. *See* Birifor
Malcolm X, **4**:199
Malebo Pool, **1**:514
  slave market, **3**:164
malguetta, early trade in, **2**:592
Malherbe, Daniel François, **3**:381
Malhundo. *See* Lunda
Mali, **3**:461–467

profile, **3**:466
agriculture
  floodwater, **5**:195
  irrigation, **5**:198
  plow farming, **4**:240
antiquities legislation, **1**:135
Arabic in, **3**:225
archaeology, **4**:224
architecture, **1**:120
art, **1**:131
balance of payments, **1**:47
and CFA franc, **3**:577, 585
cinematic tradition, **3**:517
community radio stations, **3**:526
in Economic Community of West
  African States, **2**:161–163
education, **2**:218; **3**:152
famine, **2**:358
female genital mutilation, **4**:399
forest management, **2**:396, 412, 413,
  414
geography and economy,
  3:461–463
history and politics, **3**:468–469
Koteba performance, **5**:36
labor migration to Côte d'Ivoire,
  1:522, 526; **3**:184
language policy, **3**:212
livestock, **5**:196
local government, **2**:493
manuscript collections, **3**:302
map, **3**:*462*
as member of Casablanca Group,
  4:91
mining, **3**:539; **4**:249
museums, **3**:626
music, **3**:648–649
  modern popular, **3**:666–667
neocolonialism, **4**:25
relations with Burkina Faso, **1**:278
rise of, **2**:592
river basin planning in, **5**:196
significance of salt in, **4**:365
socialism, **4**:461
society and cultures, **3**:463–467
textiles, **5**:27
  mud cloth as symbol of national
    pride, **1**:252
  printed cloth, **1**:252
Timbuktu, **5**:51
under Touré, Amadou Toumani,
  5:69
vigilantism, **1**:423
war with Upper Volta, **5**:192
women in, **5**:241
Mali empire, **2**:504, 514; **3**:49, 465,
  468; **5**:205–206
cavalry, **2**:572
creation, **2**:592; **4**:546

death and mourning and, **2:**14

in Djibouti, **2:**133

economic history of, **2:**168, 169, 171–172

in Equatorial Guinea, **2:**279

forced labor, **3:***175*

in Gabon, **2:**426

health care in, **2:**543

HIV/AIDS in, **2:**126

in Igbo Ukwu, **2:**592

industrial archaeology and, **1:**107

in Kenya, **3:**98

in Mauritania, **3:**501

mining-compound system, **4:**344; **5:**263

in Namibia, **4:**5, 6

nationalization in, **2:**171

neocolonialism and, **4:**23–24, 24

in Nigeria, **4:**40, 45

occupational health in, **2:**118

peasants and, **4:**105

precolonial, **3:**179

production strategies, **4:**247–250

railways and, **5:**86

refugees in, **4:**302

in Republic of Congo, **1:**507

sexually transmitted diseases and, **2:**112

in South Africa

Pretoria, **4:**226

Zambian migrants in, **5:**315

in South America, **2:**71

in southeastern Africa (1600 to 1910), **4:**495

in Swaziland, **4:**550

trade and, **5:**76

in Uganda, **5:**120, 125

urbanization around, **5:**156

women and, **5:**262, 263

in Zambia, **5:**309–310, 314, 318, 319–320, 321

in Zimbabwe, **2:**520; **5:**332

The Minister's Daughter (Ruheni), **4:**191

Ministry for Trade and the Colonies (France), **1:**450

Ministry of Colonies (France), **1:**450

Ministry of Colonies (Italy), **1:**460

Ministry of Foreign Affairs (Italy), **1:**460

Ministry of Overseas Development (Britain), **2:**457

minkisi lumweno, **2:**92

Minority Rights Group, **4:**529

Minshat Abu Omar (Egypt), **2:**242

minstrelsy, **2:**88, 89

Mintz, Sidney, **2:**79

Minyanka, **3:**486

Mirambo, **3:**36, 564; **5:**59

Miranda, Carmen, **2:**88

Mirau (Tanzanian healer), **2:**526–527

Mirau and His Practice: A Study of the Ethnomedicinal Repertoire of a Tanzanian Herbalist (Harjula), **2:**526

Mirghani, Muhammad 'Uthman al-, **3:**3, 61

Mirza, Sarah, **3:**344

Misani, Daniel Owino, **3:**655

Misrati, Ali Mustapha al-, **3:**366

Mission d'Aménagement du Sénégal (1983), **5:**196

Mission from Cape Coast Castle to Ashantee (Bowdich), **3:**633

Mission terminée (Beti), **1:**238

Mission to Kala (Beti), **3:**344

missionary enterprise, **1:398–408**

abolitionism and, **2:**216

and Afrian languages, **3:**329

African American immigrants and, **3:**6

African Christians in, **5:**270

on African medicine, **2:**533

Aggrey, **1:**20

in Angola, **1:**79, 80

anthropological studies by, **1:**84, 85; **4:**317

archaeology and, **1:**105

art collected by, **1:**133, 135

artisan production and, **4:**251

beginning of, **1:**382

in Belgian Congo, **1:**432

in British Central Africa, **1:**436

in Cape Colony, **1:**310

Catholic, **1:**384

in Chad, **1:**359

civilization by, **2:**569

clitoridectomy and, **4:**265

clothing and, **1:**172

conflict with Islam, **3:**56

in Congo Independent State, **1:**513

criticism by John William Colenso, **1:**431

Crowther, Samuel, and Yoruba Mission, **1:**532

early Catholic, **1:**402

education, **1:**471; **2:**201, 202

in eastern Africa, **2:**207

elitism in, **2:**204

higher, **2:**239

in Lesotho, **3:**286

technical, **2:**208

in western Africa, **2:**211, 216

in Ethiopia, **2:**299

ethnicity and, **2:**320, 337

ethnomusicology and, **2:**345

and European immigration, **3:**12

extension of imperial influence inland, **1:**475

and gender roles, **2:**445

health care by, **2:**544–545

help to slaves, **4:**454

historical research sources from, **4:**331, 333

influence on southern African music, **3:**662

informal evangelization, **1:**382

in interlacustrine region, **3:**36–37

introduction of journalism, **3:**513

Islamic, **2:**562

in Kenya, **3:**105

in Lagos, **3:**193

in Lesotho, **3:**285

liberated slaves and, **4:**448

limited role in French North Africa, **1:**449

and literature, **3:**376

in medicine, **2:**542–543

missionary councils, **1:**389

music and, **4:**195

in Nigeria, **4:**48, 54

in Nyasaland, **3:**458

orders of, **1:**404

Philip, John, **4:**123–124

photography and, **4:**138, 142–143

plow farming and, **4:**240

and press, **3:**521

prophetic movements and, **4:**257–258, 271

publications published by, **3:**523

Quaque, Philip, **4:**288

returnees in, **2:**73

ritual objects removed by, **2:**553

in Rwanda, **4:**352

in Sierra Leone, **2:**600

and sports, **4:**508

Swahili literature and, **3:**379

taboos and, **5:**2–3

Tempels, **5:**23

and translations, **3:**209, 344

tribes and, **5:**103–104

witchcraft and, **5:**227–228

in World War I, **5:**270

writing and, **3:**322–323

Missionary Travels and Researches in South Africa (Livingstone), **3:**413; **5:**101–102

Mister Johnson (Cary), **5:**34

Mitchell, J. Clyde, **1:**85; **2:**324–325; **5:**316

Mitchell, James C., **5:**224

Mitchell, Philip, **1:**441

Mitchell, Timothy, **1:**141

Mitoko sculpture, **1:**152

Mittloti (Tlali), **3:**355

The Mixers (Gicheru), **4:**192

idiophones, **3:**673–675
  use for communicating messages,
    3:237
influence of, **2:**84
introduction of Western instruments,
    3:648
  in Ethiopia, **3:**658
  in northern Africa, **3:**661
  in southern Africa, **3:**662
  lamellophones (mbira), **3:**633,
    673–674
  lute, **3:**672
  lyre, **3:**672
  mouth-bow tradition, **3:**632
  in northern Africa, **4:**194
  pluriarc (bow lute), **3:**633
  shapes and components, **3:**634
  tradition, **3:**671
  tuning, **3:**641, 675–676
  xylophone, **3:**639, 670, 671, 675
    log, **3:**631, 637
Musicians Union of Ghana
    (MUSIGA), **3:**536
Musinga, Victor Eleame, **5:**31
Muslim Brotherhood, **3:**45, 62, 63
  in Egypt, **2:**259, 261
  Nasser and, **4:**12
  political systems and, **4:**178
  in Sudan, **3:**62; **4:**537
Muslim northern Africa, history of
    (641 to 1500 CE), **3:**676–679;
    4:71–73
Muslims. *See* Islam; Sufism
Musnad (Ahmad ibn Hanbal), **3:**266
Musokotwane, Kebby, **5:**320
Mussafar, Mohamed Siddiq, **2:**68
Mustaghanmi, Ahlam, **3:**364–365
Mustansir, al- (Fatimid caliph),
    3:678–679
Mustapha, Mukhtar, **3:**333
Mutabaraka, Migambi, **3:**396
Mutahi, Wahome, **3:**388; **4:**193
Mutapa state, **1:**401; **4:**495, 496, 501
Mutara (king of Rwanda)
  Kagame, Alexis, adviser to, **3:**87
  and peace, **3:**126
  Tutsis under, **4:**352
Mutare for Jesus Rally (1995), **1:***384*
Mutebi II (Buganda), **3:679–680**, *680*
  Amin Dada and, **1:**69
Mutende, Samuel, **1:**385
Mutesa I (Buganda), **3:**680–681
Mutesa II (Buganda), **1:**441; **3:**56;
    4:86
Mutharika, Bingu wa, **3:**455, 460
Muthirigu dances, **5:**29
Mutiiri (journal), **4:**28
Mutswairo, Solomon, **3:**323, 330
Mutu, Wangechi, **2:**92

mutual aid associations
  of colonial workers, **3:**187
  sports clubs as, **4:**509
Mutukudzi, Oliver, **3:**663
Mutulu, Tshibumba Kanda, **1:**155
Mutwa, Vusamazulu Credo, **4:**315
Muwe, Chabala, **5:**317–318
Muzorewa, Abel, **5:**337
Mvemba Nzinga (king of Kongo),
    1:400, 402; **3:**163, **681**
Mwadi, **4:**291
Mwakenya (Union of Patriots for the
    Liberation of Kenya), **3:**573
Mwale, John, **3:**649
Mwali. *See* Comoro Islands
Mwali cult, **2:**130. *See also* Mwari cult
Mwalyosi, Raphael, **1:**49
Mwambutsa Bangiricenge, King,
    1:282–283
Mwan, **1:**522
Mwanawasa, Levy, **5:**321
Mwanga, Kabaka (Buganda), **3:**84,
    681–682
  British war against, **5:**122
  deposition of, **3:**87
Mwanga II (Buganda), **3:**680
Mwangi, Meja, **2:**373; **3:**387
  urban novels by, **4:**191
Mwari cult, **5:**334. *See also* Mwali cult
Mwase, George Simeon, **3:**385
Mwase-wa-Minga, **5:**317
Mwata-Yamvwa, **5:**307
Mwenda, Jean Bosco, **3:**649
mwene mutapa, **3:**612
Mwera, **5:**397
Mweru. *See* Meru
Mwezi Gisabo, **1:**282
Mwimbe, **5:**397
Mwindo Epic, The, **3:**345
Mwinyi, Ali Hassan, **3:**564; **5:**15
Mwitanzige, Lake, **3:**31
My Berber Horse (Kahena), **3:**88
My Children! My Africa! (Fugard),
    2:*419;* **5:**49
My Command (Obasanjo), **4:**85
*My Country, Africa: Autobiography of
    the Black Pasionaria* (Blouin),
    3:350
My Dear Bottle (Maillu), **4:**192
My Life in Crime (Kiriamiti), **4:**191
My Life in the Bush of Ghosts (Tutuola),
    5:116
*My Life in the ICU: The Autobiography
    of a Black Trade Unionist in South
    Africa* (Kadalie), **3:**86
My Odyssey: An Autobiography
    (Azikiwe), **1:**209
My Son's Story (Gordiner), **3:**355
Myasembo. *See* Ogot, Grace

Myene, **2:**423
Myeni, P., **3:**377
Myrdal, Gunnar, **2:**453
myrrh, **4:**166, 469, 472, 477
Mystery Smugglers (Gicheru), **4:**191
Myth, Literature and the African World
    (Soyinka), **4:**503–504
myth and cosmology, **3:**682–691
  Islamic historiography and,
    2:561–562
  myths
    about kings, **3:**125
    royal myths of origin, **4:**292
  pottery and creation myths, **1:**351
  in religion, **4:**307–308
  witchcraft and, **5:**220
Mzab, **5:**397
Mzamane, Mbulelo, **3:**208
Mzilikazi (Ndebele leader), **2:**599;
    3:414, 691; **4:**495
  refugees and, **4:**304
  Zimbabwe under, **5:**333

N

Naba Saaga, wives of, **1:***276*
Naba Tigré, **1:***276*
Nabdam, **2:**470
Nabta Playa (Egypt), **1:**204
Nachtigal, Gustav, **1:**263, 481; **5:**101
Nachtwey, James, **4:**144
Nadel, Siegfried Frederick, **2:**365
Nador, Mustapha, **3:**661
Nafana
  overview, **5:**397
  in Ghana, **2:**470
Nagada I, II, and III pottery, **2:**241,
    242, *242*
nagana, savanna ecosystems and, **2:**194
Nagira, Jared, **3:**333
Nago. *See also* Yoruba
  overview, **5:**397
  diasporas and, **2:**85–86
Nagui, Effat, **1:**186
Nahda movement, **3:**45, 62
Nahhas, Mustafa al-, **2:**363
N!ai, the Story of !King Woman (film,
    Marshall), **2:**372
Naigiziki, Saverio, **3:**396
Na'im, 'Abdullahi Ahmed An-, **3:**66
naira, **3:**577, 587
Nairobi (Kenya), **4:**1–2
  AIDS education in, **5:**242
  air transportation in, **5:**82
  architecture, **1:**120, 165
  bombing of U.S. embassy, **3:**58
  death and mourning in, **2:**23

protectorates
  and avoidance of European law, **4**:453
  in British West Africa, **1**:443
protein-energy malnutrition (PEM),
    2:379–380
Protestant Alliance, **2**:207
Protestantism
  and childbearing, **1**:366
  in Democratic Republic of the
    Congo, **1**:504
  Freetown as entry point, **1**:380
  in Lesotho, **3**:285
  missions, **1**:386, 396
  in Mozambique, **3**:611
  in Nigeria, **4**:204
Prothero, Mansell, **2**:454
Protocol on the Rights of Women
    (2003), **2**:628; **3**:426; **5**:264
proverbs and riddles, **3**:336, 342–343;
    375
Providence Industrial Mission, **4**:258
Provision of Education in the RSA, **2**:205
Provisional Military Administrative
    Council (Ethiopia), **2**:297–298
Provisional National Defence Council
    (Ghana), **2**:475; **3**:168
  Aidoo and, **5**:32
  Rawlings in, **4**:300
Prussin, Labelle, **1**:123
Psamtek I (king of Egypt), **2**:248
psychology and the study of Africa,
    4:283–285
  concepts of sickness and misfortune
    and, **2**:525–526, 528
  dreams and, **2**:140–141
  warfare and, **5**:178
Ptolemy (Claudius Ptolemeus), **2**:149;
    3:496
Ptolemy I (Egypt), **1**:335; **2**:250
  Alexandria under, **1**:57
  on eastern Africa, **2**:149
Ptolemy II (Egypt), **2**:250
Ptolemy V (Egypt), **2**:250
Ptolemy VI (Egypt), **2**:250
public health
  African medicine in, **2**:533–534
  economic history and, **2**:172
  and education about female genital
    mutilation, **3**:30
  HIV/AIDS and, **2**:123–124
  structural adjustment programs and,
    1:43–44
public opinion, discovery of, **1**:420
public-private partnership hospitals, **2**:536
Public Salvation Government of
    Democratic Republic of the
    Congo, **3**:85
public sector, **1**:332–333
  in Botswana, **1**:260

cutbacks in the 1980s, **2**:459
leading employer in Mauritania,
    3:501
social services and translation, **3**:344
urbanization and, **5**:141
Pufina (Tanzania), **1**:110
Puigaudeau, Odette du, **3**:498
La puissance de Um (Liking), **5**:35
pula, **3**:588
Pulaar language, **3**:500
Pungwe songs, **4**:190
Punic script
  historiography and, **2**:565
  on stele, **1**:167
Punu language, **2**:423
puppets
  masquerades, **2**:364; **3**:493
  theater, **4**:200, 201
purdah, **5**:246
purity, sickness and, **2**:525
Pushkin, Aleksander, **2**:70
Putnam, Robert, **1**:422
Pygmies. *See also* Baka (Pygmies);
    Batwa (Pygmies); Binga Pygmies
  overview, **5**:401
  anthropological work on changing
    music of, **1**:342
  in Democratic Republic of the
    Congo, **1**:497
  ecological impact of, **2**:153, 154
  in Equatorial Guinea, **2**:283
  land tenure among, **4**:242
  production strategies of, **4**:230
pyramids
  Egyptian, **1**:183, *183;* **2**:243–244
  as monumental architecture, **1**:123
pyrethrum, **4**:347
python symbolism, **4**:557, 561

Q

Q-FM (Zambia), **3**:528
Qader, Ahmad Weld Abd al-, **3**:364
Qadesh, Battle of, **2**:247
Qadhdhafi, Muammar, **3**:304, 307,
    308, 309; **4**:*287,* 287–288; **5**:104
Qadī 'Iyād, al-, **2**:563
Qādir al-Jilani, 'Abd al-, **3**:59
Qadiriyya-Mukhtariyya Sufi order,
    3:624
Qadiriyya Sufi order, **3**:13, 55–56, 61
  in Egypt, **3**:59
  Mukhtar, Sidi al-, shaikh of, **3**:624
  in Senegal, **4**:389
  in Sudan, **3**:60
qadis, **3**:266; **5**:327
Qairawan (Tunisia), **3**:676

Qalasadi, al-, **3**:496
Qalawun, Sultan, **2**:540
Qaramanli, Ahmad, **4**:98
Qasr Ibrim (Nubia), **2**:253
Qatrawani, **3**:496
Qemant, **5**:401
Qho (!Xõ), **1**:257
Qimant. *See* Qemant
Qine Bet, **2**:225
Qohaito (Aksum), **1**:55
Quaque, Philip, **2**:70; **4**:**288–289**
quarries, **5**:284
Quartier Mozart (film, Bekolo), **2**:375
quartz crystals, in early human society,
    2:145
Qubee script, **5**:278
Queau de Quinssy, Jean-Baptiste, **4**:406
Queen of Orango. *See* Correia, Mãe
    Aurélia
queens and queen mothers, **2**:448,
    489; **3**:118, 127; **4**:**289–293**
  Afua Kobi, **1**:12
  Amina, **1**:70–71
  anthropology on, **1**:87
  Candace, **1**:307–308, 398
  Nandi, **4**:11
  Njinga Mbandi, **4**:61
  photography of, **4**:140
  Ranavalona, Mada, **3**:373, 443, 449;
    4:297–298
  slaves as, **5**:251
  in Swaziland, **4**:551
  Taytu, **5**:*17,* 17–18
queer theory, **4**:397, 401
*The Quest for Fruition through Ngoma:
    Political Aspects of Healing in
    Southern Africa* (Schofeleers), **2**:531
A Question of Power (Head),
    2:522–523
quilombos, **2**:72
quinine, **2**:548; **4**:165
  discovery of prophylactic action of,
    3:10
Quiwonkpa, Thomas, **3**:295
Qur'an
  amuletic necklaces and, **1**:160
  Arabic script and, **5**:277
  in Islamic education, **2**:202
  in Islamic literature, **3**:327
  on medicine, **2**:539, 541
  memorization of, **2**:202
  as source of Islamic law, **3**:267
  translations, **3**:344
  witchcraft and, **5**:231–232
  woman scholars on, **5**:262
Qurashi, al-, **3**:496
Qutb, Sayyid, **3**:44, 63
Quwayri, Abd Allah al-, **3**:366

S

U

X

Y

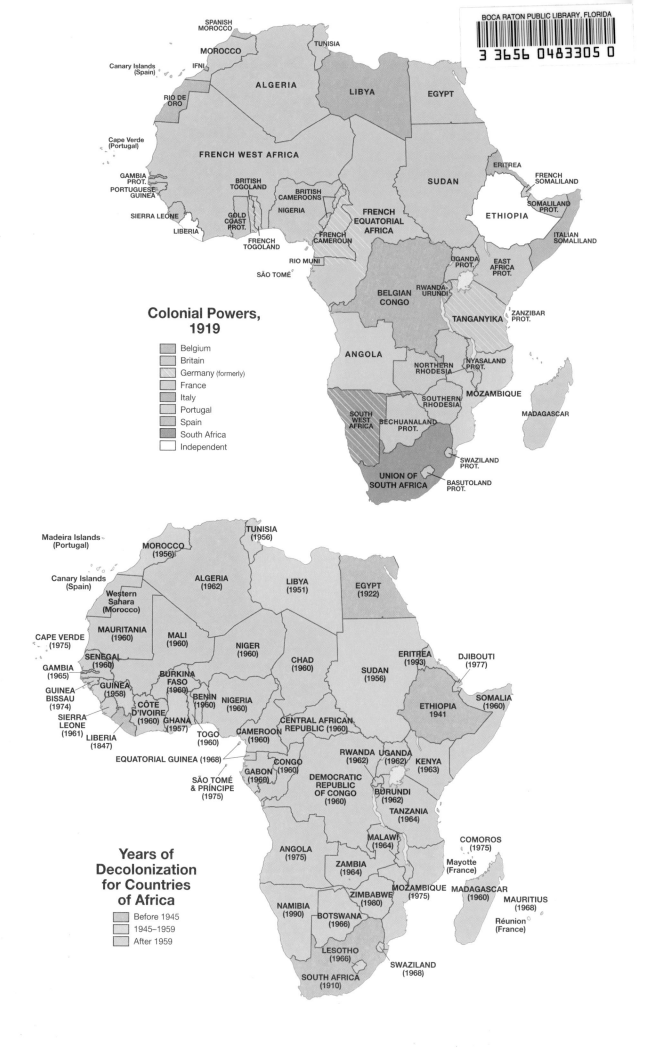

SPANISH
MOROCCO

TUNISIA

MOROCCO

Canary Islands
(Spain)

IFNI

ALGERIA

LIBYA

EGYPT

RIO DE
ORO

Cape Verde
(Portugal)

FRENCH WEST AFRICA

ERITREA

FRENCH
SOMALILAND

GAMBIA
PROT.
PORTUGUESE
GUINEA

SUDAN

SOMALILAND
PROT.

SIERRA LEONE

BRITISH
TOGOLAND

BRITISH
CAMEROONS

ETHIOPIA

LIBERIA

GOLD
COAST
PROT.

NIGERIA

FRENCH
EQUATORIAL
AFRICA

ITALIAN
SOMALILAND

FRENCH
TOGOLAND

FRENCH
CAMEROUN

RIO MUNI

UGANDA
PROT.

EAST
AFRICA
PROT.

SÃO TOMÉ

BELGIAN
CONGO

RWANDA-
URUNDI

TANGANYIKA

ZANZIBAR
PROT.

Colonial Powers,
1919

ANGOLA

NORTHERN
RHODESIA

NYASALAND
PROT.

MOZAMBIQUE

MADAGASCAR

Belgium
Britain
Germany (formerly)
France
Italy
Portugal
Spain
South Africa
Independent

SOUTH
WEST
AFRICA

BECHUANALAND
PROT.

SOUTHERN
RHODESIA

SWAZILAND
PROT.

UNION OF
SOUTH AFRICA

BASUTOLAND
PROT.

Madeira Islands
(Portugal)

TUNISIA
(1956)

MOROCCO
(1956)

Canary Islands
(Spain)

ALGERIA
(1962)

LIBYA
(1951)

EGYPT
(1922)

Western
Sahara
(Morocco)

CAPE VERDE
(1975)

MAURITANIA
(1960)

MALI
(1960)

NIGER
(1960)

CHAD
(1960)

ERITREA
(1993)

DJIBOUTI
(1977)

SENEGAL
(1960)

SUDAN
(1956)

GAMBIA
(1965)

BURKINA
FASO
(1960)

GUINEA
BISSAU
(1974)

GUINEA
(1958)

BENIN
(1960)

NIGERIA
(1960)

SOMALIA
(1960)

SIERRA
LEONE
(1961)

CÔTE
D'IVOIRE
(1960)

GHANA
(1957)

CENTRAL AFRICAN
REPUBLIC (1960)

ETHIOPIA
1941

LIBERIA
(1847)

TOGO
(1960)

CAMEROON
(1960)

EQUATORIAL GUINEA (1968)

CONGO
(1960)

RWANDA
(1962)

UGANDA
(1962)

KENYA
(1963)

GABON
(1960)

SÃO TOMÉ
& PRÍNCIPE
(1975)

DEMOCRATIC
REPUBLIC
OF CONGO
(1960)

BURUNDI
(1962)

TANZANIA
(1964)

MALAWI
(1964)

COMOROS
(1975)

Years of
Decolonization
for Countries
of Africa

ANGOLA
(1975)

ZAMBIA
(1964)

Mayotte
(France)

MOZAMBIQUE
(1975)

MADAGASCAR
(1960)

MAURITIUS
(1968)

ZIMBABWE
(1980)

Before 1945
1945–1959
After 1959

NAMIBIA
(1990)

BOTSWANA
(1966)

Réunion
(France)

LESOTHO
(1966)

SWAZILAND
(1968)

SOUTH AFRICA
(1910)